Praise for Internet Marketing: An Hour a Day

Matt Bailey is one of my favorite speakers at industry events because he delivers insights with intelligence and wit. He brings that same approach to this book in what is quickly becoming the next must-read for anyone interested in improving their business online.
    —BRETT CROSBY, Director, Product Marketing; Google

I've seen Matt wow crowds at Internet marketing conferences for years. He wows, because he has a gift for making a subject that many find daunting and complicated, sound accessible and eminently doable. The fact that he's been asked to write a book about his wisdom and experience speaks volumes. I hope to see many more volumes of Matt's written work in bookshops and on slate devices for years to come.
    —MEL CARSON, @MelCarson – Microsoft Advertising Community Manager

If you are a small business owner, this book is for you. Even the most time-strapped technophobe can understand Matt's easy-to-follow steps, implement his suggestions and drive qualified website traffic. You can pay someone thousands to "SEO" your site—or you can read this book and do it yourself. My advice: buy this book!
    —HEATHER LLOYD-MARTIN, Past Chair, DMA Search Engine Marketing Council
      CEO, SuccessWorks Search Marketing

Internet marketing is one of the highest ROI channels a business can utilize to grow it sales and drive its earnings. It is however a path many misunderstand. With Matt Bailey as your guide you are guaranteed learn the basics through to the more advanced techniques and find your way to mastering this high ROI marketing channel. Matt is an accomplished speaker, trainer, practitioner and now author and this book will most definitely educate you on everything you need.
    —MATT MCGOWAN, Managing Director, North America, Incisive Media
      (ClickZ, Search Engine Watch and the SES Conference and Expo Series)

What a great book! I've taught direct marketing to over 10,000 professionals as educational director of the DMA Direct Marketing Institute. So many of my attendees are "accidental marketers"—business owners, middle and upper managers who were given marketing responsibility, and career changers hoping to update their relevance in today's online world. This book will definitely be on my recommended reading list for future attendees. Matt makes the concepts easy to grasp and entertaining to learn.
    —BETH SMITH, Board of Directors, Direct Marketing Association;
      Owner, Smith Browning Direct; Educational Director and
      Instructor, Direct Marketing Association

Matt Bailey unpacks the mystery of SEO, site design, data and much else, in step-by-step directions, and plain English for the rest of us. No one else has approached the plain-English demystification of building an effective Web presence as cost-effectively and time-effectively as has Matt. This work is built on top of something like 15 years of experience in helping global majors and backyard amateurs be the best that they can be on the Internet. And maybe 5 years of teaching US Direct Marketing Association classes, and helping hundreds of students be the best they could be for themselves or for major companies in the US and abroad. If you have a struggling site and can't figure out why it isn't performing better, or if you just got your first PC and know your new business needs a Web presence, this book will more than repay you. It will build your business.

    —CHARLES PRESCOTT, Editor Prescott Report;
       Executive Director, Global Address Data Association;
       Director, Direct Marketing Association;
       Chair, Consultative Committee, Universal Postal Union

This book should be required reading for all business owners. At a time where everyone claims to be an Internet marketing expert, Matt is the real deal. He has provided a clear and concise guidebook containing all the tools and knowledge to help business owners quickly unleash the power of Internet marketing, In the sea of Internet marketing books, Matt's book rises to the top for its clarity and focus on generating ROI for business owners.

    —ERIC GREENBERG, Faculty Chair, Center for Management Development
       Rutgers, The State University of New Jersey

So many people launch websites but lack basic technical and marketing knowledge to make them succeed. Don't fall into this trap! Before you get started, read Internet Marketing: An Hour a Day. *It's a comprehensive resource filled with proven tips, tactics and marketing tools you can use to become an online success. Business owners large and small will benefit from this solid resource and the real-world advice Matt Bailey offers, you'll find yourself turning to it constantly!*

    —DEBRA MASTALER, President, Alliance-Link.com

If you're new to Internet marketing, you don't know what you don't know. Matt Bailey not only helps you understand what you don't know, he also manages to take subject matter that can be very complex and breaks it into easily digestible pieces for a newbie. Reading this book is like going to kindergarten on page 1 and finishing the last chapter with an MBA. This book should be required reading for all online marketing managers and small business owners.

    —ADAM PROEHL, Managing Partner, NordicClick Interactive

Internet marketing opens the door to business opportunities. It also an open door to potential pitfalls. The trick is to read Internet Marketing: An Hour a Day *by SiteLogic's President Matt Bailey so you can avoid the pitfalls, seize the opportunities, and get back home by six o'clock. Bailey's book tells you what works, what doesn't and provides a practical, day-by-day, do-it-yourself plan for success. It's the first thing that I hand to new employees to get them up to speed. And I can't believe that I'm praising a book written by a fan of The Ohio State University Buckeyes. I'm a Wolverine from the University of Michigan. But Bailey's book is that good. So, I urge you to read it, despite the author's tendency to remind me that we've lost "the game" for seven years in a row.*

—GREG JARBOE, President of SEO-PR and
author of *YouTube and Video Marketing: An Hour a Day*

I've known Matt as a terrific speaker at the Search Engine Strategies conferences, and someone whose opinion truly matters to me. He has always amazed me with his ability to take what might otherwise be complicated material and make it easily digestible for not only beginners, but also very engaging to those of us who've been in our Industry for years. In Internet Marketing: An Hour a Day, *Matt does not disappoint. It's truly a page-turner, delivering very sound advise that will save readers thousands of dollars from having done things "incorrectly", by taking the time to read this book, first. I cannot recommend Matt's advise strongly enough. It's practical, easy to follow and understand and—should you follow the things mentioned here—lead you to the "promised land" of success from your Internet marketing endeavors.*

—MARK JACKSON, President / Chief Executive Officer, Vizion Interactive, Inc.

For years I've watched Matt enthrall audiences by presenting complex material with an engaging, easy-to-understand style. I'm happy to say that style imbues Internet Marketing: An Hour a Day. *Matt takes a holistic approach that any site owner will easily grasp. By the end of the book, the reader has a complete picture of the tools and techniques that can supercharge the effectiveness of any website.*

—DAVID SZETELA, Owner and CEO, Clix Marketing

This book represents an easy-to-read, step by step guide to effective Internet marketing. Whether you are a small business owner, a marketing manager, or an aspiring entrepreneur, Internet Marketing: An Hour a Day *provides you with much needed direction and insight from one of the most respected and accomplished Internet marketing experts in the world—Matt Bailey.*

—KRISTOPHER B. JONES, Internet Marketing Expert and Founder of Pepperjam,
Author of *"Search Engine Optimization: Your Visual Blueprint to Effective Internet Marketing"*

Matt Bailey is truly a marketer's marketer, known by tens of thousands of conference attendees and speakers all over the world, for offering years of clear and actionable advice. Suffice to say we've been looking forward to this book for a while. In it, Matt systematically illustrates the holistic, interconnected nature of all things online marketing. I particularly like the focus on achieving actual ROI, defining business goals, and targeting sales as well as basics like keyword research, social media and SEO fundamentals. Run don't walk to pick up this book. There's something in it for anyone ready to invest in heightening their understanding of the online marketing space as a whole. aimClear® plans on shipping them to our clients, so they better know how to work with our team.

　—MARTY WEINTRAUB, President, aimClear®

Internet marketing in just one hour a day? Surely it can't be done! Maybe most people couldn't teach the broad topic of Internet marketing in just an hour a day, but most people aren't Matt Bailey. Trust me, walk to the counter and buy this book. Your approach to Internet marketing will never be the same again!

　—ANDY BEAL, coauthor of *Radically Transparent: Monitoring & Managing Reputations Online*, CEO & Founder, trackur

Matt's new book is a perfect marketing campaign building tool for the new Internet marketer. Not only does it show step-by-step how to implement successful campaigns online, but it's written in straightforward language that anybody building a business can understand. I only wish I had this when I started. I recommend highly that you buy this book today!

　—JON ROGNERUD, SEM Author, Blogger at JonRognerud.com and seoworld.entrepreneur.com

Matt has an intuitive knowledge of how to market online. The fact that he was able to corral his wisdom and turn it into a hands-on book that clarifies, simplifies and justifies marketing decisions is remarkable.

　—NEIL FEINSTEIN, Director, Brand & Creative Strategy, True North Inc.

In a world of trivial taglines, meaningless marketing-speak, and unmeasurable noise-making tactics, Matt Bailey's comprehensive guide to connecting online with real customers, on their level, with language, messages, and tactics they actually respond to, is like pure oxygen for your truth-deprived marketing brain. Matt knows what works, and how customers think. And he has the numbers to prove it.

　—ANDREW GOODMAN, Page Zero Media

I really love the way this book is written. It's accurate (more rare than you think), conversational, and you can whiz through it like a good piece of fiction. I've been working in Internet marketing for as long as anyone can claim to be and Matt Bailey is still taking me to school. Internet Marketing: An Hour a Day is a triumph and perhaps one of the best compendiums of Internet marketing knowledge I have seen.

　—JEFF FERGUSON, CEO, Fang Digital Marketing

Most Internet marketing books are full of fuzzy techno-speak and even fuzzier business ideas. This book contains neither. Matt Bailey has the gift of simplifying Internet marketing without oversimplifying, honed from over a decade of public speaking and consulting. You won't turn a single page without understanding exactly what to do to make your Internet marketing a success. I can't recommend Matt's book highly enough.

—Mike Moran, Co-author, *Search Engine Marketing Inc.*, and author
     Do It Wrong Quickly

I feel that Matt's book gives a comprehensive and holistic approach to all of the little details on Internet Marketing. It's a phenomenal overview of best practices to remember while working on programming, content writing, usability and accessibility, and optimizing conversions by focusing on calls to action, design and overall ROI. I highly recommend this book for anyone engaging in SEO, site design, development or overall marketing on the Internet.

—Benu Aggarwal, Founder and President, Milestone Internet Marketing Inc.

Matt Bailey's new book had me at "holistic". A small business site owner wanting frank, logical, accurate and easy to understand help for their design and marketing efforts will enjoy this book. Bailey avoids the fluff and over-glorification of site management. Beginning with business goals, this book teaches, day by day, the reasons for adding usability and accessibility to search marketing practices. There's instructions for those who hesitate to try PPC. With a constant tie back to sales and conversions, the book's greatest strengths lie in the analytical sections. You'll learn where, why, when and how as well as what to analyze. Each chapter topic is part of the whole Internet marketing wheel. If you're new to online marketing or wish to brush up on certain areas, this book is designed to offer support, instruction and insider tips from a seasoned professional.

—Kimberly "Kim" Krause Berg, Usability/SEO/IA Consultant, Cre8pc;
     Search Marketing/UX Manager, LiBeck Integrated Marketing

In Internet Marketing: An Hour a Day, *Matt Bailey goes back to the basics on why a company should be on the Internet, which business goals should be established and how they can be achieved. Even with significant experience in Internet marketing, you will find great insights in this book to make your business more profitable on the Web.*

—Nicolas Malo, Web Analytics Consultant, Hub'Sales & co-author of
     "Web Analytics: mesurer le succès et maximiser les profits de votre site Web"

Matt Bailey provides a clear road map with step by step procedures to unravel the complexities of online marketing for small and medium sized business owners, all tied up neatly with a holistic overview of online marketing that anyone can understand.

—Anne F. Kennedy, International Search Strategist; Founder, Beyond Ink USA

Although we all know that the fundamentals of marketing really haven't changed over the last few years, we still get drawn to new marketing toys and caught up in the "I have to have that" mode when, maybe, we really don't. Matt's book brings us back to reality and forces us to look at creating a strategy and analytical tools to really understand each channel's possibilities and limitations. And, just think, we can do it in an hour a day!

    —MATT SALT, Executive Director, Specialized Information Publishers Association

Matt stands out among Internet marketing professionals as one of the few who can teach effectively. He explains difficult concepts with grace and ease. You'll love this book.

    —JOHN MARSHALL, CTO, Market Motive

Anyone who tells you Internet Marketing is easy is lying to you. It is extremely complex, with lots of factors to consider. Matt Bailey does a phenomenal job making the complex simple. He give you the master plan to follow so you can develop the core skills to drive traffic to your website, analyze what that traffic is doing and what you can do if you want to get that traffic to be persuaded to take more actions on your website. Good athletes develop good skills, great athletes master and practice the fundamentals over and over again. Internet Marketing: An Hour a Day *is a must read and practice if you want to be great at Internet marketing.*

    —BRYAN EISENBERG, Best selling author and professional speaker

Matthew Bailey has one important gift and critical talents. The gift is his tremendous ability to communicate. He has honed this over time, but it was given to him at birth—as a gift. On the other hand, he can take full credit for his talents: an unerring enthusiasm for online marketing, his dogged determination to stay current yet practical and his appetite for hard work. He has put in his 10,000 hours—and then some—to become a true expert in this field. His advice is not assumption or conjecture but the sort of knowledge that comes from one who has done the work, made the mistakes and has a desire to help others benefit from his experience. Buy this book and enjoy his gift, while you profit from his talents.

    —JIM STERNE, Founder eMetrics Marketing Optimization Summit
      Chairman, Web Analytics Association

Matt Bailey has been educating audiences for many years with his conference speaking, seminars and workshops. As a thought leader in the space, his expertise and understanding of search engine optimization, usability and information architecture has helped many companies (large and small) to succeed online. This book encapsulates his vast knowhow of what it takes to market your products and services on the internet. Your journey to online marketing success is about to begin.

    —MIKE GREHAN, Global VP Content:
      SES Conference & Expo - ClickZ.Com - Search Engine Watch.com

Internet Marketing

An Hour a Day

Matthew Bailey

Wiley Publishing, Inc.

Senior Acquisitions Editor: WILLEM KNIBBE
Development Editor: CANDACE ENGLISH
Technical Editor: MICHAEL STEBBINS
Production Editor: ERIC CHARBONNEAU
Copy Editor: KIM WIMPSETT
Editorial Manager: PETE GAUGHAN
Production Manager: TIM TATE
Vice President and Executive Group Publisher: RICHARD SWADLEY
Vice President and Publisher: NEIL EDDE
Book Designer: FRANZ BAUMHACKL
Compositor: JOANN KOLONICK, HAPPENSTANCE TYPE-O-RAMA
Proofreader: NANCY BELL
Indexer: TED LAUX
Project Coordinator, Cover: KATHERINE CROCKER
Cover Designer: Ryan Sneed

Library of Congress Cataloging-in-Publication Data

Bailey, Matt, 1969–

Internet marketing : an hour a day / Matt Bailey.—1st ed.

p. cm.

ISBN-13: 978-0-470-63374-8 (pbk.)

ISBN-10: 0-470-63374-3 (pbk.)

ISBN: 978-1-118-08719-0 (ebk)

ISBN: 978-1-118-08722-0 (ebk)

ISBN: 978-1-118-08721-3 (ebk)

1. Internet marketing. 2. Marketing. I. Title.

HF5415.1265.B295 2011

658.8'72—dc22

2011005433

This book is not dedicated to my wife.

As I thought about the dedication, I realized that I cannot dedicate something to someone who is such a part of everything that has culminated in the writing of this book. Stacey, my wife, is the core of the success of our business (SiteLogic) and of my success as a speaker, writer, and teacher. Without her, none of this would have been possible. She deserves as much credit as I, because I would not even be in this business had it not been for her sacrifices and belief in me.

No, it isn't dedicated to her, because it is hers. Any success I have experienced is only because of her selflessness, sacrifice, and generosity. Thank you for all you have done, Stacey.

This book is dedicated to three men who have shaped me to be the person I am. Each one was instrumental at specific times in my life and taught me many things that would become part of how I speak, how I run a business, and how I treat people.

The first man is John Geib, my college professor.

John challenged me. He challenged me to think differently and find context to everything. When I thought I could coast through his classes, he made it difficult and yet also took the time to work with me and get to know me. His joy and passion in teaching is infectious, and I can only hope to be as enjoyable and engaging a teacher as he is.

The second man is Dennis Drennan, my former broker and employer when I sold real estate.

I like to say that Dennis taught me sales, but in reality, Dennis taught me about people. Dennis' sales meetings were more about becoming better salespeople in character, rather than by tactics. His lessons in honesty, motivation, discipline, and humility have stayed with me.

Dennis, I still have the notes from almost every sales meeting you ran, especially when we used "The Greatest Salesman in the World" as the text. Your lessons have been guiding principles in building my business, and I only hope that I can run my agency half as well as you have run yours.

The last and the most influential is my father, Dr. Earl Bailey.

As a pastor, he taught me exposition: breaking down large concepts into words and feasting on their meanings, and understanding the verbs and the structure of the language, all of which enable a better understanding of the primary concept.

As a father, he taught me discipline and love and provided an example for me to follow, even though I didn't always follow. It's amazing how time changes your appreciation of lessons heard and lessons learned.

As a man, my dad teaches me perseverance in the face of unthinkable pain, every day of his life. Dad, I don't know how you endure, but you do. What's more amazing is that you don't just endure; you flourish in the face of circumstances that would make even the bravest man crumble. You are my example and my inspiration.

Of course, I can't mention my father without mentioning my mother, Judy. Mom, you instilled a love of reading in me, and it has been one of the most valuable gifts you've given. I thank you for the hours helping me with schoolwork, your gentle patience when I made bad decisions, and your unwavering support of my hare-brained ideas. I can't thank you enough for your countless hours of babysitting your grandchildren in order that I could get this book done. I hope you are so proud of me and you'll forgive me for that time I wrecked your car.

Acknowledgments

As with any project, this was done with the help of many people, all of whom have been amazingly patient and helpful.

First, to my family, Stacey and the girls. You have put up with so much absence in the past year between my traveling and writing. Thank you for your patience. I am looking forward to fishing with you again this summer and enjoying our time together. To Callie Ann, who was born about the time this project started, my name is Matt, and I'm your father. Stacey, sorry about being so busy the past year; I'm looking forward to regular date nights again!

I need to thank my colleagues at SiteLogic: Ben Bailey, Jackie Baker, Rich Grisak, Jerod Heller, Scott Norquest, Beth Kaboth, and Sheila Miklos. Your tireless efforts while I have been distracted with this book have been nothing short of amazing. I could not ask for a better group of people. You love what you do, and it shows—thank you for keeping the business running (and profitable) while I have been so busy!

A huge thank you to Avinash Kaushik, whose friendship I have valued over the past few years. Thank you for introducing me to the great people at Wiley and getting me started in this amazing process of writing a book. Thank you for agreeing to write the foreword; you're the one who got me into this, so it seemed fitting!

Thank you to the great people at Wiley and Sybex for all of their help in this process, especially to two people who have been instrumental to this work: Willem Knibbe, you've been a great guiding hand throughout this process. Simply getting this book to happen took enough time; but you were patient, helpful, and a joy to work with. Candace English, thank you very much for your tireless editing. I can only imagine the amount of suffering my editor has to endure at the hands of my writing. Candace is able to communicate well with grace and candor, and I look forward to working with her again.

My technical editor, Michael Stebbins from Market Motive, was superb. Mike, I picked you because I knew you would be tough, make me cite my sources, and clarify areas where I simply assumed people knew what I was writing about. Thank you!

Chapter 12's content on information architecture was developed with the help of Scott Meier and Jay Oldaker. Scott also produced the wireframe that is shown on the computer screen on the cover. Thank you for your assistance and helpful advice! You not only helped clarify my thinking on this chapter but helped me communicate the concepts much better and more efficiently.

Chapter 13 could not have been as effective without the willingness of Lee Laughlin, Glenda Jackson, Chris Hofstader, and Google's Dr. T.V. Raman. Thank you for the input, the interviews, and the wonderful content that has helped educate thousands of web developers about accessibility over the years! Your time was invaluable.

A lot of content and examples in this book are a result of my time consulting with South Dakota Department of Tourism and Black Hills Tourism agencies and associations. I had some of the most fun I have ever had working with clients. In fact, I still refer to you as my friends, not my clients. Your hospitality and pride in your work provided some of the most enjoyable experiences in my professional life while visiting and working with all of you. I hope that some of my examples inspire more than a few visits to your beautiful state!

To the many others who I look forward to seeing at SES and other search conferences, you provide great conversation and brilliant ideas to consider. This is an amazing industry because of the people in it: John Marshall (who is always at the top of my list!), Brian Eisenberg, Jeff Ferguson, Annie Stickney, Andrew Goodman, Greg Jarboe (you too Jamie O'Donnel), Todd Malicoat, Christine Churchill, Sage Lewis, Chris Caputo, Ian McAnerin, Aaron Kahlow, Andy Beal, Ann Kennedy, David Szetela, Jessica Bowman, Jim Sterne, Joe Morin, Kim Krause-Berg, Li Evans, Mark Jackson, Rand Fishkin, and so many more. It's at times like this that I need a roster, because I can't possibly name the number of people I love to see at these conferences.

Of course, the SES conferences could not be what they are without a great team of people at Incisive Media that run a great show. You give me an amazing platform from which to speak, and I wish you the greatest success: Matt McGowan, Mike Grehan, Marilyn Crafts, and Jackie Ortez—thank you!

I also want to thank the fine people in Educational Services at the Direct Marketing Association: Ana Chernis, Michelle Tiletnick, and Jodi Sangster. Developing the two-day online marketing training for you helped me think through the structure of this book and use examples that have been tempered with great classrooms!

Finally, there are two women through whom I can trace the bulk of my business and success: Heather Lloyd Martin and Jill Whalen. Both of you recommended me early in my SEO speaking career, and I hope I have not disappointed. Because of the references and referrals you both provided, I can trace most of my current business and speaking opportunities back to the ones you offered me in the "early days." I couldn't ask for two better friends.

About the Author

Matt Bailey is the president and founder of SiteLogic, an online marketing agency. Teaching is his passion, because educated clients make the best clients. Matt accidentally discovered the SEO industry in 1995 by realizing that his websites were ranking well and drawing in visitors from all over the world. It was a natural fit, because he was already training local business owners in sales and marketing.

Prior to starting SiteLogic, Matt developed online marketing departments at two different agencies and also worked as a software sales engineer, which enabled him to learn technical skills that would merge with his marketing experience.

Heather Lloyd Martin of SuccessWorks says Matt has "an incredible ability to explain high-level search marketing concepts in a way that even 'nontechies' understand. Additionally, he has an excellent grasp of the various nuances that surround search marketing and clearly understands how to create a powerful, effective strategy." According to Rand Fishkin, CEO and cofounder of SEOMoz, "Matt is one of the smartest, fastest-moving people in the industry. Matt is the type of guy who knows everything that's taken place in the world of search and how to apply that information to achieve success."

Bailey is a frequent speaker at many conferences and seminars. He is usually on the docket at the Search Engine Strategies conferences and also serves on the Advisory Board. He is a regular speaker at the Direct Marketing Association, Online Marketing Summit, Specialized Information Publishers Association, Specialized Equipment Marketing Association, and many international conferences.

Bailey teaches for multiple business education outlets. He is an adjunct faculty at Rutgers University, teaching multiple modules of the mini-MBA program in online marketing. He also teaches regularly for the Direct Marketing Association's Direct Marketing Academy for Online Marketing.

Additionally, Matt is a member of Market Motive (www.MarketMotive.com), an online marketing training resource for professionals and businesses. Market Motive has been called the "Internet marketing dream team." Matt has created many instructional videos covering multiple subjects of online marketing but focuses on teaching the fundamentals.

Bailey has also provided in-house training to many businesses and organizations. Google, Proctor & Gamble, Hewlett-Packard, ADC, Intuit, the State of South Dakota's Department of Tourism and Black Hills Tourism agencies and associations, Randall-Reilly Publications, American Greetings, and Eaton Corporation are just a few of the organizations that have benefited from Matt's expertise.

Matt attended Malone University in Ohio with a concentration in journalism and communications and also served in the Army National Guard for 11 years. After graduation, he worked in selling real estate, where he first started to develop websites and learn online marketing skills that would form the rest of his career.

Matt resides outside of a small town in rural Ohio with his wife, Stacey, and his four daughters, Caitlin, Madeline, Miranda, and Callie Ann. They also have four cats, one dog, a turtle named Vera, and a yet-to-be-named goldfish. The favorite family activities are fishing and swimming in the backyard pond and watching the surrounding wildlife.

Contents

Chapter 7   **Week 4: Leverage Principles of Sales and Marketing**   **129**

Foreword

John Wanamaker famously said, "I know half of my advertising is wasted; I just don't know which half." I have always believed that this sentiment finally will be obsolete in the age of digital marketing where we have a near-magnificent capacity to measure the return on investment. Yet that is not so. We remain a people largely driven by faith, surrounded by horrible websites and so-bad-I-would-rather-jump-off-a-building customer experiences.

That reality is also the reason for my childlike delight at Matt Bailey's beautifully written book on Internet marketing. In specific, strategic, tactical ways it helps us deal with Mr. Wanamaker's conundrum.

Many books cover Internet marketing in silos (both of mine focus just on the pure joy of Web analytics). Matt has done a wonderful job of covering the space from end to end. Search engine optimization? Check. Usability? Check. Technical solutions? Check. Social-media strategies? Check. Conversion optimization? Check. And so much more. As a small, medium, or large business owner, you'll—finally (!!)—get the end-to-end view of what it takes to be truly successful on the Web.

Matt is uniquely qualified to write this book, primarily because of his deep, long list of in-the-trenches, pull-up-his-sleeves-and-roll-with-the-pigs successes. He has delivered his life lessons, igniting the passions of hundreds of conference attendees. He has consulted with some of the top companies on the Web and helped them rethink their digital strategies. In this book, he shares his hard-won intelligence with grace and uncommon wit.

There are three things I hope you'll take away from the book:

- God created the Internet so that we could fail faster. Our offline existence makes us risk averse because in that world it is expensive to fail, and it takes a long time to figure out that we did. Not on the Web. Take the advice from this book, no matter how strange you think it is, and implement it. It takes just hours or days to fail or succeed on the Web. Leverage that gift to glory.

- If you don't know where you are going, any road will take you there. Leave that for the lame. Put in the blood, sweat, and tears required to create business objectives, drill down to specific goals, identify marketing strategies that have a direct line of sight to those goals, and measure outcomes. Rinse. Repeat.

- Embrace customer centricity like it was your long-lost love. On the Web you can accomplish the impossible: delight customers *and* get high conversions! You don't have to pick either/or. Learn to solve for both because it is good karma and it is a fantastic long-term business strategy.

The Web presents an incredible opportunity to fulfill your personal professional goals and achieve remarkable results for your business. With this book in hand, I am confident your journey will be smoother, faster, and more productive.

Good luck!

Avinash Kaushik

Author: Web Analytics 2.0 and Web Analytics: An Hour a Day

Analytics Evangelist, Google

www.kaushik.net/avinash

Introduction

While I was growing up, my father was the pastor of a large church. I learned my teaching style from watching him preach week after week. He was known as having an expository style of teaching, meaning that he would cut away large portions of information and focus on a small amount of text, thereby allowing careful analysis of each part and an understanding of how it makes up the whole. He would prepare by studying that small text, researching the verb forms and language construction. When he taught, he drilled down into the details of what the author was writing, and by focusing on such a small text, it made everything else clearer. I took the same approach when developing my teaching style, because my father's example enabled me to grasp technical issues and break them down into understandable parts.

As I became more involved in online marketing, I quickly saw that this field was full of so many factors that were necessary for online success. When surveying all of the factors, most people become intimated or even overwhelmed by the sheer amount of information that one needs to know.

I found that many marketing managers and website owners simply wanted an understandable guide to help them know what is important and what they need to do in such a fast-changing online marketplace. Most explanations were too technical, when all they wanted was a "what do I need to do" approach. As a result, most marketers' goals were not clear or were immeasurable. If there is no clear purpose in strategy, tactics, or even the primary goals of a web strategy, then the goals are unclear, misunderstood, or simply nonexistent. This book is my response to that.

Like my father, I find that the best way to understand an overwhelming amount of information is to focus on a small part at a time—to evaluate and learn one discipline and one technique at a time and then understand the role that it plays and the importance and relevance to the overall campaign. As one gains an understanding of each part of online marketing, a clear pattern emerges, you begin to see similarities and consistent patterns that were previously hidden. However, these patterns and similarities were hidden because they cannot be seen when considering the whole but only by examining each piece.

As the patterns emerge, marketers can then begin to understand the factors and tactics necessary for successful campaigns and understand that the roles they play provide context to the big picture of marketing. Once the context of each part in relation to the other is in place, the intimidation factor disappears. The holistic development of the online marketer is developed by understanding the small roles that make up the entire process.

As the marketer starts to operate in this new understanding of the smaller factors, they will begin to see a strange consistency among them. Even though there is so much information, so many details, there is an overarching familiarity. There are consistent themes among each discipline, and those consistent themes will contribute to a fresh understanding of the entire process. Understanding the smaller factors enables you to understand the priorities from a high level, because one can now understand how each part may be affected by a single, small change.

I hope this book helps to reveal the smaller factors and place them in context. By scrutinizing the major factors in online marketing and comparing them, marketers can better understand the business of online marketing. It is my sincere hope that this book will make people better marketers, not just marketers who can do better online marketing.

Who Should Read This Book

I am making certain assumptions regarding the reader:

- You have a website or are getting ready to build a website.
- You are responsible for marketing that website.
- You "wear a lot of hats" in your company, or you run the entire business and do not have the time to dedicate to running a site full-time.
- You are familiar with basic analytics and website terminology.
- You want to make more money with your website.

This book is intended for the business owner or a marketing manager who needs a comprehensive overview of how everything works together in the marketing, design, development, content development, link building, and analytics strategy.

Somehow it all has to make sense, and priorities need to be placed on these activities, but how does you know what to make a priority and when? This book will cover how to make everything come together into a simplified, strategic plan to improve your Internet marketing campaigns, your website, and your marketing skills.

What's Inside

Here is a glance at what's in each chapter:

Part I: Understand Today's Internet Marketing

Chapter 1: A Holistic Approach   sets the stage for how the book will unfold and introduces some of the concepts for the following chapters. All parts of Internet marketing are related and affect one another.

Chapter 2: How Search Engines Work   provides an overview of the technical requirements of search engines. Myths are also dispelled so you understand what you can do to improve your rankings.

Chapter 3: Rankings or Profit? Establishing Your Business Goals   starts with the most foundational part of marketing, creating the goals for your campaign. Without goals, there is no measurement and no ROI.

Part II: Month 1: Evaluate and Research

Chapter 4: Week 1: Evaluate Your Situation   helps you perform a self-diagnostic on your website. Get familiar with tools that can help you identify problems on your website and test search engine friendliness.

Chapter 5: Week 2: Understand Basic SEO   introduces you to how you can increase your search engine rakings, which increases the number of visitors you can attract. This week's discussion breaks down the structure and elements of website pages and how to develop consistent information.

Chapter 6: Week 3: Jump into Keyword Research   is the foundation of nearly every Internet marketing venture. Keyword research helps you find relevant search terms, find the voice of the customer, uncover market trends, and gain an advantage over your competitors.

Chapter 7: Week 4: Leverage Principles of Sales and Marketing   presents important techniques to implement into the content development of your site. You can increase your sales and leads by implementing a few simple writing techniques that will lead your visitors to action.

Part III: Month 2: Develop Content That Converts

Chapter 8: Week 5: Understand That Content Comes First   continues with the development of active content that engages visitors. Case studies and examples show how any type of business can find effective ways to communicate benefits, tell a unique story, and improve their marketing.

Chapter 9: Week 6: Connect Your Content to Users and Search Engines ties together the importance of effective content and search engine visibility. Well-developed and structured content can appease both the needs of the search engines and the visitors. This week you'll learn how to increase sales and rankings with an understanding of human factors.

Chapter 10: Week 7: Master the Science of Online Persuasion offers the classic persuasion techniques of logic, emotion, and credibility. Implementing these techniques online results in a convincing approach to change your visitors into customers and clients.

Chapter 11: Week 8: Improve Conversions goes to the bottom line of improving Internet marketing performance. Sometimes simple changes—making clear calls to action and considering visual contrast, for instance—can have big results.

Part IV: Month 3: Develop Good Site Architecture

Chapter 12: Week 9: Create Effective Navigation covers creating effective navigation in your website, because this is the primary means of developing a clear structure of information for your visitors. Both usability and technical factors are explored as a means to increase the effectiveness of a navigation scheme.

Chapter 13: Week 10: Design for Accessibility covers the aspects of accessibility in your website design. By accounting for assistive technology, color blindness, and contrast, you will also create a more search-friendly site that is easier for all of your visitors to use.

Chapter 14: Week 11: Identify Technical Roadblocks discusses factors that may inhibit or prevent search engines from "seeing" your website. As one of the more technical chapters, it explains to marketers the value of understanding technical factors in website management and marketing.

Chapter 15: Week 12: Remember the Important Details covers all the small items that tend to be left behind or forgotten in developing and managing a website. This chapter emphasizes tools for promoting a locally based businesses, as well as on opportunities for additional visibility in the search engines.

Part V: Month 4: Expand Your Reach and Measure Results

Chapter 16: Week 13: Build Links covers the importance of various link types, because they are the foundation of your visibility. Links are like word-of-mouth referrals online and will contribute to your credibility, as well as increase your search engine rankings.

Chapter 17: Week 14: Add to Your Business with Blogs gives you ideas about how a blog can enable your business to reach visitors far beyond the traditional website. By engaging with visitors on a personal and active platform, blogs generate more visitors, more search engine ranking, and more links to your website.

Chapter 18: Week 15: Get Friendly with Social Media addresses the concerns many marketers have about utilizing social media. Social media may scare or concern some marketers, because the ROI is largely undefined, and so many opportunities are available.

This chapter focuses on building a campaign that is specific to your business and developing for the social media site that best suits your marketing message.

Chapter 19: Week 16: Develop a Complementary Pay-per-Click Campaign further builds your marketing efforts and increases your reach. The simple steps to starting your pay-per-click campaign and mistakes to avoid in this chapter will enable you to be confident as you set up a paid campaign to assist in or become a major part of your overall marketing.

Chapter 20: Week 17: Measure, Measure, Measure is based on the fact that measurement is the only sure way to know whether you are successful in your marketing efforts. Every change that you make to your marketing, design, and programming can be tracked for results in your analytics. However, most people track the wrong numbers or have no idea what reports are important. This chapter covers the "what do I track?" question.

Chapter 21: Week 18: Analyze for Action gives you a clear understanding of what analytics can do and of how to start taking action to find what works and what doesn't and how you can develop a specific plan for improvement. Suggested reports for segmentation, content evaluation, and technical troubleshooting will provide the starting blocks for you to customize Google Analytics to your business.

How to Contact the Author

I welcome feedback from you about this book or about books you'd like to see from me in the future. You can reach me by writing to Matt@SiteLogic.com. For more information about my agency and marketing advice, visit my website at www.SiteLogic.com.

Sybex strives to keep you supplied with the latest tools and information you need for your work. Please check the book's website at www.sybex.com/go/internetmarketing, where I'll post additional content, updates, and corrections to this book should the need arise. There you can also find a presentation on analytics that I presented at Google.

Understanding Today's Internet Marketing

I

Developing a book on Internet Marketing is a tricky prospect. There are so many "flavors" of internet marketing, and this is no exception. The purpose of this chapter is really to introduce you to the flavor of the rest of the book, the over-arching theme that will resonate throughout each chapter. That is, everything starts based on your business goals, all of the "parts" of online marketing are interdependent, and everything must be measured in order to have a complete view.

A Holistic Approach

Marketing is evolving at lightning speed with website design and usability advances, search engine optimization, and pay-per-click marketing techniques, website analytics, and social media initiatives all competing for a busy marketer's attention. But one important core principle remains constant: the need for an integrated approach. In this chapter, you'll learn the core tenets of a successful, coordinated, integrated approach that involves not just marketers but your whole organization.

1

Chapter Contents

The Fundamentals of Marketing

Marketing online doesn't start or end with search engine rankings. It isn't solely dependent upon how well your website is built. It certainly doesn't depend on how beautiful your website may be. It is a combination of many factors that not only work together but depend on each other in order to provide your company with more visibility online, better customer experiences, and an understanding of proper visitor measurement.

Therefore, the principles outlined in this book are not simply based on a single activity. A single focus, such as search engine optimization, is effective only when paired with additional disciplines. Effective search engine optimization requires analytics, which shows the effectiveness of the optimization, the return on investment, and necessary adjustments to the keyword strategy. Another paired discipline is usability, which tests and analyzes to see whether your website visitors are seeing what they expect and are taking the actions you desire.

Simply put,

- Make it right the first time.
- Search engine optimization, social media channels, and pay-per-click marketing help people find you.
- Content makes people stay and gives them a reason to return.
- Usability ensures that your message and visitor tasks are clear.
- Analytics tells you what just happened.
- The combination of analytics, usability, and testing will tell you *why*.

So, although there are thousands of books explaining search engine optimization, analytics, website design, and hundreds of other marketing-related subjects, this book is intended to show how each discipline must work together to create a specific strategy. I call that strategy (strangely enough) *marketing*.

Marketing is the underlying force of this entire book. This is reflected in the rest of this chapter, because the foundation of your website marketing strategy is the key to building a successful presence online.

My definition of marketing, which is based on the classic definition of direct marketing, is this:

> *Giving the right people the right message with the right offer at the right time*

I like the direct marketing definition, because that is the closest to what we are attempting to do online. Much of online marketing is rooted in 100 or so years of the direct marketing industry. The most compelling factor in online marketing is the ability to measure the effectiveness of this definition. In addition, there are many different methods, or *channels*, with which to use this formula.

What I love about this foundation is that the level of metrics employed by direct marketers would make some website managers cringe. There is a science in persuasion, and understanding that science can help you market your website far beyond getting high rankings in a search engine or two.

The Measure of Success

I learned this lesson in the early days of the Internet. I was in selling real estate at the time and specialized in commercial hospitality properties, such as bed and breakfasts and inns. I started building websites in order to get beyond the local marketing in the newspaper and Multiple Listing Service (MLS) database. The only other option was taking out full-page color ads in magazines, which was a very costly proposition.

At the end of a very profitable year, I reviewed the performance of the website to see where I should invest my time and efforts in the next year. In that review, I found a concept that would change my life.

I averaged about 40 leads a month from visitors who found the website via search engines. I learned to rank well very early and applied these practices to rank for hundreds of terms in the search engines. Search engines provided about 80 percent of the traffic to my website and hundreds of subscribers to my content. However, I did not make a single sale from those thousands of visitors. They were nice, big numbers—impressive but ineffective and unprofitable.

My sales were all traced back to a single advertising link that I had purchased. That link was an advertisement for my website on a bed-and-breakfast website directory. I purchased that link for $35 a year. A small investment yielded a thousandfold return.

The lesson was reinforced as I learned to apply more marketing principles toward this new online channel. The right message in the right place to the right person can be more effective than high rankings, high visitor counts, and a great conversion rate:

What counts, more than anything, is profit.

Make It Right

One of my favorite shows to watch has been the Home & Garden Television channel's *Holmes on Homes*. Mike Holmes is a contractor who fixes the additions, repairs, and incompetent work of other contractors. In doing so, he educates the homeowner and the viewer and advocates for better consumer rights against poor contractor workmanship.

I am inspired by this show, because it mirrors my job in the online world, even to the point where I use many of the catchphrases of Holmes in my everyday work of evaluating and fixing websites:

- "Make it right."
- "Get it right the first time."

- "Rip it all out."
- "Gut it; start over."
- "Bring in the right people for the right job."

When evaluating how websites were programmed and built, it became apparent that so many were not built with marketing in mind. The misunderstanding of what *search friendly* meant and how it was interpreted made for a mess of code that never helped the companies that paid thousands of dollars for a website.

Unfortunately, and unlike the home improvement industry, there is no licensing body overseeing website development and marketing. If someone builds a bad website, there is no way to recover, much less a decision-making authority that can judge a bad website.

As Holmes has preached, the best way to protect yourself from a bad investment is to educate yourself and learn all the questions that you should ask. This book is designed to help you do the very same thing: prepare you to ask the right questions and have the right information with which to make better and more informed decisions about your website and marketing strategy.

Who's at Fault for Website Problems?

Now, don't get it in your head that website problems are the fault of the development agency or the programmer. No, the majority of problems can be reduced to a single problem: communication.

I find that the relationship between a company and its website developers becomes tenuous very quickly, and after being in the industry since the near beginning, I think I understand why.

Clients, or the "website buyers," need a website. The problem is that they don't know what to ask for or how to ask for it. Beyond something that "looks nice" or goals that focus on the visual, there is usually very little understanding of what creates a successful presence for a company online. Therefore, the developers do what they think is best. They fill in the gaps with what they know, and if the client doesn't ask for it, it doesn't get done. Programmers need specific instructions, and clients usually aren't in the position to understand, much less provide those instructions.

Two companies are trying to collaborate to produce something, but they are speaking two different languages. The scope of the project grows, the development company puts in more and more hours than budgeted, and the clients grow more and more dissatisfied because they want something but cannot communicate what exactly they want.

When the website is delivered, the development company tends to see it as "done" and moves on to the next project. Meanwhile, the customer already has a list of things they want to change. Many website developers and development companies see websites as a project that has a completion date. To companies that use their website to conduct business, the website is never done. So, not only is the language different between these companies, but the expectations and goals are completely different as well.

Bringing It All Together with Analytics

I cannot understand why there are so many businesses that do not use analytics. Analytics is the key to most of what you need to know in order to make intelligent decisions about your website in terms of marketing, search engine optimization, social media, and pay-per-click advertising. Even design changes can be improved and measured by simply using your analytics.

Without analytics, you cannot put dollar signs in front of improvements. You can't know for sure whether that new design works better or worse. You won't be able to tell whether that new copywriter is connecting to the audience. All of these questions that are vital to determining profitability are founded in the proper applications of analytics.

When you bring it all together, here's what I have found:

Search Engine Optimization (SEO)   SEO yields a drastic improvement based on the desired metrics. For websites measuring pure visitor numbers, the number can be exceedingly high in bringing "eyeballs" to the site. For ecommerce and lead-generation sites, I have witnessed increases in conversion rates between 200 percent and 400 percent, because not only does SEO increase the number of visitors, but it also increases the quality of visitors, resulting in better visitors who need what you may have. The big difference in numbers depends basically on how old the website is, on whether SEO has ever been performed, and on your desired metrics (visitors, contacts, conversions, and so on)—there are a large number of dependent factors.

Design Improvements (Usability)   Once you get people to the website, the next goal is to get them to do what you want them to do. Unfortunately, there are usually design obstacles, content issues, or unclear steps in the process. The process of improving the visitor's path through the website is called *usability*.

Usability transforms a website from the corporate vision of what it should be to the user's vision of what they need. By changing the information, graphics, and organization of a website to meet the needs of the user, the ability of the website to gain new customers and retain old ones will increase dramatically. Jacob Neilson, a usability guru, estimated that the average website can experience an 83 percent to 135 percent improvement in metrics, though he has seen improvements far beyond that. (See Jakob Nielsen's Alertbox from January 22, 2008: www.useit.com/alertbox/roi.html.)

Analytics   Analytics tells you what happened and why. A survey of Forrester Research's Web Analytics Peer Research Panel showed the companies that hired a full-time analyst experienced a 900 percent to 1200 percent return on their investment. From my experience, that can happen well within the first year of an analyst working on a website, because they find many of the largest issues first.

Without analytics, you cannot put dollar signs in front of improvements. You can't know for sure whether that new design works better or worse. Essentially, of all the tools in your online-marketing kit, analytics is the toolbox. Without the toolbox, you cannot carry all the tools you need, and you can't justify adding more. It's a poor analogy, but I hope you get my meaning.

A Team Approach

A single method of marketing online will not survive. I work with many teams of people who approach projects from various disciplines, but all have to work together to be successful. That means a corporate website will never reach its full potential unless marketing and IT can kiss, make up, and get along in order to develop dynamic solutions that will enable a company to lead the market. Until these departments get along, the website will always suffer.

I have lost count of the companies where I have consulted on their websites only to find that the marketing department blames the IT department for the failures of the website. IT blames marketing for having unrealistic goals. The sales force is simply dismissed as not having relevant information, and those who actually work on the product or have customer interaction have very little to do with the decision making.

It's a common theme to be working with a company and seeing all the finger-pointing, only to realize that no one in the meeting has ever tried to purchase a product from the company's website. That, my friend, is a marketing problem, not an IT function. IT's job is to make sure the website is up and it functions as specified. If people can't figure out how to get to the next step in the site, that's a marketing problem.

Businesses need to build an integrated approach to marketing the website and assigning roles based on an understanding of the disciplines needed. The beauty of a holistic approach is the understanding that everything can be measured. If there is a disagreement, then great! Make two versions, and test to see which one is most effective. There are no more assumptions on how the user will react, because the tools are available to get the user's opinion, not someone's assumption.

Is This for You?

This is why I subscribe to a holistic approach. Building a successful business online is more than chasing the latest social-media site, more than a number-one ranking in Google, and more than a fancy new website.

Building a successful website is about strategic planning, understanding your market, and concentrating on a specific message. When you know your message, how you spread it will be easy.

This book is intended as a guide for marketing managers who are struggling to "do it all" and keep on top of the latest information. As such, this is also intended for small-business owners who are expected to figure out how to run a website rather than run their business. I hope that it answers questions that you didn't know to ask.

I find in my consulting practice that even after nearly 15 years of Internet marketing and building websites there is still a lot of myth, skepticism, misunderstanding, and flat-out crappy advice in circulation. The best defense is common sense. The best answers in this industry tend to have a lot of common sense. If something doesn't sound right, then chances are it isn't.

So, this is our road map to the next few weeks of going through this text in an hour a day. I will focus first on understanding how search engines work and then on understanding how searchers work. In later chapters, more technical issues will be covered, because even the best targeting and optimization won't overcome technical problems.

How Search Engines Work

Prior to beginning any website marketing activity, it is critical to understand how search engines work. This chapter covers the basic aspects of how search engines find and catalog websites and documents and how they determine what is displayed in the search results.

Search engines will be one of the highest referrers of website visitors to your business and search engines greatly affect your ability to gain visibility and market share.

Making sure the search engines can "see" your website and that they have downloaded the most recent, accurate, and complete version of your website is where search engine optimization starts.

2

Chapter Contents

The Big Picture

Search engines have transformed marketing. If they didn't have such an impact, you would not be reading this book.

A little less than two decades ago, all marketing was considered a "push" medium. TV commercials, billboards, radio ads, yellow pages, magazine ads—all advertisements were meant to be there regardless of whether you needed the message. It was all meant to reach that person who might need the service at that time.

Enter the search engine, the revolutionary technology that meets people at the point of their need. At the time, it was the only technology where the consumer told someone what they wanted at that specific point in time. If your company could be found in that decision point, your chances of gaining a new customer were very high. Your company met the customer at the point of their need, and thus an industry was born.

This has changed significantly from the early days of search. I'll explain the early days later in this chapter, because those early days are the source of a lot of current misunderstandings and bad habits.

Let's start with how things work right now. Figure 2.1 shows the search cycle.

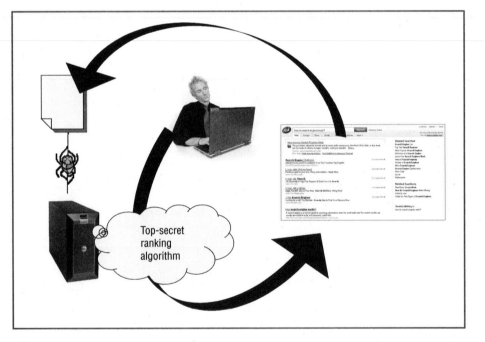

Figure 2.1 How search engines work

Simply put, a search engine makes a copy of your web pages and stores that copy into a data center. This is the first obstacle in website marketing—making sure that the search engine has your website in its database. If it doesn't, it will never show up in the rankings.

When a user performs a search (regardless of the search engines, because they all run on this basic premise), the search is made of the documents contained in the search engine's database. That search returns a list of links to web pages and documents based on the factors in the ranking algorithm. The results are then displayed on the search engine results page (SERP).

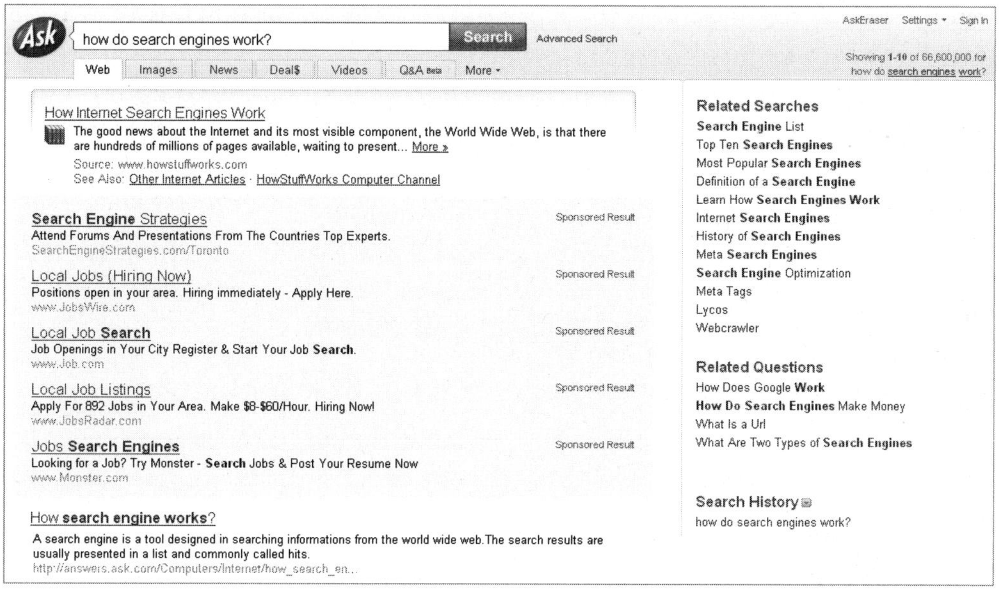

Figure 2.2   Search engine results page from Ask.com

What the searcher is being shown on the results page are links to web pages. However, those links are the product of archived data; the document (or page) that the search engine lists in the results, from its database, may not be the actual document (or page) that is live on the Web. The distinction is critical, and you may have experienced it. Have you ever clicked a result in the SERP and received a "page not found" error? (See Figure 2.3.)

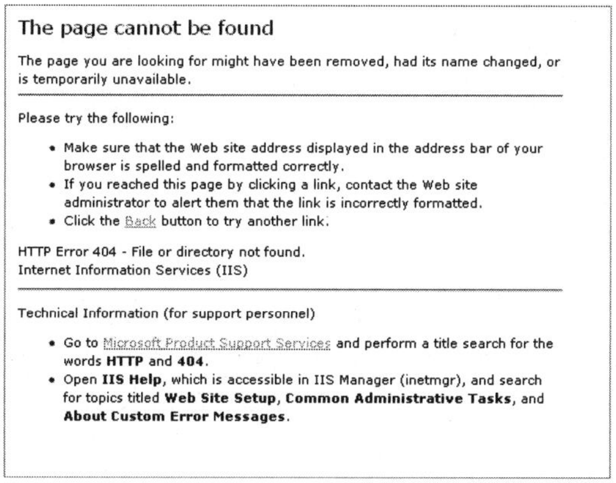

Figure 2.3   Error 404, "page not found" message

You get this error page, or something very similar, when you choose a link from the SERP but the live page is not available. What has happened is that the page is downloaded into the search engine's database and is relevant enough to gain rankings; however, for some reason, that page no longer exists or has been removed from the live website.

You do not go to the live page until you click the link; your browser then requests the actual document, and then you see the live page. *The main issue is that the search engines download a copy of your website to their server.* They need that copy in order to rank your web pages according to their algorithm. If they are not able to download a copy of your website, then your site will not show up in the search engines.

And that is really what the search engines are—massive data banks that store a duplicate copy of all the websites they can find. The ranking algorithm is used against all the downloaded copies of web pages, not the live pages.

In the past few years, SERPs have changed and will continue to evolve past the typical text-based list of sites recommended for your search. Currently, the search results will change based on what you might be searching for.

People

A search for *Bing Crosby* on Microsoft's Bing shows the integration of search results beyond the simple text-based website list. The official website of Bing Crosby, accompanying images, and a song list are readily accessed from the results page (Figure 2.4).

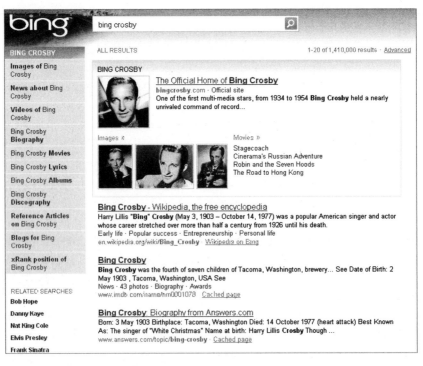

Figure 2.4 Bing search results: *Bing Crosby*

Search engines are integrating more multimedia and allowing deeper access to documents and media earlier in the search process. However, once again, they are attempting to determine the intent of the searcher and deliver results accordingly.

Places

If you are searching for a restaurant, the search engines are focusing on your intent to find and eat at that restaurant, so the results focus on providing as much information as possible (Figure 2.5).

Figure 2.5 Google search results: *st andrews NYC*

By simply narrowing a search to a business and location, Google determines the intent of my search and provides a map, address, phone number, bus route directions, and links to scores of reviews for the restaurant.

Things

Figure 2.6 shows one of my favorite results examples, a search for a PDF scanner.

This is an example of having more than one type of result on the results page. The number-two position is held by a video on YouTube by Tiger Direct. Rather than competing head-to-head in the results, Tiger Direct leveraged the popularity of YouTube to gain significant rankings visibility for its video. Just from the results, you can see that it is a seven-minute video, it is rated highly, and it provides a link to the product page. Yes, I bought the scanner—I couldn't help it. I was so impressed by the strategy that I had to support it.

After the YouTube video on the SERP, there is a product image and three results from Google Products. These are direct shopping results that provide retailer information for products and direct links into the listings. Retailers can upload a listing of their products to Google Products in order to gain visibility in this area.

Figure 2.6 Google search results: *PDF scanner*

Search engine results are being broken up by multiple media, all based on search terms. Searches for movies (Figure 2.7), restaurants, and maps will yield unique results based on the location and search.

Figure 2.7 Bing results for a movie search

Product-based searches show "how-to" videos and product results. News topic searches produce real-time results from Twitter and latest news feeds from all over the world (Figure 2.8).

With each search, the search engines will customize the results specific to your need, attempting to provide you with the best and most relevant experience possible.

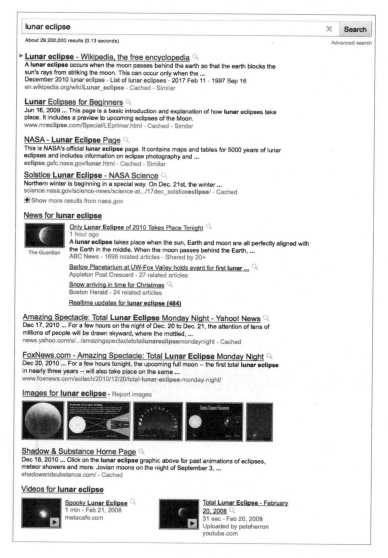

Figure 2.8 Up-to-date search results and real-time updates within the news results.

Understanding the Vocabulary

If you have ever spent any time in the presence of a search engine optimization specialist, then you will know that they tend to rattle off an impressive vocabulary of amazing words and acronyms. To the uninitiated, it is very easy to become overwhelmed by a series of familiar words that are being used in unfamiliar contexts.

Starting out with defining search engine terminology, we find that not only are the words unfamiliar but there are also multiple words that mean the same thing. This is a result of a largely decentralized industry that was born out of self-discovery rather than a university course. Early search engine optimizers found out how to rank well in the search engines largely by accident, and they researched for themselves how and why it happened. Many shared their findings on message boards, and multiple communities sprang up around the Internet for these self-taught practitioners. Because this industry was based on discovery and reaction, there was no centralized authority in place that designated official terms, practices, or guidelines. Essentially, Internet marketing has always been a "Wild West" sort of activity, and it remains that way today.

Bots, Crawlers, and Spiders

The first term you need to know is probably the most widely used and interchangeable word in the industry. The software program that search engines run in order to find websites and gather the content of those sites is called a *spider*. It is also called a *bot*, short for "robot" but much cooler. It is also called a *crawler*, because it "crawls" the Web, searching for documents.

Our very first lesson provides many difficulties for people, because it involves various words that essentially mean the same thing. I've been in many conversations where people will refer to the spider but then call it a bot, even in the same sentence!

Understanding the behavior of this software is the first critical component of understanding how search engines work. The spider requests documents and downloads them for processing. By *documents*, I am referring to web pages, PDF files, Word documents, spreadsheets, image files, and so on. Anything that is linked on the Web is considered a document. The most common form of document that we are working with in this book is the web page.

Information Retrieval

People tend toward anthropomorphism when dealing with search engines. Anthropomorphism is a fancy way of saying that we label nonhuman or abstract concepts with human-type emotions, actions, or features in order to better understand them. This is great if you understand the concepts initially. If you don't, well, then you will be confused. By giving search engines human characteristics, we blur the line between technical and emotional, which makes even more complicated explanations necessary for understanding this process.

The concept that is being communicated when someone says a search engine "sees you" is *information retrieval*. A search engine uses the spider (or bot) to request documents across the Internet. It then stores these documents in the data center—as explained earlier. The process of finding, cataloging, and then presenting those documents in a search result is called *information retrieval*.

Simply put, if someone tells you that the search engine can't see your website, it means the search engine spiders have not found and cataloged your website and stored it in their data center. This can be the result of multiple issues, most of which will be presented in Part IV of this book, but the main point is that something may be preventing the search engine spider from finding, indexing, and storing your website's pages.

Index

The *index* is where the requested documents are stored. It is the search engine's database, kept in a data center full of computers dedicated to maintaining copies of all documents found online. Search engines have multiple data centers around the world, because they have cataloged millions of documents from the Internet and they need someplace to store those documents for the retrieval process.

The first part of search engine optimization is to ensure that the website and all of its pages are being *indexed*. That is, the website has been requested and is cataloged in the search engine's database. This is verified by simply searching for that page in a search engine in order to verify that it has been downloaded and stored.

The second part of this process is to ensure that the indexed document is in a complete form, that is, that the information on the web page is the version that the search engine has cataloged.

All search engines need the three elements shown in Figure 2.9—architecture, links, and content—to properly find your website, follow links, and read the content. It is a mix of all three elements that will provide a search engine–friendly website. The architecture of a website has to be built properly, allowing the search engine to find and follow the internal links from page to page. As the search engine downloads all of the pages, the content has to be on the page and in the programming in a format that will be easily read and evaluated by the search engine. Without these three elements, your site will not be found by the search engines. We will deal with specific technical issues in Part IV of this book, along with some checklists for discovering your current situation in Part II.

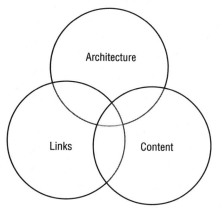

Figure 2.9 What search engines need

Snippets

The *snippet* is a critical piece of information presented to the user. Essentially, *it is the first marketing message a searcher will ever see about your website.* The snippet is composed of a few simple elements: the link to the website, a description of the page, and the filename and location of the document. A snippet of the San Diego Zoo (see Figure 2.10) also incorporates active links into the website, such as hours of operation, live cams, jobs, and local hotels.

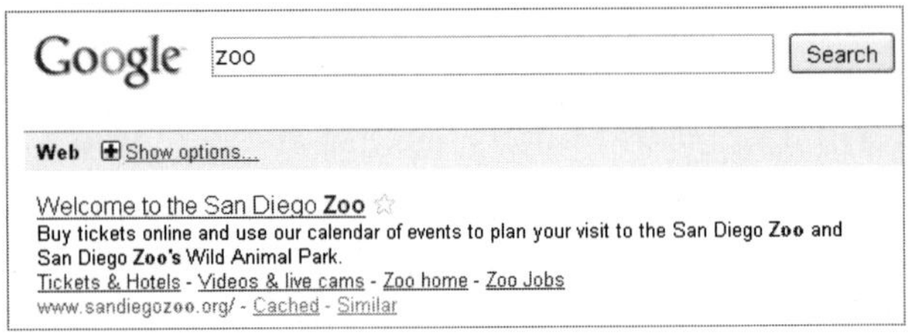

Google | zoo | Search

Web ⊞ Show options...

Welcome to the San Diego **Zoo** ☆
Buy tickets online and use our calendar of events to plan your visit to the San Diego **Zoo** and San Diego **Zoo**'s Wild Animal Park.
Tickets & Hotels - Videos & live cams - Zoo home - Zoo Jobs
www.sandiegozoo.org/ - Cached - Similar

Figure 2.10 Google search snippet: San Diego Zoo

This snippet is a critical part of getting people to click through to your website, because it must have three criteria for success:

- Be clear
- Be concise
- Be compelling

There should be no question as to what the searcher will find on the other side of the link.

HTML or Code

The HTML, or *code*, of the website contains the instructions to display the content through the browser. The code consists of directions, written mostly in Hypertext Markup Language (HTML), that specify the alignment of the content, the text size, the color, and the font. Image placement, background color, and all of the elements on the page are defined and arranged through the HTML.

The code also contains elements for server data, scripts for tracking visitors, scripts for animated functions, and other instructive data. The search engines "read" this code to find the content and also "read" the HTML to find the layout instructions for the text. In a sense, the search engines read the HTML to find out what content is in the headline, subheading, image captions, and more.

The search engines do not see the site the same way as you do through the browser. The best way to see what the search engines "see" is to right-click with your mouse on a web page and select View Source. That is the code, the content, and the set of instructions for the layout of the content that the search engines copy.

Analytics

There is a difference between website statistics and analytics. Website statistics are provided usually by an automated program that displays charts, graphs, and basic visitor information. Statistics are static information. *Analytics* is the practice of taking website-produced data and using it to improve your website.

Just about every activity on a website can be tracked—how visitors arrive at your website, what page they first see, the link they choose to move to the next page, how long they stay on that page, and how they move through the rest of the website. Analysts love to track visitor behavior from the entry to conversion, because that provides a spectacular amount of data and information that can be used to advance the website and the processes required of the visitor.

If you are looking at website data and just reporting the numbers that are published each month, you are simply reporting website statistics. Analytics takes a complete view of the website and is an active searching and questioning of the behavior and activity that takes place on the website. In other words, analytics is questioning and answering; statistics are simply reporting.

Part VI will cover analytics much more and will focus on specific tactics you can implement that will improve your overall marketing, SEO campaigns, usability, copywriting, content development, and advertising campaigns.

Conversion

The word *conversion* has been used at a few points already in this text, and it is a critical word, because it is the purpose of your website. Your primary goal for the visitor is the conversion.

The conversion can be whatever you define—a purchase, registration, phone call, download, lead form, ad click, donation, newsletter subscription, or page view. It is all based on the type of website you have, the business purpose, and how you make money. The conversion is the point that the visitor takes an action that leads to your business profitability.

It isn't bad to have more than one conversion goal; in fact, it is encouraged. It is best to have a primary conversion goal and then secondary conversion goals. For example, on an ecommerce site, if the visitor does not purchase, then the secondary goal is for the visitor to subscribe to the newsletter, so at the very least there is a new name to add to the mailings and there is potential for a primary conversion later.

How Search Engines Used to Work

Most of the confusion about search engines and how they work comes from the drastic changes that happened in the search engine industry around 1999–2000. Prior to that time, search marketing was a very different process than it is today. Articles written about gaining rankings in the 1990s reflect a different market from today's;

however, those articles and documents are still floating around online, providing an endless source of both frustration and amusement to online marketers. If you have ever searched using a search engine for information about search engine optimization, then you know what I mean. For a search engine, relevance is everything; however, a search for content about search engine optimization yields very unsatisfactory results. The information is outdated, conflicting, sometimes dangerous, and rarely cohesive.

With the distinct change in search engines around the turn of the millennium, there was a change in tactics. In addition, there was a change in mentality. It crept in silently, as SEO specialists realized that rankings weren't the pinnacle of success. When analytics started being used to measure business goals, the point of getting a site to rank well became secondary. Business goals and increased sales or leads quickly became the desired metric for success.

When I started to understand search engine optimization, it was because of a website that I was operating and marketing, and it was my primary source of income. When I had the time to work on this website, I was faced with a choice. Do I work on all of these techniques that my users won't see and may help my rankings? Or, do I spend my time on the content that the users *will* see? When your time and resources are limited, you find out very quickly which activities lead to increased revenue, and you work on those activities. That was the choice that I made, and in looking back, it was the right one. It taught me that regardless of all the shortcut techniques and advice that SEO specialists shared, the longest-lasting and most rewarding thing you could do to your website was to build quality content that searchers actually wanted to see and provide a compelling reason for them to take action on your website.

All of the old-school techniques had something in common. They were shortcuts at gaining rankings, and one-by-one they all fell out of favor with the search engines. It became easier for search engines to discover these techniques as the technology improved, and your website could be penalized and possibly dropped out of the rankings for utilizing some of these techniques. The sites that focused on their message and the user maintained their rankings and their profitability and survived.

The following are some of the "old-school" optimization and search engine tactics that used to be employed. When you see an article about these tactics, simply laugh and remember the good ol' days of search engine trickery—or, as we in the business call these tactics, "partying like it's 1999!"

Old-School: Submitting to Search Engines

Back in the mid-1990s—or in Internet terms, the "caveman days" of search engine optimization—the search engines did not use spiders (bots, crawlers) as the primary means of finding new websites on the Internet. Because of this, webmasters had to submit their URLs or even all the URLs of their entire website in order to be included in the search engine's database of websites.

To complicate matters even more, some search engines would give you a boost in the rankings based on how recently you submitted your website into the index. Simply based on this premise, you can imagine the activity that resulted. Webmasters flocked to these engines and continually submitted their pages so as to maintain their rankings. In short order, software was developed that would enable a program to automatically submit all the pages on a continuous schedule.

Essentially, the search engines operated on a principle that was exactly opposite of how they operate today. Today, they will find your site on their own and download your content and evaluate it. Back in the stone age of SEO, you would tell the search engine what your website was about, tell it the keywords that you should be found for, and submit the pages of your website that you wanted in the index.

Many businesses were built on this early practice of SEO. Unfortunately, when the practice of submitting your website was no longer necessary, there were still many companies that were able to sell website submission services. Many of these were unsolicited emails that claimed you could be found in the search engines by paying them $39.95, and they would submit your website to the top 20 search engines. Once in a while I still run into this claim today, but it is completely outdated. For one, I would like to hear how many people can name 10 search engines, much less 20.

Bottom line, there is no longer any reason to submit your website to the search engines. Google's Webmaster Guidelines even state, "The vast majority of sites listed in our results aren't manually submitted for inclusion, but found and added automatically when our spiders crawl the web."

Old-School: Keywords in Metatags

Another of those "rock-solid" pieces of advice that seems to have held on past its time is the SEO technique of adding keywords into the metatags. At one time, this was the bread and butter of the SEO specialist's website work. Search engines utilized this tag in order to rank sites according to the relevant words that were written into this element.

Just as an aside, metatags, which will be explained more in Chapters 5 and 6, are elements within the code of each web page. *Meta* is a Greek word meaning "after" or "behind," which is a great way of picturing this element. Metatags are not visible to the website visitor, because they are behind the scenes and written into the code. They are "behind" the web page. Metatags were originally intended to be the card catalog to the Internet, allowing documents to be neatly organized into logical groupings by author, keyword, subject matter, and so on. Unfortunately, nothing about allowing webmasters to promote their own websites on the Internet is organized, logical, or neat.

Of course, as with every other early SEO technique, this was abused to the point of disgrace. As soon as the word spread that the keyword metatag was the primary factor that search engines used to rank your site, site owners started to utilize it to their complete advantage. Perhaps the most egregious use of this was using words such as

Disneyland, *Mickey Mouse*, and *Britney Spears* as the metatag keywords for adult sites simply as a means of gaining rankings for those terms, which resulted in some very surprised people.

The failure in this system is that for the most part, the search engines believed what was written in the metatags and did not verify it against the content of the website. This made for unethical uses of the technique, because many webmasters were paid by visitor numbers, so simply getting people to the website was the goal. You could get a lot of people to your website if you ranked for a lot of terms, even if they weren't relevant.

Of course, time went on, and the search engines wised up. Fewer and fewer search engines relied on keyword metatags as the knowledge of their misuse became legendary. Today, the keyword metatag is not used as a rankings factor for any of the major search engines. My advice is that there are things more worth your time than stuffing a bunch of keywords into the code that no one will look at.

Old-School: Background-Colored Text

This technique was formed out of the search engine improvements of spidering and evaluating the content that was actually on the page, not in the code. By taking content, basically a paragraph or list of keywords, and then adding that content on the page in a very small font and coloring the text the same color as the background, you could hide this very ugly paragraph of stunted phrases and keywords from the user. The nice side benefit of that was the search engine would "see" it and count it toward the amount of times you used the keywords. This technique, of course, would add to the number of times that your primary keywords occurred on the page, thereby giving you more leverage to rank well for those terms.

There were many variations to this technique. Some recommended using very tiny text for a paragraph of content at the top or bottom of the page. After the use of text that was the same color as the background started being penalized by the search engines, the recommendation changed to making it a slightly different shade of color than the background. See the sneaky themes by now?

It's not that hard for an algorithm to figure out what color the background color is, the text color, and so on. In the grand scheme of online marketing, this was a very small but prevalent technique. The main issue I had with this technique is that it takes away from the content quality. I found that webmasters and site owners were more intent on disguising text from the visitors than they were about crafting a compelling and persuasive message.

Old-School: Keyword Density

Keyword density was a "magical" formula that was based on older search engine algorithms, namely, AltaVista, which would look for the number of times that a word was used within the text on the page. The keyword density formula was created based on the percentage of occurrences of that word, which created a sense of relevance.

Of course, that sense of relevance was completely false as soon as word traveled throughout the Internet that there were specific keyword-density percentages for specific search engines. Webmasters and search marketers immediately created software tools that measured keyword density, and practical "hints" for strategic keyword placement became the fashion on the day.

Of course, much of this was done without regard to actual users reading the content on the website. If you were unlucky enough to have visited a web page that was created by an SEO specialist who was attempting to satisfy a 5 percent to 8 percent density formula, then you might be reading the same word repeatedly, which just becomes obnoxious.

Even worse, there were some who erred on the side of overkill and just overloaded their pages with words in an attempt to create relevance through repetition. This leads directly into the next old-school technique, keyword stuffing.

Old-School: Keyword Stuffing

This technique was marginally successful but rarely effective in terms of actually doing business, because most users who found this type of content simply left the site in search of higher quality.

Figure 2.11 shows a page that employed keyword stuffing. Keywords were stuffed into every imaginable place on the page, hidden or nonhidden, in an attempt to improve rankings. This figure shows keywords listed in alt attributes (behind images), in the content itself, and hidden by making the text the same color as the background. It can easily be found by simply highlighting the content, which shows any hidden words.

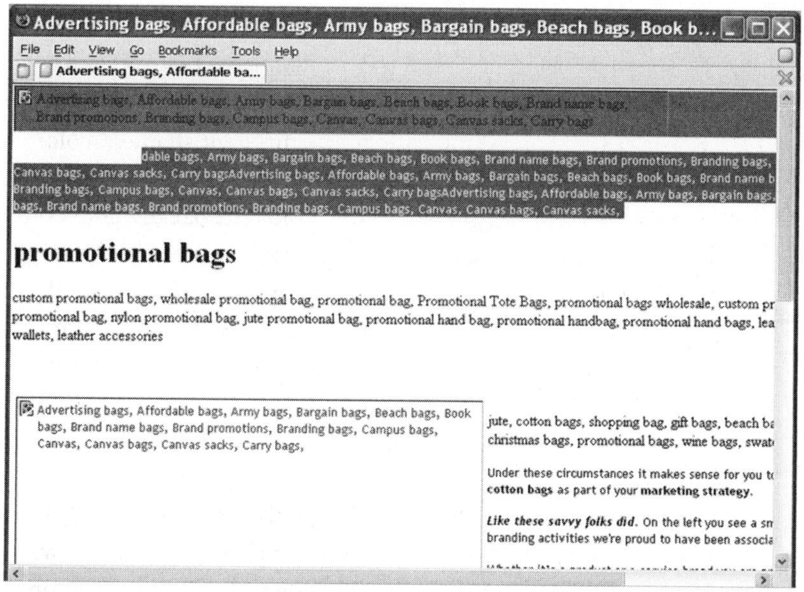

Figure 2.11 Keyword-stuffing techniques

All of this was done in the name of gaining rankings, yet the user was consistently the most overlooked factor in the marketing equation.

This technique is still used by many search engine optimizers and marketers. Somehow the old thinking of getting that "magical" percentage of keywords repeated on a single page of content will result in better rankings. It doesn't. It is overkill to your readers, and it is overkill to the search engines, which have gotten a little smarter over the years and can recognize when an overly aggressive optimizer is too repetitive. One of the best copywriting tips I received was from Karon Thackston at Marketing Words, who said, "Read your copy out loud; if it sounds too repetitive and unnatural, it probably is." Great advice.

People tend to be able to read sentences much faster and process the information easier than scanning through groups of keywords. Sentences offer a more complete thought and have the benefit of creating a context for the keyword, rather than simply regurgitating words. When convincing a searcher to click a link, purchase a product, or take action, well-written sentences that provide a strong context and a compelling message will always be more effective than repetitively "stuffing" words together.

In Part III, I'll be providing instructions on copywriting and stressing the importance of this important craft. In my experience, the ability to write well is the most underestimated task in online marketing.

Rankings or Profit? Establishing Your Business Goals

Many companies believe that the right mix of keywords, technical tricks, and tactics will result in great rankings, which, in turn, will result in good business. Nothing could be further from the truth.

High rankings do not equal profits. Nothing replaces a good business plan. Having your business goals in place and a proper understanding of what will create a profitable business is where an online business starts.

This chapter focuses on the importance of creating clear business goals. Whether you are an individual business owner, marketing manager, or entrepreneur, you have to start by establishing the goals for your business. Everything falls into place as a result of establishing your priorities.

Chapter Contents

Web Design by Alice

Many websites are caught up in what I like to call "Alice in Wonderland web design." I liken the strategy to the exchange in Disney's famous movie between Alice and the Cheshire Cat:

> *Alice: Would you tell me, please, which way I ought to go from here?*
> *Cheshire Cat: That depends a good deal on where you want to get to.*
> *Alice: I don't much care where....*
> *Cheshire Cat: Then it doesn't matter which way you go.*
> *Alice: So long as I get* somewhere!
> *Cheshire Cat: Oh, you're sure to do that, if you only walk long enough.*

Too many companies continually add pages, products, and press releases to their websites with no thought as to the direction, strategy, or primary purpose of their website. There is no specific business goal or visitor goal. As a result, our visitors wander through the content without a clear direction or goal as to what they should do—all because the business has not defined its purpose.

At the outset of my seminars, I always ask the attendees what their goals are. What is your number-one business goal? And, what is your number-one visitor goal? I'll never forget that one attendee spoke up and said that her goals were too simple. When asked what the goals were, she answered, "Make money; sell shoes." I was ecstatic. This is exactly the type of goal that every business owner or marketing manager should have readily in their mind. The simpler it is, the easier it is to communicate throughout the company.

The goals need to be written down, displayed, and advertised throughout the organization. These are the operating principles of your website, and every decision about your online-marketing strategy needs to be evaluated and measured according to those goals.

Every page of the website needs to be evaluated according to those stated goals. If a page does not reflect those goals, then it needs to be changed. If images, content, and design do not reflect those goals, then they need to be changed. If the primary call to action on the page does not reflect the goals, then it needs to be changed.

If the goals are not clear, then the organization of the website, its content, and it design will be fuzzy, and the visitor may never take your intended actions. Getting people to your website is one task, but getting them to do what you want keeps you in business. Too many businesses focus on acquiring visitors to the website but don't measure the factors that make a business successful.

Lack of Goals Shows in the Design

Being involved in website development projects for almost 15 years, I've seen any number of website design strategies and have become convinced that most companies design websites backward. The typical method of designing a website is to retain a web design company that then uses a graphic designer to produce a few versions of what your website should look like. Essentially the entire process is composed of an artist looking at your current site, creating a pretty picture of what they think your site should look like, and the company selecting which pretty picture will be the basis of its new website. This is backward. The website must be an extension of the business goals and support those goals with every page. This means that before any design is created, the purpose of the site, the focus of the content, and the goal of the visitor need to be established and developed into a marketing plan. That plan will determine how the website should look and feel but, more importantly, how it should be organized.

In Part IV, the content will go deeper into creating the information architecture and user interface, both of which are critical for good usability; building a successful marketing presence; and, as a nice side benefit, getting good rankings. In this chapter, the point is to focus on the purpose of design, which is to enable your website visitors to know who you are, what you do, why you are the best choice, and how to take action. If those elements are not immediately available because of the "prettiness" of the website, then you have lost your visitors.

A great architecture with clear navigation and obvious and readable clusters of content and links that help answer the visitor's questions do more to enable good rankings and good usability than an artist's initial vision of a website. The artist, while a critical part of the design process, should not be the architect. I liken it to moving into a new office building. I hope that the building was designed and built by the architect, not the artist. The architect understands the foundations, weights, human factors, and logistical layouts. The artist will add the touches that make the building human and connect with the tenants on a different level. The same is true for your website; an information architect will scope the website with a knowledge based on research, human factors, and business principles. Once that part is established, then the artist can be used to create a look and feel on top of the established architecture and business goals of the website.

Lack of Direction Becomes Evident in Marketing

The problem with unclear business goals isn't limited to site design; it extends to the entire organization's view of marketing. From content to function and from blogging to the entire social-media gambit, a lack of stated goals becomes more and more evident.

In no other area is an organization's lack of business focus more evident than in social media. If the marketing message is not clear, then it becomes even more diffused by the many reflections in each social-media application. When companies build a blog mainly because they heard it will increase their rankings, they neglect to make it a sales or acquisition tool. I find that the vast majority of business blogs neglect to integrate their business message or their website into the blog. The blog is developed as a stand-alone presence, and the marketing message is lost, simply because the purpose was not established prior to the practice.

I was reviewing some articles on analytics when I caught the DM News Special Report on Analytics on August 14, 2006 (www.dmnews.com/cms/lib/6502.pdf). I was impressed at the amount of information contained about the business case for analytics, all coming from some very intelligent people. The great thing was the consistent thread of thought throughout the entire report: analytics is growing, and it's more than web stats—it is marketing intelligence. Unfortunately, the gold mine is sitting untouched, because many businesses are unaware of the untold riches sitting just a few feet away.

However, this grabbed my attention more than anything else in the report:

Web analytics works best when measurement expectations are clearly defined in advance, not after the fact or on an ad-hoc basis.

—Eric Peterson

This is not only the essence of analytics; it is the essence of business. How can you expect a business to succeed when there are no measurements along the way to provide correction and guidance? I cannot count the numbers of marketing managers who are overwhelmed in their jobs and have no clear measurement expectations. The reports they request have only to do with the "window dressing" of visitors and nothing to do with the bottom line profitability of the website. Those marketing managers are the ones nodding their heads in agreement whenever I show that quote. They understand the circular path of reporting random events, rather than focusing on a specific goal and measuring according to that goal.

If businesses were to simply state their goals and to measure website performance according to those goals, the improvement would be revolutionary. Before there can be any improvement, the first step is to set a well-defined business goal. Those who practice goal setting are those who tend to succeed in business. The same is true of websites. They must have a goal, both for the owner and for the visitor. Unless that goal is declared, there is no way to determine success or failure. The only way to sift through the mountains of data, the hundreds of charts and graphs, and the pages of "top 10" lists is to have a specific set of goals to measure. By measuring against specific goals, the data will suddenly fall away as you remove what is not necessary to the overall goals. Good analytics programs allow you to strip away the stuff you don't want or need to see. They allow you to focus on the key indicators that are relevant to your site's performance.

Bottom line, if you don't have clearly defined goals for your online-marketing strategy, then no amount of analytics will assist you in making the right decisions.

Lack of Consistency Backfires with Social Media

It becomes very evident in social-media marketing when companies don't have a clear vision or goal of how they want to be perceived or their primary purpose. It results in Facebook pages that are bland, Twitter messages that are overly promotional rather than conversational, and YouTube accounts that contain a 20-minute employee training video from 1977. Without a clear goal and strategy, the rush toward social media becomes one with a directive of "We need to be there!" rather than evaluating "What can we do there?" The social-media message becomes disjointed, because there is no clear message, and the purpose becomes lost.

Non-goal-oriented social-media presences also tend to be stand-alone, because they neglect to drive visitors to a particular destination. As businesses rush to get into social media, they forget to take visitors back to the primary website in order to fulfill their goal. Companies see social media as a confusing and overwhelming necessity, especially when consultants are constantly extolling the many virtues of social-media reach. However, their hesitation is justified. So many companies question the time involved and the results returned. Time management is tough enough already, so what will Twittering a few hundred times a month do for a company? The answer is that different social-media outlets bring different results, so businesses need to focus on different ways to use each channel. Simply throwing time and interns at new social media will not produce results. The social-media efforts need to be tied into the company marketing strategy so that a clear message is always consistent.

The famous Marshall McLuhan mantra "The medium is the message" means you cannot treat all social media the same. Each social-media channel is completely different, so the message and tactics used need to be adapted for each medium. Many companies are more suited to a YouTube strategy, because they need the visual video medium to better communicate their unique advantages. Other businesses that require a pulse on early adopters and masses of opinions find Twitter to be an ideal (primarily) text-based tool. Dell tech support is a great example of this, because Twitter allows Dell to find those early adopters and touch them as soon as a user tweets a complaint about their Dell computer. Within minutes, a Dell rep is in contact with the user (I say this based on personal experience). This strategy does not work in a YouTube environment, only in the fast, text-based world of Twitter.

Facebook provides a safe method of reaching fans and allowing them to take part in your marketing. Volkswagen, for example, allows fans to upload pictures of their VW vehicles, and there is a strong subgroup of classic Beetle fans. The conversation on VW's main Facebook page is primarily fan-driven, and at the time of this writing, there are more than 175,000 fans. The photo gallery contains more than 1,700 pictures, again, mostly uploaded from fans. Volkswagen is able to utilize Facebook's fan interactions, which plays to its strength of creating a loyal customer base that reaches back for decades.

Your company does not have to spread efforts among all the social-media services if it doesn't make sense. Find what works and what spreads your message the most effectively, and focus on that channel. However, developing a strategy that works for your company requires that your business goals be clear and concise and that social media will assist those goals, rather than becoming a goal in itself. If a business is clear in its message before delving into social media, then that business is most likely able to retain that message and adapt it to the media. Otherwise, as is so common, businesses try social media and are not able to adapt their strategies to it, and the masses end up controlling their message and draining their time.

I appreciate the companies that know enough to slow down and ask questions. Be aware of the time invested, and develop a strategy. Make sure that strategy fulfills the goals of the business. Without taking the time to coordinate your message across a variety of media, your efforts will be disjointed and discouraging. Again, it all comes down to the basic principles of clearly defining your goals. What do you want to accomplish, how will you accomplish it, and what do you expect visitors to do? When the goals are established, measurement becomes clear, and a clear strategy will emerge.

Search Rankings Are Not a Goal

Leads, sales, and subscriptions are goals. Rankings are one of many means to those goals. They are an influence but not the measurement of success. Too many businesses think that as soon as they have a few keywords ranking number one in Google, they will be successful. In reality, there is much more to being successful, such as designing what customers will see on the other side of the search results. If your website doesn't reflect the quality implied by your rankings, then visitors won't stick around to contribute to your success.

Great rankings won't support a bad business model. Gaining rankings for your website is a goal to have, but it is not the immediate path to success. There are many websites that are having great success without ranking for one or two "winning" terms. This is where I like to refer to *visibility* rather than rankings. I would rather have hundreds or thousands of terms ranking well than a single term in the top spot. When evaluating the traffic patterns of visitors, the broad search terms (such as *cars*, *cameras*, and *computers* tend to bring in a lot of visitors but not *conversions*, which is more of a factor in success than rankings).

Rankings Do Not Equal Sales

In the same way that more visitors do not equal more business higher rankings do not necessarily provide better visitors. The key is to measure the factors that directly contribute to success. Of course, rankings and visitor numbers are good factors, but they are not the *only* contributions. Unless there is also a factor of quality or accomplishment tied to those visitors, then you have succeeded in only part of the equation.

This goes back to the account that I related in Chapter 1, where my website ranked highly in multiple search engines for many terms, yet the sales came from a direct link. The decision to invest time and money in rankings and search referrals would have been the wrong decision, because that was not the direct cause of profits. This is the point where we realize the principles of marketing and, even more, direct marketing apply also to online marketing. There is a difference between *visitors* and *qualified visitors*. Finding the qualified visitors and investing in those channels will provide a better use of time and resources than the scattered "shotgun approach." More doesn't equate to better. *Better* is better.

Your Rankings Reports Are Wrong

In later chapters, I will cover analytics and measuring your business goals, because the task of building an equation of rankings, visitors, effectiveness, and goal completion will provide a better analysis of true success in your marketing efforts. Take your marketing beyond the rankings, and find the true factors in your success. Otherwise, you could be wasting valuable hours in optimizing and rankings for words that don't work for you. But now, I would like to outline a few examples of why rankings reports are outdated and the wrong measurement for success.

Ranking-Report Software

Search engines do not like ranking-report software. Period. Software-automated search queries drain resources and bandwidth and inflate ad impressions, which are used to compute quality for pay-per-click ads. Therefore, Google is particularly aggressive about blocking repeated queries from the same computer or business. Google would rather keep advertisers happy than serve overly aggressive search marketers who check their rankings incessantly.

To satisfy marketers who need to check their rankings, search engines have allowed access via an application programming interface (API) *key*. It is a code that tells the search engine who is accessing the database and the program accessing the data. This allows the search engine to direct automated software using the API to specific data sets and resources. Without utilizing the API key for the reports, you could be temporarily blocked from accessing the search engine. (Google in particular is aggressive about these types of programs taking resources away from its core service of serving search results to "real" searchers. When Google detects that too many searches have been requested from the same source and at regular intervals, it simply shuts down your access. You get a page that nicely tells you that you are blocked from further access as the result of too many automated queries, from either a computer virus or other software program.)

If you do use the API key to check rankings, what will be immediately apparent is that the results from the rank-checking software will show rankings for your website that are not consistent with the live results. It is more accurate for a client to simply open a browser and search for words and rankings manually. Having someone run a rankings report to share with others is inaccurate by nature. Be sure to explain to anyone involved the expectations that the results from automated rank-checking software may be different from what they will see in their own searches. However, rank-checking software is good for checking trends at the outset of a project. Tracking large jumps in rankings after optimizing multiple pages of your website is the best use. Tracking the movement in rankings is unreliable when tracking small changes (such as a move of a web page from a number-five ranking to a number-three ranking).

Personalized Search

With the advent of users creating accounts with the search engines, personal search histories have been accumulated. Personalized search is important to the search engines in many ways, not the least of which is personalized advertising that can be crafted solely for you, based on your preferences, search history, and associated accounts. Personalization will affect search results based on your past searches, location of your access, click-through rates, and other behaviors. After all, the search engines are attempting to provide the best, most relevant results to the searcher, and using a person's search history will enable the engine to adjust the results as necessary to create that personal relevance. As a result, the rankings you see may differ from those your neighbor sees, simply based on your interaction with the search engine. I expect this practice to continue to grow as the line between privacy and advertising desires becomes increasingly blurred. Many people choose to give up privacy in order to receive more relevant advertising and do not see the risks.

Results Promotion

Google recently instituted a search-results feature called *promote results* (Figure 3.1). It's simple. If you like one result over another, simply promote the result by clicking the up-arrow button next to a result. That moves the result to the top of the page, where it will appear whenever you search for the same keyword. Many webmasters see this as a means to affect rankings, but if it does so at all, it is on a very minute scale.

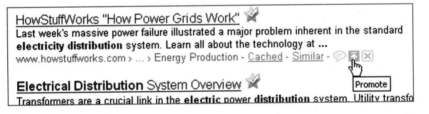

Figure 3.1 Promoting a result

I have seen results promotion used very effectively by marketing managers who are able to go into their boss's computer and promote their website for specific search terms. That way, to the boss, the company seems to be ranking as number one, so the boss leaves the marketing department alone and stops demanding to know why the website is not ranking first. This is a good illustration of ranking results being misleading!

Multiple Search Engine Data Centers

Each search engine has data centers located all over the world. This makes it effective to serve the millions of simultaneous searches that take place all of the time. For efficiency, each search engine query is routed to the most appropriate data center, which will return results based on its snapshot of the search index. Your co-workers may be sitting right next to you, send the same search query, but see different results because the query was sent to a different data center. Data centers are consistently being updated, and it is very easy to see different results, usually only within a few rankings, from a search of different data centers.

Regional Weighting

A New Yorker searching for the term *zoo* on Google is likely to get results that show the Bronx Zoo as being the most relevant result. A Google searcher in Southern California will see the San Diego Zoo as number one. Regional searches are being weighted and slowly implemented by the search engines. Obviously, this doesn't work with all terms, because many are worldwide in scope. However, within the past few years, Google has placed a heavy emphasis on local results, maps, and business listings. Offering searchers local-based results creates more advertising inventory and also connects users to locally based providers. Intentional or not, Google is turning the world market back into a local market. Locally based searches provide a more relevant result to a local searcher.

Social Network

One of my recent searches turned up a surprise, as Google rolled out another beta program that affects the search results. Google showed articles from friends of mine in the first page of results (Figure 3.2). The reason that my friends were in the first page was because I was logged in, had a Google social profile, and Google was recommending other friends' articles as a result of our social profiles being linked. Without being logged in to my Google account, my friends' articles would not have appeared in the first page of results.

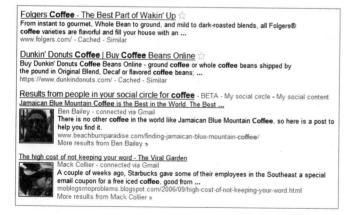

Figure 3.2 Google Social Circle Beta, showing connected friends' articles

Continual changes like this Social Profile Suggestion Beta program show the direction that a search engine like Google is heading. Google is integrating social recommendations, multimedia, personalization, and regionalization as a way of customizing search results specific to a person. The more information you provide to Google through your account, the more Google can customize your search results. The days of gaining the number-one ranking in Google and knowing that everyone searching will see that number-one ranking are over. ∎

Set Better Goals

The typical duties of an online marketer working with no established goals are simple:

1. Open the analytics panel.

2. Take the numbers of unique visitors, total visitors, and other "important" numbers, and copy them into a report.

3. Distribute the report.

   Then one of two things happens:

- No one reads the report.

- Someone reads the report and wants to know why visitors are down from the previous month. Then the analyst spends the rest of the week attempting to offer some reason or excuse for the visitor numbers.

This is what I call hamster-wheel analytics (Figure 3.3).

©ISTOCKPHOTO.COM/OHIOPHOTO

Figure 3.3 Hamster-wheel analytics

With hamster-wheel analytics, there is no progress made—only reporting of past performance. Even then, the past performance is usually limited to the larger numbers gathered from the report. If the goal of the website is to increase visitors, then wonderful—report visitors. However, there should at least be some kind of analysis of effective visitor sources that can provide insight to future campaigns.

If the goals are to sell products, generate leads, gather subscriptions, or meet other action-based goals, then measuring total visits and visitors is an incomplete picture of the actual business of marketing. It is equivalent to a brick-and-mortar store owner counting walk-ins rather than receipts. You can't make money based on walk-ins, and you don't stay in business long without analyzing receipts.

Too many marketing managers get locked into this endless cycle of reporting numbers that change consistently based upon hundreds of factors: seasonality, search engine changes, website changes, email campaigns, and press releases are just a few of the factors that can affect website traffic. Unless a marketing manager is measuring the performance of the website according to goals of the business, these factors will be external and rarely included in the "big-picture" view of why things change. Mike Moran, author of *Search Engine Marketing Inc.* (IBM Press, 2005), wrote this:

> *If you say to yourself that you are working on search optimization because you believe it will make you money, that's not a business, that's a religion. Instead, put search on the same footing as every other business decision and optimize your business instead of your search campaign.*

Mike and I see eye to eye on this. Measuring your business goals through analytics is not just about numbers; it's about improvements, processes, experience, and planning. You don't have to be doomed to repeat the same failed campaigns. History teaches powerful lessons, and analytics are a primary tool for learning those lessons.

To get started, ask yourself the following questions:

- *What is my primary business goal?*
- *What is the visitor goal for my website?* List the revenue-generating actions that visitors can take on your website. Consider everything from direct sales to leads, newsletter subscriptions, downloads, registrations, contact forms, and so on. The most definitive step in analyzing the goals of the website are creating those goals and understanding the value of each goal.

Calculate the Value of a Lead

Even lead-generation websites need to establish the value of a lead. Think of the valuable business intelligence you could have if you were able to calculate the value of your leads from different sources: trade shows, direct mailings, website, or sales calls. If you were able to calculate the return and see the value of each lead source, you'd be able to adjust your marketing strategy to go after the best source of profitable leads.

I learned this lesson in telemarketing. It was the worst two weeks of my life. In college, I took a job at a local telemarketing firm for some extra Christmas cash. I was miserable. I hated to interrupt people's dinner time and try to sell them something they didn't need, want, or ask for. Making 30 to 40 or more cold calls in an evening created more than enough "no" responses than I could stand. I didn't enjoy this job that paid me a measly $6 an hour.

However, across the cubicle was an employee who loved his job. He happily made his calls, was extremely cheerful, and felt that he had the greatest job in the world. I finally had to ask him what made this job so wonderful, because I was languishing in misery. He explained that he made $3.50 every time he picked up the phone. Well, that got my attention! I'm making $6.50 an hour, and he is making $3.50 for every call? Why was he getting paid so much? And what kind of payment plan is that? He explained." If I make 50 calls a night, I know that on average, 10 people will listen. Out of those 10 people, I average 2 people who will make a commitment. If I average those numbers for a week, then I will get a bonus. If I average those numbers for the month, I get another bonus. Add in the top closer bonus, and I average $3.50 for each phone call...." I was stunned. I saw the call as the problem. He saw the call as already-earned value, which contributed directly to his success.

Calculating the value of a lead can provide an amazing insight into measuring success on the website. I find that as soon as marketers place dollar signs next to their website reports, it gets interesting, and people take notice.

Measure According to the Goal

Strangely enough, although most businesses are focused on making money with their websites, they settle for reports that focus on data that does not provide recommendations for improvement. I am generally surprised at the level of data that businesses will settle for.

At this point, I like to paraphrase one of Socrates' famous sayings as, "The unexamined website is not worth hosting." Unless a business is reporting business value focused on continual improvements, the site is in a state of stagnation. Problems go unaddressed, and the website underperforms. I'll address analytics in greater detail later in the book, as well as the dangers of the "typical" reporting cycle. At this point, though, you should write down your goals for your website. Write down the current and potential conversion points, and assign value to them—or, at the very least, a means of developing value in the near future.

Primary Goals

- What is the business purpose of your website?
- What is the primary action that you want visitors to take?

Secondary Goals

- If visitors do not take the primary action, then what do you want them to do?
- List supplementary conversion (visitor action) points that contribute to your business, marketing, or building your email list.

Month 1: Evaluate and Research

In order to know how to improve, you will have to assess your current situation. The conflicting part is that in order to diagnose important parts of your website and marketing strategy, you will have to be exposed to some concepts and terminology that may be unfamiliar. Don't be intimidated by this. Latter chapters will explain these things more in-depth. So, if you come across content or words that just don't seem to make sense make a note on the page and come back to it later. You should even come back to this section after completing the book, and after you have made improvements to your website, as the checklists and evaluation methods should always be part of a periodic review of your website.

Week 1: Evaluate Your Situation

4

Once you've written your goals, you can work toward achieving them. First you need to diagnose any current problems. Evaluating all the issues will enable a knowledgeable approach, which will result in high-return areas building momentum for low-return changes.

Create a standards document based on your business goals to make any new website search-friendly and user-friendly from the start. By clearly defining the purpose and goals of your business and how you want people to use your site, you will be more equipped to respond to design and development suggestions. Every issue that comes up in the development process can then be evaluated against the primary goals of your marketing.

Chapter Contents
Monday: Find your Search Engine–Friendliness
Tuesday: Use Search Engine Tools to Check Your Website
Wednesday: Use Firefox's Free Tools
Thursday: Follow the W3C Accessibility Checklists
Friday: Find Human-Friendliness

Monday: Find Your Search Engine–Friendliness

As covered in previous chapters, search engines make a copy of your website that resides in their servers. Today's activities represent the initial exploration into the technical world of the search engines and how they see your existing website. Primarily, this section will teach you how to see whether the search engines have found your website or whether they have downloaded the pages.

Check the Number of Pages Indexed

The fastest way to check on the number of pages indexed by a search engine is to do a simple search. By typing the command **site:yourdomain.com** in the search box of the major search engines, the search engine will show a list of the pages indexed and cataloged in the database.

Of course, for this check to be meaningful, you need to have an idea of the number of pages in your website. If you have a larger website or one that has multiple publishers or has grown over the years, knowing the number of actual pages can be a tricky prospect. What you are looking for in this query is for the number of pages indexed by the search engines to be close to the number of pages in your website. One sign that there is trouble right away is if only two or three pages appear in the list. Sometimes, for websites that are built with Flash, you will see a few pages, the Flash movie file, and that's about it. Obviously, the search engine has not been able to get beyond the main page of Flash programming.

Having significantly fewer pages appear than you expect also happens with some programming issues that cause the URLs to be too long or difficult for the search engines to follow. This is happening more and more infrequently and tends to be the result of a programming resource more than it is the fault of the search engine. If this is identified as a problem for you, Chapters 13 through 15 will explore more technical reasons you may be having problems and how to fix them. If you are designing a new site, then those same chapters will help you avoid big problems with the search engines by knowing specifically what to avoid and why. By educating yourself to be able to respond competently to programming and development questions before the process, you will avoid a lot of frustration after the site launches.

If no pages appear in the list, that means the search engine has not "seen" or downloaded your website. This could be happening for many reasons. The primary reason is that there may be no links to your website from any other websites. Search engines use links from web pages to find new pages and new websites on the Web. If no one is linking to your site, then the search engines may not have found it.

A secondary reason for your site not to show in the search engines is likely a technical issue that prevents the search engine from properly accessing the pages of your website. Chapters 13 and 14 address typical technical traps that keep sites from performing well.

Perform a Snippet Check

Just as important as checking to see whether the search engines have downloaded a copy of your website is making sure it is the correct copy. Therefore, you should check the snippet of information that shows up in the search engine results page for your website (see Figure 4.1).

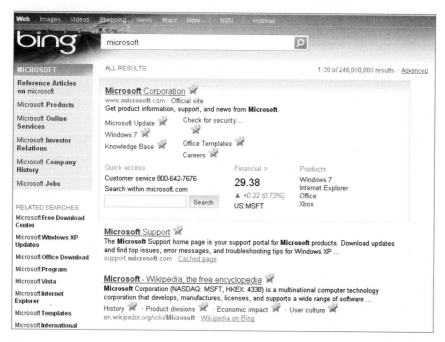

Figure 4.1 Bing: the search engine results "snippet"

The snippet is a critical piece of information about the page and about your company. *It is the first marketing message a searcher will see about your company.* It must be compelling, congruent, and clear about the content that the searcher will find on the page. Simply because a website is ranked at the top does not mean that it will get the clicks. Many sites have great rankings but do a very poor job of compelling a searcher to click.

Perform a search for your company name or brand name. Check your snippet two ways. First, search for your company or brand name, and evaluate the snippet you find. Second, search for a general term, one that you know you have rankings, and evaluate the snippet. You will see that the snippet changes based on the words being searched. Is the company name in the title field (the blue underlined text)? The text content in the snippet will change based on the search. For example, a brand-name search will result in snippets that contain the brand name, and the search term will be highlighted in bold. If your website ranks for an important search term, the term will be bold in the snippet (Figure 4.2).

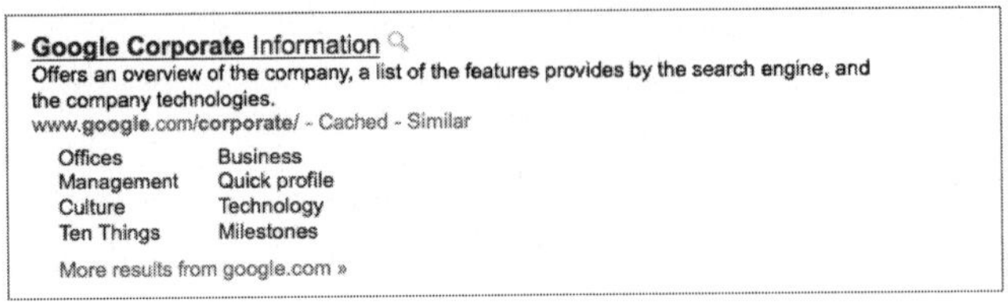

Figure 4.2 Google: the search engine results "snippet"

The text content is pulled from various sources; the meta description tag in the page header (in the code), the content on the page, or in the case of Google from the Open Directory Project (www.dmoz.org) if there is no other content available in the meta description or on the page.

Most search engines tend to build the text content of the snippet from the page's meta description (though the text content may be pulled from the page as well). Marketers can impact the text content of the snippet but not control it. It is still arranged on-the-fly by the search engine in order to show the most relevant content from the page. Although the content in the meta description does not count as a primary field for rankings and relevance, it is used in the snippet, which is the primary information a searcher will use to evaluate your site against the other results in a search. The power of the text content in the snippet can draw more clicks to your website by showing the comprehensive content of your website.

Remember, searchers have a question, and they will click sites that appear to have their answer. Well-crafted titles and snippets can draw searchers to your website. In rare cases, the snippet will show content from your website's listing from a directory, usually the Open Directory Project. This is not recommended, because you can better control the snippet with the content from the meta description.

Both Google and Yahoo! will honor the HTML instruction in your page's code that will prevent the descriptions from these directories. These are called the `"noodp"` or the `"noydir"` attributes and are used in the header of your page's code. Using the code `<metaname="robots" content="noodp">` in the heading of your code will prevent the search engines from generating the snippet from the Open Directory Project description. Using `"noydir"` will do the same but for the Yahoo! Directory.

Creating the Meta Description

The meta description tag is in the code of every web page and is contained in the heading of each page. In a simple website, it can be modified by editing each page's source code. In larger sites, content management systems allow you to manipulate this tag and make it unique to each page. However, not all content management systems or ecommerce software carts allow website owners or managers to edit this tag or control the content. Many times, the content management software simply repurposes the first few lines of product or article content, repeats the same description on every page, or shows nothing altogether.

If you are using a newer content management system (CMS), one that is open source, or one that is custom-developed, you should have the ability to create or edit the meta description. If not, the development company or a programmer may be able to write the functionality into your website. My experience with larger CMS providers is that they do not respond quickly, if at all. If you are developing a new website, consider the ability to create or edit custom page titles and meta description to be a key requirement in your CMS.

This description should be unique to the content and unique for every page of your website. It should contain two or maybe three sentences that describe the content of the page. The search engines will typically display between 160 and 200 characters in the snippet. And remember, this is for marketing! Do not be over-promotional in the description, but be clear, compelling, and concise, inviting searchers to learn more.

Tuesday: Use Search Engine Tools to Check Your Website

Each major search engine provides diagnostic features that allow website owners and managers to track search engine spider activity, errors, and recommendations. Years ago, this was something that only a few diagnostic or analytics programs provided and rarely in the same toolset. Now, the search engines provide wonderful technical diagnostic tools that help you troubleshoot your website's presence in the search engines, if there are any issues. Even more impressive, many issues can be remedied prior to any ill effects being felt by losing search results, so long as someone is monitoring these tools on a regular basis.

Google Webmaster Tools

Whenever a website is having troubles being found in the search engines or having problems getting crawled, I find that in the vast majority of cases, it is an issue with the website. Programming, scripts, and changes by some well-meaning programmer can create a problem if the search engines are not considered. Once in a while, I find that the site has not done well because of some remnants of "spammy" code that was meant to trick the search engines. In cases like this, a "reconsideration request" needs to be made once the offending tactics have been removed. Only in very rare cases have I found the search engine to be the problem.

The Google Webmaster Tools are a significant resource for diagnosing, tracking and receiving important messages from Google. This toolset provided by the search engine allows site owners to view how often their site is crawled by the search engines, the pages downloaded and if there are any pages or sections that are not being found. The tools provide the health of the website by showing rankings, click-throughs, typical keywords and other tracking tools that provide a unique insight into the performance of your website.

The Google Webmaster Tools are a significant resource, and the tools and reports are being changed, updated and improved constantly. This is not a one-time log in and check-up. It should be made a monthly or quarterly check in to ensure that everything is working as intended for the search engines. While this is a Google-only toolset, you can be assured that if your site is performing well in Google, then you will most likely perform well in the others.

Although this section is not meant to be a comprehensive view of the webmaster tools from each search engine, it will focus on the most important technical diagnostics available from these tools.

Troubleshooting Errors

The crawl error report provides instant insight into the comparison between your live website and the search engine's index. Any errors that Google receives while crawling your site will show up here. You will see a report of specific page URLs that are not being found by Google. This can be a result of added plug-ins, pages removed, new pages added, changes in programming, or any combination of odd factors (see Figure 4.3).

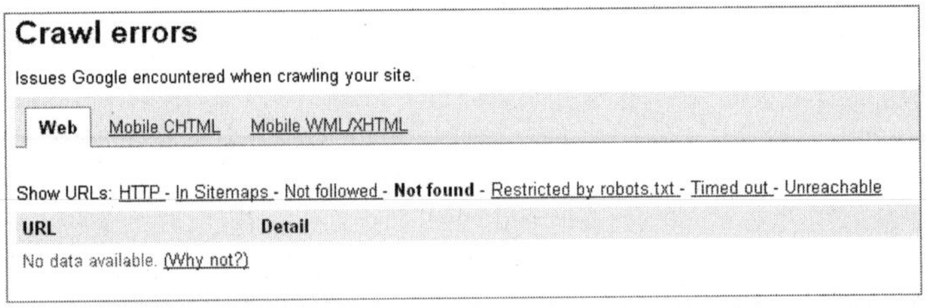

Figure 4.3 Google Webmaster Tools—crawl errors

If you are going through a website redesign and your site structure has changed, this report will help you find pages that have been "lost" in Google's index. In other words, when the new site went live, Google could no longer find the old page that was copied into the index. Unless you use a redirect to tell Google where the new page location is, the page will be deleted from the server. Chapter 13 will go into much more detail about technical troubleshooting, especially for redesigning a new website. Google Webmaster Tools will be your best tool for ensuring a smooth transition between your old website and your new one, should you redesign your website.

The page not found report will report broken links on your site. As the search engine is following links to old pages or to newly added pages, sometimes the links within your site may not publish properly. Sometimes this is also human error, usually by mistyping a URL when managing pages on the website. Checking the page not found report daily or weekly will notify you of linking issues as they happen, rather than waiting until there is a problem and diagnosing afterward. Although most errors are simple programming issues, there are cases when this report can be your best tool. Seasoned web marketers understand that there are many things that can happen, even with the best managed websites. Mistyping URLs in links, creating a nonfriendly URL, not formatting page links properly, moving pages (which causes the URL to change), or deleting old product pages are all typical activities that can "break" links. So, it's best to be proactive and check the status of the broken link report every week or every month, depending upon your level of activity with the website. If you are adding content and articles a few times a day or more, then check the broken link report actively. If you rarely update your website or add content, then it won't be as necessary to use this report as often.

Crawl Stats

Crawl stats allow you to see how often Googlebot, the name of Google's spider, visits your site and downloads new versions of your pages. Many website managers are surprised to see that Google actually visits their websites multiple times throughout a day and potentially thousands of times during a month.

The process of "submitting your website" to a search engine and waiting a month for inclusion or for changes to be picked up is long gone. Many times I have seen changes to a website show up within hours in the Google results. My, how things have changed.

If Google is not crawling your website, then there are a few issues at hand. The primary diagnosis would be that your website does not have any incoming links from reputable websites. That is primarily how the search engines find new websites, and it is a primary key in the frequency of Googlebot's visits. Popular sites are spidered more frequently.

If your website is being crawled but not many pages are being updated or downloaded, then I would compare that to the number of pages indexed by the search engine. If only a small number of pages are indexed, then there may be programming issues preventing the Googlebot from moving forward.

Note: Just because your site is spidered by the search engines and has been downloaded into the search engine's server (index) does not mean that your site will automatically rank well. There are many other factors that affect rankings. Getting your site spidered and indexed is just the beginning of this process.

Search Queries

The Search Queries tab in Google Webmaster Tools gives you an excellent idea of the visibility of your website (see Figure 4.4). This report shows the keywords where your website has appeared in the search results (Query) on the left. In the middle (Impressions) is the number of times your website has appeared to the searchers for the specific keyword. The next column (Clicks) shows the number of click-throughs your listing attracted for that keyword. Click-though rate (CTR) means the percentage of clicks compared to impressions. The far-right column shows the average position of the keyword in the search results.

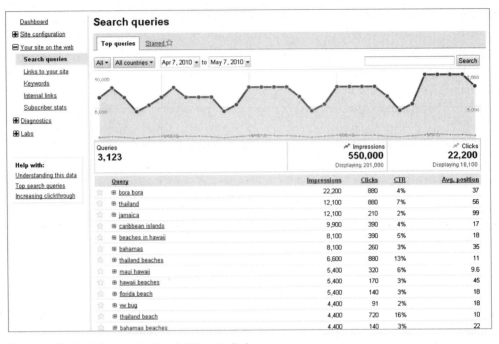

Figure 4.4 The Search Queries tab in Google Webmaster Tools

The Search Queries tab can help you diagnose your current situation and provide a seasoned SEO professional with a task list. By organizing the report based on Avg. Position or by CTR, you can see the words that rank the highest and compare them to the click-through rate. Evaluate this against the title and snippet of the results and the surrounding snippets, and you can see what the searcher sees. This will help you determine whether your title or snippet can be better written and optimized to provide a better description of your website in order to improve your CTR.

Here are some questions to ask:

How many of the Impressions keywords are your company name?

How many of the top 100 keywords on either side are company or brand-name keywords?

Are the keywords that you're ranking and getting click-throughs for relevant?

What ranking position are these keywords typically found? Less than 10? Less than 20?

If you can see that the majority of keywords on both sides are your company name or your brand name, then that signifies your need for search engine optimization. Search engine optimization brings your website up in the rankings for more terms that are critical for your business. Right now, if you are found only for your company name, then your website is being found only by your existing clients or those who know about you.

It is vital that you research keyword relevance to ensure that you are being found for what it is that you do! Being found for misleading or irrelevant terms is a waste of time for both you and the searcher. Your research will help you refine your keyword list, which is covered in Chapter 6. Do you have pages ranking in the second or third page? Can you find immediate actions that will improve those rankings?

Congratulations. You've taken your first step to developing a plan of action! At this point, feel free to click around the rest of the tools available and see what they provide. They change frequently. If you don't understand what some of the tools are or the terminology, be patient! Google offers definitions for all the main heading terms and also offers helpful guides throughout the toolset. After reading this book, you will be able to understand the terminology, the application, and the purpose of these technically mystifying areas of website programming.

Yahoo! Site Explorer

One of my favorite back-link tools is Yahoo! Site Explorer. It enables you to view the incoming links to specific pages on your website and track back to who is linking to you and the context of the link (Figure 4.5). Linking is an important part of increasing your website's visibility, and it also counts toward the search engines' evaluation of your website's credibility and relevance. Chapter 16 covers linking in much greater detail, but for now use this tool to get a picture of the number and type of websites linking to your website. Site Explorer will provide information about any domain, regardless of whether you have an account. However, for more accurate link information, I recommend getting a Yahoo! account to manage your website. As with Google, you will have to claim your website through the use of a metatag or script. The information is more accurate when you are logged in and viewing your own website's information.

Figure 4.5 lists the sites that are linking to the page www.thesaurus.com/fun/. Under Results in this example, there are four pages under that URL and 55 inlinks (links from other websites). By clicking the Inlinks tab, you can see each of the websites that link to the specific page.

Using Site Explorer, you can easily browse your own web pages and see the incoming links from other websites for each specific page. Or, you can do more of a surface check and look at the incoming links just for your domain. Then, compare the incoming links to your competitor's domains and get an idea where you stand in terms of the number of links and the types of sites linking to you and your competitors.

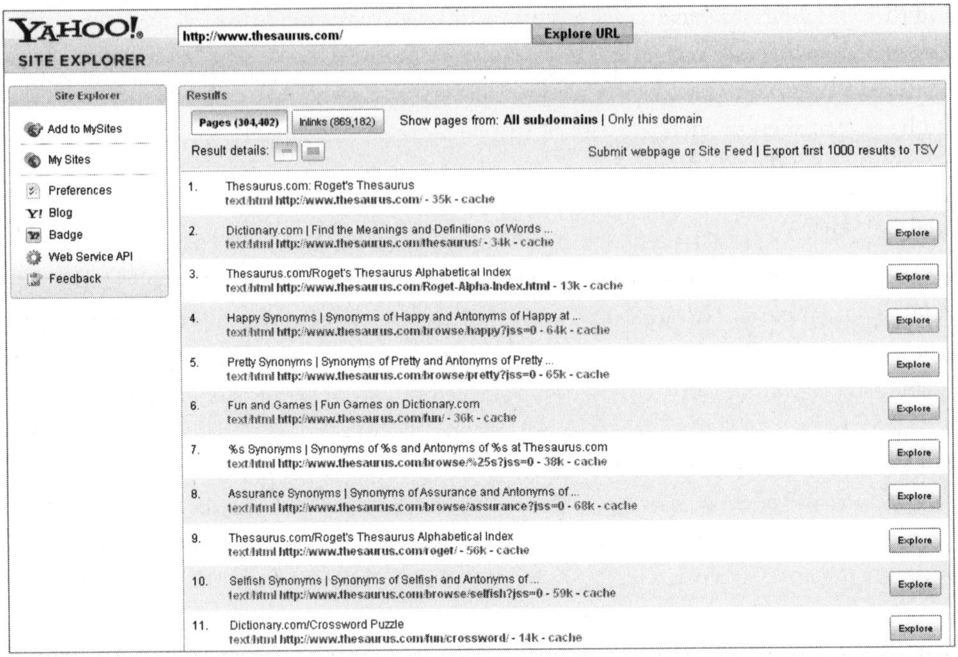

YAHOO! SITE EXPLORER

http://www.thesaurus.com/ — Explore URL

Site Explorer

- Add to MySites
- My Sites
- Preferences
- Y! Blog
- Badge
- Web Service API
- Feedback

Results

Pages (304,402) — Inlinks (869,182) — Show pages from: **All subdomains** | Only this domain

Result details: — Submit webpage or Site Feed | Export first 1000 results to TSV

1. Thesaurus.com: Roget's Thesaurus
   text/html http://www.thesaurus.com/ - 35k - cache

2. Dictionary.com | Find the Meanings and Definitions of Words ...
   text/html http://www.thesaurus.com/thesaurus/ - 34k - cache — Explore

3. Thesaurus.com/Roget's Thesaurus Alphabetical Index
   text/html http://www.thesaurus.com/Roget-Alpha-Index.html - 13k - cache — Explore

4. Happy Synonyms | Synonyms of Happy and Antonyms of Happy at ...
   text/html http://www.thesaurus.com/browse/happy?jss=0 - 64k - cache — Explore

5. Pretty Synonyms | Synonyms of Pretty and Antonyms of Pretty ...
   text/html http://www.thesaurus.com/browse/pretty?jss=0 - 65k - cache — Explore

6. Fun and Games | Fun Games on Dictionary.com
   text/html http://www.thesaurus.com/fun/ - 36k - cache — Explore

7. %s Synonyms | Synonyms of %s and Antonyms of %s at Thesaurus.com
   text/html http://www.thesaurus.com/browse/%25s?jss=0 - 38k - cache — Explore

8. Assurance Synonyms | Synonyms of Assurance and Antonyms of ...
   text/html http://www.thesaurus.com/browse/assurance?jss=0 - 68k - cache — Explore

9. Thesaurus.com/Roget's Thesaurus Alphabetical Index
   text/html http://www.thesaurus.com/roget/ - 56k - cache — Explore

10. Selfish Synonyms | Synonyms of Selfish and Antonyms of ...
    text/html http://www.thesaurus.com/browse/selfish?jss=0 - 59k - cache — Explore

11. Dictionary.com/Crossword Puzzle
    text/html http://www.thesaurus.com/fun/crossword/ - 14k - cache — Explore

Figure 4.5 Yahoo!'s Site Explorer

Webmaster Guidelines

If you are in the business of online marketing and have any responsibility at all for a website, then you need to be more than simply aware of the webmaster guidelines for each major search engine. These should be printed out, read, understood, and practiced.

I continue to be amazed at the number of online marketers, web designers, programmers, and agencies that are unaware of or, at worst, ignore these guidelines. The guidelines are a direct pipeline into the needs of the search engine and instruct users how to create a website that is easy for the search engines to access. In addition to access, the guidelines recommend usability practices that make a better experience for your visitors. The search engines care deeply about the searcher's experience as it pertains to relevance and reaction.

I have found that Google's Webmaster Guidelines are the most extensive and provide the best guide for new site owners or website managers. Although I do my best to be search engine–agnostic, I have to give credit where credit is due. So, good job, Google. The following sections outline some principal elements of Google's Webmaster Guidelines. Interestingly, the information in Google's guidelines is relevant for any search engine. The technical quality issues that are addressed are typically necessary for any search engine. The design and content guidelines are good for both users and search engines alike. This section is not meant to be a regurgitation of the already organized and written guidelines that are freely available to anyone who searches for them; it is more for the new website owner or marketing manager to understand the purpose behind the guidelines. When a person understands the *why*, then the *how* becomes easy. Understanding why certain elements are important to Google's Webmaster Guidelines helps all hands in the website development and marketing process. If more companies would have read these guidelines, millions of dollars of development could have been saved simply by understanding what search engines need from websites.

Text and Text Links

Text and text links are critical elements for the search engine. When downloading your website, the main parts that the search engines need to evaluate are the content in the text and the links on the page. As such, Google places a good amount of attention by instructing webmasters about the structure of text and the linking relationships necessary.

This involves a clear and accessible navigation scheme that also includes text links in the content. As good practice, many programmers will repeat important links in the footer (bottom) of the page. This provides alternate means for spiders to access content.

Google also prompts webmasters to utilize a *site map* for their users. A site map helps people find specific information. It also helps the search engine, because it provides a centralized page with links to the primary content pages and subject areas of a website. Typically, the links are very short and clear, allowing easy access to the search engine spider. In addition, Google recommends no more than 100 links on a page, which is a bit overwhelming, even for humans.

Technical Issues

Technical issues will be explained more thoroughly in Chapters 13 through 15, but this is a good place to introduce a few concepts. Especially critical to search engines is the ability to follow links. The majority of Google's technical guidelines focus on the ability of the spider to follow links.

Broken links are of particular concern, because those stop the search engine spider, and they also stop humans from finding content they need. Too many broken links results in a very bad visitor experience, as well as a bad search engine spider experience, and your site will suffer in the rankings.

The length of the URL and the characters included can be detrimental to the search engine's ability to follow links. The best rule for URLs is that shorter is better. If your URL is longer than the browser window, then chances are the search engines will have some spidering problems with your website (Figure 4.6). Shorter URLs containing actual words are favored more than longer ones with strange characters and computer jargon. The more characters in the URL, the more problems you may experience.

a) http://www.babydirect.com/c-22-baby-cribs.aspx

b) http://www.target.com/Cribs-Baby-Furniture/b/ref=nav_t_spc_3_inc_7_4/180-6267612-4636734?ie=UTF88node=3145001

Figure 4.6 a) Good URL: short and to the point; b) bad URL: too long and too complicated

Browsers

Google makes it a point in the technical guidelines to test your website in multiple web browsers. This is an important issue, because many developers tend to favor a single browser but do not test or have access to multiple browsers and computers for testing.

There are multiple browsers in use; Firefox, Opera, and Safari are available for both Mac and Windows. Many Mac users complain that there are still far too many websites that simply do not work well using the Safari browser on their Mac. There are differences between versions of the same browser. Websites perform differently between the different versions of Internet Explorer 6, 7, and 8. They also perform differently when they are running on a Windows XP, Vista, or Windows 7 operating system. Designers have an uphill battle when designing for multiple users, because even in the Windows market, there are multiple combinations that are used by the searching audience, and all must be accounted for.

It is wise to test in all of these scenarios. Knowing that your site is available and works for the vast majority of users, regardless of operating system, computer type, browser, and software, will help you rest a little easier. However, those who recognize the fast approach of mobile search will not stop there and will test their websites in mobile devices.

It is also well worth your time to test your website in multiple mobile devices and ensure that your message is available to the widest audience possible. The iPhone is very forgiving and renders websites very closely to using a standard browser, but there are still some design issues that may prevent easy browsing and access to the content. Other phones are more finicky from the start. The mobile trend is growing, and it will not slow down for websites that simply do not work in that environment.

Wednesday: Use Firefox's Free Tools

One of the best tools available for a quick analysis of your website is the Firefox browser. Because it is open source, many programmers contribute plug-ins that extend the functionality of the browser. The beauty of this is that the browser becomes customized to your particular needs as a user and contains many of the tools you need as a website manager.

Web Developer Toolbar

My primary plug-in is the Web Developer Toolbar. I can't live without it. Simply calling up your website in the browser and then using the functions easily available in the toolbar will show you the compatibility of your website. Essentially, you get to see your site as the search engines see it. It's a completely geeky exercise, I'll admit. But once you start seeing the purpose, you will channel your inner geek on a regular basis.

You can download the Firefox browser at www.mozilla.com and the Firefox Web Developer Toolbar at https://addons.mozilla.org/en-US/firefox/addon/60. Once you have installed the browser and the toolbar, open the browser to your home page or any page on your website. The very first thing to do is to disable JavaScript (Figure 4.7). If your navigation is written in JavaScript, then you cannot depend on the search engines to be able to see the links in the JavaScript. If the link code contains <a href="destination URL">, then the search engines should be able to see the links. However, if you have no destination URLs in the JavaScript, it can just be a load of nonsensical code. It's best just to disable this and see what works and what doesn't.

Figure 4.7 Start with a web page for these tests, and then disable JavaScript.

Next, disable the images. If you are particularly daring, choose the option to replace images with alt attributes (Figure 4.8). alt attributes are the text that appears when the image doesn't load, which happens frequently. You have to account for website visitors on mobile devices, bad conference hotel connections, and getting download speeds of 1Kb per hour on the subway.

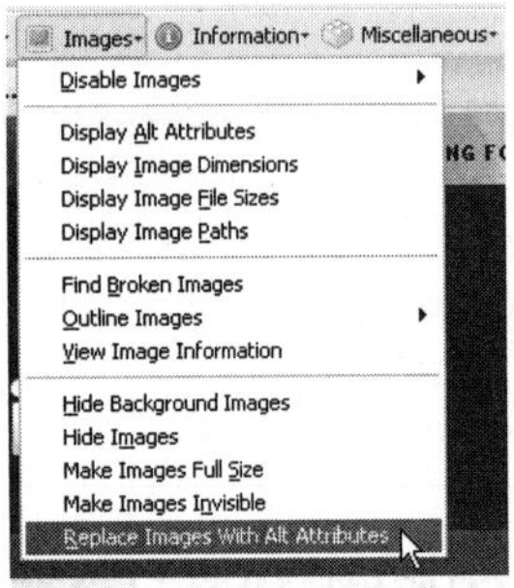

Figure 4.8 Disabling images

After you have disabled the images and replaced them with alt attributes if you so choose, you should start seeing the content that the search engines see (Figure 4.9); however, it is still too "pretty." The W3C guidelines suggest that your site should be understandable and viewable without the CSS. Cascading Style Sheets (CSS) is a fancy way of referring to the design template for your website. Disable the CSS (see Figure 4.10).

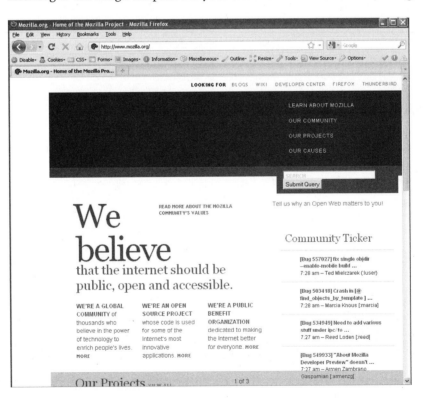

Figure 4.9
Mozilla.org without images loaded

You should start seeing a very different

Figure 4.10 Disabling CSS

layout and style for your website. This is very close to how the search engines see your site. By stripping out the images, scripts, and templates, you can get an idea of the base level of your pages, the actual content in those pages, and their structure (Figure 4.11).

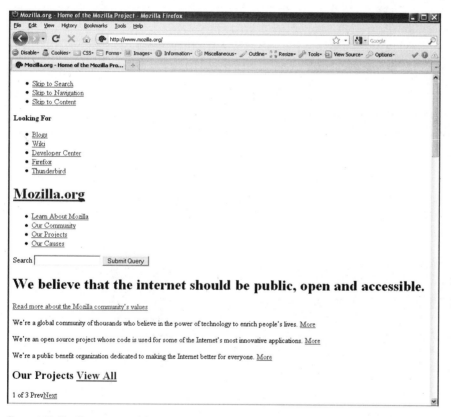

Figure 4.11 Mozilla.org, stripped down to the basics. This is what the search engines "see."

Search Status Plug-In

Another handy free tool in the Firefox browser is the Search Status plug-in, and it gets updates frequently to allow for search engine changes. Although this great little tool has many features (see Figure 4.12), on a regular basis I rely on the few discussed here.

Figure 4.12 The
Search Status plug-in

Search Status provides a quick way to find the websites linking to a specific page or domain, as reported by the major engines (see Figure 4.13). This is a fast way to get from the web page directly to the resources at the search engines.

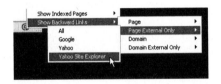

Figure 4.13 Backward links reports in Search Status

Search Status also provides the ability to find the page counts in the search engines (see Figure 4.14). This allows a fast method of accessing the page count of your website as reported by the top three search engines from a single click. This will let you know whether the search engines are indexing the website, as addressed on Monday of this chapter.

Figure 4.14 Search Status page count tools

Search Status additionally provides some very handy tools. Viewing and recognizing the Robots.txt file and Sitemap.xml file is important and will be covered in Chapter 15. The purpose of highlighting NoFollow links is covered in Chapter 16. NoFollow is an attribute that is placed on an outgoing link. By adding that attribute, you tell the search engines that the destination website is not trusted, nor should the link be counted in the popularity assessment.

The link report gives a quick status of the number of internal (within the website) site links and external (going to other websites) links on the page. There are also a number of options to view the rank of the page measured by Alexa, Google, and a few others. These are meant to provide some measure of importance per page; however, these measurements are largely unreliable because they are based on limited data. It is best not to focus a strategy around these measurements, but they can be helpful as you gain more experience in marketing online. As your comfort level with online marketing increases, you'll find your understanding and application of these tools growing as well.

Thursday: Follow the W3C Accessibility Checklists

The World Wide Web Consortium (W3C) is a standards community that develops goals and recommendations for accessibility and programming. Its accessibility guidelines are a wonderful evaluation for the technical programming of your website. The current (2.0) guidelines are very open and leave a lot for interpretation. The old guidelines (1.0) were developed in the form of a checklist, which I still prefer today as a healthy check-up for any website.

The 1.0 checklist for accessibility is at `www.w3.org/TR/WAI-WEBCONTENT/full-checklist`. The 2.0 guidelines are at `www.w3.org/TR/2008/REC-WCAG20-20081211/`. Finally, a quick-reference guide for the 2.0 guidelines, with links and resources, is at `www.w3.org/WAI/WCAG20/quickref/`.

Checking the accessibility of a website is a very relevant practice. As you review the Webmaster Guidelines and the W3C accessibility guidelines, you may notice a lot of crossover. That is because accessibility and search engine–friendliness are the same. Search engine spiders are the most "disabled" users that will come to your website. They cannot "see" your images or movies, "hear" your music files, or follow convoluted programming; they error out with certain JavaScripts, and they don't eat cookies (a tracking tool). As such, when your site performs well in accessibility tests, it will also perform well by allowing search engines to find your content and download your website.

The checklist will provide specifics, as will Chapter 15, which is more relevant and important than you may think, so don't skip it! For this review, I want to focus on the user's view of your site. Focus on the graphics and the readability.

Contrast Is Critical for Readability

Of specific interest are the checkpoints of using color to communicate information and measuring the contrast level of the text and the background color. These elements are almost always overlooked, because there is no automated test that will cover this area. It needs to be properly evaluated, tested, and audited. If you ignore this area, you could lose business, even with good rankings, powerful persuasive content, and award-winning design. Contrast problems are a killer.

This really jumped out at me when I worked on a website that was designed to target affluent women, ages 65 to 80. Of course, the designer chose pink as the primary color, and in doing so defaulted all the text color to gray. It was a beautiful site. I was struck by the color scheme and the softness of the approach. However, the target audience reacted very strongly and negatively. Unfortunately, they did not take kindly to the color scheme. Gray text on a muted pink background was very difficult to read, especially when the text was made a smaller font size in order to fit the content.

Continues

Contrast Is Critical for Readability *(Continued)*

The target audience could not read or understand the content, because it blended together. At that age, the retina naturally absorbs more blue, and areas of low contrast become yellowed and more difficult to discern. The result of a beautiful design that worked for younger eyes was a pinkish mess with blobs of gray for the intended audience. The contrast was so low between the pink background and the gray text that no one in the target audience could make it out.

I even had to admit that my 40-year-old eyes were tested with this design. The artist showed me his basis for the design. It was a magazine ad that pulled a great response, so the artist used the same color combination for the website. So, the company relied on taking the printed piece that worked well and using the same color combinations for the website. Unfortunately, you just can't re-create color combinations that work in a printed document and repurpose them for digital media. The intensity of a monitor blends the contrast, making it much more difficult for the eyes to read.

Look at your website. Is the most important information contained in an area of high contrast? Or is your most important information hidden or disguised in a low-contrast array of muted colors (gray on green, red on yellow, blue on black, and so on)? High-contrast text gets attention.

Friday: Test Human-Friendliness

The W3C accessibility checklists lead directly into the evaluation of human-friendliness. By considering accessibility, the W3C is at its core defining human interaction with websites and web-based applications. I find these checklists to be some of the most instructive and informative for developing websites. The amazing side benefit to accessibility is that it benefits everyone. By making functions easier to see, everyone can benefit. By adding captioning in your videos, the search engines can index the content while others can watch the video without sound being necessary. Accessibility raises the interaction of a website for everybody, not just a small percentage of people. Beyond simple checklists and guides, the best information you will ever get about your website is a human test. Most of the W3C checklist items can't be tested with software; it requires human interaction for the final assessment.

I find that most managers and website owners make many decisions based on assumptions. These are assumptions of what their users need, of what choices people will make, and how those users will view their website. The best way to get over assumptions is to get the opinion of someone else, especially someone you can't fire when they disagree with you but whose opinion carries some weight. For me, it's my mom.

Conduct Tests with Real People

The fastest, least expensive, and most honest opinion I can get is from my mother. Maybe yours is the same way. I find that when I show her a website and ask her to perform a task, she has no problem letting me know about any problems she has. She grew up in a generation without computers and websites, but she has a disposable income, which makes her a target for many companies. However, if she can't find your site or use it, you have the problem. She doesn't. She knows how to easily find another website that might be easier.

Watching someone use your website and asking them about the experience can be a moment of clarity that many marketing managers need. Website owners can gain a significant understanding of how searchers view their website, simply by having a third party, disassociated with the website or the development project, use the website.

I find that too many website owners have a "proud papa" complex and believe that their website was created to do the job. However, when it is a site that you see every day and when customers call because they cannot find things on the website (or much less find the website), you have a problem.

Start with a Task

The simplest and most effective test is to set a clear goal for your testers. Simply showing someone a page on your website and asking what they think is not only ineffective, but it's out of order. That's not how people browse websites. They go with intention, so measure intention.

Find a specific task, such as purchasing an item or finding a specific bit of information. If there is a process involved, such as filling out a lead form or a purchase path, add that to the task list. If you want to raise the level of difficulty (for you), find additional test subjects and test their path through the site with different starting points. After all, not everyone enters your website through the home page.

Measure the time, observe the mouse movements, and, above all, do not help! You can ask what they are thinking or searching for. You can ask what they see. You can ask what they expect to see or ask whether anything is missing. But restrain your desire to help or point out information. Otherwise, you won't learn anything.

Simple testing like this is cheap and easy and will result in some very basic improvements. Once you see how that works, then you can move up into the rankings of usability audits, eye-tracking, and high-end user testing. But until then, find the easy stuff and start there.

Set Up a Persona Walk-Through

A very effective method of assessing your content is to see it through someone else's eyes. By considering another person's abilities, needs, and background, you can also develop the skills necessary to evaluate your website on an entirely different level. This method begins by establishing a typical user persona. There may be three to four actual persona types, based on your audience, but if this is your first time, just start with a single persona. I described a persona in my example a few pages earlier. The target audience of the website was affluent, retired women who wanted to travel. After the basic demographic information is developed, we now develop the persona.

I find an effective method of doing this is to go to a stock photo website and find a picture that fits the person you are describing, ideally in the context of your target audience. If your target audience consists of engineers who are drawing specifications and they need to know about your product, then find the demographic of your engineer, probably sitting at his workstation; surround that person with context so that everyone on the project knows the persona.

Next, give your persona a name. This makes it personal. You may even find yourself saying that " Mildred wouldn't like that!" Everyone knows that Mildred doesn't exist, but giving your persona a name makes them more human, more understandable, and sympathetic. Programmers have a tendency to consider website visitors as stupid, but once a persona is established, there tends to be much more respect for the user. For travel-based websites, you can even go so far as to name the children and the dog; those are important factors for the family that has to locate and book a pet-friendly hotel. Go as in-depth as you feel comfortable, all to give you a human view through the eyes of your visitor.

Now, through the eyes, needs, and psychology of your user, view the website. You may find that the music file that plays automatically, which was meant to set the mood, now shatters the concentration of the older user, and the controls are not only hard to find but too small for someone who does not handle the mouse with great dexterity.

The key for this test is to look at your website and empathize with those who have never seen or experienced your website. The ideas you or your company utilized to communicate information may not be effective with this visitor. Second to an actual user test, the persona walk-through is one of the most effective means of discovery on your website.

Review and Hands-On

Start with simple searches for your company's website. Check the title and description that appear on the search engine results page. Ensure that the information is correct and optimal for persuading people to click on your result.

Sign up for the webmaster tools on the major search engines, such as Google, Yahoo!, and Bing. Click the tabs, and learn how the information presented in the reports can assist you in troubleshooting and improving your website. If you need, open this book to the index pages to find the relevant information to explain specific reports or functions in the available tools.

Download and print the checklists at www.w3.org/TR/WAI-WEBCONTENT/full-checklist, www.w3.org/TR/2008/REC-WCAG20-20081211/, and www.w3.org/WAI/WCAG20/quickref/, and identify any issues that would prevent users from fully accessing the content on your website. Don't worry about completing any tasks that might seem complicated or use unfamiliar terminology. Just start with what you know and understand. The more you read in this book, the more those tasks will become clear and have more purpose in the big picture.

Set up a walk-through on your website. It doesn't have to be a large-scale production. The easiest method is to simply provide a person with a task to complete on your website. Then listen. The feedback you receive and the problems they encounter will provide some of the best feedback for site improvement.

Week 2: Understand Basic SEO

A basic understanding of search engines and search engine optimization is necessary to achieve visibility online. To compete now and in the future, online marketers need a good understanding of how search engines rank, relate, recall, and determine relevance. Even more critical is the understanding of how consumers think, speak, read, and decide, because that knowledge can be used in any media and beyond search.

This chapter will remove the shroud of mystery that surrounds search engines and what they look for on a web page. After learning about the factors that search engines use to develop relevance and how they "see" your web pages, you can employ strategies that make sense to you, the searcher, and your customers.

5

Chapter Contents
Monday: Distinguish Bad Information from Good Advice
Tuesday: Optimize On-Page Factors
Wednesday: Optimize Content Structure for SEO
Thursday: Explore the Power of Off-Page Ranking Factors
Friday: See SEO in Practice

Monday: Distinguish Bad Information from Good Advice

Anyone who has managed a website or run a small business knows how hard it can be to get good marketing advice. Everyone from the high-priced consultant to the IT guy can give you advice on how to get ahead online. The typical advice is a mixture of half-truths, technical voodoo, and seemingly irrelevant instructions about filling pages with keywords. Unfortunately, the search engine optimization industry suffers from a multiple personality disorder; you'll rarely get the same tactical advice from any two practitioners. It can leave someone so desperate for advice that they'll take it from anyone, even the guy sitting next to them on the airplane. Every once in a while, I happen to be that guy.

On a late night flight to Cleveland, I was sitting next to a woman and her young daughter. We were having a nice conversation when she mentioned she had started her own business but was frustrated with her website. Of course, my ears perked up, and my attention was captured. I've heard my fair share of stories of bad advice, but this woman's story was right up at the top of the worst. She spun a long tale of woe, recounting bits of advice she'd endured during her short career with this website. I sat amazed as she shared with me the advice she'd been given and the things she'd been told to do.

I realized that many people offering advice about website marketing must have read an article or two years ago and now think they understand one or two "tricks" that work magic in the search engines. Others seem to be coming from plain ignorance. And the person who pays for the bad advice? The business owner, who is usually on a shoestring budget and just wants to run her business. Or, it's the website manager who can't afford to make a bad decision, because it will cost the company tens of thousands of dollars, maybe more, and possibly their job. This lady beside me on the plane doesn't have time for unfounded advice that could destroy her business.

Unfortunately, I cannot educate those who think they know everything already. But I can do everything in my power to be sure that website marketers have the information they need to correctly build and market their website. All they want are straight answers in a language they can understand. To start this week's activities, take a look at some of the misleading advice this business owner was given. There is a common theme to it all—that there is a "trick" to having success in the search engines.

Conflicting Technologies One consultant told her she needed to move her website to GoDaddy's platform. She transferred the domain registration, her email accounts... everything. Unfortunately, it took a few weeks of frustration before GoDaddy's support team realized she was Mac-based. GoDaddy's site-builder program was incompatible with the Mac operating system. GoDaddy's advice? Buy a PC. Needless to say, it took just as long to get everything off GoDaddy and back to her original registrar as it did to transfer things over in the first place. The result? Countless hours and dollars wasted from very bad advice.

Search Engine Submission The next thing she was told was to pay for a submission service to search engines. This is where I had to bite my lip to keep from exploding. No one has had to submit a site to the search engines since 1999. Submitting your site to search engines is a thing of the past. It's not necessary and usually is a rip-off offer. Seriously, $29.95 to submit your website to 100 search engines? Name *10* search engines...nope? Most people can't.

Search engines will naturally find your website. Read the Google Webmaster Guidelines. In fact, anyone who has anything to do with creating, programming, developing, and marketing a website should read those guidelines. Search engines want your website, and they work hard to get it. Just by picking up a few links to your website, you can ensure that the search engines will find your pages.

Domain Registration Amazingly, all the advice to this point was enough to make me scream out in frustration, but that wasn't the best part. Her Mac guy, who helps her computer run smoothly, tells her that the "trick" to getting into Google is to register her domain for 10 years. I remember that bit of advice when it was first floated as a tactic in the late 1990s.

There is a debated element of Google's ranking algorithm where search engines may evaluate the length of time that a domain is registered. Anecdotal evidence suggests that domains registered for a year are not as invested as domains registered for 10 years, which is based on the idea that the owner has made a commitment to the domain. However, domain registration alone is not a primary part of the algorithm! Many other intricacies are much more important than the years of domain registration that you purchase. Logically, if everyone went out and reregistered their domain for 10 years, what then? Who would be the most relevant? It just doesn't make sense to center a strategy on this.

Register your domain for a few years—whatever you think will make sense and as long as you are willing to invest in it.

No wonder the Internet is such a mystery and business owners make what they think are good decisions based on advice, only to have zero results. With this kind of advice, the absence of a result would be preferable to the hundreds of lost hours and ill-spent money. The basis of website visibility in the search engines is your programming, site structure, content, and incoming links. Those are the fundamental principles of building a website marketing strategy. Everything else supports these principles.

A Short History of the SEO Industry

The seemingly conflicting nature of SEO information is based on the backgrounds of those who formed the early years of the thought and practices of this fledgling business. The search engine optimization industry was born out of two very different areas; there are those who learned SEO contextually from a marketing background, and there are those who learned it mechanically from a technical background.

Those with a technical background were able to reverse engineer search engine–ranking algorithms within days of a new update. By finding out the weight given to certain on-page and off-page factors, the methods to "game" the search engines spread very quickly online. Within weeks, most SEO specialists were aware of the changes in the algorithm and how to change their websites accordingly to gain rankings.

A little more quietly, marketers learned SEO as a persuasive skill in writing and developing content that resulted in rankings, and SEO copywriting became one of the earliest areas of focus in the industry. Coupled with technical knowledge and resources, many small businesses that retained SEO specialists and larger businesses that had people learning SEO while on the job were successful in gaining immediate results in the search market.

The early days of SEO (1995–1999) saw innovation and tactics driven primarily by the technical side of the industry. Search engine submission software, doorway pages (pages that are developed for search engines to find and rank but not for people to see), keyword density, IP detection (another way of showing search engines content-filled pages, but users do not see), and many more tactics were designed to fool the search engines and inflate relevance. As search engines improved to the point of spidering pages and refining algorithms, fooling them became much more difficult, and it became something that only a gifted few did very well.

Three Factors in SEO Information

Remember that no SEO expert with more than 10 years of experience has learned their practices in a school or from a book. There are no degree programs or schools for the first few generations of SEO practitioners, because everything was learned through testing, trial, and error. This brings us to why searches for SEO advice yield odd and usually contradictory advice. There are three main factors, explored in the following sections.

Factor 1: Experience as the Teacher

Every top-level SEO specialist has learned their trade through countless hours and late nights of personal and client work. In turn, SEO specialists who learned from the first generation of SEO authorities learned the style and philosophy of their teachers and then refined it with their personal experiences.

As a result, there are many "flavors" of SEO information and specialties. There are SEO specialists who have a strong technical and programming background who think nothing of developing scripts that will provide a mechanical answer to a problem with a website. There are SEO specialists who came from a marketing or copywriting background who look to content to solve most problems. Then again, there are other professionals who have integrated SEO into their existing specializations in analytics, graphic design, and other disciplines. Accordingly, articles, information, and research written by each SEO specialist will be unique to the particular approach or philosophy of that person. Because information tends to be freely shared in this industry, articles based on people's experience and the results have flooded the Internet. Because of this, SEO specialists can agree on basics but debate endlessly on tactics.

Another issue is the industry in which the SEO specialist provides services. *Certain* industries (affectionately referred to as PPC—pills, porn, and casinos) require cutthroat SEO tactics that few marketers could ever imagine. The competitive atmosphere in those industries results in an SEO "arms race" that involves targeting competitor websites with underhanded techniques, technical wizardry, and over-the-line short-term tactics. These areas are so competitive and abused that Google has even stated that they rarely enforce their own quality guidelines. (PPC is also used as an acronym for pay-per-click marketing, so the double meaning caught on within the industry.)

The SEO practitioners in these industries will occasionally write an article about the latest sneaky tactics designed to unseat a competitor or build their rankings. In those businesses, improvements in rankings can be the results of minute tweaks in linking strategies, development of thousands of "fake" sites that link to the main site, and the use of "disposable" domains. These tactics in the majority of other businesses can easily go unused, because the competition is nowhere near as intense or scrutinized, and most businesses are focused on a long-term approach to their online presence and domain name. As such, many of these articles that focus on the tactics employed at that level can be just as misleading for a website manager or a small-business owner, because they can detract from the basics and focus someone on a minute detail or advice that may yield little results.

The catch to working with an SEO specialist is to understand their background and areas of specialty. This will greatly affect how they approach your project and the results they expect to deliver.

Factor 2: Content Written before 1999

Two things were evident to search engine optimizers in the early days. You needed content to rank in the search engines, and if you got rankings, you got customers. Because of those two things, SEO specialists wrote an inordinate amount of content in a very short amount of time.

Tactics

Following most of the published advice written prior to the year 2000 could land you in some trouble with the search engines, because many of the tactics and software utilized at the time relied on "bait-and-switch" techniques. That means showing the search engine pages that were developed primarily to gain rankings and then showing the visitor another page. The pages built specifically for search engines were typically nonsensical if you ever tried to read one. These pages were built to accommodate the algorithm, not to persuade the visitor.

Still available online are thousands of articles for creating these infamous "doorway pages." There are more than enough articles debating the use of commas to separate keywords in the meta keyword tag. There are articles for detecting the search engine spiders using IP detection and serving alternate pages specifically to them. There are articles advising webmasters to join discussion forums and put their website URL in their signature line, just to help inflate link text to their website.

The problem is context. Although the articles may have had some truth to them at some time, the subject matter seems contradictory when compared to other articles. Unless the reader understands the industry as a whole, past and current tactics, and the goals, developments, and purposes for these isolated tactics, the specifics seem random.

Events

The first major event in SEO was the change of search engines to a more intelligent method of gathering website data and applying an algorithm that was not dependent upon word repetition or metadata. The specific event date is hard to identify, because each search engine changed at different times and in different stages (and some disappeared altogether); however, the difference between performing SEO in 1998 was drastically different than just two short years later in 2000.

A second event that filled many SEO specialists with dread took place on November 16, 2003. This was the infamous Florida update (at the time, the monthly Google algorithm updates were given names, much like hurricanes). The Florida update targeted a wide swath of website factors, specifically low-quality back-links and over-optimization practices. There are many theories as to what the algorithm penalized or favored, but nonetheless, it affected nearly all websites that previously held top rankings for years prior to the update.

Articles written before or around this time period can offer very different perspectives on developing tactics for an online marketer. Reading some of the articles online now, you can see how both search engines and SEO marketers have evolved for the better in the development of tactics and with a focus on the user and conversions rather than just rankings.

Measurement

The turn of the century was the beginning of the understanding that rankings were only part of the overall equation. Design, sales, calls to action, and measurement demanded that SEO specialists become more accountable and provide business value other than a single stop for increased rankings. As businesses utilized SEO and saw increases in sales and leads, many desired to take the next step and quantify the value of the increased rankings and a return on their spending. This allowed many agencies and SEO specialists to integrate the various related backgrounds in the industry. Those SEO specialists with marketing backgrounds focused on content, messaging, and creating effective calls to action. Those with direct marketing backgrounds developed skills in targeting audiences, testing messages, and direct-response actions. Others with more analytical backgrounds saw that simple website statistics were not going to be effective measurement criteria and started to develop methods of tracking searchers to sales.

Overall, the search marketing industry evolved as a necessity in order to provide business value beyond just rankings. Design, programming, analytics, content development, marketing, and a multitude of other skills added to the ability to craft an effective website. Organic search optimization became a binder that drew in all of the elements necessary to build a website that was search engine–friendly and utilized customer-based language for increased rankings.

As the millennial decade wore on, analytics became more evident as the standard measurement of success. The bottom-line profitability and justification for marketing campaigns were preferred rather than a simple rankings report. Defining success became a lot more complicated, and the articles published in that decade spanned a wide gamut of definitions.

Factor 3: Rankings Tend to Improve over Time

Unfortunately, older content online tends to get rewarded for its longevity. As old content "seasons" over time, it also enjoys the incoming links from other websites that have been in place for years, so that content tends to do very well in the search engines. This seasoning principle is simply a factor of an algorithm that is based on typical human judgment. We tend to judge the businesses more favorably that have been established for a long time. We admire longevity in business, and it helps develop trust.

I equate this principle to comparing two restaurant choices. One restaurant has been there for years, and you know you will get a quality experience and a great meal. The other restaurant opened last week, and you have not heard anything about the food or the atmosphere from any of your friends. Most people will choose the trusted experience over the newcomer. This tends to happen with older established websites and links online. It is a way of showing longevity in this volatile industry.

This principle is not a governing principle for all content or rankings. There are areas of content where the newest content is the most desired, specifically in the news cycle. People want the latest news on events, and it is in the search engine's best interest to serve fresh news and content as it happens. So, you can see both principles at play, based on your intended searches. The best piece of advice is to find the date on any article you read about SEO advice. Finding an old article that is no longer accurate for today's online marketer is a typical experience for those searching for SEO advice.

Tuesday: Optimize On-Page Factors

A handful of primary on-page factors affect rankings. Everything is about building the relevance of a page's context. Small items are not going to mean a lot individually, but taken together in context, they add up to provide the total relevancy of the page. The most important on-page factors are discussed here.

Create a Compelling <title> Tag

Of all on-page elements, the page title is the king. I liken it to the beachfront property of your web pages. If you edit your existing titles to be more accurate and descriptive, you will see a drastic change in your rankings and visitor numbers, especially if you have never done anything with your page titles on your website.

The reason that the page title is held in such high value is that it is a multitasking element of the page structure. It is used by the search engine to determine the primary content of the page, much like a newspaper's headline. In addition, that headline is used as the link to your website in the search results.

In Figure 5.1, you can see that the page title on the individual page for Brooks Brothers is also the blue, underlined text used as the link in Google's search results. This doesn't happen only in Google; all search engines use the <title> tag in this manner.

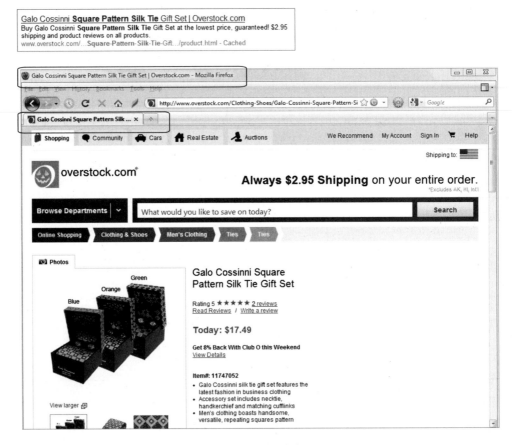

Figure 5.1 The <title> tag is used both in search results and in the browser.

The <title> tag must be crafted in a way that draws the searcher's attention but also provides topical relevance. Using keywords that match your most important search terms for the content on that page is important. However, the <title> tag also does double duty by providing a compelling reason for visitors to click your website instead of other matching results. Consider both of these tasks when writing your page title.

The <title> tag is contained in the heading of the page code. If you were to look at your pages' code, the title is contained in the area after the <head> tag. The heading contains the title, metadata, and a few other "housekeeping" items.

Avoid Using the Business Name as the <title> Tag

One thing that businesses and programmers seem to do with <title> tags is to use that space as the name of the company. It makes logical sense to do this in a development environment, because the business name is important. However, when it comes to search, your goal is to reach searchers who are searching for what you have, not exclusively who you are. Those searchers who are searching for your business name will find you. The title is best developed with a concise, clear, and compelling message in order to capture the searchers who are searching for what you *do*.

Brand names work well in the <title> tag, especially at the product level, because that may match a very specific search. However, business names are a different story; leave the company name for the end of the title or leave it out altogether. Don't worry about ranking for your business name. If you do half of the items contained in this book, you will rank for your business name, maybe even without using it in the <title> tag at all. However, just to alleviate some concerns, use the business name where it makes the most (relevant) sense—on the About Us page, company contact information, and similar business- and company name–focused pages. But allow your product, services, and article titles to be keyword focused in order to match the searches as closely as possible.

Consider the Length of the <title> Tag

The optimum length of a <title> tag is best illustrated by simply looking closely at the two places where the <title> tag is displayed: the search results page and the browser interface (Figure 5.2). <title> tags in the search results show a consistency in length. There are very short page titles, and there are longer ones. The longer ones all tend to truncate around 60 to 65 character, including spaces. The practical application of this is clear. Searchers will see only about 60 or so characters of your web page title. You have that limited space to give the searcher a relevant reason to click the link.

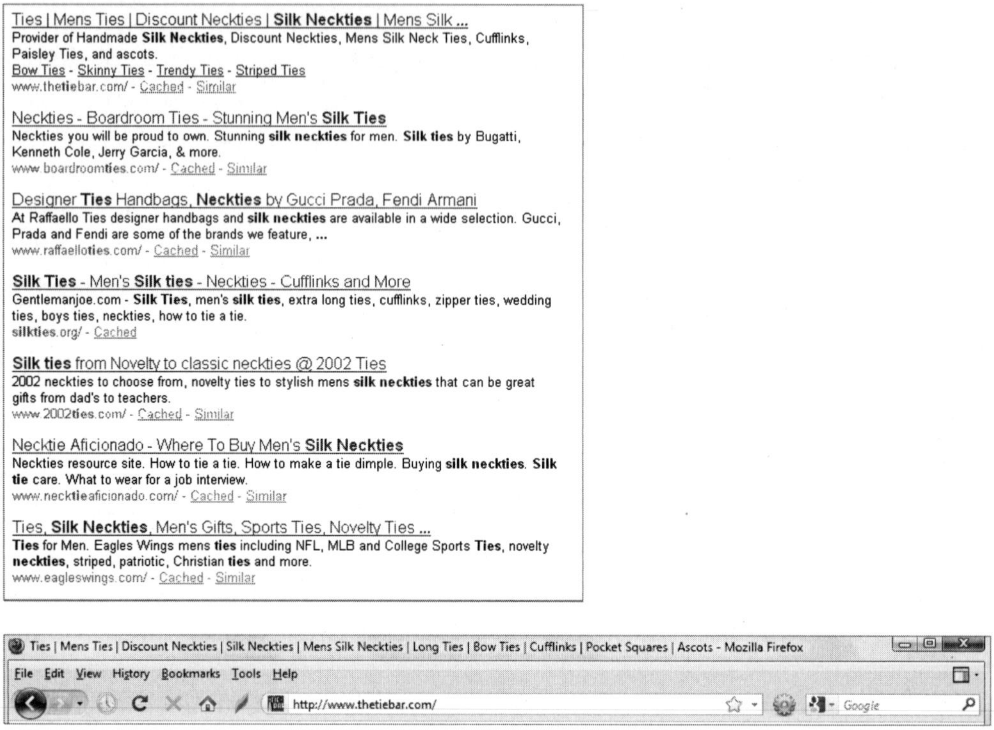

Figure 5.2 Title lengths between the search result and the browser interface

In the browser interface, the title of a page can display in 120 to 140+ characters, depending upon the size of the window and screen resolution. It is estimated that search engines will index more than 200 characters in the <title> tag. However, only 120 or so characters are visible to the searchers. Using that as a guide, the most important words to the search engines are the first words. The following are three good options for developing your titles:

Keep It Short Don't use anything too verbose—just a simple description using as few words as possible. Many SEO specialists subscribe to this tactic, because the distilled words offer much more relevance than spreading out the keywords across multiple words that aren't necessary.

Use a Complete Thought At this point, I recommend writing in a sentence format rather than groups of keywords. Humans are very well equipped at reading sentences; it is a skill that we develop and use every day. We can quickly glean the important information from a sentence with a quick scan. Some people recommend groupings of keywords separated by a comma or other separator. I don't subscribe to this tactic, because I find humans tend to read through groups of keywords slower than reading a sentence. In addition, the context is lacking from groups of keywords that are intended to reach a broad range of subject content. When comparing them to a sentence that describes the particular answer to a question, the sentence is more easily understood and provides more context to the query.

Use the <title> Tag Fully This is best done by writing two sentences—one that will fit in the search engine result page and a second that will appear afterward in the browser bar. This is best when developing two complete thoughts. I find this works well on a specific product page, where the product brand, name, type, and feature is the first sentence and the category and company name are contained in the second sentence.

Any of these can be used, but it is best to experiment and see what works best for your website. In a competitive environment, tweaking these titles can help your site gain a few rankings, but ultimately, you are after more clicks than rankings. Those sites with the highest rankings don't always get the most clicks if they show low-quality or irrelevant information in the title.

Use Metatags to Your Advantage

Meta is a Greek term meaning "behind" or "after." Metatags are located in the page code, behind what the visitor sees in the browser, or hidden from their view.

The original intent of the metatag was to provide an organizational tool for online documents, much like the card catalog in libraries (if you remember those days). The card catalog provided a systematic method of organizing the books in a library by subject, author, title, and category. The intent of this function was to provide a similar organizational structure to documents on the Internet. Unfortunately, this organization method was caught in the crosshairs of the SEO industry. Once SEO specialists figured out that you could gain rankings by cramming keywords into these fields, it was all over for the metadata. The attempt at document organization was lost by the lack of organization, influence, and a centralized data authority. Even more, the quest by zealous SEO practitioners to become number one in the rankings overruled any other use of this tag, regardless of the original intent.

Unfortunately, metatags suffered from overuse and bad information. In the early days of SEO, the metatags were the primary elements for optimization. Simply using your keywords in the metatags could boost your rankings. Unfortunately, you could also boost your rankings for words that were irrelevant to your website, because even nonrelevant terms in the metatags could gain rankings.

Why would someone do that? It all had to do with page views. Many sites at the time were selling advertising based on hits or page views. If you could gain rankings for a term such as *Disneyland* even though your site was not about Disneyland, you could gain thousands of page views from frustrated searchers who clicked your site and contributed to the page views. Fortunately, we've grown up since those days.

What about Meta Keywords?

The meta keyword tag has fallen on such rough times that it is barely even used by any of the major search engines, if at all. The keyword tag was so abused by webmasters and SEO practitioners that the function of the keyword metatags is well beyond the original intent.

For years, I have not even used the keyword tag in site optimization or development. It can help your site if you utilize an internal search engine or an intranet search, because it can be defined as a factor for a site's internal search, but very few search engines (if any) use this tag. The primary focus is on context and semantics, rather than a strict keyword match in a metatag. My advice for marketers is there are much better things to do with your busy day than spending time stressing over this outdated tactic.

As discussed in Chapter 4, the snippet check outlines the importance of the meta description. The meta description is not used as a ranking factor, but it is very visible to the searcher as an important key to the content on your pages. The meta description tag usually shows up in the search results as the "snippet" of information below the page title link. This changes in the search results based on the search terms and can sometimes look like a random sampling of words and phrases. Because of this, it is best to write a two- to three-sentence description of the content of each unique page. This will improve your chances of providing relevant content in the snippet, which can attract the click-through.

This was evidenced by a research white paper published by Enquiro (Enquiro Eye Tracking Report, July 2005; http://pages.enquiro.com/whitepaper-enquiro-eye-tracking-report-I-google.html). Enquiro used eye-tracking technology to study searcher behavior when evaluating search results. There were interesting behaviors throughout, but one of the more specific areas when it comes to meta descriptions was the snippet of information in the search results. Searchers exhibited a behavior called *fixation points*, which are areas of the page where the searchers eyes stopped, if only for a split-second but ideally long enough to read a word. Typical fixation points in the search results page were the bold text (your search terms are bold in the search results), brand names, prices, and icons (see Figure 5.3).

The impact of this behavior is clear. Your snippets need to contain as much specific information as possible, not just for the keyword, but for all the information related on the page. For example, in Enquiro's eye-tracking study, a searcher for the term *digital camera* would fixate on brand names such as Sony, Fuji, and Samsung. Sites that incorporated prices and product features were able to gain visibility. In a sense, searchers may type in only a few search terms but have a whole mind full of additional product questions. Gord Hitchkiss, CEO of Enquiro, referred to this as the *semantic cloud*, referring to the related terms that were not typed into the search box but are part of the search query. The more relevant terms and features that show up in the snippet, the more you can encourage clicking.

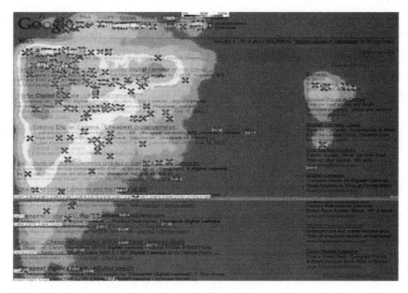

Figure 5.3 A heat map from Enquiro's eye-tracking study, 2005

Use Hypertext Links

One of the main factors in SEO is links, including links coming to your website, links within your website, and links to other websites. Links are the currency of authority in the search engine ranking formula. Why? We link to information and content that helps, provides answers, or entertains. We link to it as a recommendation to others because they may appreciate the information contained on another website. Really, a link is a word-of-mouth recommendation!

Here is the basic format of the link:

```
<a href="destination URL"> linked anchor text<a>
```

The link anchor text is the text that typically shows up as blue, underlined text. When website visitors see blue underlined text, they know automatically that it is a link. It is one of the earliest learned behaviors of Internet users.

Now, I'm not saying that all your links need to be blue and underlined. However, every degree that you vary from the "universal behavior" is another degree of difficulty that you create for your visitor. This is especially true if you create links that do not use underlines, are a vastly different color, or are combinations of these. Again, I am not saying that all links have to be blue and underlined. I am just saying that blue underlined links are understood by everyone! As a corollary, if you have content on your site that is blue and underlined and it isn't a link, you should change that immediately and stop frustrating your visitors.

Chapters 16 and 17 will deal with the importance of incoming links from other websites, as well as navigational links. In this section, I want you to evaluate how your pages link to each other within the content, not the navigation.

A good example of how this can apply to your content is the Lenovo Olympic website from the Beijing Games in 2008 (Figure 5.4). There is a paragraph of content that reads as follows:

Lenovo is offering limited-edition notebook PCs inspired by the Lenovo-designed Olympic Torch for the Beijing 2008 Olympic Games. <u>Learn more.</u>

Figure 5.4 Ambiguous link text

There are a couple of issues with this paragraph. The first issue is that there are three independent thoughts and one call to action. If you were to click Learn More, what would you learn more about? The laptop, the torch, or the games? This is why I hesitate to use link text like "learn more" or "click here" or "read more." Granted, most SEO specialists would tell you to hyperlink any amount of text with keywords in order to gain rankings. I tend to take the reader's side of the equation. If I see that "Lenovo laptop" is the link text, then I automatically know that if I click that text, I will go to a page about the Lenovo laptop. Contextually, it makes sense to the reader, and it helps the search engines determine the context of the linked page.

Coordinate Miscellaneous Page Elements

After the page title and headings, everything else counts minimally by itself. The idea is that all of the on-page factors work together in concert to create a context of the page. Repetition of keywords does little to create the same effect. As search engines improve, more emphasis is placed on the sum total of relevant content, even when using alternate versions of words. The semantics of words and concepts is the future of search and matching results with a searcher's intent.

alt Attributes

alt attributes are content that will be displayed when an image used on your website fails to load. Regardless of the cause, the alt attribute shows as an explanation or instruction for the visitor (Figure 5.5). If the image is used as a link and the image contains the only call to action or instruction, the visitor can be left without any information to move forward in the process of there is no alt attribute.

alt attributes on linked images provide a very small fraction of relevance toward rankings. alt attributes on nonlinked images may provide little relevance, if any at all.

Most SEO specialists agree that alt attributes are important but provide a negligible boost. Again, it is about the orderly arrangement of elements on the page and the factors being used cooperatively rather than using each factor as an independent bludgeon for rankings.

Figure 5.5 The original page with images loaded and the same page showing the alt attributes

Filenames

Filenames also help develop the overall context of the information. Filenames cover a wide gamut of information, including page names, images, documents, files, multimedia, and any other element contained on a page.

For instance, many people will add an image to a page and leave the filename intact. Many times it is the typical digital camera naming convention, such as DSC1100037373. Instead of simply uploading the image with the default image name, change the filename to be descriptive of what the image is. Figure 5.6 shows the results of a Yahoo! image search for the term *laptops*. The vast majority of images in Figure 5.6 contain the word *laptop* in the filename of the image, such as laptops.jpg. To improve the visibility of images on your site showing up in search results and image search results, be sure to rename the image.

Use this tactic in naming your website pages, PDFs, website images, downloadable files, and other elements that make up your website.

Figure 5.6 Yahoo! results for an image search of *laptops*

Wednesday: Optimize Content Structure for SEO

Many times, SEO advice seems to be given and implemented as a blunt force instrument. "Use this word, this many times, along with this many other words, etc." Fortunately, search engine optimizing is less about trick formulas and forcing words into content and more about creating a consistent context of the information. Yes, utilizing keywords is important, but so is utilizing additional words and concepts that add to the understanding, content and development of your marketing message and the information that users need.

Use Headlines to Get Attention

My first attempt at building a website was amateur, to say the least. Coming from a journalism background, I used the page layout techniques that were familiar to me. By using the newspaper layout as a guide, my first website focused on the layout starting with the following:

Headline This informed the visitor about the page's specific purpose.

Subheading Additional content was grouped into subheadings.

Captions Images were presented alongside a caption to explain the image.

Bullet Points These were used to present important content and sum up information.

Paragraph Headers These summarized the paragraph.

Although I was proud of my creation, I kept tweaking the layout and image placement and learning new techniques to display information. About that time, someone remarked to me that they found my website on Yahoo! It was number one in the results for a very good term. It didn't take long to figure out the relationship between the term I was ranking for in Yahoo! and the content that was presented on my site. The page that was ranking was using the primary keywords in the headline, subheadings, captions, and paragraph headers. The words I used were from some simple keyword research and logical search behavior of my target audience.

From those early days, much has changed in the search engine algorithms, but the on-page factors have been consistent. Good layout in the code helps show the important concepts and terms on the page, because it differentiates the keywords in the headings from the regular text. Just as a headline grabs a reader's attention, the <h1> tag communicates to the search engine that the text in this tag is important, and it is more important than the other text on the page. The words in the <h2> tag are secondary in importance, and so on.

Simply having paragraphs of content on a page does not provide the search engine with the necessary information to distinguish which keywords are the most important or relevant on the page. The markup in the code helps communicate to the search engines the important phrases, just as the markup changes the font size of the headline for the reader.

Use HTML to Build Context

As the page structure develops, both the user and the search engine rely on the subheadings <h2>, <h3>, and <h4> to understand the hierarchy of the content and article structure. Bullet points break up the content by providing quick, readable information bytes. Typically, features or important content is contained in bullet points, as searchers browse for fast information cues.

As a side note about other markup languages, Cascading Style Sheets (CSS) layout techniques can be used to mark up content as well. However, the HTML <H> tags need to be utilized in order for search engines to understand the structure of the pages. Continuing growth of HTML5 will slightly change the tagging semantics, but it will still be an understandable hierarchy of headline, heading, subheading tags that all work together to show the importance of content areas on the page.

Employ Layout Techniques That Provide Context

Many sites do a wonderful job of presenting content in an effective way that allows visitors to quickly scan the content and grasp the subject matter. SitePoint (**www.sitepoint .com**) is one of the standards, because their presentation of content is one of the best in providing a clear path for the eye to follow and find specific information (see Figure 5.7).

Figure 5.7 SitePoint.com article layout

The simple beauty of this payout is contained in the high-contrast text to background colors, allowing for an ideal online reading situation. With the difference in headline, main heading, and subheading, the reader can quickly surmise the structure of the document along with the outline and flow of information.

From a search engine perspective, the markup in the code allows the engine to do a similar survey of the content, because words that are contained in the header elements are usual indicators of the content. By writing descriptive content and blending keywords as part of developing the article and content structure, the search engine will "see" the importance of the headings. Figure 5.8 shows the markup use of the headings, hypertext links, and bold text.

Figure 5.8 SitePoint article layout with markup elements

Each of these markup elements provides context. The visual elements appeal to the human reader and provide structure to the page. The markup functions in the code provide context to the search engine and provide structure to the hierarchy of content.

Regardless of the type of company that you might be running online, you can take advantage of these layout techniques. For example, BuyDesign, a business-to-business website, impressed me with the layout techniques in redeveloping its website, because BuyDesign took advantage of the reading styles discussed in this chapter (Figure 5.9).

The page utilizes contrasting text space, text sizes for communicating the content outline, bold text, and bullet points. In addition, there is also an element of color used consistently throughout the website in order to communicate a specific visual element. I find that many website designs are not that disciplined in their use of color. Many tend to use it liberally, but this design uses the color orange only for specific areas designed to attract the eye in a very gentle persuasion.

Figure 5.9 Content arranged for effective presentation

In addition to the format, the development of the bullet points and bold text points to a very simple yet effective means of communicating information. Each bullet point is a product benefit. There are benefit statements used throughout the content;

however, the beauty is in the content of those benefit statements. The verb describing the benefit is the first word or phrase in those statements, and the verb phrase is bold. Even if the reader reads only the first one to two words in each bulleted phrase, they have read the important benefit statements critical to selling the product. This is a very elegant means of using website content structure to communicate marketing concepts within seconds!

How does your content communicate your benefit statements? What content attracts people as they survey your pages? Do you have more than four paragraphs on a page with no heading, subheading, image, or visual cue? How have you formatted your text for easy reading? Within a few moments of review, you may see that there is substantial work to be done in utilizing these important headings to not only increase rankings but to also increase the sales and leads provided by the website.

Thursday: Explore the Power of Off-Page Ranking Factors

The primary component of off-page factors is incoming links from other websites. Links are factors that you can affect but not control as you can the on-page elements. The search engines rely heavily on the incoming links (or back-links), because these indicate your website's reputation. My father always had this bit of advice about reputation: "There is what you say about yourself, and then there is what others say about you." You can sell, position, create, and persuade all that you can on your website. However, a significant portion of the ranking algorithm depends on how other websites link to your website. The best way to explain this in human terms is that a link from another website is like a word-of-mouth referral. Business owners all know that the best business comes from referrals. Referrals are the best marketing available, because they are free and largely based on your reputation and performance.

The same applies to websites and search engine value. High-quality websites that link to your website are providing a strong word-of-mouth referral. Sites that do well in gaining those referrals will be considered to be more relevant and trustworthy. This brings us to a primary factor in search engine optimization—the benefit of high-quality referrals in the form of links from other websites. This section covers the *why* of linking, while Chapter 16 will cover the *how*. It might seem like a leap in time to wait that long, but it all comes together in a logical flow, once the basics are covered.

Benefits of Links

Link building has never been described by anybody as "fun." In fact, it is one of the most tedious and time-consuming tasks in website marketing and SEO. Finding link partners and link opportunities is very much like cold-calling in sales. However, it's a necessary task for many websites and one that needs to be done when rankings need to be improved.

There are three primary benefits of links. Although gaining rankings is the primary purpose of many webmasters, other aspects tend to be overlooked. The "golden link" is the link that provides high rankings, great sales and leads, and a powerful branding agent that increases your visibility and credibility. If you can gain a link that provides visitors, sales, and increased rankings, you can reward yourself for a job very well done. Those are valuable links and will provide many tangible benefits for your work.

Rankings

Of course, most online marketers are after rankings. It is a known fact that a great lead from a high-authority website can boost your rankings in a matter of days. Sites that are considered authorities carry weight in the ranking algorithm. While all search engines evaluate link in different ways, Google tends to be the center of attention because it provides the market share of searchers. In the early days of search engines, Google gained notoriety based on the relevance and great results provided to searchers. Much of this was because of the linking aspect of the algorithm. Most other search engines were only concerned with on-page factors and not evaluating links. Even to this day, the other search engines still seem to use links from other websites and links within a website, but not much attention is focused on understanding that aspect of their algorithm.

In Google, this link value measurement is called PageRank. Gaining a link from a site high in PageRank will carry some of the linking "weight" from the authority site to your website.

The PageRank is displayed in the Google Toolbar, and when it was first launched, both site owners and webmasters pursued anything they could do to increase their PageRank value. Links were traded and valued based on the PageRank of the linked page. People compared the PageRank of their home pages. Webmasters tried to crack the PageRank calculations to see which other pages on their sites were more valuable than other pages. Within only a few short months, many webmasters and site owners were more concerned about gaining PageRank than rankings or even business. The SEO community was focused on gaining links in order to increase PageRank. When it got to the point that site owners were beginning to buy and sell links to each other on the basis of PageRank, Google stepped in and changed the PageRank calcuations. Since that time, the PageRank display is rarely accurate and rarely updated. Many believe it was a public relations ploy to publish this part of the algorithm, because it did create an amazing amount of interest within the online marketing community.

The lesson learned from that entire stage in search marketing was that there were too many who followed the excitement of chasing their page ranking rather than focusing on getting more sales and leads out of their websites. People refused to link to low PageRank sites (because they may lower the linking site's PageRank) and therefore didn't link to sites as they normally would. This behavior seemed to be the opposite of what Google intended.

PageRank is still around, in some form, but it is one of dozens of ranking factors for websites. Links from other websites are still considered a valuable type of currency online, because the authority from high-value websites can pass to your site and increase your authority in your niche or industry.

Brand Exposure

A benefit of getting other websites to link to your website is that it increases your visibility online. By your website or business name having links on other sites, readers see you associated with specific topics and can begin to develop an idea of what your business is, which may also enhance your credibility within an industry. If your website is consistently cited in research, articles, and information within an industry, your brand credibility improves.

There are many times an article, video, or topic goes "viral" online. Somehow, the topic or information resonates with a particular group of people, and the article or video is shared, passed along, or emailed to others within a social circle and beyond. You may not get much business out of this type of referral network, but it does increase the number of people who see your brand or company name and are exposed to the information you provide.

Sales and Leads

As mentioned, a link is an online word-of-mouth referral. Getting referrals is important, because many links can provide a significant part of your business. When evaluating a website, I always search for the links to a website that produce a very high percentage of conversions, be they leads, sales, or engagement. By identifying these high-conversion links, a business knows that they should continue to develop the relationship with the business that is the source of that link and also look to create relationships with other similar businesses.

This is a necessary evaluation when looking for link partners and for evaluating the links currently sending traffic to your website. How valuable are your links? Knowing your high-conversion links will help you define a strategy for building more high-conversion links by understanding their source.

How Search Engines Use Links in Rankings

Links play an important part in establishing your website's credibility in terms of the ranking algorithm. Beyond simply getting a link from another website, the next level of value is to get a link with a keyword in the anchor text, which will enhance the link with context. There is a large difference between the following links if they were presented within the content of an article:

```
www.wallstreetjournal.com/analysis
WSJ's financial analysis
```

The first option is simply the URL of the website. Although there are many links like this around the Internet, they simply link to a page by its URL address. There is no context to the reader other than the surrounding content and the context of the URL itself. The second option provides the context of the content on the linked page. It is developed by the author of the linking site to convey an additional level of meaning to the link by presenting it with intent and purpose, in relation to the content of an article. This type of linking provides more information to both the user and the search engine. The user sees and understands the intent and the context. The search engine finds the pattern of keywords being used to provide "outside" context to a page through using anchor text.

Content Links

Some factors the search engines use for evaluating links are the types of the link that is being used on the linking site and the surrounding content around the link on the page of that site. Essentially, they ask, where is the link to the site on the page? What part of the page contains the link, and what is the surrounding text? Is it a navigational link, an editorial link, an advertisement, or a comment link? Different types of links are given different values. Editorial links tend to be valued very highly, because they are links that fall specifically under the word-of-mouth category.

Purchased or advertising links are assigned very little value, because the advertiser can control the link text, and the link is purchased as advertising, rather than part of the natural content of the website. Banner ads and other advertising links that are purchased through an advertising server do not count toward link popularity. They are simply a method of advertising and considered a separate type of link.

Image or Text Links

Search engines also view the type of link to determine whether it is a text link or an image link. Text links count very highly, so many optimizers opt for text-based links. However, image links contain a product image or some other eye-catching graphic. Using alt attributes, as explained on Tuesday, will enable the search engines to determine the context of the image link and apply that to some level of link popularity benefit. However, it is generally agreed that the level of value of an image link from the alt attribute is not near the value of a text link. Although by itself an alt attribute does not count for much, it is one of those hundreds of tiny factors that add up over time.

There is still much debate about the value of a text link compared to an image link containing an alt attribute—which is most effective for SEO, and which is most effective for persuading visitors toward action? Of course, since websites vary, the answer to this debate is to test different methods for your site. Some ecommerce websites have tested using text links and image links (and various combinations). The surprising result was that their visitors clicked image links more. Even though they held little SEO value, they attracted more attention and gained more sales. While this may work for one website, it may not work for others. This is why measuring the results is always more profitable than measuring rankings. Decisions like this should only be made on a case-by-case basis after measuring the outcomes. Sometimes, site managers decide to scale back SEO in order to do things that might result in higher sales. This should be done based on testing and not rash decisions. These types of decisions need to be carefully weighed.

Association Links

Another factor of link assessment by search engines is the reciprocity factor. In the day when more links equaled more success, this was effective. Website owners would link to each other with the typical "I link to you and you link to me, *wink, wink*" understanding that they were assisting each other in building links.

Now, the sheer quantity of links is not valued; the quality of that quantity is the most important factor. Because of this, reciprocal linking ("I link to you and you link to me") is not valued as much as a simple, one-way, incoming link from another website. The best way to explain this is to use an offline situation. If I were to ask for a friend's recommendation on where to eat, they would probably give me the name of a restaurant that they enjoy. If I go to eat at that restaurant, who benefits from that exchange? Financially, the restaurant benefits. If I have a good meal, then both the restaurant and my friend benefit from an increased reputation. My only benefit is that I had a great meal. Linking follows the same path. A true link referral is where the site that is the destination of the link benefits from the searcher who needs an answer. The site benefits from the incoming visitors and possible business. The website that linked to that destination grows in the searcher's mind as a trusted resource. This is the perfect world that search engines envision when calculating links as a source of website authority.

Reciprocal linking implies that there is a kickback on the referral. As soon as we find out that our friend recommended the restaurant because he gets financial compensation for his referrals, his advice is now suspect. Did he recommend the restaurant out of our best interest or his? This is why reciprocal links simply do not count as highly, because it shows there may be an established relationship involved.

The Source of the Link

Beyond what is in your control on your website, the search engines place a significant amount of importance on the content of other websites that link to your website. Those other websites are third-party, ideally not related to your company but are recommending it in some manner, which provides the search engines with an independent view of your website.

Site Content

Search engines evaluate a number of factors in the source and destinations of the link. On the page that contains the link, the search engines factor the surrounding content around the link, the content of the entire page, and the relevance of the linking site. The search engines are attempting to assess the relevancy of the link in accordance with the overall content of the website. In short, does the content of the link reflect the content of the website?

Search engines may use the following questions in determining a link's value:

- Is the linked page relevant to the linking page?
- Are the two sites relevant?
- What is the content of the overall linked website?

Obviously, if you have a website about vintage car restoration, it follows that many of your links will follow along with the content of the site, with links to parts suppliers, links to articles or "how-to" videos, and links to pictures of other people's cars. If, on this vintage car website, you have a link to your friend's wedding cake website, it probably won't carry much weight. Your website has shown content and authority concerning one subject, yet the link is far outside the contextual spectrum of cars. The two subjects do not match well, so although the link will pass some measure of popularity, it most likely won't pass as much as when you link to another auto-oriented destination.

Regional Content

This is a ranking factor that has been added in the past year or so in the search results. Sites that gain a number of links within a region will rank well within that region. This is especially evident in country-based websites where links gained from within that country make a website much more relevant than a foreign website with few native links. This is another level of measuring relevance based on regional content, country-specific content, and language-based searches.

Applying regional weighting now makes it possible for a search query made in France, using French language, to direct a searcher to the French version of an international company website. It is something that most people take for granted, so it may not sound impressive. However, years ago, this was not as smooth a process as it is today. The search engines are getting better at this process and saving international companies many headaches in developing workarounds to accommodate any fault in the progression. This is based on the regional weighting of links and the focus of country-domains and language-specific links making the search results more relevant to the searcher.

Age of Links

Another factor in evaluating links that counts toward the quality of the link is the age of the link. This is a factor that rewards longevity to websites that have been valuable resources of content for many years.

Offline, many people will establish a business's credibility by asking how many years the business has been in operation. Longer seems to be better and is more trustworthy. This same evaluation is framed online, because sites that have older established links tend to rank highly based on the age of those links. It shows that they have been around longer and have survived the many tribulations of the online world.

Optimizing and Evaluating Your Link Text

On Tuesday we covered the importance of link anchor text. The anchor text that is used in displaying the link provides the context for the page and content that is the destination of that link. The same follows for websites linking to you.

Naturally, most anchor text links to your website will be the text of your domain address, not using keywords, but just the simple hypertext URL. This is the most common form of linking from one site to another. Site owners linking to your site are not usually motivated to use anchor text.

Making the most of link text requires two specific actions. First is optimizing the current links to your website, that is, asking those site owners who are linking to you to use words in the link rather than just the URL. Second—and more difficult— is developing new links from other websites with your preferred anchor text being used in the link.

This is where available link survey tools can be of great assistance. By spidering the sites that link to you, many tools can provide you with the page that links to your site, the destination page of that link, and the text that is being used in the link. This gives you a very substantial starting point in developing a plan for optimizing your current links and pursuing new ones. You may also want to include a few competitor sites in this survey in order to view the links acquired by their sites. This way, it may help in finding additional sources or directories for links.

Tools for evaluating links are endless. In Chapter 4, we covered how the webmaster tools provided by the search engines are a place to start. You can always move into the realm of some paid or subscription-based software or services that will monitor your links as well.

Friday: See SEO in Practice

Learning the basics of SEO is always a very elementary task—it seems easy, and it makes sense. Using keywords in prominent content areas on the site and in links isn't rocket science. But in my opinion, it is both an art and a science. The science is the mathematical part of the algorithm that accounts for all the keywords in conjunction with their locations, placement, frequency, and related topics on the web pages and in links. The art is in using these factors and placing them together to create a page that visitors find persuasive enough to take the action you want them to take.

Gaining rankings is only the first part of marketing your website. Getting people to your website is just the beginning; getting them to take action is the second part, and it requires both the art and science to create to right circumstances for your visitors.

SEO Examples

In a health-related search such as *tinnitus*, the results from the different search engines are fairly consistent. There are sites that are regularly in the top few results. In examining the consistencies among those sites, you can begin to see the patterns of SEO emerge. In Figure 5.10, the results from Google and Bing show the rankings based on the on-page and off-page factors.

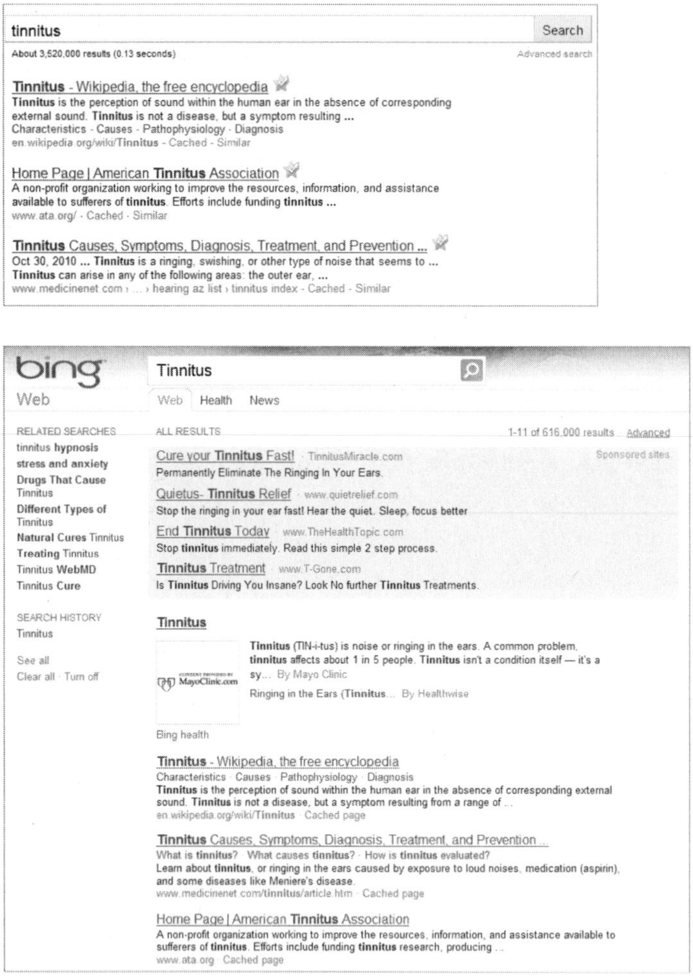

Figure 5.10 Google and Bing results for *tinnitus*

The results are remarkably similar; Wikipedia is one of the top results. The main reason for this is that Wikipedia fits many of the criteria for good search engine rankings—prominent placements of keywords and lots of incoming links from other websites; as such, it is considered an authority site.

Figure 5.11 is the Wikipedia page for "Tinnitus." You will see that there is an extraordinary amount of well-developed content organized in specific subject areas with citations to many other health and research related sites, as well as other pages within Wikipedia. The content uses markup to distinguish headings, subheadings, and topics within the content of the page. This markup is consistent throughout the site and for every one of the topics contained on the Wikipedia domain. The code shows that the headline Tinnitus at the top of the page is contained within an <h1> tag. The next level of headings is contained in <h2> tags, and <h3> tags are used for subcontent within the <h2>headings. Although on their own the heading tags will not be the magical key for rankings, they provide a specific order and architecture to the content of the page, which provides support to the major ranking factors.

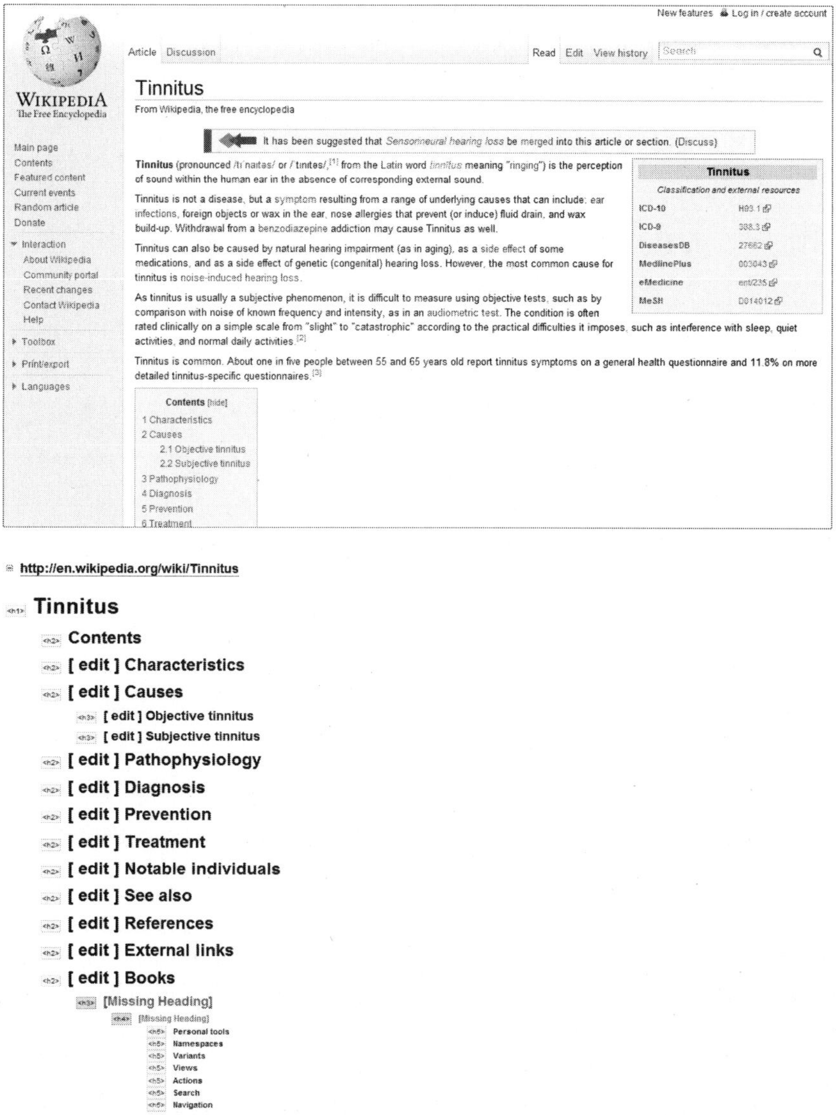

Figure 5.11 Wikipedia page for "Tinnitus"

In addition to all the on-page factors, the off-page factors support this as an authority site. A quick search on the number of links coming into this page shows Google counting more than 21,000 incoming links from other websites and Yahoo! reporting just more than 6,300. The number of sites linking to this page, the types of sites linking to this page, and the well-structured content and keywords throughout the text of the page create ideal conditions for a consistently high ranking in the search engines.

For a product search, such as *cool science gifts*, the more detailed the search phrase, the more specific the results will be. The sites in these results have to implement some sort of optimization to show up for a search that is this specific (see Figure 5.12).

a

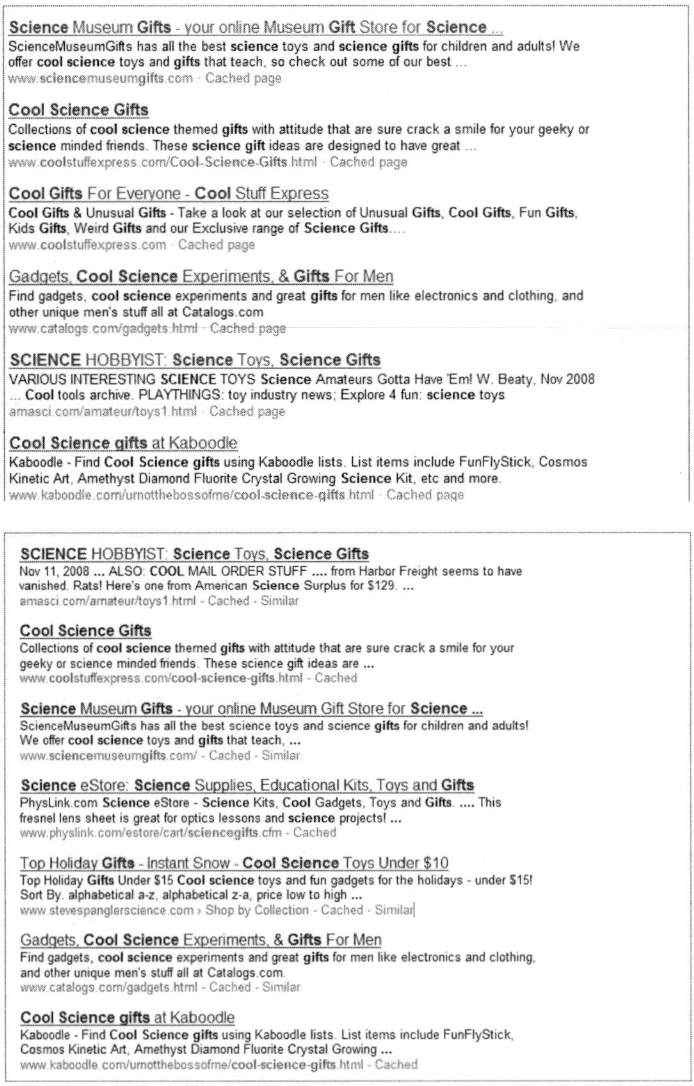

Science Museum Gifts - your online Museum **Gift** Store for **Science** ...
ScienceMuseumGifts has all the best **science** toys and **science** gifts for children and adults! We offer **cool science** toys and **gifts** that teach, so check out some of our best ...
www.sciencemuseumgifts.com · Cached page

Cool Science Gifts
Collections of **cool science** themed **gifts** with attitude that are sure crack a smile for your geeky or **science** minded friends. These **science** gift ideas are designed to have great ...
www.coolstuffexpress.com/Cool-Science-Gifts.html · Cached page

Cool Gifts For Everyone - **Cool** Stuff Express
Cool Gifts & Unusual **Gifts** - Take a look at our selection of Unusual **Gifts**, **Cool Gifts**, Fun **Gifts**, Kids **Gifts**, Weird **Gifts** and our Exclusive range of **Science Gifts**....
www.coolstuffexpress.com · Cached page

Gadgets, **Cool Science** Experiments, & **Gifts** For Men
Find gadgets, **cool science** experiments and great **gifts** for men like electronics and clothing, and other unique men's stuff all at Catalogs.com
www.catalogs.com/gadgets.html · Cached page

SCIENCE HOBBYIST: **Science** Toys, **Science Gifts**
VARIOUS INTERESTING **SCIENCE** TOYS **Science** Amateurs Gotta Have 'Em! W. Beaty, Nov 2008 ... **Cool** tools archive. PLAYTHINGS: toy industry news; Explore 4 fun: **science** toys
amasci.com/amateur/toys1.html · Cached page

Cool Science gifts at Kaboodle
Kaboodle - Find **Cool Science gifts** using Kaboodle lists. List items include FunFlyStick, Cosmos Kinetic Art, Amethyst Diamond Fluorite Crystal Growing **Science** Kit, etc and more.
www.kaboodle.com/urnottthebossofme/cool-science-gifts.html · Cached page

b

SCIENCE HOBBYIST: **Science** Toys, **Science Gifts**
Nov 11, 2008 ... ALSO: COOL MAIL ORDER STUFF .... from Harbor Freight seems to have vanished. Rats! Here's one from American **Science** Surplus for $129. ...
amasci.com/amateur/toys1.html - Cached - Similar

Cool Science Gifts
Collections of **cool science** themed **gifts** with attitude that are sure crack a smile for your geeky or **science** minded friends. These **science** gift ideas are ...
www.coolstuffexpress.com/cool-science-gifts.html - Cached

Science Museum Gifts - your online Museum Gift Store for **Science** ...
ScienceMuseumGifts has all the best science toys and **science gifts** for children and adults! We offer **cool science** toys and **gifts** that teach, ...
www.sciencemuseumgifts.com/ - Cached - Similar

Science eStore: **Science** Supplies, Educational Kits, Toys and **Gifts**
PhysLink.com **Science** eStore - **Science** Kits, **Cool** Gadgets, Toys and **Gifts**. .... This fresnel lens sheet is great for optics lessons and **science** projects! ...
www.physlink.com/estore/cart/sciencegifts.cfm - Cached

Top Holiday **Gifts** - Instant Snow - **Cool Science** Toys Under $10
Top Holiday **Gifts** Under $15 **Cool science** toys and fun gadgets for the holidays - under $15! Sort By. alphabetical a-z, alphabetical z-a, price low to high ...
www.stevespanglerscience.com › Shop by Collection - Cached - Similar

Gadgets, **Cool Science** Experiments, & **Gifts** For Men
Find gadgets, **cool science** experiments and great **gifts** for men like electronics and clothing, and other unique men's stuff all at Catalogs.com.
www.catalogs.com/gadgets.html - Cached - Similar

Cool Science gifts at Kaboodle
Kaboodle - Find **Cool Science gifts** using Kaboodle lists. List items include FunFlyStick, Cosmos Kinetic Art, Amethyst Diamond Fluorite Crystal Growing ...
www.kaboodle.com/urnottthebossofme/cool-science-gifts.html - Cached

Figure 5.12 (a) Bing results for *cool science gifts*; (b) Google results for *cool science gifts*

Again, there are sites showing up in both the Bing and Google results. There are some slight variations in the results that are based on nuances in each search engine. For example, the result for CoolStuffExpress.com is a page in Google's rankings but the domain in Bing. Google tends to put more emphasis on specific pages that are more relevant within the domain, rather than the domain itself.

In examining the ranking page in Google for CoolStuffExpress.com (Figure 5.13), a similar structure is evident. As an ecommerce site, there is less content, but the navigation and content structures within the site reinforce the keywords and content of *cool science gifts*. Although the specific phrase may be used only once on the page, the words can be easily found independently on related product names, navigation, and product descriptions.

Figure 5.13 SEO on CoolStuff Express

Specifically, look at the page title for Cool Science Gifts. In the search engine results pages in Figure 5.12, there were only a few, if any, sites that had this exact phrase used as the title link to the website. This is the power of the page title. By using a specific phrase that matches the search query, you can increase both your rankings and your click-throughs. A quick check on back-links shows that Google estimates around 50 incoming links to that specific page on CoolStuffExpress.com and more than 1,700 to the entire domain.

Compared to ScienceMuseumGifts.com, CoolStuffExpress.com ranks ahead in Google but a few spots behind in Bing. This happens frequently, because not all search engines will match up rakings. There are nuances in the algorithms that account for these minute differences in rankings across the engines. Consistency of rankings within a few rankings, such as 1–4, is the best goal to strive for in rankings, because things change frequently.

ScienceMuseumGifts (Figure 5.14) provides a different navigation style but only an infrequent use of the word *cool* when compared to CoolStuffExpress. CoolStuffExpress uses the word *cool* frequently in the navigation elements and products displayed, whereas ScienceMuseumGifts uses the word *cool* a few times in the text.

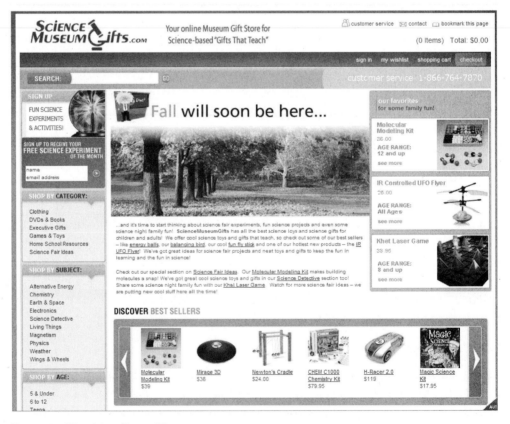

Figure 5.14 SEO on ScienceMuseumGifts

One could infer that the basic root phrase *science gifts* is most likely the most relevant, and these sites are showing up from the additional search term *cool*. Most likely both of these sites would still rank well for the root phrase *science gifts*. However, as noted earlier, the specific phrase being used in the `<title>` tag provides a significant amount of weight for this page to be ranked well in comparison with other, similar websites.

Using Comparison as a Guide

When evaluating the sites that rank ahead of your website for your intended phrases, look at the similarities shared among the sites ranking on the first page. In addition, check out the links coming into these sites. The links will not always be the primary indicator, even though they are important. In some cases, sites with thousands of back-links do not rank well against a well-optimized website with only a few back-links. Everything has to work together for successful rankings.

When evaluating competitive sites, make note of the important text areas on the pages and throughout the site, such as the `<title>` tag, headlines, headings, navigation links, text links, and other miscellaneous areas. Also, evaluate the incoming text to the domain and to the page in particular. In addition to the incoming links, look over the sites that are linking to the domain, and see whether there are any well-known sites that could be considered as an authority site. Sometimes, one of these links can be found, which provides a logical reason as to the value given to your competitor site.

By evaluating the sites that have rankings, you can begin to formulate some of the more well-known ranking factors that the sites have in common and can begin to develop a strategy to gain rankings for your own site. This comparison may also show you where your site stands in comparison with the back-links from other websites. If your site has only a few dozen incoming links from other websites and your competitors have a few hundred, then you can see where the bulk of your work will lie over the next weeks or months and what type of campaign may be necessary to gain more visibility.

Model the websites that are doing well, and observe how their sites are built and optimized. This is a good method to simply mirror what they are doing in order to become competitive. After becoming competitive, then you move on to gaining market share. A good marketing campaign not only can bring additional visibility and market share, but may also bring some valuable links as well. SEO is not just the beginnning of gaining rankings; for the marketer who understands SEO, it can be a side benefit from other online marketing activities.

SEO Is Just the Start

Just as the SEO industry had to evolve in order to be relevant, your skills will need to expand in order to grasp the complexity of skills necessary to develop, manage, and market a website. Future chapters will cover keyword selection, website architecture, programming, content development, persuasive content, analytics, and marketing.

The basic SEO skill set is necessary for many reasons, because it is something that can easily become a part of the editorial process when adding new content. It is helpful in developing the programming of a website to make it search-friendly. It means taking keyword research beyond content optimization and using it as business intelligence and better understanding the searcher. Link building becomes part of marketing; future chapters will show how you can market your content to gain links, credibility, and visibility. The basics of architecture, server settings, and programming will always be a necessity because these skills are always needed for troubleshooting and maintenance.

Understanding how information works online and how it is viewed by both humans and machines will help you create an understanding of the online marketing world. Understanding the history of online communications can help a marketer realize that the lasting power of electronic communication as online marketing will last much longer than other types of campaign. So, be ready for the long-term investment, rather than a short-term campaign, when it comes to marketing your website.

Simply focusing on a single element of marketing, such as search engine optimization, without including other factors of usability, analytics, design, marketing, and customer testing, neglects the necessary components of building a successful campaign. Everything must be done in context in order to effectively reach a targeted audience and build a long-term association.

Review and Hands-On

Review your site by looking at pages that are about specific ideas or topics. Have you used the keyword in the prominent text areas of the site, such as the title text, headline, headings, and body copy?

In evaluating the incoming links from other websites, who is linking to you, and do any of those sites use anchor text in their linking?

Run a comparison between your site and sites that are ranking ahead of you for some key phrases. Don't be too general in your keyword selection. Select something a bit more detailed (sometimes three to four words), and see who is ranking ahead of you. Create a spreadsheet and begin to make comparisons of the structure and primary text areas of the pages in the rankings and the most logically relevant page of your website. Compare the text areas, back-links, back-link anchor text, navigation, and recurrence of words.

Chapter 6 will go deeper into selecting and using keywords on the page, so don't get locked into thinking that simple repetition of a keyword on a page is the key to rankings; there is much more to all of this, and SEO is just the start.

Week 3: Jump into Keyword Research

6

SEO is a great foundation, keywords are the foundation of optimization. Many people understand the concept of keywords but neglect the simplest method of understanding how to develop the words that are most important.

As with the rest of this book, this chapter is focused on developing the skills necessary for online marketing, rather than being a survey of available tools. The tools are only as good as the person performing the research and analysis.

This chapter focuses on the types of keyword-research analysis and on understanding searcher behavior. By developing skills to gear the keyword research toward your business goals, you'll be able to attract searchers and persuade them to take action.

Chapter Contents

Monday: Call It What It Is
Tuesday: Develop Keyword-Research Skills
Wednesday: Understand the Buying Cycle
Thursday: Find Searcher Behavior Types
Friday: Organize for Optimization

Monday: Call It What It Is

The first rule of keyword research is simple: call it what it is.

Get rid of the corporate jargon; remove the fancy PR "fluff" and the marketing hype. Searchers don't have your internal language on their mind. They have questions and problems and are searching for solutions and answers.

Searchers Search Based on Need

Here is one of my favorite examples of what happens when a web page delivers content too focused on brand and not enough on what the product actually is. Diapers.com sells a product known as Boudreaux's Butt Paste (see Figure 6.1).

Figure 6.1 Diapers.com's Boudreaux's Butt Paste page

This begins our first foray into keyword forensics. There is a distinct difference between brand names and functions. If your brand name does not mirror the function, then you have an issue to overcome. Searchers are looking for an answer, in other words, a function, and your brand name may not be known to them. Because of this, when a search is for the function of a product, the results do not match the brand name.

This is the case of Boudreaux's Butt Paste. The typical parent is searching for diaper rash ointment, but that phrase appears only once on the Diapers.com product page. In the navigation, the product appears under the category of *Creams & Ointments*. The headings, descriptions, images, and context of the page all surround the concept of the brand name and not the function of the product.

This brings us to the purpose of calling things what they are: people search based on their need. Brand names are rarely the top search phrase; the general term describing what people *need* is the top searched phrase. It is a significantly common phenomenon. People type into the search box what they need and then refine their search from that initial query.

Searchers Rely on Simple Phrases

Another typical searcher behavior is the generalization and simplification of the search term. This is not necessarily the simplification of the term itself but the simplification of the concept. The searcher, even using multiple terms, is looking for a solution-based or needs-based answer. Content that is brand-based or overly descriptive may not include the same language the searcher uses, and the site will not be found. What may seem a logical marketing description could decrease your website's visibility.

Color

When looking for any products based on color, marketers and retailers tend to rely on flowery, beautiful product descriptions that will create an image in the searcher's mind. However, if your description does not match the early, simple search of the searcher, you may be removing your content from the search.

For example, in a search between *red sofa* and *wine sofa* (see Figure 6.2), there are more than twice as many results for *wine sofa*. By the way, the number of search results tends to change frequently, so it is only a guide, not a true measurement.

However, when looking at the keyword search data, the Google Keyword Tool shows that *red sofa* is the preferred search term of searchers by more than 3,500 percent (see Figure 6.3).

A similar difference is shown when comparing *green sofa* and *olive sofa*, because they have about the same number of results in Google, but *green* is searched for as a primary term five times more often than *olive* each month.

This is a distinct issue in retail optimization; advertisers and marketers tend to employ vivid language designed to provoke an emotional response. However, in doing so, the product becomes irrelevant to the search query.

In this specific case, thousands of retailers are competing for a phrase that doesn't have enough search volume to appear in keyword-research tools. They are missing the market by not being aware of the primary phrase being used by the searcher.

Figure 6.2 SERPs for *red sofa* (2,440,000 results) vs. *wine sofa* (5,190,000 results)

Keywords	Global Monthly Search Volume ⑦
Keywords related to term(s) entered - sorted by relevance ⑦	
red sofa	110,000
green sofa	40,500
red wine sofa	320
wine sofa	2,900
burgundy sofa	12,100
burgundy sofas	1,000
olive sofa	8,100
red and white sofa	390
wine sofa table	590
contour burgundy reclining sofa	46
burgundy reclining sofa	320

Figure 6.3 Google Keyword Tool data for couch colors

Function

Another form of keyword misdirection is the corporate jargon or established descriptions within a company or an industry. Typically found in business-to-business marketing, these keywords are always at the mercy of established methodologies or internal reliance.

In the landscaping industry, for example, a few companies sell stump cutters. Despite customers and salespeople calling the equipment *stump grinders*, the literature, websites, and descriptions all employ the *stump cutter* phrase. A quick check in Google Keyword Tool and Keyword Discovery showed that *stump grinder* is the only phrase used by the searcher. *Stump cutter* doesn't even show up in the list.

A survey of internal conversations, literature, and client-customer communication can help a company self-diagnose the disease of misdirected nomenclature. Avoid employing the internal jargon used within a company's corporate culture or business-to-business exchanges. Internal conversations reinforce the use of adopted or adapted words or, even worse, acronyms. Take an honest look, listen to the names and words being used, and match them to the needs expressed by your customers and searchers.

"Enterprise Solutions"

One of the most over-used phrases in the online business culture is "enterprise solutions." In my opinion, it is one of the most over-stated, under-descriptive phrases a website could utilize. With hundreds of millions of search results in each search engine, it is a phrase that does not provide a searcher with clear direction, and it necessitates further refinement.

One company that was able to get beyond the easy label of "enterprise solutions" is TDCI in Columbus, Ohio. In a beautiful bit of evaluation, the website evolved from the typical business-to-business website reliant on overstuffed terms and over-arching content (see Figure 6.4) to a site that provided a very specific, solution-based architecture and content structure.

The terminology of the earlier home page focuses on the corporate-style language, and the solution is unclear. Even in the "what we do" paragraphs, the content does not provide a specific descriptive phrase that can be distinguished within a few seconds of evaluation.

The new page provides a repeatable, descriptive phrase—"Guided Selling & Product Configuration Software"—that is immediately available to the reader. The content structure also supports the primary purpose and benefits the searcher. Within seconds, a searcher can quickly discern that they are at the right destination for their search, because this page ranks significantly better in the search engines for the services the company provides.

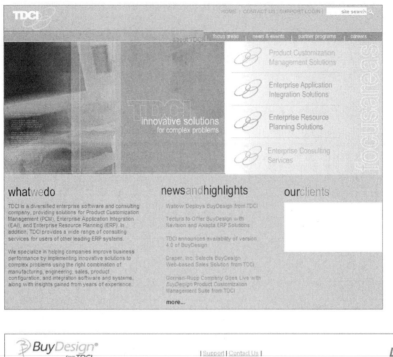

Figure 6.4 Corporate jargon (a) vs. customer-focused solutions and clear language (b)

Tuesday: Develop Keyword-Research Skills

Some basic principles underline the goal of your keyword research. The primary principle is to find the phrases that are popular search phrases; utilizing those phrases in your SEO will naturally increase your website's rankings, thereby increasing visitors to your website.

Beyond rankings, keyword research also provides insights into the mind of the searcher by providing context and themes to the searches. By looking beyond simply popularity, a good researcher can find opportunities and trends that will provide business intelligence beyond the rankings. Used properly, keyword research provides insights for more effective online and offline marketing, content development, product development, and better response to market trends.

Initial Evaluation

A number of tools are available to online marketers (see the "Keyword Research Tools" sidebar). It is really a matter of finding the tool with which you are most comfortable. I always recommend using at least two separate tools, because there will always be differences in reporting, and some words will need to be double-checked.

Keyword Research Tools

An amazing number of keyword-research tools are available online. Although this list is not meant to be exhaustive and I certainly don't want to leave out many good tools, I have decided to limit the list to the primary tools recommended by many people in the online marketing industry.

Google Search-Based Keyword Tool

www.google.com/sktool/

The premise of this keyword tool is simple; type the keywords or phrases relevant to your business, and Google will display keyword ideas for your site. Even more, if you already have an AdWords account, the keyword list will be customized to your website. I find this an extremely quick and easy tool for fast searches. In addition, you can easily manipulate the columns to list the suggestions in terms of popularity, suggested bid, or competition.

Google AdWords Keyword Tool

www.adwords.google.com

This tool is the next step to working within the AdWords system, but it provides slightly more data insight with the "Global v Local" monthly searches and the "Local Search Trends" reports. The Global number is the 12-month average of searches, while the Local number is the 12-month average based on your match-type selection. The Local Search Trends reports show the number of searches as a 12-month trend. Again, the columns are sortable, which provides many different approaches to the data.

Continues

Keyword Research Tools *(Continued)*

Google Insights

www.google.com/insights/search

When Google released this tool, I didn't get any work done for a week. This allows you to compare the search demand for up to five terms. In addition, you can also filter the results by the type of search, country and region (state), timeline, or category. The country and region are highly useful for developing regional-based AdWords buys, especially for highly targeted areas. In addition, there are also slight nuances in keywords between regions; finding them and effectively marketing that difference can be like discovering a nugget of gold in your market.

This tool provides a number of data points that really help establish context to the keywords, news events, regions, states and metro areas, and related keywords and keyword trends.

Keyword Discovery

www.keyworddiscovery.com

This program has been in my arsenal for years and is one of the first places I go for data. The strength of the data is also knowing search trends, by week, for specific terms. This provides valuable insights for marketers who have to report traffic fluctuations and prepare for wide swings in high- and low-demand cycles.

Microsoft Advertising Intelligence

http://advertising.microsoft.com/learning-center/downloads/
microsoft-advertising-intelligence

Microsoft Advertising Intelligence created a keyword-research tool, primarily aimed at PPC advertisers. The integration of Ad Intelligence as a tab in Excel made this tool one of the most intriguing and functionally intelligent tools available. Being a spreadsheet junkie, I'm excited about the prospect of having Microsoft Excel tied directly into the Microsoft adCenter.

Using the commonly used functions in Excel to manipulate the data is easy, and the data includes query time, demographics, and geolocation. You can extract the keywords from an existing website or create your own list of words. A very nice feature that distinguishes the Microsoft product from the rest is the number of tutorials to help you sift through the data and put it to use.

The first concept when working with a keyword-research tool is to realize that the keyword counts are rarely, if ever, accurate. The keyword counts are usually based on aggregate data from ISPs, search engine API data, third-tier networks, installed toolbars, and other sources. As such, you will never get the exact number of searches made on a particular search engine for a specific word.

The second most important thing is the ability to find, filter, and focus on the data. Lists of search words are a fine place to start. Use those lists to develop a strategy and an understanding of the searcher and the market. The next most important function of a keyword-research tool is the ability to view the data in different ways. Having the ability to manipulate the data in a way that helps you understand the concepts will help you better organize a strategy and find important trends.

One of my primary keyword tools is Keyword Discovery (`www.keyworddiscovery.com`). Most tools work similarly: type in the desired word or phrase, and all the variations including that word are listed in order of search popularity (see Figure 6.5).

Query ?	Searches ?
soccer	6,202,745
soccer betting	224,850
soccer ball	204,327
world cup soccer	201,094
soccer equipment	143,946
slime soccer	137,968
soccer bet	134,653
soccer jersey	125,396
soccer shoes	93,558
pro evolution soccer	84,288
soccer jerseys	81,553
soccer training	81,489
soccer electronics	77,119
soccer games	74,510
history soccer	74,263
history of soccer	70,622

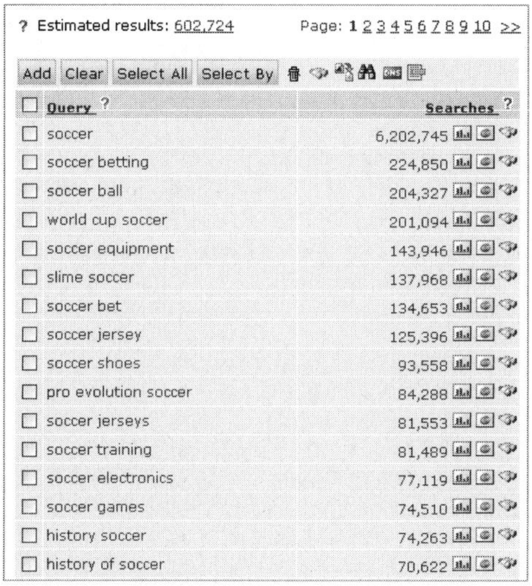

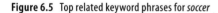

Figure 6.5 Top related keyword phrases for *soccer*

In this simple graph, keywords are listed in order of the search phrase that is used the most to the search phrase used the least. In Figure 6.5, the numbers of phrases used by searchers number in the thousands, because all the combinations that use the word are shown. This not only shows the magnitude of the number of search phrases employed by searchers but shows the multitudes of motivations for the search.

The majority of keyword-research tools all start this way, by listing the most popular search phrases first and then subsequent phrases by decreasing numbers.

Focus on Ratios, Not Number of Searches

One important thing to remember is that keyword-research tools are not going to be accurate. There are a number of reasons for this, because most gain their data through third-tier search engines, ISP data, and other sources. Even getting keyword search data through Google or Bing will provide estimated data only for that specific search engine, not the actual volume of search queries. Even though Google provides larger numbers than most keyword tools, the numbers are typically rounded off. Remember that Google is an advertiser as well, so getting businesses to bid on popular terms is part of the advertising strategy.

The number of searches on a specific key phrase is going to be largely inaccurate. Some keyword tools are going to be closer than others, but ultimately, there is no way to truly know the actual search volume of a particular keyword or phrase. Instead of looking at the actual number listed next to the keyword phrases, the best evaluation method is to view *the ratio between the numbers*, rather than the actual numbers.

For example, in the list of vacation-based keywords in Figure 6.6, several ratios are going to be important depending upon your website and your strategy.

Query ?	Searches ?
family vacation	2,062,546
inclusive family vacation	62,388
family vacation idea	31,751
family vacation florida	25,333
caribbean family vacation	23,081
family adventure vacation	19,993
family vacation resort	18,850
all inclusive family vacation	16,803
family vacation package	16,610
johnson family vacation	14,041
family beach vacation	13,368
familyvacation	13,162
family vacation deals	11,540
hawaii family vacation	11,127
cheap family vacation	10,969
lake tahoe family vacation	9,314
bahamas family vacation	8,483
family vacation ideas	8,296
family vacation destination	8,001

Figure 6.6 Vacation-related keywords

When evaluating ratios, you can see that *vacation packages* is searched more than twice as much as *vacation package*. *Hawaii* is the first destination-based search, *Orlando* is second, and *Florida* is third. *Vacation rentals* is the preferred term over *vacation home* or *vacation homes*.

The point of evaluating ratios rather than focusing on the larger numbers is that we are evaluating the trends and search patterns. Too many businesses get lost in the popular, high-volume search keywords and miss the action and understanding that comes from a deeper evaluation of the trends.

The next step in digging into the keyword research is to find the specific areas of information related to your business. Find specific repetitive words that are associated with the primary term. If the primary term is *vacation*, then the associated terms that one typically finds are *beach*, *rentals*, *cruise*, *family*, *resort*, *luxury*, and *cheap*.

Finding the associated terms is important to identifying your marketing strategy. Include the associated terms that are specific to your marketing strategy, and remove the terms that are not in your strategy. If you are selling luxury vacation condos in the United States, then remove the terms *cheap*, *Disney*, *France*, and *cruise*—they are not part of your strategy and will result in unqualified visitors to your website.

To take the vacation theme further, the next topic for more in-depth research would be going back to the search phrases for *family vacation* (Figure 6.7); the keyword searches are refined to only include phrases that include *family vacation*.

Query ?	Searches
vacation	8,133,562
vacation ideas	5,777,639
hawaii vacation	3,590,326
orlando vacation	3,562,881
vacation rentals	2,760,897
vacation rental	2,409,249
family vacation	2,062,546
vacation packages	1,864,552
ski vacation	1,536,157
florida vacation	1,528,009
south lake tahoe vacation rentals	1,368,781
kauai vacation rental	1,269,136
cruise vacation	1,222,954
tahoe vacation rental	1,143,430
maui vacation	1,010,397
disney vacation	960,634
costa rica vacation	930,982
vacation package	857,130
beach vacation	824,178
caribbean vacation	730,465

Figure 6.7 Family vacation–related keywords

By filtering another level into the content, additional segments and trends appear. For example, Figure 6.7 shows that *vacation packages* is searched on significantly more than *inclusive* or *all-inclusive* vacations (refer to the earlier Figure 6.6). This helps not only in optimizing your content but in labeling and presenting your information. You can more effectively market your information when the words more closely match that of the searcher.

If you are looking to increase the marketing content on your website, then this exercise will help you develop a specific direction for content development on your website. Finding the direction of the market and the needs of the search is critical in creating a successful website.

Spot the Trends

Don't stop at the list of numbers. Another world of data is available to you, and that is the trend. This is why I only use keyword tools that provide a trend line of demand.

If you stop only because you found a popular keyword that attracts a lot of searches, look again. A number does not tell the full story by itself; the number is made up of people making searches based on need, and many times that need is on a specific trend. The numbers you see listed are only the numbers for a particular month, quarter, or annual total, but they do not tell the story of the trend throughout the year.

The keyword research for *digital camera* keywords (see Figure 6.8) results in a very top-heavy list of searches for the term.

Query ?	Searches
digital camera	16,748,576
camera digital	448,292
olympus digital camera	361,459
sony digital camera	338,587
nikon digital camera	328,116
digital camera reviews	303,497
cheap digital camera	286,494
canon digital camera	280,613
best digital camera	255,404
kodak digital camera	249,254
fuji digital camera	228,924
digital camera review	227,399
digital camera accessories	205,079
digital video camera	167,742
digital pc camera	125,617
digital camera prints	118,445
buy digital camera	114,242

Figure 6.8 The list of search phrases for *digital camera*

Although the number of searches for *digital camera* is impressive compared to the other terms in the list, you need to see how that number is created. This is where the trend line (Figure 6.9) is just as important as knowing the popularity of the term.

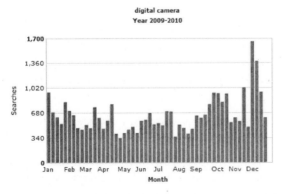

Figure 6.9 The annual trend for the keyword *digital camera* from KeywordDiscovery.com

In examining the annual trend, another story emerges. You can see that the bulk of the searches take place in the last three months of the year and is most intense in the first two weeks of December, presumably as people search for the perfect Christmas gift. A similar trend can be seen in many product-oriented searches; the trend for *tennis rackets* in the United States shows a significant spike in interest in early September (see Figure 6.10), which is about the time of the U.S. Open tennis tournament.

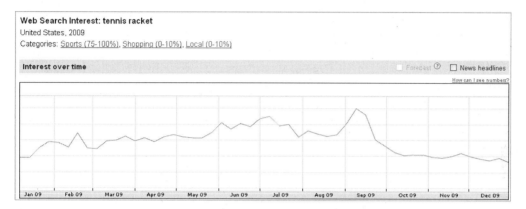

Web Search Interest: tennis racket
United States, 2009
Categories: Sports (75-100%), Shopping (0-10%), Local (0-10%)

Figure 6.10 The annual trend for *tennis racket* searches from Google.com/insights/search

Alternate Spelling and Plurals

One of the hurdles to effective keyword selection is deciding between the uses of alternative spellings and plural versions. For instance, there are two different spellings for some keywords, such as *tennis racket* and *tennis racquet*.

In instances like this, I am very glad to have the Google Insights for Search tool, `www.google.com/insights/search`. The tool allows keyword investigation for multiple words and combinations, allowing you to compare spellings, plurals, and regional variances. The Insights tool shows that *tennis racket* and *tennis racquet* are nearly equivalent to searchers (see Figure 6.11), but *tennis rackets* (plural) receives more searches than *tennis racquets* (plural). This makes it very difficult for online retailers, because consistency would dictate to target one or the other as a primary marketing focus for rankings. This is also an area that can be explored when using pay-per-click advertising in the search engines. Advertisers can bid on both terms and measure their sales accordingly to find the most profitable choice.

The Insights tool will also show regional variations; you can see this in the Filtering options. Simply by choosing United States in the filtering options, the choice between the two spellings becomes even more fascinating. The spelling option *racket* (represented by the top set of bars in Figure 6.12) is highest in Hawaii, Georgia, and California, but only California has more searches for *racket* than *racquet*. The option *racquet* (represented by the bottom set of bars in Figure 6.12) is strongly favored in New Jersey, New York, Massachusetts, and Connecticut.

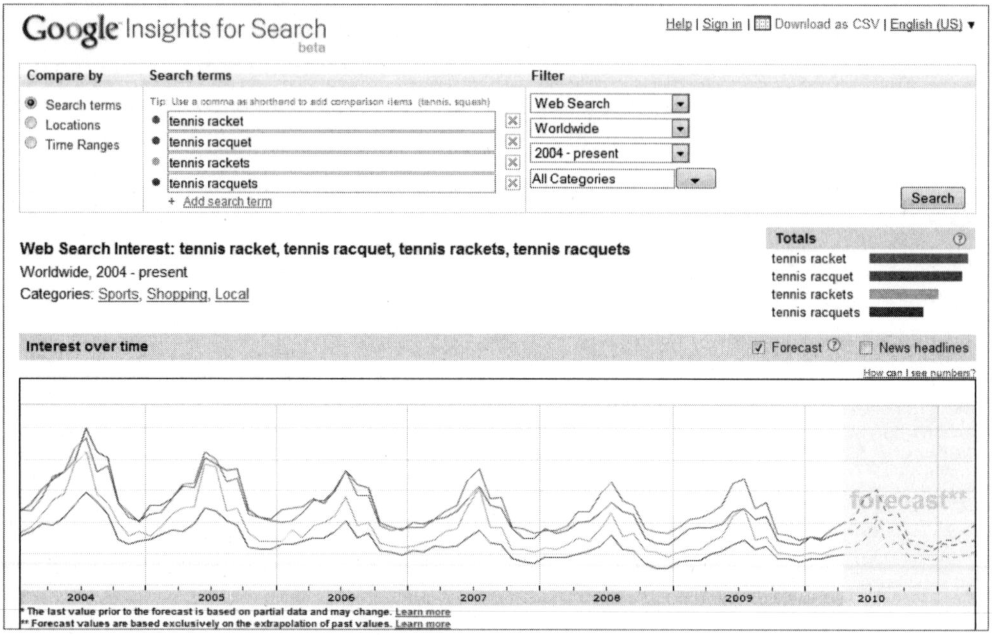

Figure 6.11 Google's Insights for Search tool comparing *tennis racket*, *tennis racquet*, *tennis rackets*, and *tennis racquets*

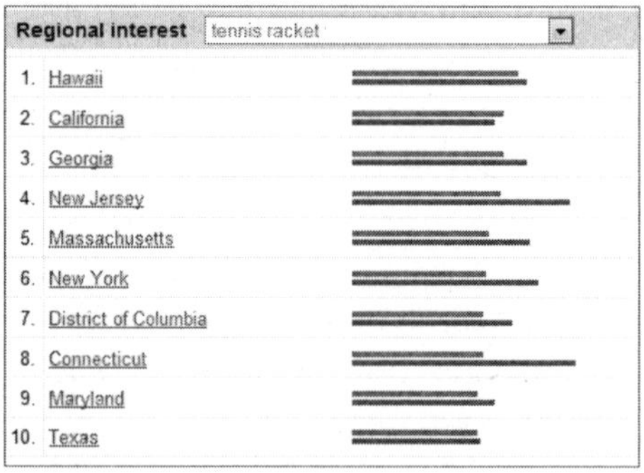

Figure 6.12 States favoring the spelling *racket*
(the top bar) vs. *racquet* (bottom bar)

Along with spelling options, plurals can be a headache for marketers. As an example of this, consider the negligible difference between *cruise vacation* and *cruise vacations* (Figure 6.13).

When choosing between spellings and plurals, test what works for you. Although rankings can be attained for each treatment, most likely you will find that one version performs significantly better in providing conversions of sales or leads or just traffic in general.

Selecting and researching your keywords is only the first step to effective marketing. Measuring keyword performance is critical to maintaining momentum. Constant measurement of keyword choices and performance is the only indicator of success and judgment in your selection of keywords. Measurement analytics and tactics for keywords will be covered in Part VI of this book, "Month 5: Measure, Measure, Measure."

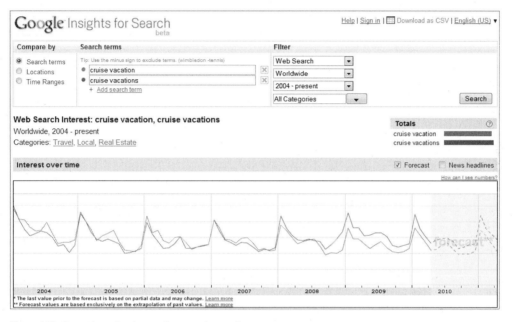

Figure 6.13 Comparison of *cruise vacation* vs. *cruise vacations*

The Keyword Long Tail

One of the most interesting phenomena to arise in the online marketing world was the labeling of the "long tail." Initially presented in an article by *Wired* editor Chris Anderson, the concept was expanded upon in his book *The Long Tail* (Hyperion Books, 2006).

In my mind, the image of the long tail is that of the prehistoric Brontosaurus—the tail itself was just as long, if not longer than the body of the animal. If you were to visually graph the number of search referrals to a website, you'd see that most people are enamored with the "head" of the graph—the left side that shows all of the words and phrases that brought the most visitors (the big numbers—managers love those). However, the long tail focuses on the quantity of search queries overall, and in most cases, the number of search terms that refer only one or two visits to the site add up to be more in number than the search referrals of the "popular" (top 10) terms. To sum up the long tail in its simplest form: Thousands of people are searching for things, and they use thousands of different words in forming their questions.

The technology of search has created nearly endless queries that can be typed by searchers in order to find your website. In fact, in 2007 Google's VP of Engineering, Udi Manber, presented that 20 percent to 25 percent of search query terms "we have never seen before." Nearly a quarter of search terms had never been typed into the search box before! Now, that could make your head explode if you dwell on it too long. More recently, Crystal Semantics managing director Ian Saunders said, "Language changes about 5 percent annually" (MediaPost, June 22, 2010). Our language keeps adding new words through new constructions, names, and technologies.

Digital distribution and search technology have created an endless amount of information that can be searched, which allows people to develop very targeted queries, specific to them. Anderson's book details the finding that simply because something is in the top 10 (books, music, blogs, websites, search terms, and so on), that doesn't mean it is the most popular. The ultimate lesson from learning about the long tail as applied to keywords means that ranking for a single, general term isn't going to be the best strategy.

Typically, marketing managers look at website statistics and get the list of top referring terms. However, because of the keyword long tail, this approach does not truly reflect the visitors who came to the website. Consider an example of an ecommerce website to understand how and why the long tail is good news and how it affects your keyword strategy. For that website, the top 10 keyword terms brought 2,000 visitors to the website (Figure 6.14). However, more than 4,600 keywords brought traffic to the website from the search engines. That means that even though 10 terms generated 2,000 visits, the next 4,600+ terms generated 9,400 visits, more than four times the top 10 terms that are typically displayed and reported by most website statistics.

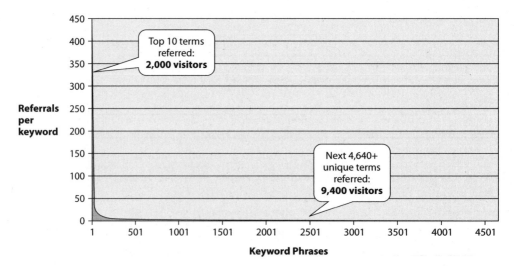

Figure 6.14 The long tail of keyword referrals

The number of visitors generated by the top 10 terms, added up, usually will not come close to the sum of visitors generated by the rest of the terms. In addition, the top 10 terms tend to be the more general keywords. Because they are general, they tend to result in a high concentration of search visitors, but both by numbers and by percentage, they also bring in the fewest conversions. However, because of the top 10 nature of a typical web stats report, those keywords tend to be the focus of many companies, because the ranking for a general keyword is highly desired, either because of business ego or simply because of the perception that a high-ranking, high-traffic term equals success.

When visits are tied to conversions, a more interesting finding arises. The majority of conversions come from the keywords outside the top 10. In fact, in most cases, the top 10 referring keywords will provide only 10 percent to 20 percent of conversions. The majority of conversions come from keyword referrals that are more specific, detailed, and directed than general keywords, which leads us to Wednesday's topic: understanding the buying cycle.

Wednesday: Understand the Buying Cycle

As you go through the thousands of variations of keywords and see all the words associated with them, you will begin to see certain patterns arise as to the intent of the searcher. This day covers how you can construct your optimization and website content based on the patterns in the buying cycle.

I find the best way to show the buying cycle is to use the example of someone buying a large-screen TV and entertainment system. Informally, I like to ask audiences about who has recently purchased a big-screen TV and how long it took them to make the decision. Most times it is about three months, and usually it is men who have taken the longest amount of time in deciding which type of TV, how large, and what brand. In fact, I would estimate the men spend longer deciding upon a TV purchase than they spend on purchasing an engagement ring.

Need

When researching keywords, we see that the general keyword is always the most common and highest referred term, which isn't a surprise. It's the point of need. When a laptop computer breaks, people go in search of a new one. Chances are, brand names are not top of mind. If they were, I believe that there would be many more brand-based searches. Instead, what we see is thousands of searches for the general term and then clusters of brand-based searches. In the middle are comparisons, features, and some very specific needs expressed.

In the case of laptop computers, the point of need is top of mind (see Figure 6.15). By far, the primary word *laptops* is the most searched term in the category.

Query ?	Searches
laptops	10,117,192
cheap laptops	415,688
dell laptops	145,067
refurbished laptops	138,399
used laptops	136,690
toshiba laptops	130,248
buy laptops	95,405
discount laptops	68,084
laptops pda	63,719
sony laptops	50,264
computing computers laptops	47,438
apple laptops	33,433
hp laptops	29,696
computer laptops	23,374

Figure 6.15 The general term is the most searched term: *laptops*.

This isn't limited to one particular category; in almost every aspect, the general term is the first word searched (see Figure 6.16).

Query ?	Searches
digital camera	16,748,576
camera digital	448,292
olympus digital camera	361,459
sony digital camera	338,587
nikon digital camera	328,116
digital camera reviews	303,497
cheap digital camera	286,494
canon digital camera	280,613
best digital camera	255,404
kodak digital camera	249,254
fuji digital camera	228,924
digital camera review	227,399
digital camera accessories	205,079
digital video camera	167,742

Query ?	Searches
tennis racquet	62,294
prince tennis racquet	7,470
head tennis racquet	6,546
wilson tennis racquet	6,178
racquet tennis clubs	4,351
dunlop tennis racquet	4,098
yonex tennis racquet	3,709
discount tennis racquet	3,387
tennis racquet string	3,231
tennis racquet review	2,315
tennis racquet store	1,834
tennis racquet reviews	1,691

Figure 6.16 The search demand for *digital camera* (left) and *tennis racquet* (right) terms

This is the very beginning of the buying cycle—the point where there is a need, and the need is the primary term that is searched. From here searchers take one of the following approaches:

- The searcher becomes overwhelmed with the amount of information and realizes that further search refinement is necessary.
- The searcher begins to search through all the available products and information and realizes that there is more to learn before making a decision.
- The searcher sees strong opinions written by other users and decides to research the decision more.
- The searcher buys the first thing they see from the website that ranks first.

As much as marketers wish the last approach were the most common, it isn't. Further research and refinement is the typical activity. As searchers start based on need, they refine based on available information, feedback, articles, comparisons, and opinions.

Gathering, Research, and Exclusion

This refinement of the search query is the part of the buying cycle that deals with gathering and evaluating information. This is where searchers learn about the basic benefits, the expected features, the typical service, and the experiences of others.

In the business-to-business world, this activity is typically performed by someone researching and gathering information in order to present to a decision maker or committee. Activities such as researching new vendors, upgrading systems, or sourcing parts, resources, or materials are part of the business-to-business searching process, just as much as they are for information-based and ecommerce-based buying cycles.

This is where brand names tend to get pitted against each other in mortal combat for the searcher's attention. Reviews of consumer products are available in almost every corner of the Internet. From Amazon.com to blogs, YouTube videos, discussion forums, Yahoo! Answers, and numerous other sources, Internet users have never been shy about sharing their experiences and opinions about products, businesses, brands, and services.

Your company website will most likely be used as part of the research. Knowing this, especially if you know the buying cycle is more than a few weeks or months, information on your website must be easy to find and download or print. Make it easy for researchers to find the specific features they need and the desired benefits. Customer testimonials are always great methods of providing a benefit statement to prospects. Be sure that any downloadable information contains your web address, a minimal number of graphics (to save printer ink), and compelling testimonials.

Make sure your information is presented in a way that makes it easy for searchers to do side-by-side comparisons. This research part of the sales process is an area where your salespeople cannot ask questions or get a feel for the prospect, so your content on the site must anticipate any objections and deal with retaining the prospect in a one-sided conversation.

Exclusion has become easier with the increase of social interactions online. User feedback and ratings have helped immensely as people make decisions online. A February 2009 Jupiter ResearchRichRelevance/BazaarVoice study found that 77 percent of consumers use rating and reviews to make a purchase decision (`www.bazaarvoice.com/press-room/39-press/309-pressreleasephpid97`).

That also means consumers can be swayed into knowing which products, suppliers, or companies they do not want to do business with. Negative reviews will impact a potential sale or lead, because if searchers see too many negative reviews or comments, they will decide to exclude that vendor or brand from their search.

Decision

The decision is the point that the prospect turns into a customer. At that point, the search they perform is highly targeted. For example, after performing research, a buyer for a digital camera knows for sure that they want a Fuji Finepix J10 that will cost between $115 and $130. From there they will search using that long string of terms and look for retailers offering the best price, terms, and shipping for the price.

The "long tail" terms consist of millions of these refined, deliberate phrases. These phrases are designed to filter out as much unnecessary information and filter in specific required information. They are the results of searchers drilling down into the important information that is critical to their decision making. Once the decision is made, the search terms tend to include features, brand names, and heavily worded phrases, all designed to produce the most relevant specific group of results.

Your Role in the Buying Cycle

To take full advantage of the buying cycle, you need to ensure that your website has content that will persuade searchers based on where they are in the buying cycle. There should be content on your site geared toward the initial focus of need. These are the general-type search phrases that initially present the purpose of your company.

There should also be content that enables searchers to find information they need to develop judgments, draw on comparisons, and find testimonials that help them verbalize and empathize. You want to help your prospects find answers, compare benefits, and refine their information. At the end of the buying cycle, having enough information that allows multiple-word phrases that describe specific benefit statements, targeted questions, and full product titles will enable your website to be much more visible for these very detailed search phrases.

For retailers and business that sell to businesses, it is prime placement to appear in general term searches, research searches, and final decision searches. The reinforcement of brand name and the recurrence of your website will help sway the searcher to use your website as the final decision-making destination.

In addition to evaluating your content based on the buying cycle, the next step is to evaluate the conversions on your website for the buying cycle. I interviewed a company that had estimated a savings of more than $15,000 every year in postal mailing costs. The company evaluated which documents tended to be requested at specific stages of a six- to eight-month buying cycle. In that time, it was able to identify early-stage requests, mid-stage requests, and final-stage requests. By identifying the requests and the typical mailings that went to each prospect, the company could now identify first-contact prospects and estimate what stage of decision those prospects were in by the content they downloaded from the website. In this way, when the sales representative contacted the prospect, he could ask very specific, targeted questions and drive the sale from the downloaded documents; he would not have to wait to send the documents by standard postal mail. This saved the company thousands of dollars in mailings and even more in developing a highly targeted lead tracking system based on the buying cycle.

By developing conversion points, key phrases, and content based on buying cycle, you'll help your website become a powerful tool in reaching prospects and customers in multiple points in their searching.

Thursday: Find Searcher Behavior Types

Another interesting facet of keyword research is to evaluate what kind of searchers will be most likely to use your website. Is your website an "impulse" website, where you can get a quick sale? Is your website a content-based website where searchers can research and learn more, which will help them make a decision? Is your website focused on answering or presenting a single purpose to the world, such as a hobby or passion that you want to share? Each of these sites has a purpose to a specific searcher, and understanding what types of searchers you attract can be very important in both keyword selection and evaluation.

In the book *Information Architecture* (O'Reilly, 3rd Edition 2006), Peter Morville and Louis Rosenfeld explain the information needs of searchers and how specific patterns emerge based on the types of information that are searched. I highly recommend the book to anyone who manages a website or is involved in website design.

I've adapted the fishing metaphor originally used in *Information Architecture* into a marksmanship metaphor based on three types of search types: sharpshooter searches, shotgun searches, and artillery searches. Essentially, the answer to a question is the shooter's target. The type of search is the weapon used to hit the target, based on how precisely the searcher seeks the answer to their question.

In this keywords exercise, you can see that searchers using certain types of keywords will inherently display different types of behaviors. Knowing which types of searchers will need your information is critical, because it will enable you to better understand how to match your information to the searcher's needs. Of course, what follows are very general descriptions of user behaviors, observed in different situations. There are always exceptions when describing types of user behavior interacting with information. These are mainly starting points to begin your analysis of your own website and the types of users requesting information.

Sharpshooter Searching

Searchers who use this method have a specific question and have little time for anything else. I observe this behavior almost daily in personal interactions. For example:

- "Who is that actor? What other shows has he been in?"
- "What '80s new-wave bands had a song title that was the same as the band name?"
- "What's the address of that restaurant?"
- "What is the number of smartphone users in the United States compared to Japan? What is the percentage compared to population?"

These are targeted questions for a specific knowledge need. Whether it is for trivial, investigative, or research purposes, the searcher for this type of information exhibits very little patience. This is when the relevance and appearance of the answer within the content are critical. Searchers who are sharpshooters want to focus on a tiny bit of information, and everything else is unnecessary information.

These users exhibit a kind of tunnel vision, because there is not much to distract them from their task. Usually, there is either a time restriction or immediacy to the question, and spending more than a few minutes is too long. In addition, the commitment level of these users is typically as low as their attention span. They need an answer, and when they get it, they are done.

Shotgun Searching

The next level of searching involves the shotgun searcher. They have an idea of the type of information they need but not a specific target. Like with a shotgun, the "shooter" simply has to aim in the general direction to hit the target, but the shot will be scattered, and the likelihood of hitting targets other than the principle one is very high.

- "We need a new vendor—find some information on ones that offer what we need."
- "I need to find a plumber."
- "I need some basic statistics on smartphone usage."
- "Let's vacation out West this year—and find some things to do on the way."

An example of this behavior is people who are researching vacation destinations and activities. Although they have a destination in mind, they are very open to suggestion when searching for additional activities. I equate this to a family driving to Disneyworld—they know where they are going, but they are very open to stops along the way, activities to do within the park, and a multitude of other options.

Seeing results that are related to the primary intent but provide additional information and alternatives can be appealing to this type of searcher, because they are not solely focused on a particular object; they are very open to additional options. Unusual or unconventional may even be appealing, depending upon the personality of the searcher.

I also equate this behavior with a man who is on his way home from work, and his calendar reminds him that today is his wedding anniversary. He typically has no idea what to purchase as a gift, but he's in a time crunch, needs to find something, and is very open to suggestion. A smart sales associate will realize the potential for a good commission when they see a searcher like this. He knows he needs to find something that looks like he was being thoughtful, but he has very little time, money is not usually an object, and he wants to look like a hero.

This type of searching behavior also crosses over into the research and gathering phase of the buying cycle. As searchers are researching, comparing, and gathering, they are also introduced to alternatives and multiple pathways to information. Something that may have started the research down one path may have led the searcher into another path of information. The reason is that the commitment has not been made, and the searcher is open to finding the best deal for the money they intend to spend.

Artillery Search

This type of search behavior took on a very personal understanding a few years ago. After my (then) pregnant wife's ultrasound appointment, we received a phone call. The lab found what looked like cysts on the brain of our unborn daughter. Of course, they couldn't get us in for further tests until four days later. They told us the name of the condition and left us with little else as we set the phone down, unsettled and afraid.

We then did what so many people have done upon returning from a doctor's office or hearing lab results; we entered the name of the condition into the search field. When seeing the results, our behavior was unlike any I had ever observed. It didn't matter which result was first, second, fifth, or twentieth. We visited every document we found in the results and read *all* of them.

Just as battlefield artillery is designed to cover as wide an area as possible, so our searching was designed to find as much information as possible, regardless of source. It didn't matter if it was a discussion forum, information site, personal blog, or parenting site; we wanted information, and the content of a single site was not enough to satisfy our need to learn.

My wife and I found ourselves looking at search results five to eight pages deep as we tried to find more and more information, experiences, and information about this condition. Especially valuable to us were the experiences of other parents. I am not sure that we were unique in this respect, but we trusted the information written by other parents more than we trusted the information on medical sites. The experiences of others counted much more in our view, because we learned that most likely the advanced scans would not produce anything.

We learned from the other experiences that this type of diagnosis is usually incorrect and is the product of doctors and technicians being overly careful. Unfortunately, people are not told this until a subsequent appointment. It was the content we found in an exhaustive comprehensive search online that alleviated our fears and educated us more than the doctors and the information provided by the hospital.

This provided a valuable experience as to the emotional state that can drive people in their searching. Sometimes events come upon us that drive an incessant searching for information. In that case, rankings do not matter, but content does. During the search, we are swayed in many directions, based on the content, and we start to make emotional attachments based on others' experiences and the content we find. People in this state will read more of the content they find, and patience is not an issue; comprehensiveness is the issue.

Realize that searchers are not a single entity of behavior but are made up of different motives, needs, and emotional states as they search. It will drive the keywords they use, the behavior they exhibit on the site, and the patience level for finding content.

Friday: Organize for Optimization

Now that you have been researching with keyword tools, surveying the information on your website, and developing buying cycles for your content, the next step is to organize this data. Based on needs, long tail terms, and buying cycles, one of the best ways to organize keywords is to start with the *anchor* term (or core term).

Today's example will focus on cars, specifically the Chevrolet Corvette, as the anchor term to illustrate how you can organize keywords to better utilize the breadth of terms and popularity for easy implementation to the website.

Visualize the Data

At the highest level, your keyword research provides a basic list of keywords and their popularity. This is the primary way that results are presented in most keyword tools. At that point, you can export the results into a spreadsheet so that you can move the fields and data into a more manageable format.

The second level of organizing keyword data is to arrange the keyword terms into a display based on words that come before the anchor term (prefix) and words that come after the anchor term (suffix), as in Figure 6.17. This is where a tool like Microsoft Excel is indispensable.

Anchor Term: Corvette

Average Monthly Count	Prefix	Anchor Term	Suffix	Average Monthly Count
				210819
			parts	12187
11126	chevrolet			
			s	10710
			passenger vehicles	9993
			z06	5964
			parts accessories	5373
			c6	5230
4900	1973			
4862	1968			
			wheels	4797
			c5	4636
			stingray	4412
4406	c5	corvette		
4288	1982			
4241	2006			
3821	1980			
3641	1962			
1967	3609			
			cars	3487
3459	1969			
			rims	3094
			seats	2797
2648	427			
			forum	2614

Figure 6.17 Use a spreadsheet to arrange keywords based on associated terms.

As shown in Figure 6.17, the anchor term is *corvette*. The most popular term associated with *corvette* is *corvette parts*. The term *parts* is in the Suffix column, and the average monthly searches for the phrase *Corvette parts* is shown in the rightmost column; you can see that this phrase is the most popular of all the related terms.

The second most popular search phrase is *Chevrolet Corvette*; however, Chevrolet is used as a prefix, so it is listed in the second column from the left, next to the monthly search count. Other terms are arranged according to the popularity of the associated phrases. In arranging the keywords in this manner, searcher behaviors begin to exhibit themselves, which will help you in your optimization.

First, searchers tend to place the years of the Corvette first or in the prefix. Second, the model names tend to be associated after the *corvette* term. Third, the refinement of associated terms becomes more evident. When looking down the Suffix column, the top term is *parts*, followed later by *parts accessories*. After those very general terms, more specific ones are used—*wheels*, *rims*, and *seats*. Another interesting observation is the search for *corvette forum*, which shows a desire to share information with and learn from other Corvette owners. This is an important part of learning about your market, finding their needs, and learning their social behaviors.

Another interesting comparison is between *corvette* (singular) and *corvettes* (plural). The plural term has only the *s* listed in the Suffix column. This shows that the singular term is searched significantly more than the plural term. However, simply consider what the typical difference would be in the searcher's intent. A plural search would imply a desire to see many Corvettes and maybe images, whereas a singular search would imply a desire to purchase or research. The only way to know for sure on your own site is to measure the similarities and differences between the singular and plural. You may find that the smallest difference in spelling makes a large impact in behavior.

Break Down the Large Numbers

Don't get completely distracted by the large numbers. Realize that those large numbers consist of general searches and many more needs than are singularly expressed. By digging into the most popular terms and finding the terms that are refined and associated, you can expand your keyword targets exponentially, which will make your site much more visible online.

The most popular associated term in our Corvette example was *parts*, but knowing that the long tail will provide many more associated terms and needs, the best practice is to further investigate the phrase *corvette parts*. Doing this, we find much more data that makes up the phrase, which also opens up an understanding into the searcher's intent and needs.

The next step is to build a similar spreadsheet matrix for the anchor term *Corvette parts* (see Figure 6.18).

Anchor Term: Corvette Parts

Average Monthly Count	Prefix	Anchor Term	Suffix	Average Monthly Count
12187	corvette			
	1957 corvette		accessories	728
504	corvette	[part]		
413	1985 corvette			
	corvette c5		accessories	385
	corvette		car	366
314	corvette body			
296	1984 corvette			
	1976 corvette		accessories	222
	1978 corvette		accessories	165
	1975 corvette		accessories	157
	corvette wheels	parts	accessories	156
149	1976 corvette			
146	corvette performance			
	free		catalogue corvette	120
109	1963 corvette			
109	corvette auto			
	corvette c4		accessories	108
105	corvette car	[part]		
103	c5 corvette			
103	c4 corvette			
	1979 corvette		accessories	101
100	corvette z06			
	corvette 1984		accessories	95
91	1978 corvette			

Figure 6.18 Digging deeper into keyword phrases

Starting with the most popular term from the prior spreadsheet, *Corvette parts*, the further breakdown of associated terms begins to show another behavior exhibited by Corvette searchers. For one, the year of the Corvette owned by the searcher becomes a major prefix component of the search term. Second, the word *accessories* is the primary associated word (a suffix).

In delving into alternative phrasings, the research focused on *parts* as an anchor term, which provided consistent associations with the term *accessories*. The next step was to see whether the associations change when using the anchor term *Corvette accessories* instead of *Corvette parts and accessories* (see Figure 6.19).

The exploration of the *accessories* term shows and reinforces the *parts and accessories* phrase that appears throughout the search terms. *Parts* is used independently of *accessories* in many searches, but *accessories* is rarely used independently of its association with *parts*. Terms that *bridge* the anchor term should also be noted. For example, in Figure 6.18, the term *free parts catalogue corvette* contains both prefix terms and suffix terms, so they are listed on the same line along with the search count. This helps you see which terms contain both prefix and suffix associated terms. In the case of *free parts catalogue corvette*, it is also the only occurrence of the word *free*, and it is associated with the search for a catalog. This is very important in the content development strategy and optimization. The company using this keyword research will recognize the need to advertise the free catalog because it is in demand, and the company will attract future customers to the website as a result.

Anchor Term: Corvette Accessories

Average Monthly Count	Prefix	Anchor Term	Suffix	Average Monthly Count
5373	corvette parts			
914	corvette			
728	1957 corvette parts			
433	corvette clothing shoes			
385	corvette c5 parts			
222	1976 corvette parts			
165	1978 corvette parts			
157	1975 corvette parts			
156	corvette wheels parts			
108	corvette c4 parts			
101	1979 corvette parts			
95	corvette 1984 parts	accessories		
86	1977 corvette parts			
84	corvette 40th parts			
78	c5 corvette parts			
74	corvette parts parts			
66	1958 corvette parts			
65	corvette top parts			
64	ebay c6 corvette parts and			
58	corvette parts and			
54	corvette c6			
52	1974 corvette parts			
51	1957 1958 and 1959 corvette 283 engine parts and			
50	1967 corvette parts			
48	1969 corvette parts			

Figure 6.19 Exploring term associations

In the case of the phrase *free part catalogue corvette*, there is usually a red flag on that term for two reasons. The first reason is the spelling of the word *catalogue*, which implies a British searcher. Understanding variations of English words used throughout the world is vital to your strategy as well, especially if you are doing international business. Further research is recommended in cases like this to be sure you are able to reach additional audiences by including the variations of words that are native to specific regions.

However, the use of this word coupled with a four-word phrase just seems a little out of place. This is one of those words that I would double-check in another keyword-research tool to see whether it is consistent or simply a quirk in the data. Sometimes, automated search engine rankings tools will cause a quirk like this. Because some webmasters or companies are stuck on knowing their rankings for terms all of the time, they continually run searches on a very specific term. All of those queries can sometimes get picked up by a keyword tool and be reflected as a high-demand search term when, in reality, it is a company or group of companies creating an artificial popularity by checking their rankings.

Learn What Searchers Want

In analysis of the demand, using the previous Figure 6.18, it is interesting to see that there are significantly more searches for *1957 corvette parts and accessories* than *1975 corvette parts and accessories*. This could be an indicator of many things and could be used to compare to market research data, current purchasing trends, and any annual purchasing trends.

Keyword research is much more than finding terms for optimization. It is also a window into searcher intent and market trends. Finding these trends can help businesses find a competitive edge by adding an additional facet to their market research. By viewing search trends throughout the year and also the content of those trends, companies can get an understanding not previously found through typical market data.

Many companies are using old market data to understand trends, and the search trend data is beginning to show that with the Internet, behaviors change. One business in particular (we'll call them "Company X") was able to change its offline marketing campaign, which typically kicked off in April. By researching keywords and their trends, they found that their business-to-business prospects were searching for their products two to three months prior to the "regular" marketing schedule. By moving up the marketing schedule to coincide with the research that was being done by their prospects, Company X was able to significantly increase sales by meeting the searchers in an offline direct mail campaign that matched the online search behavior.

Find Alternative Phrasings

The next stage of organizing keywords is to find alternative spellings, nicknames, slang terms, or shortened versions of words. In the case of Corvettes, the term *vette* is also a search term that could not be overlooked (see Figure 6.20).

This also shows the value of understanding your audience enough to find the shortened or abbreviated words within the market. In most cases, one can find the alternative versions or misspellings by researching a "root" phrase. In this case, a root phrase would be *vette*, which would then show all the misspellings and variations that contain the root *vette*. I have also found this to be a particularly effective method of capturing all the various misspellings of searches for the word *chandelier*—by first searching on the keyword root *chand*.

By finding the most commonly used root letters that are spelled correctly, you can gather most of the referrals. I find that there are always some that slip through. If you still need to be convinced, take a look at the hundreds of misspellings of the name Britney Spears that Google gathered for only three months: `labs.google.com/britney.html`.

In this case, we found significantly different behavior being shown through the search terms of those searchers using the term *vette*. The searchers using the abbreviated phrase tended to be focused on the experience of the Corvette—magazines, pictures, and performance—but not concerned about parts, accessories, or engine parts.

They were not as targeted as the conventional spelling of the phrase, and knowing this trend helps in understanding the different motivations of the searcher.

This is another area where the comparison of behavior based on the search term will be an important analysis. As always, ranking for terms is not the goal; profit is the goal, so rankings should be a consideration, but the primary measurement is the profit-generating capability of those terms and focusing on the most profitable terms, not the ones that simply rank well.

Anchor Term: Vette

Average Monthly Count	Prefix	Anchor Term	Suffix	Average Monthly Count
173	67			
			auto's	133
			magazine	122
			parts	115
92	1969			
87	1962			
84	rent a			
84	lingenfelter			
79	62			
76	78			
75	69			
		vette	pics	67
	69		convertible	66
			brakes	65
64	z06			
			wheel wheels rims lug lugnuts bumper	60
58	90			
57	black			
			autos	52
			for sale	52
50	03 cobra vs 05			
50	performance			

Figure 6.20 Find the other terms being used in your niche.

Start Optimizing

Now, with your keyword-performance spreadsheets nearby, you have a guide to optimizing your pages, based on the content, to meet the needs of the searcher. The owner of a Corvette-parts website would be able to use the spreadsheets' content to develop phrases based on popular searches and trends. If there is a page about the 1957 Corvette, then the prefix columns, anchor term, and suffix terms will provide the structure for the titles, meta-descriptions, and important headings in the content.

The next step is to organize your web pages, based on your content structure, into a hierarchy that provides a systematic development of the information that is in the website and the pathway through the content. Start with the category information and then drill down into the detail pages, using associated terms throughout the process, but avoid over-repetitiveness. It is a fine line but one that is carefully created and measured for effectiveness.

Page titles based on content hierarchy *could* be developed like this based on the research:

Category: Corvette performance parts and accessories
- Subcategory: 1957 Corvette Parts and Accessories
    - Detail category: 1957 Corvette body parts
    - Detail category: 1957 Corvette wheels and rims
- Subcategory: 1957 Corvette performance parts
    - Detail category: 1957 Corvette engine performance parts: Carburetors
        - Page detail: Carter Brass Bowl Carburetor for Chevrolet Corvette

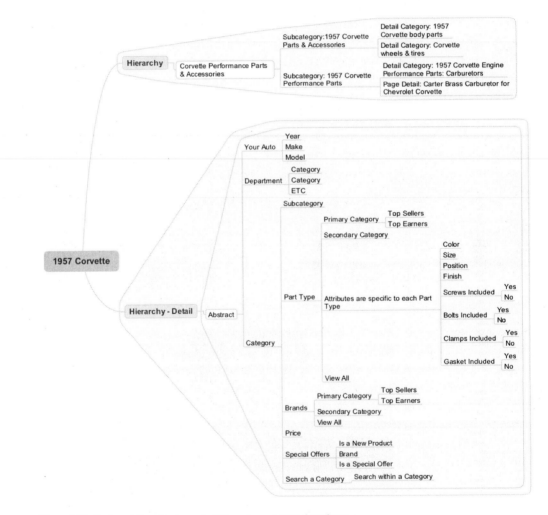

Figure 6.21 Site layout hierarchy for product hierarchy, content and attributes

Create terms that associate prefix words, anchor terms, and suffix words. In doing this, you are able to use the anchor term in many different ways, based on the content of a particular page. This will enhance your ability to rank for the anchor term, as well as the associated terms.

Developing well-written and comprehensive statements for your on-page optimization provides strong contextual relationships for the search engines. Using associated terms helps increase the ability to rank for similar terms that may not even show up in the title tag or headings, simply based on the association and context of the information.

Typically, the information on a website starts out as general in the primary pages, develops into additional information and education about the company and products/services, and then branches out into specific details. This is the same methodology of building content, especially in the page titles. Start with the general terms, and add some strong associated term. Content or category pages can branch out into more detailed information that can integrate specific content based on the information on the page; is it instructional, research, white papers, or an additional type of information? Then add those associated concepts into the page titles, meta-descriptions, and content heading.

It isn't necessary to repeat the same phrase in each on-page area (page title, description, and headings). In fact, using alternative and additional terms will make the page easier to digest, because repetitive use of the same phrase will limit the effectiveness of the optimization and visual interest of the page (See Figure 6.22).

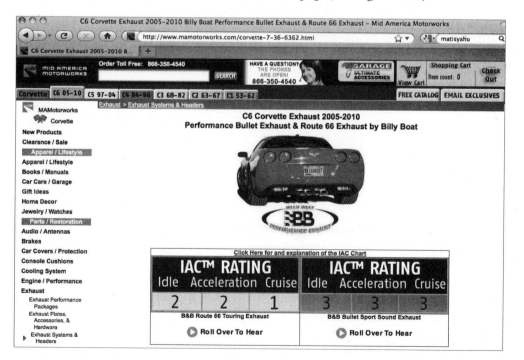

Figure 6.22 MidAmerica Motorworks Corvette Exhaust page uses multiple key phrases throughout the navigation and product information.

Here are a few simple guidelines for optimizing based on your keyword research:

- Don't be repetitive; be compelling.
- Ensure that the optimized phrase accurately reflects and reinforces the content on the page.
- Always go back to see how the title tag looks in the search results after it has been updated in the search engine.
- Test and measure for effectiveness, based on profitability, always.

Review and Hands-On

Begin by selecting a keyword tool, such as Keyword Discovery, Google Keyword Tool, or any number of available programs. Whatever you select, be sure that there is an export function that allows you to export your selected keyword list into a spreadsheet. This will be important for organizing your keywords into multiple ways of analyzing and sorting.

Start by finding all the available keywords within a subject area. Be sure not to get distracted by the large numbers for very general keywords. Look more at the ratios between search terms, subjects and specific phrasings in order to find the trends. Look at the relative difference between the reported volumes rather than the actual count. The ratios give you a better idea of popularity, because the numbers are largely inaccurate or heavily rounded.

Download as many terms as you think necessary to a spreadsheet. The number of terms will vary according to your market or concept. Start dividing the keywords in multiple ways to get a better understanding of the types of search behavior exhibited by your target audience.

Dividing the prefix and suffix words will enable you to find consistent behavior among your target searchers and realize how search phrases are constructed for specific subjects. In addition, dividing keyword phrases like this will help you write better titles and descriptions, because the prefix and suffix words can be strung together with your primary keyword to provide a comprehensive sentence that will reach across multiple search terms. This will also enable you to reach far into the "long tail" of search terms.

Divide your keywords into a typical decision cycle. Which keywords are general and typically searched first based on need? Which keywords are exploratory and research-based? Which keywords are focused on the decision point? These will help you direct specific searchers to specific points of your site that answer questions for searchers in those parts of the decision cycle.

Week 4: Leverage Principles of Sales and Marketing

The Internet has become an integral part of our lives, transforming our daily routines in just a few short years. This change brings new ways of doing business, evaluating messages, reaching prospects, and making sales. In fact, it is typical to hear that the Internet has "changed everything."

Because so many believe that the Internet has changed everything, they tend to throw out years of business knowledge that simply needs to be applied to the new medium. Human behavior hasn't changed; it has only been modified to accommodate a new medium, and we as marketers need to adapt the traditional principles of sound sales and marketing techniques to our online marketing.

Chapter Contents

Monday: Know Your Market

The foundation of all sales is to know and understand the needs of your market. By understanding their needs and motivations, you can better understand how to approach those needs in a more effective way. Simply starting a sales pitch without understanding who your customer is or what they need will result in your alienation. Customers want to like and trust the one who is selling to them, but if there is no genuine interest or understanding, the customer is turned off.

Research Is the Key

This day of learning sales principles focuses on knowing your customer. In doing this, you must take the time to research what *they* want, not what *you* want. You already know what you want as a business, but you have to take the time to understand what the customer wants. I have been in so many meetings where the company has had an amazing product—one that should be simply dominating the market. However, the main restraint was the approach to the consumer and the lack of knowledge about what they want and need.

True customer research is invaluable. With the availability of online surveys, customer research, and mountains of data, companies should have no problem finding the best message and approach to their customers. However, this takes time, work, and most of all humility. Those companies that have learned the most from customer research also tend to be the ones that are able to admit their mistakes, realize the customer is the one who makes the final decision, and are willing to change their approach.

Many times, it is the resistance to changing branding techniques online that prevents success. Other times, it is simply following the accepted business practice that has been established over the years. When utilizing keyword research, a company is faced with a stark choice—use the data to adjust your marketing or resist and reduce your visibility.

A personal experience shaped the importance of keyword research as more than a simple optimization tool, because it became a business marketing tool. When sharing the keyword research with a local company, they were highly interested in the search trends more than the search terms. In nearly every case, the search trend started in February and March. I learned from the owner of the company that the marketing cycle started in April and May, a full two months after their business-to-business market started researching for purchases. Because they were marketing the same way they had marketed for the past 50 years, they were missing the early market, and most decisions had been made by the time they were sending their direct mail campaigns and following up with sales calls. The next year, they moved their marketing schedule up to coincide with the search trend, resulting in one of the best years ever and capturing a significant percentage of the market.

In this way, the keyword research is a strong first step. It is searchers telling you, in their own words, what they need. It also supports one of the most important sales principles I have ever learned:

Listen more than talk.

Online keyword research is inherently a quiet activity. The researcher is reading, listening to thousands of searchers, and quietly analyzing and drawing conclusions. Activities that force quiet analysis are the ones that tend to be the most effective. The primary obstacle to that quiet analysis is your own assumptions.

Listen to Your Customer

Those who want to persuade must understand the impulses of the audience. Well over 2,000 years ago, Aristotle understood the value of knowing the motivations of the audience:

> *It may be said that every individual man and all men in common aim at a certain end which determines what they choose and what they avoid. This end, to sum it up briefly, is happiness and its constituents.*

—THE RHETORIC AND POETICS OF ARISTOTLE, Book 1, Chapter 5

To know what makes the customer happy in their own words is a pursuit that requires businesses to leave ego and branding behind. Simply, this activity is gaining an understanding of what the customer thinks about you or your product. Even more deeply, what need do you fulfill, in the customer's own words? You may be surprised to learn that the need you believe you fill as a business is not the same need perceived by the customer.

Businesses that have performed these types of surveys and research find how they are perceived by customers and can learn from and adjust to meet these expectations. Perceived benefits of the customer may not be the same benefits espoused in marketing copy or messaging and can be used to refine that message.

The more you listen to the customer, the more you can increase your website's "salability" (see Figure 7.1). Learning more about the needs and concerns of the customer, in their own language, can help your marketing campaigns take on a new light as you develop around the customer, rather than develop around corporate-speak or directives.

This is where involving salespeople in the process of keyword research and content development can assist a company. Sales departments are on the first line of finding and selling to the needs of the customers, and they may have a keen ear as to the immediate feedback of the client and apprehension of the prospect.

Online survey resources such as Survey Monkey and Zoomerang are accessible for any budget and can be used to provide amazing levels of insight. Any investment in survey work and setting up the survey with the proper questions will pay off with fast, insightful, and marketable information specific to your enterprise.

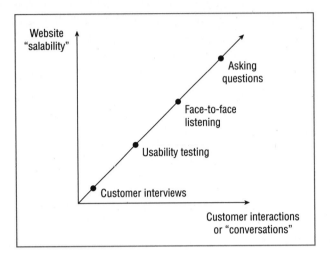

Figure 7.1 "Salability" and conversations—linked for success

The market can have very different needs. A site that is built to meet the owners' needs is not a site that will meet the visitor's needs. If you are developing a campaign to a specific market and you have not done research on that market—such as actually talking to that audience or conducting surveys, customer interviews, or more—you could be missing a large part of the marketing message.

Regardless if you are marketing to a B2B or B2C audience, simply talking to a group of your target audience about the information they desire, the needs they have, and the answers they seek can provide you with directed content and multiple strategies. You will learn that a market is a group of people with varied interests that cannot be sold the same way all the time.

The more a business listens to its customers and market, the better decisions it will make when creating a website to suit their needs. Through usability testing, interviews, and most of all listening, a site will have clear direction for growth. Additionally, there will also be a clear pursuit in the analysis of those goals. By finding what is important to the users, the analytics will either support or disprove that goal. Either way, it provides an analytical framework to judge the activity on the site.

Build Rapport

Building rapport is the foundation of building human relationships. In sales terms, it is finding something in common with someone else on their terms—not *what they have in common with me* but *what I have in common with them*. In this way, I have let them do the talking, and I show that I have listened to them by finding shared values or commonalities that I have learned from listening.

For the online application, if a searcher uses specific phrases to find a site and those words are not on the page where they land, they won't be there long. The site needs to meet the expectations of the searcher in order to be successful. Establishing rapport online is just as critical as establishing it in person.

This is the primary reason that your search terms are bold in the search engine results page—to help establish that connection. The terms you requested are returned in a visible format. Research shows that searchers tend to click results that show a bold term that mirrors their search. In addition, the odds of getting the searcher's click increases with each additional bold term. (See *Beyond Position Bias: Examining Result Attractiveness as a Source of Presentation Bias in Clickthrough Data* by Yue, Patel, and Roerig, 2010.) The more your website matches the search query or the needs of the searcher, the more apt that searcher is to click your site listing.

To get someone interested, you have to appeal to their needs first. Satisfy those needs or show that you can, and then they will be interested in more information. Visitors leave sites quickly when they see no reason to stay. If your site does not reflect the reason they came, they are gone!

Too many websites are focused on what *we* can do and *our* products, *our* services, *our* staff, and *our* mission statement. In focusing so much time and words upon *their* business, they forgot to build rapport with the searcher, who has already gone back to the search results and clicked the next link.

Tuesday: Create the Need

Most people who are great at sales will tell you that they aren't salespeople; they are merely matchmakers. They are merely matching people to the products they need. A good salesperson spends very little time closing the sale because they have already provided all the reasons to make the decision, by creating the need first.

Search is a different animal from any form of advertising. All other forms of marketing—radio, TV, billboards, magazine ads—are all based on chance; it's the chance you may have that need when you see the advertisement and then act on that need. TV goes a long way in creating the need with visuals, but it doesn't come close to the power of search marketing. In search marketing, the consumer types their need into a search box, advertisers are lined up in the results, and the consumer decides which message to explore further.

In this way, creating the need doesn't stop because the searcher expressed the need in the search box. Creating the need is a necessary part of compelling the searcher to stay on your site because you are able to meet a need that is deeper than the one searched.

Beyond the Initial Need

Fisher-Price (Figure 7.2) is a well-known toy company. However, when a searcher goes to the Fisher-Price website, they will quickly see that this is not just a site about toys; it is a site about being a good parent. Fisher-Price creates the need to be a good parent while entertaining your child. The information is based on educating parents about early development stages and finding the right toys that will aid in learning and development. Toys are secondary, because being a good parent or grandparent is the primary focus of the website.

Figure 7.2 Fisher-Price website—more about parenting than toys

Similarly, a searcher for a vacation may come across the Colonial Williamsburg website (Figure 7.3). However, this is not just a site about a historical village; it offers educational research, teachers resources, essays, and articles about colonial life in early America.

Figure 7.3 Colonial Williamsburg website—more about history than vacationing

Connect to the Need

As the Fisher-Price example demonstrates, a company does not always have to focus on the primary economic activity to make sales. As with many companies, educating the consumer is what produces more and better results than an outright sale. An educated consumer is a better consumer, because they are more likely to purchase more, more frequently, and to be loyal.

The Fisher-Price content goes deep into providing information about raising children and the developmental needs of infants and toddlers. By providing significant amounts of information by growth and development stage, Fisher-Price can then recommend specific activities rather than toys (they just happen to sell the toy that's tied to the activity).

The site goes into great detail helping parents who desire to help their baby. By speaking to the emotional nurturing aspect, recommended toys are positioned as the key to building that growth needed by the baby (Figure 7.4).

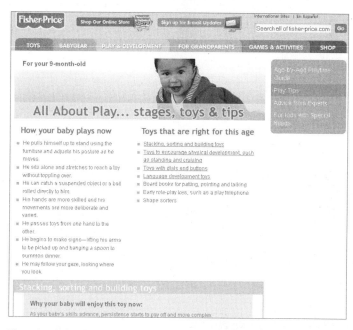

Figure 7.4 Fisher-Price positioning toys by development stage

After the introduction of the recommended toys is a content area showing the products available from Fisher-Price, with links to the products (Figure 7.5). The products are not able to be purchased from this page—that isn't the primary objective. The primary objective is still to educate and reinforce the need to be a good parent. Fisher-Price goes on to provide guides for how to play with the recommended toys. For instance, the site provides methods that caregivers can use instead of just giving the baby the blocks, which will provide care, nurturing, and better development skills.

Figure 7.5 Fisher-Price product recommendation and play advice

Connecting to your customers' needs doesn't always have to be educational or emotional. Finding a different way to position your product against the thousands of other alternatives can connect to a need in a compelling way as well. U.K.-based site Paramount Zone does this very well with its product descriptions (Figure 7.6).

Figure 7.6 Paramount Zone's humorous take on products descriptions

As you can see, the content does not focus on the typical voltage and size features but develops an emotional connection with the reader. It does so by finding a common theme (rapport) upon which to build a specific need. Rather than simply showing the product, using a two- or three-line description direct from the manufacturer's website, and listing the specs, Paramount Zone creates content that is designed to connect with the searcher. Reading the product description creates nods of agreement; people identify with getting a cup of coffee in the morning, getting distracted, and returning to their desk and to a cold cup of coffee. Once that mental imagery is in the reader's mind, they have created the emotional connection and the need. It just so happens that the answer to this need also has a spare USB hub.

Create Additional Need

Using humor, the parenting drive, the desire to save the earth, or the urge to be a better citizen are all methods of creating a need beyond the original need. However, sometimes it just needs to be refined into a simpler message, such as making life simpler.

37signals provides multiple products for project management and collaboration. Its latest entry is a "simple CRM," and it is certainly positioned in that context (Figure 7.7).

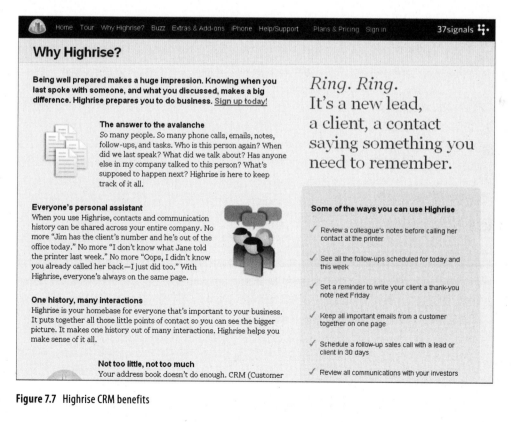

Figure 7.7 Highrise CRM benefits

The concepts are simple. The need is specific, and the answers are presented in short, memorable phrases that mirror the needs of business. Quickly scan through the content and see the points of rapport and creating the need:

- "The answer to the avalanche."
- "A contact saying something that you need to remember."
- "Everyone's personal assistant."
- "Not too little, not too much."
- "Good business is about people."
- "Be prepared and keep in touch."

The need created beyond the need for a CRM system is simplicity, which is what 37signals is offering. The Highrise product is positioned as just the basics that you expect and need to be successful. It doesn't offer more than you need, and it's not overloaded with features you'll never use—it's just a straightforward answer to your problem by focusing on the benefits and making the emotional connection to the overwhelmed salesperson.

The Payoff

Although this additional content and creating the need may sound great, here's the tangible benefit for the website owner. More content on the page equals more rankings for related phrases and concepts. By creating additional needs, you've created beneficial content that will be found by the search engines and may appear for related searches.

For example, all of the developmental content at www.fisher-price.com increases the chances of the website appearing in the results for searches such as *baby development*. This drastically increases both the visibility and the credibility of a company when they are consistently found for terms related to those additional needs.

By creating educational content that creates additional needs that are satisfied by your business, you are educating the customer and teaching them the answers to questions they didn't know to ask. The great side benefit is that it increases your rankings in those areas for great terms related to your business!

Wednesday: Anticipate the Objection

An advanced sales technique is for salespeople to overcome the objections posed by their prospects. Objections are typically seen as frustrating roadblocks to new salespeople, but seasoned sales experts are able to take an objection and turn it into a benefit.

By listening, you can uncover the typical objections that prospects have to your offering, whether it is a product, subscription, or service. Understanding the objections and planning for them can change an excuse into an eager conversion.

Today we'll examine typical objections that customers present and discuss ways to overcome those objections.

Time and Money

In the online tourism world, people tend to spend hours gathering and researching before making a decision or booking their plans. SeaWorld understands the typical objections and offers the "Benefits of Online Purchase" next to the package plans and prices (Figure 7.8). This helps alleviate the objection of purchasing online or waiting for a later date.

Figure 7.8 SeaWorld's benefits of online purchase

By publishing the benefits of the online purchase, it creates a sense of urgency for the searcher, because many of these benefits may not be available if the trip is booked through another source. In addition, the benefits may change and not be available later, so the objection becomes converted into action.

One of my favorite impulse purchase sites is Woot (Figure 7.9). Its premise is simple. It sells one product every day. When that product is sold out, too late! You have to wait until tomorrow to see what the site will sell. You have to act fast if you want what it is selling, because you don't know when the product will sell out.

Every so often, Woot will run the infamous Woot-off. Instead of selling one product for one day, Woot will sell multiple products. As soon as one sells out, the next one goes up for sale. Buyers have some idea when the next item will go live, because there is a temperature gauge reading to show the remaining amount of the current item.

Figure 7.9 Woot single-product sales—act fast!

One of the prize purchases on Woot is the Woot Bag of Crap. Seriously. When the bags of crap go on sale, the server slows to a crawl, and you can only hope that you were one of the lucky purchasers. Although most bags of crap have random items such as USB cables, dorky sunglasses, or a cheap computer mouse, some random purchasers have been known to get a very high-priced electronics item with their purchase. All of this creates a cult-like community of Woot followers. "Wooters" brag about the number of purchases as status symbols in the Woot community forums.

Many sites can take advantage of limited-time offers, and when coupled with saving money, these offers become a powerful combination and justification for a response. In fact, showing the price, the amount of savings from the original price, and the draw of the limited-time offer become a strong method of persuasion. A limited-time offer implies scarcity—once it is gone, it's gone. And you were too late to act.

The most powerful persuasion is the persuasion that you do not do. The best persuasion is when the visitors have the tools, reasoning, and justification to persuade themselves. By allowing the visitors to draw their own conclusions of value and scarcity, they can convince themselves of the good sense to act.

Cigar.com (Figure 7.10) uses this very effectively with a pop-up screen on the first visit. Act now, or lose the offer! By promoting "today only" and the amount of savings, coupled with a can't-miss product, the cigar fan will feel compelled to act for such a ridiculously high-quality product for a low price.

When combining time, money, and simplicity, financial budgeting site Mint.com (Figure 7.11) offers visitors a number of benefits specifically aimed at overcoming their objections. People tend to be very protective of their money and financial information, but at the same time they need help in managing finances. It's an emotional need but one that requires a careful approach in order to present information. Mint.com's simple benefit statements that target typical objections include the following:

- "Easy setup."
- "It's free!"

- "Get started in 5 minutes."
- "Simple one-time set-up."
- "No bookkeeping required."

In a very easy-to-read format, the major objections to a financial services website are overcome and turned into benefits.

Figure 7.10 Cigar.com "today only" offer

On another side of financial dealings is FreeCreditReport.com, which is *not* free. There is a trial period and then a monthly membership, and with additional government regulations, there is now a $1 fee to check your credit report.

FreeCreditReport.com deals with this change in operations in a very appealing manner. Pay the dollar, and they will donate it to charity. This helps appeal to two very different motivations in order to overcome the objection to paying *anything* for something that is advertised as free. The first motivation is fear—fear of a poor credit score, which is created in the message on the FreeCreditReport.com website (see Figure 7.12).

However, by mixing a message of self-preservation with a message of donating your fee to charity, these two usually exclusive motivations are now paired for a powerful result: help others by helping yourself. The implied message? If you have a problem with spending a dollar, you have a problem helping underfunded schools. Well, it may not be that extreme, but it certainly plays a part in the decision making.

Overcome the objection of the fee by making the fee a donation so that the visitor can feel good about themselves—even though they want to check their credit score (most likely because they want to purchase a big-screen TV). This example also illustrates an interesting way to address the objection to free trial offers, discussed in the next section.

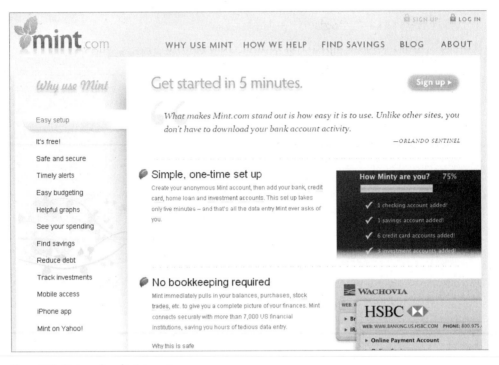

Figure 7.11 Mint.com benefit statements

Figure 7.12 FreeCreditReport.com: mistakes can cost you thousands!

The Power of the Syllogism

A *syllogism* is a means of structuring an argument or reasoning based on a major premise, a minor premise, and a conclusion.

For example:

Major premise: Our product saves you time.
Minor premise: Time savings means more productivity.
Conclusion: This product will make you more productive.

By stating the major premise, or the initial need of the searcher, and then providing the minor premise, or the additional need that you provide (the need beyond the initial need), you then create the correlation to support a conclusion.

A powerful means of persuading is allowing your audience to reach the conclusion that you want them to realize, through the guidance of your message.

The visitor can be easily persuaded when they convince themselves of something in line with your goal before you state your goal. Because they are satisfied at their ability to deduce it before it is said, read, or heard, their emotional and intellectual states are satisfied and more open to the persuasive message.

Using the earlier example of FreeCreditReport.com, we can structure the presentation like this:

Major premise: I can save thousands of dollars by knowing my credit score.
Minor premise: My fee for knowing my credit score goes to charity.
Conclusion: I am a good person for giving to charity in order to know my credit score.

For SeaWorld, the "Benefits to Buying Online" provide the same structure:

Major premise: I get more for my money by booking online.
Minor premise: I will save money for things I will pay for anyway.
Conclusion: Booking online saves me money and time.

Additional conclusion: The same benefits may not be available tomorrow, so I should book today.

Using Mint.com, the setup is similar. The goal is to make the visitor feel empowered by their decision.

Major premise: Mint.com gives me the ability to manage my money.
Minor premise: It's simple and takes five minutes to set up.
Conclusion: I can easily manage my money today!

Free Trials

Free trials are rarely free. If you've ever applied for a free trial, you know that a credit card is going to be required. That's the first objection, and it is usually encountered in the sign-up process. Handing over credit card information is always a major objection point. You can't always bet that the visitor knows that the credit card request is coming, because this was advertised as free.

The Motley Fool (www.fool.com), one of the first popular online investment and financial sites, is known for their humorous and sometimes extreme takes on financial matters. By offering a 30-day free trial along with a 30-day money-back guarantee, they are meeting the objection of price in two methods—a free trial and a guarantee—both very powerful sales techniques for gaining the conversion (see Figure 7.13).

Figure 7.13 The Motley Fool—overcoming price objections

GoToMeeting has one of the best objection-handling methods. When asking for credit card information, there is a sidebar of objections, using the voice of the visitor (see Figure 7.14). These are not written *to* the visitor; they are real questions and real concerns at this stage of the process. By asking these questions, in the visitor's voice, GoToMeeting is able to unassumingly instruct about how the free trial works and how one can easily cancel after the trial period ends.

GoToMeeting®

Your Trial Is FREE for 30 Days

Finalize your account setup and start holding unlimited online meetings now.

Step 3 of 3

Free Trial Summary

GoToMeeting for 30 days	$49.00
• Unlimited meetings — each with up to 15 attendees	
30-day Free Trial	-$49.00

| **Total Amount Due** | **$0.00** |

Please enter your future billing information.

Name on Credit Card

First (and Middle Initial)   Last

You will not be billed today.

Use GoToMeeting free for 30 days. After your free trial ends, a GoToMeeting Monthly Plan with up to 15 attendees per session will start and this credit card will be charged $49.00/mo. You will receive a reminder email before your free trial ends. You can upgrade, downgrade or cancel online at any time.

Why do I need to enter my credit card?

Providing your credit card ensures that your service will continue uninterrupted at the end of your 30-day free trial.

How do I cancel?

You can easily cancel online from your account or call toll-free 1-800-263-6317 (direct dial +1-805-617-7000) at any time during your free trial. You will still be able to use GoToMeeting for the rest of the 30-day period.

Figure 7.14   GoToMeeting free trial—objection selling

Complexity

37signals uses the objection to price, complexity, and time as an obstacle to overcome into a sales point. With its call to action of "30-day free trial, sign up in 60 seconds" (see Figure 7.15), 37signals is able to provide the user with a promise that its Basecamp product is able to be set up quickly and tested for free.

Figure 7.15   The 37Signals.com call to action overcomes objections.

In less than 10 words, 37signals takes away any excuses the visitor may have by overcoming the three objections of time, difficulty, and pricing.

User Registration

One of the most frequently ignored objections online is the request for users to register or create accounts. When a visitor is faced with the request to register on the site, they tend to avoid the registration. In Jakob Nielsen's book *E-Commerce User Experience* (Nielsen Norman Group, 2001), he mentions that sites requiring user registration for purchases account for so many uncompleted transactions that Nielsen recommends against required registration completely.

This type of required registration is being used on Target.com at the time of this writing (Figure 7.16). By requiring registration or tying into the visitor's Amazon.com account, Target leaves no other option available for the visitor. They have to create an account, or they are not able to move forward.

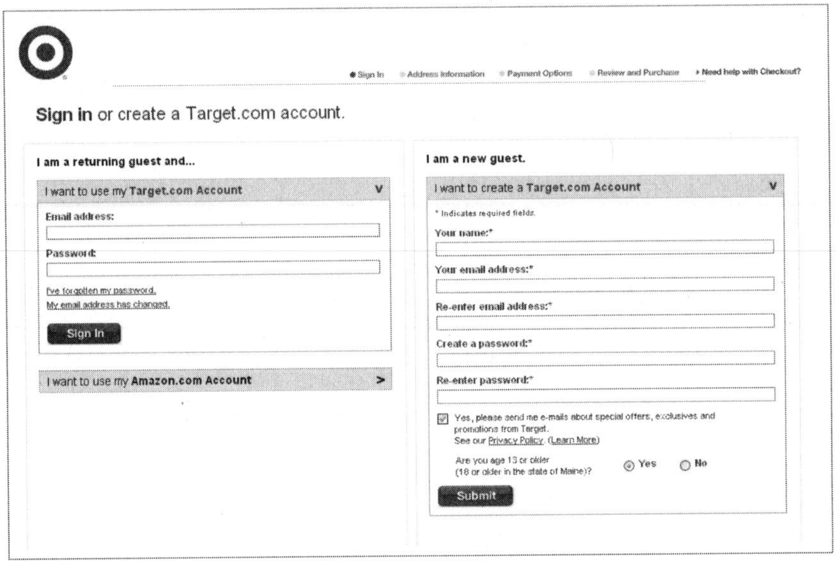

Figure 7.16 Target.com requires user registration in order to purchase.

The two biggest objections that users have to a required registration, according to Nielsen, are as follows:

- Users are reluctant to join anything or complete a registration form.
- User didn't expect or don't want to create a password.

I know that in my own experience, creating a new password is one of the most inconvenient aspects of using websites. It is an interruption in my day, because it forces me to create, record, and attempt to remember a password that I will only have to search for later.

Many retailers have read up on this obstacle to the process, and some make registration optional, but very few use this obstacle to their advantage. For instance, OfficeMax presents the options at the beginning of the secure checkout page (Figure 7.17).

The objections of creating an account are not addressed; they are simply passed to the end of the purchase, and the visitor is let "off the hook" for registering on the website.

Figure 7.17 OfficeMax user registration

This seems unobtrusive to the process, but look a little deeper, and there a missed opportunity to get the registration. Most sites ask for registration but provide little or no visitor benefits for registering! Of course no one registers; there is no reason for it!

Newegg.com (Figure 7.18) presents compelling reasons for new customers to create an account. The benefits of the new account are listed, and the process is presented as a short and simple convenience.

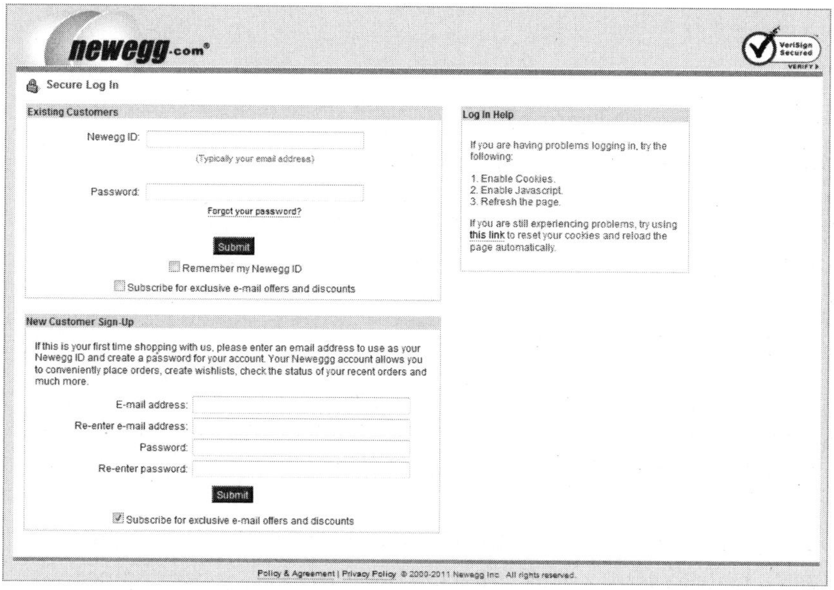

Figure 7.18 Newegg.com provides compelling reasons to register.

Thursday: Ask for the Sale

Once the need is created and the objections are overcome, the next move is to simply ask for the sale. Too many sites present their information but don't ask for the sale. I too often hear complaints from user groups and test subjects that they cannot find "what they are supposed to do" on a website. This, of course, makes them want to give up.

What is most frustrating to people is that they were persuaded and wanted to take action. After investing the time and effort, they really wanted to use that site; however, it was too difficult to find the point of action.

This is where many salespeople simply aren't able to close a deal, because they forget one of the most important aspects—which is simply asking for the sale. In Internet marketing terminology, you can define asking for the sale as the *call to action*. This is the action you want visitors to take, regardless of whether it is a sale, registration subscription, or simply clicking through to another page. Visitors must be clearly shown the request or obviously invited to take the next step; otherwise, they may not find it. By inviting a customer to take action and specifically telling them which action to take, the sales process is streamlined into the specific steps necessary for the visitor to become a customer (or a member, subscriber, or other type of long-term goal you may have for your site).

Harvest, a project and time tracking tool, very clearly asks for the sale with two large green buttons that simply state Sign Up Now and Try It for Free (Figure 7.19).

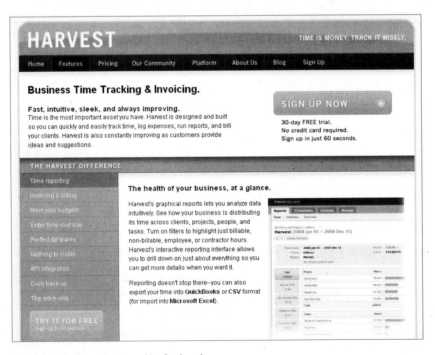

Figure 7.19 GetHarvest.com—asking for the sale

When placing a product in front of a shopper, it is best to be very clear about the product when asking for the sale. In the case of Dynamism (www.dynamism.com), the product is USB sushi drives. If you like sushi and you like USB disk drives, then this is certainly your thing (Figure 7.20).

However, when looking at this page, there are a few hindrances. The first is the lack of a clearly visible point of sale. There is no "asking for the sale." In addition, there is no clear distinction made of how this product will be sold—by the piece, by the pair, or by the entire set. The product copy goes on to describe two very different versions of the product, but there is no clear direction provided to the visitor and no clear request for action. A Buy Now button along with a pull-down menu indicating which version is desired would go a long way toward converting shoppers to buyers.

Figure 7.20 Dynamism's USB sushi. Very cool, but there's no "asking for the sale."

Start with Just a Little Information

Asking for a small amount of visitor information early in the process is one sales tactic that is related to asking for the sale. Research discussed in *50 Scientifically Proven Ways to Be Persuasive* by Goldstein, Martin, and Cialdini (Free Press, 2008) shows that people can be more easily persuaded to agree to an action when they have already made a smaller, less committed action. By inviting visitors to give a "small" yes, it is easier to get those same visitors to commit to the bigger "yes."

Continues

Start with Just a Little Information *(Continued)*

Consider the case of DentalPlans.com; right from the home page, the visitor is focused on two primary means of finding information. The first is finding available plans available in the area. The second is finding a specific dentist. There are other informative links on the page, but those are not the primary destinations. DentalPlans.com is inviting the visitor to take the next step by having them enter information first.

By asking for small decision, a savvy salesperson can prepare the visitor for a larger decision. Once people agree to provide information, such as ZIP code, size of organization, type of industry, and so on, they will be more willing to invest additional information or commitment later in the process, because they have already invested personal information in the progression through the website.

Friday: Don't Muddy the Water

This was a lesson I learned personally as a technical sales engineer. When I had a prospect who was ready to make the commitment, I made the mistake of continuing to sell and adding more to the discussion. I kept introducing new products and other options available in our line. Because I did not let the prospect commit to the sale, when they were ready, I nearly lost the commitment entirely.

When a visitor is ready to commit, let them.

Don't "muddy the water" with more information than the prospect or visitor already need. If they have need or heard enough to make the decision, don't make then view six more pages or loops of Flash movies and animations. Let the visitor get to the commitment and complete their initial task.

There are two distinct areas of online marketing in which people tend to muddy the water: getting the commitment and closing that commitment.

Get the Commitment

With the advent of the social media frenzy, I find that many businesses simply haven't fully developed their online marketing agenda. This is evident in the calls to action on many websites. The phone number, contact form, Facebook, and Twitter links are all presented. In the same place and the same size is the same call to action. All elements are competing with each other for the visitor's attention.

Ask any business what their primary call to action is, and they will jump to tell you to call or to contact! However, this strategy is not always evident on websites—all conversions are often visually treated the same. All conversions are not equal! Some make you more money than others, so the ones that make you the most money need to be the clearest, largest, and boldest visual conversion requests on the page. All other conversions need to be ordered in terms of the priority to the business, to the customer, and to the value that they provide. When web managers realize this and resize, recolor, or remessage their calls to actions accordingly, they find that their conversion rate increases significantly. That is because the "water" is no longer muddied. The content is clear, the focal point of the content is found, and the visitor knows without question where they are to go.

I recommend businesses rank their conversions according to different methods. First, rank them by profitability. Which conversions make the most money for the business? Second, rank them by purpose. Which conversions are for new customer/member/subscription acquisitions? Which conversions are for current member or customer retention? When ordering conversion points by those two methods, the placement and prominence of the conversion on each page and in each section of the website becomes apparent. For example, in my business, I am not going to promote my Facebook page to a visitor who has never had any interaction with my business. What is the point of getting someone to like my business's Facebook page if they have never experienced the business? My goal is to make them a subscriber to our newsletter or to contact us. On the other hand, I push the Facebook subscription to stay in touch as a retention and networking tool.

It is up to each business to decide how to use these tools but then to realize also how to best promote these tools at the right place and at the right time. Getting a visitor to call or contact your business should never be obscured by a call to subscribe to your Twitter stream (or any of the latest social media trends).

Close the Commitment

If a visitor to your site has to pick among multiple choices that define their needs (beyond the information they just read), they are less apt to go through the process once more. If there are multiple levels of membership, different types of products, or separate packages, then the commitment needs to be localized to the information.

This is seen in sites that try to define the customer by their business categories. These categories might make sense within an organization but not to the customer or prospect. I find this problem on the Dell website. From the choices of home office, small business, and medium business alone, I believe that I could choose any one of them (see Figure 7.21).

Figure 7.21 Dell defines its customer categories.

However, then I find out from my Dell rep that my company was considered a large company because of the volume of our purchases that year! That made no sense to me, because I would have never put myself in that category. However, these were Dell-defined customer categories and not customer-defined categories, which cause hesitation from the onset of using the Dell website. This causes muddiness in the water, because hesitation based on confusion is not the desired reaction of your website visitor.

In a similar business-to-business site, AT&T's small business portal offers many options but very little direction (see Figure 7.22). In the Manage My Account options on the right side of the screen, there are four different options; all have a registration link, but there is no clear explanation which one is for the type of business, account, or program a small business should be in.

Figure 7.22 AT&T's small-business account options

In an ecommerce setting, the closing process is often marked by overwhelming options within the cart pages and "pushy" product pages that go along with the process. By trying to push more products and more information to the customer while they are in the commitment process, you stand the chance of losing them entirely, either by their exasperation with the process or by critical "next step" links being overwhelmed by other page elements, causing the confusion for the visitor and the loss of a sale.

Take, for example, At-A-Glance calendars (Figure 7.23); the call to action is buried somewhere at the bottom of the page—one has to scroll down to see it, because it is "below the fold." (This is a newspaper term for content that is below the fold of the newspaper page. The most important content is above the fold in the main headlines. In web terms, *below the fold* applies to any content that requires the user to scroll to see it.) In the example for purchasing a calendar, there are many other calls to action, other buttons that look important, and plenty to distract the eye. The user must scroll to the bottom of the page and pick out the Checkout button among a variety of other options.

Figure 7.23 At-A-Glance's checkout page

Review and Hands-On

First, review your customer research, and compare it with the lists of words and phrases from your keyword research. Include salespeople and customer service managers in this exercise because they have direct interaction with your customers. If you are "wearing all the hats," then talk to others about your business and seek their perceptions of what you offer. Either way, find what people think of you and how that matches up with how you think of your business.

Second, review the content in your marketing and on your website. Are you building rapport with the searcher by showing your concern with their needs and their searches? Is your content too focused on what you want from them?

Think about what need you are creating beyond the initial need. What do you offer that is different or unique in your market? How do you support, educate, or develop your customers to provide an additional benefit beyond what they purchased?

Answer this question from the visitor's perspective: "What's in it for me?" List the typical objections to your business. Is it price, commitment, terms, or complexity? How can you make the objection a benefit in as few words as possible?

Review your calls to action (or commitment). Are there other options, instructions, or conflicting information that prevent a clear call to the highest profitable action? Are all your calls to action the same size or the same color, resulting in an unclear priority?

Review your commitment process. Is the process clear of obstruction? Is the path clear, or does it require visitors to ignore information, search for the next step, or sift through constant visual interruptions? Conducting this review may require someone outside your business or organization to fully review with an honest evaluation. Sometimes being too close to the process creates blindness to obvious issues.

Month 2: Develop Content That Converts

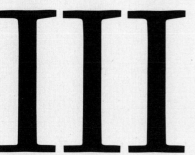

Getting people to your website is one thing, getting people to do what you want is another. Great rankings can get you visibility and visitors, but people are looking for information beyond a price tag. They need to be persuaded to take action, and when you only have seconds to make a good impression, it is your content, and the presentation of that content that will keep people on your website.

Week 5:
Understand That
Content Comes First

All of the hard work you put into optimization and rankings won't mean much if your content does not connect to the reader, provide compelling and persuasive reasons to work with you or your company, or offer creative ways to display and communicate that content. It is one thing to get people to the website, but it is another to get them to do what you want them to do, and that is based on the amount of attention and work you put into your content.

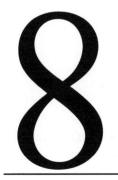

Content is an investment. It is not something you simply copy and paste from a brochure or from an old website. Content is a way to actively engage the reader, lead them through a process, and then bring them to a decision point.

Chapter Contents

Monday: Make your content explode
Tuesday: Create a customer experience
Wednesday: Tell your story
Thursday: Provide a return on the customer's investment
Friday: Test your message

Monday: Make Your Content Explode

We as marketers need to learn and utilize the emotional connections to words that our readers need in order to be properly persuaded. As playwright Tom Stoppard wrote in *Rosencrantz and Guildenstern Are Dead*, "Words! Words! They're all we have to go on." This is the mantra for online marketing. In the limited time and attention that a visitor allows us to promote our companies and businesses, we cannot waste the opportunity. Words, be they read or heard, are all we have to make a connection, position our business, and create action. Becoming familiar with those words and the emotional meaning they hold for our audience is critical to creating profitable websites and internet marketing campaigns.

Words can connect with the reader and have the potential to create an emotional response. When our information matches the needs of the visitor, there is a connection. Once the connection is made, the visitor will allow you more time and attention to make your case for their staying on the site. As the visitor senses an imminent answer to their questions, they will stay longer and click through to more pages. This is referred to as *information scent* (Jakob Nielsen, 2003; `www.useit.com/alertbox/20030630.html`) and presents Internet users as hunters on a trail. When a trail grows cold, the hunter will give up—much like an information seeker who receives no feedback on a page about their need. Using words that match the intentions of the searcher is the way to keep them on the hunt for their information.

Unfortunately, the value of words tends to be underutilized by many company websites. As mentioned in Chapter 1, there are many times that content is forgotten until the website is ready to go live. This is both unfortunate and unforgivable. Content is the key to reaching people and promoting your business. Sites need to be built around the content and support it, rather than the content supporting the design. When content is a low priority compared to the rest of the marketing elements, it results in a dry, boring, and unfocused presentation.

Before and After

Watching the evolution of design and content on certain websites is a nice way to keep the pulse of the evolution of marketing on the Internet. I've been watching the following websites over the past few years. Read on to see how they've changed over time.

John Deere Tractors

My interest in the John Deere site was spawned by Nick Usborne (*Networds*, McGraw-Hill, 2002), after listening to his Writing for the Web presentation in 2004 at Search Engine Strategies in Boston. He showed the John Deere website that had promotional copy for the 4000 series tractor that was some of the softest, most spineless, noncommittal, and vague content one could ever find (Figure 8.1). Don't take my word for it; Nick's caption for this example was "What has the reader learned?"

The content reads as follows:

Underneath their familiar green and yellow exterior isn't just a redesign of the compact tractor, but a transformation. Where power is no longer measured by horsepower. Where implements practically attach themselves. And comfort is no longer at odds with productivity. One hundred and twenty improvements. Zero gimmicks. And countless firsts. These tractors are ready. 120 Improvements. Countless Firsts. Zero Gimmicks.

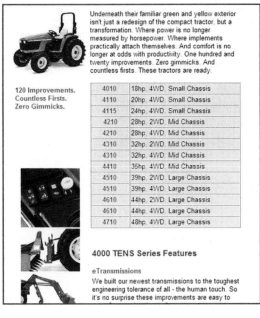

Figure 8.1 John Deere—noncommittal content

This content has no depth and no benefits. It's boring and borderline ridiculous. The company isn't selling luxury cars here; it's selling tractors to people who have very specific needs. The funny thing is that I was in the market for a tractor, and this hit home. I was looking for something that I could get dirty tilling, mowing, digging, and landscaping—not something that looks nice on a glossy brochure. Plus there's the fact that no attachments *attach themselves*—that's just an out-and-out overstatement. Power is no longer measured by horsepower? What is the measure of power then? Can this tractor tow large objects? How large? How heavy? Specific needs are not addressed. No connection is made.

Fortunately, things change, and usually they get better. The new product page for the 4000 series tractor makes so much more sense—the page in Figure 8.2 speaks to people's needs.

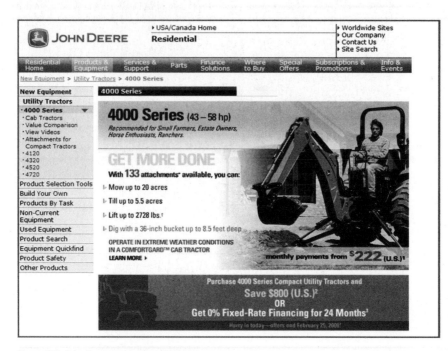

Figure 8.2 John Deere—need-based content

This page offers the following content:

GET MORE DONE
With 133 attachments available you can:
Mow up to 20 acres
Till up to 5.5 acres
Lift up to 2728 lbs
Dig with a 36-inch bucket up to 8.5 feet deep

Now that's action! Those factors speak to my needs for a tractor! This makes me excited, this allows me to envision the possibilities of what I can do, and this creates the need for me to own this tractor, and helps me to justify the purchase to my wife!

On the downside, this amazingly explosive content was tied up inside an image, rather than allowed to live on and propagate in HTML text format. Placing this content inside a graphic keeps it contained to those who see the graphic. Allowing it to be HTML text would have allowed it to be searchable; published in search results; and copied, sent, and highlighted by those people who, like me, love this tractor stuff.

As the John Deere website continues to evolve, I hope to see more transitions into consumer needs–based content. For large commitment items, a nice picture and a few paragraphs of content do very little to move the decision-making process along.

PetSafe

Another site that found the power of words is PetSafe (Figure 8.3).

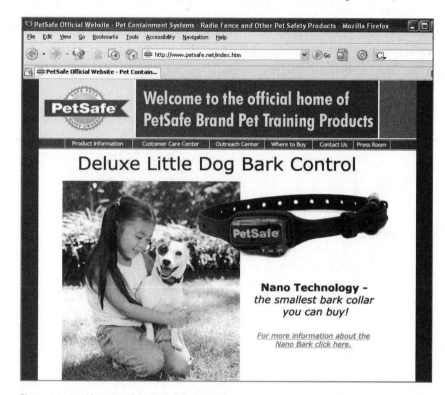

Figure 8.3 An old version of the PetSafe home page

The home page just struck me as soon as I found it, because it was very generic and totally image-focused. The main problem is that it was focused entirely on one image. Unfortunately, the navigation did not help this site, because the first navigational choice was Product Information. Now think about this for a second. The word *product* does not carry any power at all; it's a generic word. The second problem is that the word is singular. There is no visual or contextual indication that there is an entire catalog of pet supplies. The large image dedicated to one product and the noncontextual navigation stop any user who does not have a need for that particular product. Nothing draws the viewer into the website.

Fast-forward a few years, and the new PetSafe website is miles ahead of the prior installment (Figure 8.4). This home page provides a clear explanation of the website: "Safe Pets. Happy Owners."

Figure 8.4 Improved PetSafe home page

What a fantastic tagline! This is another example of the syllogism explained in the previous chapter:

First premise: Owners love their pets and will ensure their safety.

Second premise: Pets make their owners happy.

Conclusion: I show my love for my pet by ensuring their safety, which makes me happy.

You know what PetSafe sells and what they are about after only a split-second glance at the page. The text links and content groupings allow people to instantly get into the deep content of the website, either through the pet product finder or through specific product links.

Thankfully, the navigation was changed to Products, which is still generic but plural, implying many more products are available through that link. The new page has much more emphasis on content, not only the connection of the content but the presentation of the content and key benefit statements.

The customer testimonial is a nice bonus, and the content directs people to the importance of loving their pets. This connects on a different level, since you will buy products to protect and benefit your pet because you love them, not so much because you need to be sold on that.

Interestingly, the site has undergone a few more revisions, and the latest site features many more product categories and less of an emphasis on the owner-pet relationship (Figure 8.5).

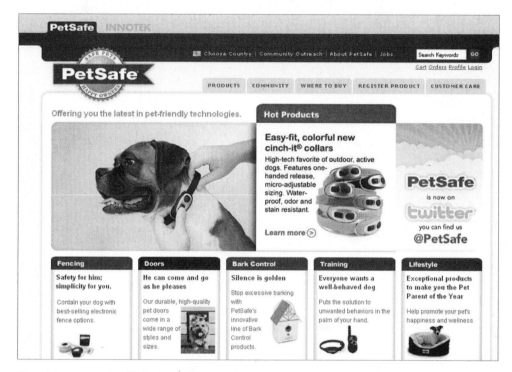

Figure 8.5 Latest version of PetSafe: emphasis on products

I am sure that the change in this site to this new home page has made a significant impact in increased traffic and search engine rankings. Implementing more HTML-based content with clear benefit statements gives the search engines more ammunition for contextually classifying your website. But the best result of creating content that connects with readers is that it works. It provides benefits, ideas, and answers. And that's what people are looking for.

I love seeing companies get the content right on their websites. I don't want your site to explode from the bulk of content but to explode in relevance and power. Too many companies rely on spineless, filler content in the place of real words that have actual meaning. Customers aren't looking for filler; they are looking for explosions that will motivate and inspire them to action.

Tuesday: Create a Customer Experience

While browsing websites for gift ideas, I am constantly seeing the awesome potential of multimedia. Now that there are multiple social websites for almost every kind of media, the potential for customers to be exposed to your experience is limitless and really inexpensive. Text and static images have been in use for a long time, but savvy marketers are now employing audio, video, and customer reviews as well.

Audio

One of my favorite features in marketing items that require more than a visual image is the use of audio. My wife loves wind chimes, and I found some very interesting and different types of chimes. However, as most ecommerce sites go, there is usually a picture and a small description of the product. This is hardly enough to go on when looking for a gift that goes beyond a static visual image. The chimes I found were made of ceramic bells rather than metal or wood, so I was very interested in hearing them. This is one product where the lack of sound is a deal breaker—I can't imagine that many people purchase wind chimes based solely on looks. I wanted to hear what they sound like before I place them permanently on my patio.

Similarly, when shopping for a performance exhaust system for a Corvette, for example, a car owner is going to be very interested in what the exhaust sounds like. Mid America Motorworks (www.mamotorworks.ccom) added an audio gallery of exhaust systems, allowing customers to browse by the sound of the system (Figure 8.6). This also allows for researching other systems that may not have been top of mind but have a great sound. For this audience, hearing the product is everything in making the final decision.

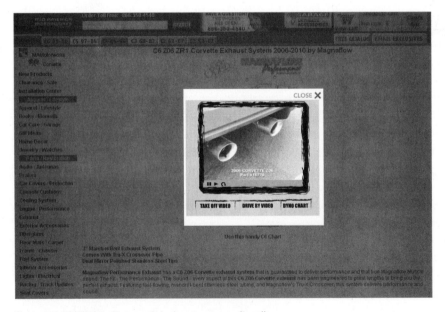

Figure 8.6 Mid America Motorworks' exhaust system audio gallery

Video

Fireworks, are, as my father likes to remind me, the only product that literally burns your money. My friends and I love a 4th of July celebration, and we host large parties to celebrate this holiday. A few years ago, my shopping for fireworks took on a whole new level of education.

How do you shop for fireworks when all you see at the store are brightly colored boxes? Well, you go to a company's website and see a video of what the box will produce.

One of the favorite displays of the night was a box called Guns of Navaronne, which we were able to preview on the Phantom Fireworks website, `www.fireworks.com` (Figure 8.7). Sound and video! All of that resulted in a very happy viewing audience. I also know that I will be getting the Strategic Air Defense display next year!

Figure 8.7 Fireworks.com video fireworks gallery

For selling a product that cannot be seen until after the purchase, these videos are critical. At the fireworks store, it was obvious which people were buying based on researching the website and which were simply wandering the store. It is a great exercise in consumer behavior to see people purchasing fireworks based on so many different factors such as price, name, and color of the package, yet very few buyers knew what exactly they were buying and what it would look like when they used it!

How much more can you create a customer experience by adding additional audio or video of your products, production process, or products results? In many cases, amateur video uploaded to YouTube has created a demand and an awareness of a product long before a company was able to produce the same results. Bloggers who review products have all written about amazing reactions by people who purchase the product after they have seen someone use it and can see for themselves the benefits of how to use it properly.

Customer Reviews

In one extreme case of a consumer review sparking a full-fledged run on a product, even so much as to create a subculture of Internet humor, is the Three-Wolf Moon T-shirt review on Amazon.com (Figure 8.8). One enterprising reviewer took the time to explain the virtues of a black T-shirt with three wolves howling at the moon. He made claims of women unable to resist him when he wore the shirt, which led to others making similar claims such as wearing it for weeks without the need to wash it, supermodels throwing themselves at the wearers, how it boosts self-confidence, and its power at the local Wal-Mart.

Figure 8.8 Three Wolf Moon short-sleeve T-shirt

Within only a few months, the number of additional reviews grew significantly, increasing the sales of the shirt. As of this writing, there are more than 1,700 reviews for the Three Wolf Moon T-shirt. Interestingly, the one-star reviews are just as entertaining and promotional as the five-star reviews. In addition, YouTube videos have been made as a tribute, as have additional shorts to complement the numerous requests of customers.

The user-uploaded images of people wearing the shirt are entertainment alone. From before/after photos to Photoshop-tweaked pictures of the shirt on Superman to an entire Marine company, all sport this phenomenon of a T-shirt. That proves you never know how these things will happen or why. The buzz created by the reviews created momentum, and the T-shirt spent nearly 200 days on Amazon's Top 100 List. It was also written about and linked from user-created YouTube videos, Wikipedia entries, hundreds of blogs, and hundreds more news sites. Six months after the original comment, Amazon was selling the T-shirt at the rate of 100 per hour. Sales increased 2,300 percent. The State of New Hampshire's

Division of Economic Development designated the shirt as the "official T-shirt of New Hampshire Economic Development" in honor of the company responsible for the shirt, The Mountain, located in New Hampshire.

Travel

The travel trade has been turned upside down since the 1990s with the growth of the Internet and social-sharing networks. Currently on Flickr, I can view hundreds of geo-tagged photos of almost every location on Earth. Photos from all over the world have been uploaded by travel enthusiasts, photographers, and people who are simply sharing their experiences. Before embarking on any type of vacation, you can go to Flickr and see the exact location, down to the square foot they were standing upon when they took their pictures! (See Figure 8.9.)

Figure 8.9 Geotagged pictures on Flickr

Travel and tourism agencies can take advantage of this type of "conversation" that happens on photo-sharing sites while people are comparing, commenting, and creating common interest groups for these images.

Of course, this is not just limited to the travel and tourism industries. Any business that has a product that simply needs to be seen can use Flickr as a marketing vehicle. In fact, there is probably a group already dedicated to it! There are classic car restoration companies, custom boat builders, cake decorators...the list goes on. Simply by finding your audience in the places they are comfortable sharing and discussing their interests, you can increase your reach.

There are multiple stories of everyday people discussing products they have either enjoyed or been disappointed in. Those consumers have been far ahead of corporate marketing departments and have had a far greater reach. They are setting the stage for the customer experience rather than the company that produces the product.

Wednesday: Tell Your Story

Stories sell. People love good stories, success stories, company stories, and startup stories. Stories can communicate information about a business that a fact sheet never will. Stories involve building a personality and a unique voice; they connect people to knowing who you are, rather than viewing a faceless website.

One of my favorite experiences in consulting was my time with Mid America Motorworks. When I met the president of the company, Mike Yager, his name badge read "Chief Cheerleader." That gave me an indication of what I would be in for over the next few months. He saw his job as being the one who motivates, cheers, and allows his people to be their best. He doesn't like the title of president—or any title for that matter. His management philosophy is empowering others; as he says, "I'm not more important than anyone else in my organization; I just have different responsibilities."

After seeing Mike in action, "cheerleader" definitely suits his management style and the enjoyment he gets from going to work every single day. In his words, "I could be president or cheerleader—who do you think is going to be more approachable?" In talking with his employees, I was amazed how many people had worked at the company for 18 years, 15 years, 12 years, and so on. The employees are excited about their work, and they share an amazing sense of purpose, instilled by Mike (Figure 8.10).

Mike started his company by using a borrowed car and a $500 loan and selling his collection of Corvette parts and accessories from the trunk of that car at car shows. He was able to take that passion for Corvettes and build one of the most recognized names in the Corvette aftermarket parts industry. He also hosts an annual Corvette Funfest, which draws more than 15,000 Corvettes and more than 40,000 enthusiasts. His personality drives the business, and his customers feel a part of his success, because they share his story, his humble beginnings, his passion, and his joy in celebrating with his customers.

All of the company's online advertising shares Mike's excitement and passion for Corvettes and air-cooled VWs. Mike uses the platform of his blog to share new products, industry news, attractive automobiles, friends, and history (both personal and automotive), as shown in Figure 8.11. Mike spotlights some of the friends that he has made throughout his years in the industry, seminars, auto ownership, and automotive clubs. He provides information, education, and a point of meeting for his friends and the marketplace. In touring his offices, the décor of the meeting rooms, café, and museum are all driven by his magnetic personality and love for classic Corvettes. In fact, the website, product catalog, and mailings all fit the brand, because the brand is driven by the story.

Figure 8.10 Mike Yager (left) of Mid America Motorworks

Mike's communication and empathy with his marketplace is driven by his own passion for the product. As a hobbyist and owner of classic American and German-made automobiles, he shares his customers' passion and enthusiasm for these classic cars. As the face of Mid America Motorworks, Mike shares his story and his passion for the industry, and customers are drawn into a relationship more so than simply buying products. Stories and personal empathy are very effective in that they create the connection to the customer by tapping into their empathy. The person listening to a story can identify with the thoughts and feelings of the speaker.

Figure 8.11 Mike's blog

Thursday: Provide a Return on the Customer's Investment

How can you distinguish a product as practical and as pervasive as a pen? Wooden Pen Works (www.woodenpenworks.com), which creates wooden, turquoise, and malachite pens, created a humorous video using the characters Statler and Waldorf from *The Muppet Show*. The video was uploaded it to YouTube, and the clip received thousands of views (Figure 8.12).

Finding that spark of creativity that helps educate and entertain customers about your product or business makes you memorable. Beyond that, it also provides your customers with a story to relate to others. In this case, you are not just purchasing a pen; you've become tied to the relational aspects of familiar characters explaining how the pen was made.

Figure 8.12 Wooden Pen Works video

There is much more emotional and entertainment investment in the purchase, which not only assists in the decision to purchase but the satisfaction and emotional benefits as purchases can link the purchase to the "infotainment," which is an additional return on investment for the customer.

This sparks the question of how many other products would benefit from interested purchasers seeing the manufacturing process. Food Network has remarkable success in showing the processes of making our favorite foods in shows such as *Unwrapped*; *Diners, Drive-ins, and Dives*; and *Good Eats*. People are fascinated by knowing the behind-the-scenes work that goes into developing products. Many times businesses are so focused on their own sales and return that they neglect the very people who provide those sales.

Defining Value

Do companies realize the return on investment for their customers? What are the intrinsic values shared by your customers beyond the monetary investment?

Information on some sites is so company focused; I have no idea what it can do for me. On other sites, the information is simply presented in a "here it is, now buy it" format, with no persuasive content to convince me to purchase. The winners are those companies that realize that if they sell to the benefit of the customer, they will create a lasting impression:

> **Fisher-Price** sells parenting advice more than toys on its website (www.fisher-price.com), as discussed in the previous chapter. It provides age-appropriate toy

selection advice and information about how you can educate using toys—the company helps you be a better parent.

Woot makes it fun to buy impulse items that you really don't need, as covered in Chapter 7. The goal is to buy it before they run out, because many products are sold at discounts or they are hard-to-find technology toys.

Wine.com doesn't just sell wine; the site helps you become a little more intelligent about wines—you may be able to even hold your own in a discussion about a Pinot Gris.

ThinkGeek (www.thinkgeek.com) sells fun in the office and products for distraction or enjoyment. Its product benefits often include stress relief or even (gasp) self-improvement. This is how it positions a shower curtain decorated with the periodic table of the elements:

How many times has this happened to you? You're showering, lathering up your hair, and as you read the ingredients, you notice Sodium Laureth Sulfate. Of course, you know it's a straight-chain alkyl benzene sulfonate (I mean, who doesn't?), but you forgot what Laureth is! The horror!

If only you had paid more attention to your Chemistry professor!

This might not remind you what Laureth is (it's a contraction for laurylether, made from the sulfation of lauryl alcohol, but you knew that), but it's hard to deny the Periodic Table Shower Curtain's usefulness. All the time you spend in the bathroom, you might as well brush up on your transition metals, and your lanthanide and actinide series. Jog those brain cells with some steaming hot water, and a giant six-foot tall periodic table.

The Periodic Table Shower Curtain is 71 inches square, and made from 100% EVA Vinyl (Ethylene vinyl acetate, but you knew that), and is semi-transparent with the Periodic Table of Elements printed in large friendly letters and colors.

The willingness for a customer to purchase more products, buy from a company repeatedly, and recommend products to friends increases as they realize more benefits. Sometimes that realization takes days, weeks, or maybe months. Additionally, the more benefits realized over a longer period of time, the greater the return will be, including a personal ROI of an investment in a good company and the increased positive perception of the company that provided the product or service.

Here are some examples:

- A family vacation creates bonding and memories for a lifetime, and you can see your children marvel at the world, which is invaluable.

- Toys are more than toys; they are educational opportunities.

- Software is a time-saver, relieving hours of stress and work, while increasing productivity.
- A hotel is a relaxing and rejuvenating experience—not just someplace to sleep.

Interestingly, the reverse holds true as well. The worse a product is or is found to be, if it ends up costing a customer more time and money than they intended, then the brand loyalty will diminish.

Friday: Test Your Message

Apart from testing your website, it is important to test your message. Testing your message prior to building a product, a campaign, or a purpose can save hundreds of hours in developing a misguided campaign. And it can save you from a bad message that may create animosity, anger, or outright attacks on your company or brand. A wrong message can damage your reputation, it can offend your target market, and in terms of the Internet it will be there forever.

The Negative

An example of this happened with Motrin, a brand of pain reliever. Motrin went live with a television commercial that sparked an outrage within the very market it was targeting: new moms. The ad features a text-based flow of the remarks made by a young woman's voice (Figure 8.13). The commercial targeted women wearing baby carriers, and the voice-over made statements about babies being worn as a fashion accessory, and that while being close to your baby, it causes pain. The mommy market exploded.

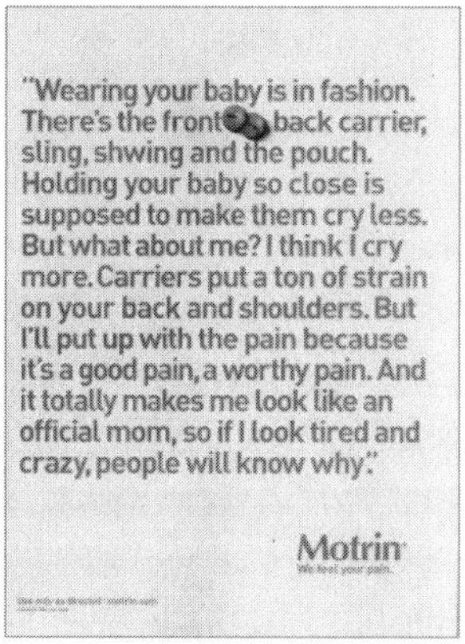

"Wearing your baby is in fashion. There's the front, back carrier, sling, shwing and the pouch. Holding your baby so close is supposed to make them cry less. But what about me? I think I cry more. Carriers put a ton of strain on your back and shoulders. But I'll put up with the pain because it's a good pain, a worthy pain. And it totally makes me look like an official mom, so if I look tired and crazy, people will know why."

Motrin
We feel your pain.

Figure 8.13 Offensive Motrin campaign targeting baby-sling wearing moms

Between YouTube and Twitter, thousands of angry women, most being new mothers, expressed outrage at being insulted by this commercial. Comments about the commercial ranged from the woman's voice being that of a teenager's view of babies, the immaturity of the message, that properly worn baby carriers do not cause pain, and that babies are not fashion statements. The consensus was that the commercial was not respectful of the love between a mother and her new baby—that, in fact, it was insulting. Women made videos of themselves speaking their minds to Motrin (Figure 8.14). Over a single weekend and into most of the following week, the Motrin commercial was at the top of Twitter messages. As women found out about the commercial and then watched it on YouTube (linked frequently in Twitter messages), the anger grew, and the infuriation deepened. A question that was asked frequently was, "Did they even test this message on new moms?"

Figure 8.14 Videos incorporated Twitter responses to the Motrin campaign.

Within days, the CEO of Motrin offered an apology for the commercial. The home page of the Motrin website was changed to display the letter of apology. The target market had spoken, and the message was received loud and clear. As with most social media–sparked outrage, it died quickly. Once the company apologized, the furor subsided, and people went about their normal lives. However, for a brief time, mothers were passionately outraged and took it upon themselves to make a company understand their anger. This is not the type of attention that companies, brand managers, or their lawyers enjoy.

This highlights the importance of closely identifying your audience and crafting a message based on their needs. It is possible to have an offering that meets people's needs, but if the message is presented in a way that condescends or gives people the perception of arrogance or insult, then the message can hurt you. At best, a bad message is simply ignored or never noticed. Obviously, there is no connection made.

The Positive

In working with one of my consulting clients, I was impressed at the amazing amount of research and customer interaction that had been performed prior to developing a new marketing campaign and website. In their words, "What we have been doing is not working, so we need to do everything better." They knew that their message was not effective and did not properly communicate clear benefits to their customers.

They developed a questionnaire to send to current and previous customers and, in doing so, found out valuable and unique information that challenged their conceptions of marketing their own product. They used the Net Promoter Score analysis of Loyalists, Passives, and Detractors to identify trends in usage, experiences, and perceptions of the company and the product. Net Promoter Score is based on the response of the question; on a scale of 1 to 10, it measures how likely you are to recommend this product to a colleague or a friend. Those who answer 9 or 10 are Loyalists, 7 or 8 are Passives, and 0 to 6 are Detractors. Matching the response to that question to the other responses helps identify common experiences of loyalists and common experiences of detractors and passives that explain how the company can become better at reaching those groups.

By examining the benefits espoused by the loyalists, the customer's words were benefit statements that the company had never made. In fact, the customers made statements about the viability of the product that the marketing department would have never developed. Their perception about the benefits created additional marketing content, opportunities for testimonials, and specific benefit points that needed to be brought out in the marketing. Many companies have a conception of what they bring to the market and the benefit they provide to the customer. However, I wonder how many of those companies actually have checked with the customer to be sure their benefit statements match the customer's actual benefits,

In this case, the benefits that the company touted in the marketing materials were far more complex and involved than the simple messages that the customers were providing in their feedback. As a result, the marketing messages were reworked to be simpler and concise. In addition, the benefit statements went into the development of the new website and incorporated the primary benefit categories as high-level navigation items in the menu. Additional benefit statements were implemented throughout the navigation, using the customer's own feedback and words to assist other, potential customers in solving their problems and finding answers.

Within weeks of the new website launch, the results were clear. Benefit-based searches were bringing new customers to the website. By restating the benefits of the customers, the website was able to rank for and draw in new prospects that were trying to solve the same issues. By testing the marketing message and refining the message to be simpler and using the same language as the customer, this company saw their website traffic increase by 800 percent and leads increase by 400 percent, just within the first five months.

Beyond the website, a new marketing campaign was launched, with the goal of creating a simpler message that was easier to communicate. The customer research showed that the majority of loyal customers found out about the company through word-of-mouth. The majority of Detractors found out about the company through more traditional forms of advertising. Based on these findings, a campaign was launched as the centerpiece of the company to reward and promote the loyal customers and encourage word-of-mouth. Loyalty breeds loyalty as they learned, and encouraging your promoters provides the best kind of customers.

Use Real People, Not Groups

Chapter 4 introduced the concept of developing a user persona. Personas are the art of developing an internal conversation with someone who fits your target market and using that mind-set to see your marketing as they see it. When it comes to messaging, testing with an actual member of that target market needs to be done. My personal preference is not to use focus groups, because a herd mentality tends to take over and people are less inclined to share their personal opinions if they differ from that of the group. In general, people want to be accepted by a group, and that desire allows them to be persuaded in order to be accepted. Because of this, I tend toward recommending properly constructed online surveys and one-on-one interviews and observation.

Do not rely on the persona to test your message, but find actual members of the market that fit the persona. Either through personal interviews, online surveys, or user observation, this is your key to understanding the psychographic profile of your persona. Record their words, phrases, thoughts, and reactions, because these can be used in further developing the persona and better understanding how you can meet their needs with a good message.

When asking a person to review your website, simply showing them a page and asking their thoughts is not enough of a test to get an accurate assessment of your website. The processes need to be tested. To test a process, give your subject a specific task to accomplish, such as a product to find and purchase or a piece of critical information and then a registration process. Either way, the process of a visitor coming to the website for a specific purpose is the tested procedure, not the opinion of the design and layout.

Be sure to test processes and watch the time and accuracy of the process. When using more than one subject to test the website, the time and accuracy of the process can be compared and evaluated to ensure that one test wasn't simply over-thought or not valid. By developing a standard process test and metric goals, you will then be able to compare multiple subjects according to a single goal, which allows for additional insights and analysis.

Review and Hands-On

Just as engineers test equipment before it goes into production or new medicines undergo trials, take the time to test your message to ensure that your message connects to your audience in the right way. Ask yourself the following questions:

- Do you have content on your site that is simply a block of text? Does it have a clear purpose and benefit? If so, rewrite your content to display clear benefit statements that will connect with your audience's needs.

- Have you verbalized that value in any way; is it clearly communicated? Additionally, how can you help them realize a return on their investment from working with you? Assess the value you provide to your customers, readers, fans, or clients.

- Can you create an experience? Anything that has a visual or auditory aspect can be used to develop another means of reaching new customers and enhancing the experiences of your current customers.

- Do you have a process that can be explained or used as education in order to show the difference of your company as compared to others? Are there resources within your company that you can use in explaining benefits more clearly or in different ways?

- Do you make a living in providing information based on a news cycle or timely events? Do you analyze the market and provide a response? How can you develop content based on these areas to provide both education and a means of entertainment, value, or necessity?

This is an area where developing an accounting of the benefits you provide and a clear message of value will assist you in then developing the best way to communicate that to your audience. Develop the message first so developing the creative communication will be easier.

Week 6: Connect Your Content to Users and Search Engines

Just as critical as writing good content that educates, informs, and answers questions is how you present that same content. Web users tend not to read long paragraphs. Quickly moving from area to area on a page, the visitor's eyes take a seemingly random approach to moving through the content. However, you can develop a few tactics with your content to ensure that visitors will see and absorb a lot of your message without much effort.

Understanding the factors that play into how people absorb content from a web page and how search engines use those same factors in determining relevance for your content can help you develop effective content that will rank well and increase conversions.

9

Chapter Contents

Monday: Understand Human Factors in Scanning

Studies by the Nielsen Norman Group explain the online behavior of people as they search for information on a page or in a website. Human interaction with content online is very limited. This led researcher Jakob Nielsen to comment on the way online users read. He concluded, "They don't" (Jakob Nielsen's Alertbox, October 1, 1997).

What people do is scan. In one study, nearly 80 percent of users would scan a new page, whereas only 16 percent of users would read the new page line by line. This presents a very large obstacle to online marketers. The content is critical to introducing the company, the purpose, and the marketing narrative. How can this be accomplished when users are not reading the content thoroughly?

The interesting observation is that many marketers, upon learning about this, are not fully surprised. All they really have to do is to consider their own habits when browsing online. It is a foraging type of reading—looking for elements on the page that speak to what we need. If we see enough evidence that the information we need is in a paragraph, we may slow down enough to scan the paragraph for the keywords that are important. Many people simply do not slow down enough to fully read a paragraph. Nielsen outlines many of the predominant behaviors and reasons in his article at www.useit.com/alertbox/whyscanning.html.

Scanning is most likely the result of a number of issues:

- Time to target: Reading online takes time, especially during a workday. Finding specific information often requires wading through pages of data, paragraphs of information, and large websites. Finding visual clues on pages helps us navigate to other pages that may assist in our discovery.

- Monitors: Nielson Norman Group also found that reading online demands time; people read about 25 percent slower on a monitor than on paper. In my own experience, I find that the contrast level of a monitor simply cannot compete with the printed page. On the printed page, the colors are less intense, and the contrast is much easier for long reading sessions. Monitors do not lend themselves to easy study.

- Search availability: Ten other web pages are a click away from a search engine query. A user can simply click the Back button, return to the search engine results page, and find more options.

- Progress: Nielsen notes that the Web is a user-driven medium, and people think they have to be actively clicking and navigating to have a sense of progress.

- Overload: In addition, Nielson reasons that life is hectic, and the number of emails, voicemails, and information overload many people experience leads to a disjointed content experience with a web page.

What Do Humans Scan?

The primary elements used by people as they scan web pages are very interesting. It depends upon the presentation and layout of the content almost as much as the content itself.

People depend on headings, subheadings, topic headings, bullet points, captions, inline text links, graphics, bold and italic formatting, and colored text in order to scan a page. The concept is simple. These are techniques used to indicate that certain text is more important than regular text, so people use those as markers for quickly surveying the information available.

Think of a newspaper. When I travel, one thing that I can count on is the newspaper lying in the hallway outside my room door. In only a few seconds I can quickly browse through the major headlines, subheadings, bylines, and images and quickly grasp the major new stories of the previous day. The same concept applies to web pages; in fact, online publishers can learn much from their aging print counterparts. Looks matter.

Headings

Use headings to communicate specific information, utilizing a keyword or additional related keyword concept to maintain relevance. The headline is the primary indicator of content on the page, and the subheadings help show the organizational flow of content. Essentially, build an outline using the headings, subheadings, and paragraph headers. The reader should be able to get a sense of the page's content by using this outline, even without the paragraphs of content.

When using HTML to format these elements, the current recommendation is to use the <h1> tags to create the headlines and <h2> and <h3> for subheadings. Although many use CSS for the markup, there is little consistency in defining headings, and search engines still need to see <h1>, <h2>, <h3>, and so on, as contextual indicators of the important content. However, as HTML 5 amasses wider adoption, the code will become much more semantic and logical, using similar tags such as <headline> or <header> to denote the layout elements.

Bullet Points

Bullet points, when used wisely, can increase readability and retention by readers. To make them more effective, any benefit information must be placed in the first few words of the bullet point, because visitors will also scan bullet points, usually only the first few words.

Bullet points go wrong when too much information is packed into the bullet point, making it more than a short sentence, or when more than four or five bullet points are used. Stacking more than five bullet points creates a repetitive layout block, which makes it very easy for readers to ignore.

Text Links

Text links within the content are an important navigation resource to the visitor. By placing them in the content, the contextual value of the text link is much higher than when presented in the typical navigation elements. While readers are scanning the content, the text link is an element that gets their attention, because the color and underlined element is the universal sign for a link. This is also why I recommend that link attributes (color, underlined) be clear in a website design.

Everyone knows what blue underlined text denotes. Now, I am not saying that all link text on every website needs to be blue and underlined; I am simply stating that every web user learns very quickly what blue underlined text will do. Every degree that your design varies from blue underlined text links is another degree of adaptation you are requiring of your visitor to understand your design. Be aware of the color and attributes of the links in your design, because it may be difficult for users to immediately recognize the text links.

The words used in a link point to the information contained on the linked page. Readers are particularly focused on these links within the content, because they help them quickly determine whether the information they need is on this page or on the next page, on the other side of the link. As such, text links within content have a very high relevance for information, and users depend on them.

One of the first tests I ran when I first had access to ClickTracks, a visual analytics program, was the click overlay report. This report showed which links were clicked by visitors on a specific page. I could easily see which links received no activity and which links were clicked the most and then compare the different link activity. I consistently observed that website visitors clicked the text links within the content more frequently than the links in the navigation. This supported the idea that visitors were scanning the content, not the navigation, and found the link that contained the information they needed.

Layout

By building a good heading structure and bullet points to support the logical outline of information, the page will start to build itself with a logical layout. Similar to the old grammar-school writing technique of building an outline of a story, a web page is most effective when there is a logical development of information.

Heading size, with the most important headings used as a headline and then ordered sequentially in smaller fonts, helps the reader perceive the importance of the text headings. Differentiating the headings and the important features from the regular text helps readers distinguish important benefit statements and the structure of the content. The structure of the information is as important as the information itself.

By creating an outline of information on the page, the reader can quickly determine the relationship of the content. Ideally, the size and font of the headline are immediately noticeable. The subheadings related to the primary information are all consistent in style and weight, allowing an easy visual pass over the information. This allows the reader to digest the content available on the page simply by font size, color, and weight. If there are multiple content areas, they are easily identifiable. Of course, there are always expectations based on presentation and design selection, but you must also consider the reader, as well as their ability to determine the content of the page and the availability of additional, related content on that page.

In my own accessibility testing, I was able to observe behavior noted in one of Jakob Nielsen's accessibility tests: website users who were using screen readers scanned page content by listening. Users who depend upon screen readers to listen to the page content did not want to sit and listen to each page being read to them word for word.

The main program for screen reading, JAWS, was utilized with keystrokes that mimicked the scanning of sighted users. The screen reader users quickly attempt to ascertain the content of the page by listening to the headers on the page by pressing the number keys that correspond to the HTML heading. Pressing 1 will read the level-one heading, pressing 2 will read the level-two heading, and so on. The next thing that the users will do is press Insert+F7, which is shortcut for the links list, and all the text links will be read in order for the listener to determine which link has the content they need.

This also brings up the importance of creating clear and concise text links within the content. Too many links that are duplicated cause problems for this type of browsing. Imaging if you were listening to the link list on a page and all you heard was "Click to read more" seven, eight, or more times.

The commands in JAWS duplicate the scanning that sighted users exhibit, even down to a command that will read the first line of each paragraph. Face it, we all scan pages. It's just a matter of how much.

Bringing It All Together

In considering the needs of website visitors, especially in areas of business-to-business marketing, there is a need to be quickly and easily understood and allow the user easy access to the information. In these next few examples, the headings, bullet points, text links, and layout become obvious when comparing different layouts within the same business niche.

In this comparison, two websites offering the same service can instill confidence or confusion, simply based on layout techniques. DecisionRisks (www.intellisec.com) utilizes a very clear content layout structure. There is a clear logo, navigation space, headline, and clear subheadings. At the comparison site, the Fraud Detectives (www.frauddetectives.com), there is a similar structure, but the layout detracts from the information. There is a clear logo, but after that, all the subheadings are presented with the same font, the same size (with the exception of the business name), and the same color. The layout actually takes away from the communication, as opposed to enhancing the information (see Figure 9.1).

Figure 9.1 Just the difference of utilizing clear headings, navigation space, and content layout can mean a substantial difference in the perception of credibility.

In a similar respect, using these elements of headlines, bullet points, text links, and category headings poorly can work against you, especially if you employ them too much. By overloading the page with too many of these elements, you overwhelm the visitor, and there is no emphasis on importance. The old adage of "less is more" is certainly true in website design and information architecture. The less information that competes for the visitor's attention, the clearer the page will be in its central message.

Camelback Displays (`www.camelbackdisplays.com`) uses the layout techniques you've learned about, but too many items are competing for the visitor's attention. The overloaded navigation, competing text links, and excessive category layouts all work against a clear focal point (see Figure 9.2).

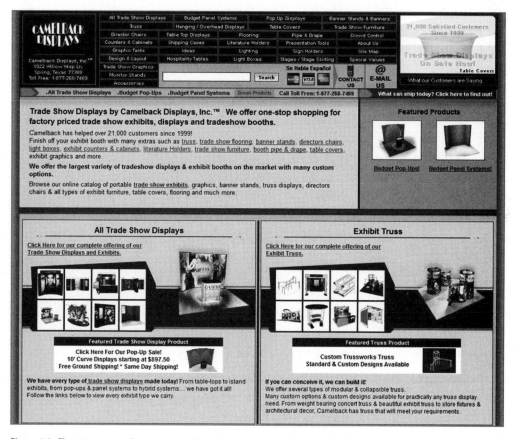

Figure 9.2 There is structure, but excessive information takes away from a central focus.

A competing website, Smash Hit Displays (www.smashhitdisplays.com), is able to coordinate these elements into a cleaner presentation that reduces the amount of information and provides clear paths to additional information. The headline is clearly larger, and the category headings are consistent, along with the category layouts. The navigation is available but unobtrusive for the visitor (see Figure 9.3).

Figure 9.3 The structure allows an easy view of the information, provides a focal point, and provides easy access to subcontent.

However, some designs can be much bolder and edgier, especially market leaders, because they can afford to provide a more visual impact; however, in this category, there is still an emphasis on clear content layout. Nimlok (www.nimlok.com) is able to provide a very strong focal point for the layout with a short paragraph of information about the company. The rest of the information is clearly defined categories of services, information, and navigational elements. By taking away some content, there is more visual impact and clear navigation choices (see Figure 9.4).

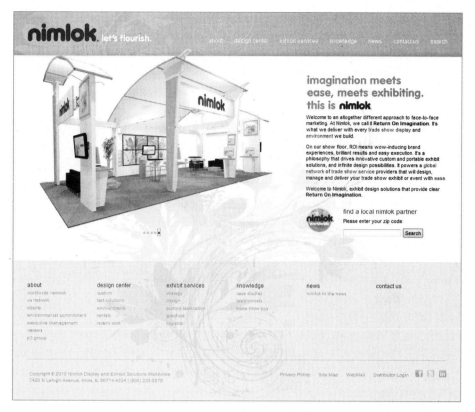

Figure 9.4 Brand leaders can be bolder in design and function, but they still assist users by providing clear content areas within the structure.

Tuesday: Create Concise and Memorable Content

A Nielsen study of Measuring the Effect of Improved Web Writing was focused on improved usability of content by making it more understandable and memorable. The results of the study are published at www.useit.com/papers/webwriting/writing.html.

The study started with a promotional paragraph of tourist attractions in Nebraska. The goal was to find the best rewriting and reformatting of the paragraph to result in better usability and comprehension of the information. Four different versions were created:

- The Concise version used about half as many words to communicate the same information.

- The Scannable version introduced the content with a few sentences and then utilized bullet points to highlight specific phrases.

- The Objective version removed any promotional language.

- The final version combined all three to create content that was short, scannable, and objective.

Interestingly, the Concise version performed very well, which supports all the direction I received while studying journalism at college. My journalism professor constantly requested that we write the same content but in half as many words, which is a journalism school mantra. The Concise version improved the usability of the content by 58 percent. None of the other *single* improvements came close to that level of improvement.

The combined approach of half as many words, a scannable format, and non-promotional language resulted in a 124 percent improvement in the usability of the website. This relates to the scanning behavior outlined in the previous section. Fewer words, presented in a scannable format, will result in better retention for the visitor.

Nielsen also found that visitors read only the first few words in a paragraph and then move on. This shows the importance of online copywriting, not just for the search engines but for the unfocused, unlinear, and unpredictable visitor to your website. The content needs to be not only scannable but also presentable and arranged in a fashion that allows for a quick assessment of value and relevance. Only then will the visitor slow down to read the information they believe is there through the deduction of content elements presented on the page.

Another study evaluated online behavior and found that online readers will read about 20 percent of the content on an average page (about 600 words). As content is added, only 18 percent will be read. (See Harald Weinreich, Hartmut Obendorf, Eelco Herder, and Matthias Mayer's "Not Quite the Average: An Empirical Study of Web Use" article in *ACM Transactions on the Web*, vol. 2, no. 1 [February 2008], at http://portal.acm.org/citation.cfm?id=1326566.) This creates a very transitory experience among you, your website, and your visitors. In this medium, in-depth content that requires consideration and careful parsing will be overlooked. Whatever your message, it must be carefully scripted and presented in order to be grasped and understood within seconds. Whatever your persuasive argument for using your company, it must be preparsed for critical information and clearly presented without distraction in order to be culled.

Unfortunately, this process is not without critics. Educators, cultural critics, and futurists all see a dim future in students' acquisition of knowledge from the erosion in their learning habits. The careful study of multiple sources is being quickly exchanged for the website with the clearest bullet points.

Neil Postman, a former professor at NYU, has written many books on the subject of communication and education. I believe every marketer should read his book *Technopoly: The Surrender of Culture to Technology*. Postman outlines many of these issues and the cultural movement in that very prophetic book written before the modern Internet. In an even more prophetic book from his earlier works, Postman refers to the attention divide as follows:

"consciousness of the process of abstraction." That is, consciousness of the fact that out of the virtually infinite universe of possible things to pay attention to, we abstract only certain portions, and those portions turn out to be the ones for which we have verbal labels and categories.
—NEIL POSTMAN, *Teaching as a Subversive Activity*, Delta, 1971

Granted, Postman is explaining the human ability to refine information on a large universal scale, but even on our small scale of considering the online reader's attention, it explains the behavior of filtering out unnecessary or slow-paced information in order to quickly find the abstractions of words and short concepts that fit the semantic picture of our information need.

From an educator's standpoint, this trend of dividing information into small labels and information bits is troubling, because the move to embracing technology in the classroom has not produced better students but more disengaged students. These new students are more adept at speedy browsing of social media sites and have no patience for the slower pace of the participatory, isolated experience that deep reading requires. Professor and author Mark Bauerlein puts it like this:

That's the drift of screen reading. Yes, it's a kind of literacy, but it breaks down in the face of a dense argument, a Modernist poem, a long political tract, and other texts that require steady focus and linear attention—in a word, slow reading.
—MARK BAUERLEIN, *"Online Literacy Is a Different Kind,"*
The Chronicle Review, Volume 54, Issue 31, Page B7

As both a parent and a marketer, I am torn, just as I am torn in the subject of marketing to children. I find myself both fascinated and repelled by the concept. While understanding how information is derived from websites and building information accordingly, am I contributing to a lower form of literacy? While performing activities that improve profits, are we also reducing levels of engagement with critical content?

As a marketer, how do we react to this, understand it, learn it, and then apply this knowledge? Postman answers this very question:

The way to be liberated from the constraining effects of any medium is to develop a perspective on it—how it works and what it does. Being illiterate in the processes of any medium (language) leaves one at the mercy of those who control it.
—NEIL POSTMAN, *Teaching as a Subversive Activity*

As a marketer who desires to utilize these concepts, I believe the best means of using and benefiting from developing persuasive content online is to study it. Know and understand how it works, and command it, rather than being commanded by it; in doing so you also become aware of when it is being used to persuade you.

The first step is to be self-aware of your own reading and scanning habits. What websites do you tend to visit more than others? Is it because of the arrangement of scannable content? How often do you find yourself scanning headlines, bullet points, and paragraph headings rather than the content? Do you find yourself reading only the first few words in a paragraph and quickly moving your eyes through the rest of the paragraph?

The second step is to follow up this text by utilizing the resources cited in this chapter and others to develop an understating of human behavior in information interaction. As Postman recommends, if people do not understand the process, then they are at the mercy of it. The only way to liberate yourself from the effects of this scanning is to develop an understanding of it, its applications, and eventually its implications on society at large. Once you understand it, you can then use it more effectively to reach your audience and communicate clear concepts through the efficient use of fewer but more powerful words.

Wednesday: Consider Your Site's Credibility

Today's content is based on a study performed by Stanford University's Persuasive Technology Lab, `http://captology.stanford.edu/pdf/Stanford-MakovskyWebCredStudy2002-prelim.pdf`. I turn to this study often, because it is supported by Nielsen's findings and my own observations.

Performed in December 2002, the study asked participants to rate website credibility. The respondents rated credibility factors such as navigation, language, professionalism, and content as the elements that they consider to be high on the list of creating credibility and trust for a website. However, the respondents were very quick to judge a website by the visual design. According to the researchers, the subjects "made credibility-based decisions based on the website's overall visual appeal." Regardless of the policies and security factors that may have been noted prior, the respondents overwhelmingly made assessments based on visual factors. However, those visual factors and visual appeal may not be what you'd expect.

The visual factors specifically noted were typography, font size, color scheme, and layout. This is not about pretty pictures and fancy Flash movies. This is more about *readability*. At a basic level, typography, font size, color scheme, and layout are simply factors in developing content to be easily organized and read. This is about layout factors and using text effects to communicate important information.

Coincidentally, when looking at the top visited sites on the Internet, not many of them display an amazing graphical interface. The main "design" could be summarized as a pleasing combination of typography, font size, color scheme, and layout. Consider Google, Amazon, eBay, The New York Times, Yahoo!, YouTube, Facebook, Craigslist, LinkedIn, Bing, BBC, AOL, and Apple. Very few of these utilize a bleeding-edge technology for navigation, and none utilizes a graphic-intensive display. Instead, they all focus on the layout and presentation of information, supported by the typography, font size, and color scheme. This creates credibility and, reduced to its simplest element, the readability and consistency of the information structure and architecture of a website. A logical navigation is supported by a content hierarchy (using text size and color scheme) of clearly defined categories, labels, and information. These elements create credibility in a user's mind, because there is nothing hidden, confusing, or at cross-purposes with the quest for information.

To achieve good readability on your web pages, it's important to consider the following topics.

Text Size

Tiny text is the primary complaint I observe in usability testing. Test subjects continually mark this as one of their most hated obstacles to using websites. Tiny text creates work for the visitor, because reading becomes much more difficult, slower, and labored. From my background in design, I have seen a lot of young designers in their early 20s with large monitors and high-screen resolutions. Despite what they may say, you are in charge of your website, and if you think the text is too small, it is.

Funnily enough, if you have grown up watching television in the United States, you have been conditioned to distrust the fine print. Small text in a television commercial creates distrust, because it is typically the disclaimer information, which reduces the impact of any claims made by the advertisement.

On a website, small text is difficult to read and can create a negative experience for the visitor, because it may imply distrust. Although website visitors can easily use a few keystrokes to increase the size of the text, the majority of users are unaware or unwilling to use these readily available functions. Instead, they leave your site or complain about its presentation.

For example, newspapers for years have had reader surveys asking for feedback of how to make the newspaper better. For decades, readers have always asked for the same thing as the number-one request: a larger font size. However, a larger font size means more pages for the newspaper, which means more cost and less profits, so the text size has never changed.

Easy reading of online content is intrinsically tied to the size of the text and readability of the font. To purposefully use small content in order to accommodate graphics elements is at cross-purposes with the credibility and readability of the site and will cause a problem with your visitors. Even though your visitors could use their browser to increase text size, I've observed that many do not know how, and will simply complain and leave.

Text in Motion

I am still amazed to find scrolling text on websites. Scrolling text is used on nearly every cable news and sports channel. Just from my own observation, either you can listen to the news reader or you can read the scrolling headlines. You cannot do both at the same time and take in information by hearing while reading something different. Although multitaskers seem to love this over-stimulated input, it is hardly an exercise in efficiency. One has to do one or the other in order to fully grasp a single message.

With websites, it is an even more difficult proposition. On television, there is only one other competing factor: the news reader. In a website, the competing information is the rest of the page. If the scrolling content pulls the reader's attention from the page, then the rest of the page makes up the competing elements, and the reader is distracted from your own content, resulting in less retention.

Text Contrast

Using low-contrast text on a background color is one of the main obstacles to communicating information online. This affects the primary content areas, as well as navigation, subnavigation, headings, calls to action, and other critical areas. On a digital screen, while people's eyes are moving rapidly to ingest bits of information at a high rate of speed, low-contrast text combinations are usually overlooked.

By nature, our eyes are drawn to areas of high contrast. This is why white space plays an important role in design. White spaces help define contrast by allowing our eyes to easily flow from one content area to another.

If you want some content to be ignored, place it in a low-contrast presentation such as blue on black, yellow on white, red on yellow, or gray on green; all of these are combinations that are killers to a reader's attention. There are many gifted artists who are able to make some of these color combinations work, but unfortunately, some are simply trying to apply a print design to the digital world, and it does not translate well. Digital colors have much more intensity, and the colors compete much more than a print advertisement.

The best contrasting color combination for reading online is simply black text on a white background. It's not sexy, but your visitors will read it.

Even more, your accessibility will be enhanced. Much of the past and current accessibility guidelines (see www.w3c.org) deal with presenting a suitable color contrast for users. Color combinations must provide enough contrast for someone with low vision or color blindness. As with any accessibility developments, including this emphasis in your designs will make the site more readable and of sufficient contrast for everybody, as well as ensure that your message is findable on your web pages.

This is an area where you can simply ask a friend or relative to help who will be completely honest with you about your website. Review your site on your own, and then ask others for their opinions about the readability of your site. Is the main point readable and primary on that page? What items distract from the overall message or make reading difficult?

Create a checklist for your testers, asking them about the specific elements contained in the Stanford University study (http://captology.stanford.edu/pdf/Stanford-MakovskyWebCredStudy2002-prelim.pdf). Ask each tester to rate your site in terms of credibility, readability, contrast, and text size. Feel free to add a few more rating categories after you've read the study.

Thursday: Create Accurate, Attention-Grabbing Headlines

In Monday's content, headlines and subcontent headings were covered as a way of assisting in the layout of the page. Today we will cover the words used in those headings. This is the one thing that people will use to judge the page they open. Get it right, and they'll stay longer. Get it wrong, and the Back button just became your enemy.

Headlines are meant to communicate as much information in as few words as possible. In newspapers, headlines are meant to be catchy, attention-grabbing information, with the intent to draw the reader to the story. In considering search engines, however, the writer must take into account the relationship that the title will have to the subject matter and the relevance of the information.

The important thing to remember is that there are multiple audiences that will see these pages and information. Your regular readers or website users are one audience, search visitors are another significant audience, and visitors from links, social news sites, and blogs are another audience. If you use this page as a landing page from a newsletter, email, or promotion, the context of the audience can change significantly, depending upon their expectations of the information. Basically, the headline needs to be concise and needs to present the information in the best context to meet the information needs of a wide array of visitors.

Heading Phrasing

Online publishers that have roots in magazine or print publication typically have an obstacle in developing headlines that speak the same information to both humans and search engines. Print publishers have a long-standing history of creating snappy headlines that grab a reader's attention. They use puns, witty observations, and story-dependent headlines. However, that same talent that works wonders in print does not translate well to the Web.

Print publishers have the luxury of presenting to an audience that already understands the context and the presentation. Readers are typically subscribers or purchasers, and as such, they understand the context of the medium. Headlines are more meant for entertainment and flow, rather than doing double duty of reminding the reader of their purpose in reading the entire text. Internet publishers do not have this luxury. Readers find their articles from a vast array of sources, and as such, they need the context of the publication and the headlines to communicate much more information for their purposes.

Two anecdotal situations bring this to light:

One article titled "Why Brazil is so hot!" was about the commodities from Brazil and the why the Brazilian market is ripe for investors. However, the interpretation of the title may cause a reader to infer that the content is about the weather and Brazil's proximity to the equator. In the context of an investment site or a newsletter, the title may be effective. For an investor seeking information about international investments, this headline will not rank well in search engines. For a searcher or browser who stumbles across the headline, it does not carry much contextual relevance.

The second situation was a publisher that wrote an article for the Christmas season titled "Holiday Time Travel." Although the article was one of the most read articles online, when digging further, they found that the majority of people who found this article were actually searching for *time travel*!

Headline Structure

Ideally, the main heading on the page is different from the page title. Many content management systems will simply duplicate the page title and the page headline (heading). Although some may be locked into this option, I always recommend utilizing separate text for the headline and the page heading.

Utilizing a separate heading structure allows for a broader keyword reach, utilizing long-tail keywords (if you need a refresher on the keyword long-tail, go back to Chapter 6: Tuesday), and it can be used to broaden or restrict the focus of the content on the website. Properly used headings in relation to the page title can direct users to understanding whether this is a broad categorization of content, directing them to deeper pages, or it can provide comprehensive information about a specific subject, showing the visitor that they have reached the specific page for that information.

Readers may read only the first two to three words in the headline, so develop the information accordingly. Use action verbs and keywords to make the best use of a reader's scanning time. Making the headline too long will also distract from the reader's time. A shorter headline, usually a single line with a single purpose, can be digested very quickly and set the tone for the flow of content through the rest of the page.

Friday: Connect Human Factors to Search Factors

Here is where things get really interesting. Search engines use all the information you've learned this week about human factors as a means of determining relevance. The search engine's primary goal is to satisfy the human searcher and ensure them that they have found the most relevant results for their search. The only way that a search engine can satisfy a human search is to build the algorithm on human factors.

This is where building attention-grabbing headlines (from yesterday) assists in developing both great rankings and the visitor's attention. Searchers have questions, and they are searching for answers. The amazing thing about answers is that those answers are usually benefits. Saving money is a benefit; saving money by switching service providers is both an action point and an attention-grabbing benefit.

This is where understanding the needs of the searcher and the needs of your audience are critical to your success in marketing online. What exactly do you offer? What benefit is there to the visitor to take action and use your service or purchase a product from you and not a competitor?

Offering the lowest price is always a tangible benefit. However, competing on price will only net you as much loyalty as long as your price is low. Competing on service can bring you a little more loyalty, and you need to have a lot of established credibility to be able to sell and position that on a website. Competing on benefits is a method of providing that "need beyond the need": the need to make a safe decision that won't backfire, the need to feel confident, and the need to show competence and aggressiveness. These are benefits that can be communicated in content and are full of the additional search terms that searchers utilize. Searchers are searching for answers, and the best answers meet a need.

For example, to use some examples from earlier in the week, Nimlok makes trade show booths, but it also offers consulting for developing a campaign around the trade show and maximizing the marketing investment. Similarly, Nomadic Display offers free PDF trade show marketing guides. These benefit statements within the site speak to a primary benefit of doing more with the trade show budget than having a nice booth; they speak to the overall marketing of the event and how companies can make more from their investment. Clear benefits provide better sales solutions (see Figure 9.5).

Figure 9.5 Clear benefit statements add more than just the answer; they provide additional credibility and impact to a company.

When developing a benefit statement that is compelling both in terms of the benefit and in visual impact, the impact reaches into both technical and emotional levels. As the clear visual impact of the statement reaches the eye of the visitor, the programming markup also employs factors that make the benefit statement stand apart from the rest of the content on the page.

Clear headings, high-contrast colors, and large font sizes work together to create a string of text that is meant to be more than the rest of the content, thereby making it unique on the page and more important. To the visitor, the call to action and the benefit are visually clear and appealing, matching both the intent of the search and the intent of the action. This is when clear benefit statements work to your advantage.

Using human factors in reading, scanning, and credibility, the search engine algorithm utilizes all of these on-page factors to determine relevance for a page:

- Scannable content presented using HTML or CSS markup
- Keywords in titles, headlines, page headings, and bullet points
- Accompanying key phrases and related concepts in pages
- Key benefit statements that are visually appealing

This results in the mantra "Do what is right for the visitor first, and the search engines will follow." From more than 15 years in managing, promoting, creating, and assessing websites, I've learned that time is much better spent improving the readability and salability of the website and the content rather than chasing minuscule search engine changes. Bigger profits are attained by understanding your visitors, understanding the information they need, and satisfying their questions than by constantly tweaking the number of keywords in a headline. Rather than attempt to chase the search engine's algorithm and adapt to the minuscule or, sometimes, major changes in each search engine, your time is better spent understanding the needs of the visitor and optimizing your content for their ingestion.

Although it is true that the search engines adjust their algorithms frequently, the basics rarely change. The on-page optimization factors covered so far in this text are still the same. There may be a small percentage of changes here and there or some factor that outweighs another by a fraction, but the basics of on-page factors remain heavily consistent. The bulk of search engine changes focus on an accurate judgment of incoming links, which is a primary means of showing credibility and, as such, is generally abused more than other factors. This will be covered more in depth in Chapter 16.

Review and Hands-On

Review your headlines for context. Consider the different audiences and the different methods that people may use to find your site and the information contained, and then answer the following questions:

- How do your titles rate? Do they communicate the primary intent of the page?

- Are they sufficient in communicating the correct message in a clear and concise format?

- Are your keywords properly used and associated with concepts that are specific to the information?

- Does your headline stand alone in defining the content of the article or the page?

Browse through the content on your website. Do you have paragraphs of content? Although paragraphs make sense in printed literature, most website users are looking for the important elements of information and will not give a paragraph a first look, much less a second. More paragraphs mean that fewer of your visitors are reading your content, which also means they are absorbing less information and fewer key indicators of relevance.

Review the content on your website to find the large content blocks of paragraphs. Find methods of breaking up large content blocks that are visual "black holes," and rework the content in order to present a more scannable, objective, and concise resource of information. Reduce the amount of words by at least half, and create more visual cues to key benefit statements, such as bullet points or text boxes.

Review and remove content that contains overly promotional language. This includes overstatements, noncommittal, brochureware, and empty content that do not promote a better understanding of key factors.

Ask a friend or relative to help who will be completely honest with you about your website. These areas are particularly difficult for people, so review your site on your own, and then ask others for their opinions about the readability of your site. Is the main point readable and primary on that page? What items distract from the overall message or make reading difficult?

Create a checklist for your reviewers, asking them about the specific elements contained in the Stanford University study (http://captology.stanford.edu/pdf/Stanford-MakovskyWebCredStudy2002-prelim.pdf). Ask each tester to rate your site in terms of credibility, readability, contrast, and text size. Feel free to add a few more rating categories after you've read the study.

After reviewing the changes you have made and the assignments from this week, understanding how search factors play along with human factors should show that there is little difference. There may be slight changes in keywords and wording of benefit statements, but the process is remarkably similar.

Week 7: Master the Science of Online Persuasion

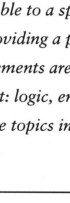

Of all the books, recordings, and videos concerning persuasion, all the original ideas can be traced back to a single volume, Aristotle's Rhetoric. *Often, the older, established wisdom is simply accurate and more deeply rooted in understanding than modern business literature.*

Rhetoric scientifically breaks down the modes of persuasion available to a speaker, and the necessary elements of providing a persuasive message. Ultimately, three elements are critical to making a persuasive argument: logic, emotion, and credibility. We'll cover those topics in the first three days of this week.

Chapter Contents

Monday: Build a Logical Proof
Tuesday: Use Emotion to Convince the Reader
Wednesday: Communicate Credibility
Thursday: Test Your Persuasive Message
Friday: Plan for Misspellings and Plurals

Monday: Build a Logical Proof

The beginning of persuasion is the logic or proofs of your argument. If you are selling software, your selling points must be clear. What is it that makes your product, service, offering, or organization a better choice than the rest? This is the heart of the logical proof, providing reliance upon a good decision based on facts and a convincing argument.

The foundation of reasoning effectively is understanding the issues that are facing your audience. Attempting to sell something without understanding the true needs of the searcher will cause them to ignore your message. Building a message on the understanding of your audience and the education and reasoning necessary to inform and develop an educated decision and understanding of your company will not only develop solid content for your marketing but also provide multiple benefit statements.

Consider the Voice over IP (VoIP) company Vocalocity. The company's marketing content introduces the VoIP product but understands that many searchers know something about VoIP but not enough to have specifics on how it works or how it can improve a business. By introducing the concepts as well as the products, the website builds on the logical proofs of reason to show a case first for switching to VoIP and second for purchasing its products (Figure 10.1).

The sales process for this type of product can be extensive. Many commitments and levels of commitment are involved, so there are multiple levels of education and information necessary to build trust and decision points for a conversion. By educating the searcher with logical arguments (see the following list), Vocalocity builds trust and, in turn, credibility with its approach to selling phone systems:

- "A phone system you won't outgrow." While small business are looking at small budgets to start, no one wants to get locked into a system that will be outdated in a few short years or won't grow with the business.

- Overcoming fears of VoIP technology through testimonials and benefits of the less expensive service.

- A powerful phone system that helps small business perform like a big business.

- No on-site equipment, eliminating hassles and maintenance.

The prospect uses the available information to deduce that the VoIP phone system will offer a quality, scalable system that won't get outdated, restrict growth, or create maintenance hassles.

Salesforce takes a similar approach (see the following list) to its presentation of the reasons businesses should choose Salesforce over other CRM providers. Figure 10.2 shows how Salesforce uses logical proofs based on the track record of thousands of companies, the low-risk approach of a free trial, and the constant updates to the system, resulting in a safe choice for managers.

- More than 77,300 companies use Salesforce CRM—a market leader, which means a solid product that has been established and tested.

- "Say goodbye to complexity." Businesses don't have time to troubleshoot and install complex software. Businesses want to do what makes them money.
- Salesforce allows you to focus on what's important—selling.
- Salesforce provides faster, more responsive service.

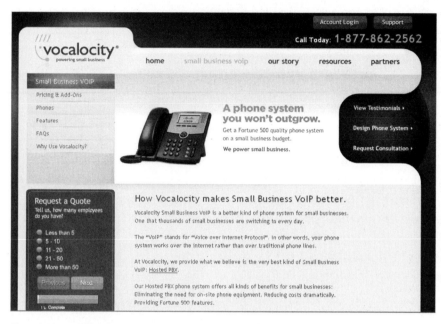

Figure 10.1 Vocalocity: taking a reasoned approach to marketing

Figure 10.2 Salesforce: logical proofs built on performance, creating a low-risk decision point

These benefit statements speak to the need of a business to control information and streamline contacts into a consistent sales channel, without the time necessary for setup, training, and troubleshooting. It's something that "just works" and increases sales. The number of companies utilizing the software is a solid indicator of trust and experience, which assists the decision-making process.

The website for Caliper, which provides personality assessments for employers (Figure 10.3), focuses on two proofs on the home page messaging:

- A logical fact: "For nearly half a century, Caliper has helped over 25,000 companies…"

- A client testimonial: "Caliper can double your ability to hire top performers."

Figure 10.3 Caliper marketing proofs

By showing logical facts of competence and reach in the marketplace, Caliper has started the persuasive process with clearly labeled proof of its business capabilities. Having a customer testimonial as proof and as a primary message is a powerful tool, because a client experience is an experiential fact.

Claims need to be substantiated information, whether through documentation, testing, or client testimonials. For example, if a software product is proven to be easier to use than other competitive products, then that proof can be used as a logical argument. However, if the software company simply makes a claim of it being easier, without presenting facts or tests, then making a baseless claim of overstatement could damage the company's credibility.

The Danger of Overstatement

Overstatement is a disease that has spread throughout millions of websites. Overstatement is making a claim without meritorious facts to support the proposition. If that happens, "The reader will be instantly on guard, and everything that has preceded your overstatement and everything that follows it will be suspect in his mind because he has lost confidence in your judgment or your poise" (*Elements of Style*; MacMillian, 1935).

By overstating your case, you may cause the exact opposite reaction than you intended. The desire for overstatement is based in the intent to impress; however, it tends to result in suspicion. Usability guru Jakob Nielsen has found that "promotional language imposes a cognitive burden"
(www.alertbox.com/alertbox/9710a.html).

Searchers immediately challenge overly promotional language and are skeptical of exaggerated claims. Almost subconsciously, people are wary of the "too good to be true" type of selling and will look for an opportunity to find a hole in the logic. The best course is to argue your case on the established merits and accomplishments of your organization.

Another course of action when using the logical approach is to make comparisons to other providers. Sylvan Learning Centers uses this approach for its SAT test prep marketing (Figure 10.4).

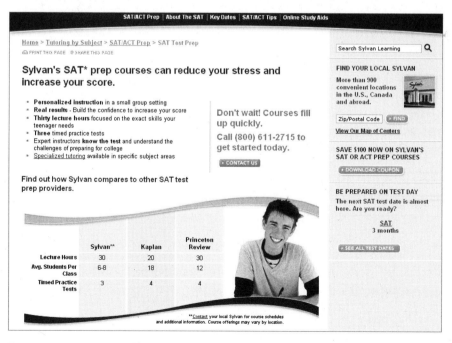

Figure 10.4 Sylvan's proof by comparison

Sylvan makes a claim that its prep course will reduce your anxiety and increase your test score. It backs up this claim by bulleting how this will happen and then presenting a chart showing the advantages of the Sylvan system compared to the other test prep providers. By making the claim and backing up that claim on the same page, Sylvan has established a logical proof, which will enhance its credibility.

Tuesday: Use Emotion to Convince the Reader

Of all the tools available to the persuader, none is more effective than the use of emotion. Aristotle thought much of the use of emotion, but he warned against its overuse in persuasion, especially at the expense of credibility or logic, because, eventually, people will tire and will not respond favorably over time.

In *Greek Rhetoric and Literary Criticism* (Longmans, Green, 1928), W. Rhys Roberts summarizes the topics in Book II of Aristotle's *Rhetoric* as follows: "Study human nature. Observe the characters and emotions of your audience, as well as your own character and emotions." Book II is a fascinating exposition of the many emotions that can be used for persuasion. Aristotle explains groups of emotions and also addresses how to use the emotional proof differently with each type of audience, such as young men vs. older men.

Chapter 7 introduced the sales technique of building "a need beyond the need." This is most effective when the "need beyond the need" is an emotional need. Selling to the emotions and creating the emotional need are critical parts of developing a connection and getting a more immediate conversion. Your search visitors are searching to satisfy a need, so by meeting that need logically and then creating an emotional need that can be satisfied with your product, service, or content, you strengthen the persuasive abilities of your marketing to gain a faster conversion. When researching your audience, one of the most critical activities is to build the psychographic understanding of the character of your audience. By understanding the needs and roles that are important to this audience and tapping into this need, your product goes beyond a commodity and into a valued part of life.

By associating strong emotions with the goal, it actually makes the sales process deeper. Well-established brands and companies can sell solely on the basis of emotion, because they are so tied to an emotion, and the product sale is secondary. When you can turn the decision to purchase or use your company to an emotional satisfaction, you can then build that into a long-term relationship with a customer (so long as you deliver what you promise). Let's take a look at some companies that are using emotion to great effect in their marketing.

Western Governors University: Offering Self-Improvement

To start off, let's compare two websites selling the same thing: online degree completion programs (Figures 10.5 and 10.6).

Figure 10.5 Western Governors University uses the emotional draw effectively.

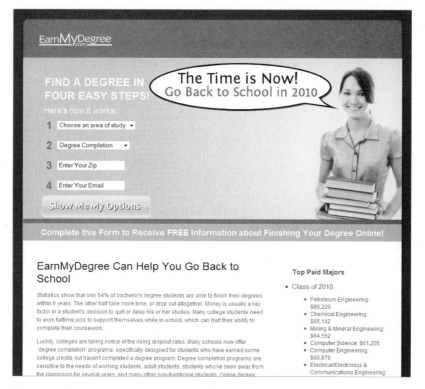

Figure 10.6 EarnMyDegree.com does not use an emotional association.

The website for Western Governors University develops a message of "becoming more" and uses images of nontraditional students graduating and receiving degrees. The visual emotion is built by connecting with people in similar life situations and the desire to "become more." "Becoming more" is a powerful concept, because it is developed in large part by the receiver of this message. The advertisement simply plants the seed of "become more," and the more the receiver hears and dwells on that message, whether it is simply completing the degree, getting a new job, starting over in life, or starting a business, the "more" is defined by the customer, not the company. The open-ended message is designed to put the onus of the emotional proof into the mind of the visitor.

EarnMyDegree.com simply offers a how-to message. There is no emotional plea and no sense of satisfaction or accomplishment communicated. As a result, the message falls flat, because there is very little persuasive content for the visitor.

Harley-Davidson: Emphasizing Freedom and Independence

Perhaps no other iconic product or brand has been marketed as well as and has increased in influence with the advent of the Internet as much as Harley-Davidson motorcycles. Beyond selling motorcycles, Harley-Davidson has captured the American spirit by selling freedom. By this simple emotional draw, Harley-Davidson is able to sell cross-culture, cross-demographic, and cross-socioeconomic boundaries and signify the same intangible emotional draw to each segment of its audience.

Freedom, especially grounded as the American ideal, is captured so well in the marketing of Harley-Davidson and is reinforced throughout the marketing of the brand. With stores across the United States, factory tours, Harley Owners' Groups (HOGs), and rallies around the world, the riders of Harley-Davidson identify strongly with the spirit of independence and freedom. The content on the website and the online marketing reinforce this attitude (see Figure 10.7). Toughness and freedom shadow the content, the calls to action, and the camaraderie that one will find as a Harley-Davidson owner.

By creating communities of riders, Harley-Davidson is able to reinforce the "freedom of the open road" mentality, and the website offers much more than the bikes themselves. There are trip maps made especially for motorcycles, along with insider tips and local dealers noted on the map for service or parts along the way. The interactive trip planner becomes a resource beyond the initial sale that simply helps to extend the brand into the emotion of the community.

By providing dealer shops, factory tours, rewards at Best Western, and photo galleries, recognizing the custom styles of different riders; and focusing on groups such as women, Latinos, veterans, and military, Harley-Davidson brings together different groups for a singular interaction, not just with the brand but with the ideal. Everything aligns with the brand, which just happens to be part of the more powerful, larger emotional draw of freedom and independence.

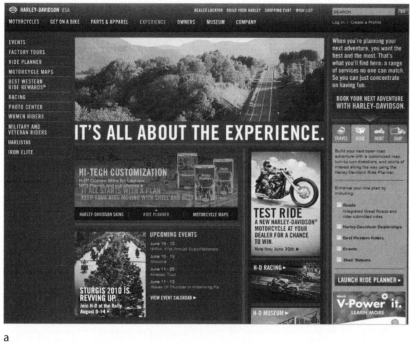

a

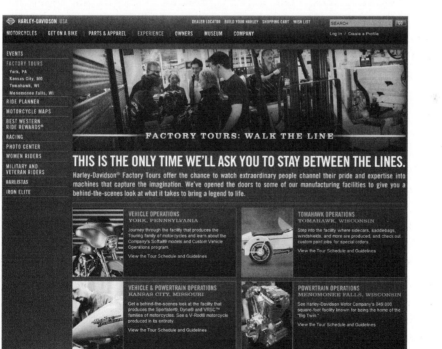

b

Figure 10.7 (a) The Harley-Davidson website associates emotion with the product. (b) Even in promoting factory tours; it recognizes the spirit of independence and freedom.

Creative Memories: Focusing on Fond Memories

Having been introduced to this product by the hoards of local crafters and scrapbookers, this was an easy emotional proof to spot (Figure 10.8). Scrapbooking is not about buying photo cutters, about buying line-free paper, or about buying all of the supplies (of which there are many). Scrapbooking is about memories—reliving, rediscovering, organizing, and displaying the memories from photos buried in shoeboxes.

Figure 10.8 Creative Memories is about telling your story with your photos and keeping memories alive.

In the literature, the products are not presented as products but rather as aids for your creativity in documenting a story. After all, who wouldn't be more creative when using photo sorters, cropping, and photo-mounting tools. These aren't positioned as typical scrapbooking commodities; they are keys to inspiration for unusual shapes, arrangements, and color schemes.

When reading the company literature and the recruitment for sales representatives and for home shows, the narrative of the company continues to concentrate on stories. The company has a story, every person has their own unique story, and both the company and its products are simply vehicles to allow you to communicate your story more effectively.

The emotional plea is to save memories. By focusing on the emotional value of saving and telling stories, it focuses on a very deep-seated emotion within the human race—remembering those who went on before and passing stories to the next generations. By providing the tools to enhance those memories and stories, Creative Memories taps into our hardwired human nature to recount stories through generations of oral tradition that will be generated by a new way of seeing our photographs.

Aflac: Emphasizing Security

Knowing that Aflac was a supplemental insurance company, I was prepared for an emotional plea. However, when viewing the content of the website, I was even more enthralled to see the stories that are the focus of the content (Figure 10.9). The stories are the central focus of the content. Rather than relying on the typical corporate style of communication ("We have what you need; buy it!"), Aflac relies on the powerful emotional impact of people who are alive and have their health, home, and family because of their decision to purchase supplemental insurance.

Figure 10.9 Aflac's focus is on people and their stories.

Sure, insurance companies have reputations for over-using the emotional plea, but Aflac's approach brings in the logic and credibility factors of providing proof from a testimonial. You can't tell the person who is giving the testimonial they are wrong, because they lived the experience that is their testimonial. By providing these pictures and stories, the site makes an impact.

Wednesday: Communicate Credibility

Establishing a credible identity is completely dependent upon the presentation of a website and content used to persuade. No amount of well-written content will save a poorly designed website. Neither will a well-designed website persuade well, if there is no emphasis on providing compelling, persuasive content. The two are interdependent upon each other. Poor site design alone can cause people to question credibility. A professional presentation is critical to online business success. A pleasing design, arrangement of content, and clear reading presentation will make a website stand above others. (For more on this, refer to Stanford University's "Stanford Guidelines for Web Credibility" at www.webcredibility.org/guidelines.)

Even Strunk and White's *Elements of Style* addresses the factor of credibility, because even the design of the content is an important factor:

> *Before beginning to compose something, gauge the nature and extent of the enterprise and work from a suitable design. Design informs even the simplest structure, whether of brick and steel or of prose.*

In developing credibility, the website must be usable in the way that the visitor expects usability to work. If text looks like a link and it is not a link, then the visitor becomes frustrated, because the visual cue indicated that the text was "clickable." By reducing the perceived functionality of the website, credibility suffers.

The following are a few examples of how websites create credibility through the presentation of the content. It is remarkable how the same content can be perceived differently, simply based on the presentation. However, there are consistent factors in creating the credible presentation of content, as the following case studies show.

Online News: Critical Credibility

Of websites that need to communicate credibility, news organizations are near the top of the list. Built on decades of creating that same sense of credibility in print, the media have now shifted to meeting the needs of an online audience.

When evaluating the top news websites online, one realizes that there is very little "design" in these websites. The focus is on the layout, typography, font size, and color scheme in order to present the information in a credible and understandable manner.

In evaluating the top news sites in Figure 10.10 (wjs.com, usatoday.com, cnn.com, foxnews.com, and nytimes.com) in the United States, a clear pattern of content arrangement and presentation emerges:

- The most "designed" element is a thin header, which contains the logo, current weather, and date.
- All content is presented as black text on a white background.
- Primary headlines are black or dark blue.
- Headings are ordered in terms of size.
- Every time blue body text is used, it is a link.

Figure 10.10 Online news websites use the same content presentation and arrangement techniques, which are all credibility mechanisms.

Figure 10.10 *(Continued)*

Figure 10.10 *(Continued)*

This makes the content easy to scan and digest, and it makes it easy to quickly locate articles of interest. Also, the reader rarely has to guess the purpose or location of a link, because every site makes the links operate almost exactly the same.

Saunders + Silverstein: Implied Credibility

A search for the term *IP lawyer* produces two different results that emphasize how design, content presentation, and clear messaging contribute to credibility.

The website for Sanders + Silverstein is very simple in its presentation, design, and message. The navigation is clear, the content is organized, and the call to action is succinct (Figure 10.11).

Immediately following this result was the listing for a patent attorney (Figure 10.12). This site, while presenting a lot of information, appears overwhelming, which is the main problem when not designing the arrangement of the content.

Even small amounts of text can appear overwhelming when there are no visual cues that help the user scan the information. Even more, just some simple design elements would greatly improve the presentation of the content, creating additional credibility. When seeing these two sites site by side, the differences are clearer. People generally like areas of white space in designs, because it makes the content clearer and provides greater contrast when reading. Even if there is more content, and better content, just through the information design of the presentation, it does not communicate it well, according to persuasive studies. People tend to trust more professional sites, despite the actual credibility of the organization.

Figure 10.11 Saunders + Silverstein LLP, a very clean and clear message that builds credibility

Figure 10.12 Patent attorney website with a lot of information but more difficult to read based on the presentation. This diminishes credibility.

Apple: Earned Credibility

Few companies can use overstatement to their advantage, and Apple is one that has used it in the past. In fact, Apple once made the claim that the iMac "changed the world." This was met with a winking skepticism by critics who recognized Apple's bold claims but also criticized the tendency for overstatement.

However, with the more recent releases of the iPod, iPhone, and iPad, the first release was a winner, and the iPhone and iPad have done more to raise the bar of mobile devices than any other products (see the overstatement there?). In fact, given the trend over the past decade, Apple has done more to create credibility with market-leading innovations that have transformed the digital, personal, and computing landscape. When it comes to innovative personal computing devices, everyone is chasing Apple.

Having spoken to many businesspeople about the impact of the iPhone and the iPad in such a short amount of time, I found that most will agree that the iPhone was a distinct game-changer and was such from the first day it was offered. Because of this, it is not with false swagger that Apple opened the marketing of the iPhone 4 with a complete overstatement (see Figure 10.13); based on recent performance, not many critics will argue with that statement today.

Figure 10.13 Apple iPhone 4, banking on earned credibility

Interestingly enough, it is not just the legions of Apple fans who agree with this statement. The industry agrees that Apple hit a home run with the iPhone, and by all accounts Apple has done it again with the latest release. When you have a strong recent track record like Apple, marketing statements with such bravado are received with much more acceptance.

Earned credibility is like money in the bank. You have something to prove your performance and available credit in the mind of the consumer. When you have delivered consistently in the past, you can make bold statements about the future. However, this type of credibility is usually as good as the last performance. Consumers tend to have short memories, and a bad quarter or a bad performance can take away the credibility very quickly. In the long run, a company that is perceived well by the customers and has a great track record of success and performance can use the earned credibility, but only if the performance is maintained.

Thursday: Test Your Persuasive Message

Too many times it is assumed that taglines and benefit statements, especially when new, have been crafted well and are effective. However, without user feedback, there is no way to know what major flaws may rest just under the surface or if the words being used are not emotionally powerful enough to create action. Everything may look pretty and work on paper, but nothing can substitute for actually getting customers' opinions and feedback.

I've worked with many firms to establish testing and measuring programs. Few, if any, regularly talk and interact with their end users in order to improve their marketing. Only a few have actually tested their benefit statements and sales copy with users. Just because it is a website does not mean that user testing is not necessary. Unfortunately, most website owners are more willing to criticize their users for being ignorant than assuming responsibility for a poorly crafted marketing message. Unfortunately for them, the Web is very democratic; users vote with a simple mouse click. If they can't understand your tagline or decipher user benefits, they simply will not respond. The value of user feedback and surveys is to learn their expectations and respond to their concerns and expectations. This will enable you to develop a clear tagline and valuable benefit statements based on actual user feedback and supported by analytic data.

If your site is being "improved" by a company without data to back up the changes or without data in place to measure the changes, then there is really no reason to continue. Why pay for changes that will not or cannot have effective measurement to determine whether the changes were worth the price?

User testing is destructive by nature. It first destroys your preconceived notions about your marketing; it then destroys parts of the marketing and website itself in order to make it better. Simply marketing a website live as soon as it is finished does not mean that your marketing message is correct and complete. This is the most dynamic media in the last millennium because it offers a constant feedback and refinement capability. By testing your message, layout, or offer, a business can grow market share within weeks, just by adjusting to visitor behavior and feedback.

Consider the case of one of my consulting clients, Freedom Health, who provides health products for the equestrian market. Its online marketing strategy was based primarily in education. Visitors to the website would see studies, medical tests, and product information that was nearly overwhelming to the casual horseperson. Despite the dozens of high-profile industry testimonials that were available on the site, users tended to be on the site for short amounts of time and rarely contacted the company.

Freedom Health sought to improve its messaging, because it realized its message was not being heard, nor was it building business. Its message was made up of attempting to educate horse owners on equine digestion, diets, and health concerns, which was not producing effective results online. The company conducted online surveys with current users, past users, and nonusers to gain insight about their message and customer perceptions. In doing so, they realized their audience perceived a different value of the product than what was being marketed.

This is where listening to the customer can make a significant impact on your marketing. Freedom Health took the time to consider the customer attitudes toward its product, and in doing so, the company learned more about its current customers and its target audience. Freedom Health took this information and refined its message to a simpler, targeted emotional statement that would resonate with the expressed needs of the customer base.

Even changing their tagline from "Success from the inside out" to "My horse at its best" resonated much more effectively with the audience, because it captured the relationship between horse and rider, as well as the competitive spirit that most riders possess. Although the earlier tagline was a nice tagline, it did not communicate an emotional value to the customers. In addition, it required much more explanation of how it was a benefit than the new tagline. The new tagline communicated the benefit statement and reduced the need for more in-depth communication of the medical studies and tests that justified the product purchase.

The customer base was passionate about their horses, and the traits that stood out were partly competitive and partly relationship, but all concerned the health and demeanor of their horses. Rather than reading through pages of medical research that supported the claims and effectiveness of their nutritional supplement, the customers wanted justification for the product. The health benefits and the testimonials, simply presented, made it easier for them to communicate to their friends.

Freedom Health then went about changing the entire website to communicate this message. Incorporating the message into the navigation, primary information architecture, and structure of the website refined every sales point into a simply communicated, content-rich statement. The testimonials were powerful, because they communicated the benefits of the product in customer-specific terms. They used the primary benefit statements that addressed the concerns of prospective customers and matched the testimonials to the specific content of the pages.

Simplifying the tagline and the marketing focused on giving Freedom Health's loyalists a simpler message to tell others. The surveys found that the best and most loyal customers came from word-of-mouth marketing. By providing the loyal customers with a simpler message and rewards, it would make it easier for customers to spread the word to their friends.

Freedom Health took the feedback of the customers, reworked both the value proposition and the sales message, and redesigned the website around the words and influence of the customer feedback. In doing so, they improved their visibility, attracting 800 percent more visitors to the website from search engines and social media within three months of going live with the new website. More than that, the leads from the website increased 400 percent, which reinforces the concept of listening and testing your message with your audience.

Friday: Plan for Misspellings and Plurals

Many of the questions I receive in my seminars deal with keyword selection. It has to do with how to rank for both singular and plural versions of words, misspellings, and word variations. Many times, this leads to a larger discussion, so I will address it here, because this is also related to credibility.

Misspellings

A Canadian friend of mine, Ian McCanerin, alerted me to an interesting phenomenon. Ian worked with Canadian companies that did a lot of business in Quebec, where by law information has to be presented in both French and English. He noted that searchers, particularly in the Latin-based languages of French, Spanish, and Italian, tend to leave out accents in their search terms. I mentally filed this away for future use. A few years later I was working with a French company and recalled this valuable piece of information. In developing a keyword strategy, the research shows that typing in search terms without the accent marks was a strong tendency among searchers. This immediately prompted questions about how to address misspellings in an optimization and marketing strategy. Fortunately, in this digital marketing business, there is no shortage of information, and the research always takes you to the information that you need.

When researching keywords, we immediately noticed that most people searched with the incorrect spelling of the term, because they were not searching with accent marks. So, while many companies were optimizing for a memory card in French, *carte mémoire SD*, French searchers were overwhelmingly searching for the grammatically incorrect version without the accent mark, *carte memoire SD*. This was also a case where Google did not offer a spelling correction of the word (which has improved drastically over the past few years, especially for non-English terms).

There were distinct differences in the search results for the two versions of the search term. One little accent mark could change the rankings for four websites, and one site dropped off the first page completely. Interestingly, the majority of the websites in the top results used the grammatically correct accent version of the word. The top result used both versions in the page title. However, the majority of SEO copywriters recommend against using misspellings or variations of words in the same sentence or on the same page, because it lacks professionalism, to which I agree.

In the paid advertising at the top of the terms' search-results pages (shown in Figure 10.14), an interesting opportunity presented itself. Memory card maker SanDisk was aggressively bidding on the phrase *carte mémoire SD* but was not bidding on the overwhelmingly more popular search phrase without the accent mark, *carte memoire SD*.

Figure 10.14 SanDisk bidding on (a) the lower-volume, grammatically correct version of the phrase (*carte mémoire SD*), but not (b) the higher-volume, grammatically incorrect version of the phrase (*carte memoire SD*)

As search engine spelling correction features continue to improve, I recommend that site managers avoid optimizing for misspelled words. Including misspelled words in a bidding strategy for pay-per-click advertising, however, is a recommended strategy. There is usually significant opportunity, because your competitors may not have opened up their bidding on misspelled terms. However, for organic SEO and the content used on your site, I will always recommend proper spelling and grammatical construction.

Plurals

The choice between singular and plural versions of words was more difficult when analytics programs were not as agile as they are today in tracking search terms all the way through to conversion. Prior to analytics, the basis of decision was the popularity of the search term. Plural versions tended to have higher search volume, which made them more desirable phrases. However, as analytics became better at tracking conversions, it became apparent that in many cases the singular version of the word tended to drive more business than visits, while plurals tended to draw more visits than business.

In one case, a travel business recognized that for its primary destination term, *vacations*, the plural was ranking very highly but drawing few conversions. On further analysis, it was found that the singular version of the term, *vacation*, ranked on the 4th page of Google, at #34, but was driving more than double the number of search visitors with a 2 percent conversion rate (see Table 10.15).

▶ **Table 10.15** Analytics Information for the Search Terms "vacations" and "vacation"

Metric	Data for "vacations" (plural)	Data for "vacation" (singular)
Ranking in Google	#3	#34
Search referrals	600	1800
Conversion Rate	0%	2%

The approach was clear; develop the ongoing campaign around the singular version of the word, as if the phrase was already profitable and would continue to increase in profitability as the rankings and visitor numbers increased.

What was determined in this case was that plurals show an interest, but singular terms denoted a stronger motivation. A searcher searching with plurals tends not to be committed, is open to suggestion, and may not be motivated to make a decision that day. A searcher using the singular version of a word or phrase tends to be more intent on finding the object, and they tend to convert at a higher rate. This searcher-based language behavior has been observed in other types of businesses as well, but I hesitate to consider it an across-the-board behavior. Only by examining your analytics will you know for sure. Analyzing behavior and motivation with your analytics will be covered in much more depth in Chapter 20.

In recommending a keyword strategy for an existing website, I always defer to the analytics. Making a decision without all the information will result in an incomplete strategy. Rankings alone cannot be the final determination, because measuring the intent and behavior based on words and then, ultimately, the profitability of each choice is best done in your analytics.

Review and Hands-On

Review your website and advertising content for statements of fact. Eliminate overstatements or unsubstantiated claims that do not have proof of fact or information readily available to back up your claims. Answer these questions:

- What logical, factual claims are you making in your marketing?
- What logical, factual claims are you making on your website?
- How do those claims align to your primary marketing message?
- Do you have client testimonials that provide proof as well as a primary marketing message?

Redevelop any promotional claims into factual statements that will provide a logical or emotional basis for prospective customers or clients to form an accurate opinion and basis for judgment. Ask yourself the following questions:

- How can you translate the "need beyond the need" you identified for your business in Chapter 7 into an emotional draw that is larger than your business or your product?
- What emotion or need can be satisfied or met by using your business?
- How can you rewrite your advertising message with that emotional message?

To figure out how you can build a connection with your visitors that will keep them as a loyal customer rather than a one-time transaction, evaluate your pages on the following criteria:

- Are the fonts consistent? Are they readable?
- Is the level of contrast between the text and the background sufficient?
- Is your color scheme pleasing? Is it consistent?
- How effectively does the page use font size when presenting headlines, headings, and content?
- Is your link text consistent in appearance and behavior?
- Is the information designed for easy scanning?

In comparing your website marketing against some of the examples used in this chapter and in Chapter 9, what are steps that you can take to develop a more credible approach with your website?

Week 8: Improve Conversions

11

Now it's time to convert visitors to customers, subscribers, and registrants, or they simply take an intended action on the site. The science of conversion deepens every day as new technologies are continually developed to help marketers better understand the digital consumer. The technologies seek to understand both the mind-set of the consumer and the technology of the online medium.

On average, the conversion rate for all types of websites is 2 to 3 percent, which is a very small number of people. However, it is important to remember that this is only an average—the number is not great, just average*. It is easy for businesses of all types to exceed this average number by focusing on the conversion process and continually measuring, analyzing, and optimizing the process.*

Chapter Contents

Monday: Call Visitors to Action
Tuesday: Make It Attractive
Wednesday: Overcome Obstacles
Thursday: Promote the Next Step
Friday: Implement Testing

Monday: Call Visitors to Action

The goal of marketing your website is to get visitors to your site. The second goal is to get them to do what you want them to do; otherwise, the first goal has been for naught. The number-one problem with website conversions is that people are not able to find the appropriate place to convert. In testing, the primary hindrance is the ability for the visitor to find the contact form, purchase link, or "next step" in a process. It is imperative that visitors find what they need on your website. To do that, there has to be a number of clearly visible options available to them. Such options are called *calls to action*.

The call to action on your website should be the most obvious and logically placed link or object on the page. The call to action must be clear and specific. Anything else will dramatically reduce your ability to do business online.

Understanding the Three Kinds of Visitors

Regardless of the intentions or decisions made by your visitors, the bottom line is that if the visitor doesn't see it, it doesn't exist.

If a visitor cannot find the conversion point on your website or the next step in the process, the problem is yours, not theirs. If your website needs a manual in order to understand the process, then you have a bad website. Steven Krug's wonderful book *Don't Make Me Think* (New Riders Press, 2005) was aptly named, because visitors need to have the call to action in front if their eyes and in their field of view; otherwise, once they stop to think about what to do and how to do it, chances are that you have lost them.

Using a website is almost a stream-of-consciousness activity. The user has a goal, and once that goal is in sight, they will continue to take the actions necessary. Once that goal becomes cloudy or out of sight, the entire process comes to a standstill.

Simply having a link or graphic to convert is not enough. It must be a focal point for the visitor.

Visitors have one of three mind-sets:

- "Yes! I'm ready to purchase, register, or interact."
- "Maybe. I need more information."
- "Probably not. I haven't found what I'm looking for."

Given the low average conversion percentage, it's vital that you appeal to visitors in all three of these categories. The following sections cover how to cater to each kind of visitor.

"Yes! I'm Ready to Purchase, Register, or Interact"

To cater to visitors who are at your site because they're ready to make a purchase, you must make that purchase exceedingly simple. Simply put, if there are no options available, none will be taken.

For visitors ready to make the decision, the focal point of the page must be the biggest, boldest, and most obvious graphic on the page. If this is the primary method that you monetize the website and the business, then it shouldn't be a difficult decision, right?

The primary conversion action that you want visitors to take needs to have a significant visual impact apart from the rest of the content and the rest of the links or graphics on the page; otherwise, it blends in and becomes part of the overall page design. By not distinguishing the call to action, the visitor is not able to easily find the obvious next step. Simply by making this action obvious, you can increase the conversion rate in your website.

This interaction should also lead the decision-making process concerning which calls to action to place on the page and their specific placements. The primary action concerning the content on the page needs to have the biggest visual impact. Smaller actions should not compete with the primary conversion. For instance, I have seen too many websites that have "print page" as the most visual call to action on the page, while the "request information" link is smaller, lower on the page, and less intuitive. Which action makes you the most money and is related to the content on that page? That is the one that needs to be the primary visual focus of the page.

Consider another example of an unclear call to action—Frys.com (see Figure 11.1); the product image and information are at the top of the page, but there is no clear instruction to add the product to the cart. It is not until the visitor scrolls to the bottom of the page (*if* they scroll down to the bottom of the page) that an "add to cart" button is visible. Even then, it is small and very lonely on the right side of the page, apart from the rest of the content.

A website I always point to as a clear example of making the conversion obvious is Woot.com (see Figure 11.2).

The call to action is a large, gold graphic with the words, "I want one!" A highly unmistakable graphic, it easily communicates to the visitor the purpose of their visit and the next step to take. Your calls to action need to reflect this type of bold intent. It needs to be an easily seen object that allows visitors to make the next step in the process.

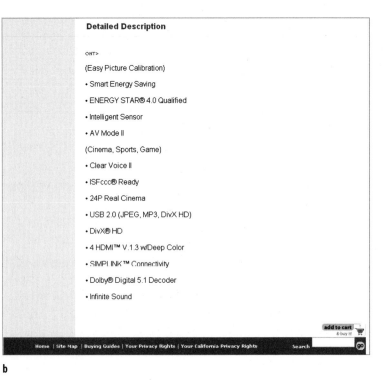

Figure 11.1 Frys.com's ecommerce call to action

Figure 11.2 Woot.com's "I want one!" button

"Maybe. I Need More Information"

There may be a sizeable group of visitors to your site that may have an interest in your content and your business. For them, it is critical to be able to "bounce around" within the content of the site. Related products, related articles, top blog posts, and links within the content allow visitors to quickly find related or more in-depth content. This is very important for the visitors who need to see more information before making a decision. And in their case, it is all in the presentation.

For content-rich sites, there must be enough related information and topics of interest within visual proximity to make the visitor click to more pages. Usually, side topics or related topics are sidebars or callouts within the article itself. Many times, one can find lists of related articles and topics at the end of an article. My preference is to work these into the sight lines of the visitor through the sidebar or in the content. The primary reason is that if the article on that page is not the information they are seeking, the related content will help a visitor quickly get to the next page. Although I do like to see related content at the bottom of the page, I know that many readers are too impatient to scroll down to the end of an article simply to see what might be there, especially if the article isn't relevant.

The *Wall Street Journal* uses this effectively in the articles on its website (Figure 11.3). The right sidebar is full of additional options intended to attract the reader's attention in a variety of content groupings.

For business-to-business (B2B) sites, the lead form should be handy at all times, and if a visitor is not quite ready to fill it out, related information and additional sales content need to be readily available. Plan an intended information path, and continually interlink pages to show important concepts. Both the conversion point and the related information are critical for those who need more information and those who have enough to make the decision.

Still, making home-grown investments part of a well-diversified portfolio could be a prudent long-term move.

Here are some ways to invest in the U.S.A.:

1 Focus on the U.S. Consumer

Investors looking to invest in U.S. companies that cater almost entirely to the U.S. consumer should look to utilities, telecoms and regional banks.

Unlike blue-chip giants like General Electric and Coca-Cola, which get "40%-plus of their revenue from outside the U.S.," the customers of companies in these sectors "are in the neighborhood," says Todd Rosenbluth, a mutual-fund analyst at S&P.

American Leadership
The U.S. continues to face obstacles on its path to economic recovery, but this year hasn't been as bad for the American stocks as it has for those in Asia and Europe.
Cumulative year-to-date return of diversified stock funds'

U.S.: down 4.4%
Asia/Pacific: down 10.3%
Europe: down 12.1%

*Through end of June
Source: Lipper

Tim Foley

For utilities, he points to the Franklin Utilities Fund and the American Century Utilities Fund. They have expense ratios of 0.8% and 0.7% of assets, respectively, below the 1.5% average for their peer group. The American Century fund, which is off 7.3% this year (through June), holds utilities and some telecoms such as Edison International and AT&T. The Franklin fund, down 7%, includes Sempra Energy and American Electric Power.

U.S. utilities and telecoms don't have exposure to problems and risks in other countries and they have high dividend yields, says Mr. Rosenbluth. Also, they provide core services, which aren't as affected by a decrease in discretionary consumer spending.

For financials, he likes the John Hancock Regional Bank Fund and the Fidelity Select Banking Portfolio fund. Up 2.3%, the John Hancock fund includes PNC Financial Services, BB&T and Bank of America. The Fidelity fund, up 4.8%, includes BB&T, Comerica Bank and Fifth Third Bancorp.

With business models that could be less affected by regulatory reform and more capital, regional banks may be in a better position than their small community bank and larger bank counterparts, says Erik Oja, a banking analyst at S&P Equity Research.

Figure 11.3: *Wall Street Journal* (www.wsj.com) information links

Visitors who might not commit to a contact form may subscribe to an email newsletter. This is where defining and measuring your secondary conversion points can help you understand the visitor trends on your website. If they won't subscribe to the newsletter, maybe they will sign up for a webinar. If they don't sign up for a webinar, then maybe they will register to download a free white paper. Just because a visitor won't take the bait for the big conversion, that doesn't mean you have lost them entirely. Provide additional methods for visitors to convert on your website by making it easy for visitors to gain information the way they are most comfortable.

Related products, related articles, white papers, case studies, free downloads— all of these are persuasive content that can keep a visitor on the site and improve the chances of them contacting your company. Customers online are not simply looking to see who is out there in the industry and then call for more information; they won't take that action. Customers are looking to see who is competent in the industry and will provide answers to what they need. They are looking to be persuaded and have reasons to back up their choice.

This is where tracking visitors to your website is critical. In a study from eMarketer, most social media visitors to a B2B sites went to the About Us page for a company, and that was the final destination. There are many interpretations of this data; my interpretation is that there wasn't enough interesting information taking them somewhere else. Most B2B companies place very little thought in the About Us page, so there is no wonder that this may be is the final resting place for site visitors.

"Probably Not. I Haven't Found What I'm Looking For"

If there are too many of your visitors that are the one-page wonders (those who visit only one page of your website and then leave), then there may be a problem with your content. Most likely, these types of visits are the result of content that carries meaning across multiple industries or concepts. Words that may mean one thing in your market may mean something completely different in another market.

An example of a crossover term like this is *nested tables*. In my coding days, this was a term we used to explain tables coded inside of tables in order to lay out pages for the Web. They are also an accessibility nightmare! However, when my wife heard me talking with another coder about nested tables, she thought I was talking about furniture. Figure 11.4 shows why. A quick Google search for *nested tables* brings up content on both applications of the term.

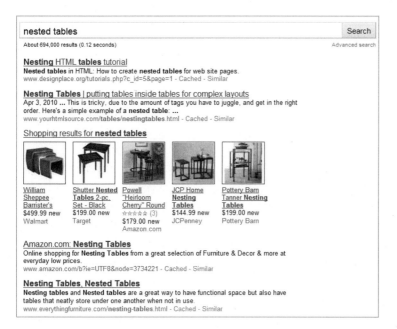

Figure 11.4 Google results for *nested tables*, which shows two very different results

These terms are quickly found comparing your search rankings to your analytics. By looking at the search results, you may find that a word or two specific to your business is also a crossover term. In addition to your ranking reports, reviewing your referral terms in your analytics will help you identify specific phrases and pages that may be causing confusion.

Perform a search in the search engines, using your top referring term in your analytics, and see what websites appear in the rankings. Browse through the sites in the results to see whether there are any sites that are also using your industry term but may not be related.

Tuesday: Make It Attractive

Just having a conversion point in a logical place isn't enough. Just having the Subscribe button available doesn't mean people will give it a second glance. Just because you offer a newsletter isn't reason enough for someone to be interested. Instead, you actually have to sell the action. That's right, persuasion doesn't stop with the content, and you actually need to sell the conversion tasks on your site as being attractive options.

Benefits beat instructions, and here are some examples to show how you can better position your conversion points to increase business.

What's in It for Me?

Recreation.gov will not let you book a national park camping trip unless you register for a membership on the website (Figure 11.5). However, there is nothing on the registration page that tells the site visitor about this requirement. It is the equivalent of being told "because I said so," rather than asking politely and providing substantive reasons for the request.

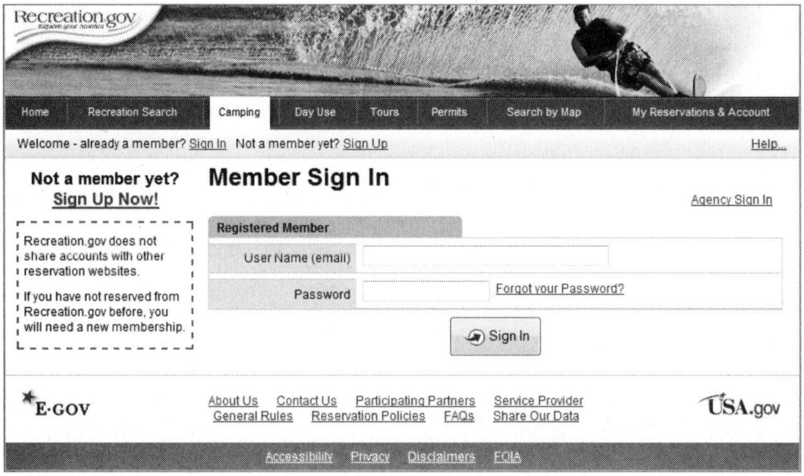

Figure 11.5 Recreation.gov requires membership but doesn't tell you why.

One of the biggest reasons for a lack of registrations is that visitors mainly receive instructions to subscribe rather than benefits. Companies forget that they still have to sell that subscription, and if it isn't attractive, no one will want it. When faced with a request to subscribe, register, or any other type of action, users either ignore it or wonder "What's in it for me?" If the site does not answer that question, then there will be no action.

As another example, an article page on MySolutionSpot.com (Figure 11.6), a subscription option is presented to the visitor. However, no reason is listed or presented as to why the visitor should even consider registration. There are no benefits, actions, or accompanying reasons that will help the visitor make a decision to even consider the registration.

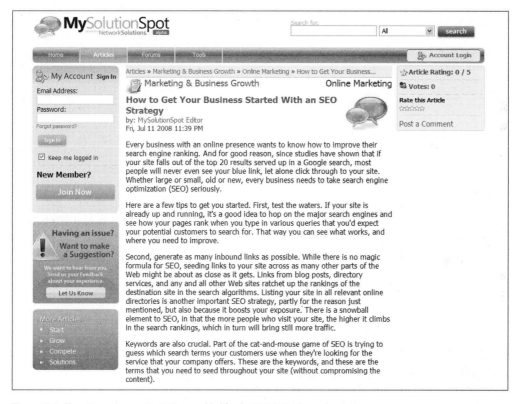

Figure 11.6 There is no reason or invitation provided for the MySolutionSpot subscription.

In contrast, the historic city of Deadwood, South Dakota, offers visitors an attractive message that helps persuade them to action. Instead of simply placing a graphic requesting visitors to subscribe or request vacation information, the graphic is accompanied by a simple explanation that is focused on the searcher's needs: information, updates, planning, and events (Figure 11.7). By focusing the message of the benefits to the visitor, the subscription and lead form become a friendly means to accomplishing the task. (See Thursday's discussion under "Check the Length of Forms" for more on lead forms.)

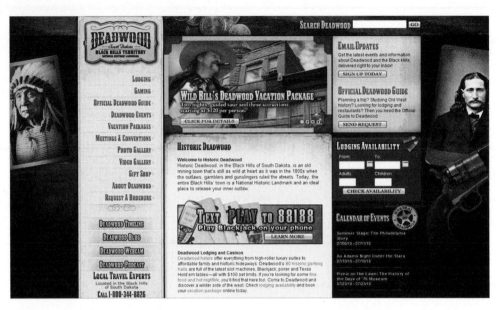

Figure 11.7 City of Deadwood: benefits are explained as both email updates and the visitor guide.

As you can see, sometimes even a very simple sentence with a few visitor benefits may be all it takes to show the visitor "what's in it for them." Placing a subscription or request with no tangible benefits communicates a very high expectation from the company but results in very low expectations from the visitors.

One of the easiest benefits to promote is savings. TigerDirect.com utilizes this very effectively by promoting the email subscription to visitors at the very top of the website (Figure 11.8). With the simple benefit statement "Sign up for our deal alerts," TigerDirect has covered two very critical benefits to the customer: money savings and limited-time offers. These are two of the strongest benefits for giving a business an email address; there is a strong level of perceived value in that statement, so the visitor is more likely to respond.

Figure 11.8 TigerDirect.com direct benefit statement for an email subscription

Even offering similar conversion points can be done effectively when the message and the design both follow a similar convention. As shown in Figure 11.9, First Class Flyer provides three primary conversion points to the visitor: Learn More, Start Free Trial, and "Sign up for a free trial issue of *First Class Flyer*."

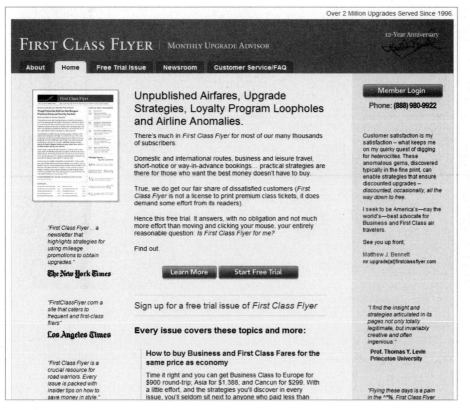

Figure 11.9 First Class Flyer presents three clear conversion points to the reader.

The two blue links go to the same place; one is a graphic link, and the other is a text link. The size, content, and color of the text link indicate that it is a link, because it is considerably different from the rest of the content format. The other conversion point is a button that is easy to see and labeled with a clear purpose of gaining more information, which is exactly what the visitor receives. The calls to action mirror the content and are all clear in function and behavior, giving the reader what they expect to see.

Provide All the Information

In addition to providing a reason for a visitor to take an action, you must remember to provide the necessary information. Dynamism.com (Figure 11.10) has a link to buy that is bright red and in the lower right of the page, which is a logical place considering the layout. However, there is vital information missing that the visitor needs to know prior to making the decision to buy. What is the price of the item? Do you have to purchase the entire set? Is the board included?

Figure 11.10 Dynamism.com presents an unclear purchase link.

Unfortunately, the answer to those questions is located under the image as a gray "pricing" link. In context of the page, this is a very low-interest area of the page, and the gray-on-white color combination creates an understated "blob" of content. Visitors will see the purchase link prior to the "pricing" link because of the red call to action.

The layout used by ThinkGeek, on the other hand, is exceptional, considering all the information packed into a small space yet easily scanned by a user (see Figure 11.11). The information is presented in a way that allows the user to gain the important benefit points and also to see whether the item is in-stock, shipping restrictions, a user-generated video, and a quick description. By designing the content on the page in a logical and quick presentation, the critical information is quickly presented, and a decision can be made even faster by the reader.

This page uses elements of layout techniques presented in Chapter 9 about font size, color scheme, and layout; these are all important aspects of communicating trust and credibility, and the content is designed to point your eyes to the bright orange Buy Now button. Nothing else on the page is that bright or contrasting.

Similarly, Highrise CRM (Figure 11.12; www.highrisehq.com) allows users to select a package that is right for them. Rather than the user having to page through multiple options, the page presents all of the options in a single graphic, complete with pricing. This allows the visitor to see the option that is recommended and what is right for their needs.

Figure 11.11 ThinkGeek presents a clear display of product information and conversion point.

Figure 11.12 Highrise CRM options display

Remove Bland Imperatives

Imperative sentences are commands, and no one likes being told what to do. Anyone who has children knows the first question after being told what to do: "why?"

Through my own testing, I tend to see that users simply ignore bland imperative sentences in calls to action. However, when the imperative is replaced with an assertion (see Chapter 7) or an invitation, the visitor looks more favorably upon the action that you want them to take. For example, replacing the word *submit* with *sign up* or *subscribe* is much more inviting. Simply changing a few words in your content can result in a much broader appeal and a better draw for visitors. In a test on the site Which Test Won? (a wonderful usability resource at http://whichtestwon.com/test-4-results?pollid=4), the Cabot Heritage Foundation improved its subscription rate by testing two calls to action:

```
Send My Free Report
Start My Free Subscription
```

Cabot replaced the original text (Send My Free Report) with the second version (Start My Free Subscription), and the conversion rate dropped by 23 percent. The choice of a few words, which may seem innocuous, can significantly affect your business. Using words that describe the action and the benefit can make a call to action more inviting, more accessible, and friendlier to your audience.

Using the visitor's intention to reinforce the call to action is a particularly powerful presentation. The popular blog-software provider, WordPress.org, uses this because the page presents the call to action as a bold blue link that says Download WordPress 3.0 (see Figure 11.13). The primary action meets with the purpose of the website and the expectations of the visitor.

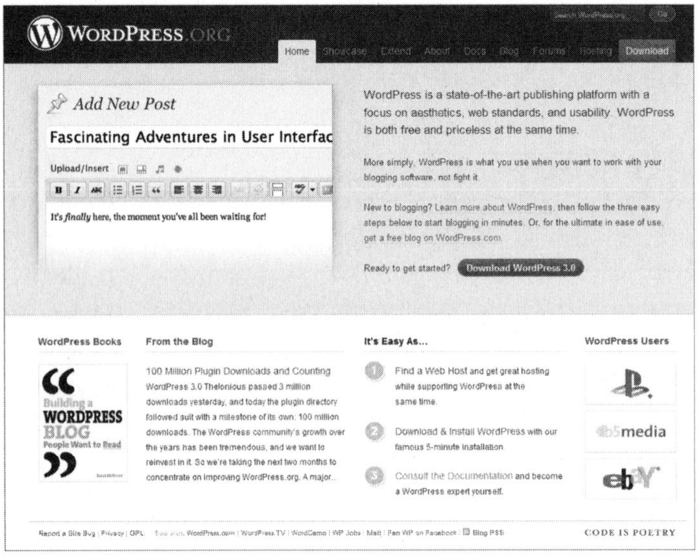

Figure 11.13 WordPress.org: call to action link label

Don't Focus on RSS

Really Simple Syndication (RSS) is a web-feed technology that marketers, journalists, technophiles, and news junkies absolutely love. However, the broader audience has no idea what RSS is, means, or even looks like. To the rest of us, RSS is a means of sending information from one source to many sources. This information can be displayed on another website, a news feed, or a news website and can be displayed in any customized format. Marketers like RSS technology as a means of allowing readers to subscribe to content.

However, the broader population has very little idea what RSS is. In a 2008 report, Forrester found that only 11 percent of consumers used RSS (What's Holding RSS Back? Katz, 2008). However, half of online marketers used RSS. Even the RSS icon (Figure 11.14) is used as a conversion point on thousands of websites—sometimes by itself and sometimes with "What is RSS?" text. Either way, it is unfamiliar to the greater population of Internet users. Yet, thousands of websites rely on this icon to promote their website or blog.

©iStockphoto.com/[Angelhell].

Figure 11.14 RSS icon

This is a simple example of how online technology far exceeds the abilities of the average consumer base. Marketers and programmers are far out front in the technological race and the applications, but the larger consumer market is still far behind in adopting, understanding, and applying these technologies.

If your audience can't recognize the RSS symbol or has no idea what a reader is, don't waste time in explaining these objects and functions. (If the visitor doesn't have an RSS reader already, they'll need to get one in order to subscribe. If a visitor is not using a reader already, what do you think the chances are of retaining a visitor when they subscribe with an unfamiliar technology?)

Diminishing RSS

As of late 2010, ComScore shows that readers accessing website content via RSS feeds has been dropping significantly. Google Reader's visits are down 27 percent, and Bloglines (another RSS reader) has dropped 71 percent over the past few years.

There are a few reasons for this drop. The first can simply be summed up in only a short sentence. My parents don't understand RSS. I've explained it, and I've demonstrated it, but they don't get it. Now, they are both very highly educated and intelligent people. RSS just doesn't compute for them. This is not to deride anyone's intelligence, because my own usability testing has shown that the majority of Internet users don't understand what RSS is, or what it does, nor do they desire to take the time to learn about it.

Second, RSS depends upon a significant knowledge level of the visitor. To subscribe to the RSS content of the blog, they have to know what that means and how to do so. Also, it means that they have a reader (or RSS feed aggregator) either installed or available to them to add the RSS feed. They also would have to know which RSS feed to subscribe to for the reader (ATOM, XML, comments, posts, and so on). Unfortunately, this does not describe the average Internet user.

Third, RSS is mainly a delivery mechanism. RSS readers are rarely pretty; they were mainly functional. With the rise of Facebook and Twitter, which accept RSS feeds, the information can now be delivered in an attractive and understandable format, but most readers have no idea how it was transmitted or sent to their social media services. Social media not only took away the popularity of RSS; they co-opted it as a delivery mechanism to their own publishing platforms.

Visitors know what email is, and they understand how it works. Also, as a marketer, I would much rather have email addresses than RSS subscribers. Email addresses are worth much more, because they are a qualified list that I can approach and have value specifically as a list generated from the website or other form of marketing.

The old sales adage "Sell to the customer how they want to be sold" holds true in this instance. *Don't waste your visitor's precious time by selling a technology; use technology to sell your company*, and allow potential and current customers to access information the way they are comfortable accessing it.

USAToday's sports blog Game On offers two very clear ways for users to subscribe to information (Figure 11.15). Those who do not understand RSS do not have to search the site for alternatives.

Figure 11.15 USA Today's Game On subscription block

One of my favorite blogs for entrepreneurial inspiration is Pamela Slim's Escape from Cubicle Nation (Figure 11.16). On her blog, she shows clear icons to subscribe to her updates via RSS, Facebook, or Twitter. However, she also provides a specific area for email sign-ups by inviting visitors to receive a monthly newsletter.

Figure 11.16 Escape from Cubicle Nation provides various ways for readers to be updated.

Having an RSS option is good, but realize that only a small percentage of users know what it is. Based on your market or industry, the percentage could be higher or even lower. If you are in the technology or journalism industry, then the usage of RSS is more prevalent than in any other markets. Other than that, the percentage of users who have readers will now place your RSS feed in competition with every other blog and website to which they subscribe. The fight for the visitor's attention still takes place, whether in the reader or in the inbox.

Wednesday: Overcome Obstacles

One of the most valuable tools in the arsenal of the marketer is the ability to overcome objections or to take weaknesses and make them strengths. In verbal communication, this is a true gift to those who have to sell in one-on-one situations. Online, this ability needs to address the obstacles in the persuasive process. What marketers tend to forget is that sometimes your own website may be its own obstacle.

If your message is not clear or if there are graphical elements competing with the purpose of the site or the ability to clearly communicate the content, then the site is creating an obstacle to the visitor. Your job is to find those obstacles that are creating confusion, blocking the purpose, or distracting the visitor from the information they need.

Communicate a Clear Purpose

It is a good idea to conduct regular visual assessments your website. A visual assessment is the technical term for gaining a colleague's opinion about the page or about the website. My preference is to ask people about the purpose or to identify the focal point of the page rather than simply asking for an opinion about how it "looks." In other words, rather than asking someone what they think of your page, ask what they think your web page is about. You may be in for some astonishing answers. You'll most likely find that the largest, most contrasting area on the page is the part of the site that people use to determine the context of the page and possibly the entire website.

This is why it is critical to have images that fit the narrative of the content and the company. The same goes with taglines and headlines; they must immediately make sense within the context of the content and the company.

Using taglines that promote the benefit of the company or the product can aid the user in quickly accessing the content. GoToMyPC (Figure 11.17) has a very easy-to-spot purpose thanks to the tagline Access Your Mac or PC from Anywhere. Within seconds, both the name of the company and the tagline are able to communicate a clear benefit to the visitor. The visual acuity of this page is consistent with the message, the images, and the content.

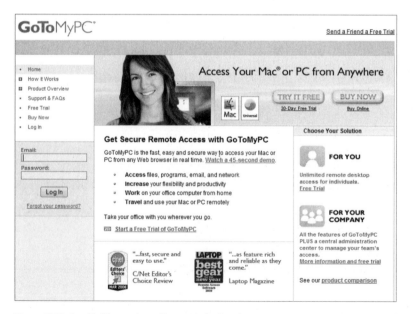

Figure 11.17 GotoMyPC.com: the tagline states the function.

Consider Readers' Visual Acuity

Visitors will freeze immediately when presented with too many options, especially if those options are redundant, are unclear, or have similar labels. Figure 11.18a is a prime example of this type of over-presentation.

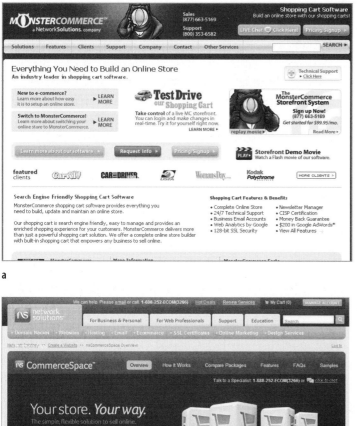

a

b

Figure 11.18 a) The old Monster Commerce over-conversion page; b) Network Solutions' simpler rework of the ecommerce software page

In a very small amount of space, there are 10 calls to action on the Monster Commerce page. Some are clear to the purpose, such as "Click here" for tech support and live chat; however, the organization of this page renders it very unclear. There is very little color consistency, because there is liberal use of the orange, green, and purple colors, but they are not consistent in purpose or content. In addition, the calls to action are all different sizes, so there is not one that looks more important than the other.

To make matters even more complicated, there is no specific link that drives users to more information; instead, the information seems scattered: three variations of "Learn more...," "Request Info," two "Pricing/Signup" buttons, a test-drive, and a demo movie. This large-scale presentation of multiple options presents a confusing array of options and could easily be revised to the critical information that the visitor needs to move forward.

Network Solutions has since revised this content (while also eliminating the Monster Commerce brand). The newer version of this content is presented in a vastly simpler presentation (Figure 11.18b).

The new page limits the visitor's choices to very clear, relevant topics. The information is presented in a contextual format, with article content presented as text blocks and calls to action as high-contrast graphics on the right side of the page. Rather than inundating the visitor with an information overload, a clearer path to information is presented.

Present a Clear Contrast

A sure way to help the visitor see your conversion point is to use contrast. Contrast doesn't depend only upon color for a communication scheme but is a clear feature that draws the eyes to a specific area of the page. Human eyes are drawn to areas of high contrast, because they are easier to read. Those areas should contain your most critical information and invitation to action.

If you are using subtle contrast to communicate importance (shades of gray, black on blue, red on yellow, and so on), you are losing the attention of the visitor to other areas that have a higher contrast. Low-contrast areas provide a higher difficulty of reading and thus are typically scanned over or ignored by readers.

This is an area where many businesses fail to understand that there is a major difference between colors from print design to web design. Colors that work well in a glossy print piece may not necessarily translate to a digital format, especially when there is no control over the settings on a user's monitor. Pleasing contrasts between colors in print become lost and nearly blended together in a digital format, because colors are a much higher intensity.

A clear example of this is the old Miva home page (Figure 11.19a). The colors work very well together and are used in all of Miva's advertising. However, the color red in a digital format is so intense and vivid that it grabs the user's attention. When there are multiple words, objects, or images using red, the user will constantly scan the red objects, and the rest of the page tends to drop out. Users tend to look at red objects as important elements or action words, and any objects and text are subordinated.

Unfortunately, in this design, the call to action is white text in a light blue gradient. In conjunction with the red text, this creates the illusion that the rest of the menu labels are more important, because they are red and have more contrast, and the calls to action are less important, because they are presented in low-contrast elements.

The current Miva home page (Figure 11.19b) uses the opposite approach. Calls to action are red, high-contrast features, and the color red is used much more sparingly. The blue is used to highlight objects and more effectively uses contrast for better communication of important information.

a

b

Figure 11.19 a) The old Miva presentation; b) the redesigned Miva home page

Thursday: Promote the Next Step

A level of customization is necessary to improve the business goals of your online marketing. Regardless of the ecommerce software or lead form generator/code that you have selected, the default settings are rarely the best settings. Every process that requires a visitor to click a link or go to another page is another step in a process. Each process needs to have its own call to action, not just the initial call to action but throughout the entire conversion process.

Provide Clear Instructions

One of my most interesting consulting engagements carried me to a company that was close to a civil war between the IT department and the marketing department. This company, we'll call it Infighting Inc., was having growing pains because they were expanding their ecommerce presence and taking the necessary steps to streamline the process through inventory, sales, shipping, and advertising.

As I was auditing the process, I kept hearing the same story from the marketing department. They constantly complained that sales would be better on the website if IT would fix the website. They claimed that the site would break, and it needed to be redone and that the current IT staff just wasn't up to the task. This was a consistent story and one that was even repeated throughout the company. Everyone pointed to the IT department as the culprit of the company's inability to grow online.

In the audit that I performed for the company, my team and I found something very interesting. We found that we couldn't break the site. No matter how hard we tried and all of the combination tests to see whether we could create errors and breaks, it just wouldn't happen.

In our report to Infighting Inc., we asked the marketing department how many of them had ever attempted to purchase anything through the website. Not a word. In the four years of this company's current website, no one from the marketing department had ever attempted to use the online shopping cart to purchase a product.

The following were the findings and recommendation of me and my team. The website was not broken, it worked well, and the programming was solid. What was broken were the instructions to users through the process and elements in the design of the cart that impeded progress. This was not an IT problem, because the function of the cart was fine, but a marketing problem, and the instructions and design were the responsibility of that department. The website was not broken; rather, the design of the process was broken, and users were unclear as to the steps, process, and functions available to them. IT keeps the site up and running, while the marketing department is responsible for getting the visitor from the entry to the conversion and beyond and for communicating the message and instructions throughout the website.

Just because your website works correctly doesn't mean it is set up correctly. The function of the programming is only the beginning. The function of the instructions and the process for the user are where you need to be intimately involved in observing, testing, and analyzing. This is where you lose sales, because customers become lost in the process, unclear as to the next step.

Think Through Your Multistep Conversion Process

If your business requires multiple steps to convert, then your first step is the most critical. Getting the conversion is important, but the worst thing you can show the visitor is an error message, especially when they took the most logical action shown to them based on the layout, contrast, and call to action label. 1-800-luggage.com based a conversion action on a call to action of "add to cart." However, the primary step was to choose the color of the luggage (see Figure 11.20). Adding the luggage to the cart produced an error message, which required the visitor to go back and select a color.

Figure 11.20 1-800-luggage call to action: add to cart or select color?

Cases like this make the user think they did something wrong, when it is all based on the presentation of the website. Usability, at its essence, is making the task easiest for the visitor. What stands in the way of that task is usually the design, the label, or the lack of clear instructions.

In addition to required tasks, there are also unrequired tasks that seem to make their way into ecommerce applications. So, if your product has only one option, then you need to default to that option. Don't require the visitor to take more steps than necessary to complete a simple task. In Figure 11.21, the visitor to Manhattan Fruitier has to check the item first (even though there is only one option) and then click the Add to Gift button. If the task is not performed in this order, an error is generated.

Figure 11.21 Get rid of useless steps.

PetSmart's Add to Cart feature for a dog collar also requires a number of steps (Figure 11.22). However, PetSmart is very clear about the required information and the order in which it is needed. Rather than focus the design and therefore the visitor's attention on the final conversion point, contrast and layout are used to bring the attention to the necessary steps needed to add this product to the cart. The visitor clearly sees the priority of actions, understands the steps, and is able to take them, and the process is clear.

Figure 11.22 PetSmart.com multistep conversion process

Assess Your Checkout Steps

In ecommerce sites, the lack of clear "next steps" or a specifically labeled action point to move forward in the process will hurt your sales. When the process is unclear or the next step is hidden, the visitor leaves. Unclear steps result in low sales.

Using a "temperature bar" that shows the visitor which step they are on and how many steps are left is critical to showing them what kind of time and commitment will be required to complete the conversion. The Hilton website uses the temperature bar at the top of the page to inform visitors of the stages in the process and where they are in the process (see Figure 11.23).

In a typical session, the visitor will go to the shopping cart in order to view their items. So, what is the next step after viewing their items and the final price? The checkout. Unfortunately, this is where many ecommerce companies just simply fail in this step.

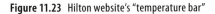

Figure 11.23 Hilton website's "temperature bar"

Figure 11.24 shows Manhattan Fruitier's checkout page. The steps are not only unclear, but there are no differences among the button options. The most critical in this placement is that the Cancel Order button is on the far right where the checkout button usually is! The danger of visitors accidentally deleting their entire order is highly likely with the placement and order of the buttons and no distinguishing differences among them. The Checkout option needs to be larger, more contrasting, and prominently placed. If there is no difference in the buttons, then they are all of the same importance, and there is nothing leading the visitor to the step they need or want to take.

The best practice is to associate the final price and the Checkout button. These two functions are "married" in a sense, because they should never be apart. The final price leads to the Checkout option, and because it is the next logical step in the process, it needs to be the most obvious contrasting element on the page.

Figure 11.24 There is no clear "next step" button; all the buttons are the same size and same importance.

To repeat an earlier point, just because you have ecommerce software does not mean that the software accounts for these "next step" actions or is built specifically to make the conversion process simple. The default settings and graphics are meant to get the action completed, rather than provide the best possible user experience. Customization is necessary to ensure that your cart software works for your store and your website.

eCost.com takes no chances in this regard (see Figure 11.25). The Checkout link is a large green graphic in a high-contrast presentation and is located to the right of *and* below the final price.

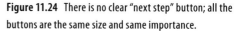

Figure 11.25 eCost.com's bold checkout steps

There is no need to guess about the next step from this page, and yours should be as obvious. You have nothing to lose but more sales.

Check the Length of Forms

I love lead forms. I think lead forms are the easiest conversion to get and are completely overlooked, especially in the ease of programming it requires to get great data from very short forms.

In most cases, companies are only looking to get a name and an email address. If you are using a customer relationship management (CRM) system, then you can build from this basic level of information and grow it every time you build a relationship with that contact. The majority of problems with forms is based in a single issue. They are too long.

Value

The more information you require from a visitor to complete a form, the more value you need to offer. For access to a white paper, for example, an email address and maybe a company name are all that would be expected as part of that value transaction. However, how about requiring a user to set up an account, create a password, provide business information, and provide their first pet's name? You've asked for too much information, and visitors will not see the value in providing that information, especially when they can simply go back to a search engine and find more information for less investment.

Your form needs to match the perceived value to the visitor. If you want to capture a lot of business data from a lead form, then your offering needs to be of equal or greater value and communicated well. Otherwise, visitors will abandon your form.

This was exemplified a few years ago when I joined a fantasy football league on CBS Sportline's website. My league received an invitation to register and create our team from an email. Unfortunately, this email link brought us to a landing page that had 18 fields for registration. And all of them were required fields! Even more, no one wanted to take the time to create a password, and no one really saw a purpose in giving their address, zip code, phone number, and gender (see Figure 11.26a). Suffice it to say that only one of the 12 participants took the time to fill out the form.

A few days later, another link appeared in the email reminding the rest of the 11 participants to register. This link brought everyone to a different page (Figure 11.26b). This registration page required only the most basic information necessary to set up a team, and by the end of the afternoon, everyone in the league had signed up. A simple matter of value kept even the most hardcore fantasy football player from registering on the website, because the perceived time and effort was more than they were willing to provide.

a

b

Figure 11.26 a) An overly demanding CBSSportsline.com Fantasy Football registration; b) a simplified version of the form

Tracking

One thing you can do to get a better handle on your website and marketing is to start adding small registration or contact forms throughout your marketing. You should not only add the forms but also integrate tracking codes through the programming so that when a form is completed, the salesperson (or whoever receives the forms) is able to know which page the visitor was on and what they were looking at when they sent the form. This little bit of programming enhancement can help your sales force be much more prepared when contacting a website visitor.

Adding tracking codes to forms can also help you tie together the search terms or the advertising that brought the visitor to the site, what they saw, and what persuaded them to take action and contact you. Tying together search terms and actions on the website can be a powerful way of optimizing your content and positioning information to be better understood by the visitor. Additionally, receiving a form and knowing the page, content, and specific context of the contact form will enable a better contact and answer to be provided the visitor.

Encourage Actions after the Conversion

In Chapter 7, old sales axioms were applied to new marketing methods. This concept is along those very same lines. It is one of the foundational sales truths and very effective in its execution, and that is to follow up after the sale.

There is a phenomenon experienced by consumers or purchasers called *buyer's remorse*. It is the second guessing that takes place in the buyer's mind after making a commitment. Buyers wonder whether they made the right decision, whether maybe there was a better product, or whether this is the right company to do the job. Either way, once humans have committed to something, there tends to be a creeping doubt about that commitment. The sales advice to follow up after the decision is based on the behavior of people to accept another person's opinion that they have made a good decision. Reinforcing the commitment is a powerful way of ensuring the visitor that they have made the right decision. This is why a car salesperson will call you a week or two after you purchased your car, telling you that you made a great decision.

Unfortunately, this great sales technique has made very little inroads to the online world. Once a visitor makes a conversion on a website, they are typically left with a black page that says "thank you." What a horrible way to start a new relationship.

This visitor just gave you some of the most valuable time and information that they could give. Their email address is a thing of value, and it should be treated as such, with graciousness and appreciation. If the conversion included the credit card, then it also required a high level of trust. Either way, the visitor converted on your site by giving items of high value, only to be shooed away with a simple thank-you message.

Instead of languishing with mediocre thank-you messages, this is your opportunity to express sincere gratitude, compliment the decision, and start developing that new relationship. Replace the boring and bland thank-you page with valuable information, related products, downloadable information, and links to other items that they may find of interest. Just because a visitor converted doesn't mean they have to leave the website!

This is particularly effective in B2B applications, because the thank-you page from a contact form could provide a checklist of information to have handy when the sales rep calls or information to gather for the next stage of the purchase process. In either application, prepare your new customer with information that will reinforce their decision, prepare them for the next contact, and provide them with more than they ask for. You just may see your retention rate and long-term sales rate increase as a result.

The process at site Czech & Speake, www.czechandspeake.com, follows this type of handling of the new-customer relationship. A thank-you page is displayed to confirm the order, along with a call to action to *continue* the process. After clicking the Continue link, the new customer is presented with a few specials related to the product they just purchased along with an offer "just for you" (see Figure 11.27).

This handling of the customer experience maintains the process beyond the sale. Simply because a customer has checked out does not mean they are not buying.

Friday: Implement Testing

At the outset of this chapter, I quoted the typical statistic of the "average" conversion rate. When I was in the Army, our physical fitness tests were graded on the ability to run 2 miles and perform a certain number of push-ups and sit-ups. You received 100 points for performing to a specific goal based on your age and height. A 300 was a perfect score for the fitness test, which a few could attain. On the other end of the spectrum, you could also pass by attaining the "minimum acceptable standard" of 60 points in each event. There were some for whom this was good enough.

This is how I view the "average" conversion rate, which is the minimal acceptable standard. If you set your goal to reach the "average," you are setting very low goals. I find that many businesses are happily content to meet or slightly exceed the average conversion rate or the rates within their industry. As a result, they become fixed upon rates that are irrelevant and largely out of their control.

What *is* in your control is your conversion rate. Regardless of the average or of the industry or market, your conversion rate is within your control. The best standard of measurement is your own marketing performance. Did you meet or exceed what you did last year, last quarter, or last cycle? Constantly comparing your website's performance to others leads to a myopic view that stifles creativity and innovation within your own company. Comparing and analyzing your own marketing and website performance on a constant basis is the only way that you will develop online marketing skills and wisdom that will exceed the "average."

a

b

Figure 11.27 Czech & Speake provides additional information to the new customer, rather than ending the process on the Thank You page.

One of the examples used in Tuesday's readings was the example of Cabot Heritage Foundation and how the company affected its conversion rate with only a simple two-word change in the subscription text. The website, WhichWestWon.com, is a fantastic resource for getting ideas for your own website. Testing doesn't necessarily mean creating large, wholesale changes to your website. It is, however, identifying small iterative changes that can be measured and compared.

A website is never "done" because it is the most dynamic marketing tool at your disposal. With the ability to track minute changes to content, graphics, placement, headlines, and hundreds of other small changes, you can significantly increase your conversion rates.

Consider Alta Colleges, which developed and executed an exemplary testing plan (`www.searchenginemarketingstrategy.com/wwcs09/`). This case study of Alta College and their agency of record, Location3 Media, shows the development and execution of an exemplary testing plan (`http://www.location3.com/projects/westwood-college-case-study-2009`). Location3 Media tested multiple styles of ads in both Yahoo and Google, and they were able to improve conversion rate by 57 percent by using geotargeting by state and region. Another layer of geotargeting was implemented by developing a local campaign wherever there was a physical campus location. This increased the conversion rate another 80 percent.

The most impressive testing developed in the landing page testing. The idea developed that more "right-brain" degree programs might respond better to a contact form on the left side of the page, while "left-brain" program applicants would respond to a page with the contact form on the right (see Figure 11.28).

Figure 11.28 Alta Colleges A/B test of right vs. left-side forms

The degree programs were divided along the lines of right-brain and left-brain stereotypes, and an A/B test was performed. Overall, the conversion rate improved 44 percent, which is impressive. Most degree programs showed a slight improvement with the right- or left-justified landing page, and only half provided enough data to prove the hypothesis.

Two "left-brain" programs in particular responded strongly to the form on the right side of the page, the MBA and the HVAC programs. The HVAC landing page improved conversion by 83 percent, and the MBA program landing page improved conversions by 91 percent, lending credence to the assumption that some respondents in a left-brain field would respond better to a right-side contact form (Figure 11.29).

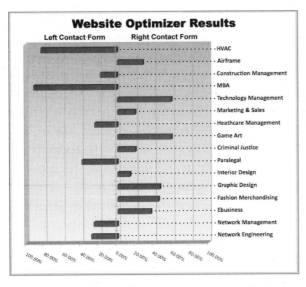

Figure 11.29 Alta Colleges college landing page testing results showing the conversion improvement for each degree program

Review and Hands-On

Chapter 3 was about establishing clear business goals, and here is the place where the goals come into practice. In evaluating your website, *does every page communicate the goals for the business and the visitor?*

Every page should be asking the visitor to convert in some way, either a direct conversion to a sale, lead, or subscription or an indirect conversion to more information, related topics, or other noncommittal activities.

Review your calls to action. Simply presenting a subscribe function will not suffice. What reason are you giving your visitors to invite them to subscribe, purchase, move forward, or click to additional content?

- Explain what is in it for the visitor.
- Remove bland imperative statements from your conversion points.
- Create more active button labels.
- Test simple messages.

Just from an initial glance at your pages, use the principles of visual acuity, purpose, and contrast to determine the most critical information on the page. This is also an activity where you may bring in a third party to get an outside opinion of the messaging of your marketing, the purpose and clarity of the tagline, the arrangement of the content and images on the page, and also the purpose for the page.

Review your content and design to identify areas of low contrast. Ideally, those are not areas of importance or targeted conversion points. If they are, you know what to do.

Outline the steps in the process that you require your visitors to take. List every check, form field, link click, and step in the process. To be completely honest, bring in a third-party to record all the actions necessary simply to go through a conversion process.

After you have compiled the list of actions, evaluate which are necessary, which can be optimized or combined, and which should be left out entirely.

Evaluate your contact forms, your request forms, and your usage of them. Are they asking the right questions for the right conversion point? Are they too long and do they have too many required fields? Do you really need to ask all of that information in order to get the contact?

Afterward, look at your landing page after the conversion. What does it say? What can you do to provide follow-up after the conversion that will assist in building a relationship with the new customer or in moving along the sales cycle?

Testing produces results. There is no lack of testing tools available online, with most of them being free. With the pervasiveness of Google Analytics, the step up to Google's Webpage Optimizer takes only a few hours to a few days for a business to acclimate to a testing program.

The amazing thing about testing is that the time invested in testing is earned back very quickly, because questions about the process and the website can be answered with user-based behavior data, not opinions.

Month 3: Develop Good Site Architecture

Any true craftsman uses tools to create a master-piece. In the hands of an internet craftsman, the information architecture is the result of knowledge, experience, skill, and the right tools, used correctly. Developing the architecture of your site is critical to visitors that need to access your information. Get this wrong, and both your rankings and your business will suffer. Get it right, and your visitors may never notice it, which is a compliment, as they will be too busy finding what they need.

Week 9: Create Effective Navigation

The information architecture of a website is a critical component in assisting visitors and developing more in-depth search engine optimization techniques. Visitors rely on both the navigation and the structure of the information presented on the website in order to find the information they want. Search engines tend to reward sites that have a consistent information hierarchy that develops a specific context to the page, the surrounding section, and the site as a whole. If your site's navigation is confusing, visitors will be confused, your conversions will suffer, and your success in the search engines could be limited.

Chapter Contents

Monday: Consider the Home Page as Direction Rather Than a Destination

Website development has come a long way since the early days. Usually, a business would go to a web agency and ask for a new site, and within days the business would be reviewing three options for the new home page. That style of development had a number of problems, because it put the power completely in the hands of the artists' interpretation of the information on the website. (But of course, when you don't do more than the typical navigation options of About Us, Product, Services, and Contact Us, I guess you don't need much.) What I mean is that the focus of the information was limited to the understanding of the business by the agency and its artists and would not typically exceed that point. Maybe some research was done into the market and the business and a value proposition established, but the process was typically driven by the aesthetic of the design rather than developing information structures focused on the business goals.

Fortunately, the design process has become more about understanding the visitor's interactions with the information, measured according to the business goals. The design process has become one of designing "informationally" and creating the aesthetic to enable interaction with the information.

One of the main contributors to the previous way of thinking was the view that the home page was a destination in itself. To visitors, the home page is anything but a destination, and when these two views collide, the business loses. Visitors want to know where to go and how to get there, and they expect the home page to provide that direction. If the information isn't available, then they leave and go to the next search result or available link.

The Dangers of the Home Page as a Destination

When a business thinks of its home page in terms of a destination, an almost egotistical view arises that this should be a source of entertainment, which led to the insidious "splash page" theory of home page development. With the advent of Flash in the early 2000s, businesses flocked to have animation and mini-commercials running on their home pages. With lots of animation, and maybe even a dash of sound, it was a recipe for visitor abandonment. Rarely did an analysis of visitor behavior show that anyone was willing to watch and wait for the commercial to end. Coincidently, Skip Intro tended to be the most utilized link on the page.

Even today, it is common to run across a home page that focuses more on a celebration that you navigated to its URL than a helpful guide to the information contained within the site. This view hinders visitors in their searches for the content they need and the content that will help you, as the business owner, be more profitable. It is in your best interest that the information on your website be easy to find, because it is the *information* that creates the conversions.

Additionally, some SEO specialists over-optimize the home page in an attempt to have it rank well for as many keywords as possible. Unfortunately, this tactic results in a cluster approach to gaining rankings. By placing all the keywords and subjects on a single page (the home page), the result is a page that attempts to meet the needs of thousands of visitors with only a few words and concepts but little clear direction. The result is a home page that ranks for many general terms but provides little context for direction. As Seth Godin points out in *Meatball Sundae: Is Your Marketing Out of Sync?* (Portfolio Hardcover, 2007), "No one visits a website's home page anymore—they walk in the back door." Basically, every page on your website is a home page. Every page is an opportunity to gain a conversion or help the visitor find related information. Simply getting a visitor to the home page is not good enough because visitors want and are able to enter at the appropriate page and the most relevant page to their interests. When they don't see the information they want, the visit does not last long. Getting visitors deeper into the website, based on their interests, creates better visits and, in turn, better sales and conversions. In analytics studies for research and for clients, the findings are consistent. When compared with the visitors who search on the same word but who enter at a "deeper" page in the website, they tend to stay longer, do more, and convert at a higher rate.

A research project for a client brought this into a clearer focus. Visitors who used the same keyword for their search entered the website at one of two primary pages: the home page or the category page. The home page of this website typically ranked in the top three results in the search engines. The visitors entering at that home page had a significantly higher bounce rate and a lower conversion rate when compared to the site average. The category page was on the second page of results and averaged a ranking of #13 in the same timeframe. The visitors who entered at this category page (for a search on the exact same term) stayed longer, looked at more content, had a lower bounce rate, and doubled the average conversion rate!

Once this behavior showed itself on one website, it became a template for analyzing visitor behavior on other websites. Consistently, visitors tended to convert at higher rates when they entered the website closer to the destination than if they had entered at the home page. Although there were many theories as to why this behavior was taking place, the most logical theory that fits the most evidence was that the navigation on the home page was not clear enough to help visitors quickly find the information they needed to make a quick decision to find the direction of the content.

For visitors who do enter at the home page, whether by search, by direct navigation, from a bookmark, or from a link, they are expecting direct cues to the deeper content. Visitors on your home page typically have a mission in mind, and the construction on your home page must show the purpose of the business and a clear, understandable structure of content. Without clear information architecture utilizing clear language and easy-to-read content, a visitor will grow wary of the visit, especially if they cannot trust the layout of the content.

Using the Home Page for Direction

The 1970s sitcom *M.A.S.H.* had an iconic symbol in the center of the camp: a road sign with the destinations to the hometowns of those serving in the camp. The home page should be like that sign: it should point the way to the information the visitor needs (see Figure 12.1).

Figure 12.1 The home page points the way to the content.

The tools to point the way are typical; it's the global navigation, because it gives more detail to its placement and purpose. It includes the subnavigation, footer links, header links, and links grouped by context. By understanding the purpose of each of these elements, you can more effectively direct visitors to their desired content while also showing related and available content nearby, which allows for the serendipitous discovery of valuable content.

Navigation is not just limited to a single bar of links, using rollouts, flyouts, or whatever. Navigation is much more than this. In many well-designed websites, many users do not even see or identify the main navigation, because the rest of the information structure presented on the page is much more relevant and functional to their purpose. Developing clear navigational structures that speak to the visitor in many different ways is the method by which you can effectively lead them into the content of the site.

Figure 12.2 shows an example of a website for USB-rechargeable batteries. You can see that the main navigation is secondary to the benefit statements on the right side of the image. In fact, thanks to only a few well-written benefit statements, the visitor has the basics of the product's advantages and available information within seconds.

The main navigation across the top, while helpful, is not the primary source of information on this page. Other, more informative links and graphics are used to direct the user to the information that suits their needs.

Figure 12.2 USBCELL's use of navigational items other than the main navigation is helpful and designed well.

The advantage of well-designed information architecture is clear. You do not have to rely upon the main navigation to be the sole information gateway. Rather, allow the multiple benefit statements for your business to draw in visitors. Bring out the "need beyond the need" as an information device. Provide groups of related links; as in the case of the previous figure, there are two clear groups of linked information: support and where to purchase. By bringing together elements of contrast, persuasive content, clear benefit statements, and calls to action, this design allows visitors to access multiple areas of content without feeling overwhelmed.

Tuesday: Categorize Subjects with Card Sorting and Tree Testing

Two very easy tools are available that will enable you to better develop website navigation as well as understand how visitors view the information on your website. These two tools, which can be employed by anyone, can help with a lot of content on the website. Better organization means better navigation.

Card sorting is a method of organizing subjects into categories. Customer involvement at this stage can help you explore how customers group and organize information into categories. What you learn from card sorting can be put into practice in developing the first few levels of navigation and grouping your content.

Tree testing tests the effectiveness of your navigation and information hierarchy. By giving a task-based test to your users, you can evaluate the effectiveness of your organization or navigation scheme. Mainly, this tests the words and labels for your navigation to see whether they are understood. Better content labels means better communication with your visitors.

Card Sorting

At its most basic level, card sorting is a great content organization tool. At the most complex, card sorting is a testing tool that allows developers to test the organization of content on a website. Before moving forward in the development process, or as a continual test during the development process, card sorting tests provide immediate feedback from testers about the type of content and its organization.

You can do card sorting anywhere with very little investment. This can be administered remotely by a computer, which allows input from clients and customers. In person, card sorting can be done on whiteboards, on walls, or even on floors using sticky notes or index cards. Whatever the medium, it cannot be permanent. It must allow you to be fluid in moving the subjects around, constantly reorganizing.

The card sort test is simple. Take all the subject matter you have on your website—each page, along with the specific content of that page—and write each bit of information on a different card. Now, organize those cards into a hierarchy of information. What is a major category? What is a minor category? Should this information stand alone? The primary question is, how can this information be grouped logically?

By organizing your content through a visual method, you can grasp the importance of how content should flow. You may also see how visitors could become confused when subject matter is closely related but not relevant or, if it is relevant, easily found. Card sorting helps you find logical categories, establish relationships between the content, and develop a better strategy for organizing the content. In addition to finding consistencies, the card sort will also expose areas of your navigation that are not clear or have no logical placement.

Card-Sorting Tools

For online card-sorting tests, I recommend two primary options. There are a few others, but they don't compare in terms of features and flexibility. Optimal Sort from Optimal Workshop (www.optimalworkshop.com) and WebSort (www.websort.net) are the two leaders in this area, but expect more to join them in the coming years!

Card-Sorting Tools *(Continued)*

For in-person card sorting, I have been using an application for the iPad called iCardSort. It is a very clean drag-and-drop interface, and because it is on the iPad, I have no problem getting people to perform the card sort—simply because it is alluring by being on the iPad. iCardSort can then email each respondent's results with all of the categories defined and an image of the final sort. It's perfect for later analysis!

If you don't have an iPad or just want to save money, then the old-fashioned method of sticky notes or index cards is still the most reliable standby. People are familiar with them and seem to respond better to the tactile sense of holding and organizing cards.

Careful, though! Most people will organize the content differently each time it is performed. And of course, not everyone will have the same opinions on that organization! The best method for card sorting is to build a level of consensus based on enough tests that consistencies arise. My preference is to have 12 to 20 customers or nonemployees. That number should provide enough trends to develop a plan of information development.

Card sorting is a good method to help include customers and get their opinions on content organization; however, it is critical to keep customer tests apart from internal or employee tests. It is surprising how different the tests can be from the internal view of a company when compared to a customer's input. Employees tend to spend much more time and be much more careful about classifying information compared to customers who may be taking the test.

Enticement and Rewards for Customer Participation

For getting customers to participate in a card sort, especially an online card-sorting exercise, I like to provide incentives or drawings for those who complete the task. When sending an invitation to customers or others to be part of the card sort (or any type of survey), I recommend to ask them for less than 10 minutes of their time. In doing so, I try to make the test require less than five minutes. The worst thing you can do is create an extremely long test that does not reward people for their assistance.

Remember that this is customers helping you, and you need to provide an incentive and show gratitude for their willingness to provide their time and effort in these tests and surveys. Gift cards, gift certificates, branded logo clothing, and future discounts can work well as incentives.

To get a good sample of responses, you need to be gracious, accommodating, concise, and generous. Keep in mind you may also have to perform the card sort a few more times during a development process, so make sure you have a good pool of willing candidates to invite.

There are two methods of building a card-sorting exercise: the open card sort and the closed card sort. With an *open card sort*, there are no predefined categories or groups. The open card sort is really a free-range activity allowing the most freedom for testers to interpret and group the information without restriction. Testers are asked to group the cards into categories and label those categories.

The *closed card sort* starts with predefined categories and then asks testers to assign the cards to each category (Figure 12.3). This helps if you have to fit information into a predefined structure. Performing the open card sort will help find the consistencies among testers to build top-level categories, and then the closed card sort can then be used to reinforce or verify those categorizations.

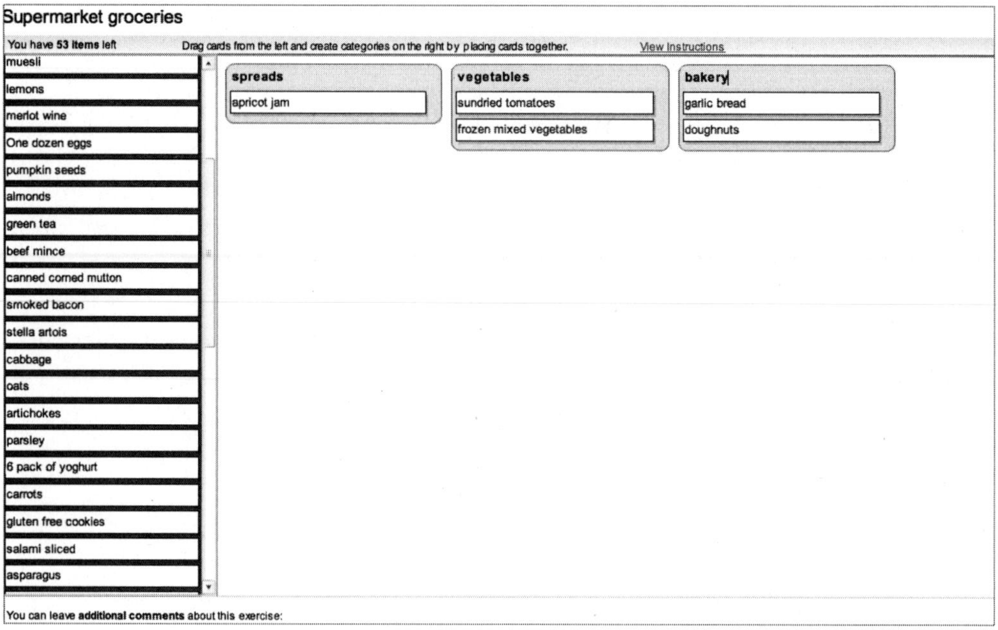

Figure 12.3 Closed card sort using Optimal Sort

The key in the overall card-sorting exercise is organization. Card sort testing provides the ability to understand how customers organize information and match that thinking in your website's information architecture. However, bear in mind that visitors will rarely ever see your website in this manner. Maybe a site map would reflect this two-dimensional view of the structure, but it is not the typical view of a user. The card sort only provides a formative view of the data from a surface view. It does not take into account the needs of users once they enter the website, nor is it a task-based evaluation of the ability to use the website. Card sorting is mainly for quickly testing the organization of information on the website.

Tree Testing

Although card sorting is more of a high-level informational organization technique, it lacks a task-based level of engagement. This is developed through the tree test. Tree testing gives testers a subject and provides multiple choices as to the most logical place to find that subject.

The tree test is a method of ensuring that your information is findable based on the information labels utilized in your site. By asking participants where they would find specific products, information, or important items, a site owner can quickly discover whether their categorization and labeling scheme works for visitors as well as the organization.

A typical tree test would provide a test question similar to the one in Figure 12.4.

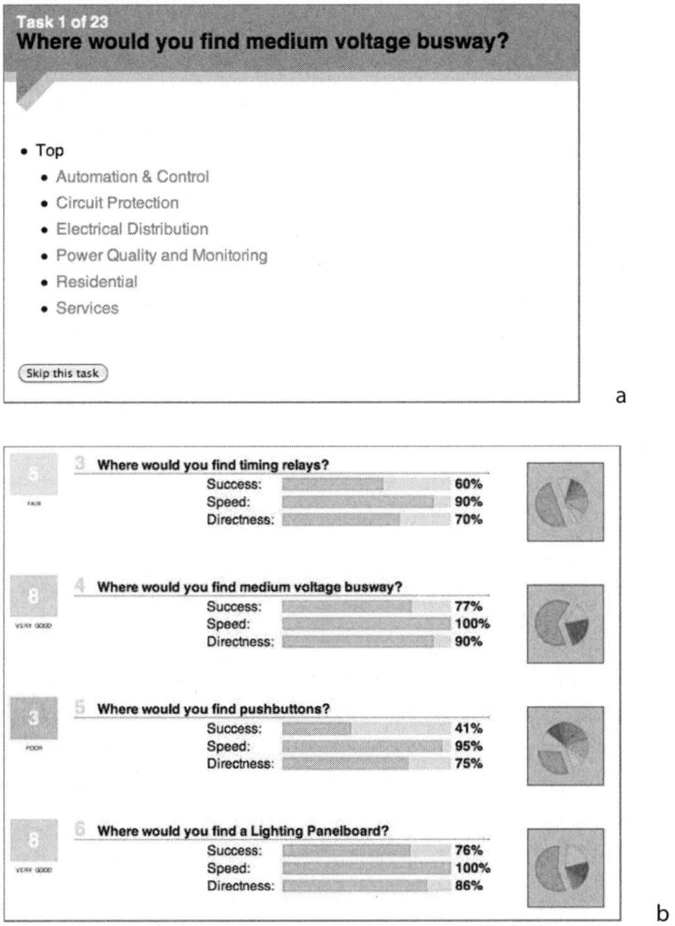

Figure 12.4 Tree test and results from Tree Jack

By asking the question in a task-based format and providing the typical top-level structure and labels, you can see whether testers are of the same mind-set as the developers in organizing content and understanding the purpose of the keyword labels in the navigation. Also important is the speed at which testers are able to identify and classify the content into the relevant area. Results that show the testers taking too long to decide upon a category signify that the content groupings might be too confusing or too similar, therefore causing hesitation.

As with card sorting, there are many levels of this type of exercise. This can be administered on paper or electronically using a simple web-based test offered. Regardless of cost, medium, or scale of the testing, employing these tests helps you better develop your website and your overall marketing in the language and the perceptions of those who will be depending upon your website to find information. By better understanding both the language and the thinking of the visitor, you can better organize your website and use the correct terminology that your users will understand. Tree testing will also provide guidance and specific data that will enable your ability to make good decisions.

Wednesday: Support Navigation with Information

Navigation typically has two problems. It's either too little or too much. It can have too little choice, too little information, and too few options. Conversely, many sites overwhelm the visitor with too many choices, too much information, and options that all look the same. This tends to happen when there is more of a corporate-speak approach to building the website. It's a "This is how we organize our information and so the customer must do the same" mentality.

To understand how to support your navigation with information, let's look at two tourism destination websites. Using two western U.S. cities, whose websites and appeals couldn't be more different, we find that the navigation is treated differently as well. These examples illustrate the importance of surrounding your navigation with information that enables the visitor to understand their *location* within the website, the *relation* to other content, and a clear *destination*. Otherwise, there will be a high level of *frustration*.

Case Study: Confusing Navigation

The first city is Breckenridge, Colorado (see Figure 12.5). The navigation is positioned in the middle of the page, which is a bit nontraditional, but it's definitely not a big issue. There are navigation elements at the top of the page, but they are not major visual elements, and they are not intuitive enough to capture a visitor's attention. Using the primary evaluation elements of pictures and contrast (people look at pictures of people, and our eyes are naturally drawn to areas of high contrast), the attention on this site will naturally settle on the large image of the woman fishing and the high-contrast content at the bottom of the page.

Figure 12.5 Breckenridge, Colorado, home page

However, since every page is a home page, let's look at another page from the same site (see Figure 12.6). Here we start to see the site's navigation fall apart and become undependable. Starting at the top of the page, the URL bar (which is part of the user's interface) shows this page as being `http://gobreck.com/page` `.php?pname=summer/events/ISSC`. The URL matters in terms of visitor navigation. When words are used in the URL, they assist visitors in understanding their location within the site and the content of that page. When the words in the URL bar match the content of the page, it helps develop the overall search engine optimization relevance, and it helps as a navigational anchor to assist visitors with content recognition.

The image on the page is somewhat indistinguishable, and the entire navigation bar has changed colors from green to blue. Being on an inside page, the navigation bar should change only in a way that informs the visitor as to the section of content where they are located. Since this page is in the Events section (which the breadcrumb links suggest), then the Events tab should be highlighted or distinguishable from the other in some way. Highlighting the current section of content by using the navigation bar is one of the primary elements that gives a visitor a sense of location.

Figure 12.6 Breckenridge, Colorado, events page

The next two elements develop additional confusion, because the headline on the page is the "Budweiser Select International Snow Sculpture Championships," but the breadcrumb trail navigation (those are the links that are meant to help you find your way back home) located just under the main navigation tell a different story:

> Home > Summer > Events Budweiser Select International Snow Sculpture Championships

Why are we taken directly to the text for this one event instead of a list of all the summer events?

The subnavigation (on the left of the page) offers little help because it contains links to other events by week, by month, and by holiday. There are very few cues as to how to navigate to an actual summer event.

In moving through the site, there tends to be a breakdown in the subnavigation's ability to provide a location to the visitor and a clear relation to additional content. On another page (see Figure 12.7), the breadcrumb navigation reads > Home > Summer Activities, but the subnavigation provides choices of Winter, Summer, Breckenridge Golf Course, Kids Activities, and Activities Information Form. The conflict of information will cause hesitation as the visitor attempts to complete information-gathering tasks, because the instructions to access information are unclear.

Figure 12.7 Breckenridge, Colorado, activities page

Further, the heading of the page is Activities. However, in both the breadcrumb navigation and in the URL bar (which reads `http://www.gobreck.com/page.php?pname=summer/activities/`), Summer is the key navigation term. This is a primary example of the navigation not being supported by the surrounding information. In addition, the usage of white text on a light gray-green background for the breadcrumb navigation creates a very low-contrast element, which nearly hides it from vision. The breadcrumb is a major part of the navigation structure and should always be clearly visible.

When evaluating all the navigational tools available on the page, there is a lack of consistency:

URL: `http://www.gobreck.com/page.php?pname=summer/activities` is displayed on a page that seems to be about activities as a whole, not just summer ones.

Page title: The page title—Breckenridge, Colorado | The Official Web Site for Breckenridge Colorado—is too general, especially when the content is about sporting and outdoor activities available in Breckenridge.

Page heading: Activities.

Subnavigation content heading: None.

Breadcrumb navigation path: > Home > Summer Activities.

The last page in this site example site is a click deeper from the Activities page. By clicking the actual Summer page link from the left navigation bar, something different happens (see Figure 12.8). New visual elements are added to the subnavigation. At this deeper level into site's structure, introducing a new visual cue in the navigation will only serve to confuse the visitor. In addition, the format of the visual cues does not aid the visitor, because the active page is the Summer Activities page, but in the subnavigation, the label for this active page is gray-green text on the green background, another low-contrast presentation. The active page needs to have an active state label (bolder and more contrasting) that shows it as being the most important label in the hierarchy of the navigation, not the least important. Making elements low contrast takes away from their importance.

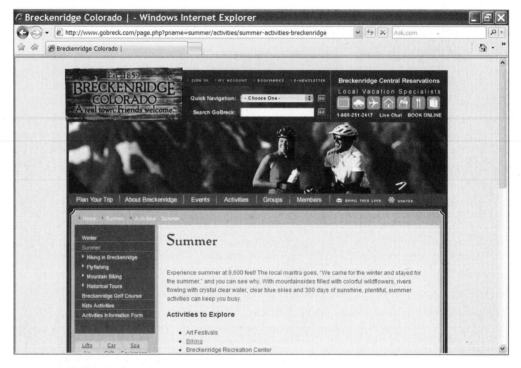

Figure 12.8 Breckenridge, Colorado, summer activities page

Again, the breadcrumb navigation provides a confusing path presented in low contrast: > Home > Summer > Activities Summer. With the URL reflecting a similar structure, it is clear that these two elements are somehow tied together in the site structure and are simply reflecting the direction of the content that has been entered through the content management system. A few corrections in both the content and the site structure could make a major difference in the ability of visitors to navigate the site.

Case Study: Clear Navigation

The second city on the tour is Rapid City, South Dakota. Another tourism destination, it also employs very graphical elements along with a similar type of information such as events and activities. However, the naming convention here provides a more active approach to the navigation labels (see Figure 12.9). The navigation and the words in the navigation are much larger than on the Breckenridge site, allowing for easy viewing and creating a level of importance, because the font size is larger compared to other elements on the page. The heading in the center of the page is the largest size of text, so in the page hierarchy, this is seen as the most important content, "Unpack in Rapid City. Unwind in the Black Hills." The image of the buffalo creates a striking impression of what you might see in Rapid City. Above the main navigation are other choices that are much more specific to the B2B travel and events industry, but the design does not overshadow the primary consumer-focused nature of the primary navigation. The text size is smaller; it blends with the design and provides clear utility for that specific audience.

Figure 12.9 Rapid City, South Dakota, home page

As the visitor navigates further into the website, the usage of both the breadcrumb trail and the subnavigation provides an accompaniment to the content and information on the website (see Figure 12.10). The heading of the subnavigation panel on the left side of the page is repeated, and the options are all listed. Although I would like to see the main navigation heading highlighted in some way on the brown bar, the repetition of the heading on the subnavigation helps.

Figure 12.10 Rapid City, South Dakota: What to Do

Repetition is an important part of reinforcing the content. The information on the What to Do page repeats the subnavigation topics, and the information is presented within a high context of related images. All of the navigation information is consistent and directed:

URL: http://www.visitrapidcity.com/whattodo/

Page title: Rapid City Things to DO – Family Attractions, Shopping, Dining

Page heading: What To Do in Rapid City

Subnavigation content heading: What to Do

Breadcrumb navigation path: Home page > What To Do

In the next level of content, the subnavigation becomes an even more useful tool to help the visitor know their placement within the content structure of the website and the relation to other information. The selected Arts and Culture link becomes bold, indicating that it is the active page (see Figure 12.11). In addition, the content structure of the navigation tools is still consistent because the URL, breadcrumb navigation, page heading, and subnavigation all change to reflect the visitor's location in the Arts & Culture section.

Figure 12.11 Rapid City, South Dakota: What to Do – Arts and Culture

An important note at this point is the subnavigation text feature while on this page. The Arts and Culture text in the subnavigation is larger and bolder, which also makes it more contrasting in comparison with the rest of the navigation choices. This is a visual cue to visitors that this is the active page they are viewing, and the rest are related pages.

As with the earlier pages, the content on the age is then supported with features of the Arts and Culture content, accompanied by links within the content that take the visitor to more information about each activity. The links are provided in context, with a clear separation between content areas, and all of the links utilize clear text in the link. Using text within the link notifies the visitor that further information about the linked text is only a click away. This is important to note! Chapter 16 will go into much more detail about the value of these text links, and this is a great example of presenting links in a highly contextual format.

Utilizing simple layout techniques such as text size, text button contrast, and text color can help visitors easily locate themselves within the content as well as utilize the visual cues for finding related information and the calls to action.

Case Study: Navigation as Beautiful Function

The trends in developing navigation are based on providing the most information that will appeal to the most visitors. This is accomplished by providing multiple paths to information within the site (using the home page as a directional hub, not a destination) and relying less upon the main navigation bar as the only navigation tool. Visitors are able to navigate the site and find important content as it is presented on the page and in various other navigational tools. The primary navigation has had to evolve and provide clear direction to the content within the site but also be tastefully presented in context of the website. Too many drop-downs or flyouts in a menu can cover up the content and create usability problems. One of the more impressive examples of overcoming with these factors is the National Public Radio website, www.NPR.org (see Figure 12.12).

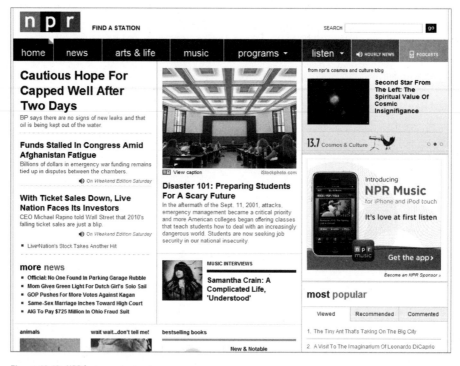

Figure 12.12 NPR home page structure

On this page, the information and top stories are easily visible, because the headlines are bold and larger than the body text. The headlines are different sizes, which relate importance and a hierarchy to the articles. The global navigation runs near the top of the page but is not a primary element of the immediate information display. It is not until a visitor specifically selects one of the main navigation options that a large field of links appears with the specific information (see Figure 12.13).

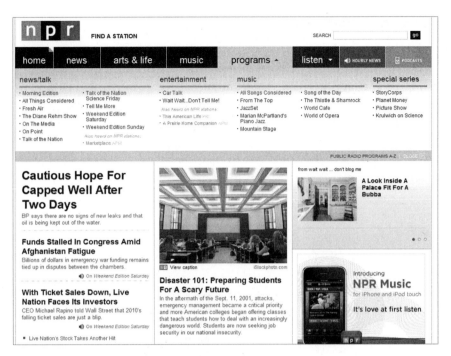

Figure 12.13 NPR "drop-in" navigation

This is a wonderful usability technique, because it exposes information as it is requested by the visitor, rather than taking up valuable page space with links that may not be used or needed by other visitors. The rest of the page is pushed down so that the navigation does not cover up the content but instead displaces it from the top. From a technical perspective, these links are in the code and can be found and followed by the search engines, but to the visitor, they are not presented until requested.

As the Programs tab is selected, the subnavigation element is revealed to show the content separated into groups, accompanied by the relevant links. If I were going to the site specifically to find more information about the show *Car Talk*, I would click Programs and easily find the Car Talk link listed under Entertainment. The global navigation becomes a very functional tool that expands as necessary to allow for a traditional view of content, but it does not supersede the content of the page.

Thursday: Lead with Links, Labels, and Alternative Navigation Techniques

The sites that are developing navigation tools beyond the traditional main navigation bar are employing layouts that allow for more information to be shown on the page but in a way that utilizes space more efficiently and is not overwhelming. By employing the knowledge attained from the card sort and tree test exercises, site owners can develop content associations to create groupings of similar content, presented as links, that speak more directly to visitor needs and to create clear labels that allow those visitors to find their information faster.

Links and Labels

One of my favorite sites for showing grouping, labeling, and linking is Wine.com (see Figure 12.14). With the rotating main image providing clear calls to action, the information surrounding the image is classified into specific groups: Shop for Wine, Send a Gift, Wine Clubs, Wine Accessories, 90+ Rated Under $20, 2009 Bordeaux Futures, and Wedding Gifts. Within each of those groups, there are at least three links of specific content.

Figure 12.14 Wine.com: lots of direction to lots of information

The grouped classification of these groups of links, along with a clear group label, provides an easy visual path through the information. The group labels are clear enough to view quickly and then return to explore topics further. The main navigation at the top of the page becomes nearly obsolete by the amount of topical information displayed on the page.

As a visitor goes further into the site, the content is broken down further, becoming more granular but also increasing the amount of information packed into a relatively small visual space (see Figure 12.15).

The classification of wine is a tricky process, because people tend to shop for wines in various ways. Besides the basic red and white differentiation, people like to see choices but tend to be easily overwhelmed when they see those choices. By

breaking up the amazing amount of information and inventory into practical groupings of links, the information becomes much more tangible and can be easily scanned
and processed by a visitor.

Figure 12.15 Wine.com: more groupings in deeper pages

Again, on the Wine Shop page, there are major content groups with clear labels:
most popular links, price, type, style, region, ratings, best deals, and more. These topics
are clear based on the bold text and the font size, which establishes a topical hierarchy.
There are nearly 200 links on the page, but the organization, presentation, and clear topical labels allow the visitor to quickly make sense of the amount of available information.

Alternative Navigation Techniques

For sites with a lot of product content, providing filters has become a space-saving
method for allowing visitors to navigate to specific content. Both Lands' End and
Brooks Brothers provide tools for filtering through the ties, rather than simply browsing through hundreds of images (see Figure 12.16). The tools provide alternative navigation tools for drilling down into the content, which is very helpful for those visitors
who know exactly what they want or need.

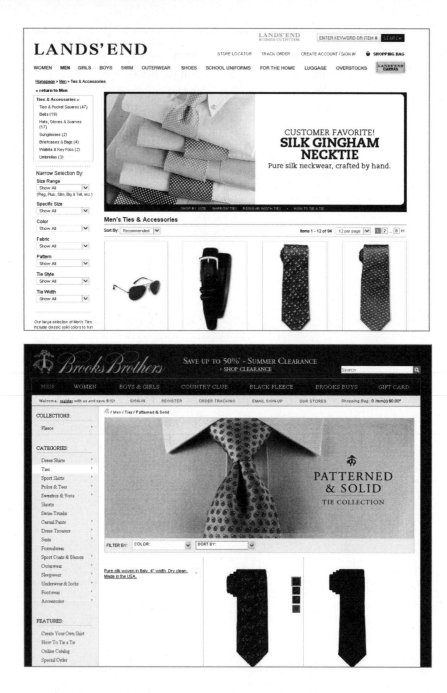

Figure 12.16 Land's End and Brooks Brothers navigation elements

By providing these tools alongside the ability to browse rather than replacing the browsing fully, the sites give both "browsers" and "hunters" the ability to shop in the way that is most comfortable to them.

Interestingly enough, both of these websites do something different once a visitor has browsed to the product content. The subnavigation on the left side drops out entirely but is replaced on the right side with suggested matching shirts at Brooks Brothers. On Lands' End, there are other suggested tie options (see Figure 12.17).

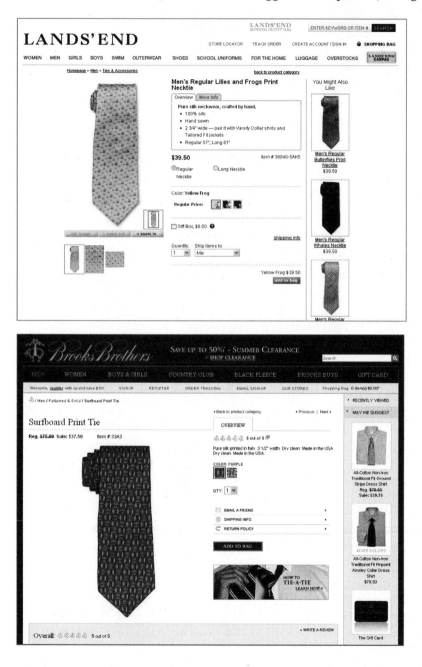

Figure 12.17 Lands' End and Brooks Brothers: both sites drop the left-side subnavigation once a specific product is chosen.

Despite the absence of the left-side navigation, the breadcrumb navigation underneath the main navigation on both sites is in a very obvious place, which allows the visitor easy access to go back to main area content. Even if the visitor goes to a previous page, they are doing so without using the Back button. When visitors use the Back button, it is mainly because there is no visible option that will take them ahead, so they go backward. Providing tools for the visitor to continue going forward, even though it is back to a previous page, the visitor is still making progress. Research shows that the use of breadcrumb navigation improves site efficiency (*Proceedings of the Human Factors and Ergonomics Society 46th Annual Meeting, 1315-1319*, Maldanado & Resnik, 2002; *Navigation bars for hierarchical websites*, Bowler, Ng & Schwartz, 2001).

AT&T uses multiple navigation styles in its home page (Figure 12.18). Because of the amount and the different types of customer segments and shoppers, the information on the home page is designed to "catch" as many people as possible. There is tabbed navigation across the top for market segments. The "main" navigation is along the top of the large graphic that is used for time-sensitive or other offers. The bottom two rows offer a significant amount of information and choices of offers, bundles, local service, and Internet access, all with graphical elements. On the bottom row of the page, the links are mostly functional for existing customers but are grouped in six columns of no more than four links. This allows for customers to quickly scan the column labels, find their need, and locate it quickly by the relevant link.

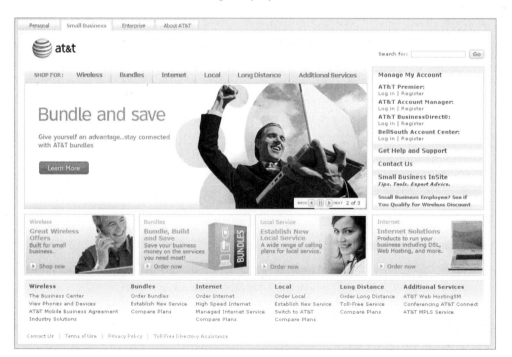

Figure 12.18 AT&T's website segments customer and shopper needs

Friday: Develop Using Wireframes

Wireframing is a design function that can increase the speed of creating or changing your websites, online marketing, and other landing pages. Wireframes are a visual development tool used to show the basic visual elements and interactions on a page. Similar to card sorting and tree testing, it has a very basic element that starts simple and then moves on to very complex layouts. However, just the simple act of developing wireframes can begin to communicate important elements and functions of a website, rather than leaving them up to interpretation.

The essential task of wireframing is quickly communicating the layout and interaction points of a web page. This can be done on paper, whiteboard, or software developed specifically for this task. Either way, this enables a team of people to see the layout, assign content categories, add labels, and do various functions prior to the design of the website.

As mentioned earlier in this chapter, not too long ago the focus was mainly on a graphic artist to build a site based on the direction and information they were given, which was typically none to very little, and interpret that information into a vision for how they envisioned a typical user entering the website. This has changed in recent years as good designers have added interactive development to their skill sets. By developing skills in information architecture, web and application developers/designers can translate complex information into a skillfully designed interface for users. As the online marketing industry has matured, the emphasis on the information as the cornerstone of development has started to replace the emphasis on solely aesthetic design. The emphasis on type of business, nature of the visitors, and goals of profit and conversion have started to develop multiple niches of expertise in understanding the structure of the website focused on the goals. Both are necessary elements, but the goal of the websites is always paramount, because all measurement is based upon the final goal.

To put it in practical terms, the first step in developing or improving your online marketing effort is to identify your business goals. Second, know your customer. This is developed by implementing the tactics outlined in earlier chapters, including interviews, questionnaires, persona development, and keyword research. After those steps, apply card sorting and tree testing to better understand how your customers see and organize information and apply keywords in developing content groups.

The Business Case for Wireframing

From an investment standpoint, wireframing focuses on the development of the information flow, and the process of developing that information is a critical communication process between those developing the website and those commissioning the website, whether they are in the same business entity or not. The guesswork and interpretation of the business goals are developed with the business integrated in the entire process, rather than the old model of an agency interpreting the website and providing a product to the business.

Wireframing is a design tool that enables the design process. By clearly defining the layout, function, and textual elements for layout and communication, the time and investment for development decrease significantly. Endless iterations and edits are reduced significantly, because wireframes provide the structure and detail first, rather than structure and detail being afterthoughts added as the website is developed.

By providing the details of the layout up front, the flurry of changes and surprises that typically preclude a website launch are reduced, or maybe eliminated, as all parties involved in the process have agreed to the wireframes and all are starting with the same goal in mind. The wireframe is the design document that drives the process.

The more detailed the wireframe is developed, the faster and less expensive the site-design process becomes. Investing in the predevelopment of the website pays off large dividends in time and processes. As any developer can attest, endless iterations cost everyone in the process hours and over-budget stress. Reduce these expenses drastically by investing in development of a wireframe goal first and then developing from the wireframe. You'll find that the process becomes smoother and streamlined as everyone understands the final product at the beginning of the project.

Start Simple

Wireframing applies all the knowledge and findings from the testing and develops structure to the knowledge. My preference is for everything to start on a whiteboard so that changes can be made quickly and easily. Using a whiteboard allows multiple pages to be outlined quickly, and many people can be part of the process, bringing needed information to the dynamic.

In the whiteboard process, I find that speed and repeated changes are essential. Perfection is not the goal; this is simply an initial method of gathering important information and ideas into the initial formation of particular pages. Typical key pages that are outlined in this manner are the home page, category page, product page, article page, search result page, and conversion process (checkout or lead generation form). The key pages are defined by the business goals for the visitors and will change based on the purposes of your website.

This process ensures that important information is included from the start such as in the calls to action, footer information, related articles, or related products. These are the typical design elements that tend to be afterthoughts, but when developed into the wireframing process, they are not a surprise and are included early, thereby making the entire page flow with the information with a focus on the business goals of the website and the calls to action that fulfill those goals.

Building Blocks

The next stage of wireframing is to use blocks to designate important areas of pages, such as text blocks (primary, secondary, related, footer, and so on), navigation areas, calls to action, and graphic elements. This stage develops the size of the page and the size of the elements from the initial layouts. This is where the first set of guidelines is established as the size of the blocked areas and the relationships between those block sizes are analyzed and measured to fit the screen width (see Figure 12.19).

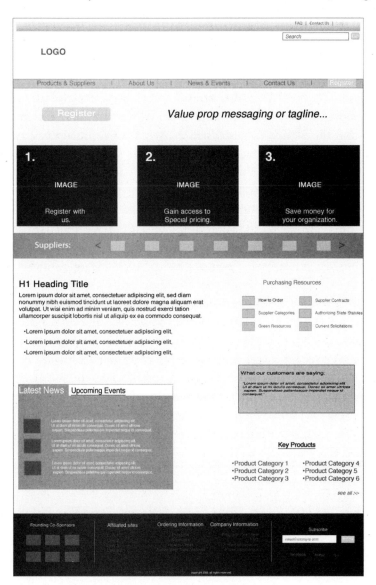

Figure 12.19 Develop size relationships between elements.

Different block areas can be designated by different colors. This wireframe uses combinations of black and gray for text areas, green as action items, and blue as linked content or images. The primary purpose at this stage is the layout and size of the page elements and developing clear relationships between the elements in order to ensure that the message and purpose of the page is clear and that the calls to action are in place.

Iterations at this point consist of placement and size changes, and the beginnings of the labeling scheme can be developed at this point. Content is being developed behind the scenes, because the pages and structure have been defined, and the content can follow as the wireframes become more detailed.

Functional Layouts

Once the spatial relationships have been defined, the wireframes can move on to the final stages. Some prefer just to provide the layouts with specific function labels rather than put content in place, but the more clearly defined the wireframe, the more efficiently the development of the site will progress.

In this stage of wireframing, details are more developed. What follows is the development phase in which programmers implement function and artists apply graphics, color schemes, and layout. That isn't to say that font sizes, color schemes, and white space can't be defined in these stages; in fact, it may help the development as more detail work is applied and approved prior to the coding of the website.

If any special functions are necessary for navigational aids, visual cues, or other behaviors, these are noted in the functional layout specification. Scripts that will be necessary to expose text, tab-based navigation, or other functions on the page should be defined regarding how it will be developed and scripted and any specific language necessary for the function. By identifying these scripted tools on the website, any roadblocks to search crawlers or accessibility can be identified early and dealt with by change or adaptation.

A finished wireframe can provide enough detail that it can look and feel exactly like a website (see Figure 12.20). Many wireframes in the finished state can be easily coded into the live site, and the function and flow of the site can be witnessed and tested.

As mentioned, investing in this process saves both time and money. Defining layouts, functions, content paths, content arrangement, and flow are all handled in advance and can be agreed upon prior to developing a design and suffering through endless iterations. When goals are clearly defined and interpreted through the wireframes, the iteration process is limited because the business case has been made early, and all decisions are focused on the end result of conversions and profits.

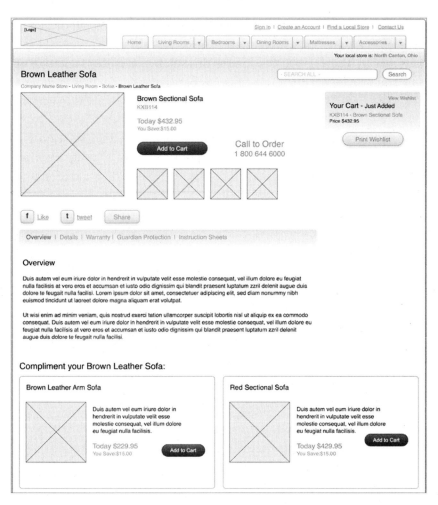

Figure 12.20 Functional wireframe providing all necessary elements for the next stage of design

Review and Hands-On

Take a second look at your home page. Do you view it as a destination for your visitors or as a direction to the information contained on the website? Are visitors able to quickly see your business benefits and the available content in a fast, friendly format?

Previous assignments have asked you to get third-party opinions of elements on your site. Ideally, some of those have remarked about the home page and the navigation used in your website. What have people said? Have their comments reflected your page as a destination or as a direction to the content?

Is your main navigation the only function available to find information? Are you limiting visitors to a single tool for exploring your website? How many navigational aids are you providing, and are they understandable?

Start with just a basic card sort by yourself, and then invite others to participate. After you start to understand how people are generating groups, ask a few customers if they wouldn't mind helping you improve your website. Again, this can be as easy as starting with index cards or sticky notes and as complex as subscribing to an online service. Either way, you will learn more about your website and the organization of your content.

Evaluate your main navigation:

- Does it employ visual cues that show the hierarchy of information from within the website?
- Do the words within the navigation support the section of content and the content presented?
- Are all the navigation tools consistent in the presentation?

From an interior page on the site, complete this quick evaluation to check for consistency among the navigation elements:

- URL (What words are used in the URL, if any? Do the words match the content of the page?)
- Page title
- Page heading
- Subnavigation content heading
- Breadcrumb navigation path

Are you using elements of text size, contrast, and text color combinations to show a clear relation of the current page in relation to other pages and topics available?

How can you take important information and package it into a visually impactful container that utilizes a clear topic label and four to six clear links to deeper information?

Have you looked at your analytics to see the popular content or popular pages within your site based on topics?

What are people looking for when they come to your site? Is it easily shown on the home page and throughout the site in the form of related or topical content?

Wireframe the key pages of your current website. You don't have to be exact, and don't get fancy—a simple sketch will do. If you would like to make wireframes on your computer, simple programs such as Microsoft Word or PowerPoint and Apple Pages contain the basic elements necessary to get started.

Wireframe the key pages of a few other websites to get an idea of how they are arranged by content area and functions.

When adding a new landing page or page, section, or advertisement to your website, start by wireframing, and answer as many questions as you can early in the process, rather than afterward. Make sure that your business goal and visitor goals are primary elements in your designs.

Week 10: Design for Accessibility

Accessibility is one of the most overlooked and misunderstood issues for online marketing and website development. This chapter focuses on the basics of accessibility and its business value. The serendipity of accessibility is simply amazing because issues addressed by accessibility actually make websites easier to use for everybody. Not only that, but search engines rely on the very same things that assistive technology needs for full accessibility.

Chapter Contents

Monday: Get Familiar with Accessibility

Accessibility, to most people, is making sure your site can be used by visitors who are blind, deaf, or reading impaired. The technology that is used to help people access the content on your site is called *assistive technology*. This allows people to access the content, functions, and abilities just like any other visitor. However, in order for the assistive technology to work properly and allow the same level of access to everyone, there are required programming elements. These programming elements are sometimes seen as intrusive or expensive modifications, but in reality, accessibility is simply good business. The same needs that assistive technology users have are also the same needs of and functions used by search engines. The bottom line is that accessibility for people benefits your search engine visibility as well.

National Federation of the Blind vs. Target

In February 2006, the business case of accessibility was thrust into the public eye. The prominent American retailer Target became the focus of a lawsuit brought by an individual and the National Federation of the Blind. The president of that organization said, "Blind customers should have the same access to Target's online service that Target offers its sighted customers." A judge deemed that the website could be sued just as the physical store could be sued.

Alternative Attributes

There were three primary areas in which the Target website failed to serve those who were blind and using assistive technology. The first issue was a lack of *alternative attributes*, also known as alt attributes or alt text. As discussed in Chapter 5, an alt attribute is the text that shows up on a web page if the image is not available. This may happen for a variety of reasons such as slow connection speed, server timeout, or heavy network traffic. I've been at busy conventions where the Internet has slowed to a crawl because of all of the trade show vendors, mobile devices, and laptops trying to access the Internet from the same location.

alt attributes are critical, especially when the replaced image is a call to action, such as a subscribe action, add to cart, or simply an instruction for the next step in a process. If the image is not available and there is no alt attribute, then there are no instructions provided to the visitor.

The primary assistive technology device used by blind users is a screen reader, of which JAWS by Freedom Scientific is the most pervasive. Assistive technology takes the information from the text of a web page and translates it into a device that is usable for nonsighted or low-sighted users. JAWS will read the text of a web page so that a blind visitor can hear the content, make selections, and continue the process.

The collision in usability comes when assistive technology cannot access the required information to communicate to the visitor. In that case, the visitor is left to either troubleshoot and navigate the website without instructions or leave and go to another website to accomplish their task. When alt attributes are not used for images, important instructions may be unavailable to assistive technology users.

Figure 13.1 shows a page from the Baby section of the Target website in 2006. It covers a lot of content. For sighted users, this page is very easy to navigate and understand.

Figure 13.1 The Target website's Baby section

However, because the majority of content of the website is actually pictures and pictures of text, there is very little information available to the visitor if the images do not load into the browser (see Figure 13.2). When the images do not load, there is nothing other than navigation links. A visitor cannot understand what content is available on the page, where they are, and what they can do. There is no instruction, content, or any information that helps the visitor.

To anyone using assistive technology, this is especially frustrating, because the screen reader is mute. There is no content on the page, so little content is read. Only the links are read to the assistive technology user, so they are the only content on the page.

What makes this style of website development even more egregious to the nonsighted user is the amount of calls to action, sales, discounts, and free shipping offered that are available only through images (see Figure 13.3). The image links are made to look like text but are not text and, thus, not available.

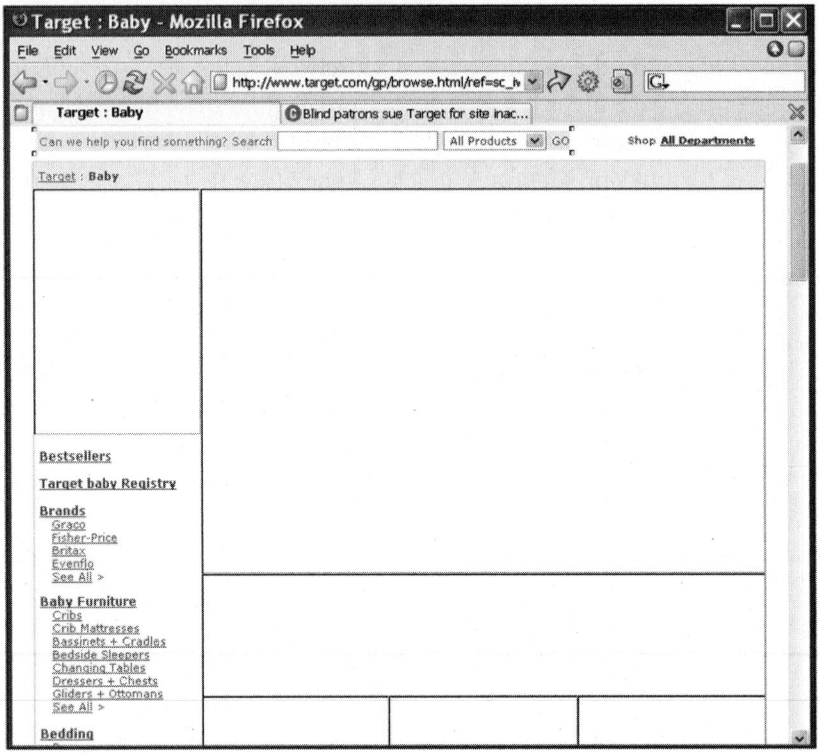

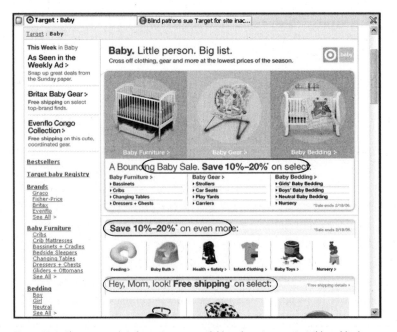

Figure 13.2 Target.com Baby section with no images

Figure 13.3 Target.com sale information was available only on images, invisible to blind users.

Image Maps

A second main issue addressed in the lawsuit (though closely related to `alt` attributes in this case) was *image maps*. Image maps are images that provide links to multiple destinations based on where the visitor clicks the image. If a visitor cannot see the image, then the image map and the links provided are useless. None of the images maps on the Target website provided alternative attributes.

Mouse-Only Programming

The third issue raised was that part of the website was programmed specifically for user interaction through a mouse. Only a mouse click and mouse navigation could navigate through a section of the website. Though rarely deployed by sighted users, most websites allow for keyboard-based navigation using the arrow, Tab, and Enter keys. This may come as a surprise to some, but the mouse is a vision-oriented tool, because it relies on eye-hand coordination. Blind assistive technology users "read" by hearing the content read to them and navigate by using the keyboard as the primary interface tool. When a command is programmed to execute only by a mouse click, then keyboard users cannot continue in the process.

This lawsuit brought a number of issues to light and also provided a means for the accessibility community to voice their needs for using websites. However, all three of the major issues raised by the lawsuit were not issues solely for the benefit of the accessibility community. For instance, any number of circumstances could cause the images on a website not to show, and any user, sighted or otherwise, would be at a loss for further instructions.

Contingency Planning

I was staying at a busy hotel during a large technology convention. The speed of the connection was so slow that when I attempted to connect to the Internet in my hotel room, I wasn't sure I was successful. The connection timed out, only a few images loaded, and none of the images had alternative attributes. I was left to guess which area of the site to click in order to gain access. This is a helpless feeling and one that assistive technology visitors experience often.

Providing alternative attributes and keyboard navigation, rather than mouse-only, allows visitors, regardless of vision, easier access to a site's functions. Developers always should make contingency plans for something being out of their control. Part of that contingency planning is the use of the alternative attribute in images. No one can control how their website will be rendered on a device, which browser will load it, how fast the connection speed will be, or what other programs may be running to help the visitor understand the website. When making contingency plans for these types of situations, alternative attributes are simply smart business.

Search

The improvements that the NFB was asking from Target would have ultimately made the Target website better for search engines. Outside of the lawsuit, one could make an argument for the business case of fixing these issues for the site to be more search engine friendly. Adding alt attributes to images would enable the search engines to get more context from the pages and images on the Target website. In addition, replacing more of the text that was contained in pictures with HTML text would have helped even more—for both assistive technology users and search engines.

This is one of the most amazingly overlooked issues in accessibility. That is, that the needs of search engines and of assistive technologies are often the same need to be able to gather the HTML text from the page and interpret the markup of the text: headlines, headings, linked text, bullet points, content, and image alt attributes. Both need to be able to read, interpret, and output the content. Search engines need to store it and use it for the ranking algorithm. For assistive technology users, it needs to be read, processed, or manipulated and output for various devices. Either way, if a designer or website owner neglects the principles of accessibility, they are also neglecting the very things that search engines need. This is discussed in more detail in the next section.

Search Bots and Assistive Technology

Have you read Google's Webmaster Guidelines yet? If not, then you need to do so. Chapter 4 outlined some of the important aspects of the guidelines, so it is well worth it to refresh yourself on the content. Here's the link:

www.google.com/support/webmasters/bin/answer.py?hl=en&answer=35769

Three areas are specifically outlined to help webmasters assess their websites for search engine friendliness: design and content, technical, and quality. For accessibility, I am going to focus on the first two.

The factors I want to emphasize from the design and content section are as follows:

- Make a site with a clear hierarchy and text links. Every page should be reachable from at least one static text link.

- Create a useful, information-rich site, and write pages that clearly and accurately describe your content.

- Think about the words users would type to find your pages, and make sure your site actually includes those words within it.

- Try to use text instead of images to display important names, content, or links. The Google crawler doesn't recognize text contained in images. If you must use images for textual content, consider using the alt attribute to include a few words of descriptive text.

- Make sure that your `<title>` elements and `alt` attributes are descriptive and accurate.
- Check for broken links and correct HTML.

Interestingly, the Google guidelines have included the use of the `alt` attribute since they were first published. Simply following this list in the development or maintenance of a website could save many business owners and developers from troubles with search engines.

From the technical section, the following issues have accessibility at the core:

- Use a text browser such as Lynx to examine your site, because most search engine spiders see your site much as Lynx would. If fancy features such as JavaScript, cookies, session IDs, frames, DHTML, or Flash keep you from seeing all of your site in a text browser, then search engine spiders may have trouble crawling your site.
- Allow search bots to crawl your sites without session IDs or arguments that track their path through the site. These techniques are useful for tracking individual user behavior, but the access pattern of bots is entirely different. Using these techniques may result in incomplete indexing of your site, because bots may not be able to eliminate URLs that look different but actually point to the same page.
- Test your site to make sure it appears correctly in different browsers.

The next list of pertinent checkpoints is from the W3C Web Content Accessibility Guidelines (WCAG):

`www.w3.org/TR/2006/WD-WCAG20-20060427/Overview.html#contents`

- Guideline 1.1: Provide text alternatives for all nontext content.
- Guideline 1.3: Ensure that information and structure can be separated from presentation.
- Guideline 2.1: Make all functionality operable via a keyboard interface.
- Guideline 2.4: Provide mechanisms to help users find content, orient themselves within it, and navigate through it.
- Guideline 2.5: Help users avoid mistakes, and make it easy to correct mistakes that do occur.
- Guideline 3.1: Make text content readable and understandable.
- Guideline 3.2: Make the placement and functionality of content predictable.
- Guideline 4.1: Support compatibility with current and future user agents (including assistive technologies).
- Guideline 4.2: Ensure that content is accessible or provide an accessible alternative.

When you read the content of these guidelines, you'll notice similar themes in both sets. Themes of using text alternatives include `alt` attributes and transcripts for podcasts or captioning for video. Both sets of guidelines address using proper HTML coding, using content to meet the needs of site visitors, and testing the website with various browsers, interfaces, and operating systems in order to test the accessibility for both users and search engines. The list of needs for users and for search engines is amazingly similar. In fact, the old WCAG checklist was more restrictive and detailed in the checklist but nearly mirrored the Google guidelines. This link provides a comparison between the old 1.0 guidelines and the 2.0 guidelines. I still recommend businesses and site developers become familiar with both, because they are invaluable throughout the development and assessment processes.

www.w3.org/TR/2006/WD-WCAG20-20060427/appendixD.html

The bottom line is that search engines are the most disabled users that will ever come to your website. They can't read images, view video, hear audio files, or understand the hierarchy of content without HTML markup being used. They are simply looking for text and rely upon the same technology as most assistive technology. Make your site accessible for all users, regardless of computer, operating system, browser type, and device or any assistive technology, and you have made a website that is clearly open for business for the search engines.

Tuesday: Learn the Intricacies of Accessibility

Accessibility is not a horizontal approach where one single technique is used on a sliding scale to meet the needs of a group of people, and the higher you move the slider, the more people are provided access. Unfortunately, it doesn't work that way. What does exist is an amazing testament to the human will to overcome a variety of unique factors.

Interestingly, most low-vision or assistive technology users prefer Google or Ask as their primary search engine. Overwhelmingly, it is because of the interface. Both Google and Ask feature a stripped-down interface rather than a portal-style interface, such as Yahoo! and MSN. Portal interfaces do not score well with low-vision, blind, or assistive technology users because of the "noise" it creates in the experience.

Google's Accessible Search Project

In the summer of 2006, Google released an Accessible Search Beta through its Labs projects. The Accessible Search was the personal project of Dr. T.V. Raman, who came to Google about a year prior. The move by Google to release the project came on the heels of Google changing from the visual-based security device of the CAPTCHA, where users have to type the letters that they see in an image (Figure 13.4). Blind users were not able to access many Google services, such as Gmail, Blogger, Google Groups, and a Google account because the visual-based security kept them from participating in Google's services. Google added an audio component as a response to online petitions and outcry from the visually impaired users.

Dr. Raman comes from a background of advocating standards-based programming and structured data on the Web. This made its way to the Accessible Search algorithm that favors WCAG standards-based websites. This was a natural method of creating the accessible focus of the search.

Figure 13.4 The CAPTCHA is designed as a test to screen out human visitors from undesired "bots."

The Accessible Search was received positively by the blind community, yet many low-vision users took issue with the tagline used in the search interface of "Search for the Visually Impaired." This was typical of larger issues faced by the accessibility community that many sites are accessible for blind users, yet the same amount of accessibility is not available to low-vision users, who require different methods in order to access the content. Low vision users require high levels of contrast and increased text size, while blind users do not require any contrast or text size controls or information.

Despite the contention among the different groups, Google is widely accepted as the search engine of choice for accessibility. The main reason is the uncluttered interface, which makes it easy for users using magnification interfaces, screen readers, or joystick interfaces. The reception to Accessible Search was positive overall. The end result was that users found this to be a useful tool. "And that's our goal," said Dr. Raman. See the "A Chat with Google's T.V. Raman, Developer of Google's Accessible Search" sidebar for more detailed insights from Raman.

A Chat with Google's T.V. Raman, Developer of Google's Accessible Search

Work hasn't stopped for future development of Google's Accessible Search. Recently, the Accessible Search has been improved to give blind users access to the same advanced search features that are available in the regular Google search.

Dr. Raman, who has been intimately involved with building speech-enabled interfaces for many years, sees the Google Accessible Search as "a good first step in delivering the most accessible information online" and believes that Google will continue to develop ways to be more accessible. He welcomes any user feedback; he says, "We get better when we know what works for the user and welcome feedback on everything from improving taglines to adding new features." Based on this, there are thriving discussions on the Google Groups Accessible topic.

Dr. Raman thinks the impact of the Accessible Search will go beyond a simple service and one that will affect the development of the Web. "I hope that as we continue to improve Accessible Search, we'll have a long-term positive impact on increasing awareness of the need to create clean, accessible web content."

Continues

A Chat with Google's T.V. Raman, Developer of Google's Accessible Search *(Continued)*

In evaluating the sites that ranked highly in the Accessible Search, it was obvious that there were elements of standards-based programming (W3C and Accessibility Guidelines) that favored more text-based websites. Dr. Raman noted there are consistent factors that contribute to this observation. "For accessibility, clean, well-structured semantic markup is the best thing you could hope to have," he says. The three key words *clean*, *well-structured*, and *semantic* are all important. Adherence to specs definitely makes checking easier. He notes that it is entirely possible to create web pages that could pass the automated accessibility tests but could also end up not being truly accessible, which could then be used to "game" the system. But he also stresses the importance of creating "clean, well-formed XHTML content" in that "over time, websites will find it significantly easier to serve all their users better—simply because their content will be easier to manage and evolve."

The big question was how helpful the `alt` attribute was for rankings. Most Google engineers are very tight-lipped about any search factor and its value in the algorithm, but Dr. Raman explains the importance of this small factor for both users and search engines, "Google scores alt attributes appropriately, and things like stuffing a 14-page essay into an `alt` tag won't help you rank better and will annoy your users. We encourage users to use `alt` and `title` tags in the best way for users, and that work well for Google as well."

The Moving Target of Accessibility

When working on large accessibility projects, I have been amazed at the varying attitudes and comments that are made, usually off-handedly. Most attempt to marginalize the importance of accessibility by rationalizing the need to overlook the stringent programming factors with the reasoning that "We only have to make this accessible for less than 1 percent of people." The motivating factor for being accessible seems to be, simply, not to get sued.

What amazes me the most is the ground that has to be covered in creating a comprehensive accessibility plan. The very moment you dismiss something as being "irrelevant" or "a small percentage," you've missed the entire point of the project. Accessibility is a matter of allowing people to access information in a method that is understandable and usable. The difficulty intrinsic to the project is the variance among assistive technology and the access methods, as illustrated in the following sections.

Factors in Vision Accessibility

It is best to consider vision accessibility as a continuum; you can start with low vision as a starting point, because that is the beginning stages of assistive technology. Usually low vision can be overcome with screen magnifiers or, at minimum, increased text size within a browser. Both also benefit from high-contrast settings. Low vision can be the result of multiple factors such as age, health, eye disease, cataracts, and other various health factors.

On the other side of low vision is no vision. This group uses screen readers, Braille displays, or a combination of the two. (Note that not all blind users know Braille.) For the interface to a website or system, the assistive technology devices are usually Braille keyboards and speech-to-text programs.

In between these two ends of the continuum are various factors that affect vision, such as color blindness and dyslexia. Color blindness will be the subject of Wednesday's content. Even color blindness has different factors and levels of visibility.

Case Studies in Low Vision and Blindness

To better understand some of the issues that people face and the assistive technology that they use to browse and interact online, I interviewed a series of people with widely different experiences. When hearing their stories, I am amazed at the innovation in the digital industry, and I also understand better the things that I can do to make my website a better experience.

Lee: Low Vision

Lee has albinism, and one of the main factors is low vision. Lee is a long-time computer and Internet user and has had extremely low vision since birth. She says search engines, and the Internet in general, have been a boon to her:

Growing up, there were many things that I had difficulty reading (e.g., phone books). The Internet has opened up a whole new world for me, and search engines have helped me organize it.

She relies on Apple's built-in magnification software in her daily browsing. *She prefers to view yellow or white text on a black background for added contrast.* She prefers to use the search engine Big.com, which is powered by Yahoo! Big.com is built specifically for low-vision users, enabling them to read the large-font results without eye strain.

Lee explains how she sees:

I have a difficulty seeing details at a distance. I also have problems reading small print and light and glare are issues as well. I have nystagmus (an uncontrollable and irregular motion of the eyes). The world doesn't move, but my brain has to work harder to provide a stable image. Eye fatigue is an issue. Compared to most people with albinism, I have fairly good vision and am able to get by with minor modifications.

Continues

Google's accessibility search is based on blind readers who rely on screen-reading software; Lee relies on high-contrast text to read. However, she also uses Google Search but not as much. "I'd love to see the ability to store interface preferences in a cookie. I want to go to Google and automatically have it show up as light text on a dark background. I can do it through the OS, but in many applications, it is a hindrance. So, if Google would let me do it, that would be great."

Lee is very active in the albinism community. She thinks search engines respond to the accessibility community very slowly and that information passes slowly as a "trickle-down" effect.

Chris: Blindness

Chris is a JAWS power user; in fact, he had a major hand in its development. He is blind but is able to use the Internet and related technologies faster than most sighted persons. He has been online long before HTML was the protocol and used to use Emacs as an interface to a chat program.

Chris prefers Google and Ask, mainly for the clean interfaces they offer, but also likes using search pages designed for hackers, especially when searching for technical information. No matter which search engine he uses, he is able to use all of the tricks in JAWS to filter out the noise and find specific information.

Chris understands the frustration of users who don't understand how to use JAWS:

Unfortunately, most users don't know about or care to invest the time in learning how to access such things quickly, so [they] struggle with "accessibility." I think, on search engines, the greatest accessibility problems are no longer issues that can be corrected with the WAI [Web Accessibility Initiative] or [Section] 508 guidelines but, rather, are design principles for usability. What is "usable" to people with varying levels of vision impairment has hardly been studied and those of us interested in doing so are few and far between. So, in my opinion, moving from "accessible" to "usable" will take another decade.

To Chris, and many others, it is a factor of usability, which is why Google and Ask get high marks for their simple interfaces. Yahoo! and MSN searches are not rated highly because of the portal-style interfaces loaded with information and links, which is "too noisy." Search engines that use the Turing test to filter bots (CAPTCHA) are also a huge obstacle to enjoying many of the custom features.

Overall, Chris says that search engines have improved as a whole, mainly by integrating more accessibility and standards-based programming into their results pages. But no matter what anyone says, he still finds Flash to be an "accessibility nightmare." He seeks information that "is best expressed as text or audio."

Cognitive

Screen readers are not just used in the assistive vision realm. Many people with dyslexia, which falls into the cognitive disorder category, use screen readers to assist in reading and interpreting the content. These users rely on the design, colors, and overall presentation of the site as cues, but the reality is that most of these users have excellent vision but still use a screen reader to reinforce their reading order of words.

This is important to note, because many programmers would simply dump anyone using a screen reader into a text-only version of an application or website. However, knowing that not all users of screen readers can be lumped into the vision category interrupts this line of thinking.

Physical

Perhaps the most amazing category of assistive technology devices is in the physical category. I am always amazed to see the amount of creativity in this area, from large-key keyboards and speech-to-text programs, both of which are also used by low-vision users, to laser pointer keyboards, headset pointers, and an amazing array of similar devices. There is so much crossover in the types of access that to lump accessibility into a small percentage of specific users is to ignore the bigger picture.

A Case Study in Cerebral Palsy

Glenda has an inspirational story and wrote a book about overcoming cerebral palsy and building a life for herself. Glenda uses a combination of assistive technologies to interact online.

Her main input device is a keyboard on a nonslip mat. This is critical as she slides her hand along the top of the keyboard and uses her left thumb to hit each key. Any movement or involuntary jerk would move the keyboard if not for the nonslip mat. This also affects her use of a standard mouse. In its place she uses a joystick to control the cursor movements. Along with this, she uses word prediction software that predicts the words that she is typing, which saves on keystrokes.

Glenda does not have any vision impairments, but she relies on interfaces that are clear, are simple, and have a consistent design. The consistent design makes it easier for her to find information, while cluttered pages and flashing animation distract her from easily navigating the page. She prefers the Google Toolbar because of the simple interface and availability for searches.

Even though she is a 10-year Internet user, she relies on simple interfaces to use websites, read pages, and interact. She does not need the low-vision or blind accessibility features but rather features that enable her to input information easily and do not distract her by moving or flashing elements.

Global

To put it simply, anyone who complains that the text they encounter on the Web is too small can benefit from assistive technology. Anyone who has arthritis or other physical limitation to typing or using a mouse can benefit from assistive technology.

Many accessible tools are built into Microsoft's Internet Explorer browser, as well as Windows operating systems. The Firefox browser has multiple extensions that create additional layers of accessibility as unique as the users themselves. Apple Macs and PowerBooks are very well known for their assistive technology abilities and tend to be preferred by those who are extremely active online. A multitude of Internet users employ accessibility tools, and creating accessibility resources and an accessible website serves those users as well as your business.

Wednesday: Understand Color Blindness and Contrast

Most people tend to think of accessibility as a blind-only issue. However, color blindness affects a large number of the population and affects the ability of people to distinguish between various colors. The most common is red-green color blindness. The accessibility issue facing color-blind visitors is that colors that are used as primary information devices are simply lost or unclear, because the colors are indistinguishable. The only way to ensure that a feature of importance is communicated effectively beyond color is contrast.

Color blindness is something that affects about 8 percent of the male population. Color-blind women tend not to be as affected as men, and color blindness among women is not as prevalent. Estimates are far-ranging on this issue, because rates of color blindness seem to be higher in certain countries, mostly the United States and Europe.

In addition to color blindness, the simple process of aging creates numerous vision issues. As we age, our vision naturally loses acuity. Colors dim as our vision becomes less sharp and blurrier. For adults older than 40, the ability to focus is more difficult, because the lens in the eye naturally hardens. People compensate for this with reading glasses, bifocals, or even surgery.

The definition of accessibility increases all the time when you consider the amount of vision issues and difficulties of people as they grow older and also attempt to do more online. It is critical that pages provide enough contrast in order to make content easier to read and tasks easier to accomplish.

On Monday the Web Content Accessibility Guidelines (WCAG) were used to show the importance of keeping search engines in mind. For this emphasis on contrast, I am going to go to both the earlier version of the WCAG 1.0 and the later 2.0 version. The earlier version is much more specific in terms of contrast. But the 2.0 version provides some very clear testing procedures for contrast ratios.

Guidelines for Contrast

WCAG 1.0 introduces contrast like this:

2.1 Ensure that all information conveyed by color is also available without color.

2.2 Ensure that foreground and background color combinations provide sufficient contrast when viewed by someone having color deficits or when viewed on a black and white screen.

I can't say enough about high-contrast text online. I seem to be able to find at least one website a week using blue text on a light blue background or, even worse, blue or grey text on a black background. I am also noticing a lot more light gray text on white backgrounds, which maybe seems "artsy" but is much more difficult to read. The text on the site needs to be big enough and contrasting enough to allow for easy reading. Unless you want to hide your message, make it easy to read.

WCAG 2.0 increases the responsibility but also provides specific information for measuring contrast.

Guideline 1.3 : Ensure that information and structure can be separated from presentation

1.3.2 Any information that is conveyed by color is also visually evident without color.

1.3.4 Information that is conveyed by variations in presentation of text is also conveyed in text, or the variations in presentation of text can be programmatically determined.

1.3.5 Information required to understand and operate content does not rely on shape, size, visual location, or orientation of components.

Guideline 1.4 : Make it easy to distinguish foreground information from its background

1.4.1 Text or diagrams, and their background, have a luminosity contrast ratio of at least 5:1

1.4.3 Text or diagrams, and their background, have a luminosity contrast ratio of at least 10:1.

Essentially, contrast needs to be at the heart of the information architecture and the design of the website. Poor color combinations could cause visitors to overlook important information and critical tasks. Unfortunately, both the business and the visitor lose when this happens. Creating content that uses contrast to effectively communicate information increases the business case not only for those who need additional contrast or a larger text size in order to see the content clearly but also for all users.

WCAG offers multiple tools for testing contrast on your website and pages. I also recommend using a program to simulate what your website/advertising looks like to someone who is color blind. It is always helpful to understand and adjust to ensure that your message and calls to action are clear. Viewing this will help not only those who have color blindness but all of your website visitors, because contrast is an element that people rely on to find important information.

Designing for Color Blindness

Most color blindness takes the form of red-green confusion, while the minor forms are mostly blue-yellow confusion. Although most websites will not create large obstacles, communicating information or instructions through graphics or color codes that rely on these colors or the difference of colors will cause confusion.

A great resource for understanding how your web pages would appear to those with color blindness is Vischeck (www.vischeck.com). Any obvious problems will become apparent. If you would like to explore further, Lighthouse International (www.lighthouse.org) provides designers with color-blindness web color charts and examples. There are diagrams that show how those with color blindness perceive web-safe colors.

Here are some important design recommendations:

- Never make color the single visual cue; use font sizes to assist emphasis.
- If red, green, or blue is being used as a font color for emphasis, another cue should be used, such as an underline or bold attribute.
- Use effective color contrast in web pages and presentation materials (PowerPoint!).
- Avoid fonts that are too decorative. Script fonts used online are notoriously difficult to read.
- Label graphics clearly so that users do not have to rely solely on color keys.
- Use descriptive text near graphics, such as a caption, as well as the alt attribute images to explain the purpose of the image.

Using these elements will also create better methods for the search engines to use the information on the page. Search engines can read the color instructions in the HTML but cannot use it as a basis for judging graphic elements. Because more information is added to explain graphics and highlight specific areas of text, this will also help in naturally implementing keywords to target your specific business or venture to the search engines. It will also go far in assisting users to understand your site and your purpose.

Thursday: Create Accessible PDFs

An important component of Internet marketing is PDF files. Portable Document Format (PDF) allows additional information to be downloaded to the visitor's computer or viewed on mobile devices, regardless of operating system or platform. This is an excellent way to provide sell sheets, product information, and white papers to the visitor. Search engines are able to index the content within most PDFs, and the ones that do well in search engines will also tend to do well for the assistive technology visitor. PDF documents can be created using a tagged structure, like a web page, which allows assistive technology to provide a document structure and information hierarchy, which the search engines need as well. (However, PDF documents do pose a few marketing problems, as discussed in the "PDF Marketing Obstacles" sidebar.)

PDF Marketing Obstacles

In addition to accessibility problems, PDFs can also pose general marketing obstacles. The marketing problem arises from the expectations of users, especially when they expect a web page but instead get a PDF.

PDFs tend to rank very well in search engines. As a result, many users will click the PDF, just as they click a typical search engine result. The downside starts immediately when the user has to wait 20 to 30 seconds for the PDF reader to load and open.

Delays when trying to find information can be costly, because many users just don't want to be bothered with waiting. However, when the PDF application starts, the user is locked in; they can't stop it or leave.

The next problem comes as the user starts to look through the PDF. If it is interesting and has good content, there is often no immediate way for the user to get to the company website. This is because very few PDFs are built with hyperlinks embedded in the document, even though the hyperlink is a very valuable resource for users to get to the main website.

Most users will not edit the address bar of their web browser to get to the website, because they tend to rely on the Back button. When a user hits the Back button, they are now seeing the search engine results page again, with your result alongside competitive websites. You had them at your site, but they couldn't get any further. This is how the PDF becomes a user trap.

Overcoming PDF Accessibility Obstacles

For many users, PDFs are much more frustrating than this. Because PDFs can also incorporate many images, they lack elements that websites include, such as alt text for images or document structure. Many screen readers are unable to handle PDFs if they are not "properly" constructed and can cause frustration. For many users, the only option is to upgrade their assistive software, at a potential cost of hundreds of dollars.

Creating an accessible PDF is not difficult and can be done by changing settings in the standard PDF creation, which is typically done using Adobe Acrobat. Creators can also test the accessibility of their PDF documents. The best means of creating an accessible PDF document, however, is to start with a tagged source file (discussed next). Starting with this, any device should be able to access the document. With accessibility, the benefit of creating accessible documents is that the documents are open to be read by multiple devices. PDAs and phones are included in this list.

Many of the issues are determined by how the PDF was created. If the document was scanned in as an image, then it will not be accessible or search-friendly. If the document was scanned in using Optical Character Recognition (OCR), then the text that was recognized will be available to assistive technology devices and search engines, but there will be no markup tags to communicate the headings, links, images, and other text attributes.

If a PDF was created in a graphics program, then it becomes a bit more complicated. Text fields added into the document and populated with text will most likely be readable. Text in the form of art or images, which usually are headlines or titles or other important text areas, tend not to be translated into readable text by a search engine or screen reader.

Fortunately, *tagged* document formats are included in Adobe programs and Microsoft Office. The most basic explanation of tagging is that the document has an underlying structure such as header information, text and graphic display commands, and alt attributes, similar to a web page. Using preset or custom styles such as Headline 1, Heading 2, Heading 3, paragraph, unordered list, bulleted list, and other commands will structure your document similar to a web page and allow it to be structured for accessibility and better search engine friendliness. Each style is a "tag" that is carried through the document, its creation as a PDF, and its subsequent reading by a search engine or other document "reading" program. The tags create a logical order and structure to your document, which allows the reader to follow the document as the author intended. A tagged format also allows a PDF document to be reflowed. Reflow is an important consideration for those who have to resize the document for readability and for viewing on handheld devices. Reflow allows content to be structured for viewing without horizontal scrolling, allowing the user to only rely on the vertical scroll to see the content.

Microsoft documents embed this and will carry tagged data through PDF creation. Be sure this option is selected in the document settings setup screen. Documents created in many other design-based programs need to be converted to a PostScript file, and then the PostScript file must be converted to a PDF in order to maintain the tagged format. Web pages saved as a PDF must also have Create PDF Tags selected in the settings.

Although Adobe Acrobat does allow users to add tags within the document, the best method is to add the tags while creating the document prior to converting to a PDF. Be aware, however, that tagging within Acrobat is not always interpreted correctly and can affect the reading structure.

Not only does tagging allow you to better communicate with all of your website users, it also allows search engines to better search your documents for information and context. You can benefit, as always, by creating more accessibility options that help you market your website more effectively.

Adobe Reader is a free download and comes with a host of accessibility features for users. Unfortunately, they may be easily overlooked. The built-in accessibility features allow a greater majority of users to view documents regardless of vision or access.

Accessibility Tools within Adobe Reader

The best place to start setting up Adobe Reader for accessibility is the Tools > Accessibility Setup Assistant. This brings up a wizard to enable specific accessibility options for interpreting the document (see Figure 13.5). Choosing Set All Accessibility Options is recommended for most users, and Adobe will then move into installing the additional features.

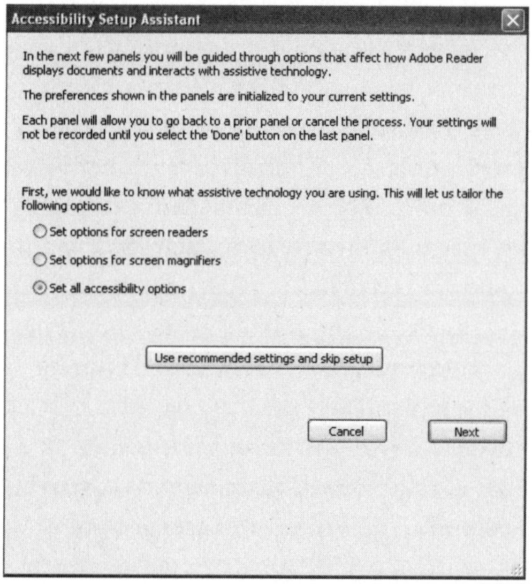

Figure 13.5 Adobe Reader's Accessibility Setup Assistant

Screen Reader

Screen readers are mainly used by blind or extreme low-vision users but are not limited to those who need vision accessibility. Many users with cognitive difficulties, such as dyslexia, rely on screen readers to help them better follow the content on the screen.

The voice option is not nearly as full featured as JAWS, Window Eyes, or other screen readers, but there are keyboard commands to provide "read full page" or "read one page" options. The Read Out Loud feature uses the Microsoft Sam voice, which can be quite monotonous. However, the voice contains many inflections at appropriate times. It is easy to listen to after some minor tweaks to the pitch and speech rate. This can be done by selecting Edit > Preferences > Categories > Reading. The user also has the option to override the tagging commands contained within the document.

Contrast

In the Edit > Preferences > Accessibility menu is another great feature that increases accessibility for any user. The first option allows the user to replace the document color format with a high-contrast format. Or, if the user already has a predefined windows color scheme to enhance readability, they can select that scheme or set up a custom scheme.

The line art feature is particularly effective, because it can render line art as a black-and-white image, allowing a high-contrast image to be seen by anyone with color blindness or someone who simply prefers to see graphs or art in a noncolor format.

Reflow

Screen magnifiers are becoming more prevalent, because they increase the text size not only in web documents but also in all applications on the computer. Screen magnifiers come in many styles; some are similar to magnifying glasses and highlight areas of content, and others "blow up" a section of the screen to the entire monitor viewing area.

Reflow is an important feature that allows readers who use large text options or screen magnifiers to view the document at a larger text size or increased document size, yet without the horizontal scrolling that is typical when increasing the document size.

Enabling reflow allows documents to be seen without horizontal scrolling. This is especially helpful for low-vision users who increase the text size of the document, but then also increase the side to side scrolling. Reflow eliminates the horizontal scrolling so that documents can be easily read as a single column of text that fits the device or viewing area. The implications for this expand far beyond accessibility, because they can be used by all PDF users. It's very helpful when viewing PDFs on devices such as PDAs, BlackBerry devices, or other web-enabled phones. There have been many times I have attempted to read PDFs on a Palm device, only to get frustrated by getting lost in all of the cross-scrolling. Access the reflow feature in Adobe Reader after you have increased the document View size by pressing Ctrl+4.

Text Zoom

The default zoom can be set anywhere between 8 percent and 6400 percent. This is done in the Edit > Preferences > Page Display menu in the Magnification settings. Again, this is a feature that is helpful to all Adobe Reader users.

Multimedia

Adobe Reader has made many strides in making accessibility options available, and the latest is through the multimedia options in Edit > Preferences > Multimedia. There are options to do the following:

- Show subtitles
- Play dubbed audio (when available)
- Show supplemental text captions when available
- Show audio description when available

Of course, these features are dependent upon creators to implement multimedia that includes these options. The main issue will be getting those who create these documents to make them easier for all users, but also they need to be aware of the features that are available. Sadly, I believe that most users are not aware of the simplest things they can do to make a PDF more accessibility-friendly, web-friendly, search-friendly, and user-friendly.

Friday: Accessibility Applied to Search

This week, while learning about accessibility, you should also see how much of the allowances and features presented can also provide better, more structured information that will help your website be more open to search engines, rank better, and meet the needs of users regardless of skill level or vision. The last area of consideration that bridges the needs of both assistive technology users and marketing is the use of link text.

Link text is important because it is used by sighted readers as a visual cue. It is also important to assistive technology users as a means of quickly scanning the content of the page through listening.

Scanning by Listening

Jakob Nielsen's usability testing extends into the realm of testing accessibility and screen reader users. The study, "Beyond ALT Text: Making the Web Easy to Use for Users with Disabilities" can be accessed at http://www.nngroup.com/reports/accessibility/ . One of the most interesting things that I found in the study was that screen reader users browse web pages similarly to sighted readers.

Sighted readers, as explored in Chapter 9, quickly scan through web pages in order to find the context of the content. This is done by scanning the page title, headings, images, and any bolded, highlighted, or linked text. A strikingly similar behavior is observed when screen reader users are listening to web pages. They listen to web pages according to the structure.

In accessibility testing of websites, screen reader users listen to the page information, typically the page title. Then, using a keystroke on JAWS, they would list the headings on the page and listen to the headings. The next step is listening to the links, and a keystroke brings up all the links on the page and reads them in order. By listening to the elements on the page, the screen reader user is able to determine whether the content they need is on the page before actually listening to every word on the page. Screen reader users scan by listening.

This is where developing a page structure defined by HTML attributes is critical in allowing accessibility for visitors because the assistive technology needs proper markup on the page to provide a significant content of information. Based on this, the user selects the link and repeats the process until getting to the page whose headings most closely matches the task. Then the user will listen to the content but only after listening to headings and jumping to that section of the page.

This reinforces the need for the usage of HTML markup language to better define elements on the page for both search engines and assistive technology. Both technologies need this information to interpret and display information, visually or aurally, in order to help visitors. When these are done properly and designed well, it helps everyone better understand the content on the pages.

Anchor Text

The old WCAG accessibility guidelines wrote it simply: "Checkpoint 13.1: Clearly identify the target of each link." WCAG 2.0 made people scratch their heads in wonder when the sentence was changed to "Checkpoint 2.4.4: Each link is programmatically associated with text from which its purpose can be determined." Don't let the big words get in the way. All it means is that people, regardless of access device, should be able to determine the purpose of the link from its context.

What I am talking about is the small but powerful concept of *anchor text*—the contextual text that hyperlinks to another page or another site. The problem is the number of sites that employ the following use of anchor text:

- Click here
- More info
- Skip intro

An anchor text link of "click here" or "more info" provides no information as to what the visitor will find on the other side of those links. The goal of usability is for a site visitor to easily find their way through a site without thinking. Each step is clear and logical; information is easily found and communicated. "Click here" provides an action but not a reason.

This is a prime oversight, especially when "click here" links are littered throughout the page. These are links that are supposed to describe what you will find when you click the link. There are three reasons for eliminating this harmful practice from your site: usability, accessibility, and search engine rankings. I tend to favor usability over search engines ranking tactics, but this is one area where there are obvious benefits in usability and accessibility, so I'll take the search engine benefits as a nice bonus. When you see this simple potential for greater success, I am sure you will spend a few hours working on removing these unusable road signs in your site.

If "click here" or "read more" were used as a proper context, it may be helpful, but the majority of time, it is a lazy alternative to constructing a clear call to action within the information. Visitors all know what blue, underlined text denotes. It is not difficult to surmise the purpose of the link by reading the linked text. If it is written well, it is effective.

For accessibility, repetitive "click here" links create a headache to anyone using a screen reader or other assistive device to access the page. Most assistive technology allows users to bypass the navigation and go directly to the content. These programs also allow users to list the links on the page, which allows them to quickly navigate to the content. Imagine hearing a page's link list with "click here" repeated five or more times in a row with no clear description to the destination or available content. Where does that leave the user?

Lastly, using anchor text for internal and external page links can have a positive effect on your rankings if they are structured properly. I can't imagine that many site managers are striving for top rankings for "click here," but it seems as though there is a competition. You can affect your rankings by changing the anchor text to be more descriptive of the content and using keywords in the description.

One of the better examples I have seen in a use of content in anchor text, especially in the light of this chapter, is WebAIM's website, www.webaim.org (a great accessibility resource). In developing its navigation, the site identified the five major groups of visitors that are targeted by the content of the site and the particular interests they have. By identifying their markets and the unique concerns of each group, they were able to formulate descriptive anchor text links into the site. This allows users to quickly find the information they need (see Figure 13.6).

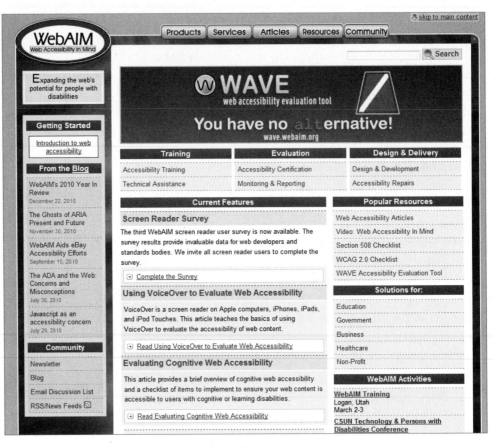

Figure 13.6 Webaim.org uses anchor text (link text) as an effective means of contextual navigation.

Nick Usborne (*Net Words*, McGraw-Hill, 2002) defined what I consider to be one of the best applications of anchor text in a website, the "action-benefit interaction." The text link should not only describe the information that will be found when clicking the link but also offer a promise or a benefit to the user.

From a search engine rankings standpoint, employing user benefits in your text, and especially your text link, is beneficial. Searchers tend to look for solutions to their problems. When a site is focused on the needs of the users in the language of their need, it increases not only the chances for your site to rank for those terms but also your site's ability to connect with those users and increase your chance to convert them to buyers.

The next time you go to write "click here" in the text of your page, stop and ask yourself, why should the user click this link? Does it properly describe the benefit to the user? Think through your strategy, and rewrite that link. This will provide a contextual relevance to the page within your own website, as well as relevance to the visitor, who will realize that more information about that particular word or topic can be accessed simply by clicking the link.

From an accessibility standpoint, users who list links to "hear" the possible information accessed from the page will hear a clear, relevant list of topics, rather than multiple links that read the same and with no distinguishing content. This will improve the user experience all around, as well as make a small impact in the search engines by creating additional relevance among your pages.

Review and Hands-On

Review your website using the Google Webmaster Guidelines and the WCAG checkpoints with both search engines and assistive technology in mind. I tend to recommend the 1.0 guidelines in addition to the 2.0 revision, because the 1.0 guidelines are a bit easier to read and understand for nonprogrammers.

- Google's Webmaster Guidelines:
  `www.google.com/support/webmasters/bin/answer.py?hl=en&answer=35769`

- `Web Content Accessibility Guidelines (WCAG):`
  - WCAG 1.0 Checklist:
    `www.w3.org/TR/WCAG10/full-checklist.html`
  - Checklist for comparing WCAG 1.0 to WCAG 2.0:
    `www.w3.org/TR/2006/WD-WCAG20-20060427/appendixD.html`
  - Full WCAG 2.0 with explanations and resources:
    `www.w3.org/TR/2006/WD-WCAG20-20060427/guidelines.html`

Explore the accessibility options available through browsers such as Internet Explorer, Opera, Chrome, or Firefox. Find the commands to increase and decrease text size. Also, within the operating system of your computer, find the accessibility options and see how they work.

The typical tools you may find are contrast settings, zoom or screen magnification settings, text-to-speech options, and mouse and keyboard adjustments. Explore these options and see how they can make browsing the Internet easier for different people with different needs. You may, in fact, find a few that will make your life a bit easier as well.

Microsoft offers an extensive learning center on accessibility and how Microsoft technology enables users to take advantage of a full range of accessible options: `www.microsoft.com/enable/`. Take time to review the information and explore the products and demos available on the website.

Download a color blindness simulator, or use an online simulator to test your site. Get a sense of the differences that people see when viewing your content.

Find any potential issues by performing tasks on your website through the simulator. Ensure that your calls to action and graphics are able to still be read and understood. Resources for this are located here:

www.w3.org/TR/UNDERSTANDING-WCAG20/visual-audio-contrast-without-color.html

Take the Ishihara test for color blindness to get a sense of the vision differences. Many tests are available online.

Go to Webaim.org and listen to the screen reader simulator: http://webaim.org/simulations/screenreader. If you feel particularly daring, download a trial of JAWS, turn off your monitor, and attempt to navigate your website simply by listening (printing a menu of commands is helpful).

Review your site for unclear text links. Take some time to rewrite the link to include a descriptive explanation of what the reader will see after the click. Take care to ensure that the context is communicated through the link alone, and consider screen reader users.

Take the following steps the next time you are creating a PDF for web use:

- When you're creating the PDF using a document to create a PDF, such as Microsoft Word, check to make sure you are using the tagging features, such as the Heading 1, Heading 2, text, alt attributes, and URLs. *Adding links in PDF documents can also provide a means of search visitors being able to navigate back to your main website instead of being trapped in the PDF file.* Many organizations have developed the styles in Microsoft Word to be custom to their business.

- Open a few of the PDF documents that you have on your computer and check the accessibility options. If you can use the Read Out Loud feature, highlight a block of text and hear it being read to you; then the search engines will be able to "see" the text as well.

- Turn on Reflow (View > Zoom > Reflow), and then increase the size of the document. This should fit the document on your screen, regardless of the size.

Understanding how these features enable better search engine friendliness as well as accessibility will enable businesses to take advantage of these easy tips. This also enables better viewing and reading for all users regardless of the various vision or assistive technologies they may need. Increasing accessibility increases ease of use for everyone.

Week 11: Identify Technical Roadblocks

As websites become more and more automated through content management systems, a simple change can result in thousands of pages of errors. Understanding how to identify, troubleshoot, and correct these issues is vital to today's marketer. IT departments are many times overwhelmed with work, and they do not have the time to constantly keep the website under surveillance. It is the business owner and the marketer's responsibility to stay current with the website and be aware of issues that could be preventing search engines from viewing the website or preventing users from seeing valuable content.

Chapter Contents
Monday: Check the Quality of Your URLs
Tuesday: Understand URL Rewrites
Wednesday: Use Redirects
Thursday: Uncover Duplicate Content
Friday: Utilize Robots.txt to Welcome Search Engines

Monday: Check the Quality of Your URLs

Many of the problems within a website can be evidenced or traced to the uniform resource locator (URL). Every document on the Internet has to have a unique address in order to be requested and displayed. Much like a residence has a mailbox, every document has a unique address that enables it to be found in order to deliver the document and receive inquiries.

Similarly, some addresses are easier to understand than others. It is very easy, for example, to look at an address from your home country and understand the syntax of the format and the words, and you can easily figure out the location of the address. Looking at addresses of another country, there may be a different syntax and additional numbers or letters that just aren't familiar.

Every page of a website has a unique address. Problems arise when that page is duplicated at another address. This is similar to having more than one mailbox for your house, because the mail carrier would become confused as to which mailbox to deliver the mail, much as you may be confused as to which mailbox would contain the mail.

The consequence of duplicated pages is that a search engine would catalog multiple pages of the same content. In doing so, it would not be apparent which version of the page was the correct version. Having these duplicated pages reduces the value of the primary content, because the search engine is not able to determine the correct page. The result is that the ranking potential of that page becomes diluted among the other duplicates.

As a rule, simple URLs are best. URLs that are especially effective are those that are also understood by humans, because they contain an address that makes sense, using words. My general rule is that the URL shouldn't be longer than the URL address box in your browser. If it is, then your site may have problems in the search engines (more on that shortly). Refer to Figure 14.1. All the letters, numbers, and characters make a complicated URL, which humans won't understand, and it may also stump the search engines.

On the other hand, a simpler URL (called a logical URL) is one that employs words rather than a combination of letters, numbers, and characters. Logical URLs use a word that reflects the content of the page. For example, Figure 14.2 shows a page on Etsy that serves up the product as the logical URL.

A simple application of the logical URL has arisen recently. In early 2010, Facebook allowed its users to create vanity URLs for their profiles. Each user can now have their name as the URL after www.facebook.com. Users stayed up late in order to be first in line to get the desired name. This makes publishing your profile and finding friends easier, as well as being able to have your name show up in search engine results for your Facebook page. This also makes company pages easier to spot (see Figure 14.3).

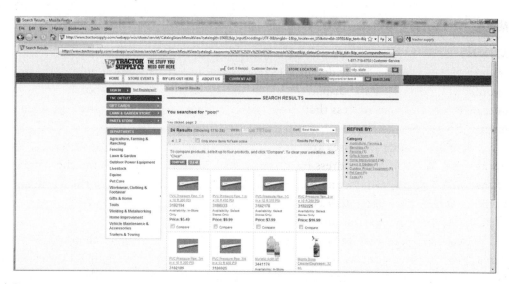

Figure 14.1 Tractor Supply Company URLs are longer than the browser address box.

Figure 14.2 Etsy uses the logical URL with the product name in the URL.

Figure 14.3 Volkswagen's Facebook page: the vanity URL is a logical URL (www.facebook.com/VW).

Sites with large inventories and multiple classifications often have unwieldy URLs. Anyone who has ever bookmarked a page on eBay may have noticed the URL (see Figure 14.4).

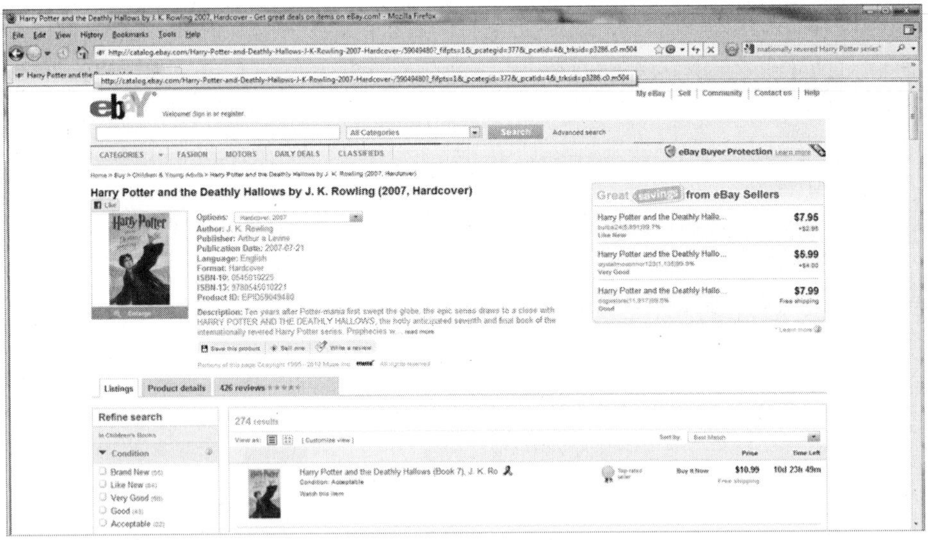

Figure 14.4 eBay's URL for a product listing

As you can see, the URL contains a hefty amount of letters, characters, and numbers arranged in a chaotic way. This is all information that communicates to the database behind the scenes of the website to arrange the page with particular information. It also may contain various tracking codes, variables, and instructions for the database.

This creates two primary problems. The first is that the more complex the string of characters in the URL, the more problems it will provide for the search engines. Search engines rely on a very simple ability to find and download pages. If the links to those pages are too complex or cause the same page to be downloaded an infinite amount of times, the search engines don't know how to organize and store the content, which prevents visibility in the rankings.

In this example, the eBay page is not indexed by Google. However, there are many similar pages that are indexed under different URLs (see Figure 14.5). The primary product page that is linked from the eBay home page is not indexed, but seller sites are being found, because they have a "cleaner" URL structure.

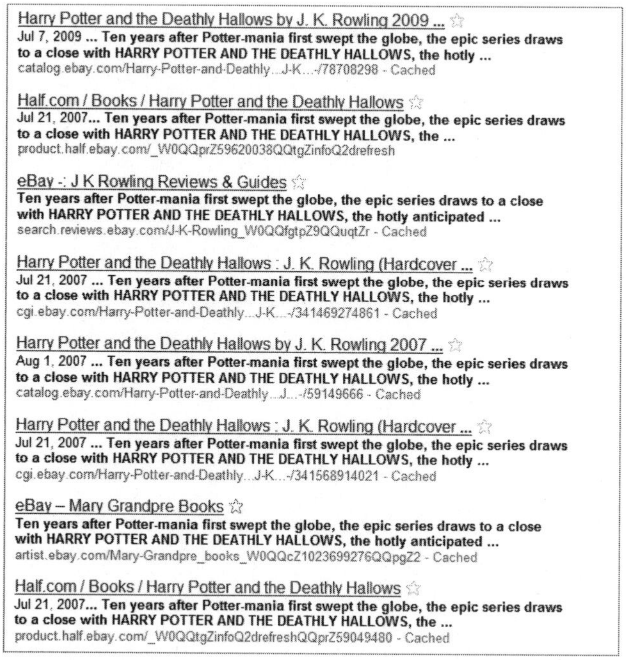

Figure 14.5 Google's index of eBay listings for *Harry Potter and the Deathly Hallows*: none of them contains the original page with the complex URL.

The second problem is that the URL is part of the user interface (UI). As part of the UI, the URL can help the user as much as hinder the user. When a website uses a logical URL and includes important category labels and keywords, it can help the visitor effectively navigate the website, because the URL can help the visitor determine location and content. Figure 14.6 shows a page from ThinkGeek, where the product and keywords are utilized throughout the content and primary headings and are reinforced by the logical URL.

Figure 14.6 The logical URL on ThinkGeek adds to the context of the page and the understanding of the visitor's location within the website.

As a pleasant side benefit to assisting the user, adding keywords to the URL also affects search relevance. Additionally, as other websites add a link to your website and to a specific page, that keyword in the URL adds context to the link and can help build additional relevance. This tactic alone is not one that will dramatically improve your website visibility, but it is one that can help, especially in a very competitive niche.

Do My URLs Need Work?

A caveat to this discussion on URLs is that the logical URL is not always necessary, especially if your site is doing well with both search engines and visitors. The evaluation methods in Chapter 4 should provide a good understanding of whether a change to your website's structure is in order.

If your website is doing well, then the search engines have indexed your website, and most of your pages are showing up in a search for your site (see Chapter 4). If your website is indexed and has good rankings, then a change to a logical URL could cause more problems than possibilities. I recommend staying with something that is working, because creating new logical URLs may create major changes in the way search engines index your pages.

Here's a quick checklist to know whether changing to logical URLs is the right move for you:

1. Your site has little to no rankings.

2. Very little of your traffic is generated from the search engines.

3. Your URLs are complicated and long.

4. Your Webmaster Tools reports shows that most of your pages have not been indexed, and none of the pages with the long, complicated URLs have been indexed.

If your site meets all of these factors, then rewriting your URLs to logical URLs may be the remedy. However, it is not a simple process, and many factors will determine how easily this can be accomplished. The method to create a logical URL is called a *rewrite* and will be covered next.

Tuesday: Understand URL Rewrites

A URL rewrite is the method of taking a complex URL and translating it using words that are understandable to the visitor. A complex URL would look something like this:

`www.website.com/?id=23678j&f=765`

A rewritten URL would take the parameters listed after the domain, "translate" them, and rewrite the URL to display like this:

`www.website.com/products/shoes`

To understand the process of creating a rewrite, it is necessary to understand a little bit about databases. I find that many marketers will read about the rewrite or hear about it at a conference and then excitedly go to their IT department, demand that it be done that day, and expect it to answer all of their problems. The problem is that the IT department will most likely respond nicely but then promptly go back to whatever it was they were doing and ignore the request.

Rewriting a URL is not a simple matter, especially if the website has been around for a number of years. Using a logical URL is one of those functions that is much easier to plan at the beginning of a development project than after the website has been launched. It requires that the database be structured in a method that will enable the logical URLs to be created.

The Basics

A simple way to understand a database's relation to the content of the site is to look at a very basic sample URL structure (before rewriting):

www.website.com/ is the root level of the website. Most often, this is where the home page is located.

www.website.com/?id=4 The *"?id=4"* is a typical database inquiry that resides in the URL. This is a variable that requests a specific data field, or record from the database, which is then displayed to the visitor. The parameter `"id="` is the instruction for the server to present the information found in record 4. Each number (or parameter) contains information from a specific record that has been entered into the database. The page that displays to the visitor is built using the information from this record in the database. Typically, the record at this level is usually a high-level or general category, like shoes.

www.website.com/?id=4&cat=17 requests additional records of information from the database to be displayed on the page. The addition of another variable (`&cat=17`) is most likely a subcategory. So, if the primary top-level category was shoes (`id=4`), then this subcategory (`&cat=17`) could be a subcategory such as running shoes.

www.website.com/?id=4&cat=17&prodid=15 reflects the additional information being requested as the visitor drives deeper into the content of the website. The database is pulling additional information to show a page that has more information and additional classification. To follow the example, this page would most likely be a specific brand or type of running shoe.

www.website.com/?id=4&cat=17&prodid=15&detail=45 would reflect the product-level page. The additional parameters in the URL at this point may be reflected in the breadcrumb trail as Shoes > Running Shoes > Cross-Trainers > Brand Name, because the URL has built by the selection of the visitor. However, at this point, there are many parameters in the URL. A parameter is usually marked by the equal sign. Too many of these, and there may be a problem with the search engines.

With a simple database like this, it would be fairly easy to construct rewrite rules to translate the URLs as follows:

- www.website.com/?id=4 to www.website.com/shoes/

- www.website.com/?id=4&cat=17 to www.website.com/shoes/running-shoes/

- www.website.com/?id=4&cat=17&prodid=15 to www.website.com/shoes/running-shoes/adidas

Of course, this is a very crude and simplistic example, but it provides an entrance to a world that digital marketers need to understand. As the URL becomes more complicated and encumbered with symbols, letters, equal signs, and various other characters, it also creates additional difficulty for the search engine. The more complicated the database, the more complicated constructing logical rules for a rewrite will become. This just isn't a plug-and-play solution, as some marketers would prefer, and giving your IT department or programmer some leeway in timing and reacting to this request is recommended.

Simply having additional characters will not make your site bad for the search engines. There are many factors, and it is always recommended to take the measurement steps outlined in Monday's assignment and in Chapter 4 to be sure that the URLs are actually the culprit. There are many factors in the technical side of marketing a website, and you need to be sure you have correctly diagnosed the primary problem before taking drastic measures.

Consider the Site's Database Type and Scripting Language

If a rewrite is in your future, than educating yourself as to the type of rewrite is a recommended activity; otherwise, your IT department will make fun of you.

You will need to know what type of database your website employs and the language used to interact with the database. There are two primary databases types that split the web development industry: there is the side of the industry that uses Microsoft technology, and there is the side of the industry that doesn't. There are a few other exceptions such as Sun and Oracle, but Microsoft SQL (the branded Microsoft database) and MySQL (the open source Linux version) make up the majority of database use.

To get the information out of the database, a scripting language is necessary to create the web pages. For sites using a Microsoft SQL database, the traditional languages that have been used to interface with the database are Classic ASP, ASP.NET, Visual Basic, and VB .NET. For these languages, combined with Microsoft SQL, there is usually a rewrite solution available. On Microsoft IIS servers, there are many options available, with IASAPI filters, a module called `mod-rewrite`, and Microsoft URL Rewrite Module 2.0 being a few of them. In addition, ASP.NET has a `context-Rewrite` module that will allow for creating rewrite rules.

In the open source world, which is dominated by Linux, the server runs on a program called Apache, and the typical database used is MySQL. The primary language used to pull the information out of the database and structure it is called PHP. The cost of developing in MySQL and PHP is much lower, because there are no licensing fees, and access to these resources is free. In PHP, there are multiple rewrite functions available, with `mod-rewrite` and `.htaccess` being the primary tools. (See the "Setting Up a Redirect" sidebar for more information on Apache and `.htaccess`.)

Although I typically don't require marketers to learn the details of programming and scripting technologies, there is a significant advantage to learning about the differences among the multiple options and why your programmers prefer one or the other. This is where taking the time to sit with your programmer and gain a better understanding of the languages and database structure of your website will enable you to better understand what goes on "under the hood" of your website.

Gaining a better understanding of the programming and selection process, purpose, results, and typical opportunities and problems generated by dynamic (database-generated) websites will enable a marketer to gain a unique perspective on how to use the database to their advantage. Instead of viewing the IT department or the programmer as an obstacle, smart marketers see an opportunity to learn and develop additional knowledge and skills that will enable them to better manage and market websites in the future.

Regardless of the database and language used, the complexity of the database is the primary issue. If the database is too complex and contains too many variables and additional factors, then other methods will have to be employed to get your website "seen" and indexed by the search engines. This will be covered in Chapter 15.

Once you gain a better understanding of the necessary steps to build a rewrite solution, then you'll need to take the next step of building redirects, which will be covered next.

Wednesday: Use Redirects

A redirect works on the same principle as forwarding your mail when you move. When you move to a new residence, you notify the post office to direct your mail to your new address. Likewise, a redirect forwards all the page requests for an old address to a new address. Whenever a page's URL has changed, such as through a redeveloped website, a redirect points to the new page URL.

Redirects can be a confusing subject but are an integral part of website management. Properly applied redirects can improve your search engine rankings and also improve your visitor experiences. Using redirects when launching a newly redesigned website will prevent many problems, primarily lost traffic and lower rankings. However, as powerful tools as redirects are, redirects are still tools and can be used improperly. Applying redirects in some situations may have unintended consequences if you are not aware of how redirects affect search engine requests.

There are multiple uses for redirects when administering a website, and I will cover some of the most common uses in this section.

Types of Redirect

There are many redirects, but the vast majority of time you will deal with only a few types. The type of redirect used has significant impact with your search engine indexing and, ultimately, your site's visibility. Knowing which redirect to apply and how search engines and browsers will react to each is an important part of website management.

301: Moved Permanently and 302 Found (Temporary Redirect)

The 301: Moved Permanently redirect is the most common and recommended type of redirect. It operates at the server level, which means that when a URL is requested and a 301 redirect is in place, the server reports that the URL no longer exists but has been permanently replaced with a new URL (usually behind the scenes). The new URL and corresponding page are loaded in the browser.

For humans, this process is virtually transparent in the browser window. However, in the URL window, the URL will change from the URL requested to new URL directed. For a search engine, the bot or spider receives the "forwarding address" and knows to direct any further requests to the new page. Eventually, the new page will replace the old page in the search engine index.

Even though this may be a temporary move or you may not technically consider a change in your site to be "permanent," the 301 is still the preferred method of managing page changes to the website. There are two primary reasons that this is the preferred redirect. The first is that the 301 redirect offers more security than a 302 redirect. (The 302 redirect was originally called the *temporary redirect* but has recently been renamed the *302 found* redirect.) There have been issues in the past where 302 redirects opened up a site for unscrupulous webmaster to "hijack" traffic from a website.

The second reason the 301 redirect is much more viable, however, is it maintains the value of incoming links from your old URL to the new URL. This is the most critical and valuable use of the 301 redirect for pages, because the search engines will be able to apply the benefit of the incoming links to a new page, rather than an incoming link going to no destination on your website.

Search engines recognize the permanent redirect as being a replacement address for a page. As such, the value of the old page will then pass to the new page, thus keeping the value of incoming links and not losing them. The permanent redirect is the only method that will retain this value. Using a 302 redirect will not pass the value of the old URL to the new URL. Using a 301 or a 302 redirect will require access to the web server, because best practice requires the status code to be generated by the web server. For Windows servers, the management panel allows easy management of redirection. Apache web servers use the `.htaccess` file to manage the redirects from the server.

Figure 14.7 shows an example using WebBug (a program used to view the server request and response). You can see that the domain www.coke.com redirects to the primary domain, www.coca-cola.com, using a 301 Moved Permanently redirect. The header of the returned document provides information about the server and the location of a redirected document, which is critical for search engines to index and apply.

Figure 14.7 www.coke.com employs a 301 Moved Permanently redirect to the domain www.coca-cola.com.

A 302 redirect will show up in the header response as well, as in Figure 14.8's example of the request to www.ibm.com. IBM uses a 302 redirect to send all page requests to another directory, www.ibm.com/us/en.

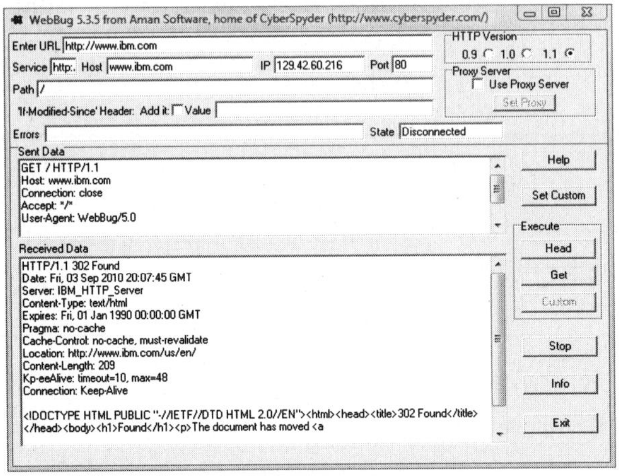

Figure 14.8 IBM.com uses a 302 redirect to forward requests from the root domain to a different location.

Using HTTP Header Response Tools

For those who need to do some troubleshooting and identify the server response for redirects, WebBug (www.cyberspyder.com/webbug.html) is an excellent tool. There are other tools similar to this, usually called *HTTP header viewer* or *HTTP header response* tools.

The header contains the information that is returned to the requester of a document from a server. The server returns information such as the status of the request, such as 404 not found, 301 redirect, 200 OK, and many more; however, those are the most common.

I find these tools valuable when I suspect that there are redirects happening at the domain level that may prevent the search engines from accessing the website. Although this knowledge isn't critical, it is handy to have some knowledge of how to troubleshoot certain problems. Finding a domain-level 302 redirect could be the key to a successful SEO campaign. Not finding it could cause an entire campaign to flop, simply because of a minor detail in the server settings. It is a minor detail, but it is a big deal— one that needs to be identified and managed. Knowing these details makes you a more valuable resource to your company and a more effective online marketer.

For large organizations where multiple people are responsible for the website and server mainte-nance, I recommend checking the redirects periodically to ensure that nothing has been changed. This is where routinely logging into a webmaster tool account or checking redirects at least quar-terly can be good preventative maintenance.

Metarefresh

The metarefresh redirect was popular in the early days of web browsing, because it was commonly used to surprise a visitor by redirecting them to a location that was not requested or expected. Many adult sites used this technique by placing a redirect script on a well-ranking page that attracted visitors for a different subject. Once the visitor was on the page, the refresh script would then forward the visitor to another website. The refresh command could be programmed to wait for a specified amount of time before sending the visitor to the new URL. Because of the application of this technique, the metarefresh was an untrusted method for redirecting URLs for many years.

Although both Google and Yahoo! are now accepting an undelayed metarefresh as a form of 301 permanent redirect, the server-based 301 redirect is still the preferred method of redirect. The metarefresh is a script that is coded into the metadata of the page, rather than managed by a server. Because there is no server management of the redirect, no information about the new URL or the change to the new URL is communicated to the search engine. On more visible note, a meta-refresh code will disable the Back button for your visitor. That breaks a strict rule of usability, because the Back button is one of the more valuable tools for browsing online.

JavaScript

JavaScript is another method of redirecting, but it is also the least recommended. Many times, website managers use alternate means of redirection, because their hosting company or technical staff has informed them that server-based redirects are not possible. It is best to research the cause for the inability to have a server-based redirect rather than implement less secure or less desirable methods of redirection.

The JavaScript redirect is rarely used or recommended, because JavaScript requires the visitor's browser to execute the script. Not all browsers have JavaScript enabled or support JavaScript, and many operating systems will not execute scripts for various security reasons. In addition, search engine crawlers do not execute JavaScript either, which will inhibit the ability to redirect the old URL to the new URL and maintain the value.

Setting Up a Redirect

Using an Apache server, access the `.htaccess` file, usually by FTP. Ensure that you are able to see hidden files, which will enable the `.htaccess` file to be seen. Open the file using a text editor, such as Notepad, and add a line with the following instruction:

```
RedirectPermanent /oldpageURL.php http://www.domain.com/newpageURL.php
```

This will redirect a file (or page) to a new file (or page). The structure of the line is the command, the old URL location, and the new URL location.

Continues

Uses for Redirects

After reading some of this information and all of the warnings on misplaced redirects, some marketers get gun-shy and feel as though redirects are dangerous. Not so! Redirects are the heavy machinery of website management, especially in terms of SEO. You shouldn't operate it if you don't know how, but you should be able to know when it is necessary.

Redirects are most effective when a site redesign project is in the works. If you have a website that is ranking well and has a lot of incoming links, then maintaining the traffic and links will be a critical part of the redesign, and that is when redirects are your best friend in the business.

Save Rankings after a Redesign

Redesigning or redeveloping a website has become a major issue for companies as they seek to refine their online presence and invest in their websites. However, more than ever, the search engines are the biggest obstacle to website improvement.

I find that in website redevelopment projects, one of the largest hurdles encountered is dealing with the transition from the old website to a newer architecture. Unfortunately, some companies do not take this into consideration, because it is never brought up as a problem. When the site eventually goes live *without* the redirects in place from old pages (with rankings) to the new pages, both rankings and visitors will drop off drastically.

Many companies have experienced this pain, only to realize afterward that the problem was that no one accounted or took responsibility for planning the redirects, and the business suffered as a result. There needs to be a clear plan for dealing with forwarding the visitors and search engines from the old pages to the new pages. This is a very important consideration and one that must be dealt with in order to maintain rankings and visitors to the website after a redesign. For larger sites, planning a transition to maintain the links and rankings held by thousands of pages that will no longer exist is quickly becoming one of the more time-consuming tasks.

Surprisingly, the main obstacle to developing improved websites (both architecturally and usability-wise) is the search engines themselves. The method of retrieving pages into a central index for an algorithm is antiquated, because it does not account for improvements and changes in a website. In short, companies are being penalized for not being aware of the limitations of search engines, Google in particular.

The following is what goes wrong:

- In a website redesign project, the page URLs of the site typically change. Companies are becoming more aware of search-friendly programming and implementing it into their development. However, when the new architecture goes live, rankings are lost because old URLs are no longer available. The old architecture and old page URLs held the rankings.

- Incoming links to the website and the deep pages within the website no longer have a destination URL. This reduces the value of the incoming links to the website, because the destination of the link no longer exists.

To remedy these situations, the formula of applying URL rewrites and 301 redirects is employed in order to match the old pages to their newer counterparts. In a server redirect, the old page is requested, and the server scans through the instructions to see whether there is a new page to deliver instead of the old page. In doing this, rankings can usually be maintained.

Redirected links to the new URLs maintains visitors and their link value, but be aware that over time, that value can diminish. The redirected link is not a direct link; the new page destination may not be the page intended as the original link destination, thereby losing value. It is always best to have a direct incoming link to a specific URL for the best long-term link value. However, for site owners with hundreds to thousands of links, they now have to go back and ask other webmasters, site owners, and companies to edit the links on their sites to point to the new URL in order to receive the full value.

The issue with redirects is that every redirect takes a fraction of server resources to accomplish. A few redirects are fine; however, when working with sites that are taking 8 to 10 years of history and thousands of pages, the redirects become a considerable drag on server resources. Different methods can be used in this case, such as redirecting an old directory to the new directory (redirect the old pages within /old-category to www.websiteexample.com/new-category-content/).

Using this method, any request to any page within the old directory of a website will be redirected to the new directory, thereby reducing the need of redirecting every single page in the old directory. It is the quickest method of capturing the most pages. However, if there are a few well-ranking pages with many incoming links directly to those pages, I always recommend redirecting those to the new corresponding page. In that way, I can manage the transition for specific pages much more closely.

A Site Redesign Catch-22

Companies are developing websites with increasing technology and more complex programming every day, using search-friendly architecture, Ajax, CSS, and other technologies in an attempt to make the experience better for their users. However, because the means of information retrieval are so outdated, these same companies are sometimes penalized for changing a site that would have been better left alone.

Essentially, Google has its own rules of website development, redevelopment, and innovation. If a company is not aware of those rules or does not invest the time and money to reverse-engineer their new website to accommodate outdated technology, then they are effectively penalized.

In short, the rule of "Would I do this if search engines didn't exist?" (Google Webmaster Guidelines: Quality Guidelines; basic principles) is nonsensical. Developers are left to struggle with increasingly outdated search engine technology in an attempt to have a new website (that is ideally better for their users) maintain rankings.

Domain Management

Typically, your website will have a www prior to the domain name. As mentioned in the prior section, the information retrieval algorithm used by search engines is still based on a very old method. As such, to a search engine, your domain with the www is a different page than your website without the www prefix. In other words, www.website.com is considered to be a different page than website.com. Because it is a different URL, the search engines consider it to be a different page, even though the two URLs deliver the same page.

This is what is considered "duplicate content," when the same page is indexed by the search engines under two or more URLs. This causes confusion in the search engines as to how to apply the correct relevance to the proper page. The best method of gaining rankings is to have unique content that distinguishes your website from others. However, duplicate content provides an obstacle because there may be multiple pages, with the same content, found at different URLs.

One of the primary places this happens is at the domain level, where the home page can show up under multiple URLs. To humans, they all look the same, but to machines (search engines) they are all duplicate pages, saying the same thing, all at different locations. So, the search engine has to choose which URL is going to be the primary URL, and it may not be the one that the website owner prefers. This is where redirects help with managing the domain and directing the search engines to your preferred home page URL, rather than allowing the search engine to determine it for you.

Potentially, a home page can be considered a duplicated page in many ways; for example, the following home page URLs all point to the same page but appear as four different pages at four different locations:

`http://www.homepage.com`

`http://homepage.com`

`http://www.homepage.com/index.php` (or `home.php`, `.asp`, and so on)

`http://homepage.com/index.php`

This is called *canonicalization*; a different page could reside at each of these locations, but traditionally, it is the same page. Search engines then attempt to find the most relevant page to assign as the best source for assigning as the default domain URL.

Major search engines such as Google provide tools that allow users to determine a preferred domain, because the domain with or without the www is considered to be two unique pages, because they are unique URLs. Also, in the Google Webmaster Tools is an area to set redirects for Google. In the Parameter Handling section, users can set specific guides for Google to avoid the long URL parameters and instead direct Google to a shorter, logical URL (see Figure 14.9).

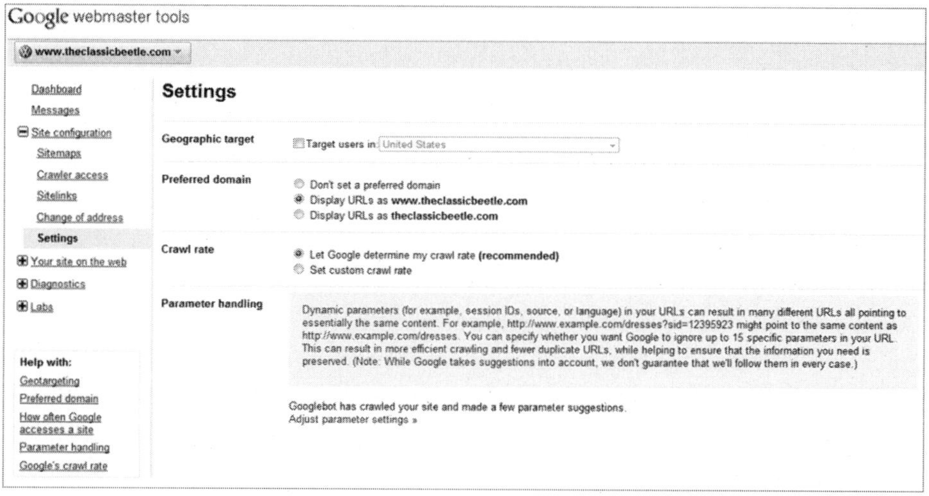

Figure 14.9 Google Webmaster Tools domain and parameter settings

Although many webmasters are very happy for the ability to manage this within Google, it is very important to realize that there are more search engines than Google. Simply making these changes in your Google Webmaster Tools settings does not change these issues for other search engines. This is why setting redirects to manage these issues at your own domain and on your own server is so important. Managing these issues for your own site will make all search engines view your site correctly, the way you want to manage them. Simply choosing to manage these issues in Google will not help other search engines, although it is a good tool to manage within Google specifically.

The redirection remedy for domain management is to choose a specific domain URL and redirect all other domain URLs to that specific domain. Choose between a domain with or without the www, and redirect all the traffic to the primary URL. This is a task I recommend; if you are not comfortable with performing, get help. This is a significant process, and having a programmer who is adept at making these instructions will help you.

Duplicate content can arise in a website in many other ways. These issues will be explored more in-depth in Thursday's lesson on avoiding duplicate content.

Beware of Domain-Level Redirects

The issues covered in this section are focused on domain management issues, but you should be aware that some programming methods employ redirects in order to manage other site issues but without considering search engine marketing.

CMS System Redirects

A content management system is a software program designed to allow a site's managers to add, edit, and manage content on the site without a knowledge of programming. As such, the interface has to be simple in order to allowing management and editing functions. The problem comes when CMS systems are purchased and employed, but the company developing the CMS did not take search engine spidering and indexing issues into account. As such, the CMS may employ redirects to manage the pages and architecture of the site, not aware of the issues it may create with search engines.

An example of this is easily identified when a visitor types in the domain of a website and is redirected to a long URL that contains additional subdirectories. An example of this was the American Cancer Society website. If a visitor went there directly by typing in www.cancer.org, a redirect would send them to www.cancer.org/docroot/home/index.asp (see Figure 14.10). What happened behind the scenes is that the content management system was publishing all of the pages in a deeper subdirectory, /docroot/. To direct all of the visitors to the new home page location that deep in the structure, a redirect was used. Unfortunately, this was a 302 temporary redirect.

Because of the 302 temporary redirect, search engines would not apply the "new" home page and home page URL as being the actual home page and URL. In a search for the website, the primary domain still appeared as the home page location (see Figure 14.11).

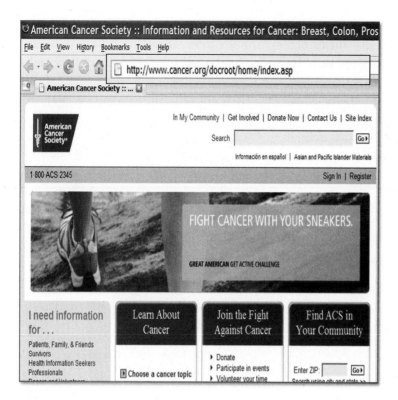

Figure 14.10 Cancer.org redirect to a deeper website structure

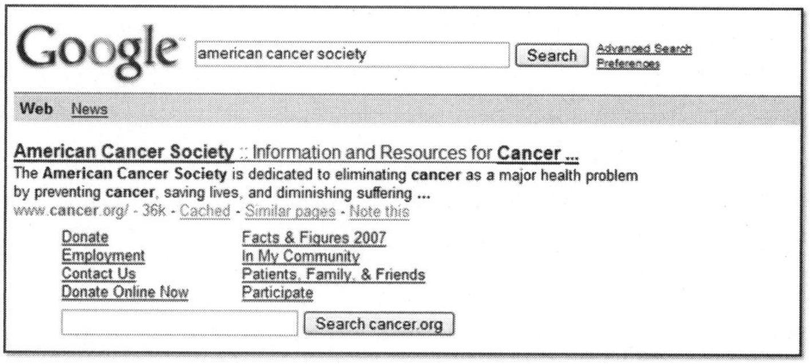

Figure 14.11 Google's result for Cancer.org still showed the location as the root-level URL and did not pick up the redirect because of the 302 code.

A redirect from the root level to a deeper structure of the site is not a recommended method of dealing with website structure. Today, the American Cancer Society has corrected the domain to be hosted at the primary URL and removed the redirect (see Figure 14.12).

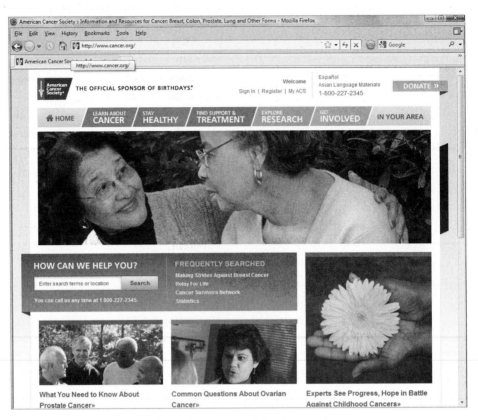

Figure 14.12 Cancer.org is now corrected to show the home page at the root-level URL.

A redirect at the root level causes a few problems with search engines. The first problem is simply one of website structure. Traditionally, the home page is considered the most important page of the website, because it is often the primary landing page for visitors, and it located at the domain level (www.domain-name.com). Visitors expect to see the home page of the website when they type in the domain address. The home page introduces the website's purpose and also contains much of the information necessary to reach all the other pages of the website.

Simply by the home page's technical location, at the root level of the domain, it is important. When redirecting the home page location to a "lower level" (such as another directory or subdirectory) of the website, the page appears to be less important to the search engines. This is simply a matter of the information hierarchy, because the most important page on the site appears to be in an "unimportant" place.

High-level pages tend to be considered more relevant and important for search engines. In the past, SEO experts would recommend keeping as many of the directories as close to the root as possible in order to assist in spidering and relevance. Much of the reason for this was anecdotal and based on experience and one's own interpretations. As search engine technology improved, deeper file structures become more irrelevant.

There is no search engine that has claimed preference one way or another, but keeping the home page on the root level is one area where SEO experts have agreed that preference and a clean hierarchical structure can assist your site's visibility.

However, when adding a 302 redirect from the root level of a website to a deep directory, there will be problems. The second problem deals with link value. The majority of links to any website are mainly domain-level links. Most people will link to the domain of a website. When a 302 redirect is employed, the value of the prior page is not applied to the new destination (because it is temporary). As such, all of the link value that was generated from other websites is now pointing to a page that does not exist.

The most optimal situation is that all of the incoming links are pointing to a page URL that has content reflecting the purpose of the incoming links. When there are incoming links but no destination page and no content, many of the relevance factors will be incomplete, and rankings will fall or vanish altogether.

Avoid domain-level redirects, as in the example of the American Cancer Society's Cancer.org, and avoid the CMSs that lock a website into a redirect-based deep site structure. By following these guides when selecting a CMS provider, you could avoid future issues with search engines.

Thursday: Uncover Duplicate Content

As mentioned many times in this chapter, duplicate content is a very real issue when managing a website. As your site becomes larger, as it becomes more complex, and as more functionality is added to provide better tools for navigation, there is always the possibility of creating multiple URLs for the same page of content.

Many consider duplicate content to cause a penalty in the search engines, but there is no such thing. Duplicate content creates difficulty in assigning unique content to a specific page. When the same page of supposedly unique content is now found on two or more pages, then the search engines are not able to identify the real source of that unique content. Rather than being a penalty, it is more of a consequence. The search engines are simply attempting to process multiple sources of information and find the primary page that has been lessened in value. By ensuring that each page is unique with its own unique URL, you can avoid duplicate content issues.

Managing duplicate content is a considerable challenge with dynamic websites, because it requires a substantial knowledge of tracking down issues and duplicate pages and then identifying the cause. Today I'll discuss some of the typical causes of duplicate content.

Use Google Webmaster Tools

Google's Webmaster Tools also includes a report that will show you duplicated title tags. This is a good first-level check, because you may find that some of your page titles are duplicated, which may lead to the entire pages being duplicated. However, if the multiple URLs are similar and you are using a content management system, then you have more investigation to do, because something may be set up incorrectly in your CMS.

Simply because the title tags are duplicated may not mean that your content is duplicated. This may also be an error from your optimization campaign, because the same title tag was used more than once. If that is the case, it is an easily remedied issue.

In using any of these tools, the key is not to panic! Stay calm and find the specific sources of the problem before you go ranting at someone from IT or calling your web developer. It is best to be calm and research the issue first.

Use Analytics

Using your web analytics program is the first place to find duplicate content issues. When examining the pages that are being requested by visitors, you can filter through all of the pages by using a word or common URL or page title feature.

In Google Analytics, the Content > Top Content report will show the pages that have been requested by visitors in that time period (see Figure 14.13). At this report, go to Filter Page Containing at the bottom of the page listing and add your parameter or page URL. It may take some refining, but you can see what pages are similar or duplicates of the URL. Typically, the duplication can be spotted in the URL extension (.htm and .html), an added parameter, or even a misplaced character in the URL.

Figure 14.13 Use Google Analytics to find duplicated URLs and pages.

Although the Google tools are being represented well in this section, it is important to remember that all search engines rely on the same types of information retrieval (at this point). Google has been aggressive in helping site owners and providing helpful information, so the tools offered are very productive. Any issues uncovered in Google's Webmaster Tools will also help fix issues in other search engines.

Use Search Results

A very easy way of determining duplicate content is to do a search with a unique string of content from your website.

To do a simple search in Google for uniqueness, type a copied block of content from your website, using quotes, into Google's search box (see Figure 14.14). In this example, the results show only pages that include the quoted content "The BDP-S370 Blu-ray Disc player features Blu-ray 3D playback, Wi-Fi Internet connectivity, and instant streaming of online video content from the BRAVIA Internet Video platform. When connected to a broadband Internet network." A portion of this text can be seen in the bold text in every result. As you can see, 51,000 websites use the same manufacturer's description for this product. Only the popular sites will have any visibility for this content.

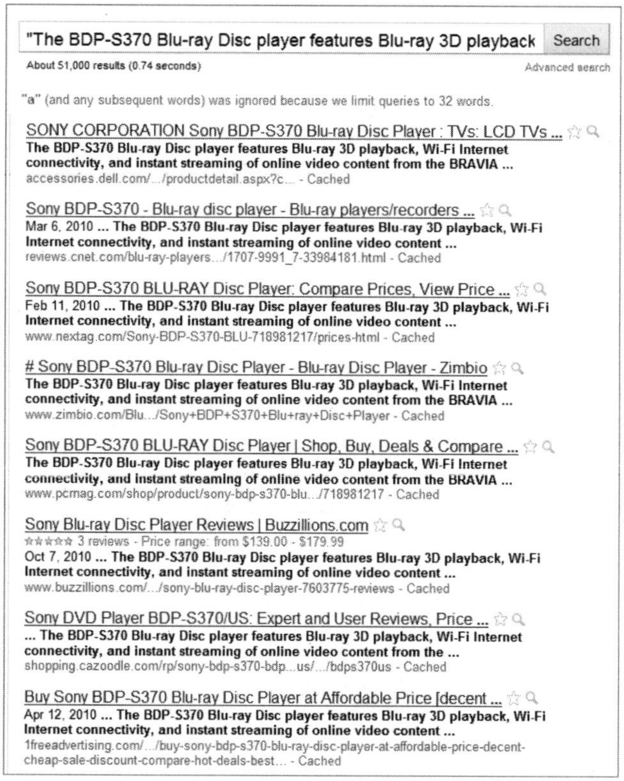

Figure 14.14 Searching a quoted sentence to find duplicate content

Keep an Eye Out for Plagiarism!

You may find that some sites are copying your content. If this happens, you can report such things to Google, if it is overly egregious, but it is a common occurrence. An additional resource to find plagiarized content on the Web is Copyscape, www.copyscape.com.

The results shown are all from your website. Using quotes means that you are searching for that exact text. Without quotes, you will get the pages that most closely resemble that phrase. If more than one page shows up in the results for a sentence or two when using quotes, then look at the URLs; if they are different, then you know that you have duplicate content happening on your website.

Identify the Culprits

Unfortunately, there is no easy way to determine how duplicate content arises on your website. There are some traditional methods that will generate duplicate pages, but many times it is the result of CMS programming. Even adding modules or additional management programming may cause duplicate content.

In one case, the popular Magento eCommerce product generated thousands of duplicated pages on a website of only 25 products. The culprit was the "order by price" function, which created innumerable versions of alternate pages as part of the programmed function. In many cases, the culprit is a function that is added to increase management, but if the programmer does not take the search engines into account, the result could create hundreds to thousands of new URLs in order to perform the function.

There are a few primary places to find duplicated URLs. One is the home page logo. On websites, the logo is typically a link to the home page of the website. Every once in a while the home page logo will be programmed to go to the home page URL (typically www.website.com/index.php), but it is a different URL than the root level (typically www.website.com/). In doing this, the link from the logo had created a link to another home page URL from every page of the website. Be sure that the logo links to the preferred version of the domain, based on the redirect instructions from Wednesday's section.

Another culprit is usually found on ecommerce websites. When the shopping cart is programmed and added to the website, it technically changes to a new subdomain, https, the secure version of the website. Visitors expect to see the security measures on the browser, such as the lock icon and the https in the URL window.

Let's take a moment to think about the types of links programmers use in building navigation. There is the *absolute link*, which includes the entire link path to the document, www.website.com/products/detail/shoe. Then, there is the *relative link*. The relative link only uses the directory structure for navigation without the full domain path, such as /products/detail/shoe. The relative link method is a time-saver in some cases, because programmers do not have to type in the complete URL in order for the website to function properly.

However, if the navigation or other links within the secure portion of the site employ the relative URL, then the entire site will be duplicated. For example, if you are in the secure shopping portion of a website, `www.website.com/cart/purchase`, and there is a relative home page link on that page (`/home.php`), then the server fills in the rest of the information for the link based on the secure setting (`https://`). As a result, all of the domains can be duplicated; `http://www.homepage.com/` is duplicated as `https://www.homepage.com`, and so on. Based on this, I always recommend using absolute URLs to manage website links, especially in the ecommerce cart or in any type of subdomains.

Each CMS has the potential to create duplicate content, and website managers have to be constantly vigilant about this. Whenever adding programming or functions, you need to be aware of how the new function will create or manage pages. The ways that CMSs create duplicated pages are as unique and as plentiful as the CMSs themselves.

If the problem cannot be corrected, then it may be managed either via a redirect on the server or by blocking the pages from the search engines by use of the `robots.txt` file, which is Friday's topic.

Friday: Utilize Robots.txt to Welcome Search Engines

Nothing is as confusing to a website owner as the `robots.txt` file. The `robots.txt` file is a programming protocol (agreed upon rules) between a web server and the search engine spider. `robots.txt` contains a set of instructions for compliant spiders to follow. Unfortunately, although search engines understand the file, humans have a difficult time grasping machine language, especially if they rarely deal with it.

The Google blog ran a two-part series on understanding `robots.txt` and the robots metatag. Both of these articles, while providing a lot of great in-depth information, are much more than any site owner or manager wants to know. Especially when you start talking technology, bots, spiders, permissions, and so on, most owners and marketers don't know where to start, nor do they even want to understand the technology behind either of these issues. What people really want to know is what to do and where to put it so they can get on with the business of the website. If that's you, just read the next section, "Just Tell Me What I Need to Know!" The following sections provide some background for those of you who are curious to know more about why this little file is so important.

Just Tell Me What I Need to Know!

The best way to explain the `robots.txt` file is that it is a "welcome mat" for the search engines (Figure 14.15). It's not so much that the file is necessary for search engine success, but it's one of those hundreds of small things that you need to consider, much like everything in SEO. If you have it, it will help your search engine success in a very small way. If you don't have it, it won't harm you; it's simply a technical issue. The downside of not providing a `robots.txt` file is that you are relinquishing some control to the search engines and leaving some issues to chance. I don't like that.

If you do have it, you might have seen a slight improvement in search engine rankings. Most experience minor improvements, but the evidence is mostly anecdotal. You won't get penalized for not having this file but are able to manage the site more closely and get some reward (even if it is a slight boost) from adding this file.

The search engines request the `robots.txt` file before or during every spidering session. Some request it before every session, and some request prior to groups of pages. Either way, search engines request this file multiple times in a session and in a day. If the file does not exist, then it shows up as a "page not found" error in your web server log files. So, if the search engines request it, it must be necessary to their purposes. That's why I believe it is important to have—it is a way of maintaining more control over your website. You can see whether you have a `robots.txt` file or what is in it by typing into your browser **www.yourdomain.com/robots.txt** (*yourdomain* is the domain of your website). I like to explain it as a "welcome mat" because some people have a welcome mat at the entrance of their house and some people don't. Either way, it doesn't prevent people from coming into the house. It's the same for the `robots.txt` file; it simply tells search engines that they are welcome to visit the site.

If you want to get fancy, though, you can tell the search engine where *not* to go on your site. Typically, these are files that are not important to the search engines or files that you don't want showing up in the search results. It's kind of like that closet where you store all your junk when you quickly clean the house. When people come over, you don't want them to use that closet. It's not vital for them to know what is in there, because it's stuff you want stored out of sight.

For a website, some people "disallow" printer-friendly pages, images, duplicated directories, and admin pages that they do not want to show up in the search results. Now, I am not saying to use this as a way of protecting information that you don't want people to see. If that is the case, then you need to put that behind a password.

The robots.txt file is not to hide information from people. It simply to tell the search engines not to index the content.

Knowing this is really what's important from a marketing standpoint; the technical standpoint is a little more difficult, because it gets into server commands, which most people don't understand. Frankly, I'm surprised how many times I run into problems with the robots.txt as the culprit. This little file has been the cause of a lot of problems for some very large websites.

However, as promised, here is what you need to do if you just want this done, without all of the technical background.

Open a text editor, such as Notepad or equivalent program, and type this in:

```
User-agent: *
Disallow:
```

Now, save the file with the name robots and the .txt extension. It should look like Figure 14.15.

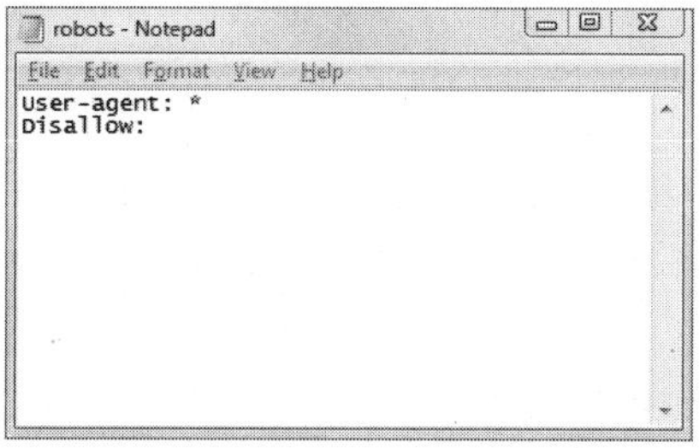

Figure 14.15 The robots.txt file, set to allow the entire website to be spidered by the search engines

Upload this file using an FTP program to the root level of your website. Congratulations! You now have put out the welcome mat for the search engines. If you are curious to know more, read on. If not, jump ahead to the review and get started evaluating and working on your site!

Learning *robots.txt* Structure

Only two lines are required for a standard robots.txt file. The first line identifies the robots you want to specifically command.

```
User-agent: *
```

The asterisk is a wildcard, meaning "all robots—follow these instructions."

The second line tells the robots where *not* to go, which is defined either at the directory level or at the page level.

```
Disallow:
```

If you don't want to disallow anything, then don't type another character! That's the typical setup to allow the search engines free reign of your website. It's as simple as that.

Now, some people get a little fancy and like to disallow certain directories. This is usually done to remove any duplicate content. So, let's say I have a directory of all my printer-friendly pages, which are really only duplicates of the HTML pages.

```
User-agent: *
Disallow: /printerfriendly/
```

I've disallowed the entire directory of printer-friendly pages by specifically naming it to the search engines.

The forward slash is an important part of this file. Where most people make their mistakes is with that slash. The forward slash indicates a directory, and anything contained in the directory after the first forward slash will be disallowed. A forward slash by itself indicates that you want to block the entire root directory and anything contained within the structure. Ouch! That would be a big mistake!

Accidentally Blocking Your Website

By adding a slash to the disallow command, like this:

```
Disallow:/
```

you are telling the search engines to "go away" with this command. This would be disastrous for most websites, and it happens often.

©iStockphoto.com/[sjlocke]

The reason that this happens often is from development projects where the robots.txt is used to block search engines from indexing the work "in progress." When the site goes live, the development team will just copy everything from a staging server or development directory onto the new server. The robots.txt file simply gets copied over with the new website and gets forgotten. Only when the rankings fall and the new site does not appear in the search engines does someone realize that there is a problem.

To remedy this, consider using an `.htaccess` password rather than `robots.txt` to block access. The password access would be nearly impossible to "accidentally" deploy on a new site, because it would be noticed immediately.

Google's Webmaster Tools has a function (under Site Configuration > Crawler Access) that will show you the status of your `robots.txt` file and all of the documents and directories that are being blocked. This tool shows you the last time that the file was requested and the pages that are disallowed from Google's index. At the bottom of the page, you can test your `robots.txt` file to be sure that Googlebot and Googlebot-Mobile (Google's search engine spiders) are able to successfully access your website. If you have set up your account using Google's Webmaster Tools, the name of the website and the text of the `robots.txt` should be shown in this resource. Click the test button at the bottom of the page, and Google will show you if it is able to access your site using the current `robots.txt` protocol (see Figure 14.16).

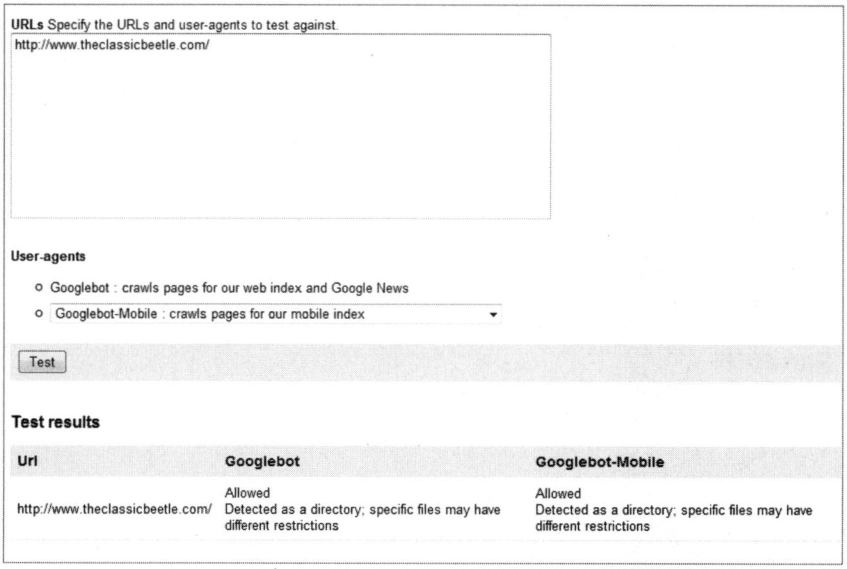

Figure 14.16 A successful `robots.txt` test in Google's Webmaster Tools

As with most of these resources, if it works in Google's Webmaster Tools, it will work with other search engines. If Google is not able to access your site because of `robots.txt`, then Yahoo!, Bing, Ask, and others will not be able to access your site either.

Additionally, the `robots.txt` is only a protocol. Not all search engines nor all bots follow the protocol. There are content "scrapers" (bots that copy your content for republication on other websites) that pay no attention to the `robots.txt` file. This is not a magical file that completely blocks access to the files you want to keep protected or out of sight. Anyone can produce a bot that will download information from a website. It is the creator of the bot who decides whether they will create a `robots.txt`-compliant bot. That is why this is not intended to be used for any type of security.

Additional *robots.txt* Resources

Ideally, this has helped a few understand the place and purpose of the `robots.txt` file. Even more than that, I hope that it has taken the fear away from dealing with this file. Many site managers are very gun-shy, because they may have had a disallowed site from the search engines with a misplaced slash at one time or another.

If you want more information about the `robots.txt` file and all the things you can do with it, I suggest the following resources:

Robotstxt.org: www.robotstxt.org

Official Google Blog: The Robots Exclusion, pt 1: http://googleblog.blogspot .com/2007/01/controlling-how-search-engines-access.html

Google Blog: The Robots Exclusion, pt 2: http://googleblog.blogspot.com/2007/02/ robots-exclusion-protocol.html

Robot.txt Code Generation Tool: www.mcanerin.com/en/search-engine/robots-txt.asp

The bottom line when dealing with `robots.txt`? Don't be afraid to ask for help. Many marketers, business owners, and large companies have unwittingly blocked the search engines from accessing their websites. It's a simple file that can cause a lot of problems, so don't be afraid to have a third party check your work.

Review and Hands-On

Learn about your server and the language used to develop your website.

- What type of server is your website hosted on? (Windows Server, Apache, other, and so on.)
- What type of database does your website use?
- What type of scripting language does your website employ?
- Do you have a rewrite function on your URLs?
- What function was used to develop the rewrite?

Provide three positive reasons that persuaded you or your company to choose that particular host server, database, and language selection for your site.

Find a software program or a website that will provide a header check. Check your page codes to ensure that mostly you have a 200 OK code for a page that was requested and delivered. If you have redirects in place, be sure to check them, and make sure that they are 301 redirects and they are going to the correct destination.

It's time to bring out all of the tools that have been discussed about content duplication: webmaster tools, analytics, and search. Look in your analytics, and see whether there are any page duplications for the same content or page titles. Search for a unique sentence from a few of your pages and see whether there are any duplicates. Beyond searching on your website, search online to see whether you have syndicated content that is being duplicated online.

Check the status of your site in Google's Webmaster Tools. Go to the Crawler Access section and the report, and test to see whether your website is accessible with your newly created (or revised) robots.txt.

Week 12: Remember the Important Details

If you have been religiously reading this book an hour a day, then congratulations—you should now be finishing up the third month of your web marketing journey. You're past the halfway point in learning about all about the development, design, content, architecture, and persuasiveness and are on your way to fully marketing your business through the use of analytics, PPC, social media, link building, blogging, and networking.

At this point in the development and marketing cycle people tend to get excited about what's to come, and they forget the important little details that can mean so much in a website. The river of marketing is very shallow yet very wide. They basic concepts are easy to grasp, but it is the thousands of little details.

Chapter Contents
Monday: Compare Tables and CSS
Tuesday: Create Better Error Pages
Wednesday: Test Your Site Search
Thursday: Consider Site Maps
Friday: Use Local and Mobile Marketing

Monday: Compare Tables and CSS

When I bring up this topic in seminars, I immediately can see who knows what is coming simply based on the reactions. Marketers who have no idea about this will stare at me with "deer in headlights" regret, thinking that they have stumbled into a programming class. Programmers and developers, who are familiar with this, know that they can take it easy for a half an hour, because this is old knowledge to them.

If you've done any amount of programming, you'll be familiar with the concepts of tables and Cascading Style Sheets (CSS). For marketers, these are layout instructions that build a page. Tables are a method of arranging content on the page. CSS does the same but goes further than simply location-based instructions; CSS includes color, size, action, and more, and it does it in a very elegant manner when compared to the traditional HTML programming, which uses tables.

Tables

Tables are a simple way of laying out content, and this was the primary method of building a page in most early What You See Is What You Get (WYSIWYG) website development tools. By making layout easy for the nonprogrammer, programs would build code and arrange the images, text, and objects into a table-based format.

Picture building a website in a spreadsheet—you can merge tables for larger fields and lay out paragraphs in the places you want them to be. However, if you add a picture, it will make that row and column extremely large when compared to the rest of the rows in order to accommodate the dimensions of the image. So, if you want to align the text around the image, you have to start merging cells, rows, or columns in order to make the content flow around the image.

Figure 15.1 shows the table-based layout of the computer content on the Costco website. When only looking at it from a layout perspective and blocking the images, you can begin to see the structure of the website's layout. You can see the block-type layout for each product and category outlined; some cells are merged, and some cells contain many other cells in order to show the information in the right order.

This type of layout is why many websites do not render well on smartphones. Until the iPhone came out with the Safari browser, most smartphones were not able to render websites the way they were intended. How the older generation of smartphones renders a website is similar to how the search engine reads a web page. Both view the code from top to bottom as a linear set of instructions. In doing so, the table-based layout is read in order from the top-left column to the bottom-right corner. The search engine and the phone read the code from top to bottom and display it likewise, even though the table-based layout creates a left-to-right design that is viewed in browsers. This is called *linearization*.

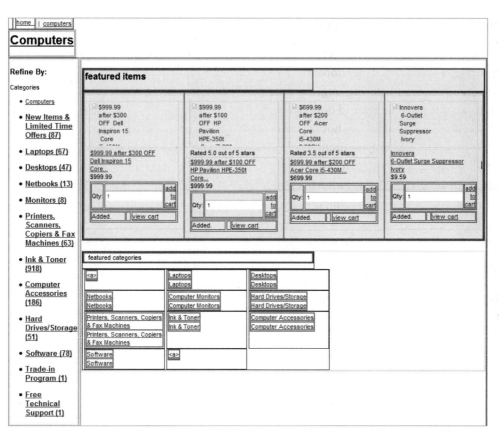

Figure 15.1 Costco.com's table-based layout

Some mobile browsers do not have the capacity to render web pages similar to what one would see on a computer. The processors just aren't able to handle the instructions. Older smartphones have trouble with sites that use tables. Navigation is hard to find, content is near the bottom, and nothing is in the right place—it all appears chunky and out of order. This is the result of a table-based layout. The new generations of smartphones, such as the iPhone, Android, and Windows phones, however, are able to render the website on the phone just as one would see it on a computer browser.

On both search engines and some smartphones, linearization will read the top-left cell first and then everything in the left column. At the end of the column, the top of the second column and everything in that column will appear, and then subsequent columns will be read and rendered (Figure 15.2).

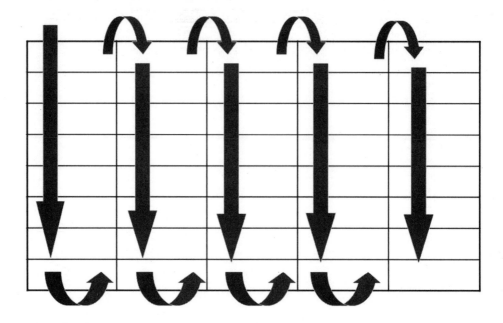

Figure 15.2 The rendering and reading of a table-based layout is column by column.

This is simply based on the code and how it is read and rendered within each device and browser. Tables, while visually showing the programmer and the end user a traditional left-to-right reading order, are simply code that is meant to render visually left to right in a browser. However, the code is written as instructions, starting with the top-left cell and the subsequent leftmost column. The instructions then move on to the next column, starting at the top, and so on. Older mobile browsers cannot render the left to right instructions on the screen, so the table columns appear "stacked" in a linear layout, which causes an appearance of an unorganized layout.

The Costco website appears to make sense when looking at the browser-based rendering and reading of the code, but when linearized, everything is then stacked up and looks unorganized (see Figure 15.3).

There are many solutions to this dilemma. One solution would be to create a mobile-friendly website that will enable visitors to access the information that is critical to them. The type of business you have and how customers interact with your information would determine the type of mobile site you would offer. Another solution would be to redevelop your website into a CSS-based layout, with consideration for mobile access. This would be a significant investment, but it is an investment that has far-reaching benefits, because the CSS-based layout enables your website to be rendered on multiple devices, multiple browsers, and multiple operating systems.

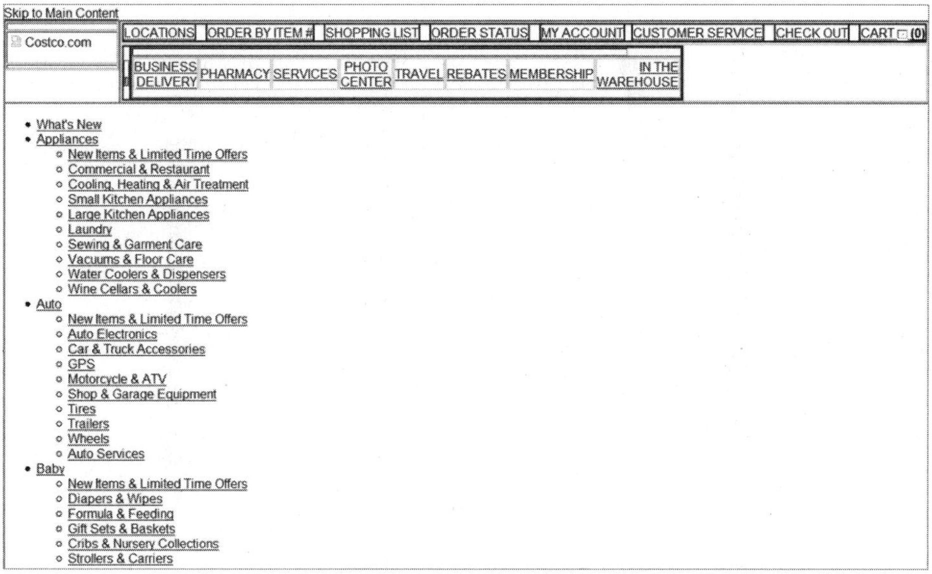

Skip to Main Content

Costco.com | LOCATIONS | ORDER BY ITEM # | SHOPPING LIST | ORDER STATUS | MY ACCOUNT | CUSTOMER SERVICE | CHECK OUT | CART ☐ (0)

BUSINESS DELIVERY | PHARMACY | SERVICES | PHOTO CENTER | TRAVEL | REBATES | MEMBERSHIP | IN THE WAREHOUSE

- What's New
- Appliances
  - New Items & Limited Time Offers
  - Commercial & Restaurant
  - Cooling, Heating & Air Treatment
  - Small Kitchen Appliances
  - Large Kitchen Appliances
  - Laundry
  - Sewing & Garment Care
  - Vacuums & Floor Care
  - Water Coolers & Dispensers
  - Wine Cellars & Coolers
- Auto
  - New Items & Limited Time Offers
  - Auto Electronics
  - Car & Truck Accessories
  - GPS
  - Motorcycle & ATV
  - Shop & Garage Equipment
  - Tires
  - Trailers
  - Wheels
  - Auto Services
- Baby
  - New Items & Limited Time Offers
  - Diapers & Wipes
  - Formula & Feeding
  - Gift Sets & Baskets
  - Cribs & Nursery Collections
  - Strollers & Carriers

a

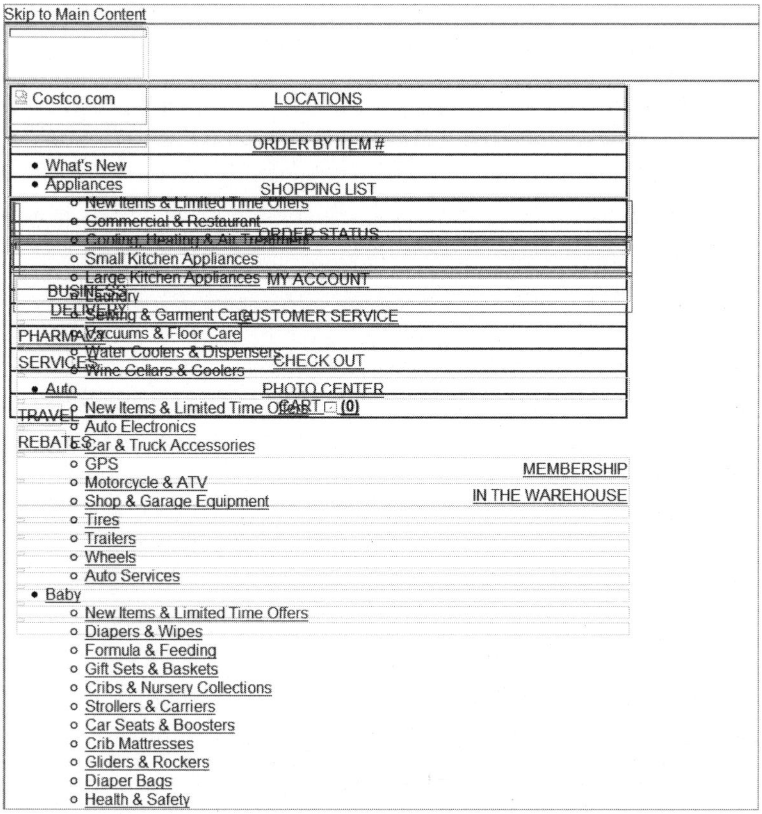

Skip to Main Content

Costco.com   LOCATIONS

                    ORDER BY ITEM #

- What's New
- Appliances   SHOPPING LIST
  - New Items & Limited Time Offers
  - Commercial & Restaurant
  - Cooling, Heating & Air Treatment   ORDER STATUS
  - Small Kitchen Appliances
  - Large Kitchen Appliances   MY ACCOUNT
BUSINESS   Laundry
DELIVERY   Sewing & Garment Care   CUSTOMER SERVICE
PHARMACY   Vacuums & Floor Care
             Water Coolers & Dispensers
SERVICES   Wine Cellars & Coolers   CHECK OUT
- Auto   PHOTO CENTER
TRAVEL   New Items & Limited Time Offers   CART ☐ (0)
  - Auto Electronics
REBATES   Car & Truck Accessories
  - GPS   MEMBERSHIP
  - Motorcycle & ATV   IN THE WAREHOUSE
  - Shop & Garage Equipment
  - Tires
  - Trailers
  - Wheels
  - Auto Services
- Baby
  - New Items & Limited Time Offers
  - Diapers & Wipes
  - Formula & Feeding
  - Gift Sets & Baskets
  - Cribs & Nursery Collections
  - Strollers & Carriers
  - Car Seats & Boosters
  - Crib Mattresses
  - Gliders & Rockers
  - Diaper Bags
  - Health & Safety

b

Figure 15.3 Costco.com: computer page table-based layout (a) and then with the same page linearized (b)

CSS

With CSS, website development took a leap forward, because the ability to separate the instructions for layout, design, text attributes, and many other visual elements were able to be distilled into single document. This document would reside on the server, and each page of the website would simply call out the instructions from the central document, and the design would be applied to the page. Figure 15.4 shows an example using www.csszengarden.com.

The same base code is used in each of the designs. The only change to the code in each page shown is the callout to a specific CSS style sheet that controls the design, layout, and text markup. This callout is contained in the heading of the code (see Figure 15.5). The callout is as follows:

```
<style type="text/css" title="currentStyle" media="screen">@import "/205/205.css";
```

a

Figure 15.4 The CSS Zen Garden website (a) shows how different style sheets can be applied to the same code, creating an entirely new layout and design. (b and c) The same code rendered with two different style sheets.

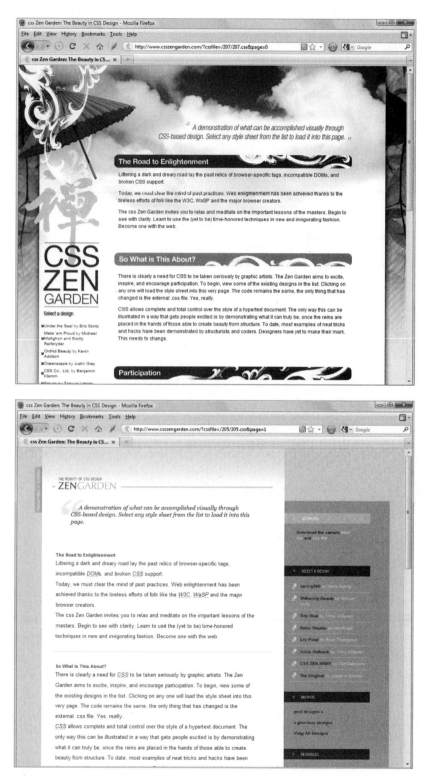

b

c

Figure 15.4 *(Continued)*

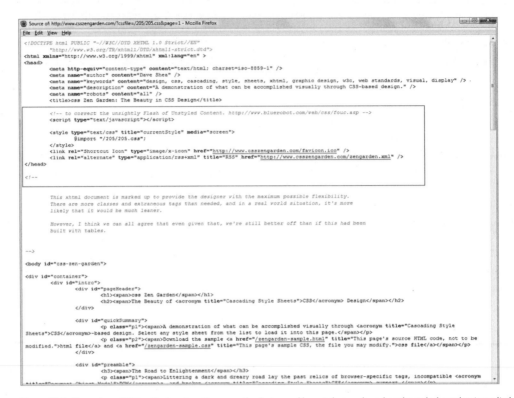

Figure 15.5 The code on CSS Zen Garden stays the same, the design and layout changes based on the stylesheet that is applied.

This allowed pages to be developed with content as the central focus within the code. Rather than building pages with hundreds of lines of code that were simply meant for layout and design instructions, those instructions did not need to be on the page, which then created shorter and simpler pages of codes. At this time, around the late 1990s through the next few years, webmasters were also fearful of too much code on the page, because there were indexing limits of the amount of code that search engines would download from a single page. This is less of a current focus, because current trends have focused on the design and the user interaction, as well as creating a faster download of the page. Google has taken steps to assist webmasters, through Google's Webmaster Tools, in creating lighter, more optimized pages that will decrease the load time of pages. While storage space and technology are still improving, lighter pages seem to be favored. Instead of the code being full of instructions, now the code is primarily content, which possibly enables better rankings.

Through CSS, the design of the page is separate from the structure and content. The code on the page is shorter, because the browser links to the reference file that provides the instructions for layout, design, and additional page information. Because of this, CSS designs are relatively easy to change. By creating the design and layout through CSS, the content and structure of the page are separate, thereby allowing a CSS template to be easily applied. Blogs especially take advantage of the CSS programming, and many blog publishers are able to change designs within minutes simply by loading a new CSS template.

The advantage to the CSS layout is that it is easily adaptable, making the CSS site very flexible, especially when loading into other devices, such as smartphones. Because a strict programming style such as tables is not used, the CSS "flows" and also makes accessibility easier, making the programming much more fluid. Websites become much more flexible across different devices, browsers, and operating systems.

Tuesday: Create Better Error Pages

One of the best investments in time on your website is to create a custom error page. An error page is a default page that the visitor sees when the page they requested is not found. Nearly every Internet user has landed on a generic, server-generated 404 error page at least once (see Figure 15.6).

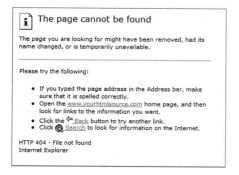

Figure 15.6 A typical 404 error page

Error-Page Basics

The reasons that a visitor stumbles upon your error page are many, and they are not always under your control. It could be an error in the code on a particular page that prevents the proper page from being delivered. Another website may have linked to your site and misspelled the URL name, or it could be a link to an older page, prior to your redesign. Sometimes, users attempt to directly navigate to a page on a website and mistype a character. Most likely, however, the page was removed altogether and no "forwarding address" was provided (remember the purpose of the 301 redirect, discussed in Chapter 14).

If there are no redirects in place after you redesign your website and the page URLs have changed, then your visitors from the search engines, bookmarks, and links will all see your error page. One of the most common times that visitors find error pages is from the search results. As you may remember, search engines download copies of your website to their database. Even if you redesign your website and create new pages, the old ones are still retained in the database for some time. If those old pages held any rankings at all and there are no redirects in place, then those searchers who click the link will go to the error page and see the generic "page not found" message.

Whatever the cause, you need to ensure that when a visitor comes upon your error page, the error page is a navigation tool and not a dead end. This is the reason for the custom error page; it is a contingency plan for when things go wrong (it is not "if" they go wrong—it is "when," so it is simply smart planning to account for anything that could go wrong for your visitors).

Consider Your Phrasing

At the very least, your error page should contain the main navigation of your website. Sorry to say, I have seen many custom error pages that simply provide the error message but no method of getting back into the website. You need to provide the visitor another means of navigation other than their Back button. If the visitor uses the Back button when finding your error page from a search, you have lost them. Keep the visitor moving forward and making progress.

Your goal is to create a friendly, helpful message that communicates assistance. Provide the main navigation as well as helpful groups of links to specific information groups within the website. Offer a search box, especially if it works well on your website (that will be addressed in Wednesday's lesson). If you offer promotions or campaigns, offer those links as well.

Be proactive by developing a report in your analytics program, checking on this page every month or quarter, and seeing how your visitors are finding the page. This allows you to correct issues as they are found, rather than letting things creep up as a surprise. In all, the error page needs to be a resource and not a dead end. Be sure you know which it is and how your visitors are finding it and reacting to it.

What's a 404?

Your users may not even know what a 404 error is. Some of you reading this book may still not know. A 404 Not Found code is a server response code (like the 301 Moved Permanently). However, web surfers may not know (or care) what a 404 code is or means. They have already landed on a page that they didn't expect, so don't confuse things even further by labeling the page "404" or "404 Error Page."

There are a lot of wonderfully creative error pages on the Web; unfortunately, many make use of the 404 code, which the primary audience of the website may not understand. Rethink your use of "programmer-speak" and server codes, especially if your audience is not tech-savvy and may not understand the usage of the 404 code designation and design into the error page. The message needs to be friendlier and more informative than the default message of "Error 404, Page not Found." This is a server code and message, which is not written for the visitor.

On the technical side, do not use a redirect to divert people from the error page to the home page, especially with a 302 redirect. Let visitors hit the error page and find their way from there. Redirecting errors to the home page or to the site map creates havoc with the search engines, which rely upon the 404 error code to know whether the page is no longer available.

Don't Assign Blame

Most of the error pages seem to imply that the visitor is at fault for discovering the error. Typical error messages reinforce this notion that the user is at fault:

- "Make sure you haven't mistyped the URL."
- "You may have bookmarked a page that no longer exists."
- "The content you requested couldn't be found."
- "Check that the web address that you entered doesn't contain a typo."
- "It is possible that you may have typed the address incorrectly?"

Now let's make this very clear. When you imply the user is at fault for mistyping an address, you are assuming the following:

- Visitors use the URL bar as their primary navigation interface.
- Visitors are typing in a page destination that is beyond the domain level.
- Your site has no broken links.

If you watch your analytics, you will find that the majority of visitors to your error pages will come from links from other websites or search engines. This is mainly from old links that have not been updated (maybe from your last redesign or two). In this case, it is not the fault of the visitor for following a link that has no destination. The fault is with you for not redirecting an old link to the new destination page.

To assure the visitor that they are in the right place and the fault is most likely not theirs, the message of the error page is critical. This is not a "blame game." Keep the message on task, which is getting your visitor to the information they intended to access as soon and as directly as possible.

I tell marketing departments that the responsibility for designing and writing the messaging on the error page is theirs and not the IT department. When the IT department is told to create an error page, they do just that, and you have an error page. Instead, the error page is the realm of the marketer, and the purpose is to clarify and assist the user experience, because it was just interrupted. This is a high-risk situation that needs to be handled well, because it could mean that visitors will leave your website.

Essential Parts of an Error Page

Typically, error pages lack even the most basic navigation tools, which is amazingly counterintuitive. A visitor has just been stranded, and very few sites offer a little help. The error page should be the most navigation-and-tool-friendly page on your website.

Every 404 error page should contain the following (at a minimum):

- Main navigation
- Search box
- Friendly message (without blame)
- Primary hierarchy of links to content

Check out the examples in the next section; they are excellent inspiration.

Great Error-Page Examples

I have always found that seeing some examples of others' 404 error pages can provide inspiration for your error pages. Here are a few that I think deserve mention:

Apple Apple has one of the best in user experiences in the business. Figure 15.7 shows an error page from Apple.com.

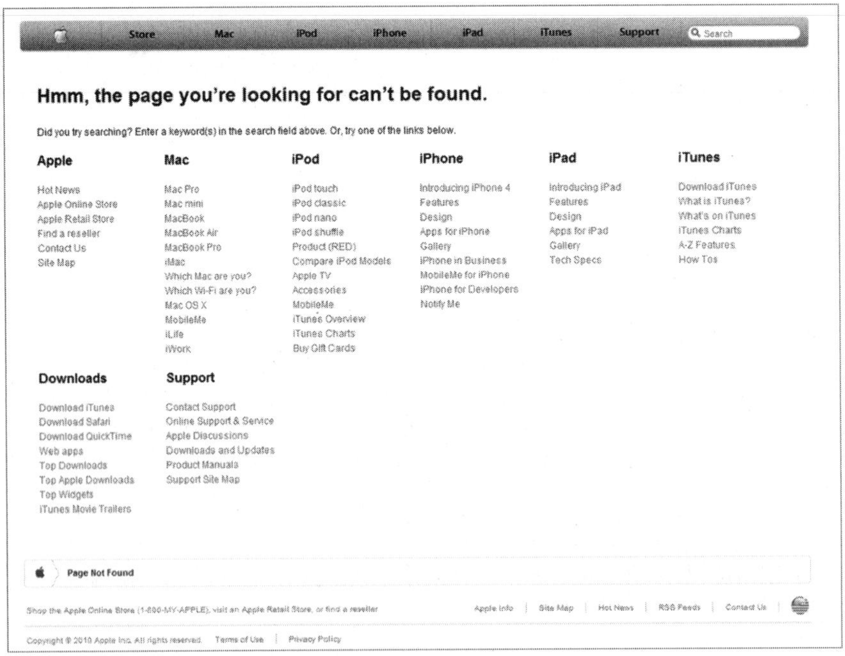

Figure 15.7 Apple's 404 error page. Simple, no 404 code, no blame, and lots of navigational assistance

A List Apart This is a technical site with a nontechnical error page, with one of the friendliest explanations (Figure 15.8).

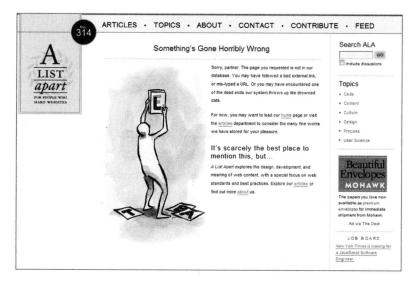

Figure 15.8 A List Apart presents a humorous look at the error page, especially since the website focuses on best practices.

Etsy This site presents a page that's friendly and kitschy. There is very little to distract the visitor, but it is effective (Figure 15.9).

Figure 15.9 Etsy fits the error page to their audience, which is crafters and those who purchase unique, handmade items.

Mozilla This site has a message with impressive friendliness and clarity, especially for a primarily tech-based site (Figure 15.10).

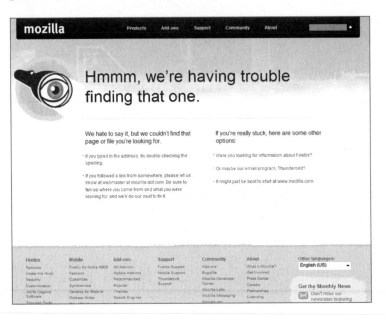

Figure 15.10 Mozilla.com provides a substantial number of links to the primary information areas but a clear focus on the three primary areas of content.

Volkswagen This site offers a friendly message, no blame, and plenty of information links to get back into the site (Figure 15.11).

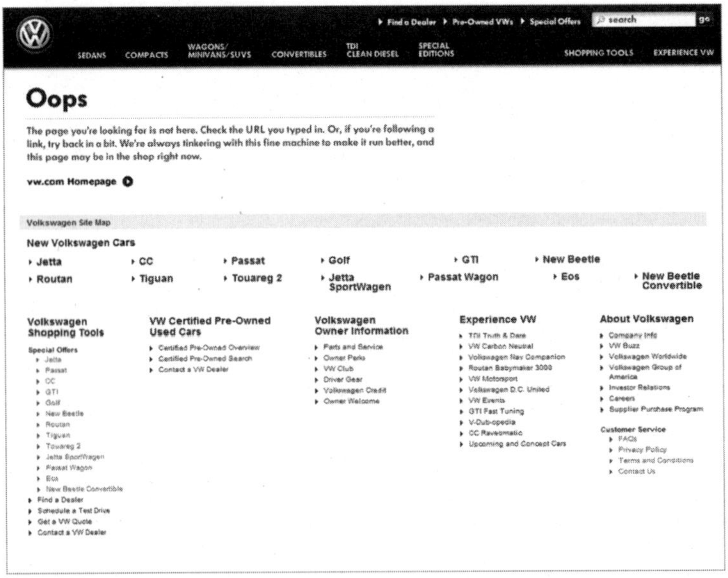

Figure 15.11 VW.com presents a slightly offbeat page, especially for a large company, but does not lack in providing links and helpful message.

The Wall Street Journal This site is very straightforward but informative; it relies on providing links back into the content (Figure 15.12).

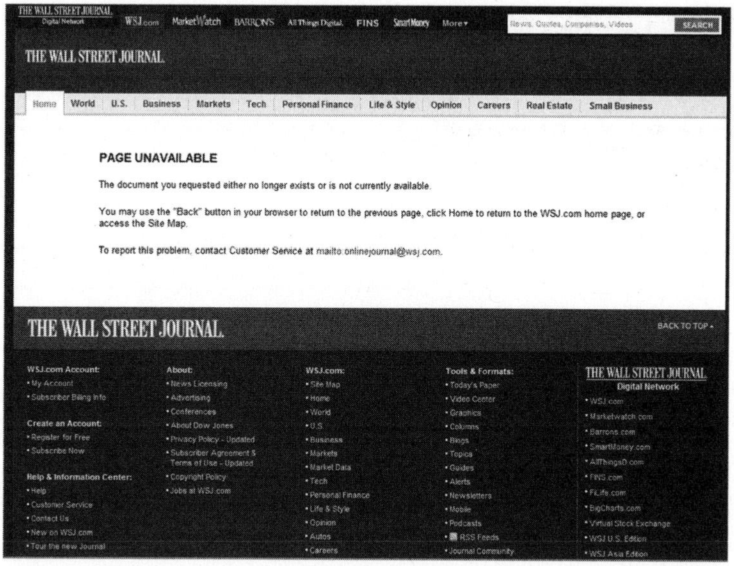

Figure 15.12 WSJ.com presents links to the major parts of the day's news, navigation to all of the properties and news areas, and a link to report any problems.

Center'd This site offers a cute and cuddly approach that is perfect for a social-media site (Figure 15.13).

Figure 15.13 Center'd goes for the cute and cuddly version of an error page. Maybe the visitor will stay because of the cuteness factor?

37signals This showcases usability and aggressive error-solving techniques. Note that although a mistyped URL is listed as one possible reason for the error, the phrasing is not accusatory (Figure 15.14).

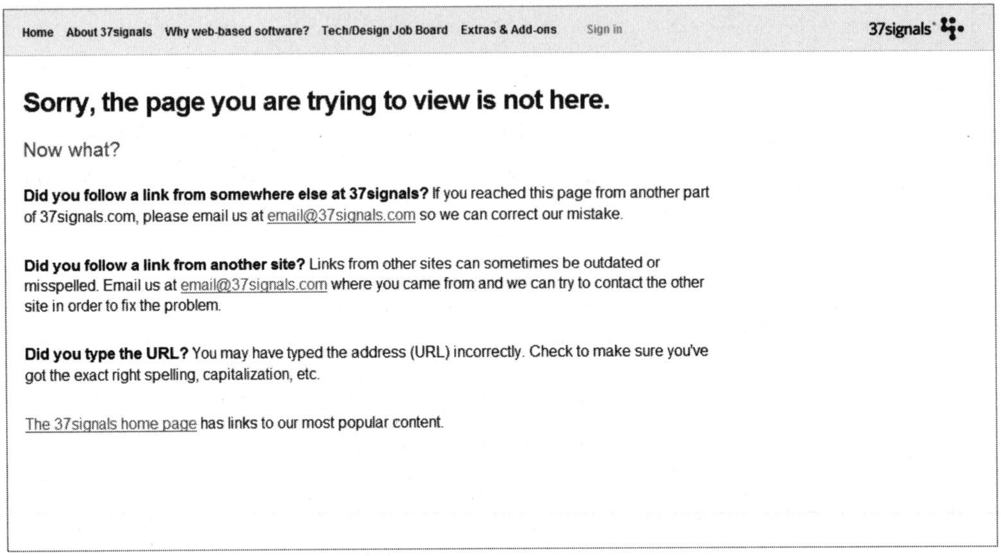

Home   About 37signals   Why web-based software?   Tech/Design Job Board   Extras & Add-ons   Sign in   37signals

Sorry, the page you are trying to view is not here.

Now what?

Did you follow a link from somewhere else at 37signals? If you reached this page from another part of 37signals.com, please email us at email@37signals.com so we can correct our mistake.

Did you follow a link from another site? Links from other sites can sometimes be outdated or misspelled. Email us at email@37signals.com where you came from and we can try to contact the other site in order to fix the problem.

Did you type the URL? You may have typed the address (URL) incorrectly. Check to make sure you've got the exact right spelling, capitalization, etc.

The 37signals home page has links to our most popular content.

Figure 15.14 37signals troubleshoots the error along with the visitor.

Wednesday: Test Your Site Search

Site search is the search function that is provided to visitors to your website. This is your internal search engine to the content within your website. Strangely, this is an afterthought to many businesses, but it is a critical part of the user experience. A recent study showed that three out of four searchers in ecommerce tend to use the site search to quickly find a product or category of product in a website. Unfortunately, most companies are unaware of how the site search helps or hinders their visitors.

The worst things that your internal site search can do are show too many results, too few results, no results, or irrelevant results. Unfortunately, too many internal site search engines have been developed internally with a goal of producing results—not presentable, usable, and relevant results.

Track

The first step in making your internal site search a productive part of your website marketing strategy is to track the searches that are made. Compare the list of keywords to the information on your website. Is there a reason people are using your site search instead of the navigation? This may expose some information architecture issues if there is a consistent theme to the words being searched and the content arrangement on the page. You can set up most analytics programs to track this action and the words that are being searched. Be sure to track the end result of the search and whether it ends in a sale, lead, or exit.

Evaluate

Once you start seeing search terms as they are being recorded, go to your site search, and type in the terms your visitors are typing in. Now you can see the results that your visitors are seeing. Answer the following questions:

- Are there results?
- Are the results relevant?
- Are there too many redundant results?
- Is the display of results understandable?
- Is it clear where to click?
- Is it clear which result is best?
- Do the results provide too much information?
- Do the results provide too little information?
- Are the results ordered in a logical manner?

Once you see the results of a search and see what your visitors see, then you may start to understand the problems that your users have when searching on your website.

If you have an ecommerce website, then this is something that you can't afford to get wrong. Searchers using your internal site search will expect to see products, and if the results are completely irrelevant or presented in a clumsy format, chances are they won't go further into your website.

Time to Hire a Specialist?

Site search can be a traffic killer. If it isn't executed well, you will lose sales. Low-quality information and information display will not be accepted by your visitors. Just as they expect relevant results from a search engine, they will also expect relevant results from your site search. If it is developed well and provides searchers with tools they need to make decisions, then it can be one of the most profitable areas of your website.

Continues

Time to Hire a Specialist? *(Continued)*

I do not recommend that site search capability be done by an internal group, a development company, or anyone else who doesn't specialize in developing ordered, usable, and salable search results. I have found that the companies that specialize in site search technology are the ones that do it well and constantly refine their algorithms and displays based on customer feedback. It may cost more, but isn't the point of using a specialist to get the knowledge and benefit of their experience?

Some companies choose to use the Google internal site search for their websites, but others do not like offering searchers the ability to search the Web from their websites. Third-party leaders in site-search technology are SLI Systems, PicoSearch, and Search Spring. There are also many open source scripts and plug-ins for those who are technically savvy and want to manage it completely on their own.

The worst thing that your site search can show is no results for a search. This tells the visitor that there is nothing on the site that matches their search, nor, it seems, is there anything that is close, because most times, there are not even any suggestions to provide a pathway to the products (see Figure 15.15). A good site search provides results based on the search keywords, suggested words, corrections for misspellings, or related products. A bad site search shows no results, because visitors will leave if you do not have what they want.

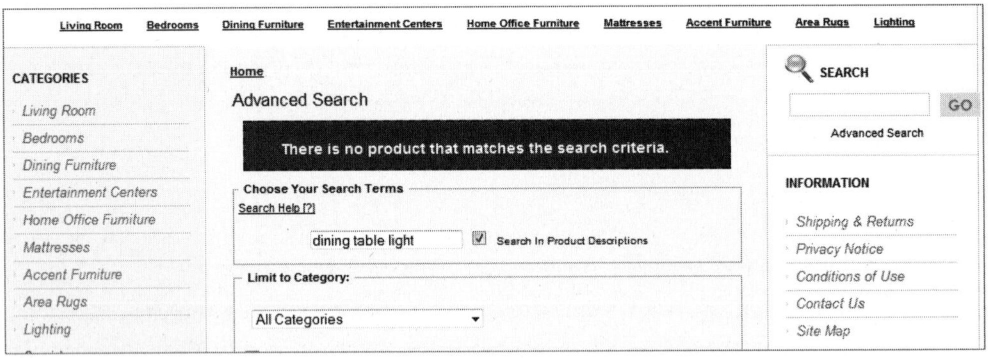

Figure 15.15 The last thing your visitor needs or wants to see when using your site search: no results

The second worst thing that you can show the visitor is too much information with no organization or context (see Figure 15.16).

Figure 15.16 Cell-Phones1.com shows too many results in an illogical format that will overwhelm the visitor.

On the positive side, well-formed results from a site search can keep visitors engaged, because they see the content they need, presented in a logical format. For both information sites and ecommerce sites, incorporating graphics into the results can be a very appealing to your visitors. In addition, the presentation of information needs to be in logical format:

- Concise title, which serves as the link to the page
- One- or two-sentence description of the content (or product)
- Date and author (if a content site)
- The product price and purchase link (if an ecommerce site)

Great examples of internal site search can be seen at the ecommerce site Stupid .com and at the content site Smithsonian.com, as shown in Figure 15.17.

a

b

Figure 15.17 Two great examples of internal site search results that present an orderly, logical and attractive results page

A clear interface relies on consistency. This is where consistent product image sizes can assist or detract from your search results. Inconsistent product images, because of size, background color, and style, produce a cluttered view of the products. In many cases, different product image sizes will also skew the rows and columns of product information and make it more difficult to read through the information.

When the product images are the same size and ordered consistently throughout the page, the horizontal reading lines allow a quick scan of the images, product information, and pricing along the same row. Vermont Teddy Bear uses the site search technology from SLI Systems that provides related searches, clear and consistent arrangement of products, and consistent product images (see Figure 15.18).

Figure 15.18 Vermont Teddy bear uses the internal site search to provide clear product images and details.

Thursday: Consider Site Maps

Two types of site maps need to be covered in this section. The first is the site map that is available to your visitors, which is a type of directory to the content of the website. The second is a site map that is developed specifically for the search engines and submitted to them as a catalog of all the documents in your website that you want included in the search engines' databases. These are distinctly different files and should not be confused.

Visitor Site Map

The visitor site map is a page that provides a structural overview of the content of the website. Some visitors may navigate this way on a website, and traditional SEO wisdom says that this is a resource page for the search engines as well. By providing a top-level page that contains links to primary and secondary categories, pages, and important information, visitors are able to see all the information provided by the website in a hierarchical structure. This enables them to make a decision about what page to select by seeing it in context with the rest of the information. As a nice side benefit, this page is a similar resource to search engines. To clarify, the visitor site map is used by both humans and search engines, but the search engine site map is accessed only by search engines. It allows the search engines a single point of access to multiple pages of the website.

The problem is that some have allowed this file to become an overdeveloped link page, with the intent of getting more pages indexed more frequently in the search engines. In doing so, it ceases to become a resource for any visitor who may use the page, which was the primary reason.

The site map page is a resource first and foremost for the visitor, and it should be structured to reflect the information architecture of the website: high-level categories, subcategories, and important information. Attempting to place a link to every single page in the website on this page just transforms it into an unwieldy, overstuffed page (Figure 15.19).

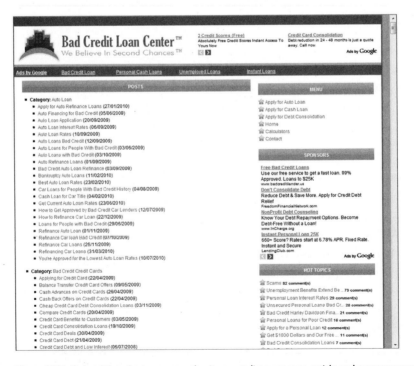

Figure 15.19 BadcreditLoanCenter.com uses the site map to list every page, article, and resource ever published to the website, rather than a contextual approach that would be easier to navigate. (The page is much longer than the screenshot can show!)

In addition, develop the categories on the page with context. Adding short descriptions to content and categories that can use additional defining will help the visitor distinguish among similar content and aid in their search for specific answers or information.

Use this page to quickly communicate the structure of the website and allow the visitor to navigate the page itself quickly and logically, finding the relevant information (Figure 15.20).

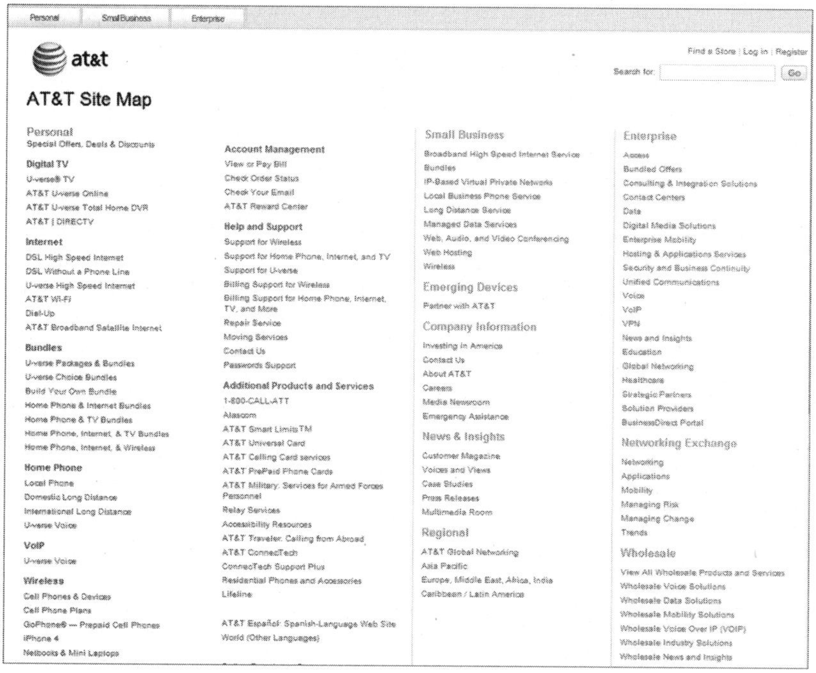

Figure 15.20 ATT.com uses a site map effectively with clear category headings and related links to the content.

Search Engine Site Map

The search engine site map file is an XML structured document that contains the typical information necessary to describe each page on a website. The document contains meta information, content, and URLs and is meant to provide the search engines with the content they need in case they have not been able to index the website.

Many webmasters have created and submitted this file via www.sitemaps.org, a joint source for the search engines, or they have simply submitted the file to each individual search engine. However, this is not a necessary task for inclusion to the search engines, and I recommend it only in special cases. Much of the following information is anecdotal and based on the observation of me and many other experts in the SEO world. Most feel that submitting a search engine site map should be done only in the case that the search engines are completely unable to index your website and there is no hope of fixing the code or the website to enable it to be indexed (for instance, if there is no available budget to redo the website or correct the programming). Only then would I recommend submitting the website via a site map.

This XML site map can be submitted at the website Sitemaps.org (which is supported by Google, Yahoo!, and Microsoft) or uploaded through the webmaster tools at each search engine, or you could even add the URL of the XML site map to the robots.txt file. Maintenance on this file is necessary, because it is not a one-time activity. Periodic uploads of the XML site map are recommended in order to provide for new pages that have been added or older pages that have been removed. If the owner of a site does not update the XML site map, they could be reporting that pages exist when they really don't.

Search engines will index your website naturally, and they generally index websites frequently and consistently. In addition, pages that are found and indexed naturally by the search engines tend to rank better than those that have been "discovered" from the XML site map feed. Logically, it follows that the same idea of the natural indexing patterns of the search engine would be preferred over a webmaster submitting content directly into the index. It comes down to a trust factor. Search engines trust their own assessment of pages, rather than the site owner's assessment.

Another factor that plays into the value of naturally found pages is that the search engines can apply their linking values to pages that are indexed, both the page with the source of a link and the page with the destination of that link. Both are necessary in computing page quality and relevance, so sites that are only found from a site map submission are not able to provide this information "naturally." The search engines trust their own assessment when they have all the information. A user-submitted site map does not always provide all the information, especially the contextual information of interlinking, which is a major part of the algorithm.

As such, the submission of a site map is always a last-case scenario, in my opinion. Some webmasters claim that their rankings decreased after submitting a site map. I haven't been able to verify such results, but I find that I don't lose much by *not* submitting a search engine site map. I'm sure that there are others who would disagree. But from my experience and the experiences of people I admire in the business, success is plentiful and not contingent upon submitting this file.

Friday: Use Local and Mobile Marketing

As mobile devices increase in usage, more and more visitors will be accessing your website via them. Europe and Japan both have had nearly a decade of prolific mobile marketing experience, and the United States seems to be finally catching up. While I was attending a conference in Europe last year, a colleague from Slovakia mentioned that more than half of the ecommerce transactions in Eastern Europe were performed on mobile devices! The United States certainly has a long way to go, but the new versions of smartphones have made it easier for the U.S. audience.

Local Opportunities, with an Eye on Mobile

Retailers, merchants, stores, and businesses can now make themselves competitive with the global search results by making their businesses appear when people most need them. Placing a local listing in the search engines is free. (However, there are some unscrupulous businesses out there that will charge you for this free service.) It can be difficult in some cases, but it is an easy process to get your business listed in the local and maps portion of the search results (Figures 15.21 and 15.22 show the local options on Google and Bing).

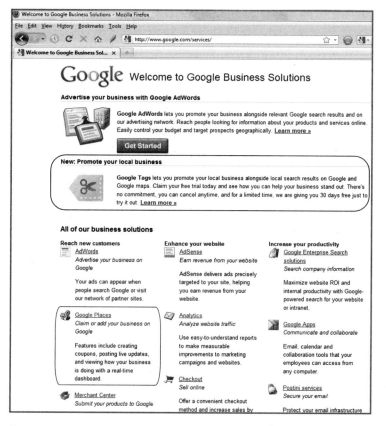

Figure 15.21 Google Places and Google Tags: local businesses can create a listing for display in the search results.

Both Google and Bing allow you to upload business information, phone numbers, hours of operation, pictures, video, and additional information that searchers may need to know. Both Google and Bing will require the business to verify ownership, and this is done through phone verification or through the mail. A verification code will be provided that the business owner uses to confirm they are the owner of the business and manager of the listing. Once that is completed, information can be edited and uploaded.

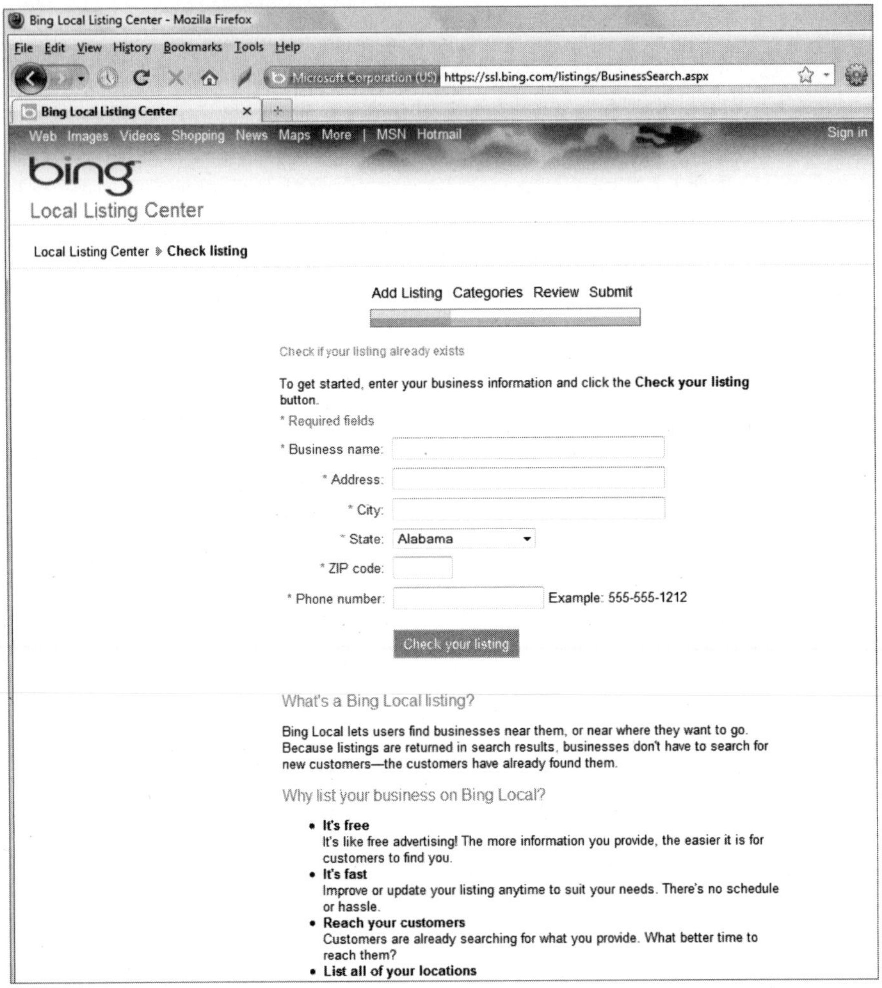

Figure 15.22 Bing's Local Listing Center is the place to create or claim your business listing.

Reports are also available of the activity that takes place once the business is listed. This shows how people saw your listing from search queries. There is also a report to show how many people clicked through to your website, clicked through to the map, or requested driving directions (see Figure 15.23). Compare that to a typical Yellow Pages listing! It's free, and you get activity reports specific to your listing.

Additionally, applications made for smartphones are changing the way businesses are marketed locally. This takes the reliance away from a typical search engine session, because users can use an app such as Yelp (see Figure 15.24) to find restaurants, stores, attractions, and other businesses based on their current location, rather than from a computer. Results are returned to the searcher based on their distance from the destinations.

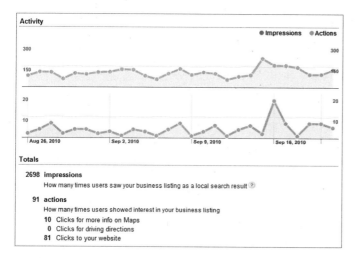

Figure 15.23 Local listing report from Google Places

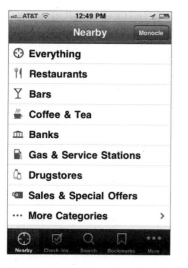

Figure 15.24 The Yelp app searches near you for local businesses.

Similarly, local searches have taken on a completely new aspect for mobile users. One personal example is from a recent trip to New York City. I was speaking at a two-day training class, and my throat was hurting already in the middle of day one. I am loyal to the Vocalzone brand of throat lozenges, and they can be difficult to find. I typed in **Vocalzones** into the search engine on my iPhone search engine, and I found out everything I needed about the company and the product. However, there were no available results that helped me to find the product and which stores carried it Manhattan. On a whim, I typed **Vocalzones** into Google Maps on the iPhone. Immediately, three locations were displayed, the nearest of which was four blocks away (see Figure 15.25). The walking directions took me there, and I was able to search, find, and purchase my throat lozenges during the lunch break.

This is the new frontier of searching. Location-based technology makes it easier than before to find that hidden restaurant that everyone recommends. Step-by-step directions point us in the correct way in any city, and we are able to find our destination.

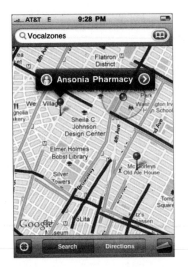

Figure 15.25 Google Maps showing where to find the store that carries the product I searched for

Mobile-Specific Opportunities

The release of the iPhone, Android platform, Windows phones, and other smartphones has enabled users to easily access the Web from any location and has clearly affected browsing habits. Applications (*apps*) that can be downloaded to these devices offer specialized information that is easily accessible.

Using Mobile Apps

Businesses are finding amazing ways of utilizing mobile applications by providing immediate access to information. In addition to the "around me" or "nearby" searches discussed already, some of the mobile developments include the following:

- Theaters that allow people to purchase tickets through their smartphone and show the scan code at the entrance.
- Banks that provide a mobile interface with easy access to the specific options that mobile bank members need. Mobile users do not have to struggle through the web interface and are able to easily accomplish specific tasks.

- News sites that provide a mobile interface to scores and headlines. This allows mobile users to quickly get the information they need in clean and mobile format.

- Airlines and hotels provide apps for easy booking features and reports of your miles, points, and status.

- Quick response (QR) codes allow an app to take a picture of the QR code (see Figure 15.26), which will open a specific destination page in their browser. A magazine reader can use their mobile device to scan the QR code in a magazine ad and be taken to a purchase page for that product. A QR app is required.

Figure 15.26 A Ralph Lauren ad featuring a QR code that will take the reader to the Ralph Lauren website

Using a Mobile Version of Your Site

By tracking what kind of device is accessing your website, you can deliver a mobile version of the website when appropriate. Mobile access to websites is rising, and the ability to deliver an interface that is specific to the needs of the mobile user is becoming more of a concern. Although some smartphones allow users to enlarge or condense the information on the screen, it still requires users to enlarge the screen to see the text and the links and navigate an interface that is designed for a large screen. The mobile interface is designed to reduce the interface to critical information and few links. The interface is easily read and navigated, because it is designed for the small screen.

One consideration to add is a link between the mobile and nonmobile versions of the website. Some mobile users prefer to view the nonmobile version of the website, especially with a normal web browser such as Safari on the iPhone, so make that choice available to them. Alternatively, some users would be happy to see a mobile version available and may choose to use or bookmark that link.

Businesses, publishers, retail sites, and others are finding that offering mobile versions can increase customer satisfaction. As established before, people go online and search when they have a question. Being found when someone is away from their office and answering that question can help develop a new customer relationship or increase the value of an existing relationship.

The difference is stark. By offering a mobile-specific site, you reduce the amount of noncritical information displayed to visitors, and you need to have a true understanding of what visitors need and want. The formatted display specific to the mobile user creates a better experience. Figure 15.27 compares the mobile-formatted and standard-formatted ESPN sites displayed on an iPhone.

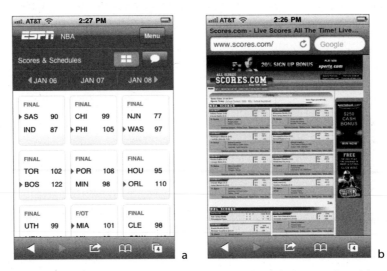

Figure 15.27 ESPN's mobile site (a) provides clear and preformatted information for mobile users. If the mobile site didn't exist, mobile visitors would have to resize and navigate through an interface that is tiny when displayed on a phone (b).

Create a Mobile Site

One of the more comprehensive articles available for those investigating a mobile-friendly website is located at Mashable.com, http://mashable.com/2010/07/13/mobile-web-optimization/. This article goes through the steps of determining the functions and information that need to be available, emulators to test your current site, and links to additional support information.

The most involved step in creating a mobile-friendly site is creating new style sheets (with CSS) for each device. This is the time and cost investment in this technology, but it creates effective and elegant mobile-specific interfaces. A comprehensive guide to developing a mobile website is the book *Mobile Marketing* (Pearson, 2010). Chapters 9 and 10 of that book go into great detail about the technical and SEO factors in developing a mobile website.

For blogs, there are plug-ins available that will automatically create a mobile version of the blog for mobile users. For websites, a business should evaluate the needs of the mobile user and the typical information they may need. Not all of the functionality of the regular site is necessary to include on the mobile site. Membership and customer sites should allow access to membership and account information. Publishers can provide access to new articles and resources specifically for the mobile user. Travel destinations can provide a completely different experience for mobile users than the website experiences.

The applications and abilities are limitless, but the challenge is to find an interface that will benefit the needs of your customers. Ignoring this fast-growing market will be at your risk.

Review and Hands-On

View the source code on your site by selecting View (found in the toolbar of most browsers) and then Page Source. Identify as many elements as you can. Find out whether you are using a CSS layout, a table layout, or some combination of the two. A good comparison is the CSS example site www.csszengarden.com. At this site, you can load a different style sheet that completely changes the layout and design; however, the source code always remains the same. Only the style sheet is different. Finally, view your site in multiple mobile devices to see how different devices will render your website.

Perform searches on your website, and evaluate the results from the questions earlier in this section. Search for critical terms that are specific to your website and company, and evaluate the results for accuracy and usability. If the results are unclear, are unrelated, or provide too few or too many results, then this is an area for immediate improvement.

Evaluate your site search. A good site search can mean immediate improvement in sales and leads, all because you are dealing with visitors who are already on your site but are depending upon the site search to help them navigate your information. Giving them what they want will increase your conversion rates.

Verify that your site is being indexed by the search engines using the various webmaster tools provided by each search engine. If your site is being indexed regularly and frequently, then submitting a site map is probably not necessary. If you have recently undergone a redesign, then submitting a site map may help initiate a spidering session from the search engines, but they will find your new site, new pages, and new information very quickly, sometimes within hours of your launch.

If your site is not being spidered and is extremely large and contains complicated URLs, the diagnosis might be that the search engines are not able to spider all of the information on your website. Your webmaster tools may provide feedback as to why this is happening or show that large numbers of pages are not being included. In this case, submitting a site map to the search engines may help your case.

For a website site map, intended for visitors, best practices say that you name the site map page sitemap (sitemap.php, sitemap.html, and so on). This makes it clear both to visitors and to the search engines the purpose of the page. Make sure that this page is designed for humans and contains the important links necessary and ordered into a logical hierarchy.

Create a local business listing on the major search engines and local business sites (Yelp!, FourSquare, UrbanSpoon, and Local.com, to name a few). Ensure that you are using as many of the opportunities available to list your information, such as images, video, coupons, and map locations.

View your website on a smartphone, and look into some analytics integration to see how many mobile users may be accessing your content. You can find the type of device, operating system, and similar information as your other, traditional website visitors. Consider how a mobile site may benefit your users and the type of information they would need to access.

Month 4: Expand Your Reach and Measure Results

Now that you have developed skills in the programming, design, content, and persuasive areas of website development, it is time to develop the multitude of options in gaining visibility with your website and measuring each to find what works best for you. Linking, blogging, using social media, and exploring pay-per-click marketing will all help build your overall online presence and attract visitors to your website. Analytics will enable you to find what works and build on each opportunity.

Week 13: Build Links

Now is the time to expand your reach and get others to notice what you have been doing.

Chapter 5 covered the basics of on-page SEO and referred to linking, while Chapter 13 covered some of the accessibility issues related to links. Links are the currency of online marketing. Gaining good-quality links to your site will enhance your reputation, increase your search rankings, and make your site more visible to the online audience. This chapter will focus on the primary off-page factor of links, which are so important to the success of your Internet marketing.

Chapter Contents
Monday: Learn How Search Engines Utilize Links
Tuesday: Distinguish Various Link Types and Their Value
Wednesday: Understand How Link Development Mirrors Offline Networking
Thursday: Find Link Opportunities
Friday: Evaluate the Marketing Value of Your Links

Monday: Learn How Search Engines Utilize Links

Links are the "nuts and bolts" of the Internet. Links are the glue that holds together the millions of documents and files in the online world, and it has been that way long before this modern version of the Internet. In the early days of the Web, links (or *hyperlinks*, as they were originally called) were the primary means of navigating from one document to another. The Internet was referred to as such because all of the documents and files available were connected by a series of hyperlinks.

The entry of Google into the search space launched a new method of determining relevance by the number of links pointing to specific websites, web pages, and documents.

Get Linked

If you're interested in the origins of Google's link-based rankings, check out Google founder Larry Page and Sergey Brin's doctoral thesis, "The Anatomy of a Large-Scale Hypertextual Web Search Engine" (http://infolab.stanford.edu/~backrub/google.html). This document became the backbone of their research in creating Google. In it, they describe the creation of PageRank to mathematically judge the relevance of pages based on linking structures.

Links mirror human factors. Links are a method of assessing the value of a web page as determined by the relationships established with other websites. Similarly, humans evaluate new business relationships based on the experiences and relationships of other business and the references of others who have used that business.

As webmasters learned about the importance of linking, especially in Google, there became a race to develop links—and as many links as possible—to their websites. This first wave of link building was based primarily on the thinking that more links made more relevance. From this thinking arose the concept of the link farm. Link farms were pages developed with no other purpose than to link to other websites. Typical link farm pages were long pages with nothing more than hyperlinks to web pages, but with no context or descriptive information. They were just lists of links.

Eventually, the evaluation of links was refined to include not just the link itself but the link text. This, of course, set off another firestorm of link acquisitions and an extreme focus on gathering links with keywords in the link text.

The next major level of refinement was the relevance and authority of the linked site. Where you get the link is just as important, if not more important, as the link itself. A link from a popular website is worth tens or hundreds of links from the sources. Beyond that, search engines evaluate the text on the linked page, as well as the linking page, to ensure relevance. The age of links, as well as the age of the domain and various other domain-related factors, are also included in the evaluation.

The content of the website of the outgoing link was compared to the content of the website with the incoming link. One page's text was compared to the other's text.

The incoming link was evaluated in context of the page, in context of the site, and in context of the physical region or location. For example, a Spanish company would benefit from links acquired from other Spain-based company websites. It helps refine the relevance based on geography.

As search engines continually refine the algorithm for relevance, the emphasis is on determining the quality of links and eliminating low-quality or "spammy" links. The on-page ranking factors rarely change in the algorithm, but the off-page link factors are the ones that are actively refined in algorithm updates.

Links Get You Found

Links perform a number of functions in assisting you in the marketing of your website. For starters, a link is the primary method that search engines use to find new websites. In the past, webmasters would submit a website to the search engine. Now, however, Google's Webmaster Guidelines instructs site owners to gain incoming links to their websites rather than submit the domain to the search engines, because the natural activity of spidering the Internet will result in the search engines finding your website.

Even though this is found in Google's Webmaster Guidelines, the principle is the same with every search engine. To find new content online, all search engines utilize a form of information retrieval—finding new and updated pages, downloading them, and evaluating them for relevance to show to searchers.

Links Provide Relevance

In gauging relevance, search engines rely upon the link text, also called *anchor text*, in order to find context. The term *anchor text* refers to the words used in the link, rather than simply linking with a URL. By using words in the URL, the person creating the link provides a contextual anchor to the reader.

Find Your Link Text

You can find the link text used by other websites that link to you with link management programs that will search online for website links to your domain. These programs will also capture the anchor text of any links that are pointing to your website.

- Link Diagnosis is a Firefox plug-in and is free: www.linkdiagnosis.com.

- Advanced Link Manager is a tool I use in my agency: www.advancedlinkmanager.com.

- LinkDex is a newer program that is very user friendly and quickly becoming a favorite: www.linkdex.com.

- Majestic SEO allows searches on any domain but also offers a subscription access for additional reporting: www.majesticseo.com.

Continues

Find Your Link Text *(Continued)*

- SEOMoz offers two tools for measuring and evaluating links; Open Site Explorer (free) and Linkscape (subscription-based for more advanced Users): www.opensiteexplorer.org, www.seomoz.org/linkscape.
- Raven SEO a subscription-based link building management tool: `raven-seo-tools.com/features/link-manager/`.

Simply by reading a website's link text, you may be able to figure out the subject matter of the linked-to website without even seeing the website. In Figure 16.1, the report shows many different descriptions used in the linking anchor text to Netflix.com. Just by viewing the anchor text, you can see keyword phrases (*rent from Netflix*, *rent this movie*, *rent the DVD*) in the links that indicate the brand and the business of the website.

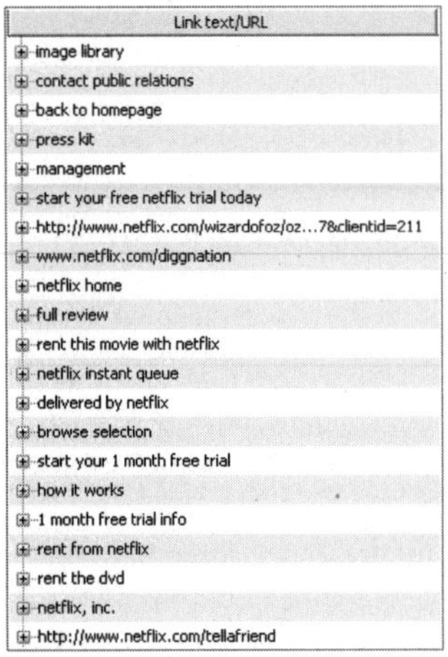
Link text/URL
image library
contact public relations
back to homepage
press kit
management
start your free netflix trial today
http://www.netflix.com/wizardofoz/oz...7&clientid=211
www.netflix.com/diggnation
netflix home
full review
rent this movie with netflix
netflix instant queue
delivered by netflix
browse selection
start your 1 month free trial
how it works
1 month free trial info
rent from netflix
rent the dvd
netflix, inc.
http://www.netflix.com/tellafriend

Figure 16.1 A few of the anchor text links to Netflix.com

You can designate the anchor text in the code (see Figure 16.2). Otherwise, the link will simply be shown as the URL to that web page. Linking with words provides context, which is valuable to visitors and search engines, because they both need to know why you are linking to that page.

When you link from your site to another site and you use keywords in the anchor text, you are designating the context for that page by the words you use in the link. This provides a clear context for your visitors, who will then know why the link is there. The anchor text lets the visitor know what information they will find on the linked page and how it can help them.

This also helps the search engines determine relevance, because link text plays a large role in rankings. The more keyword-based text links that direct to a website, the more relevant that site appears to the search engines. This is because other people have linked to that site with a judgment about its value, as shown in the link text.

```
<a href="/link.html">keyword anchor text</a>
```

keyword anchor text

Figure 16.2 Anchor text structure

Links Show History

The age of a link can show the longevity of a website. The date that the link was first found and recorded can show that a website has been around for many years or only a few weeks. Similar to evaluating a vendor's business longevity and history, the age of links to a website counts for experience.

I often equate this to the decision of where to eat and comparing a new restaurant opening in town to one that has been around for years where you always know you will get a great meal. People tend to trust their experiences more than they are willing to be the first to try something new. Often, salespeople have to be prepared to answer how long they have been in business, how many and what types of clients they have, how many employees they have, and other types of information that help establish both their longevity and their credibility. If a business has been around for many years, they must be doing something right. This carries over to the online world as well. If a website has been around for years (especially considering the relatively short history of Internet marketing), then there is some credibility. Older domains tend to be trusted more than new domains.

Some people theorize that Google gives favor to older sites—this "sandbox" theory says that Google prevents newer sites from ranking well until they are "proven" with quality links and success. I don't subscribe to this theory; instead, I see the apparent favoritism toward older sites as a matter of supply and demand. If someone creates the thousandth Viagra website on the Internet, there is no reason for Google to immediately provide the website with any credibility or favor. In fact, there is every reason that site needs to prove that it is able to compete and bring something new. The economics of search engines will favor sites that bring something new to the market and focus on a specific niche that is unfilled. In these cases, there is not a long wait for gaining a foothold in the rankings, because the market demands this new information.

It is in the search engine's best interest to incorporate the most information and as many web pages as possible into their index. Excluding pages is not in the interest of search engines, because their job is to provide access to information and provide relevant results. Acquiring as many pages as possible is critical to their competitiveness. In a competitive market, redundant sites are not necessary; new sites that provide new information where there is demand are necessary and will find visibility faster. Older sites have more links and are trusted more. Bringing a new domain to the market means that you will have to work hard to gain visibility and to achieve near-term success. It will be necessary to establish your credibility.

Links Identify Communities

One of the most amazing phenomena of linking online is the ability to track conversations and patterns among certain websites. As news articles are generated, people's interest in articles is based on certain likes and interests, and as a result, certain articles seem to be passed along via linking among communities of similar interest. In this way, search engines can track how certain information is valuable to a community of sites. In addition, there are those sites that are "bridge" sites. They may be a member of more than one community, and so articles and referrals will cross community boundaries and have relevance in other areas.

These linking patterns help search engines determine the importance of subject matter to specific sites and develop both relevance and importance of these communities. It also helps the search engines identify artificial linking communities designed solely to create the illusion of relevance for low-quality sites.

Delve Deeper into the Value of Links

Mike Grehan's work (at www.searchvisible.co.uk/Link_Equity_Explained.pdf) showcases an interview with one of the leading search scientists, Andrei Broder, about how linking identifies communities online that may not be readily available or trackable otherwise. In fact, they may not even exist apart from the Internet.

Without physical boundaries, people of like interests can find each other and share important information within that interest and create a community of publishers and consumers. In this methodology, opinion leaders easily can be identified, because the spread of information within a community will typically start with a link on their site and spread among the community. "Bridges" will emerge as the point of information between communities.

If you are fascinated by this information, check out some of Broder's numerous scholarly works on the topic of linking communities and developing link value:

- A Taxonomy of Web Search: http://portal.acm.org/citation.cfm?id=792552.
- The Web and Social Networks: http://ieeexplore.ieee.org/xpl/freeabs_all .jsp?arnumber=1046971.
- The Future of Web Search: From Information Retrieval to Information Supply: www.springerlink.com/content/u23uq83n96r25510/.

Links Are Word-of-Mouth Referrals

In all, the goal of the search engine is to provide the closest measure of human judgment as possible. On-page factors are within the site owner's full control. Links, however, are in the control of your market. As my father used to say, "There's what you say about yourself, and then there's what others say about you. People tend to believe what others say." The same principle applies through links.

Links are a method of showing value. A person links to a website when they see something of interest, relevance, or value. When this happens, the person linking to the site is casting a vote for the importance of that page, or that site, for that specific subject. In this method of analysis, search engines use the voting system to determine why certain sites are considered more important than other websites.

However, the votes are certainly weighted based on the importance of a site. In other words, not all votes are equal. Search engines evaluate the incoming links to a site and then look at the sites linking to those sites. Then they look at the sites linking to *those* sites, and so on. Sites with high authority provide authoritative approval of a website when they link and in doing so spread their "credibility" to the linked site.

Site managers can say or do whatever they want on their websites, but if the market does not appreciate or value it, then they will not link to it. It is truly a capitalistic system of gaining links to your site, because people vote with their link. If they like your site and it provides value, it will receive links. If not, it won't. The Web is very democratic in that good sites will attract attention and referrals and bad sites won't. (Some very low-quality sites are able to find methods of gaining links that make them appear to be relevant and important. You will not find those techniques in this book, because I don't recommend that business owners or marketing managers pursue those techniques. They are very short-term strategies, and search engines have allocated teams of engineers to identify and remove those sites from the index.)

The word-of-mouth aspect of linking will be explored more on Tuesday.

Tuesday: Distinguish Various Link Types and Their Value

Just as not all links from other websites are equal, not all links within your own website are equal. Site links each have a specific purpose, and the value of those links are based on the purpose they provide to your visitors. Search engines typically employ a page breakdown called *block-level analysis*. In this analysis, the page is broken down into typical "blocks" of information, such as navigation, content, advertising, footer information, and so on. This way, search engines can more efficiently determine the differences between the different purposes of site links based on their location within the page.

Navigation Links

Navigation links are the primary method of internal navigation to pages and content within your own website. The importance of these navigation links and the words (labels) used to define categories and content were discussed in Chapter 12.

The search engines block navigation links separately from the content of the website, because the navigation is the tool for both the searcher and the search engine to access the site's content. The navigation is the primary internal structure and is more closely related to on-page factors than to off-page link factors.

Footers are also part of the block analysis, because the bottom of most websites now use the footer as a means of providing links to important parts of the website and important information. In a sense, they have become mini site maps. Because of this, the footer is considered to be a navigational link structure on the page, because it is usually repeated across every page of the website.

Content Links

Links in the content can be broken down into two categories: in-site links and off-site links.

In-Site Links

In-site links are also called *internal links*. These are links to other pages within your own website, but they are contained in the content of your site, apart from the navigation. In-site links within the content tend to be clicked more often and are more useful than the navigation links. The main reason is context. If the visitor is on a page of content and needs more in-depth information that is in another place on the site, the link placement on that page provides the immediate access to that information, without having to renavigate the site for that page.

In-site links are given a more "relevance" weight than navigation links, because they are contextual by nature. They are added to assist the visitor and add to the information flow. Typically this is an editorial decision to add to the content of the site by placing helpful links within the page.

Off-Site Links

Off-site links (those to sites other than your own) integrated into the site content contain the most value for establishing relevance. Based on the concept that links are word-of-mouth referrals, links made within the content are considered "editorial" type of content—content that is on the page and developed to provide information to the visitor. If you are linking to another website within your content, then there must be a very good reason for that link.

Whether it is a citation, a reference, a resource, or just simply necessary for providing information, a site owner making it a point to link contextually to another website shows that there is value in the site being linked, and it is a resource that the visitor needs or can benefit from seeing.

Gaining a link (especially with relevant anchor text) from the editorial content of another website is the most valuable type of link, and that link carries along with it the credibility and authority of the referring site, which assists in building both better rankings and increased visibility.

Advertising Links

Another way of gaining links is to purchase them on other websites. However, this practice has undergone a lot of scrutiny over the years. In theory, links that are purchased as advertising should not provide a ranking benefit since they were purchased as advertising, not developed based on editorial-type decisions. The reasoning is that sites could affect the ranking factors by buying their way to better link development.

Based on this, Google has developed strict guidelines on buying links. If links are purchased, they should be through an advertising server. Simply buying links on another website for the purpose of gaining a link for rankings is highly discouraged. This creates a gray area for link development. The goal of any SEO professional is to gain links to their website from other relevant and authoritative websites. Ideally, a website has a link to your site because they like you and want to recommend your business to others. However, there are opportunities to purchase a text link on a site or a network of sites that are relevant to the readers of those websites. In the past, this was a method utilized by SEO experts, buying thousands of text links across thousands of websites, which gave a new website immediate link value. Like it or not, Google does not want site owners buying and selling text links to serve this purpose. Although there are aggressive webmasters who employ this technique to develop their links, they know that Google may catch them at any time and penalize them. For best practices, use advertising as advertising and purchase links through a reputable ad server or advertiser.

In the block-level analysis, search engines do not apply benefit to links to advertising, so these areas are blocked out, as identified by the ad server code or by the site manager excluding purchased links with a *"no-follow" code*—a method of noting certain links that you do not want the search engines to follow (similar to `robots.txt`, discussed last week).

Social Links

If you haven't been sleeping through the past few years, you have probably noticed additional "decoration" on web pages in the form of small "share" or "like" icons (see Figure 16.3).

Figure 16.3 Social sharing icon links

These icons represent various social-networking sites that allow you to post articles to "like" them. In doing so, you add a link to your profile that recommends the article to the people in your social network.

The social network links on the pages do not provide any link benefit, other than providing easy access for you to recommend the page, product, or article to others; in doing so, it builds external links to the website. Social networking sites have been one of the fastest-growing methods of building links to a website, because people are more than willing to share recommendations with each other.

The benefit is in the action of visitors recommending your page to their friends. So, there is additional work to be done, which will be addressed in Chapter 18.

Comment Links

Comments are a product of blogs. Blogging software allows site visitors to leave comments and questions about an article, and the site owner can directly interact with the commenters about a subject. When a visitor leaves a comment, they have the opportunity to leave a link to their website along with their comment.

This created an issue over time, because people looking to increase links realized that they could leave comments on blogs and get their link on the page of a highly authoritative blog, simply by adding it in the comment. As you can imagine, this caught on and created many problems for popular bloggers, many of whom had to deal with thousands of comments being made on their sites weekly or even daily.

The search engines then created the no-follow tag (as mentioned in the "Advertising Links" section). The purpose of the no-follow tag was for blog authors to be able to designate comment links as links that were not part of the editorial content but were comments from nontrusted sources. The development of the no-follow tag was to designate nontrusted links, which in this case made perfect sense. It gave site owners more control of the links and who they decided to give links. Trusted links were made in the editorial content. Commenters could link all they want, but no link benefit would be passed to their websites. The no-follow tag has been used in various other techniques by website managers, but the primary use is to designate untrusted links. Blog software now comes with comment links set to no-follow by default.

Wednesday: Understand How Link Development Mirrors Offline Networking

The more I study linking and link development, the more I realize that linking is remarkably similar to offline business networking. You are not going to link to a site that you have never seen or used, right? Of course not! We link to websites that provide us with value, good and timely information, or products that we recommend to others. We link to sites that we want others to know about, which is the same as offline networking and word-of-mouth marketing.

Making and Receiving Business Referrals

One of the best summaries of networking I've seen is the motto of Networking Professional Inc. Its motto is "We do business with people that we like, that we know, and that we trust." That is a great summary of how we people choose a new vendor, a new insurance plan, a used car, or a computer. A good salesperson understands that a relationship can easily trump features. People will go out of their way to do business with someone they like, know, and trust, because they feel they will get the best deal with the person or business they think best understands their needs.

The polar opposite of that is "that guy"—if you have ever been to a networking event, you know that the last person you want to get stuck talking with is the one who dominates the conversation, tries to give you the "hard sell," and won't accept no for an answer. You know who I am talking about. He just doesn't seem to have the realization that others do not want to be pressured into doing business.

How does this relate to links? Easy. We link to content that we like, we know, and we trust. We recommend products, services, and websites to our friends by referring them. When we link to a website, we are making a public word-of-mouth referral to that business. When you, as the owner or manager of a website, recommend another website, you are placing your reputation on the line. You are publicly noting that you recommend this other site for something specific and that others will benefit from it as well.

Cold-Calling

Sending link requests without a relationship or to random sites is very much like cold-calling in sales. Cold-calling is the practice of getting a list and working through the names and numbers of companies in order to get a response. Cold-calling is the least favorite method of gaining business in sales, because there are very few positive responses. There is no relationship, so it is harder to get business. Salespeople love working "warm" leads, where there is a relationship established, regardless of how thin, because there is a common ground.

You may have received emails like the one in Figure 16.4 requesting that you link to other website. These types of requests are generated automatically and are simply an autogenerated, nonpersonal request. This should be your first indicator that you can delete this email without any guilt.

We appreciate it if you will use the following information to link back to us:

URL = http://www.chiropractorsmarketing.com/chiropractic-marketing-plans
Title = Marketing ideas for chiropractors
Description = Ideas from a chiropractic practice marketing firm offering chiropractors tips, ideas and advice on how to improve chiropractor marketing and advertising programs.

You'll see that we have placed your URL, Title, and a description of your web site designed to promote your presence online. Please feel free to verify this information and let us know if you want us to change your link and related information. We will be glad to do this immediately.

If you will agree to supply a link for us, we'll maintain your link indefinitely.

You may respond to this mail in three ways:

1. You can choose to place link on your website. Please reply to this email to show your willingness for link exchange.	
2. You may unsubscribe from this web site because you do not like the linking website. However, we may approach you if you are interested in link exchange for some other web site. You will be unsubscribed within 48 hours and your link will be deactivated.	Unsubscribe
3. You may want to UNSUBSCRIBE COMPLETELY. We will never contact you again. You will be unsubscribed within 48 hours and your link will be deactivated.	Unsubscribe

I'm anticipating a positive response from you...

Figure 16.4 An autogenerated link request

Here is why this type of request can be trashed without a moment's thought. It is a cold-call link request. First, it offers no value. What is in it for me? Why should I link to this website? There is nothing in this email that shows that they understand what my website is about or how they came to see a viable relationship. It is all about their desire for a link. There is no statement of value to me or my visitors. Second, there is no relationship. I have never done business with this website, nor have I ever used it. Why then, should I offer a link on my site to this site? Why should I make a referral to another business when I have no experience with that business? My goal on my website is to provide the visitor with information they need to make a better decision—this link does not fit that goal. I am not going to recommend a company I know nothing about. Third, there's a catch. The email states that there is already a link to my site on this site. However, if I do not link to their site, then they will delete the link. Delete requests like this.

Understand Reciprocal Linking

If I am visiting in New York City and I ask my cab driver for a recommendation for dinner, I'll consider their recommendation highly, because they are a local resource. If I go to the restaurant and have a good experience, I am appreciative of the referral. In this situation, who profits the most from the referral? In terms of credibility, that cab driver. In terms of satisfaction, I do. In terms of profitability, the restaurant does. The restaurant benefits the most because the cab driver directed me to their establishment.

Now, if I find out later that the cab driver gets a kickback from the restaurant for recommending them, my opinion of the cab driver's credibility will be diminished. He obviously had ulterior motives for his recommendation. He did not have my interest at heart; he had his own.

This is why links from one site to another are so powerful. They contain credibility. Getting a link from another website is powerful that way. However, many website owners get together and decide to build links by linking to each other with the intent to get a benefit.

This is called *reciprocal linking*. It's the "I'll link to you if you link to me" approach. However, consider your website visitor. Are you providing them with value? Are you linking to another website for your own benefit or for the benefit of the visitor? This is why the one-way links are considered more valuable, because they are the resource for the visitor and primarily for their benefit.

Reciprocal linking will not be held as valuable as a one-way link. However, in many business models, especially news and content-driven industries, there will be natural cross-linking and reciprocal linking. These associations are always driven by context. The context of the subject matter and the natural patterns are always able to be established, because the communities are able to be visualized as described in Monday's content.

A good link request is personal, provides a specific reason, and builds a relationship. A good link request builds on a relationship that is already established and provides value to all involved. As an example, I was working with a company that used products created by DuPont. In looking at the DuPont website, there was a section of case studies that mentioned my client and how they used DuPont products to solve a problem. A simple email with a simple request resulted in a link from the case study to the client page. There was a previous relationship, and it provided value to both parties.

Building Business Value

On Monday I compared a new website to a new restaurant opening in town. Not many people will go out of their way to try a new restaurant, because they favor the reliable rather than the risky. However, in order to gain credibility, restaurants do something that you can learn from. They invite critics. New restaurants that want to start a buzz will invite the local media, restaurant and food critics, friends, family, and many others to have a free meal. In doing so, they are able to showcase their menu and product to as many people as possible and create a group of people who are able to recommend the restaurant to others.

This type of opening relates very closely to websites. When a new site goes live, the best thing it can do is let others know about the site. This can be accomplished by making a strong use of email, press releases, announcements, and actively searching out directories, forums, and online sources to list your website. From experience, a strong PR and email campaign can drastically increase the number of links coming into a website in a very short time. In addition, those links tend to be from trusted authority sources, so a new site is able to gain credibility.

Building links requires you to continually provide value. The value can be great products at a great price, amazing customer service, or educational or entertaining content. Whatever type of product, developing a value is critical to continuing to gain links. As those who know your site and enjoy their experience, they will share it across many different platforms.

Developing Relationships

Links don't come to you easily if you aren't active in the market and no one knows who you are. Unless people know who you are and what you bring to the party, they won't talk about you—thus, no links. Bringing new data, a twist in something that is previously accepted, or a new perspective will go far in getting attention and engaging your peers in conversation.

Good content is what makes people listen or read and stay attentive. However, content can be good but not meet the needs of the audience. If the audience finds no need for the content at that time or no personal benefit, then the content has little value. This is where adding to the conversation can get you noticed. Rather than sitting back and wondering why no one notices your website or your business, you need to give to the community in order to get noticed. Sometimes, this may mean sharing data or research that will help your competitors, but it will also persuade prospects, because they see your competency. By contributing information that educates your market and sharing links to other articles and resources (via blogs, Twitter, forums, and so on), people notice good content; they pay attention to it because it is a new perspective, new data, or something interesting. When real, quality content is brought to the market, people take notice.

The best business conversations are not in the boardroom. Most times, they aren't even official. They usually take place in the hotel bars of conferences, impromptu (or barely formal) get-togethers, via IM or email, or in coordinating travel schedules. Casual, relaxed conversations can be the greatest source of information and content and of making valuable contacts.

Thursday: Find Link Opportunities

For any web marketer, gaining important links to your website is a critical stage, especially for a new website. Developing a solid base of links at first is the easiest part. Then, work into link development based on searching and researching. Next, your overall marketing plan should include methods of attracting new links. The final stage is a constant review of the links you have acquired and methods of looking for ways to improve them or grow additional links.

Develop a Base of Links via Directories and Associations

The first place to start in link building is to go for the "low-hanging fruit." These are the easiest and quickest links that will serve the primary purpose of getting your site spidered by the search engines. For new sites, this is especially critical for getting found by the search engines. This is what we call the basic links or the "base" links that every new site needs.

In the modern day, search engines rule as the primary way to find information, but there was a time that online directories were the first resource for finding websites online. Prior to search engines, directories contained valuable lists and descriptions of websites, all classified in a particular niche.

As search engines come into existence, they needed to populate their database with as many websites as possible, especially high-quality websites, in order to have enough of a catalog of websites to provide relevant search results. The best places to find a large number of quality websites were these directories. The directories that were considered to be the most valuable were directories that were human-edited. This meant that there was a review process conducted by humans. A sort of quality review check was made on the site before it was allowed to be included in the directory. Because there was human judgment involved, search engines trusted the human-edited directories much more than automated directories where anyone could be included. Many directories are still in existence, and some—including Yahoo! Directory and Open Directory—still carry some weight.

General and Business-Specific Directories

Two of the first and foremost were the Yahoo! Directory (`dir.yahoo.com`) and the Open Directory (`dmoz.org`). Yahoo! Directory started out as a free resource, but after being swamped with inclusion requests, Yahoo! went to a paid model. One can go to the "front of the line" and pay $299 USD for expedited service and a review within seven days. Once the site is accepted, then there is an annual $299 USD fee to remain in the directory.

The Open Directory is a completely volunteer-driven effort. Because all of the sites are reviewed and in order to handle all of the requests, volunteers handle a specific directory niche and review the sites that are suggested within their category. If there is no volunteer for a particular category, then it may take a while to get listed. It takes a long time to get listed in the Open Directory, regardless, because this is a volunteer effort.

If you have a website that has been around for many years, chances are you may already be listed in these two directories. (In the early days of the directories, some editors would simply add sites that they found in order to populate a category.) If not and you have a new website, then it may be worth the cost and the wait to list your website. If you choose to do so, then I suggest reading through the website submission guidelines of both directories extremely well and making the correct submission the first time, rather than wasting time and money in submitting a site description that will be rejected.

In addition to these and other generalized directories, there are many specialized vertical directories. (A *vertical* in this sense is a business or niche-specific directory. Examples of these can be found in the travel, automotive, electronics, publishing, and many more niche markets.) Finding these directories is as simple as a web search for a business directory in your market (see Figure 16.5). Many directories exist as part of a network or a resource for a market. It is a good idea to become familiar with the networks and directories in your market, because they may also be involved in other ventures related to your business (such as blogging).

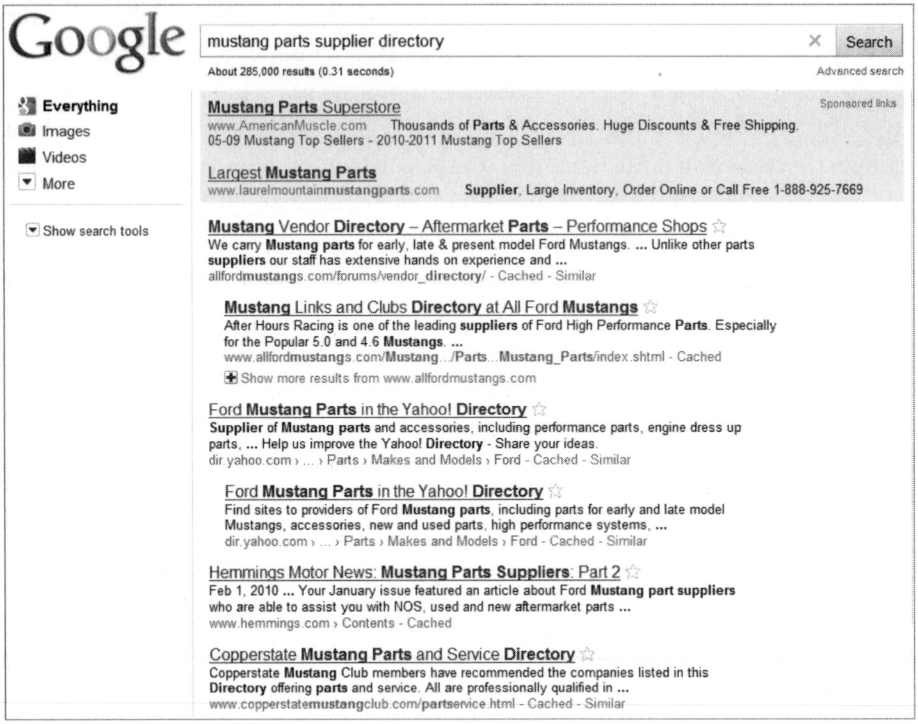

Figure 16.5 Simply searching for a directory will help you find relevant sites for including a link to your website.

As with submitting your site to the other directories, be sure you follow any instructions listed for inclusion into other directories. Also, be ready to pay a fee, because many sites require a fee as a method of monetizing their content.

Local Directories and Associations

As you use the search engines themselves to find linking opportunities, you have probably noticed a heavy emphasis on local results. The top three search engines have put noticeable resources in developing the local results and making local businesses more findable. If you have a local business and have not taken advantage of these free listings, you need to visit the local listing center at each search engine:

- Google Local Business Listings (http://maps.google.com).

- Yahoo! Local (http://local.yahoo.com) and Yahoo! travel (http://travel.yahoo.com).

- Bing Local Listing Center (https://ssl.bing.com/listings/BusinessSearch.aspx).

- Business/social websites and directories like Yelp (yelp.com) and FourSquare (foursquare.com) have found ways to reach beyond the typical directory structure. They provide business information based on distance and reviews. They allow visitors to rate and review businesses, and you can make a very good decision on using a business based on the feedback of others.

These localized resources provide great links to a business, but they are also very high visibility links, because the search engines are all attempting to push local listings for local searches. Again, the search engines are attempting to provide the most relevant results, so when local businesses are searched, the searcher had better see local businesses first. Even beyond the local search, the ability to find a local supplier rather than ordering online with a business you've never met can be a significant resource.

Getting your local business into the results is a way to push the national players further down in the results and provide your local business with more prominence. The search engines provide a lot of space on the results page for local business results, and it is a great way to help people find you (see Figure 16.6). Not only can they see your search listing, but business results provide phone numbers, hours of business, reviews, directions, subway lines, and other relevant information to help people locate the establishment as well.

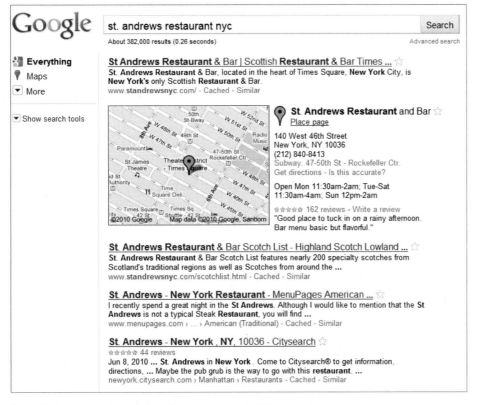

Figure 16.6 A local search result for my favorite restaurant in Midtown Manhattan

If you have a "brick-and-mortar" business, then chances are you may also be a member of a few local organizations. Chambers of Commerce usually list their members' websites along with the business information on their website membership directory. Check with your local business organizations or membership-driven associations to see whether they have websites that also list their members and provide a website link as part of the membership. Sometimes, you may have to pay for the link besides the membership or association fee, because some local Chambers of Commerce figured out that people are willing to pay extra for links to be added to their business listing.

All of these local search resources, local businesses associations, and directories are excellent ways to build up your base of links for a new business. After you have built up this base, it is time to move on to the next level of finding link partners and resources.

Research Other Websites and Blogs

Using the back-link programs listed for Monday's assignment, comb through the links to your competitor websites. There may be sites linking to them that are not linking to you. Be sure to familiarize yourself as to why that may be. Your approach will mean everything in a site's decision to link to you. There could be an established relationship or an advertising arrangement, so be sure to do your research on sites prior to approaching them.

In addition, rate the incoming links to your site and your competitor sites based on your familiarity or the authority of those linking sites. There may be a site with very high authority that could provide your site with very good visibility along with your competitor. The word *authority* in the context of linking has a few connotations. The first application of authority is based on Google's PageRank or the number of quality incoming links—the technical or objective measurement of authority. The second application of the term *authority* is meant as a recognized prominence within an industry, either by reputation, by branding, or by history. This is the subjective measurement, because a link from this type of site would give added credibility to your website.

Searching for resource sites within your market could provide a very good insight as to where certain sites are ranking and the breadth of their visibility in the search rankings. Sometimes, simply searching for other websites can be a good source of linking ideas. Do a search and look for every site that isn't a competitor of yours. You may find local resources, a blogger, a directory site, or other sites that can be a source of links. Do some digging into the company behind the website, if you can, and find out how they are related to your industry. Are they a source of news or a place for reviews and customer experiences; if it is a regulatory agency, what is their purpose, and would they benefit from having a link to your website as well?

One of the keys to building links is to ask yourself whether this website would benefit by having a link to your site. Will their readers appreciate the link, and will it make sense to them? If so, then the site owner will be more apt to list your website as a resource.

This is why I enjoy using the Blog Search function on Google (search normally and then select Blogs under More) and Bing (www.bing.com/blogs/). Finding the bloggers in a particular topic or market that is the same or similar to your business can be key to developing a very good ally in link partnerships and also in developing a credible resource.

Bloggers need content in order to thrive, so they are always looking for the freshest, most up-to-date content, as well as industry scoops and information. If you can provide the need for bloggers' content by providing them with significantly important information that their readers will want to read, then you have developed a very good source of both links and visibility.

Earn Quality Links with a Marketing Plan

Although I do consider link development to be a major part of marketing the website, I've decided to break out these next two areas specifically. Both can be incredibly useful in developing new streams of traffic and links to your website. However, both require solid investments of time and creativity to develop.

Website link development has become a much more in-depth and time-intensive process over the past few years, because site owners have had to develop newer and better links than their competition in order to gain rankings. Those that have been in search engine optimization have experienced a sort of "link arms race" over the past few years using many tactics in order to gain, optimize, refine, and develop links. Your benefit is that you can evaluate those efforts and see which tactics will work for you and your business and create reasonable expectations based on the time you can give these options.

Attract Links by Honing Your Content

Link baiting is the term given to the tactic of writing articles with the purpose of getting them to be passed on or recommended to others. Link baiting is what I like to call the "sensational" approach to link building.

These articles have the most extreme headlines or the most fear-based hooks, such as "10 things you *have* to do to your website, or hackers will steal it!" When marketing an article on the social-media sites, sensationalism works. Social-media sites make spreading sensationalism easier and faster. You have to click only a few buttons to send, post, vote, or tweet a link.

The headline is the most important part of the equation. This is the primary method that readers will judge the content and importance of the article. It has to be something that communicates an element of sensationalism—maybe the fear of being left out or the fear of being the last to know.

The headline also has to be something that communicates the time commitment very quickly. Just browsing through some of the headlines on a typical social-news site will show this tip. You'll always find articles using the "top 10" formula. This formula communicates to the reader the number of points that will be made and a sensational factor. Using the formulas to create titles such as "10 Reasons...," "5 Secrets...," or

"7 Worst…." will communicate a very quick and possibly entertaining read to the searcher. They will be able to quickly peruse the content and decide to read further, because they know that there will be a limited number of points made in the article.

A good place to see headlines using this and many other formulas is the website Digg.com. Digg.com is a website where members contribute articles and websites and add their comments and where other Digg members vote on the article (they "digg" it). As an article receives more votes (*diggs*), it trends higher on the page. High-trending articles that make it to the top of Digg.com will receive thousands of visitors, typically lasting a day or two. Figure 16.7 is a shot of Digg.com showing the headline "hook" in action. Three of the six trending articles this day are using this formula.

Figure 16.7 Digg headlines using the "top 10" formula

Of course, the other three headlines in that screenshot contain another type of headline that does well in social media: secrets. People love to find out something they aren't supposed to know. Headlines that capture that desire to know more or showcase a prurient interest will do well on a mass scale, simply because of human nature.

Other types of articles that tend to do well are those that cover topics you might see on daytime talk shows. Typically very sensational types of news articles or weird news tends to do well. The weirder the better, but that's just my opinion.

If you have a business and you are attempting to gain footing in the social-media news sites, then prepare to write articles about something this audience wants to read about. Your new hire or landing that new contract might make for a good press release, but it won't make it in the world of social news. There has to be a good hook or something that entertains, or it won't have much of a chance at all.

In addition to these things, a thick skin might be necessary. If your article does not deliver, the large crowd that frequents these sites are not typically hesitant about sharing negative opinions. In fact, in some communities, they thrive on negative comments and will encourage and compete with each other to leave the most scathing comments. Don't let this discourage you; simply be prepared by researching the community prior to targeting it.

The more votes your article accumulates, the higher up the list of popular topics it goes. If it gets to the front page of these social-news sites, then you are well on your way to getting thousands of visitors to your website. The intended result is that of these thousands of visitors, some will link to your website with their blog, social media accounts, Facebook pages, or Twitter. (Social media will be covered more in-depth in Chapter 18.)

This is an area where getting the recommendation is a way of gaining visibility. Gaining links comes when people recommend your article to others by a voting link or a recommendation. In a marketer's perfect world this happens organically and people love the article that you write.

In reality, this takes time to master and time to build a following. Simply writing articles and attaching social-media icons do not guarantee that people will recommend them, vote on them, or link to them. Although having social-media links on your articles may look nice and provide some decoration, it does not guarantee the action. As with any form of marketing, it takes trials, testing, and tolerance to understand this medium.

It all comes down to content. You have to produce something that the market wants. If you are able to do that, then you will gain some followers. The ones that have been able to do this quickly are ones that are not building a typical business or run a brick-and-mortar business. In addition, you can never predict the subject matter that rises to the top in these circles. Off-kilter, funny, and off-beat does very well on the big social-news sites. Highbrow, detailed analysis of important issues of the day typically does not attract large numbers but will attract a small number of interested readers. You need to decide how you will reach people and what type of content you will use to reach them.

For many sites, developing funny or sensational content simply isn't possible, or it is out of the question. This is where developing a community and finding the opinion leaders can be more of a targeted approach to link building than simply generating eye-catching articles. That is where online PR skills are needed.

Conduct Online PR

Online public relations (online PR) came as a natural outgrowth of developing PR campaigns based on offline PR strategies. However, it developed with a significant difference. Where PR professionals had their lists of media contacts and would pitch stories or articles to those professionals, they tended to do it on a mass scale. Hundreds of reporters, news organizations, and opinion leaders would be on the distribution list, and the press release or the pitch would go out to them all.

The Internet and the rise of free blogging software enabled tens of thousands of people to become self-published news sources within a very short time. Many well-known bloggers simply started with a love for a particular niche topic and started to write frequently about it. In doing so, they developed an audience that enjoyed their opinion and style.

Some PR professionals immediately seized upon the opportunity. Instead of pitching the same idea to hundreds of reporters, why not pitch to the blogger who has a direct pipeline of readers? Bloggers have become the new opinion leaders of the digital age. Online PR was born, as the pitch became focused on approaching a few quality news sources rather than on hundreds of typical sources.

The approach to a blogger or an online publication had to be refined. Bloggers were not people who were getting paid to report the news or publish. The vast majority were writing because of a love or serious interest in the topic. Because they took a personal investment in the topic, they responded to more personal inquiries. A PR pitch that was not crafted especially for them or even identified them personally as a valuable resource would be simply discarded. The blogger was personally invested in this labor of love, so they only responded to those who took the time to approach them on a personal level and offered value to the relationship.

This provided a highly targeted method of gaining links. By building relationships with bloggers or publishers at other online publications, businesses could gain visibility in an online article, complete with a link or two to their website. The combination of gaining an article about a company or product and gaining a link to the website creates a very high-quality link. That link provides branding, provides lead generation, and positively affects rankings!

The benefits of this targeted approach are many, but very much like link baiting, there are some common elements. The most common is the time involved to carefully craft the content that others will find compelling. The next step is to develop the pitch to the news source, a blogger, or an editor. These things take time, and hastily created content and pitches are rarely effective.

Review Your Internal Links

Up to this point, the majority of information on building links has focused on external linking. This section will cover building your internal links. Building internal links in your content pages to other pages within your website can be an effective way of helping users and increasing rankings. However, please do not get over-aggressive or eager and think that changing all of your site's content into links will increase your rankings. That's not at all what I am recommending.

Not all engines value internal site links the same. When optimizing internal links on a website, I usually have seen improvement in Yahoo! and Bing, but not as much in Google. Remember to always do what is best for the user, and the search engines will follow. Moderation is the key, and it is better to be cautious than to do too much.

There are many "overlooked" opportunities within a website that can add value to the visitor experience and help strengthen the internal anchor text of a website. The first thing to do is to simply review areas of the website that can benefit from adding links into already existing content.

One area that always tends to be overlooked is the FAQ page. The Frequently Asked Questions (FAQ) page contains questions and answers that are relevant to the website visitors. However, I am amazed that so few FAQ pages actually contain links from the answers to the section of the website that further answers the question. When you consider helping the visitor, this is an area that is sure to benefit.

Other areas are typical online publishing tools—related articles, most popular articles, most commented articles, most popular articles this month, most popular products, and so on. These are all categories that can increase visitor engagement by linking to relevant content, whatever the interest. Common themes in subject matter, popularity, and timeliness are all relevant to people, so simply adding navigation links with properly optimized titles can add to both longer engagement on your website and better rankings for your specific subject areas.

Friday: Evaluate the Marketing Value of Your Links

To focus on a campaign for link development and marketing your website, the issues of time constraints, content resources, and campaign direction need to be defined. Otherwise, there is no measurable gain and no defined path toward a goal.

Define the Goal

Knowing this, the place to start is to define the desired outcome from a link. This can be a conversion such as a sale, a completed lead form, or a registration. When comparing visitors who come from different sources, measure them by the same goal. This may sound logical, but many people miss that important point. Most marketers tend to use time on site and page views as an important measurement metric, but those two methods are a very incomplete method of measurement. By themselves, they do not provide much in the way of valuable analysis because the intent is difficult to ascertain. By measuring a goal, you measure the final product of the visit. Other data points, such as time on site and page views, make more sense when they are seen in the context of the goal completion, not apart from it.

Analyze the Data

Knowing which links provide visitors, which provide sales and leads, and which don't provide any value are all critical to helping you develop a marketing strategy.

Everything can be tracked, valued, and developed into a strategy. Analytics are able to track the value of each link to your website and show a significant difference in the sales and lead generation value of linking websites. It will also provide a clear strategy in developing a plan to approach similar sites that are able to provide a good source of sales.

Consider the Source

Simply by breaking out the visitors from the incoming links, a pattern will emerge. Figure 16.8 shows an example of a content site (we'll call it site X) with two primary conversion points: registering for a webinar and subscribing to the mailing list. These two goals were tracked together in the overall conversion rate. When comparing the conversion rates with stats such as time on site and pages viewed, there is enough comparative data to begin to assessing the value of the visitor from each source. The pattern looks the same on almost every website that is analyzed in this method.

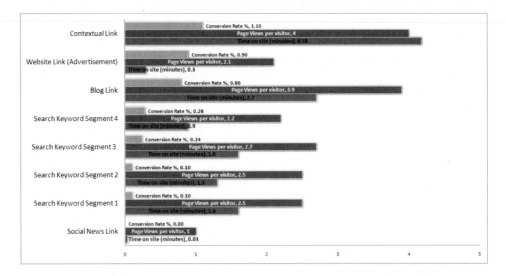

Figure 16.8 A comparison chart of visitor engagement and conversion by source, using a simple spreadsheet

What emerges when defining a goal such as "Where do my most engaged and valuable visitors come from?" is that the most vibrant source of visitors is from an article in an online news source (a contextual link). The visitors who came from this article converted at the highest rate, stayed longer, and read more pages than any other type of visitor. In the case of the link from the online news source, the article was written exclusively about site X's business and some of the issues it had experienced. The article contained a few direct links to pages on the website within the context of the article. As mentioned earlier, when another site links to your website, it is like a word-of-mouth referral. When a link is placed on an online news source to another website that is part of the story, the reader is able to follow the link and continue their desire to know more about a specific subject. Readers of the online news source were coming from a highly engaged state of reading a trusted source of news, and when presented with a link to the subject of a news story, they clicked the link.

The credibility of the news source and the context of the link were all presented with continuity. The subject matter was all related, and the news source passed credibility through the link to the website. As a result, the readers wanted to find out more about site X, the business, and recent developments in the business before they ever clicked the link to go to site X.

The next highest engagement sets were visitors who came from an advertisement and from blog links. The website link was network advertisement on other websites that advertised a webinar. The results of the ad showed a fairly good response rate. Most importantly, when compared to the ad buy and the results, it was a profitable ad buy—one that could now be justified in the future because of measured performance.

The blog links consisted of other bloggers writing about this website and recommending their readers to go to this site and find more in-depth information. Links from bloggers created the same type of engagement. Visitors from blogs were highly engaged, because of the same reasons. When looking at the links on the blog sites, the links were from articles writing specifically about that business or a similar subject matter and contained links within the article to the website. As a result, the readers knew where they were going when they clicked the links and already had familiarity with the business because of the blog article.

The next engagement set was made up of the four primary search terms for this website. All of the search visitors seemed to behave in the same manner, all with similar engagement factors of conversion, time on site, and pages viewed. The realization came when going back to the source of the visit. The search visitor defines the subject matter by their search term. The results that are shown are based on search term. If they do not see what they need after clicking any of the results, search visitors know that all they have to do is click the Back button, and they will see 10 to 15 more options for their need. As a result, they are significantly less engaged than link visitors. They are not reading a trusted source that is recommending another website; they are only being presented with a list of options as their starting point.

The last engagement set consisted of visitors from social-news websites, including Twitter and Facebook. The engagement showed a very significant trend among social-news referrals. Even though most of the visitors in this time frame were generated by the site receiving tens of thousands of visits from a very popular article, the visitors did not stay long. In fact, there was a conversion rate of 0 percent, the average page view was a single page view, and the average time on site from these tens of thousands of visitors was 0.03 minutes, which is about 2 seconds. There is not a whole lot of engagement that can happen in 2 seconds. So, even though this was the primary source of visitors, it was also the least engaging and least valuable source of immediate benefit to the business.

Visitors who clicked these links seemed to only have the slightest degree of interest, and it did not last long. In fact, less than 1 percent of social-news visitors in this evaluation moved on to read additional articles or information. This is typical behavior of those visitors and the engagement level they are presenting. When contrasting with other sources, the social-news visitor finds links to various stories in a feed or presented on a page with many other stories. In both cases, there is very little context to the presentation. All of the articles and information on social news sites tend to be very random, even within categories. As a result, the social news reader is clicking an article link with a mild level of interest. They also tend to go immediately back to the site and look for the next link, because there are hundreds of other articles competing for their time and attention.

The result of this analysis was that not all links will produce the same value to a business in terms of providing engaged and profitable visits. Another benefit of this analysis provided for future marketing decisions. By seeing the results of different marketing campaigns and their effectiveness, better decisions could be made in marketing the website, because the expectations of results could be better managed and predicted. After you analyze the sources of visits to your own site, you will see which sources of visitors are more effective and profitable compared to others. You can then maximize your effective channels of visitors and troubleshoot the less effective channels. You may need to reevaluate the focus of your link marketing, when you see all of the sources in context. The reason becomes clearer when you take a step backward in the process and evaluate the sources of those links.

A Case Study: The Benefits of Links

Linking provides many benefits to the site owner or manager. First and most obvious is the rankings aspect. The rankings tend to be the primary driver for many SEOs. However, by focusing only on rankings, the other benefits may be lost. Using a typical report that almost any analytics program can generate, I can see how visitors found an article on my website. But even better is knowing the value of each of those sources, which shows the different benefits of links.

Report Results :: Details [Where readers came from]			
Rank	Last Date/Time	Referral Site	Count
1	Nov 07, 2007 @ 22:29	http://www.stumbleupon.com/refer.php?url=http://www.sitelogicmarketing.com/blog/02-analytics-according-to-captain-kirk	22371
2	Nov 05, 2007 @ 08:16	http://www.stumbleupon.com/refer.php?url=http://www.sitelogicmarketing.com/blog/10-content-creative-customer	645
3	Sep 26, 2007 @ 09:01	http://blog.searchenginewatch.com/blog/070522-140826	341
4	Oct 23, 2007 @ 06:47	http://www.google.com/reader/view	133
5	Feb 02, 2007 @ 19:28	http://clicked.msnbc.msn.com/archive/2007/01/24/41373.aspx	131
6	Jan 25, 2007 @ 19:34	http://meyerweb.com	118
7	Nov 04, 2007 @ 18:57	http://www.searchenginequide.com/searchbrief/senews/010064.html	118
8	Oct 11, 2007 @ 10:20	http://publishing2.com/2007/01/25/not-all-traffic-is-created-equal	107
9	Nov 07, 2007 @ 12:08	http://www.ientry.com/bloggers.html	106
10	Feb 28, 2007 @ 09:44	http://www.searchenginequide.com/searchbrief/senews/009440.html	93

Rankings

The article was linked from Clicked, a blog on the MSN Network. Within days, a noticeable increase in rankings occurred. Gaining a link on this prominent blog was a significant factor in increasing the rankings of this article.

Branding

The top source of visitors to this article, by far, was StumbleUpon. StumbleUpon is a social recommendation site that sends people to random sites. However, sites that are "stumbled" (voted) on more often are weighted to appear more often in the random suggestions.

Thousands of visitors followed the link on StumbleUpon to find this article, and in finding the article, many voted on it (or stumbled it) and referred it to others. In doing so, it perpetuated the branding of the site and the article. The exposure grew to the article and in doing so put the brand in front of thousands of people who may never have seen it before.

Sales/Leads

The article was linked from a few other sites. One in particular was iEntry, which provided an excellent source of leads. Visitor referrals from iEntry tended to produce contacts and inquiries.

By having this site link to the article, it may not have provided any boost in rankings, but it did produce business and immediate leads for the business, based simply on the link to the article, which resonated enough to cause visitors to fill out a lead form and start a conversation.

Building Relationships

In evaluating link visitors, it is also beneficial to see *who* is linking to you. This is an opportunity to build another relationship in your industry or in your niche, especially when your website catches the eye of a noted expert or popular source of content. In this report, I found that Eric Meyer (of http://meyerweb.com), a noted expert in CSS programming, had linked to the article. This opened the door to having many conversations with Eric and resulted in gaining a new friend, a trusted resource, and helpful information. Another result is that as content is generated in the future, the potential for additional links between our sites is increased, because there is now a trusted relationship.

Use Context and Competition to Develop Engagement

Two specific factors determine the engagement of visitors from various link sources: context and competition. The value of the author of a link providing context is a critical factor in developing high-value visitors from their initial visit. When visitors come from a source of news with high credibility, that credibility is shared with the destination of the link. In addition, the article is about a specific product, company, or market, so the link is in the context of the article, and the informational value is very high. The competition for the reader's attention is very low, because the article is about a specific subject and the link is in the article (see Figure 16.9). Typically, the links within an article or a news source are limited to the relevance to the story (see Figure 16.10). When the link is in the article, the content is directly related to the link, and the competition for the reader's attention is extremely low. These two factors create a highly engaged reader to your website.

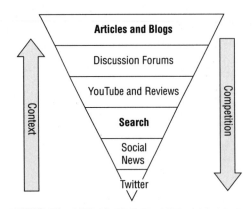

Figure 16.9 Context and competition determine visitor engagement by source.

Figure 16.10 Links from news articles, such as this one on TechCrunch.com, carry high context and credibility.

Blogs share this same type of engagement relation. Bloggers link to other articles, stories, and news sources. Because of this, the context of the subject matter is very high, and the link competition on the page is very low. However, blogs in general tend to have many more outgoing links on a page, linking to blogrolls, advertisements, and other calls to action. There is typically more competition for the reader's attention in comparison to a highly authoritative news source.

Blogs also provided another unique aspect of information in this analysis. Once a blog links to a website as being a source of information or recommendation, the chances of that blogger linking again and directing more people to the same website is much higher. Of all of the links that brought visitors to the website, not only were the links from blogs providing high-quality visitors, but they consistently brought them over greater lengths of time. Most other link sources would direct a good number of visitors to the website, if it was social media, a lot of visitors, but they all tend to drop off after the initial few days of popularity. Visitors from blog links may decrease after the initial article, but they rarely stop. The visitors from blog links keep visiting the website, and the more articles on the blog that link to the site, the more readers consistently follow the links.

Of course, not all social media can be grouped in the same generalization. Sites that have links from discussion forums and YouTube experience highly engaged visitors from those sources. Although not as highly engaged visitors as visitors from blogs and online news sources, they are engaged, the context is substantially high, and there is slightly more competition. Discussion forums are prime marketing research areas, because active forums contain hundreds of thousands of members who actively discuss products, companies, industries, and all in very niche topics. In forums, links to websites are typically from one member to another making a recommendation (see Figure 16.11).

Figure 16.11 Discussion forums provide highly relevant and personal recommendation links.

YouTube is able to provide similar types of engaged visitors but by an entirely different method. Visitors from YouTube were first attracted by the content of the video and have either clicked the link in the video description or clicked the link in the company YouTube profile page. Either way, there was an active attraction to the content of the video, resulting in the visitor wanting to know more about the company, the product, or the subject matter.

Search visitors, as mentioned earlier, are in a unique state, because they are the ones determining the context of the link from their search term. There is also a regular number of links on the search results page, creating a very competitive environment for the searcher's attention. Based on these two factors and in comparison to other visitor sources, search visitors tend to be in the middle of the engagement pyramid. They are a valuable source of visitors, but visitors from highly contextual links still tend to convert better, stay longer, and read more. However, the number of visitors from search is typically much higher than that of links.

At the bottom of the engagement pyramid are the visitors from social news and Twitter. This is not to say that this is a very low-quality or bad source of visitors. What this shows is that in comparison with other visitors from other sources, social news and Twitter bring in very low engaged traffic, mainly because the context of the link tends to be very low and the competition for their attention is very high. Both sources receive many links to choose from in a day, because there are thousands of social-news articles being promoted in a day, and whichever is available when they view their news stream or Twitter feed is one that grabs some level of interest. The context of articles in the feed is very low, because the subject matter is so vast, depending upon who you may be following and what piques your interest at the time. A Twitter or social-news feed contains thousands of links to articles, with no consistent context. Because of this, the expectation level is very low, and the engagement is low as well. It is simply based on the amount of expected information and the little bit of context provided with the link (see Figure 16.12).

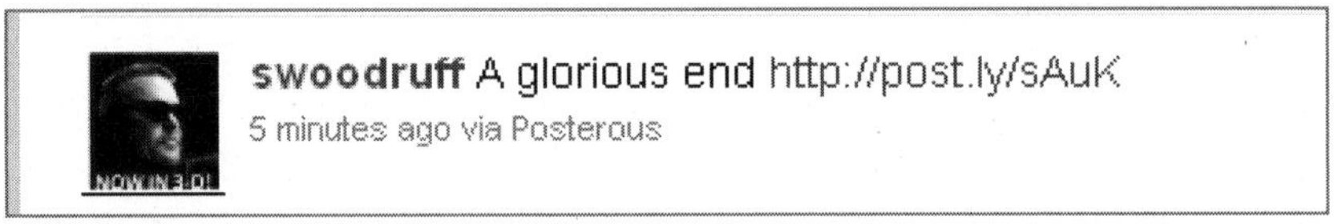

swoodruff A glorious end http://post.ly/sAuK
5 minutes ago via Posterous

NOW IN 3.0!

Figure 16.12 Twitter links sometimes contain little context for the link, resulting in a lower visitor engagement.

Based on these comparisons, which you should be performing on your website regularly, you can better judge what kind of visitor you need and what will be the best links to develop those kinds of visitors. If high-volume visitors are the need, then social media and Twitter would provide the best source of high-volume visitors, based on this behavior. If your desire is for more high-quality, high-conversion visitors, then a campaign of online PR, targeting news sites and high-profile bloggers, would be the key to building those high-context, low-competition links, which would also bring a high level of authority and credibility from the links those articles would generate.

Developing goals for your visitors is the place to start when analyzing the type of link-building campaign that will be best for your business. Not all businesses are the same, so your link-building efforts need to be planned based on desired outcome, available resources, and expectations.

Review and Hands-On

Identify the number of links coming in to your websites. Then, look at the sites that are linking to you, and find what pages they link to and the typical link text. Many tools are available for tracking and evaluating your links:

- LinkDex (www.linkdex.com)

- Advanced Link Manager (www.advancedlinkmanager.com)

- BuzzStream (www.buzzstream.com/link-building)

- Link Diagnosis (www.linkdiagnosis.com)

- Majestic SEO (www.majesticseo.com)

- Raven SEO (raven-seo-tools.com/features/link-manager/)

- SEOMoz: Linkscape and Open Site Explorer (www.opensiteexplorer.org)

In addition to looking at your links, evaluate the links to your competitors' websites. Compare the number, the link text, and the sources of those links to get an idea of additional link opportunities and the quality of links.

Evaluate your website with a block-level analysis. Print your home page and an internal page that is typical of the content. Draw a line around the block-level elements of the different navigation links (primary, secondary, product filters, content sections, footers, and any advertising).

Look at the content sections that are the most valuable, and see how you are using them. Evaluate how you are linking internally and externally and the link text you are using for each.

In your analytics, start to develop some reports that will show you the visitors you are getting from other websites. If you do not have goals or revenue tracking set up, don't worry; I will cover that in Chapter 21. However, just an initial view of the visitor sources from links should provide an interesting view of who is linking to you and the type of visitors they are providing.

Evaluate how your link-building efforts mirror offline networking. Are you relying on the cold-calling approach? Are there relationships that you can develop or build within your industry where there are common ties?

How can you contribute better education or understanding in your industry? Is there different information or interpretation that you can bring that will start conversation and get you noticed? Sometimes holding back information (for fear of your competitors accessing it) will inhibit a good conversation where everyone can benefit. Consider that when information is shared, links usually follow.

Look through your own site and find areas of opportunity that can benefit from an internal link from one page to another. From a blog entry to a product page or from the FAQ page to the page that is associated with the answer, find areas within your own site that can benefit the visitor with a direct, internal link.

Next, determine which focus of link development might be better suited for your business. Browse through the stories that are on some of the social-news sites such as Digg.com, Reddit.com, and StumbleUpon.com. If there is a strong association that you can make with the type of content you provide and the content that does well in this format, start to develop content with the goal of gaining attention and gaining votes in this system.

If your business would do better taking the online PR route, begin by identifying the bloggers and online publications in your market, and familiarize yourself with their writings, opinions, and audience. The more you know and understand the people whom you approach with your ideas, the better you will be able to personalize your pitch and provide value.

Evaluate your own site traffic on the basis of acquisition and compare the trends. If you do not know how to do this, hang on! Chapters 20 and 21 will cover analytics. Analytics programs such as Google Analytics, Yahoo! Analytics, and many others will allow you to view user activity by source. Using a spreadsheet, you can chart the different aspects of each source.

In addition, evaluate all the sources through which your site can reach visibility through the different channels:

- Search (and the various keywords)
- YouTube
- Discussion forums
- Customer reviews
- Local search
- Social news
- Twitter
- Facebook
- Links from websites
- Links from blogs
- Links from news sources
- Image search

Evaluate to see which may be bringing in the highest-quality visitors or converting visitors currently and which might be easier than others to develop and grow with your available resources.

The next few chapters will cover social media and growing your visibility in many of these channels, followed by using analytics to better measure the profitability of your work.

Week 14: Add to Your Business with Blogs

Blogging has revolutionized the Internet and has added amazing dimension to business communications. Blogs directly contribute to increased visitors, increased search engine rankings, and more pages being included in the rankings. This is because of the architecture, the management of content, the additional marketing capabilities, and the enhanced communication of blogs.

Chapter Contents

Monday: Build a Business Case for Blogs

Blogs are websites on steroids. Really, it's not fair.

Blogs are built using the best of website architecture, and they are link-intensive, content-generating machines. Typical websites just can't keep up, and it all comes down to the platform. Blogging software, such as WordPress, is free to the masses. With cheap hosting and free software, the accessibility to one of the most nimble, powerful content management systems creates a perfect storm of egalitarian competition on the Internet.

When used as part of a business marketing strategy, having a blog can attract more visitors, more links, and more pages indexed by the search engines—and that translates into more business! A recent survey by HubSpot found that businesses that blog attract 55 percent more visitors than their nonblogging counterparts (`http://blog` `.hubspot.com/blog/tabid/6307/bid/5014/Study-Shows-Small-Businesses-That-Blog-Get-` `55-More-Website-Visitors.aspx`).

Blogs satisfy the basic needs of the search engine; they have clear architecture, links, and content (see Figure 17.1). Blogs take these three necessary components and use them to an extreme level when compared to websites.

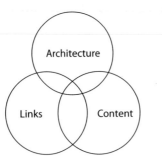

Figure 17.1 The necessary components for getting good search engine visibility

Technical Advantage

Blogging software such as WordPress, TypePad, Moveable Type, and others is typically low cost or free. WordPress, at the time of this writing, dominates the market as open source, community-developed, free software. The plug-ins developed by the community extend the functionality of the software beyond the original code base. This powerful free software competes head to head with some of the most expensive and custom-developed content management systems on the market. As a result, people have been able to use blogging software to easily create a website and start publishing, usually without any technical know-how.

Blogging software is basic, stripped-down functionality. The sole purpose is to create an understandable interface that allows nontechnical people to add, edit, publish, and manage the content of their website. Because of this, the code "footprint" of the blog is very small, because the blog relies heavily upon CSS as the design and layout tool. If you remember Chapter 14, which was about technical issues and the advantages of CSS, you'll know that CSS gives blogs the ability to change designs within minutes, without changing the code or the content in the site.

This light footprint allows the content to be the primary bulk of the code that is read by the search engines in each page. In addition, the light code provides very fast page-loading times. Because of the simplicity of the code and structure of the default settings of the architecture, blogging software makes it very easy for the search engines to access the website structure and each of the pages. This creates an ideal environment for easy indexing and inclusion in the search engines.

Websites are often developed using templates or custom programming. Many times this results in extraneous code in order to accomplish certain tasks. Many content management systems are not programmed to take the search engines into account. Even custom-developed websites may not take search engines into account if it is not part of the specification. The result is that websites are all different in code structure, code programming, and additional functions. In contrast, blog software creates a unified software approach where hundreds of contributors have developed search-friendly, light, and accessible software. The successful architecture of blogs is the result of thousands of contributors who have helped create a "lightweight" but powerful publishing software that is standards compliant, search engine friendly, and accessible to anyone wanting to start a website.

Link Advantage

Bloggers develop content by finding content. In finding content on other websites or blogs, they tend to link to the content that inspires them to add, create, or support other information. In doing so, they cite the original work and also link to any additional sources that aided them in the creation of the article. As a result, blogs do not lack external site links. In fact, blogging's intrinsic external linking was key to its growth, success, and popularity. As a result, blogs gain incoming links faster and more frequently than traditional websites, and they also link to other websites in greater number.

Traditionally, when editors link to a website, they will link to the home page. As a result, website home pages tend to be very heavy as the link destination. Blog structure made it very easy for editors and readers to link to the specific page of content for the article. As a result, when editors and other bloggers link to an article, or *post*, on the blog, they will tend to link to the full URL of the article page, not just the website domain.

This allows blogs to gain very deep links from multiple sources. This practice is very hard to duplicate on traditional websites, but because blogs are a constant source of content and active information, bloggers link deeply to each other's websites, and the tools are readily available to allow the average visitor to link to the page content. That leads to the importance of content, covered next.

Content Advantage

This is where blogging mentality is different from the traditional website mentality. Blogging encourages a constant conversation, either with the public, the customers, your market, your peers, or simply anyone who will listen. Websites encourage a very static approach with little addition.

Bloggers are constantly in search of new content to add and educate their readers. If the readers are not engaged, then they do not frequent the blog. In addition, the blog is built on a publishing platform that makes it very easy to publish via Really Simple Syndication (RSS), which syndicates the content to many additional sources.

Blog publishing structure enables the home page to show the most recent articles (or posts); in addition, each article (or post) has its own page and unique URL published online. Each post is a stand-alone page. This enables other bloggers and editors to link to the individual article rather than the home page. If they link to the article on the home page, it may not be there next week or next month, because the home page of a blog contains only the newest and most recent articles.

Here are some general observations comparing blog and websites:

- Blogs are updated frequently; websites tend to be very static.

- Blogs have more timely information; websites are rarely up-to-date.

- Blogs encourage conversation through comments; websites do not.

- Blogs constantly gain links and link to sites; websites slowly gain top-level links.

Updated content is the critical factor in this equation. It is in the search engines' best interest to have the most up-to-date content and the most requested content in the search results. To provide what searchers want, search engines are constantly hunting for the latest and most relevant information on any topic. As a result, search engines favor the content provided by blogs.

Keyword Advantage

In the HubSpot survey mentioned earlier, businesses that actively blogged had 55 percent more visitors, 97 percent more inbound links, and 434 percent more indexed pages in the search engines. A follow-up survey showed that businesses that were actively blogging drew more than 6.9 times more organic search engine visitors than nonblogging businesses. (http://blog.hubspot.com/blog/tabid/6307/bid/5506/Active-Business-Blogs-Draw-6-9-Times-More-Organic-Search-Traffic-Than-Non-Bloggers.aspx). How can something as simple as a blog develop this much additional organic traffic from search engines? It goes back to something mentioned in Chapter 6, the keyword long tail. The keyword long tail consists of the hundreds to thousands of related terms that your website will be found for. Even though you may have a keywords list you are targeting, the search engines will naturally find relevance for terms beyond your list; blogs enable that list to go even further with all of the related content that is published.

As a result, blog articles are great resources for very detailed information on deep topics. Search engines tend to favor blogs, because searchers with detailed queries will tend to find the information on a blog. Blogs enable businesses to provide very detailed information in a very search-friendly platform. More in-depth and varied content fits the needs of thousands of searchers, and the development of content on a blog creates a source for visitors looking for that information.

Engagement Advantage

In the same study cited in the previous section, based on analyzing visitors who find a business website through search vs. visitors who find a business's blog through search, actively blogging businesses see a significant benefit to blogging. Even when the blog is not providing the same numbers as the website in terms of visitors, the engagement is very different. If you remember Tuesday's discussion in Chapter 16 on the different visitor behaviors based on the source of the link, this will come as no surprise.

Figure 17.2 shows a website that is bringing in more than 1.5 million visitors. In that same time frame, the blog generated 17,000 visitors. However, the difference is in the engagement.

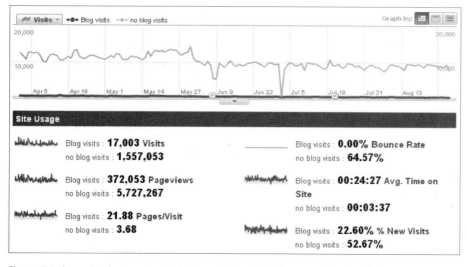

Figure 17.2 Comparing the engagement of visitors entering at the blog vs. entering the website

Two-thirds of visitors who enter the website leave the website after viewing a single page. The average time on site for website visitors is about 3 minutes, and the average number of page views is 3.6 pages. After factoring the bounce rate, time on site, and page views, the blog-generated visitors are still on the site after 5 minutes. In fact, the blog-generated visitors stay and engage on the site significantly longer with time on site topping more than 20 minutes and 20 pages per session!

This is typical behavior of blog-generated visitors. They stay longer, do more, and engage more with the website when they find content. This includes visitors who find the blog via search engines. Visitors who enter the blog from search engines tend to be much more active and engaged than visitors who find the "traditional" website through the search engines.

Blogs make it easy for the visitor to be engaged with an information architecture that is very accessible and functional. Comments, related topics, new articles, and a very clean design and structure make it easy to find more content and stay longer on a blog.

Blogs are a resource for growing your business's visibility online that you just cannot ignore.

Tuesday: Understand the Architecture of a Blog

Surprisingly, in surveys, many people say they do not read blogs. Yet when compared to the numbers of blogs that have increased rankings and increased visitors, I tend to think that the majority of Internet users do not see the difference between a website and a blog, because they are very similar and, sometimes, indistinguishable.

This section covers the initial setup, development, technical considerations, and elements of a blog. Because WordPress is the overwhelming blogging platform at this time and one of my favorites, I'll be showing screenshots of WordPress. However, many of the technical functions are the same in all blog setups.

The initial structure of a blog that make it distinguishable from a traditional website includes the following elements.

Posts

Posts, or articles, are the daily updates made to the site. Posts are the primary way of updating the blog and adding new content. The content entry interface allows even nontechnical website managers and editors to add content easily. Basically, if you are familiar with Microsoft Word, you can navigate your way through adding content to a blog (see Figure 17.3). The icons are very similar to any word processing software, and they allow you to write, edit, format, and manage the content in the post. Additionally, there are functions that allow you to add video, images (and resize), audio, and other media elements.

The page is developed similar to a word processing document and then published when the Publish button is clicked. Of course, pages can still be edited and corrected after the initial publication.

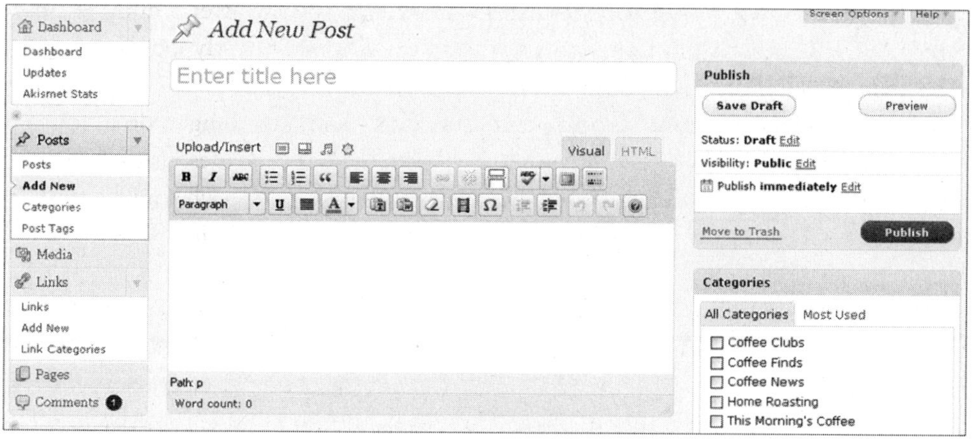

Figure 17.3 The interface for adding content to the blog through WordPress

The latest post is usually at the top of the blog home page. This can be changed, but by default, the most recent post is at the top of the list, and prior posts are listed in order. There are usually about five or ten posts on the main blog page (which is also usually the home page). In addition, the most recent post is located in multiple places on the blog. It is on the home page as the most recent post, it is also added as the most recent post in the assigned category, and the post is published as a stand-alone page.

This is where *permalinks* come into play. Permalinks (short for "permanent link") are the final destination of the blog post. As more posts are added, the home page and category pages change to reflect to most recent posts. The permalink is the URL of the stand-alone blog post. Every post has its own URL. This is where the links are directed for those who reference the post. Blogs naturally provide the most exposure to the most recent posts but then also rely on the stand-alone page as the primary destination for link traffic, references, and citations.

Pages

Pages are the most static content on the blog. Pages such as About Us and Contact Us are considered top-level content pages that do not change often but are necessary for providing immediate access to important information.

Creating the About Us and Contact Us pages is the same as creating a post, but they are not published in the same place. The pages are published as a top-level navigation selection, rather than published to the main blog page as the most recent entry (see Figure 17.4).

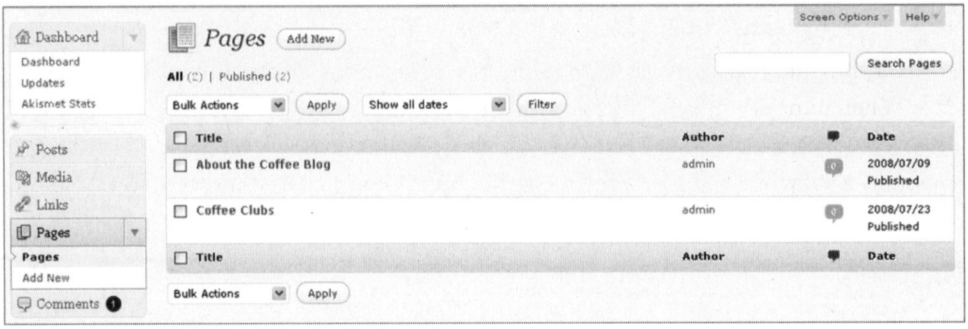

Figure 17.4 The listing of the pages created on the blog

Categories

Figure 17.5 reflects the two primary navigation lists on the example blog: categories and pages. The pages are listed across the top as top-level navigation elements, and the post categories are listed as the side navigation.

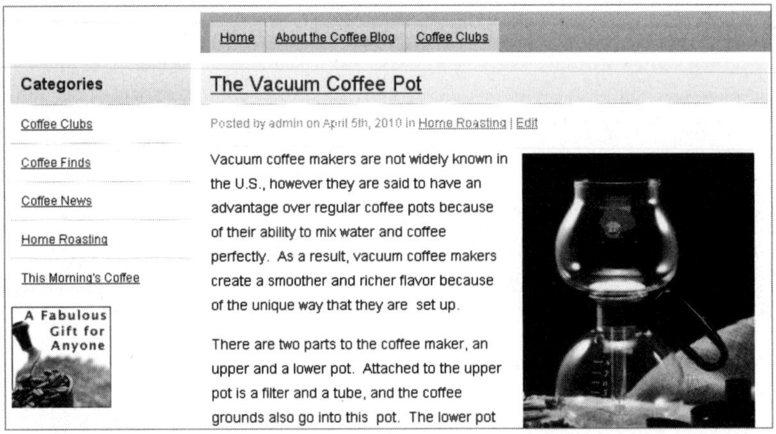

Figure 17.5 Pages are listed along the top, and categories are listed down the side. Posts are organized by category.

When adding a post, the editor is prompted to assign the content of the article to a category. A post can be listed under a single category or multiple categories; it is up to the discretion of the editor or manager. When the post is assigned to a category, then the post will show up not only on the main page of the blog but also on the category pages.

The categories are the primary method of navigation to further content into the website. This can be enhanced with other plug-ins and functions available on most blogging software. These allow for additional navigation elements such as most recent posts, most commented articles, most popular posts, or other short lists of post links.

Archive: Calendar

By default, blogging software also classifies the posts made on the site with a date stamp. When a month passes, all the posts published that month are then grouped into another category, month and year. For blogs that have been around for many years, this creates a very imposing list (see Figure 17.6). Although this may seem like a helpful default, it rarely is.

Figure 17.6 Archive listing by date

The trouble with this kind of archive is that few visitors are searching for content using the date as a reference. Visitors use words and subject matter and, as a result, rely on category navigation and the search box. The archive-by-date function takes up a lot of space and lacks context. Visitors need context, and navigation by topic will always meet their content needs, because topics and categories provide context to the need for information.

My advice is to delete the default archive setting and provide additional navigation by contextual topics (related content, latest posts, and so on) rather than by date. This will also eliminate a lot of content being indexed by the search engines in a completely different context rather than by the content. This navigation scheme allows the content to be indexed by date-based categories rather than by the content-based categories.

A calendar is another function that tends to be a default in most templates. The calendar highlights the dates that a post has been published to the blog. The date is a link to the posts that were made that date. Again, I don't prefer this method of navigation. In addition, this can also be a reminder of how you forgot to blog last week, and it will remind your readers as well.

Blogroll

The blogroll is a typical feature at many blogs, and it can be a valuable place to be, especially on high-profile blogs. The blogroll is a "roll call" of recommended blogs from the author of the blog. These typically include friends of the publisher or business or other blogs that they read on a regular basis, as well as some off-topic blogs that provide humor, ideas, or inspiration.

The advantage of the blogroll is that it is a direct link from one blog to another in a very prominent place on the page. In many blogs, the blogroll is on every page, making it another sort of navigation tool but linking to other blogs of note.

This is not a must-have feature of a blog, but it is one that is used to build networks of blogs in different markets, political groups, advertisers, or other associations. This is a default feature in many blog software applications, but it can also be easily removed from the structure.

Tags

Tags are another method of classifying content. When getting ready to publish a post, there is a field on the page that asks the writer to add keywords based on the content of the article (see Figure 17.7).

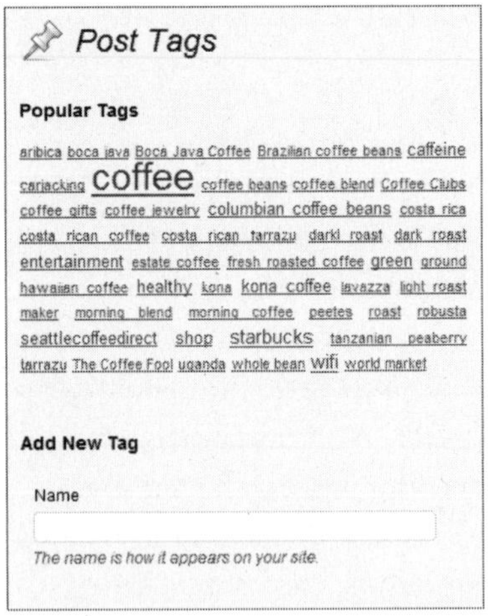

Figure 17.7 Tags are associated keywords used for additional classification and navigation on the blog.

As you can see, the tags used in this article are a way of highlighting certain concepts and keywords that are an enhancement to the navigation. If the visitor would like to see more content about sustainable coffee farms, then all they have to do is click the tag to see all the posts that have that tag associated with the article. As the author of the content, you can assign as many tags to a post as you think are relevant. Typically, if the article makes mention of a word or topic, you add a tag. As you add more content, you can select from previously created tags or add new ones.

However, the tagging can go a bit too far, because some sites create what is called a *tag cloud* and provide all the tags in one group for visitors to navigate through the keyword tags rather than as a contextual navigation. The only context provided in the tag cloud is that based on size. The larger the tag, the more it is used in association to articles. I prefer not to use large tag clouds, because they become a very large, unwieldy, noncontextual distraction on the page. As a result, it grows into a large block of text that makes it difficult for visitor to read and distinguish between categories (see Figure 17.8).

buywell coffee caribou caribou coffee christmas blend **coffee** coffee cup news coffee giveaway **coffee** how to coffee maker **coffee review** Coffee Reviews **Coffee Roasting Coffee Shop** coffee shop review **coffee taste coffee tasting** contest dark roast free coffee french roast gloria jean's **green mountain How to** jason coffee Jason Coffee TV **k-cup** Kansas City **kcup** k cup coffee keurig **kona coffee** live show music review News **news rocketfuel coffee starbucks** starbucks coffee stuff **sumatra** thank you timothy's timothy's coffee win **wolf gang puck**

Figure 17.8 A tag cloud can provide helpful topics. But unmanaged, it can become a jumbled mess of words that don't help your visitors.

Comments

What makes blogs such a foundational part of social media is the ability for readers of the blog to make comments. Although some businesses shudder at the thought of comments being made on the blog by anybody, it is a valuable contribution and a great ability to have a managed conversation about specific points.

All blog software comes with the ability to manage the comments that are being made on the blog (Figure 17.9). Comments ultimately have to be approved by the site manager. Most bloggers like to review all the comments by hand prior to approving them or deleting them. You also have the option of first approval. If an comment is made and approved, the comment author is then free to add additional comments without review. The settings you choose must be the ones you are most comfortable with. It is up to the company to develop a policy for managing and approving comments.

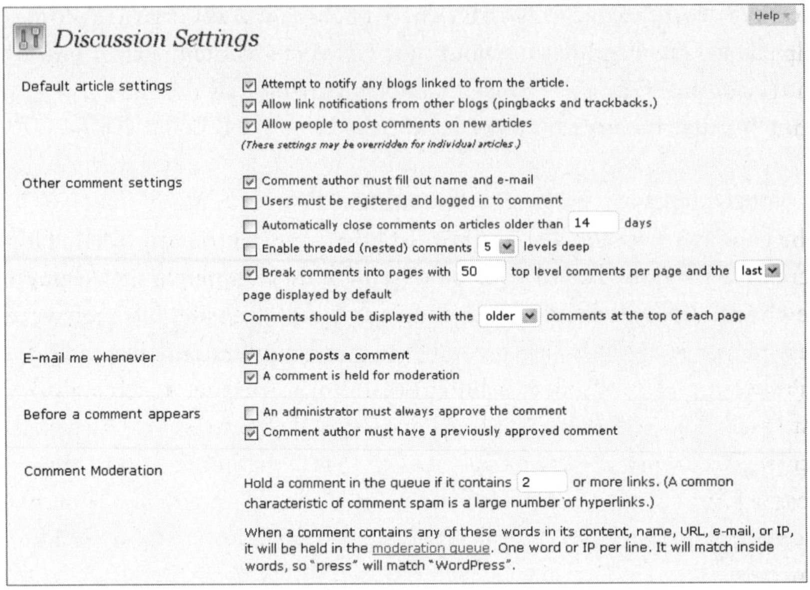

Figure 17.9 WordPress comment administration screen

The worst thing a blog can have is unregulated comments on the blog, because it makes it appear as though the manager or owner is unaware of the comments being made on the blog or has unwanted links showing up in the comments.

Managing the comments on an active blog can be a time-consuming process. However, the time spent screening irrelevant, "spammy," or link-dropping comments will only increase the relevance and quality of the comments for your readers. *Link dropping* is the practice many sites use to build their links by making very general comments that look harmless, but they are relying on the harmless comment to be approved, thereby providing a link to their site with the context of anchor text instead of their real name.

Approving comments builds your credibility, especially when you allow comments that might be critical and address them in a follow-up comment. However, critical comments that contain language that you do not approve of are fine to delete. I recommend adding comment guidelines to your website that make it very clear that any comments with profane language, insulting other commenters, or blatantly dropping a link instead of a real name will be deleted (yes, I delete comments that are using anchor text instead of a real name). You are the site owner, so it is your prerogative, and you make the rules.

One particular comment spam plug-in (a program that is made to "plug in" to a parent program, like WordPress) is Akismet, which is included with WordPress.

With Akismet, you create an account, and all comments are reviewed by the Akismet server, which helps eliminate hundreds to thousands of spammy comments. If one does get through the Akismet review, you can mark it as spam, and Akismet will "learn" to eliminate similar comments in the future.

Permalinks

Permalinks can be controlled by the blog author to reflect a more friendly URL. This is the ability to create a URL rewrite in your blog (remember Chapter 14?). Although a rewrite is somewhat complicated for a large database-driven website, blog software such as WordPress makes it easy for anyone to create clear, contextual URLs.

When you're setting up a WordPress blog, I recommend setting up permalinks as one of the first tasks. The Permalinks link is located under Settings. On the permalinks setup screen, the interface presents a very clear understanding of how this software is so powerful in the hands of nontechnical publishers. The owner or manager of the blog can customize the URL structure setup exactly how they would like it to appear (Figure 17.10).

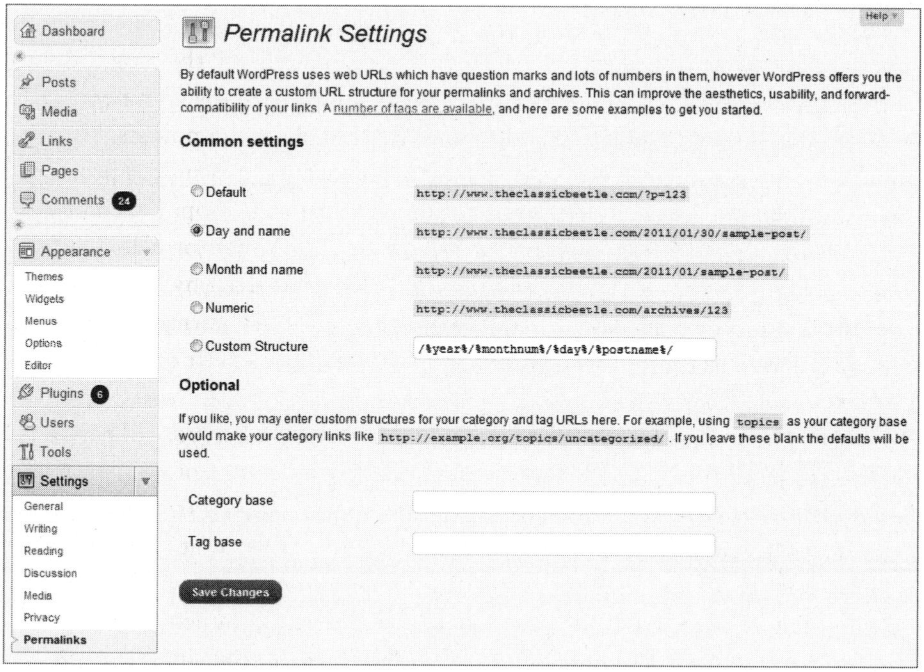

Figure 17.10 The URL structure of permalinks can be customized based on your needs.

The default setting in WordPress creates the URL that is typically seen in database-driven sites, with the ?p=*123* parameter, where *123* is a variable. This means the post equals record 123 in the database. To build the page, the template pulls the article based on the record number and displays that to the visitor.

The permalink changes the address of the URL from the record number assigned to the post (for example, ?p=123) from the database to more understandable, contextual information, such as the post title, the post date, the post category, the month, or a customized structure. Creating a URL simply based on post title, as shown in Figure 17.10, can be done as long as there are no duplicated post titles, because that would cause an error. To avoid duplicated post titles in the URL, use another parameter, such as the post number, month, or day, in order to ensure that all post URLs are unique.

Widgets

Widgets are a method of extending the functionality of the blog and customizing sidebar areas specific to your business needs. From the administration side of the blog, widgets allow you to add content and functionality to areas of the page. For example, the administrator can add advertising, links, related content links, and other navigation items to the page simply by dragging and dropping the widget, rather than making changes to the code of the website.

The widget contains the code necessary to display the appropriate content but comes in a portable format. Widgets can be activated by adding them to the page or inactivated by taking them out of the page. They can contain graphics, text links, advertisements, and many other functions (see Figure 17.11).

The advantage is that pages can be changed with a simple drag-and-drop interface, rather than getting a programmer to make these changes to the site. In addition, the widgets are completely transparent to the visitor of the website. The functions allowed in the widgets provide a better user experience by allowing the site owner to provide relevant navigation, call to action messages, and functions specific to their business, rather than getting locked into a template and dealing with programming restrictions based on how most other businesses would use the template. Widgets create a high level of customization, allowing you to develop the look and feel of the blog specific to your business goals.

Widgets are a way to extend the customization of your site and the functionality you require. For example, a blog for a corporate site may want to incorporate links to white papers and content contained on the formal website. To add this as a regular part of the blog's design, a widget would allow that customization. By creating a "text" widget and dragging it into the preferred toolbar, you can create content similar to adding content into a post (see Figure 17.12).

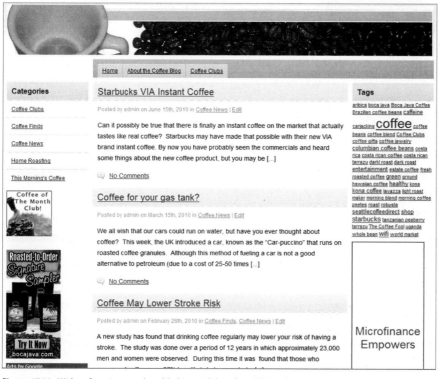

Figure 17.11 Widget functions can be added into sidebars for additional customization, as on the two sites shown here.

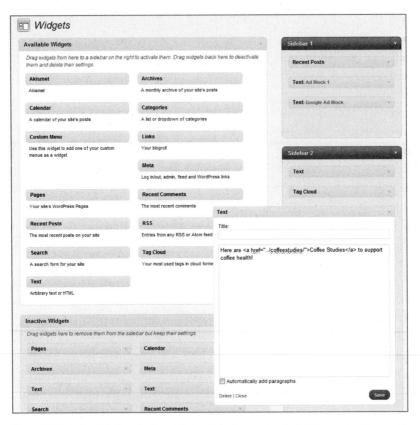

Figure 17.12 Adding links into the Text widget, which allows customized sidebar content for your blog

Wednesday: Develop Your Blogging Style

So, you are ready to start blogging. Well, be patient. That is the first word of advice. There are millions of blogs out there already. Getting noticed and drawing visitors is going to take some time, so the first four to six months are going to be the least rewarding. Having a plan will get you through those first few months of few visitors and find motivation to keep working and writing.

Build a Content Plan

The first thing is developing a content plan for the first six months to a year. Your posts don't have to be a complete novel; in fact, it is best if they aren't. Posts should be easy and fast to read. If you want to write a long educational and informational post, that is fine, and at times it is necessary to show the capabilities of your business. However, start with some simple, "bite-sized" articles that allow you to showcase your company and information.

A schedule of content will help you stay on track and develop ideas before you start, rather than getting three months in and having no ideas. Planning will eliminate much of the guesswork and help you stay on message. The plan does not have to be a strict and overbearing taskmaster; it is a guide. If you see that your visitors are responding to a certain type of information or post, then feel free to adjust your schedule and content to take advantage of the trends. Don't follow your plan so strictly that you can't allow for events and trends to help you grow.

Before you blog, I recommend taking stock of your available resources of both time and content. Is it realistic that you have the time or resources available to research and write a few times a week? If you are starting a blog, don't post articles less than once a week. If the resources and time are available, develop a content plan for the next three months. The plan should involve article ideas, contributions to the market, ideas for attracting attention from other bloggers, and prospects in your industry.

In addition, answer the question, Who are you writing for? I find that the most successful bloggers have a specific person or type of person in mind. Whether it is a client who has many questions and needs guidance, an intern who needs to be educated, a peer in the industry, or someone else, it is best to have a specific audience target in mind. This way, you are able to stay on task and ensure that your content is always directed.

For me, it is easier to write and stay on task when picturing marketing managers or a business owner. When picturing them, I answer their questions on the best ways to market their websites on a budget, regardless of whether it is a time budget or a money budget. (We are all trying to find ways to do the best things more efficiently.) In this way, I write with a business coaching style, and it keeps me from writing content that doesn't belong or fit the style of my business.

Find Your Style

One of the more important developments for new bloggers is finding out the type of blogger you are. Not everyone can write five to six paragraphs of content three to four times a week, and not all readers want to digest that much information in a week. There is a careful balance of the time you spend writing and the time your visitors will spend reading. The first few months of developing articles will help you find your writing or publishing style.

In some cases, there will be more than one author, and there will need to be consensus among the group as to the purpose, guidelines, and consistency that will be needed to meet the goals of the business. Each author could have a remarkably different style and personality, which will enhance the depth and topics of the blog, because no two people will write the exact thing but may see it from different angles. More authors mean more content and more opinions on relevant topics to your audience, but it also means more management and planning.

Beat Reporter

The beat reporter is one who constantly watches the headlines, reads hundreds of articles and websites, and always reports the latest happenings within an industry. This type of blogger provides value through being an information source. By distilling all the available news into a clear, understandable message and updates for others in the industry, the beat reporter style can build up a following very shortly.

The other aspect of the beat reporter is that by reporting the news and constantly updating everyone else, it is the most demanding of all the styles. If you are seen as the source of news updates within a niche or industry, then the content needs to come quickly and regularly. The access to the information is easier but requires significant amounts of time to peruse the latest news and decide which to report and then publish. This style requires that the blog be kept up-to-date constantly, and most blogs of this style have posts published two to four times a day. That is why this style gains visitors faster, because the content is coming faster, through numerous updates. This is a big commitment, but with big rewards as well in terms of readership and subscribers.

Analyst

The next content style is the analyst. These are bloggers who pick particular areas of information and consider the news in terms of the market. The analyst most likely will publish a few times a week, and the content will be focused on how to apply the latest information into actionable information. Analysts provide the context of the latest news into forecasts and relevance, assessing the impact on the industry and practical applications.

Analysts are not as dependent upon the immediate news cycle but are dependent upon the ability to see through the news and provide the larger picture for an industry and provide the answers to all of the activity. Opinions, trends, historical context, and past performance are all tools that the analyst uses to provide their information and build their credibility.

Building a following and subscribers will take longer in this approach, but this approach also builds credibility and authority because you are doing more than reporting the news. The analyst is considering and making recommendations based on information. People are always looking for support and decision-making advice.

Investigative Reporter

The investigative reporter typically has an assignment that takes them around the world and requires their attention for weeks or months at a time. They are typically focused on a single area and become the expert in that area as they interview, research, analyze, and witness the events that they bring to the audience.

This is an area that many established bloggers tend to develop after they have been blogging for years and find a specific area of interest or passion. The updates may come more infrequently, but they provide very deep, interesting, and informative information that can be used or inspire additional information and action.

A Style All Your Own

Although the preceding types are three typical of blogger writing styles, by no means are they the definitive styles. There are many styles that different people develop based on content, personality, opinions, and time. Many blogger personalities are formed over the course of a few years, as feedback is heard and the style emerges naturally.

There are many ways to start, and the possibilities are endless. Here are a few examples:

- A home contractor uses a blog to show before and after pictures of their work, along with notes about the project and how the improvement helps a home's value or living space.

- A local animal shelter uses a blog to show pictures of available pets and new adoptions.

- An artist uses a blog to showcase new comic strips and comments on life, including the struggle to be creative.

- Many blogs simply post resources found online for other businesses, becoming a resource and establishing themselves as experts in the industry.

The options and applications of blogging are still evolving, and many are simply developed based on an idea or accident. There are really no rules to how to blog to build your business, other than to provide content that other people want or need, whichever way that is easiest and best done by you.

Find Inspiration

The best advice about writing was provided about my university English professor. "If you want to write well, then you need to read well." That's great advice, especially for blogging. If you want to blog well and regularly, then you need to read well and regularly. In my early days of blogging, I found that reading other bloggers was particularly helpful in staying up on current events and developing analysis based on other findings and opinions.

I followed a handful of bloggers regularly, and what was most attractive about them was that they made me think. When you can find others that make you think, it is the breeding ground for ideas. Find those bloggers in your industry or niche that provide information that challenges you and makes you think. Those will be the sources of inspiration that will help provide content for your own blog.

As you develop your own content based on the inspiration of others, link to those sources of inspiration, and cite the article they write that provided the idea. This is called a *hat-tip*. Years ago, in polite society, one would tip their hat as a sign of respect or greeting. In blogging terms, you link to the article where you received the news or the idea and then provide your own analysis or opinion based on the insight you developed from their article.

Bloggers track sites that link to their articles and read what others say. Many are very active in keeping up on who is reading and linking to them. If you want to get their attention, be sure to begin the conversation by making a comment or two on their blog. Blogger etiquette at this point is that you simply leave a comment that adds to the discussion; please do not use this as an opportunity to link to your own article. At this point, you are trying to build a relationship and not advertise your own blog.

You will get the attention of other bloggers by commenting and linking to their articles. As that happens, take the next step and initiate an email conversation with them. Be sure to be respectful of their time, and be polite. You are marketing yourself, and in doing so the attention is on those bloggers and not you. Do not use these opportunities to talk about you and your blog unless you are asked. This is part of simply developing a relationship; it takes time, and you have to establish your credibility.

This is how I developed my relationship with Avinash Kaushik, who wrote the foreword to this book. He wrote a post on his blog that inspired me to write a post on mine. I commented on his blog, and he followed the link, read my article, and commented on my blog. Over the next few months, it moved into an email conversation and discussion about analytics and additional issues. Eventually, when I was in the Bay Area speaking at a conference, Avinash invited me to come visit his offices (back when he was at Intuit). We spent a few hours visiting and talking, and we developed a friendship that has lasted years as a result.

Your motivation has to be that of developing relationships, educating, and investing. Your passion about your company and your industry will show in your content. There is no quick payoff of links, recognition, or advantage. People can pick up on those motivations very quickly, and you will not get the response you desire if those are your first intentions. Approaching bloggers is like building a new friendship, and the relationships you develop will pay off secondarily in links, attention, and visitors.

Thursday: Avoid Blog Design Pitfalls

As powerful as blogs are in creating more business opportunities, there are significant areas that are overlooked in the development and execution of designing and developing a business blog. These issues are consistent enough that they inhibit the ability of the blog to properly monetize the business by preventing sales and leads beyond the initial visits. Just as I've discussed with regard to a standard website, such blog problems can easily be remedied by making a few small changes that will immediately enhance the business value of your blog.

Unstated Purpose and Benefits

Related to the lack of conversion points is the lack of a clear business focus behind the blog. While so much emphasis is usually placed on a business website's home page and the messaging on the home page, very little seems to be placed on the blog. Considering that more visitors may see the home page of the blog more than the actual website, the home page should provide a thoughtful reevaluation of the marketing on the blog.

Just by looking at the blog, can you tell the purpose of the blog or the business behind the blog? What is the benefit statement? How can the blog help your business beyond providing articles and information on a regular information?

These questions should provide an understanding of the need to have an established purpose for the blog. Too many businesses jumped at building a blog on their websites because they heard it would increase their rankings, but they forgot to actually use it as a business-building tool.

Just because this is a blog does not mean that the rules of credible design and persuasive content don't apply. In fact, they are even more important when communicating in this very social medium! The purpose of the blog, the benefits to the reader, and explicit calls to action need to stand out and be clear. Don't get caught up in using a template and assuming it does what you need. You still need to engage the visitor and show that you have their needs in mind in your design.

Just as in marketing a website, there needs to be a clear purpose, clear credibility, and a clear benefit to the blog. Otherwise, it comes across as a mash-up of content all competing against itself.

Unclear Conversion Points

Just as with any other kind of business website, having clear conversion points is a key marketing principle. A business blog isn't just a method of communicating information; it is also business development. Too many business blogs go with the default setup of the blogging software and seem to completely forget that the blog is a business tool. Too many businesses are getting a lot of visitors to their blog, but they forget to advertise the business. They provide valuable information but no conversion or call to action to learn anything more about the business. As a result, the visitors are "stranded" on the blog with no clear way to interact with the business or go to the business website. E-commerce blogs often share information about products and applications for products, which gets them a lot of visitors, but then they neglect to link to the products. Similarly, businesses often talk about their research and benefits but then forget to put lead forms on the blog.

The way to defeat this trend is to simply evaluate your blog based on the established goals for your website marketing plan. If the goal is to increase leads, sales, and registrations, then the blog needs to reflect the same business goals as the website. The default settings will not do this, because it will take customization and testing to ensure that you are meeting the needs and expectations of the visitors and persuading them to take action.

The blog Pinch My Salt is very well designed and keeps one of its primary monetization strategies well "above the fold" (you don't have to scroll down to see it). The graphic link to the store is in the upper right and in a clear visual space for the reader to find (see Figure 17.13).

Figure 17.13 Pinch My Salt keeps the conversion point clear.

Poor Navigation and Contrast

Contrast is a specific point of design consideration throughout this text. However, it seems as though people tend to forget the guidelines of good web design when adding a blog to their website. Some of this comes from the ability to find thousands of blog templates that can be easily used to change the design and layout of the blog.

Just because the template is available online does not mean it is designed well or considers standards and accessibility. Anyone can submit a CSS blog template to the list of available templates, and the designs need to be evaluated based on the same standards as websites. Contrast, layout, typography, font size, and color scheme (see Chapter 9) are just as important in creating credibility on the blog as they are in creating credibility on the website.

The same issue is seen in navigation preferences on blogs. Simply because your chosen template has a navigation style does not mean you are locked into that specific navigation scheme. The beauty of blogs and the extension of widgets allow you to customize your content and build navigation that makes sense to your readers and furthers your business goals.

The blog typically covers more information territory than the standard website and also presents it in vastly different methods. Many people do not realize that they are even visiting a blog when it is designed well, has clear navigation, and has easily findable topics. Your site may need a navigation bar with Related Content, Recent Comments, or Recent Posts links in order to keep your audience engaged and reading. Other sites may want to populate the sidebar with products that are sold on their ecommerce website. Some may want to place ads in the sidebars.

The main focus of building the blog is to style the content and the navigation to suit your business needs. That involves a focus on your audience, which then demands clear information architecture. Continue using keywords in navigation, categories, clear titles in posts, and well-designed content.

Remember also to evaluate the theme you have chosen to be sure that contrast is included in your customization. Some templates like to do things differently in order to be artistic, but we know that contrast is important in navigation and in the calls to action. Watch especially for the links contained in your blog, because many templates will change the colors of the links and the rollover effect. You want to be sure that visitors know that the links are links in both color and action.

Poor Interlinking

While blogging software makes the ability to administer a website and publish online accessible to anyone, there is still a learning curve in developing the ability to draw people into a website or blog beyond their first page. This is where interlinking pages, content, categories, and products can enable your visitors to engage much more deeply than the content on the page.

Chances are, if something attracted them to the initial page of content, be it search results or a website link, they are interested in that subject. By adding links to related content on your blog or your main website, you can offer more. This is why there are specific groups of links available in the widgets and the blog software to add Related Posts, Recent Posts, and Recent Comments links.

People are naturally drawn to conversation and to see what other people have read. This is why popular posts and comments provide a natural curiosity to readers, and a logical placement of the category and links near the content provides an easy method of gaining more page views from your visitors.

If the business has a website and a blog, then it is necessary to interlink the two. Providing information via the blog is a great means of outreach and visibility, but the business goals still need to be met, and a blog must link back into the primary goal of the website, whether it is ecommerce, lead generation, or something else. The earliest version of the GM FastLane Blog had no navigation to the other GM websites or even internal navigation to get to additional articles or related content (see Figure 17.14).

Figure 17.14 An early version of GM's FastLane Blog (a) contained no navigational links to additional content. The newer version (b) makes categories and navigation an important part of the structure.

Having an access link or navigation options to the main website allows visitors to get to the website's information and access the sales and marketing information necessary to lead development. Most blogs default to being an independent entity and, as such, need to be reworked to some degree to allow for integration of the primary website. Otherwise, visitors will come and read the content on the blog, unaware that there is an entire website of information and the possibility of finding an answer to their question or a vendor that has the products they need.

CNET does this very well, by maintaining the main navigation on the header of the blogs but also by providing blog-specific navigation for each niche blog it publishes (Figure 17.15). The main navigation to the rest of the website is always available, and the focus is on the blog as an addition to the site, rather than being a replacement for the website.

Figure 17.15 The CNET Digital Media blog maintains both the main navigation for the website and the blog navigation in the design.

In a manner of speaking, businesses need to advertise their own websites on the blog. This is where attention-getting graphics as calls to action can place people into the lead process on the website. By advertising your own services and calls to action on the blog, you can entice your visitors to go beyond being a reader of the blog to being a business prospect or customer.

One of my favorite destination travel blogs is from the Black Hills of South Dakota (www.blackhillstravelblog.com). By visiting the blog, I can be reminded of earlier experiences but also learn about new experiences and destinations that only the locals seem to know. The blog offers multiple options to interface with the writers, the content, the area, and the tourism industry—a call to action to book a vacation. The website has a specific purpose and does not vary from that, but it also is an amazing source of new visitors to the websites in the region and in the travel industry as well (see Figure 17.16).

Figure 17.16 The Black Hills Travel Blog engages visitors on many levels but keeps the primary goal in front of the visitor—booking vacations.

Friday: Manage and Increase Subscribers

One would think that if blogs are so powerful at building traffic and business, marketers would go to great lengths to use whatever means they could to develop the visitors into a strong marketing force. Unfortunately, I see many missed opportunities by blogs because they neglect to add one simple conversion point. Because of the growth of social media, the primary means of interacting with the blog is to vote for the stories through clicking the social-media icons. The next available means of subscribing to the content of the blog is usually though a strange little icon that is usually confused with a volume button (see Figure 17.17).

©ISTOCKPHOTO.COM/[ANGELHELL]

Figure 17.17 The RSS symbol

This is called RSS. Unfortunately, as discussed in Chapter 11, relying on RSS as a primary marketing tool could lose you viable customers who simply don't know what RSS is. In the past, RSS has been used by news junkies, journalists, and anyone who processes large amounts of information and news on a daily basis. Sites set up RSS feeds, and they can see which sites have new articles, browse through the articles, and read the ones they want without ever going directly to the sites. The program used to view all of the website "feeds" is called a *reader*. An RSS reader is almost like email, but each folder is the website you've subscribed to with the latest posts and articles from that website. Currently, two well-known (sort of) readers are Google Reader and the now-shuttered Bloglines, operated by Ask.com. As of late 2010, ComScore shows that accessing web content from RSS feeds has been dropping significantly. Google Reader's visits are down 27 percent, and Bloglines' dropped 71 percent over the past few years.

This is why so many Internet marketing pundits have declared RSS dead. It requires a significant knowledge of Internet familiarity and therefore creates a barrier to the average Internet user. However, when looking at the majority of blogs the primary, sometimes the only call to action is a subscription to RSS, so one would think that the technology is universal. It's not.

On blogs where I have recommended adding a Subscribe by Email call to action, the number of email subscribers has grown to at least double and sometimes triple the number of RSS subscribers. The proportion of visitors that will subscribe when given a choice of email rises substantially. This is why I am amazed so many well known marketing blogs do not offer an email subscription.

Ask any direct marketer what holds the greatest value, and they will tell you it's the list. For years, direct marketers focused on getting names and addresses; once they have them, you are on the list, and they can send test mailings, catalogs, targeted mailings, associated offers, and everything else to you, because you are on the list. Email is the same way. When building a blog, emails are valuable, much more valuable than RSS subscribers, for many reasons. When a reader subscribes via RSS, you do not know who they are. You really only know how many RSS subscribers there are, but nothing more about them. Apart from the feed, you can't contact them personally. In addition, being RSS subscribers, they are not coming back to your website. They won't see your ads, and they won't see your calls to action. Those who subscribe through email can be sent an email when a new post is made, and you can track who and how many return to the website to see the new update. You can also send additional offers and direct updates to your opted-in list of subscribers. The value is in the subscribers, in other words, the list.

Facebook is an email-like method of allowing people to receive updates. However, unless they are aware of the update by constantly watching their Facebook page or their Facebook feed, they could easily miss the update. However, Facebook allows you to contact your subscribers through Facebook mail, which also goes to their regular email. It's a double-contact email, because they are notified of the message in their Facebook inbox through email—a great way of making sure your message gets through to your friends.

Twitter allows you to gain subscribers, and you can communicate to them through traditional tweets, but there is no way to know who saw your status update and who didn't. There are a few ways to measure the feedback from your updates, but not on the personal level, like an email response rate. You can send direct messages in Twitter, but they had better be personal. Direct messages broadcasted to all of your followers pitching your service aren't popular.

Email is still a personal medium, and the majority of Internet users still list email as the primary reason they go online. For some, especially in business, email is a lifeline to all that goes on around them. Email is still one of the cheapest and most effective marketing methods available, and incorporating a strategy to build an email list is simply smart marketing.

Review and Hands-On

Make a list of the blogs that you read currently. If you don't read any, find a list of the blogs in your industry or news and information blogs. Make note of the organization and navigation of those blogs—what would work for your business? What wouldn't? By reviewing different blogs, you will find elements and styles that you like and dislike, so make notes of those elements.

WordPress was discussed heavily in this chapter and recommended as a blogging platform. If blogging is in your plans, take the time to have WordPress installed. Don't be afraid to ask for help! Set it up on a development server or a stand-alone server where you can make mistakes and see how things work. I always recommend people have a personal blog to use as a testing ground, rather than trying things on a business blog.

Develop your content plan for the next three months. Try to plan at least two short blog posts per week for the next three months. The better you plan, the less you'll be stressed when searching for a topic.

In developing the plan, read through the blogs that you have selected or bookmarked, and find the style you enjoy. The quick, short updates typical of the beat reporter? Or is your style the more thoughtful, drawn-out analysis of an investigative reporter? It is important to find a style that is comfortable and suits your personality.

As your blog comes together, review the layout and design chapters (Chapters 11 and 12) in order to make sure your blog follows the same principles as successful websites. Do not lose sight of clear navigation, contrasting elements, and clear calls to action. Ensure that your primary call to action is clear on the site and that your subscription options are visible and suited to your business.

Week 15: Get Friendly with Social Media

Social media. The sound of those words makes most marketers and business owners shudder. It's a fear of the unexpected, the unknown, and the uncertain. Everyone from trade journals, industry peers, and teenagers are telling you that you should be using social media, but no one seems to be telling you how, why, or what you can expect from it. It seems to be just one gray cloud of peer pressure, with no clear path to ROI. Take a deep breath; I promise that I will go slow. By the end of this chapter, you should have the confidence to move forward using social media.

Chapter Contents

Monday and Tuesday: Understand the Breadth of Social Media

Wednesday: Communicate Your Message Effectively

Thursday: Assess Your Resources

Friday: Enact Your Social-Media Plan

Monday and Tuesday: Understand the Breadth of Social Media

Social media has been around longer than the modern Internet. One of my geekiest claims to fame is that my dad brought home a computer in 1984. Within only a few months, inspired by the movie *WarGames*, I had a modem (where you would place the phone handset in a cradle and go online through CompuServe, a dial-up service). The only places that was really of any interest at that time were the bulletin board systems (BBSs), one of the earliest forms of chat and discussion forums.

As I look back now, the BBSs were the beginnings of the digital social-media culture. People with common interests would meet, discuss, debate, recommend, and refer each other to businesses or products. There was no marketing in this public forum because marketers were vastly unaware of this emerging form of communication.

In later forms, this communication developed into threaded conversations in newsgroups, or UseNet. Newsgroups operated on the same principles as the bulletin boards but offered abilities to upload and distribute files and participate in discussions without a high technical level of knowledge.

As technology, broadband, mobile, and social-media applications have increased, so also has the ability of people to communicate with one another through online media. The field of social media has increased dramatically both in the number of participants and in the number of media options. Depending on a person's comfort level with online communications and interaction, they will find a social-media type that will work for them.

Blogs, of course, are the foundational blocks of modern social media. Blogs dominate the social-media landscape in both accessibility and results, which is why last week's chapter was dedicated to blogs. This week's chapter provides an overview and strategy for utilizing the rest of the social-media tools.

When added to a marketing manager's daily duties within a business, the prospect of keeping up with social media and understanding how each new media works can be overwhelming. Unfortunately, many businesses feel pressured to do something, anything, when it comes to social media. If they don't have a clear strategy or understanding, the purpose becomes convoluted, the time involved and resources needed for social media seem to be too much or to be unaccountable, and there is no measurement of results. You need a solid foundation of knowledge to avoid being overwhelmed, so I will start with a basic overview of the types of social media and how they reach specific audiences.

Discussion Forums

The types of discussion contained in the early BBSs and newsgroups are typically contained in discussion forums these days. Discussion forums are still one of the most vibrant and viable places to discover what customers and groups discuss and share in terms of products, industries, and niche topics. The general rule is that the more niche the topic, the more conversation and the more active the community will be in the discussion forums.

There are millions of discussion forums, and they cater to the most niche topics imaginable. The discussion forums are not just about cars, music, horses, and dogs, but there are multiple forums for different car makes and models, music genres, dogs breeds, and horse disciplines. In short, name the topic, and there are most likely a number of forums dedicated to it (see Figure 18.1).

Figure 18.1 A sampling of parenting-related topics on a discussion forum

Most discussion forums are owned and operated by a single person. Typically out of passion for a specific subject, the person started the forum as a way to find and share information with like-minded people who have similar interests and the same passion about a topic.

It is not rare to find a very active discussion forum that is gaining members and actively growing. In addition to the membership, most discussions on a forum are publicly available. This means the topics, discussions, and information are all open to the public. The search engines are also able to find, index, and publish forum information in the search engines, which adds to the visibility of the topics.

Although a forum may have thousands of active members, the reach is far beyond the members. Most forums have an active readership that does not participate; in fact, many do not become members because they have no desire to participate in the discussion. They only want to read the information and keep up with it. These non-participating members are called *lurkers*, because they hide in the shadows but do not want to be a visible participant in the exchange of information.

Forums contain some of the best user-generated information of any social media, mainly because of the length of time many of the forums have been around, the number of members contributing, and the types of information that is shared. Because I have an affinity to old VW Beetles, I tend to read forums for advice and information when I am troubleshooting a problem, and that is when I am able to find great information and links to specific vendors and products that can assist my search (see Figure 18.2).

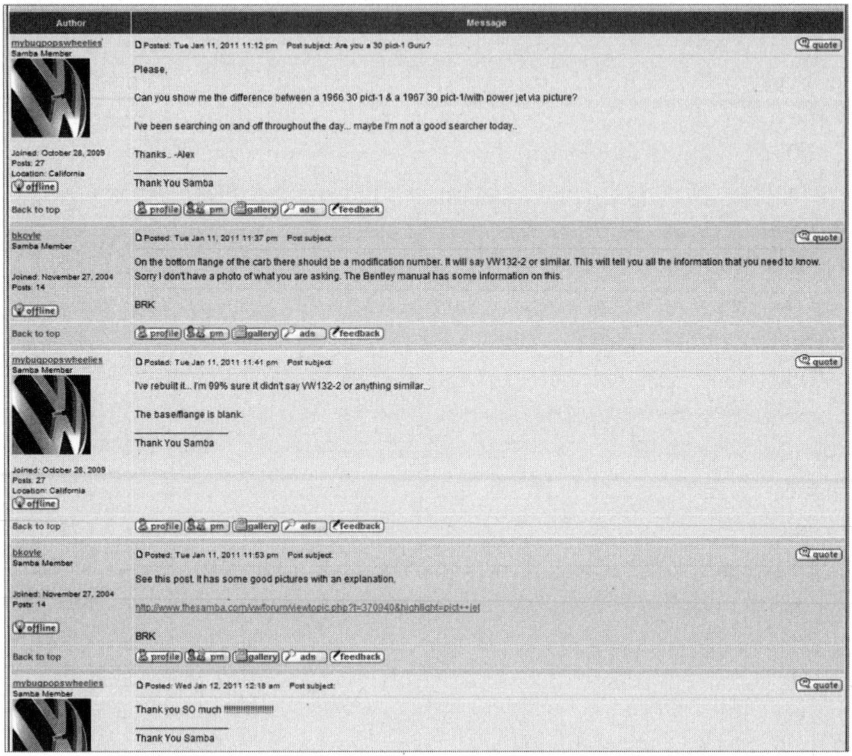

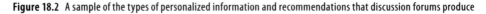

Figure 18.2 A sample of the types of personalized information and recommendations that discussion forums produce

Because of this information sharing and the level of nonmarketing influence, discussions tend to be very grassroots. For a business, this is a very solid source of research and insight into the niche customer. The typical concerns, hesitations, and objections discussed in this venue can help a vendor or a business formulate a solid strategy simply by reading and "listening" to the community.

As with any online community, there are a certain set of rules. As a marketer or a business, it is generally frowned upon for you to register as a member at the forum and immediately begin marketing yourself or your business. The forum is made up of people who like to discuss without being marketed to. Push too hard, and the forum owner will most likely disable your account, sometimes without warning. If you find a forum in your particular industry or niche, take the time to read the information posted for vendors and businesses. It is better to be informed of the forum's particular policies and understand the expectations rather than create a negative image of your company.

Media Sharing

Media sharing, simply put, is the sharing of video, audio, images, and other media. From vacation photos to videos of a blender to podcasts about grammar usage, people are placing large amounts of multimedia content online through media-sharing social media.

Video Sharing

Media sharing is currently dominated by the darling of social media, YouTube. As cited in one of the other books in this series, *YouTube and Video Marketing: An Hour a Day* (Wiley, 2009), YouTube is the second largest search engine, ahead of Bing and Yahoo!, even though it is not considered as a search engine. That is how extensive YouTube has become.

YouTube, which was founded in 2005, burst on the scene as a video-sharing service. Prior to YouTube, online users were sent videos through email. Offices would share emails throughout the office and with their friends, resulting in an amazing amount of bandwidth being used to share quick, silly, or amazing videos.

Along came YouTube, which allowed users to create an account, upload videos, and simply send a link to the video, rather than the video itself. Without having to actually send a file, the speed of sharing increased significantly, as well as the access to the videos. To make the perfect combination of events, *Saturday Night Live*'s "Lazy Sunday" (which NBC decided to remove from YouTube in attempting to direct visitors to the NBC video site) and EepyBird's "Diet Coke and Mentos" videos were released at about the same time, and the combination of the accessibility of YouTube and viral videos made YouTube an instant sensation.

After five years, YouTube's success is astonishing. Take a look at its stats:

- More than 2 billion views a day
- The third most visited website
- 24 hours of video uploaded every minute

Simply put, if you want to reach people, YouTube could be a good place to consider.

YouTube is owned by Google, and you may have seen that videos are also shown in Google search results periodically. Many times, the videos tend to be more relevant than other results and get more clicks. For some searches, multiple videos may be shown, even before the other search results. Providing video content is easier than ever, and the ability of videos to get prime placement in Google's search results can provide a significant source of traffic to your website.

Although there are other video-sharing sites, such as Vimeo, Viddler, and Daily Motion, the basics of uploading and optimizing the video are the same. Optimize your video with a keyword-specific title and description, and be sure to complete all the text fields describing the video. Use keywords to explain the title of the video, the description, and the tags. Search engines will read the content in the text fields and use that for relevance. YouTube (Google) has also developed technology that will automatically create captions based on the words in the video.

When creating a page, be sure to provide a link back to your website in your profile. When necessary, link the relevant page on your website from the particular video. The default settings won't allow you to do this in YouTube; your channel type must be changed from "YouTuber" to one of the other options. In doing this, you will be able to add a direct link to a web page in the video description box (Figure 18.3). In this example, the title of the video, the description, and the tags all use keywords of the subject and location in the important text areas. The hyperlink in the description (under the video window) allows viewers to go to the page where they can get more information.

Figure 18.3 The display of the title of the video, the description, and the tags in YouTube

Photo Sharing

Sharing sites Flickr, PhotoBucket, Shutterfly, SmugMug, WebShots, and Picasa all allow visitors to create an account and upload photos to share with their friends and the online public. There is also some overlap, because the photo-sharing sites are starting to offer video. However, people tend to think of them as pictures first, rather than strong contenders in the video space. Users can create albums and provide descriptions of the locations and the types of cameras, lenses, or filters used to capture the photograph. Although certainly not limited to professional or semiprofessional photographers, users of all types are welcome and able to upload photos from their collection to share with others.

If you are older than 30, chances are you have boxes of photographs stored away in a closet or basement. The older you are, the more you have stored away, all with the intention of organizing "some day." The problem that people have when organizing these photographs is the inability to organize them in a logical format, because this is the limitation of the hard-copy format. The same picture could be put in the honeymoon pile, the beach or vacation pile, or maybe even the relatives pile. If more than one person is helping organize these photos, then there will be even more methods of organization and disagreement over which pile the photo will be placed in.

This is the beauty of digital photo sharing. You can upload a photo and classify it with multiple tags. This way, the photo will show up in any collection where the tag is selected. A photo is relevant to many aspects of our life, so limiting one photo to one display category makes little sense. By offering unlimited categories for a photo, it can be appreciated and seen more, based on the whim of the browser. By selecting multiple categories of tags, it increases the relevance of the photo in the collection but also provides new and unique ways of browsing through collections, both yours and others' in the photo-sharing websites (see Figure 18.4).

Figure 18.4 Photos can be classified under multiple categories via tags.

One of the more interesting features in the photo-sharing sites is the conversations that take place within certain groups. This is a prime area for research and participation for a business that might be able to contribute and develop relationships in these areas. This skiing photography group in Flickr.com, shown in Figure 18.5, has active discussions about skiing venues, helmets, and photography equipment.

If your industry has related active groups in photo-sharing sites or even somewhat related groups, it is a good idea to see the images associated with your industry and also be aware of the conversations that take place within these groups.

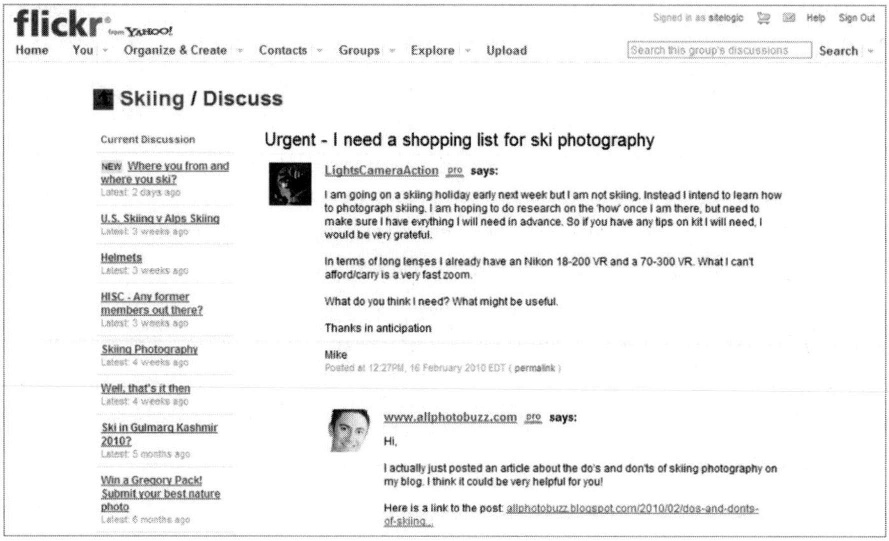

Figure 18.5 Diverse conversations happen on photo-sharing sites.

Customer Reviews

One of the earliest forms of social media is the customer review. The early days of eBay showed the necessity of having evidence that the buyers and sellers were active and trustworthy. By allowing buyers to rate sellers and sellers to comment on buyers, reviews played in important part of the development of the ecommerce industry.

Today, most sites that offer any type of transaction, in addition to business listings, offer a way to leave a testimonial or review. Travel, ecommerce, local business listings, seller reviews, and store reviews all allow customers to provide their feedback and response to the public.

When allowing customer reviews, business owners all seem to have the same objection: "What if someone leaves a negative review?" Somehow the prospect of a negative review is a paralyzing obstacle to many businesses. However, there are a number of reasons businesses need to stop hiding from reviews and handle them directly.

First, the reviews are happening anyway. Even if there are no reviews available on your website, people have the ability to leave reviews about your business on many other websites. By bringing the discussion and reviews to your site, you can meet them better than by attempting to manage the discussion on someone else's website.

Second, no amount of stifling reviews can hide a bad product. If you are confident in your service and product and people like it, then there will be good reviews. You can also ask customers to assist you by providing reviews and possibly offering them an incentive for doing so. However, if there is a problem with your product or customer service or a deeper problem, it will come out in the reviews. This is not a fault of the availability of reviews; this is a problem with the business that needs to be corrected.

Third, sometimes bad reviews can help your business. Consumers are smart and can spot a bad review for what it is, maybe a grumpy vacationer, a perfectionist, or simply someone with a grudge—they can all be pretty easy to spot. Simply having the bad reviews mixed with all other reviews can help potential customers spot the inconsistencies. Many times, bad reviews are a result of misplaced expectations.

When evaluating reviews, you can see that expectations play a large role; consider Figure 18.6, which shows such an example from Travelocity. The Milford Plaza in New York City has both a "very disappointed" one out of five rating right next to a highly favorable five out of five rating. When reading the review from the unfavorable rating, a story emerges that this was the guests' first trip to New York City, and they thought the rooms were too small. Welcome to New York City! It is not always a bad review that turns people off. Sometimes, bad reviews go good, especially when they help others manage their expectations.

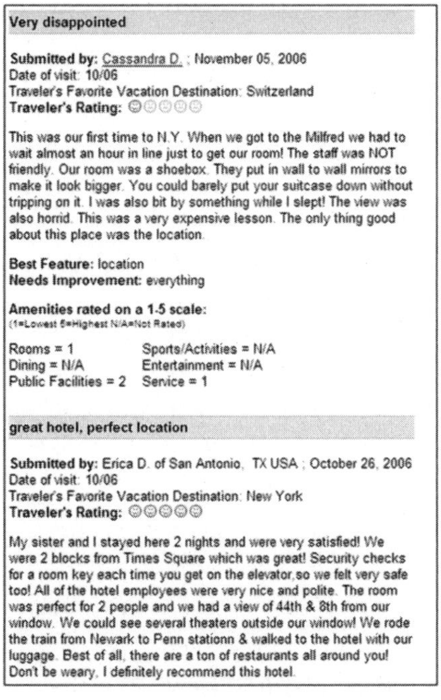

Very disappointed

Submitted by: Cassandra D. ; November 05, 2006
Date of visit: 10/06
Traveler's Favorite Vacation Destination: Switzerland
Traveler's Rating:

This was our first time to N.Y. When we got to the Milfred we had to wait almost an hour in line just to get our room! The staff was NOT friendly. Our room was a shoebox. They put in wall to wall mirrors to make it look bigger. You could barely put your suitcase down without tripping on it. I was also bit by something while I slept! The view was also horrid. This was a very expensive lesson. The only thing good about this place was the location.

Best Feature: location
Needs Improvement: everything

Amenities rated on a 1-5 scale:
(1=Lowest 5=Highest N/A=Not Rated)

Rooms = 1	Sports/Activities = N/A
Dining = N/A	Entertainment = N/A
Public Facilities = 2	Service = 1

great hotel, perfect location

Submitted by: Erica D. of San Antonio, TX USA ; October 26, 2006
Date of visit: 10/06
Traveler's Favorite Vacation Destination: New York
Traveler's Rating:

My sister and I stayed here 2 nights and were very satisfied! We were 2 blocks from Times Square which was great! Security checks for a room key each time you get on the elevator,so we felt very safe too! All of the hotel employees were very nice and polite. The room was perfect for 2 people and we had a view of 44th & 8th from our window. We could see several theaters outside our window! We rode the train from Newark to Penn stationn & walked to the hotel with our luggage. Best of all, there are a ton of restaurants all around you! Don't be weary, I definitely recommend this hotel.

Figure 18.6 A negative review among positive reviews is not always a bad thing.

Knowledge Sharing

Knowledge sharing is one of the simpler areas of social media, and it is also an area that has some level of misunderstanding. In the knowledge-sharing sites such as Wikipedia, AllExperts.com, Yahoo! Answers, Helium.com, and Ask.com, the goal is to provide as much topical information about a subject, allow people to ask questions that are answered by others, and vote on helpfulness of the answers. These sites focus on providing information and answers and allowing the social crowd to edit, amend, and contribute information to a shared site.

Although Wikipedia is most likely the most well-known of these sites, what is not typically advertised to the general user is that these sites allow anyone to contribute information or answers. Regular contributors are rewarded by their active participation and sometimes ratings from other readers. Because of this, the trust and value of contributors are based on active participation rather than actual expertise. Even if an expert in an area is a contributor, they are not accorded the same weight as an active contributor.

These sites provide authority-type links to websites when they include links as a citation or reference within the article, answer, or topic page. Most of these outgoing links are noted with a NoFollow exception to the link, which tells the search engine that this is not a trusted link. Adding this feature reduces the amount that these sites are being used by webmasters and SEO marketers to generate links to websites.

The marketing value is primarily in the visibility of the website, such as Wikipedia. In some personal marketing experience, visitors from Wikipedia tend to be high-converting visitors, and Wikipedia helped make the sale. There is still some debate on whether link value is passed, despite the NoFollow links on these sites, so I generally recommend keeping knowledge-sharing sites as part of a larger strategy, mainly because of their visibility in the search engines.

Networking

Networking is one of the most well-known uses of social media and one of the most pervasive. Social networking allows people to set up a personal profile online and connect with other people through their profiles. There have been many sites and applications throughout the years that have allowed people to do this such as Bebo, Orkut, Xanga, Friendster, Second Life, and MySpace. The most recent incarnations of social networking that are more well-known are Facebook and LinkedIn.

Facebook

Facebook is the social networking leader with more than 500 million users, as of this writing in early 2011. Competing with the likes of Google and YouTube for visitors but dominating both in terms of activity and length of time, Facebook allows users to build their own profile and connect with other users. With a profile, users can add video, images, recent purchases, status updates, location check-ins, and discussions with friends. It creates a wide-open window into the users' life for all the friends in their network. Users can share as much or as little as they want; however, privacy is always an issue with Facebook.

For Facebook to make money, the only assets they can bring to advertisers are user demographic, personal information, and purchasing behavior. Many users of Facebook do not want this information shared. However, privacy watchdogs are always reporting when Facebook attempts to change privacy settings, and the users share their disappointment of these changes through their status updates.

Facebook allows businesses to create a profile page for the business. Businesses can interact with their fans the same way that users can interact with each other. Businesses can communicate with their fans through the Facebook mail and allow fans to upload images and pictures and provide information or promotions specifically through Facebook. Loyalty, retention programs, and branding dominate the business usage of Facebook, because very few are using it to acquire new customers (eMarketer, www.emarketer.com/Article.aspx?R=1007934). Although it is not impossible, most users will not tend to "like" a business on Facebook until they have done business with them, similar to a word-of-mouth referral. People will not simply "like" a business without knowing anything about them, unless it is for a promotion, giveaway, or similar type of contest.

For retention, Facebook creates an easy communication channel by allowing businesses to send updates to their fan base, as well as send invitations and messages. The Invitation and Messages features do a "double duty" in connecting to the fans of a business, because they send a notification to the person's Facebook messages, as well as their personal email—a double notification. In many cases, this is more effective than a blast email, because emails can get caught up in spam filters or ignored. However, people make sure they are able to receive their Facebook emails and notifications. As with anything, though, this is best done in moderation. Too many invitations or messages can get you dropped by a fan, especially if the offers are not appealing or relevant.

Integrating Social Media for Marketing

For additional marketing, Facebook has become one of the most important sites for sharing links to videos. Within the context of the business fan page, videos can be hosted at YouTube, embedded on the company website or blog, and on Facebook. This is a great way of integrating social-media channels to point users to a specific destination. Too many businesses simply blast their messages and emails without a target destination or goal for their networks. Defining a target destination for the users, such as the company blog or Facebook page, is critical for integrating the numerous social-media sites available to businesses.

Continues

Integrating Social Media for Marketing *(Continued)*

One "business" that does this particularly well is the rock-metal group Blind Guardian. Its Facebook page is the center of all its communication with fans. From personal experiences while touring to inspiration for songs or playlists, Blind Guardian uses Facebook as the central information source for the band. It uses the additional features on Facebook to add video, audio, and images customized to the pages.

You may not be a rock band as a business, but you can certainly see how many forms of media can be combined into making Facebook a destination for your customers—if that works for you.

Integrating Social Media for Marketing *(Continued)*

LinkedIn

LinkedIn provides the ability to maintain a professional network of people from past jobs, universities, associations, and groups. In addition to the networking, business-oriented questions and discussions are part of the website. These discussions can be part of the entire network or limited to specific groups.

Targeted to a business audience, it is a professional networking service that does not focus on the social aspect as much as a professional networking and discussion forum. When the world economy troubles hit in 2009, LinkedIn reported increased users and increased subscriptions and revenues as a result. People who were out of work were using LinkedIn to connect with other users and companies, and businesses were using LinkedIn to find new employees while saving on professional service (head-hunter) fees.

The primary function of LinkedIn allows employers to search for potential employees by searching by job title, experience, or location. An employer can see the job history, resume, recommendations from other co-workers or clients, and links to personal websites or blogs. This is one of the most extensive lists of personnel available to an employer in one of the easiest professional profile search engines.

In addition, salespeople looking to get an introduction to a specific company can search their network to find common connections that could make an introduction. For salespeople, the ability to network millions of people within a connection or two provides an infinite opportunity to develop contacts and connections in a desired company or industry.

Microblogging

Microblogging is a term used to post a short announcement or update, similar to a blog, but within a certain character limit. Twitter is the most famous of these services; however, Facebook has placed itself as a major competitor to Twitter in this area. Even more confusing, people can also combine their Twitter updates so that they also show up on Facebook!

Twitter is a powerful communication tool at conferences, seminars, and social gatherings. It allows real-time conversations about information that is breaking or being shared. People can share in the events of a conference by simply monitoring the hashtag for that event. A *hashtag* is a method of tagging in Twitter and is accomplished by using a hash mark and a keyword for the topic. For example, if I want to tweet or follow tweets about the NFL, I would simply use a hashtag in my comment, "I am watching the #NFL" (see Figure 18.7). Any tweet that carries that hashtag can then be followed by anyone searching for that subject. This also makes the term searchable, because Twitter followers can search by the hashtag and add it as a permanent update stream.

Twitter is one of the fastest-breaking news mediums ever created (the next section talks about news in social media in more detail). Within moments, up-to-date news on earthquakes, revolutions, political movements, and weather is shared. Twitter has changed the news industry, because the ability to have tens of thousands of reporters around the globe and broadcasting news and updates creates limitless access to news.

One of the primary abilities of Twitter is the ability to get your announcement in front of thousands of users outside your immediate network of followers. This is done through the retweet. The *retweet* is when a user finds your Twitter update to be of significant importance and they want to share it with their network. They simply republish your update with the code RT (for "ReTweet"), and your message is now broadcast to that user's network of followers. By publishing valuable and informative tweets, you increase chances of being exposed to tens of thousands of Twitter users, because the more your message is "retweeted," the more exposure and visibility you receive. If Twitter makes sense for your business and you would like to explore this medium even further, then I recommend another book in the An Hour a Day series, *Twitter Marketing: An Hour a Day* (Wiley, 2010).

Figure 18.7 The hashtag in Twitter is the primary means of tagging and tracking topics, this one for the #NFL.

FourSquare is another type of this media, but it is focused as location-based microblogging. Users can update their status based on where they are, usually by checking into a business, building, or public area. Users in your network can see where you checked in, which is especially helpful if you are trying to find your friends around town. FourSquare encourages users to leave tips and recommendations for other users specific to a location. For example, a tip can be left at a restaurant to order or avoid a specific dish.

Social News/Linking/Bookmarking

Social-news sites arose as a method of sharing interesting articles with a network of other users. In addition, by setting up an account at these news sites, someone can view all the articles that you have bookmarked and created links to. Besides simply linking to the articles, users can also place comments and commentary on the cited or linked article to share with other users.

Sites such as Digg.com, StumbleUpon.com, and Reddit rely upon users to link to, or *bookmark*, articles. As articles receive more links, they are considered "votes" and are promoted in the structure of the website. The more votes an article receives, the more visibility it is awarded within the system, which results in additional visitors to the article and additional links (votes).

In its heyday, around 2007 to 2009, Digg could boast sending tens of thousands of visitors to articles that made the home page of Digg.com, an ever-changing list of popular articles based on user votes. This could also result in gaining links to an article from some of the thousands of visitors to a website. If those visitors had a website or a blog, then they would link to the article from their blog, in addition to voting up the article in Digg.com. Digg.com can still send a substantial amount of visits to your site, but other social media has replaced Digg as the center of attention.

StumbleUpon works on a similar principle yet is a bit more random, as users "stumble" upon a website rather than pick and choose from a list on a website. This is more like channel surfing, because you never were sure what the next page would contain. Users can pick a category, such as science fiction, and then be shown a series of articles in that category that has been voted on from other StumbleUpon users. Of course, you then vote on the sites presented to you.

For a few years, and even into today, these are some of the favorite link-building sources for SEO specialists, because you can quickly generate tens to hundreds of links to an article or a website by developing a catchy article, recruiting a network of friends to vote on the article, and then watching it climb in status on the social-news site. Unfortunately, many firms and specialists saw this as a prime link-building opportunity and specialized in creating articles that would be picked up and ranked highly in these services. They built extensive networks of users and services that would vote on articles in order to circumvent the traditional methods and create an artificial method of "fooling" the social-news sites, propelling articles to the top page consistently. This gave many business owners and marketers the sense that they could do the same thing, especially after reading or hearing about the visibility, linking benefits, and the potential for tens of thousands of visitors. Unfortunately, without a large network of resources, the same effects were very difficult to duplicate. Although many how-to guides were published, many of the secrets and tactics were not easily available to marketers and business owners in order to fully understand how they could take advantage of this link-building and website traffic source.

Today, Twitter and LinkedIn have done a lot to displace the power of social linking and bookmarking from the once-popular sites of Digg and Reddit. In addition, many specialized niche news sites have risen that provide readers with recommended articles within a specific industry or niche, which also provides a more focused and attractive outlet for marketers. The accessibility of gaining visibility with an article is easier, and it is presented to a more relevant audience.

Wednesday: Communicate Your Message Effectively

The primary foundation of any social-media participation is to first evaluate your business and your message. Your message is of significant importance. It communicates who you or your business is and the value that you bring to the marketplace. Your message is the hook that brings people to your website, makes them curious to know more, and persuades them to take action. The development of your message is the first step to developing your social-media campaign. Your message is what makes you unique, and it communicates the benefit you provide. The message does not change.

Marshall McLuhan was a visionary in the technology space. Just about any student in media has heard his famous phrase "The medium is the message," which was originally applied to the three big mediums, radio, TV, and print. Today, we have innumerable applications to this phrase and more than ever need to understand the implications of this truth.

"The medium is the message" is the observation that the same message will be interpreted in different ways depending upon the medium through which people receive the message. One of the earliest, most famous examples of this was in the early days of television in the presidential debate between John F. Kennedy and Richard Nixon. Those who watched the debate on television overwhelmingly thought that Kennedy won the debate, because Nixon appeared tired and worn. Kennedy was young, energetic, and played well to the television audience. To those who listened to the debate on radio, Nixon was overwhelmingly perceived as the winner, because he was well reasoned, factual, and engaging. Two very different groups of people received the same content but through two very different mediums. One was auditory driven, the other visually driven, and both mediums inherently affected the judgment of the audience, depending upon how they tuned into the debate.

A particular message, with specific intent and careful messaging, can be properly interpreted or extremely misinterpreted simply based on the medium through which it is transmitted. In terms of social media, a message that works well in one medium may not be translating well or be received well in another medium.

Target a Single Medium

Once you have your message, the next step is to determine the medium that best fits your message and your resources. The vast majority of companies that have become famous for their social-media savvy focused on a primary medium when getting started, rather than all available mediums. By focusing on a single medium that best communicates your message and then using the rest of the social-media world to support that message and medium, you can contain your marketing to a focused, supported, and directed approach. The type of business you are determines the best medium for you.

The examples of those businesses that have created amazing results in social media are well known and recounted as hero stories in many marketing venues. These are the examples that marketers see and hear and then strive to repeat when they enter the world of social media. Keep in mind, though, that for each success story there are thousands of failed attempts that are not publicized or published as warnings. Only the lucky few who have figured out the magical social-media formula are the ones canonized for their originality.

Each social medium carries with it an intrinsic depth of interpretation. Audiences apply different filters and interpretations based on the type of media and the types of messages that are broadcast using that media. Simply put, what works on YouTube doesn't always work on Twitter. What works on your blog may not work on Facebook. For your business, think of your message and your audience and the important aspects of how you can present your business and how your customers will be part of the community. Is your business best at presenting a visual or an auditory message? Does your business rely on an immediate news cycle and dispersing information to as many people as quickly as possible? Then Twitter would be an ideal choice, because blogging may be too slow.

Video-sharing sites such as YouTube tend to be a "see-to-believe" medium for businesses that have a very visual product. Product demonstrations, stunts, and comedy work very well in this medium. Videos that show processes, such as manufacturing, how-to, and other types of instructional and educational videos are also effective.

In terms of networking/microblogging–type social media, consider that on Facebook, the pace of communication is slower compared to Twitter, which is an immediate or real-time conversation. Users of Facebook spend long amounts of time updating their profiles and catching up on their friend's news. According to Nielson, Facebook users are on Facebook more than 6 hours a month (Nielsenwire, http://blog.nielsen .com/nielsenwire/online_mobile/june-2010-top-online-sites-and-brands-in-the-u-s/). Conversations can take place over a number of days, similar to email. The sense of immediacy is significantly less than Twitter, because people communicate at their own pace in Facebook. Comparatively, many of the conversations on Twitter take place in minutes and can be very old news in a period of hours. If you aren't watching when it happens, you might miss it, because Twitter is a "stream of consciousness" medium.

Social-news media relies on visitors to have accounts at the major link sources, but as Twitter and Facebook have grown, they have started to displace the "old guard" of social-news sites, such as Digg, StumbleUpon, and Reddit. There may not be as many visitors with those accounts, depending upon your industry. So, knowing the typical "hangouts" for your visitors is critical in promoting your site through social linking and social news. If your visitors tend to be Facebook focused, then many may not have accounts at Digg or StumbleUpon. Track and measure the usage of these icons and the number of new visitors that come to your website from each one to determine which should be the focus of your marketing attention.

Case Study: Blendtec on YouTube

One of the best-known business-oriented viral videos on YouTube is Blendtec and its "Will it Blend?" videos. With an investment of less than $100 and an inexpensive video camera, the first videos were recorded of the Blendtec Blender shredding a rake handle, marbles (www.youtube.com/watch?v=aM94aorYVS4), ice, and golf balls (Figure 18.8).

Figure 18.8 Blendtec experienced great YouTube video success.

Blendtec sells a very high-end blender, which starts at $400. However, these videos launched them into a realm of visibility beyond a marketer's wildest dreams. The videos were born out of the simple idea that people just have to see what it can do. How else do you distinguish a high-priced blender from the rest of the pack?

This is where the emerging factor of YouTube enabled Blendtec to become a viral phenomenon. Creating a video series blending the new iPhone and iPad, marbles, glow sticks, and many other items, Blendtec became more than a typical product demonstration; it became entertainment. Companies even pay Blendtec to blend their new products, just for the exposure. By tapping into the curiosity of the marketplace and providing simple video production, the videos enabled Blendtec to increase sales dramatically. At last count, the combined numbers of views of the Blendtec video puts it on par with the visibility of a Superbowl ad, at a tiny fraction of the cost.

The primary factor in creating the Blendtec success was the medium of embedded video. An embedded video is one where you simply need to place a script in your website, and the video will play on your page. This enables bloggers and website managers to take a video from YouTube and add the script, which then puts the video on their site or blog, allowing them to show the video on their site to their audience. A true "see-to-believe" product, Blendtec benefited from video sharing and the ability for the videos to be embedded on websites, on blogs, and in emails. People could talk about them on their blogs and websites, send to friends and discuss on the site, and also make requests for new videos. Blendtec needed YouTube and video to accomplish what they did.

Case Study: VW's Engagement on Facebook

Volkswagen has decades of experience being a brand icon. Big, gas-guzzling cars were selling and were what the American people wanted, until a little "bug" came into the picture and was embraced by counterculture, parents, teenagers, and college students everywhere, going on to sell millions in the United States.

Volkswagen actively engages its audience on Facebook and provides an outlet for their fans to openly discuss anything they want about the company. Fans can post photos, video, and comments on the company's main page. This creates a closely connected community with the brand, because VW has a dedicated following (Figure 18.9).

However, rather than simply allowing the fans to be part of Facebook, VW uses Facebook to provide significant promotions and news to their fans. Volkswagen previewed its 2011 Polo GTI to its fans in Europe on Facebook before any other outlet, rewarding fans for their dedication. In addition, while the 2011 Passat sedan debuted at the Paris Motor Show would not be available to the United States, VW posted the sketches of the new midsize sedan (which would be available to the United States) to let its audience peek at the new design.

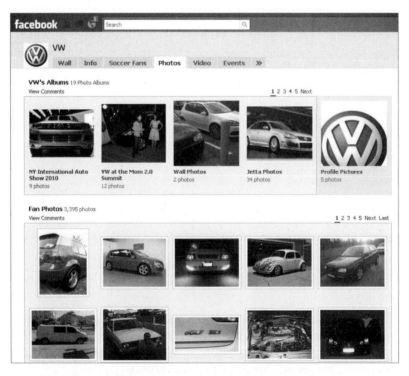

Figure 18.9 Volkswagen allows the community to develop the Facebook presence.

Case Study: Dell Support on Twitter

One of the first businesses that was able to make Twitter work for them was Dell Support. Within moments of a Twitter user making a comment about a Dell computer, Dell Support was monitoring the Twitter comments about them, and they would contact the author of the tweet. From my own personal experience, I tested to see how quickly they responded. I received a direct message on Twitter within four minutes, and they quickly handled my issue within the hour. Now that is immediate service.

This is the power of Twitter; it is an immediate medium. Twitter trends rise quickly and then tail off after a number of hours or sometimes days. Twitter is a medium that focuses on the immediacy of information. Twitter tends to be more of an in-the-moment medium than, for instance, Facebook; it allows insight into what many users are thinking and their immediate frustrations with their computer, from which they are accessing Twitter. Dell found a way to tap into the immediate frustrations of users and estimated that millions of dollars of sales came from using this new medium to reach customers.

In a 2009 Reuters article (no longer available online) about Dell's adoption of Twitter, Dell made more than $3 million from Twitter followers who clicked links in tweets and more than $1 million in the six months prior to the article. You can find the case study on Twitter at `https://twitter.com/twitter101/case_dell`.

Branch Out to Additional Media

Once you're well established in one medium and you're having success with it, you might consider integrating other forms of social media into your marketing strategy. Just like when focusing on a single medium, the specifics of your business and clientele determine the social-media options that are right for you.

Do your customers have a strong sense of community and sharing? Then Facebook and most likely a blog would be good options for building a community. In fact, developing a discussion forum that rewards the community for their involvement and ideas might be a good move that would make your business look very good and also provide great research benefits for customer research.

Suppose your business develops custom car accessories; a combination of Facebook, a blog, and media sharing could be the best way to cultivate an audience and develop relationships. In that type of industry, customers love to show off their cars and their creations, so a visual aspect is critical. The ability for your customers to showcase their own photos and video would be important as well. This can be done within Facebook or by creating a Flickr group for your business and customers. Giving customers the ability to feel a sense of belonging and the ability to contribute will grow the relationship.

Developing a company blog that showcases the ability to develop those custom accessories would be an effective way to build additional search engine rankings for specialized terms. Integrating videos that are hosted at YouTube that showcase the equipment that is at the shop will give the potential customers or prospects an inside look at your business and the quality of work. The blog can also showcase new creations and show some of the processes that went into creating the custom parts and the final result.

Thursday: Assess Your Resources

Attempting to blast your way into all of the available social-media opportunities will lead to quick burnout from making undirected efforts across numerous channels. All the while, important business issues are neglected and sometimes left behind, because the demands (sometimes self-imposed) of keeping up with social media can stretch the business on a budget or with limited resources in both time and employees.

Much of today's content is about deciding what social media you should use based on various factors of your business, whereas yesterday's focused on the nuances of each medium. The factors between these two sections should help you find the right medium for your message.

Personnel

If you are running your business all alone, then time is a big consideration. Your efforts will have to be managed and practical. Conversely, if you work with a team of people, then you have more time and specialties to use in your marketing. Either way, you have to build your social-media marketing in a way that suits your time and resource limitations.

Small Businesses

If you are a small-business owner, chances are you don't have hours to put into an extended and far-reaching social media campaign. In fact, I'm sure that given the choice, you would more likely just do your business rather than talk on Facebook or Twitter. Honestly, I don't blame you. This is why you absolutely have to assess your available resources and establish a plan, rather than attempt to do everything at once.

After developing your message and determining the right channels to reach your audience, then it is necessary to evaluate the number of hours you can put into a campaign. If three to five hours a week is all you can dedicate, then focusing on a single medium may be the best use of your time. By focusing on a single medium and doing it well, you can save yourself the frustration of attempting to do everything. Stop burdening yourself with the pressure to do everything everyone tells you, and decide upon the best course of action. If time is very strict, then one of the easiest, least expensive, and most user-friendly thing you can do as a small business is to develop a Facebook business page and ensure that you are in the local business listings in the search engines. You can use Facebook to reach your customers and fans and also use it to offer discounts, specials, or offers to grow your community and customers. Do something simple and easy to build your confidence and see some results; then grow into the larger game.

Midsize Businesses

Even if you don't have much in time or personnel resources available, you can still take advantage of social media. The ideal midsize business media option is a blog, which is very inexpensive in comparison with building a website. The blog allows you to be flexible in developing content, sharing your business's story, and showcasing your products or content. Establishing a blog is contingent on the ability to write well. The ability of someone being able to communicate important business-case information as well as provide entertaining and informative information is an important resource for establishing a successful blog presence.

There are many small to medium-sized businesses that have been able to make a large impact in their local area or industry by gaining the visibility that a blog can bring. One important factor that a blog can bring is the added search engine visibility and rankings, because the blog posts help the business be found for many key phrases and related topics. The more content is written on the blog, the more content is available for searchers to find and search engines to rank.

With building the blog, using Twitter and Facebook to link to new posts or announcements can aid in the visibility of both the blog and the entrance of your company in the social-media space. Using additional social-media outlets can aid in building links to the blog posts and assisting in the development of a readership and customer retention.

Of course, your business may be able to take advantage of additional social media, such as YouTube or the immediacy of Twitter. It is up to you and your company to decide which media will be most effective for your focus and your market. Although Twitter gets a lot of attention and buzz in the media, it is always wise to understand where your customers and prospects get their news and find their information. If your target audience is not on the bleeding edge of technology (and most are not), then Twitter may be a good way to communicate to peers in your industry but not to reach new customers.

Large Businesses

Large businesses have the capability of employing web managers, analysts, and marketing managers, and when it comes to developing a plan for the large business, the social-media manager must work in concert with the marketing team, the web team, and the web analysts. Too many businesses allow the social-media specialists to run on their own, without the broader teamwork of the online marketing team. The entire team must understand the message and the purpose of the social-media communications. If not, there is a fractured message, and the purpose is incomplete and possibly at cross-purposes with the rest of the online goals. Therefore, the company is not able to track an effective return.

Social media in a large company has to be established as part of the overall online message and focus for the company. Specific messages for new customer acquisition, client retention, and company marketing need to be developed and refined, all with a specific destination and a purpose for how the message will be sent and how visitors will follow the links. The goal for the visit needs to be clear, and the goals will most likely be different for each target group.

The social-media campaign within a large company cannot act independently. It must be tracked by the analytics and run in concert with the development of landing pages, videos, Facebook posts, and website updates. The website must match the message and present a clear and consistent message to the public. When the online marketing team is operating as a team, the social-media message is effective, because it is backed by the creativity necessary to present the message, and all aspects of the marketing are measured and analyzed for effectiveness.

A Word about Interns

When I hear that a business plans to make interns the primary line of action for social media, I shudder. The best advice I can give a business is that an intern should be the last person to manage the company's blog, Facebook, or Twitter presence. There are functions that interns are certainly able to perform, but not the function of being responsible for communicating the message of the business, developing conversations with prospects and customers, and being an overall advocate for the business. This is a job for an employee who loves the company, loves the business, and is completely dedicated to their work.

Would you rather the first impression of your company be made by an excited employee or a summer intern? As a potential customer, would you rather be talking with an employee who has a deep knowledge about the company, the product, and the industry, or would you rather be talking with an intern?

Too many businesses learned this lesson the hard way when they let interns set up their Facebook pages or Twitter accounts. In addition, when the interns then left the business to go back to school, the social-media accounts lapsed, and no one kept up on them. When the business was able to get an employee to do something with them, they did not have access, because the accounts were set up by the interns using their email addresses. In some cases, interns used their personal or school email addresses, making it much more difficult to get access to the company Facebook page.

There are many interns who are fully capable and gifted at what they do, but they are there to learn business and marketing, not to run the social-media campaign. This is a first-line marketing communication, and the care of communicating a clear message should be left to those who love their business and can communicate well.

Plan Your Time Wisely

Time is an important consideration when developing a social-media presence that works for you. The availability of mobile devices that allow access to websites, blogs, Facebook, Twitter, and FourSquare allow you to update and post content while on the road. Additionally, the ability of mobile devices to take pictures and video allow for quick snapshots and videos to be taken and uploaded quickly, providing fast updates. This can be extremely effective when providing updates to your customers from a trade show or a seminar.

Blogs

Blogs require a significant investment. Especially if you are starting a new blog, the articles must come frequently; otherwise, there will not be enough consistent information for people to take notice. To get the attention of both people and search engines, there needs to be a significant amount of information and conversations taking place on the blog in the form of comments. If you are starting a new blog, plan on making posts to the blog about three to five times a week. At the very least, do this once a week, but the growth of the traffic and the return from your efforts will come very slowly in that case.

Photo Sharing

Using photo-sharing services such as Flickr can be done periodically, because this media operates at a slower pace. Simply taking a group of photos and uploading them isn't enough, however, when using a photo-sharing service. To get them found, each photo must be optimized for visibility. By creating a title, a description, and tags for each photo when uploading photos, you increase the chances of your photos being found and shared by other users. If you don't take the time to complete all of these areas, then there is no purpose to uploading your images. It only takes a few more minutes to complete these text fields, but it is worth it to make your photos findable.

Twitter

On the other end of the speed spectrum is Twitter. Twitter is an immediate medium. While users can browse through the comments and posts of other users, the news is usually fairly old after few hours or a few days. Most active users of Twitter have programs such as Tweetdeck, Twitterific, or Twhirl (the list is endless) that enable them to keep up with conversations and users throughout the day.

Making Twitter your medium of choice is a significant time investment, because keeping up with the news as it comes across Twitter can consume a person's day. The ability to multitask managing the Twitter stream and keeping up with one's daily work takes a certain personality.

Discussion Forums

Discussion forums are one of the most low-impact methods of jumping into the social-media world, because discussion forums don't require any special software, any technical knowledge to participate, or any new multimedia integration. You just need a username and password to get started. But they also offer some of the best real-world applications and user insights. The research from being exposed to non-marketers and gaining an understanding of the joys and frustrations straight from the market will provide a significant reach for a business that is willing to be part of the forum audience.

If you are able to find an active discussion forum in your market, try to devote at least 20 to 30 minutes a day to browsing the active discussions. You'll quickly pick up how to find the most recent discussions, as well as ones that were started since you last checked. Take the time to also read through older threads and see how the community works and how they communicate to each other.

One rule in taking this approach—don't sell. Members of a discussion forum aren't interested in hearing your commercial. However, if you can bring insight into a conversation as well as some advice and education, it will be appreciated. Forums are a "soft-sell" audience, so you have to establish credibility before you can sell anything.

It is fine to have a link to your website and your title in your signature, and that is acceptable. You may notice other users have sayings, links, and titles in their signatures, and that is usually allowable so that other users know who you are and your website if they choose to know more. Actively recruiting customers on a forum is simply bad taste, and they might disconnect your account if you cross the line.

YouTube

If YouTube is your choice for social media, then be sure you have video-editing capabilities. Simply adding videos to YouTube is not enough to ensure that people are able to connect the video with your company. In *YouTube and Video Marketing: An Hour a Day* (Wiley, 2009), author Greg Jarboe shows that videos are mostly found when they are embedded in blogs and websites. This means most people will not find your video simply because it is on YouTube. They will find it on a blog or a website and, many times, on someone else's blog or website.

Because of this, your videos must be made to be "portable." The branding of your company must be on the video, either as a prevideo intro or as a postvideo credit. In addition, adding your website address and embedding comments will provide anyone who watches the video with the information they need to find your YouTube channel, connect to your business, and link to your website. By creating videos that other people will want to display on their blog, you are working to expand your visibility by providing content to other websites. When other bloggers display your video, they are showing your video to their network, which expands your reach.

In-Person Interaction as a Complement to Social Media

My favorite form of social media is face-to-face and eye-to-eye contact. This is how business has been done for thousands of years, and regardless of how popular social media is, business will still be dominated by personal relationships. Sure, you may be able to build business online through online networking, but I have found that meeting a client in person makes an impact—one that will help create a client for life, rather than a contact in my digital network.

Some of my best friends in this industry were met on discussion forums, blogs, LinkedIn, and Twitter. What was truly amazing was how meeting in person made the friendship much deeper. When actually talking with a person, hearing the inflection of their voice, and seeing their facial expressions and hand gestures, we become much more familiar with that person and can build on the digital friendship by creating a real friendship.

It is common to hear that 90 percent of communication is nonverbal. When we text, tweet, blog, and Facebook, we limit the ability to communicate effectively. We cannot determine tone by text. We cannot hear irony in typed words. Yet we limit ourselves to primarily communicating by text. Sixty percent of communication is body language.

Strangely enough, as social media becomes more pervasive, I find that more and more seminars are dominated by people staring at their laptops or iPads more than staring at the speaker. What is more interesting is that most of the audience behind the laptop would describe themselves as being "social." Yet, there is no eye contact and no association with the person next to them. The only social contact is to their network of associates outside the room.

I might be old fashioned in this regard, but I still believe that there is no substitute for the original social media, face-to-face communication. It's effective, it gets the point across, and everything digital is to imitate the original. Don't forget to use in-person meetings to solidify your social-media relationships.

Friday: Enact Your Social-Media Plan

I've often equated marketers who get involved with social media as excited dates who show up without their pants on. They are just a bit too excited and take things much too fast for anyone to be comfortable. To put it bluntly, too many marketers and companies see social media as a way to get sex on the first date (see Figure 18.10).

Social media is not a conquest; it is a journey. You'll find out things about yourself and about your market and your audience. It's a relationship. In fact, it is thousands of relationships that you are starting with other individual users. Simply because you get into social media does not mean you will instantly receive new customers, visitors, or business. Nope, you have to work for it.

©ISTOCKPHOTO/DivaNir4a

Figure 18.10 Remember the rules for dating, and don't be too aggressive.

For those just getting started, the following sections contain a quick four-step plan to get started in social media. Starting with the basics, this plan works for those who are tentative getting started and possibly slightly fearful of social media. It ends with the goal of all types of social media. Ideally, when reading "Step 4: Cultivate a Fan Base," any fear of the unknown will subside. There is a goal to work toward when entering the world of social media, and the goal of building fans definitely helps your business to succeed.

Step 1: Create a Profile

Getting started in the social-media world is as simple as getting out to the major social-media outlets and securing your account name. Whether it is your personal, business, product, or preferred name, if it is available, you should secure it as soon as possible. To see all the available social-media products and to see which have your preferred username available, there are services such as Namechk (`http://namechk.com/`) or Knowem (`http://knowem.com/`).

Ideally, your username is related to the business or your product (think keywords) so that people can easily associate your account with the company. If you are more interested in personal branding, then some form of your name can be used, though it will be difficult to secure most names unless you have some unusual spelling or a very unique name.

Start by securing your username at the more well-known and prolific social-media sites. Then move on and check into those that are listed to see whether any are niche social-media sites pertaining to your industry. It is worth the time to check into these services and see what they offer and how it might fit into your social-media marketing mix. Sometimes a more focused and targeted approach can yield good results more quickly.

Move on to completing your profile at these services. For some social-media sites, the more you present a complete profile, the better exposure you will have to the network. For sites like LinkedIn, Facebook, or discussion forums, this is especially effective. The profile is where you are able to list websites and blogs as live links to your business. Anyone who sees your profile will be able to follow those links and learn about your company.

Step 2: Start Slowly

After creating a profile, start listening. Especially with discussion forums, this is the easy part. You won't go wrong by listening first. This is also where setting up the alerts in Google News or Google Blogs (as shown in Chapter 4) can help you find other websites or bloggers who are talking about you, your company, or your products. If they are complimentary, follow up and thank them. If not, listen first. Arguing on the Internet is rarely successful.

While you are listening, look for other friends or colleagues listed on these services, and connect with them. You'll need to start building your networks in order to increase your visibility, and almost every service allows you to "friend," "connect," or "invite" others to be part of your network.

Once you feel confident enough to engage your audience with participation, the rules of social media are remarkably similar to the rules of dating. Marketers tend to be very over-active when approaching social media, thinking that this could be the magic potion to their lagging sales or a way to get some easy business. Unfortunately, social media is one of those areas where you not only get out of it what you invest in it, but you also have to be investing in the right areas and in the right ways.

No one likes to be on a date with a partner who talks all the time and hogs the conversation. People like to be able to share conversations, and when you can listen to others, you come across as caring and unselfish. Social media reacts this same way, because marketers who constantly talk and sell are a turn-off and rarely (if ever) effective.

One thing my mother taught me about dating is to be complimentary. People love to be complimented, so find areas in which to compliment bloggers whom you follow and read, compliment customers who leave a positive review, or thank someone on Twitter for posting a link to an article that you found helpful. You'll be amazed how well people respond to compliments, and they will also pay more attention to you in the future.

The next bit of advice is one of those sayings that sound well enough but difficult in practice. Be engaging. In real life, we consider this as making eye contact, paying attention when the other person speaks, and being able to recall details of the conversation. The same applies to social media. Paying attention to what people say and remembering details of conversations, posts, and tweets shows that you are an active participant who appreciates the information that is shared and received.

One of the best pieces of advice in dating is to "be yourself." Don't try to be someone else. This applies as well to companies that try to be something they are not in the world of social media. Many large brands (McDonald's, Sony, Wal-Mart, to name a few) have attempted to build a grassroots campaign by pretending to be regular users. However, it was not hard to figure out that an agency was behind the campaign, attempting to be someone they weren't. Social-media users can spot a phony pretty quickly, so it is best to be who you are and talk in your own language.

Finally, don't brag about your previous "conquests." No one likes to hear how great your company is and how successful at social media you are and how many sales you received as a result. A sure way to turn off followers in your network is to let them know that you are only there for the sale, and not for the relationship or the conversation. If you present yourself as only being there for a quick fix, then your followers will drop off quickly. Your market and your audience want to know that you are dedicated to building a conversation and contributing to the market, rather than solely taking away for your own personal gain.

Step 3: Participate Actively

Once you have gotten past the dating stage, then you can continue the relationship by actively participating in the conversations. In fact, you may even begin by starting your own conversations in a discussion forum, commenting on other people's blogs, or actively blogging yourself. The next step in this stage may also entail creating and managing a group on LinkedIn, Facebook, or other social service where you can have specific market-focused conversations.

This is the proactive part of social media, where you are learning just as much about others in the market and about those in your market as you are learning about your company and how it is perceived. You are actively applying new information to your campaign in order to help your company and build your reputation online.

This is the phase where you are very comfortable in your online social marketing and have confidence enough to try new things, develop some small campaigns, and test some messages. Of course, this also implies you are working closely with your analytics to track the efforts of your campaign and the conversations surrounding you and your business.

Tracking the Conversation

Tools that you may want to look into for tracking conversations at this point are far-ranging. Trackur, Brand's Eye, Radian6, and BuzzLogic are just a few of the more well-known applications for tracking social-media efforts. Just a simple search on *social media monitoring tools* will provide a substantial list of offerings.

Social-media tracking is a matter of finding all the places where your business is mentioned. Some programs will even take it to the next level by finding the opinion leaders in your industry and measuring the tone of the conversation. It does take an investment of your time to track these conversations and develop plans of action with all the information you will receive.

As an example of some of these tools, take a look at the images here, which show a Trackur social-media report for Pringles. Trackur makes a very easy report of topics based on keyword and has different tiers of access. The report is based on the keywords being mentioned on Twitter, News, YouTube, and other social media. You can then mark whether the mention is positive, negative, or neutral as you track the conversion around your brand.

Continues

Tracking the Conversation *(Continued)*

pringles   [Hide / Expand All] Sort: All Results | Influence | Favorites |

Date Filter: MM ▾ DD ▾ YYYY ▾ THRU MM ▾ DD ▾ YYYY ▾ [Apply] [Clear]

N Horseradish Pringles? | Flickr - Photo Sharing! - Horseradish Pringles? Really?   100 Jan 4, 2011
Source: www.flickr.com ✖
Horseradish Pringles? Really? Horseradish? Comments and faves. Add your comment here. ... This photo belongs to. pchow98's photostream (6500). Newest photo →; Horseradish Pringles? IMGP0379 · IMGP0377. Tags ...

👍 View this article   💬 Add to Favorites   ✉ Share this article   Influence: 100   ● ✓ ●

N Grace Dent's TV OD: The Biggest Loser - The Guardian - The GuardianGrace   100 Jan 8, 2011

N Abandon your resolutions. Stop looking for your soulmate. Reject positive   100 Jan 1, 2011

N Horseradish Pringles? - pchow98 posted a photo: Horseradish Pringles? Really?   100 Jan 4, 2011

N Field Commander Pringles | Flickr - Photo Sharing! - Field Commander Pringles | 100 Jan 9, 2011

N Pringles Sour Cream | Flickr - Photo Sharing! - I hope somebody enjoyed eating   100 Jan 11, 2011

N parking lot Pringles - Lizzie~Belle posted a photo: parking lot Pringles. 351/365.   100 Dec 16, 2010

N Pringles Sour Cream - I hope somebody enjoyed eating their Pringles Sour Cream   100 Jan 11, 2011

N Slimmer Pickings - Wall Street Journal - Slimmer PickingsWall Street   100 Jan 7, 2011

N pringles? | Flickr - Photo Sharing! - Don't you hate it when you bought Pringles and   100 Jan 6, 2011

N Smoky BBQ Pringles rock | Flickr - Photo Sharing! - Smoky BBQ Pringles rock | 100 Dec 21, 2010

N Pringles Xtreme Hot Paprika & Smokey Bacon | Flickr - Photo Sharing! - Pringles   100 Jan 1, 2011

N Singing for His Breakfast - New York Times - Singing for His BreakfastNew York   100 Dec 26, 2010

N Pringles Salt & Pepper | Flickr - Photo Sharing! - Pringles Salt & Pepper. Yummy   100 Jan 1, 2011

Step 4: Cultivate a Fan Base

This is the step that separates the social-media practitioners from the social-media experts. Again, just like with dating, the goal of social media is to not continually talk about yourself. The goal of social media is to build an army of fans of your business who will promote your company to their friends. (Ideally that is not your goal when dating, though!) Ask anyone—it is more powerful to hear about a company from word-of-mouth than from advertising. Word-of-mouth carries the credibility of a friend or associate, and the chances that you will purchase, use, read, or investigate a company are higher when a friend recommends it. This principle rings in my mind as clear as my father's advice: "There is what you say about yourself, and then there is what others say about you."

Social media is *not* about constantly pushing updates and content into the conversation. Social media is about identifying those fans, friends, and followers who love your business, love your products, and love your media. Social media allows you to find and identify these fans and make them better fans. They become better fans when you empower them to talk about you as a business and reward them for their passion in marketing your business.

Of course, they don't see it as marketing or as "pushing content." They see it as recommending something they value to someone else. This is where the development of a clear message is critical from the start. Developing a simple message that your fans and loyalists can easily communicate to their friends will enable your message to go far beyond your traditional advertising.

The first step in this plan is to find those active and passionate people who are already knowledgeable about your business. These are the ones who already refer business and talk up your business to their friends. These are the ones who you want to reward for their help. Identify these passionate fans and learn from them. Find out what drives them and what they love about your company, your message, and your product.

As you grow your social-media efforts, keep in mind the things that your current customers like about you, and use that as your message online. Invite the fans who you have already to join you in social media by adding comments, adding reviews, or spreading the word about your business. Their word-of-mouth approach to their networks will push your message even further.

Once you have fans actively helping you, reward them and provide them with the tools they need to communicate your message effectively. For some fans, T-shirts, mugs, and hats can be all it takes to send them over the edge into a fan frenzy. For others, developing a badge, group, or some form of public recognition for the fan to show their pride and passion for your business will enable them to respond to a question or conversation with a friend.

If necessary, provide additional rewards for fan participation. Some companies have developed ways to reward referrals and word-of-mouth by presenting gift certificates or redemption codes. Some businesses are able to make a competition of fan participation; others are more subtle and simply reward for participation.

Whatever works for your business, the point is that your message will travel farther, faster, and more effectively when fans and friends are taking it to their networks and friends. It is much more effective to have even just 10 people raving about your company online more than you alone. This is the oft-forgotten value of social media—to enable fans and friends to take your message beyond your borders and into theirs.

Review and Hands-On

Develop your message. What do you offer, and what makes your business different or unique? Blendtec never claimed to be the best blender or even draw comparisons; it simply demonstrated the product and let it "speak for itself." Rather than a message that needs to be shouted or explained, how can you quickly communicate the value that your business brings to customers or subscribers?

Do you have a see-it-to-believe-it product, software, technology, or other type of visual presentation? Do you have more of an immediate "push" of timely information to readers? Are you a service-based business that needs to react and advise people?

Each type of business has its strengths toward a specific medium. Find your strengths, and explore the medium that will best fit your business and message. Find the medium that best suits your business, showcases your product, and enables a better understanding of what you and your business can do.

Take an account of the personnel, technology, and time available to you. Time is an important consideration. If you are a small-business owner, your time in developing social media needs to be focused and directed toward specific tasks. You still need to run your business and make a profit. If you are a marketing manager, then find the strengths of your team and apply them to the media type that best suits your resources, time, and budget. Decide upon a single media focus and the best supporting media to assist in the promotion of your target media.

Secure your usernames, find people who you already know locally and in your industry, invite them, friend them or follow them, and start to build your network.

Start dating. Listen first, and don't come on too strong. Remember, you are not there to make a sale on the first try. You are looking to find and establish relationships with other people. It will take time to build your credibility.

Get comfortable. Stay in your comfort zone at first. You may find that talking about personal things is uncomfortable; it is OK to stick to business. Make a commitment to maintain an active presence on the mediums you have chosen. Budget the time during the workday to work on connecting with people or developing your videos.

Start tracking your results. Find where your audience is most active. This will help confirm your choice of primary media, and it will help you to adjust as necessary. Stay active on the tracking, because this will also be a good feedback mechanism for your efforts. It will be quiet for the first few months, but as you gain more followers and more attention, it will demand more of your time to review more feedback.

Find and empower your fans. Reward those who love your business and tell others, because they are your most important followers and your best resource. You'll know that you are winning in social media when your fans do most of the work in spreading *your* message to *their* friends.

Week 16: Develop a Complementary Pay-per-Click Campaign

Business owners need to know how to run an effective campaign and not bust their budget making a simple mistake or overlooking an opportunity. This chapter is all about strategies (some well-known, some not-so-well-known) to create effective campaigns, save on your budget, and make sure your dollars are well-spent.

Even if your principal focus in online marketing is on the "organic" side of the equation—programming, search engine rankings, usability, and analytics—pay-per-click (PPC) can be an important component in a comprehensive campaign.

Chapter Contents

Monday: Understand the Advantages of PPC

Tuesday and Wednesday: Take Advantage of Keywords

Thursday: Take People to the Right Page

Friday: Measure the Right Thing

Monday: Understand the Advantages of PPC

Pay-per click advertising is the method of placing paid advertisements in the search results. They are usually found under the heading of "Sponsored Results." They are called pay-per-click because you are charged only when a visitor clicks your ad and goes to your site or landing page. Running a pay-per-click campaign alongside your organic campaign presents multiple benefits. First, the ability to have additional branded results on the search engine results page enhances your visibility on the page and the likelihood that a potential customer will click your result. However, there is also a chance of *cannibalization*, which is the effect of having both paid and organic rankings for your site competing against each other; this can reduce your effectiveness and increase your budget. Either way, most experts agree that this small effect is worth having the additional visibility, because it can lend credibility to your site.

An In-Depth Resource on PPC Marketing

Another book in this series, David Szetela's *Pay-per-Click Marketing: An Hour a Day* (Wiley, 2010), is an excellent in-depth reference on the subject. This chapter will get you started on the right foot with basic PPC information, but Szetela's book will give you the information you need to go further with advanced PPC tactics and bidding strategies.

Additionally, Andrew Goodman's Winning Results with Google Adwords, 2nd Ed. (McGraw-Hill Osborne Media, 2008) offers very specific instruction and clear business strategies for Google Adwords campaigns.

I frequently reference both of these resources, and both authors have provided me very unique insights into PPC marketing. I consider these books to be at the top of the hill for definitive guides on PPC Marketing.

Organic rankings tend to attract more clicks. Different studies provide different results, but the results tend to favor clicks on organic results somewhere between 70 percent to 80 percent compared to PPC results; so, the volume of clicks favors the organic side. Avinash Kaushik, Analytics Evangelist, Google, in a 2008 speech stated 14 percent of clicks are PPC and 86 percent are organic on Google. A 2004 study by iProspect showed that among all engines, the click rates were around 40 percent PPC and 60 percent organic, but there were variances within each engine (www.iprospect.com/premiumPDFs/iProspectSurveyComplete.pdf). However, the volume of clicks, even though it is around 20 percent to 30 percent of search volume for paid advertising, is not something to dismiss. Enough of the available volume of clicking those ads provides a significant number of visitors to provide sales, leads, and exposure for many businesses. Additionally, as the search engines experiment with placing more types of results on the results page (videos, maps, reviews, images, and so on), the organic results are pushed down on the page, and the PPC results are able to stay "above the fold," which allows you to maintain visibility in a competitive environment.

PPC campaigns help fill in the gaps in your organic strategy and, with experience, can become a major foundation of your business. Pay-per-click is an immediate method of gaining visibility in the search engine results pages. Based on that factor alone, it should not be overlooked as a marketing strategy. In addition, PPC offers very unique methods of getting specific, targeted messages in front of the right audience at the right time. As a result, PPC provides one of the most measurable and adjustable campaigns available to a marketer. Some specific advantages of PPC are explored in the following sections.

Immediacy

PPC allows for time-sensitive advertising messages to be displayed and directed as part of a campaign. As opposed to traditional organic SEO, PPC offers the element of immediacy, whereas traditional SEO requires planning months in advance of a search marketing campaign. The immediacy of PPC allows for a campaign to be created, running, and competitive within hours. If a new trend or information needs to be shared with your market, you can craft a specific message, emphasizing the timeliness of the information. When the trend has passed, the campaign can be ended, and the "old" news is no longer being displayed. Organic SEO cannot be turned on and off like this and requires much more planning to take advantage of seasonal trends.

Utilizing PPC also provides immediate feedback on campaign performance when testing new keywords. If the PPC campaign shows promising results for targeting a new group of keywords, then you will know that investing content and optimization in an organic campaign can be profitable as well.

Tight Message Control

PPC offers the ability to control the message on the search engine results page, where the sponsored results are located. Organic SEO is based on affecting the text in the search engine results page, whereas PPC allows you to control every aspect of the advertisement. Advertisers can write multiple ads and test to see which ad produces the most click-throughs and, ultimately, the most revenue.

PPC provides advertisers with the ability to create the ad copy and messaging and to control the message. Although webmasters can affect the text in their organic listings only, PPC advertisers can create multiple versions, test what works, and constantly refine the listing in order to maximize the numbers of clicks. Advertisers can also include and test sales discounts, product pricing, offers, and other incentives that would not work in the organic listings. The ability to write the PPC message is tightly related to direct response marketing and provides a significant advantage to those who closely watch and refine their campaigns.

Customized Landing Pages

The next comparative aspect of PPC and SEO is the "landing page," the page that the prospect sees after the click. SEO practitioners have to work to make sure the most ideal and relevant page holds the ranking for a term, because sometimes a page ranks differently than what was intended. SEO can affect this process. PPC advertisers can designate a specific page as the "landing page" for the advertisement and create landing pages for specific ads, ad campaigns, and ad groups. This also allows for the ability to tightly control the campaign and quickly test different designs of landing pages.

Although SEO practitioners can test different versions of landing pages, PPC practitioners can test radically different messages, page designs, and calls to action without worrying about losing rankings. Because the visitors are coming directly through the ad, rankings do not have to be part of the conversion factors when testing PPC landing pages, which eliminates a large variable.

Quick Results and Analysis

SEO practitioners who affect results have to plan campaigns and then measure them for effectiveness when a critical mass of visitors has developed. Usually that happens about two to three months after the optimization campaign, if it is based on a specific search trend. The measurement of SEO efforts is not usually in real time (when the campaign implements). The measurement of PPC can happen very quickly, and all aspects of the campaign can be changed and tweaked as necessary to improve response rates and click-throughs.

Advertisers can see immediate results the same day that a campaign goes live and can test messages, keywords, landing pages, and positioning of the advertisement. The real-time measurement allows for these types of changes during the campaign because all aspects of the process are tracked and reported through the PPC management interface and analytics.

Smart advertisers spend a significant amount of time in the first few days or weeks of a campaign to ensure that the right message is being displayed to the right people at the right time. A well-managed campaign can consistently find ways to reduce ad spend while increasing results. This allows for immediate measurement of profitability, which provides significant allowances and advantages for PPC campaigns.

Placement

PPC campaigns allow advertisers to define placement. If you want your ad to show up in the most prominent space, then you can pay more than all of the other advertisers to gain that visibility. If you want high visibility, it is completely within your power to bid on high placement positions and increase the budget accordingly to maintain that placement. If it is hard to gain rankings for a particular word or groups of words, then PPC can nicely cover the real estate of the search results page until the organic results are able to get more visibility.

Advertisers can also scale back and do more strategic placement of advertising, such as focusing on the sponsored results on right side of the page rather than the top of the page. Instead of bidding high for the top placement, advertisers can test other ad positions that do not cost as much to see which provides better results according to the goal of the campaign.

Budget

PPC is one of the only ways to ensure that you stay within a budget for a search marketing campaign. The search engines all allow for the advertiser to place daily limits on the campaign spend, which allows advertisers to stay on budget and not overspend on a campaign. Of course, this can be made much more effective by properly managing a campaign and optimizing the budget through testing and measuring the results.

The budget is affected by multiple factors, most of which are under the control of the advertiser. The more targeted the campaign is, the more factors are in place to control the ad spend. However, the budget of the campaign can also be affected by developing ads, landing pages, and performance factors that take advantage of the quality factors that the search engines have in place. Quality factors ensure that the ads are relevant and responsible for customers, and knowing these quality factors will enhance your campaign because you will be able to achieve better results for less spend.

Finally, PPC can provide additional profitability by targeting words and phrases that have shown to be extremely profitable for your business. When evaluating your costs, return on investment, and profitability, you can use PPC and SEO to provide complementary coverage of high-profit keywords and keyword phrases.

Quality Score

Each search engine utilizes a methodology of judging campaign performance. This is called a *quality score*. Similar to the algorithm that provides relevant results in organic search results, the quality score attempts to score ads and campaigns for relevance. The quality score rewards advertisers for good performance by lowering bid rates for relevant campaigns. Prior to the quality score factor, advertisers that paid the most for clicks would get the highest visibility, regardless of relevance. The ad did not have to match the keywords that were bid on, and visitors could be taken to unwanted destinations. Someone could advertise "free iPods" for the keyword *university* and take visitors to a casino site. The search engines saw the potential of losing credibility and revenue, so they responded by creating the quality score.

The quality score for each search engine tends to fall into the same types of measurements: relevant ad copy, relevant landing page (to the ad), and good click-through performance. Ads that receive more click-throughs are generally considered to be more attractive to customers, so those ads are considered more relevant. A high quality score benefits an advertiser's campaign with lower click-through costs and better positioning.

The quality score is based on how relevant the ad copy is to the campaign keywords and then on the relevance of the landing page based on the ad copy and the keywords. Another part of the equation can be the performance of the ad itself. If it gets enough click-throughs compared to the number of impressions, then it performs well. If the ad receives many impressions but very few click-throughs, then the ad is not performing well, because it is not an attractive option for searchers. Essentially, the quality score is a logical quality assurance test for the advertising network provided by the search engine.

In Google, a high quality score reduces the price you have to pay to maintain your position, be it the top spot or the second or third. Only ads with high quality scores will show above the organic rankings on the search results page, which is a good opportunity to increase visibility. High quality scores will also provide advertisers with additional ad site links, which are additional links near your ad copy that lead to additional landing pages for your campaign.

To present searchers with the most relevant, high-quality results, the search engine has to ensure that there is some type of review policy in place. The searcher is the customer in this process, and the searcher expects that the ads will be relevant and not misleading. The more relevant and attractive the ad is, the better the advertisement will perform.

Tuesday and Wednesday: Take Advantage of Keywords

The rest of this week is going to focus on the basic functions of developing a successful campaign. These foundational building blocks are also the most common mistakes advertisers make when developing a campaign. There are many ways to bust a budget when setting up a campaign, and most of the search engines do not make it easy to cover all of the necessary details for a campaign. Because of this, it is easy to start a campaign and lose a lot of money very quickly. By following some simple guidelines, you can avoid losing a great deal of money.

Match Ads to Keywords

One of the first keys to developing a successful campaign is to target your ad to the keywords. When setting up the campaign, you select the keywords that searchers would use to find your business products or services. When you select these keywords, your ad will show up in the search results for those words. PPC also offers the benefit of creating multiple ads for different keyword subject matter. Start by choosing the keywords around a specific concept, and then you will be prompted to create an ad that will display when those words are searched in the search engine.

In developing your ads, consider your target audience, the searcher. When you bid on specific keywords, your ad needs to match the keywords as much as possible in order to be relevant to the searcher. Making your heading, ad copy, and display URL match up with search keywords enhances the visibility of the ad. This also enhances the quality score of your ad, because it closely matches the keyword.

Including a compelling offer, such as a discounted price, free shipping, or other offer will also provide a reason for your ad to stand out from the rest and capture the attention of the searcher. Consider all of these elements when creating your ads, and don't waste your money by displaying irrelevant ads with no matching keywords. You'll pay higher bid rates with a poor quality score and lose visibility at the same time.

Bold Matching Words

PPC ads are similar to organic results, in that the matched search terms are bold in both the organic and paid results. Remember the study on bold search terms and click-throughs that was referenced in Chapter 7? That study (Beyond Position Bias: Examining Result Attractiveness as a Source of Presentation Bias in Click-through Data from Yue, Patel, and Roerig, 2010) showed that results that display bold terms that most closely match the search phrase typed in by the searcher will also increase the likelihood of that result being clicked by the searcher.

Figure 19.1 shows that many advertisers don't follow this simple guideline. In these results, the number-one ad is Cabela's; however, there are no matching terms bold in the result. Neither the title nor the ad copy display any content about fishing poles. So, despite showing up at the top of the list, there is no relevant information given to the searcher that matches their intent! Of all of the ads being displayed, this ad is the only one that does not match *any* part of the search term.

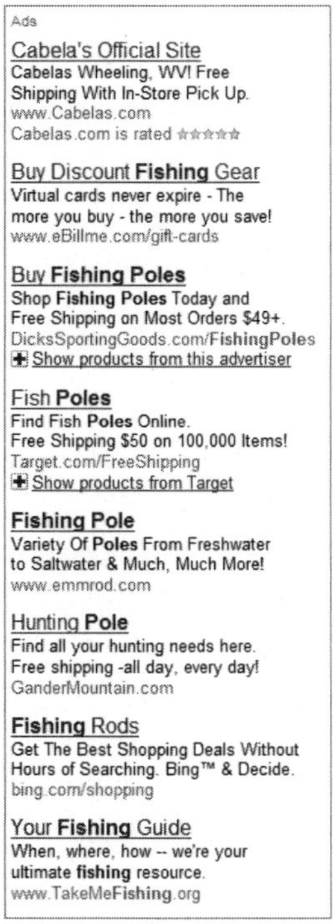

Figure 19.1 PPC search results in Google for *fishing pole*

This will affect the quality score of the ad, because it is not clearly relevant to the search term. This will reduce the quality score, because the ad also sends people to the Cabela's home page and not a page about fishing poles. Neither the ad, the landing page, nor the keyword term show consistent relevance among the campaign factors, which causes Cabela's to pay more for this prominence as opposed to another advertiser with a better quality score that may be spending less for similar visibility.

In viewing the rest of the ads for the keyword phrase *fishing pole*, only two match the full two-word phrase: Dicks Sporting Goods and Emmrod. Of those two, only Dicks Sporting Goods matches the search phrase in both the title and the ad copy. Some of the ads show only *Fishing* in the title but not in the ad copy, which shows some relevance. This lack of accuracy and focus on the keyword phrase seems very strange considering that this is a very popular consumer item. A good ad grabs the searcher's attention because it matches their search phrase and their intent.

Ad Copy That Makes Sense

Even stranger is the type of ads that appear to be strangely off the mark. The Target .com ad shown in Figure 19.2 displays results for *Fish Poles*. What exactly are fish poles? Similarly, Gander Mountain displays an ad for a Hunting Pole, which is even more confusing.

Figure 19.2 Target ad is for Fish Poles, and Gander Mountain ad is for Hunting Pole in bidding on the search term *fishing pole*

Many times, when there are distinctly weird results, like these, it is the result of an autogenerated ad based on the keyword. Even still, you would think the ads could be a bit more accurate for a common phrase like *fishing pole*. Mistakes like these reduce the quality score, because the ad is not relevant to the target search phrase, and as a result, it is not clicked as much as a more relevant ad.

The title of the ad is critical. It is vitally important to match the search phrase as much as possible to attract the attention of the searcher with the bold words that match their search. In doing so, you show the searcher that they will click through to a relevant page that matches their intent.

In addition to the title, the ad copy in the two sentences is a powerful place to create a targeted message with a specific call to action, price, or other offer that can grab the attention of the searcher. In the example results, only Dick's Sporting Goods provides a compelling message that is specific to the search phrase (see Figure 19.3). The offer is free shipping on orders of more than $49.

Figure 19.3 The Dick's Sporting Goods ad matches the
search phrase and includes a compelling offer of free shipping.

Now, although Target also offers free shipping, the offer is not specific to the
search. The offer is nonspecific for more than 100,000 items, which is not important
if I want only one item. In trying to be relevant for everything, it becomes relevant for
nothing, especially if the searcher wants only one thing.

The ad copy in the Cabela's ad (Figure 19.4) does little to further any transaction. For starters, I am nowhere near the Wheeling, West Virginia, store, nor would
I plan on driving there for an in-store pickup. In fact, why would in-store pickup be
relevant to me if I am shopping for a fishing pole? Every other offer on the page shows
me free shipping. This is another case of a boilerplate ad being shown for multiple
keywords; similar to Target's ad, this ad is attempting to reach the greatest number of
people with the least amount of targeted or compelling information.

Figure 19.4 The Cabela's ad offers boilerplate
content that is not relevant to the searcher.

Display URL

One of the last factors in developing successful PPC ad copy is the destination URL.
The advertiser can define the destination URL in the ad copy, as well as the specific
page URL in the campaign. However, it is surprising how many advertisers neglect the
issue of relevance and matching in the display URL.

Using the current example, the second PPC result for *fishing pole* is for eBillme
.com. The ad heading matches the word *fishing*; however, the ad copy displays completely irrelevant content. The content of the ad is for virtual cards. Even more distracting in this ad is the display URL, www.eBillme.com/gift-cards, because the display URL
does not match the intent of the searcher, nor does it match the search keyword; it can
compel searchers to refrain from clicking this ad, because they may infer that the destination does not match their intent.

Target does something similar. The display URL for Target's ad is www.Target.com/
FreeShipping. Although that is compelling, the Target ad is for Fish Poles and mentions
free shipping on 100,000 items but not fishing poles or gear specifically.

The search result for Bing (on a Google search—did you catch that?) has a relevant heading, which is especially surprising. Bing, a search engine, has a more accurate
heading of Fishing Rods than Target and Gander Mountain (Fish Pole and Hunting
Pole, respectively). However, the display URL is for www.Bing.com/shopping. It is somewhat relevant (more relevant than gift cards), but it does not reflect the search term.

By developing display URLs that are specific to the keyword and the ad, you develop increased relevance to the searcher, which will be rewarded in terms of gaining more attention, possibly more clicks, and an improved quality score. The display URL, when including a keyword, also enhances the perceived relevance by increasing the visibility of the search terms in the ad.

In looking at the complete ad for fishing poles provided by Dick's Sporting Goods, the display URL is for www.DicksSportingGoods.com/FishingPoles. This relevant, matched advertisement gives Dick's Sporting Goods the only ad with three matching bold terms in each text area along with a compelling offer of free shipping (refer to Figures 19.1 and 19.3). No other ad in this group competes in terms of relevance, offer, and visibility.

Understand the Keyword-Matching Categories

This may be one of the most misunderstood areas of developing a PPC campaign. When selecting the keywords for your campaign, you can also determine the matching preference for that keyword. To explain further, you can bid on a keyword, but that keyword is usually used in various forms and phrases by searchers. You do not have to bid on every version of the word, because there are always irrelevant versions of words. The search engines allow you to set your preferred level of variance and acceptance for those words. This is one area where advertisers can make big budget mistakes, because it requires a certain level of knowledge about setting up a campaign based on keywords. Although it is easy to say that you want a certain ad to appear when a searcher uses a particular phrase, it is difficult to then define the parameters of how and when your ad should show.

You can increase the effectiveness of your spend by managing these keyword-matching factors closely. You can also lose control of your budget very quickly if you don't utilize these tools.

Broad Match

Broad match is the default setting for most keyword-bidding tools. Unfortunately for advertisers, this is also the easiest way to lose control of a budget. A broad match keyword, such as *fishing*, will cause your ad to show up for search phrases that have *any* variation or phrase that has *fishing* included. It would also show up for *fish*, *fishes*, and *fishing boat*. The word you choose to broad match will cause the ad to show for any combination of words, in any type of search phrase that might match the word.

One of the best examples of this was a company that was in the silicon oil business and set the keyword campaign to broad match on the word *silicon*. As you can image, the ad appeared for any search phrase that had *any* inclusion of the word *silicon*. You can let your mind wander as to the types of keywords that use silicon and the many other industries that are well-known for silicon. Despite the ad being a technical ad for a specific type of silicon oil, the number of clicks the ad ended up costing this company $4,000 in less than 10 days.

Broad-matching keywords is a good way to cover a lot of area, but it could also lead to your ad showing up for alternate variations that are not accurate or would attract qualified visitors. This is where knowing the full range of related and unrelated keywords will benefit you as you set up the campaign specific to the keyword or phrase that is accurate to your business and your goal for that ad group.

Exact Match

The opposite of the broad match is the exact match. In this case, when you add the keyword phrase into the ad group, you include brackets around the single word or quotes around a phrase.

For the single-word exact match, you would add the keyword as follows: [fishing]. This means the ad would appear only for those searchers who use the single keyword *fishing* as their whole search phrase. Unless that word is part of the search phrase, it won't show the ad.

Using a single word as a keyword is rarely advised, because single words usually have very high search volume, which will cause your ad to show frequently. If the ad is not relevant to the many uses or associations that single word may have, then your CTR will drop, which in turn drops your quality score. Using additional terms enhances the focus of the campaign to the target searcher and their intent.

Adding quotes to the keyword as a phrase, such as *fishing tackle*, creates an exact match phrase. This means that the only time your ad will show is when the term *fishing tackle* is used by itself, in that specific order. This is one of the most restrictive uses of keyword targeting for your ad and helps target your campaign to phrases that you know are particularly effective and draw qualified visitors.

Developing these keyword targets goes back to the keyword research you developed in Chapter 6. Understanding the full range of the keywords that are relevant to your business and industry will help you decide on when to broad match and when to focus into a smaller search group but a more targeted approach with exact match.

It is a balancing act in your budget and campaign to ensure that your ad shows to the widest and the most qualified audience. The more targeted your ad groups and the more clicks your ads receive, the better the quality score will be for your campaigns.

Phrase Match

Closely related to the exact match is the phase match. This is where your keyword bid consists of a few words but needs to be focused on a particular phrasing rather than just including the words. The phrase match works for you to match the words of a phrase in a particular order, rather than simply matching the words in any order.

To create a phase match, put quotes around your selected phrase. For example, If you bid a phrase match on *fishing pole*, your ad would show up in searches for the following:

sport **fishing poles,**

fishing pole reels

kids **fishing pole**

It would *not* show up in searches for the following:

fishing tackle and pole

fishing reels for poles

poles for fly fishing

As you can see, the phrase must match the order of the words in the quoted phrase in order for your ad to appear.

This is a matching technique that requires careful execution, because you could also potentially exclude relevant traffic if you are not careful. Careful keyword research will enable you to find the particular phrases and order of words that will work best in particular searches.

Negative Match

Often overlooked, the ability to use negative keywords is one of the most powerful matching tools in developing a campaign. Few advertisers use this function, yet it is one that can maximize your budget, increase your quality score, and improve your conversion rate.

When you developed your keyword lists from your research, you should have noticed that there were some keywords that simply weren't part of your business or strategy. In fact, those keywords may have some very high search volume but just are not relevant to your business. In cases like this, a negative match would be utilized to screen out those keyword phrases that are not relevant but would use phrases that could cause your ad to show.

The quality score measures the number of impressions (when your ad is displayed) as compared to clicks. This is called the *click-through rate* (CTR), which is the number of clicks your ad receives compared to impressions. The higher your CTR, the higher your quality score, because your ad is performing well and has shown to be relevant.

The advantage of utilizing negative keywords is you can reduce the number of irrelevant impressions your ads receive, which, in turn, increases your CTR. If your ad displays for irrelevant keywords, which means that nonqualified visitors would see the ad and not click it, then that would reduce your CTR. Screening out nonqualified visitors is an advertiser's dream. By limiting the exposure of your ad to only those who are interested in your particular product or service, you are able to save more money on your budget and spend it in areas that are targeted and profitable.

Let's continue with the example of *fishing*; the keyword research for *fishing* shows a few keywords that use the phrases that I am bidding on but aren't relevant. One example, if I were a fishing-goods retailer in California, is *Florida fishing*. To make this a negative keyword, I include a minus sign prior to the word Florida: -florida. This removes my ad from rotation whenever a searcher's phrase includes the word *florida*. If I don't offer repair of fishing poles, then I would add the parameter *-repair* to the list as well.

In doing this, I can remove my ad from appearing to nonrelevant or unqualified searchers. Even more, by preventing nonrelevant or useless ad impressions to those searchers who have a different intent, you can reduce the number of unnecessary impressions. By lowering the number of nonrelevant ad impressions, you could increase your CTR and improve your quality score.

Utilize Ad Groups

One of the easiest ways to ensure that you have a targeted ad that will also increase your quality score, not to mention your effectiveness and profitability as an advertiser, is to utilize ad groups. In short, don't create one ad and then bid on hundreds of keywords. Use different ads for different keyword groups. As you've seen in the examples so far this week, often "boilerplate" ads attempt to cover as many search terms as possible without showing an ad that is specific to the search. Instead, some advertisers present a very general ad for the store, but it is not relevant to a searcher's keyword.

This method of advertising is not only lacking in matching the searcher intent; it is also a big budget buster. The lack of relevance in the ad in comparison to the keyword will reduce the quality score. Bidding on separate keywords while attempting to use the same ad will only compound the problem and significantly decrease your quality score, costing you more money.

Cabela's is an advertiser that does this type of advertising. In bidding on multiple keywords but showing the same ad, the campaign is not targeted and could be improved significantly by creating a different ad for each keyword group. You got a taste of the Cabela's approach in Figure 19.1. In Figure 19.5, the same Cabela's ad shows up for searches on *hunting equipment* and for *camping gear*.

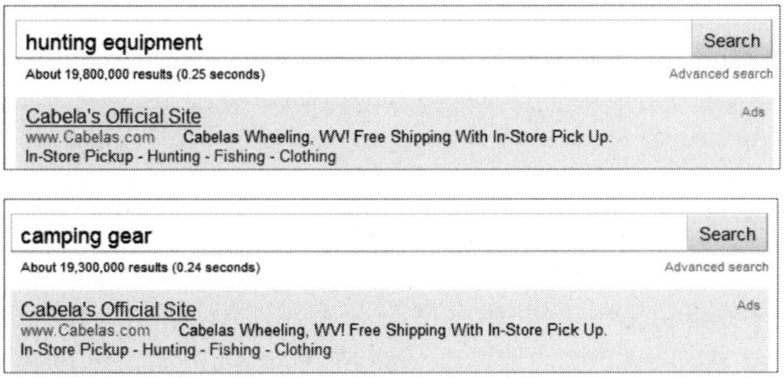

Figure 19.5 Different search terms, same ad

The advertiser is attempting to show an ad for any type of keyword but with a single ad. The campaign would yield better results with more targeted ads for each specific keyword group. Searchers respond to ads that are more targeted and specific to their search terms and intent. In addition, the quality score of the campaign increases significantly when there is more relevance and the ad group is tightly focused rather than disparate words with a single ad group.

An advertiser that is going after the same terms with more targeted ads and a higher quality score will spend less money and gain better visibility than one who takes this approach. In addition, that targeted advertiser will also most likely be sending their searchers to a targeted landing page, which will enhance conversions (which I will cover in tomorrow's content). When bidding on multiple keyword topics with a single ad, the destination page will be the same for everyone, regardless of what they are searching.

When displaying the same ad for so many different topics, the ad will lose prominence when compared to more targeted, specific ads that utilize the search terms and provide a relevant offer. For example, the Fisherman's Warehouse ad that appears for searches on *fishing tackle* (Figure 19.6) will be much more relevant for the searcher when it appears next to the general Cabela's ad from Figure 19.4.

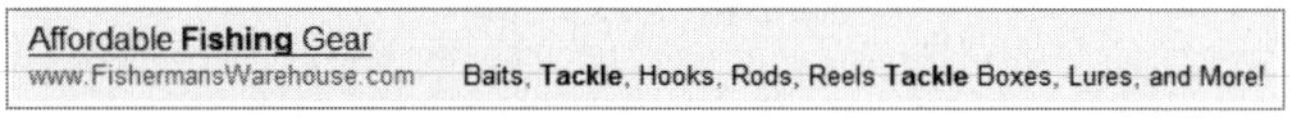

Affordable **Fishing** Gear
www.FishermansWarehouse.com   Baits, **Tackle**, Hooks, Rods, Reels **Tackle** Boxes, Lures, and More!

Figure 19.6 A targeted PPC result for *fishing tackle*

Similarly, a search for *camping gear* will yield more targeted ads than the general ads that will have to pay more because of a lower quality score. Which ad in Figure 19.7 is more relevant for a search on *camping gear*?

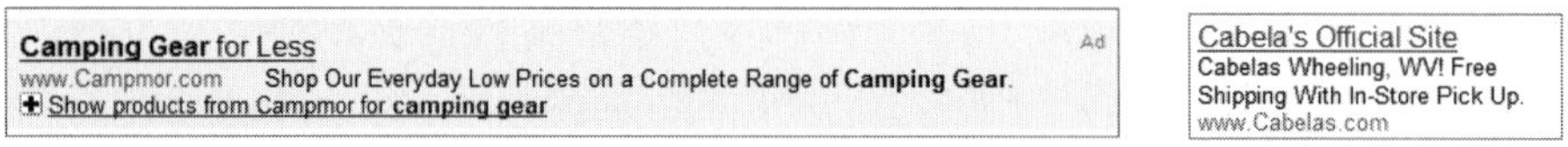

Camping Gear for Less   Ad
www.Campmor.com   Shop Our Everyday Low Prices on a Complete Range of **Camping Gear**.
⊕ Show products from Campmor for **camping gear**

Cabela's Official Site
Cabelas Wheeling, WV! Free
Shipping With In-Store Pick Up.
www.Cabelas.com

Figure 19.7 PPC search results for *camping gear*

For best results, break up your keywords into like groups and write ads that are specific to those groups of keywords. You will find that the more targeted the message and offer can be for a specific keyword group, the better the performance will be for that group, and the better the performance will be on your budget. The more targeted the keywords and ads are in each group, the better your quality score will be, which improves your campaign.

Of course, it is much more work to develop more ads and to develop multiple campaign groups and ad groups. However, more work will yield better performance and more conversions. PPC is one area where being lazy will cost you thousands of dollars in ad clicks but will gain you nothing in profit. You need to aggressively manage these campaigns and constantly improve the performance in order to get the most out of your spend.

Don't Bid Your Way to a Number-One Ranking

Another way to blow through your campaign budget in a hurry is to outbid every other advertiser for the number-one position in the PPC results. Bidding for the top spot may seem like a logical strategy, because it does have the most visible spot on the page; however, it has been shown consistently that the number-one ad receives the most clicks from searchers but also performs at a lower conversion rate than other ads.

The reasoning is simple; shoppers will click the number-one result, but then, if they are comparing, they will also click the other ads as well, and by that time, you may have lost the sale. It costs a significant amount of money to bid on the top position, and if your quality score is poor, buying your way to a better placement costs you much more than it's costing other advertisers.

In the small-scale example in Figure 19.8, a report from Google Analytics shows the importance of understanding PPC ad positioning as it relates to click and conversion rates. Figure 19.8a shows the number of clicks based on the position of the ad on the page. The first position drew the most of clicks, which most advertisers bet on for visibility. On the surface, this seems like the logical place to be on the page. However, Figure 19.8b shows the conversion rate by ad position, which tells another story. In this report, the conversion rate is the highest in the lower ad positions. Granted, the lower ad positions received only a few clicks, but the trend is unmistakable.

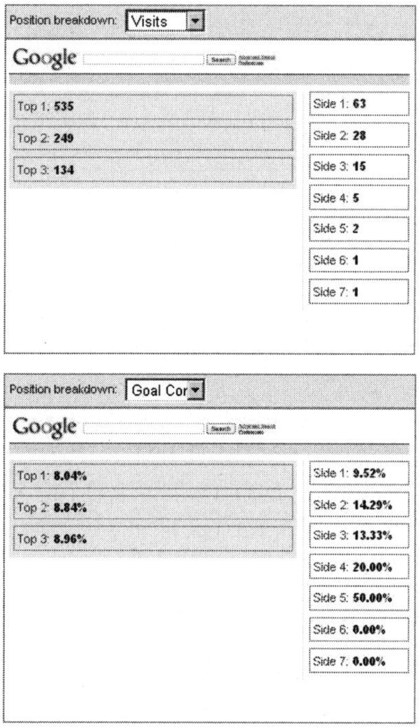

a

b

Figure 19.8 Click-through rates (a) vs. conversion rates (b) based on ad position in Google

This is where smart advertisers are able to find the "sweet spot," the ideal ad positioning for both clicks and conversions. Ad clicks are not a measurement of success; profit is. The money saved by not bidding against high-budget advertisers for the top ad position but being visible enough to gain the maximum number of conversions for when those searchers click through multiple results. Working to find this sweet spot saves advertisers money in ad clicks and maximizes the conversion ability of the keyword group and the ad.

Thursday: Take People to the Right Page

The landing page is one of the most critical tools in the development of a PPC campaign. One of the biggest mistakes advertisers make is setting up a campaign and then sending all of the visitors who click the ad to the home page. Sending visitors to the home page, especially when the home page shows no signs of being related to the PPC ad, forces visitors to navigate to the correct page that has the information they want. Visitors simply do not stand for this, especially if the navigation is unclear. If the ad was targeted to a specific subject and a specific offer, then clicking the ad must send the visitor to a page that reflects both the content and the offer of the ad. If not, then the visitor will most likely leave.

This is one of the reasons that the landing page counts into the overall quality score with the search engines. The search engines want to be sure that the visitors will go from a relevant ad to a relevant page, and in doing so, the advertiser increases their quality score.

From a sales perspective, it is simply smart business to send the visitor to a specific page that accommodates their intent. By matching the intent of the search phrase and the ad and then the page, the searcher can be satisfied in the information they see and has a high probability of converting into a customer.

Today's content will be focused on the two primary markets utilizing PPC: ecommerce and lead generation. Although many of the techniques are the same, the landing pages have the necessary elements that have been proven to be effective in each type of business.

Ecommerce

Here are two examples to consider, using the ads covered so far in this week's content. If you remember the fishing pole ads that appeared in the search results, you'll also remember that the most relevant ad was the one for Dick's Sporting Goods (refer to Figure 19.4). In addition to the great headline, ad content, and display URL, the link also sends visitors to a landing page that matches both the content and the offer of the ad, as shown in Figure 19.9.

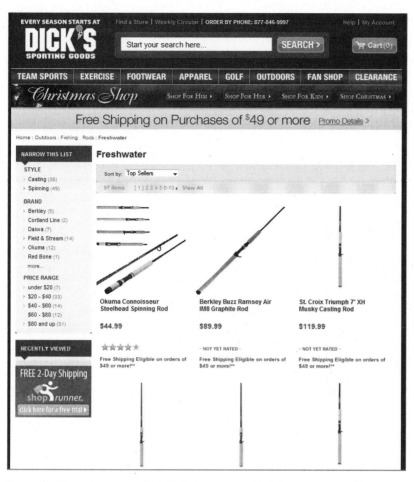

Figure 19.9 The landing page for the Dick's Sporting Goods ad for fishing poles

As you can see, the landing page matches the ad by showing products that match the search and the content of the ad. In addition, the offer contained in the ad was for free shipping. The header under the navigation reinforces the free shipping offer, so the visitor can be assured that the offer has carried through from the ad to the website.

In contrast, the ad for Cabela's (in Figure 9.4) offered no relevant content of the search for a fishing pole. The landing page from that ad maintains that lack of relevance and association (Figure 19.10). The ad directs visitors to the home page for Cabela's, which then forces the visitors to navigate the website to the fishing area, which increases the chances that a visitor will give up and shop elsewhere. (In fact, when looking at all the ads that Cabela's displays for other keywords and products, all the PPC ads send all of the click-throughs to the home page. None of the other ads takes visitors to the content that they are searching for; they are all sent to the home page, as if it is the most relevant page for everyone.) In addition, the images shown on the home page are focused on hunting, not fishing, which creates the impression of irrelevance right off the bat and has very little to do with the intent of the searcher who clicked the ad.

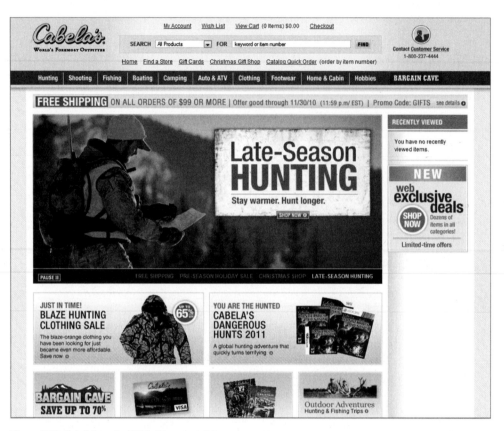
Figure 19.10 Cabela's sends all PPC visitors to their home page.

Landing pages are not a one-size-fits-all proposition! Landing pages need to be customized and developed for each ad group and tested for effectiveness. The more relevant the landing page is for the visitor's intent, the easier the conversion will be. It is simply smart business.

Cabela's certainly isn't alone in its poor marketing. Let's take another look at perhaps the most irrelevant ad for a fishing pole in Figure 19.1: eBillMe.com. Its ad was focused on gift cards (see Figure 19.11a), and the display URL was advertising that visitors were going to a page about gift cards. The landing page (Figure 19.11b) doesn't vary from this intent; a visitor who searches for *fishing pole* could click the eBillme.com result and then be shown a landing page that has no remote relation at all to the need and intent expressed by the searcher. The landing page is about gift cards, and even then, none of the gift cards in the page is related to fishing.

Figure 19.11 (a) eBillMe.com's PPC ad for *fishing pole* focuses on gift cards. (b) The landing page is a world apart from the fishing pole of the searcher's intent.

Lead Generation

For lead generation sites, the offer has to be contained within the limited space of the ad, and then the landing page needs to reflect the ad, present compelling reasons to register, and present an easy method of completing the lead form or the registration. There is not a lot of time to waste with the searcher, and within a few seconds, the message has to be easy to process and have a hook strong enough to gain the lead.

A good example of this is the search results for *CRM software*. For a sales product that has an extended sales cycle and focuses on lead generation, the top advertisers need to capture the lead as quickly as possible by providing specific calls to action, benefit statements, and compelling reasons to move forward in the process.

The top three advertisers for the term *CRM software* have all developed a landing page specific to the campaign ad group. Each also creates a landing page that reinforces the content contained in the ad and develops it further in the landing page. Each landing page also reflects an offer made in the ad and then uses it as a primary call to action on the landing page (Figure 19.12).

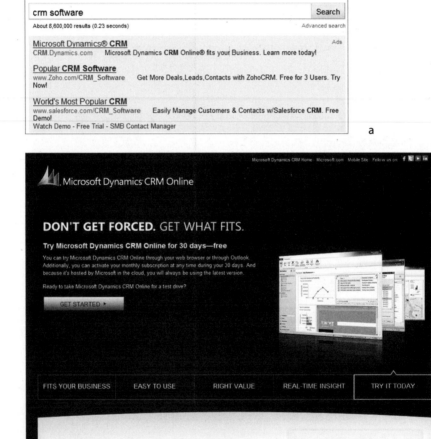

Figure 19.12 (a) PPC results for *CRM software*; the landing pages for that term from (b) Microsoft, (c) Zoho, and (d) Salesforce.com

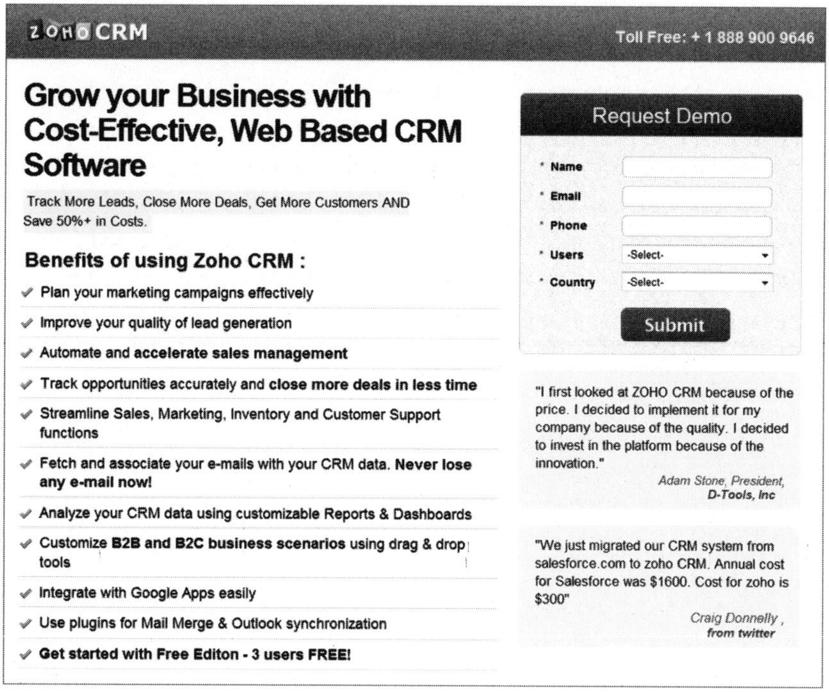

c

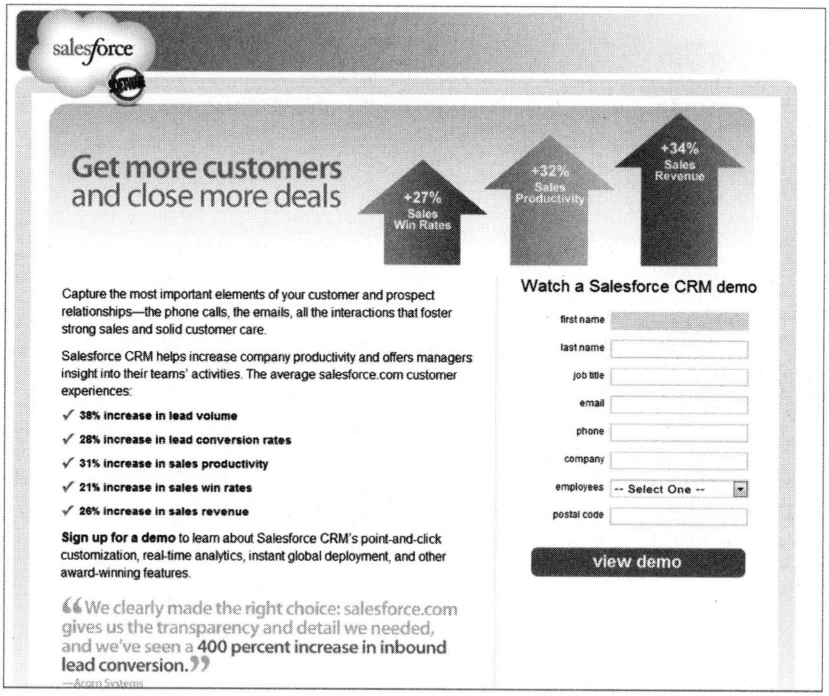

d

Figure 19.12 *(Continued)*

In order, the Microsoft CRM product is the top advertiser in the space. In looking at the landing page, the page accurately reflects the message of the ad with the focus on finding a CRM system that fits your business, rather than being forced into an oversized, over-featured system you may never use.

Important elements of landing pages are following the offer and message of the ad in the content of the landing page in addition to capturing the lead. The Microsoft CRM page does not attempt to capture the lead on the landing page. It requires an additional step for the visitor to click in order to get to the lead form.

Contrast that approach with the next advertiser in line, Zoho CRM. Zoho CRM creates a bold landing page without a lot of emphasis on graphic elements but emphasizes instead key benefit statements and business propositions that are focused on the sales process. The major difference is that the Zoho CRM landing page attempts to get the lead on the same page with a contact form in the upper right. The biggest, brightest color on the page is the red Submit button on the form, which will quickly grab the visitor's attention.

The final ad in the top three advertiser spots is for Salesforce, which is the best in class because of the design, layout, copywriting, and color focus of the page. If you've read through the earlier sections of this book, this should come as no surprise.

Google's Ad Extensions

In addition to a great landing page, you may have noticed in Figure 19.12 the additional links in the Salesforce.com PPC ad in the results. This is an example of the additional ad site links offered by Google where advertisers with high quality scores are able to enhance their campaigns.

The Google Sitelinks feature allows you to add up to 10 additional links to landing pages or website pages. The links will rotate but will favor the first four links, based on priority. The Google Sitelinks feature displays the availability of additional information that might be more relevant to the search, but even more, it increases the screen "real estate" that is accorded to the advertiser.

In addition to the Google Sitelinks feature, there are other enhancements available to add to your PPC campaign. These are accessed in the Ad Extensions tab, which is not readily available on your Campaign toolbar. Enable Ad Extensions by clicking the drop-down menu at the end of the tab toolbar in the main Campaigns screen, as shown here.

Google's Ad Extensions *(Continued)*

All online campaigns

| Campaigns | Ad groups | Settings | Ads | Keywords | Networks | Ad extensions | ▾ |

View: Sitelinks Extensions ▾   All but deleted ▾   Columns   📥

Location Extensions
Phone Extensions   r ads that have appeared with an ad extension. You'll only see statistics for the campaigns you are currently viewing.
Product Extensions   ics
Sitelinks Extensions

| ●   **Sitelinks Extension** | Campaign | Status | Clicks | Impr. | CTR ⑦ |

Automatically include additional links to your site in your ad.
Take a tour

Once enabled, you can add additional features to your PPC ads, such as a location extension, which will add your address to your PPC ads. The phone extension will add your phone number, and the products extension will enable you to feature specific inventory in the ads. The location and phone number extensions are extremely helpful for mobile users, because they add the ability to map your location or call you directly from your ad in the search results.

The page has a specific graphic at the top, which falls directly in line with communicating the concept contained in the ad and in the headline of the page. There are no graphics on the page that do not assist the process, such as stock photo images of salespeople in a generic office. The content on the page is focused on a very tight structure using bold attributes, green check marks as bullet points, and an optimal layout for scanning the text. The Salesforce.com landing page also has significantly less text on the page than the other two advertisers at 291 words. Zoho CRM's landing page contained more text at 599 words, and Microsoft CRM's landing age topped the scales at 1,068 words on the page.

By following the "scannable" layout that most visitors use when they browse web pages (refer to Chapter 9), Salesforce develops a landing page that is easily scannable, the graphics build the case and are related to the message, and the form is contained "above the fold," allowing visitors to easily complete the lead form without scrolling the page. In addition, the call to action button is not labeled as "submit." Instead, the red call to action button reinforces the purpose of the lead form, to view a demo.

Small changes and differences like this are evidence of a form that has been tested in numerous iterations and tweaked in order to convert the most numbers of visitors. Each small element of the landing page plays a part in gaining a response from the visitor, and the Salesforce.com page does an excellent job of reaching the right audience with the right message.

Friday: Measure the Right Thing

One of the more aggravating things I hear when discussing PPC campaigns with advertisers is the emphasis on clicks. It isn't difficult to find advertisers who know their click-through rate but not their conversion rates. This leads to my last point on PPC advertising, which is to make sure you measure the right thing—profitability.

Clicks and CTR will not create a profitable campaign. Sales and leads are the things that create direct revenue for a company, and they must be the central focus of any PPC campaign. This is why every PPC campaign is incomplete when CTR is the final measurement of success. CTR is not a direct reflection of revenue, only of your spend. It is the same with the number of visitors—clicks and visitors cost money. Do you know how much you made as a result?

This creates work. Tracking revenue and tracking profitability is not easy, and it is not built into most analytics programs. This is something that requires careful tracking, coding, tagging, and analysis in order to accomplish. Now, for ecommerce websites that are pure ecommerce players, this is a bit easier than for everyone else. However, it is still surprising how many are not tracking sales based on PPC campaigns and ad groups.

Even in lead generation websites, in order to properly track ad groups and effectiveness, there has to be a defining value of a goal. To track profitability or the cost of acquisition, the value of the goal needs to be defined. You can't track lead generation success without first defining the value of each lead.

This brings us back to a principle discussed in Chapter 3—knowing the value of a lead. Recall that chapter's story of my college telemarketing job. Although I despised the work and made only $6.50 an hour, an employee who loved the job mentioned to me that he made $3.50 for each phone call. The disparity was all because he understood the value of a lead. He explained that out of 50 calls he could average making 2 sales. If he averaged that production throughout the week, he would be receive a bonus. If he averaged that kind of production for the month, he would receive another bonus; if he averaged that for the quarter, he would get both a bonus and a reward. When all the bonuses, rewards, and incentives were counted, his income averaged out to $3.50 a phone call. Now he understood the value of a lead!

Unless you understand your own sales cycle and what it takes to convert a lead to a sale or a registrant to a subscriber, then you will not know the value of a lead. Smart companies know the values of leads and the differences of value based on acquisition. What is the value of a trade show lead? What is the value of a direct mail lead or a cold-call lead? When the lead can be tracked in value based on acquisition, then the entire marketing cycle can be based on measurement and effectiveness, which then affects the marketing spend of those companies; they spend smarter because they understand and know the value of a lead.

Of course, this depends on strict tracking guidelines. Lead generation companies need to tie their leads into their sales tracking system in order to find and judge lead values based on acquisition. Companies that rely on sending web visitors to a phone conversion need to implement a click-to-call or other form of call tracking. This is where having call centers that are able to track call sources, especially from the website, and then integrate into the analytics can make a world of difference in tracking advertising spend and effectiveness.

It comes down to measuring one thing: money. If you aren't tracking money, then nothing else matters. Only tracking money will help you be able to trace the most effective investments of that money by results. And that is where analytics is so vitally important for companies to not only implement but to master. Analytics is the cornerstone of Internet marketing, because nothing else can provide the tangible evidence of success, specific areas of improvement, and clear results from campaigns. Master analytics, and you will master online marketing, which I why this book has saved the best for last. See you in the next chapter!

Review and Hands-On

Start with the keyword lists that you developed from your earlier research. Divide your keywords into logical groups of like words. Develop your ad groups at this stage by finding the keyword phrases that can fit into a specific ad group. This can be by product, service, or content. The focus is to develop an ad that is closely related to the keyword group.

After that is completed, review the keywords in each group, and specify which phrases should be a strict match or a broad match. To really set apart your campaign, look again at the keyword lists you initially created and find those phrases that use the words you are bidding on, but also use an additional word or two that are not relevant—these are the negative words that you can use to refine the ad group and eliminate the nonqualified searchers from seeing your ad.

Once your ad groups are built, develop a few ads for each group. Focus on creating an ad that is clearly relevant for the group of keywords. Use those keywords in developing the title of the ad and the body copy. If there is a specific offer that you can add, such as free shipping, free demo, or free webinar, then work that into the ad as well.

It is always good to develop more than one ad for each ad group. You can run more than one, and the bidding interface will report to you which ad is performing the best. So, run multiple ads, and test different messages. Refine your campaign by tweaking the ad text in order to develop one or two that consistently perform well in attracting visitors to click your ad.

At this point, you still do not have to be part of a PPC network on any of the search engines. This is all preparation work, because everything should be in place and create a logical flow for the searcher. Of course, nothing should be actively running on a search engine if you haven't developed your landing page.

Develop the landing page. Each ad group should have a landing page that is specific to the ad. The offer needs to be reflected on the page as well as a clear call to action. These pages must capture the attention and the interest of the searcher in a very short time, only a few seconds, so be efficient, clear, and concise.

Planning is key in developing successful PPC campaigns. The other key is never to set up a campaign and leave it to run on its own. PPC campaigns can be constantly developed, tweaked, tested, and improved. Simply leaving a PPC campaign to run will end up costing you more in click rates, because you will be overlooking important signs that your campaign may be incorrect or targeting the wrong audience. Never "set it and forget it," but be constantly on guard and attempting to improve the campaign.

The final step is measurement. Clicks are not the measurement of campaign success. Ensure that the campaign is set up correctly to capture the result of the click—the conversion. Evaluate your campaign success on the conversions that the ad group and keywords produce, and adjust as necessary. You will find that some ads produce low click-throughs but high conversions; you may also find ads that produce high click-throughs but low conversions.

Ultimately, this needs to be measured in terms of profitability. Although conversions are a great measurement, the total spend of your business needs to be included in the calculations of the marketing and delivery of your business. The true calculation of profit is the ultimate measurement of a successful campaign.

Week 17: Measure, Measure, Measure

Although you'll spend these final two weeks focusing on analytics, I've touched on analytics throughout—and for good reason. The importance of analytics needs to be ingrained from the beginning of a project.

Many marketers have a negative impression about analytics because they have developed opinions based on bad information. They have no idea of the gold mine of information that is available to them through their website analytics or marketing analytics software, and as a result, most view analytics as an expensive and time-consuming way to develop a report with unique website visitors, time on site, and pages viewed. When marketers understand how to use analytics properly, it changes everything.

Chapter Contents

Monday: Understand the Terms
Tuesday: Establish Goals
Wednesday: Evolve from Data to Analysis
Thursday and Friday: Develop Segments

Monday: Understand the Terms

In many cases of online marketing analytics, there is misunderstanding of the terms that are used and what they really mean in measurement practices. For any organization to communicate properly, there needs to be a consensus on what the words mean and the information they carry.

Page Tagging

Page tagging is how most analytics data are collected. Simply put, in order to get analytics for a website, a piece of code needs to be added to every page of the website. This is both the easiest and hardest thing to accomplish for many websites. Depending upon how your website is built and what type of management system is creating your pages, it may be easy to add the code to part of the programming that will naturally reproduce the code on every page of the website. Some websites use multiple templates, and the code needs to be added to each template in order to ensure proper data collection.

The first step to gaining the best information that you can get from your analytics is verifying the code throughout every page of your website. If you do not have the code on every page, your analytics will be incomplete. Unfortunately, analytics programs do not inform you if they are installed incorrectly or missing information. It is usually a physical process of verifying the code by hand or by software that will check every page of your website for the code. All the code does is send visitor information to a server, which collects that data and reprocesses the raw data into understandable information. I like to call those the pretty charts and graphs. The code interacts with the visitor's browser and acquires information such as IP address, operating system, browser type, screen resolution, pages, and files requested and other data. All of this information is sent to the web analytics server, cataloged, and then repurposed to show the activity in some kind of relevant report.

Accuracy

In the world of analytics, there is no such thing as accuracy. John Marshall is one of my good friends in the industry and was the founder of ClickTracks, one of my favorite analytics programs for many years. I asked him once if his creation was more accurate than other analytics software, and he stopped me with his answer. He said, "We don't sell ourselves as being more accurate than our competitors; we like to say that we provide less inaccurate analytics than our competitors." That explained the dirty little secret of the world of analytics in only a few brief moments.

You see, the collection methods utilized by analytics programs are a very inaccurate science and actually full of many holes. Visitor activity can be reported different ways by different programs, simply based on the rules of interpreting the data. All analytics programs interpret the raw data differently, which is why no two analytics programs will ever report the same number, even if they use the same raw data as the basis.

The methods of acquiring visitor information are improving, but there are large deficiencies in the data and different methods of interpreting the data. This problem is based on the HTTP standard, which the current Internet has developed as a means of delivering web pages and documents to users. That protocol is simply not the best method of tracking accurate data online. As a result, much of the reporting is based on "filling in" information that is missing.

Unique Visitors

One of the core contents of any report within an organization is the unique visitors. This number is generally meant to report the number of individuals who have visited the website. It includes those who visited only once and those who visited multiple times. It is generally thought that this is a good indicator of how many people have seen the website.

More accurately, this should be called the "unique device" report. I use four computers: one at work, one at home, a laptop for travel, and an iPhone. If I visit the same website with each one of those devices, it will be reported as four unique visitors.

If I find a website using a search engine at work, then email that link to myself, and click the link from my home computer, then I will show up as two unique visitors: one visitor, who found the site from a search engine, spent a few minutes, browsed a few pages, and then exited the website. I will also be reported as a separate visitor who directly accessed the site and converted within a very short amount of time.

Although the unique visitors are very easy to interpret as unique people, they are anything but that. It is a number full of errors, inaccuracies, and assumptions. But, it's the best we have for the given situation.

Visitor Sessions

This number represents the number of times your website was visited. It represents active sessions on your site, whether the visitor viewed only one page on the site or multiple pages. This contains users whose session may have timed out, usually because they left the page on their browser and came back an hour or so later to finish their task—that would show up as two sessions. This report does not distinguish how many people visited the website. It is made up of how many times a user (as defined by the analytics software) requested information (pages) within a certain time frame.

My goal is not to completely destroy any method that you may be using to measure activity on your website. My goal is to show that many methods that people use to track success are based on numbers that may not mean what people think they mean.

Hits

One number that I am glad to see falling out of many analytics programs is hits. This is most likely one of the most misunderstood numbers in online marketing. The number of hits has nothing to do with people. The number of hits is made up of how many files have been downloaded from your website's server.

You see, each web page is made up of multiple files. A single page is a file, any images contained on the page are files, and any scripts (CSS, JavaScript) are considered files as well. A web page can have as many as 10 to 20 files or more depending upon how it was built. So, a page that contains 20 files creates 21 hits (because the page is a file as well). Hits are not people! I like to joke that a good SEO specialist can double the number of hits reported for your website within a day—all is takes is doubling the number of files included in the page.

Remove *hits* from your analytics vocabulary. If you are talking about people, *visits* or *sessions* are more accurate for what you mean.

Bounce Rate

Bounce rate is an infuriating number to casual analytics watchers but a fun and intriguing number to those who understand how to get data out of analytics. The bounce rate is the rate at which people come to your website and immediately leave. Most times, they leave because they see nothing on the page that meets their needs. The phrase implies exactly the behavior of the visitor. They see your web page and immediately bounce out.

Exit Rate

The exit rate is the rate at which people leave your site after visiting more than one page. The exit rate is usually reported by page, and you can see which pages have higher exit rates than others. This gives you an understanding of which pages may not be as persuasive as others. Or, it can help you understand whether there is information, design, or something that simply makes people leave from a certain page.

Conversion Rate

The conversion rate is the ratio between people who simply visit your site and those who do something that makes you money. This is the extension of your goals. Whether it is a sale, lead, registration, or subscription, if it makes you money, then it is a conversion. Other types of conversions that can be tracked are downloaded files (such as white papers), visited pages, subscriptions, video views, and other events.

As we will delve into next week, determining your conversation rates is an important part of developing a true measure of success. Developing and tracking all the goals within a website provides a more extensive measurement of effectiveness and the ability to gain insights into more data, visitor behaviors, and visitor preferences.

Additionally, adding monetary values to each conversion will enhance your measurements. It is one thing to count the number of conversions and report a rate of conversions, but adding the aspect of monetary value based on the actions and the activities of your visitors will add an additional layer of available analysis to your repertoire. Calculating your financial gain based on conversions will enable you to measure an amazing number of activities and measure how profitable those activities are when compared to others.

Better decisions are made when financial goals and measurements are used. Decision makers who may not have the time to listen to the majority of your analysis will be particularly interested in a "bottom-line" analysis that focuses on revenue and profit and can be quickly summed up in a statement such as "Look how much we made, and we can make more by doing this...." Adding dollar signs to your reports is a sure way to get more attention.

Tuesday: Establish Goals

Goals are critical to understanding the proper role of analytics. Most marketers spend their time reporting information rather than analyzing visitor performance. As emphasized throughout this book, you need to have the goals of the website and your marketing campaigns established, published, and understood by everyone involved. The only way to develop a clear understanding of the success of the campaign of the website is to measure the established goals, rather than inconsistent measurements of nonessential data.

Eric Peterson, who wrote and self-published *Web Analytics Demystified* (2004, Peterson) and *The Big Book of Key Performance Indicators* (2005, Peterson), explained the importance of goals in an interview with Direct Marketing News (August 11, 2006): "Web analytics works best when measurement expectations are clearly defined in advance, not after the fact or on an ad hoc basis." (You can find the article at `www.dmnews.com/from-dm-news-special-report-on-web-analytics-peterson-says-web-analytics-getting-better-all-the-time/article/92290/`.)

Unfortunately, most companies and marketers I talk with are used to developing ad hoc reports or reports that are unfocused on the primary goals of sales, leads, registrations, or other actions and more focused on activity reports that are usually heavily flawed because they are generated on-the-fly and may not include all of the relevant information. There are too many factors involved in an ad hoc reporting situation, and as a result, reports are generally inaccurate, are potentially misleading, and are a terrible basis for decision making.

So, what should be done? The very first step is establishing the goals of the website. Identify the purpose of the website from the corporate or business standpoint. In short, what do you want? To make money? To raise awareness? To increase branding? Chances are, if you purchased this book, making money is your number-one goal, and you want to make more.

The secondary goals all revolve around the visitor actions that make you money. What actions do visitors take that lead directly to making your business money? What actions are indirectly making you money? What events can lead to better customers?

The secondary goals are those where you should rank the actions of visitors and develop a priority for those visits based on revenue and profitability.

This is a significant part of analytics, and no analytics program will be successful unless goals are established and values are communicated based on all the goals for the visitor. For example, if the visitor does not purchase a product, then you want them to request a catalog or more information; if they do not do that, then you want them to give you their email address for the newsletter or offers. If they do not do that, then you want them to download a white paper, request a demo, or do something else where you can attach a value to the business.

Socrates said that "the unexamined life is not worth living." I like to modify that statement for the world of online marketing: the unexamined website is not worth hosting. If you are not measuring goals and revenue from the actions of your website visitors, then you have no idea if you are successful. Only by measuring your goals will you know whether you have created a successful online marketing presence.

Use KPIs to Grow Your Business Analytics

Business goals in analytics are called *key performance indicators* (KPIs). These key performance indicators are just that—indicators. Smart analysts understand that indicators are signposts to additional data, not specific data in itself.

For example, a report on new vs. returning visitors is helpful as an indicator. It is a quick method of ensuring that your website is continually gaining new visitors or retaining visitors, based on your goals. However, while the indicator shows an immediate signpost of success, you need to delve beyond the initial layer of data in order to see where the new visitors are coming and why. This is how you capitalize on trends and find additional opportunities.

In the same way, watching the number of your unique visitors is important, but it is still an indicator. Visitors need to be explored in context of conversion in order to find out what is effective and why. Unique visitors as a goal is good if that is how you monetize your site, maybe through advertising, but you still have to create an actionable plan to increase those unique visitors by analyzing what sources are providing those visitors and which are able to be grown more effectively. The number of unique visitors is a KPI, not a goal. It is an indicator of direction—in that you are either heading in the right direction or heading in the wrong direction. The KPI reports your progress, but it does not report a plan to improve the site.

The top pages viewed can be an important report, if it is not used as the primary report. Having a KPI goal of increasing page views is good, but it serves little purpose if the page views are not explored beyond the KPI report. Knowing which pages are being viewed, why, and where they fall in visibility, prominence, and demand by visitors, you will have no understanding of the means necessary to increase those page views.

This understanding of using KPIs to monitor goals rather than be reported as an objective will enable you to take the step in tomorrow's content. KPIs need to be associated with other KPIs and data in order to find trends and opportunities to improve the site, but marketers need to be able to read the signs provided by the KPIs in order to become analysts.

Three Obstacles to Effective Analytics

In the years of dealing with businesses, I have found that there are three consistent factors that prevent marketers and business owners from effectively using analytics in their marketing. Despite the intent of the business to improve and use the data to improve the website, there is an extreme disconnect between the desire of the business to use analytics and the knowledge of how to access or use that data. This is the first obstacle.

The Dashboard

The analytics dashboard is the first obstacle to effective online marketing analytics. I say this because when marketers open their analytics program, the very first thing they see is the dashboard, and the majority of them think this must be the most important information, simply because it is shown first. Beyond that, there are no clear instructions contained in the dashboard to allow people to know where to go to get information.

Sure, there are some tabs that say top keywords, top pages, and top content, but all that the marketer sees is more charts, more graphs, and nothing that contains any clear information that indicates a problem or clear success. Each tab brings more graphs, more information, and maybe some interesting ways of seeing the content of the site, but no clear information that will improve the marketing.

The dashboard is the initial screen on analytics programs, and it simply evolved from the earliest forms of tracking website activity in the mid-1990s. Basic programs then focused on tracking the bandwidth usage for websites, because that was a primary cost of doing business online. The earliest "stats" programs focused on how much data was transferred online. As a result, those programs grew because they were the only real "hard" data of what activity was taking place on the website. Visitors, time on site, hits, and page views became a staple of those programs because they were easy things to gather from the server. As a result of this, those measurements became integrated into the methods of reporting success of the website. Between being the only information available, the rush to be online (and the thinking that everything has changed), and the necessity to report something, these reporting metrics became the standard report of the online marketer.

The dashboards of analytics programs do not change based on who you are (unless it is custom-developed for you, which carries a significant cost). Dashboards are built to be a one-size-fits-all solution, so they report the same information and display the same charts and graphs to everyone. Unless you are able to get in and modify the information, add goals, add revenue tracking, and adjust the information to your goals, it will not change. Analytics need to be customized to meet your needs; if not, they simply report the basic information.

Velleity

An old word that has dropped out of everyday use in the American vocabulary, *velleity* carries an awesome weight to its meaning. According to the Merriam-Webster dictionary, velleity means "a slight wish or tendency" or "the lowest degree of volition." The Random House dictionary is more specific by describing velleity as "a mere wish, unaccompanied by an effort to obtain it." My definition, based on my experiences in the corporate world, is a desire to see something done but not enough desire to make it happen.

Many marketers nod their heads in agreement when they hear the definitions of this word. It describes so many corporate cultures in a single word. There is a goal to improve but no action to make it happen. There is a desire to use analytics to improve the website, the measurement, and the business, but there is no action or effort or no decisions made to get better. Rather, without the action necessary to change old habits and develop new skills, desire falls flat, and everything remains the same. That leads to the last obstacle, the hamster wheel.

Hamster-Wheel Analytics

I mentioned this in Chapter 3, but it is the typical behavior by so many online marketers that I have had to attach this behavior to any discussion of analytics. Hamster-wheel analytics is simply reporting the same numbers every month (usually a copy-paste activity from the analytics program to a report) to the same people or departments, and then nothing is done. Sometimes, you may be asked to justify or answer why the numbers are lower than last month (or higher, if you are lucky). And then you spend the next few days exploring options and reasons why the numbers changed or didn't change.

Unfortunately, most people in this situation are not aware of other marketing that is happening within the company. Marketers reporting information and in charge of analytics are usually the last to be aware that an email promotion went out earlier that month, that there was a discount published on the website, or that another department experimented with a PPC campaign.

This leads to the reason that the hamster wheel keeps companies trapped by doing the same thing all of the time. There is no new information introduced to the system. Unless the marketer or the analyst knows *everything* that happening to drive visitors to the site or draw them to convert in some way, then no insights can be developed, and certainly no measurement of success can be determined.

The analyst or person responsible for developing these reports must have access to all of this information, and it is critical they are involved at the beginning of trials, promotions, communications, campaigns, and any type of electronic communication. If it is not tracked, then there is no data that can be used to determine success. By keeping information from your analytics, nothing changes, no new information is introduced, and no goals are measured.

Instead, the same reports will be generated. The same reports will go to the same people. The same questions will be asked. And nothing will ever change, and no measureable improvements will take place.

Wednesday: Evolve from Data to Analysis

The problem that most marketers and business owners face is that they focus most of their time on recording and reporting the numbers I touched on Monday. Although those numbers are readily accessible, they are also the most inaccurate collection of generalizations one can find about a website. Developing reports based on those numbers is what I call "caveman stats" because it is right out of the 1990s (see Figure 20.1). Marketers need to evolve beyond the simple stats and into a true financial-based analysis of their online marketing. The following sections show the progression of this evolution.

Figure 20.1 Caveman analytics: evolve to better analysis!

Gather Data

The first thing you'll see from your web-analytics reports is a piece of data like this:

- Page views = 80,000

Now, is this number good or bad? The answer, you don't know. You see, this is data. Data is value neutral. It is a fact without bias; it is what it is. Data is not good or bad. It is simply data—a number.

Add Context to Create Information

What you can do to understand data better is to associate it with another piece of data. In doing so, you add context to create information.

Say you add this piece of data:

- Average page views per visitor: 8

Again, this data by itself is not good or bad; there is nothing you can do to improve a website using this amount of data. It is simply an average. All you can do is add more data, which adds more context.

- Visitors who searched for *coffee* viewed an average of six pages.

This is starting to make sense, isn't it? By associating the numbers with an action, you are able to start developing a picture. Mental images are powerful, and when you start developing the image of a particular group of visitors to a website and their particular activity, then you can begin seeing the trends and activities that take place every day. Now you're just getting started; again, you add more context by adding more data.

Synthesize Information to Form Knowledge

Say you add these bits of data about visitors who searched for *coffee*:

- Viewed an average of six pages
- Spent an average of $8
- Have a conversion rate of 7 percent

Adding more information doesn't complicate things; it clarifies things! By adding more data, you add more context. Adding more context adds more insight! By continually adding data to the problem, you have created the next level of the information hierarchy—knowledge. You have taken data, added it together to develop information, and synthesized all that information to create knowledge. You have knowledge of a specific group of visitors on the website and their activity, which results in revenue.

However, this is the level at which analytics programs stop. All software-driven analytics stop at the knowledge level in the information hierarchy.

Analytics programs are wonderful tools to gain knowledge about online marketing and the activities that take place. But to apply that knowledge takes something special, something more, something...that analytics software just can't provide. And that is you, the analyst.

Arrive at an Understanding

After the knowledge you can gain from your marketing activities, you arrive at an understanding. Analytics software can't understand the information for you; it can only answer the questions you ask. You are the missing link between knowledge of the information and the application of the knowledge—knowing what to do with that knowledge to reach understanding and, next, wisdom.

Gain Wisdom

The next step after understanding is wisdom. The experience of applying knowledge and seeing the results provides an analyst with the experience necessary to understand when and how to apply knowledge for improvements, analysis, and additional insights that would ordinarily be lost.

Although analytics software companies like to sell their solutions as being the biggest, most used, most comprehensive, and most extensive solutions, analytics software is only as good as the person getting the information out of the software. The ability of the human to get information from the computer is the critical step in all of this.

This is why the mantra exists (primarily perpetuated by Avinash Kaushik, Analytics Evangelist, Google, who wrote the foreword to this book) that you need to invest more in your analysts than in your software, because it is the analyst who will take the knowledge received from the analytics and apply it with a level of understanding. The software will not do it by itself. The missing link in analytics is the human analyst (Figure 20.2).

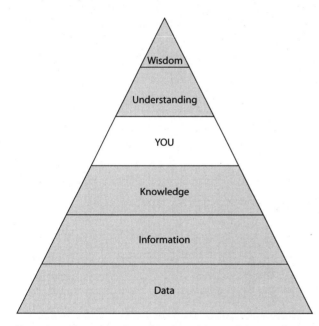

Figure 20.2 The analytics hierarchy is dependent upon human intelligence.

If you are not investing in the person, the analyst, or the marketer who is performing the analytics, then you could be spending thousands of dollars for a high-priced software package that is being used only to generate simple reports, because no one has the knowledge necessary to gain an understanding of how to use the information.

As mentioned already, context provides meaning. A number by itself provides nothing, but as soon as the number is presented within a context, it can then be used to develop a judgment. When you look at the search term that a specific group of visitors used, you develop a context, a story, and an event with specific requirements. You can then evaluate, judge, and make decisions about that particular event, because you have isolated it from the rest of the information, set it apart, and evaluated it specifically because of the particulars of the information.

Once you have developed context, then you can begin to build a powerful new way of looking at the data of the website, which then takes analytics from the realm of the mundane to the amazing—wisdom is the result.

You aren't reporting numbers anymore. Analytics is not about numbers; it is about analyzing behavior. When you develop the context of a visitor, it is based on the intent of the visitor; you are a psychologist, not an analyst. The better you understand the particular visitor, their intent, their reactions, and the result of the visit, the better you will be able to improve your online marketing. Only when looking at the motivations, expectations, and reactions of your visitors will you be able to explain the behavior with a specific understanding of that segment. The explanation will lead you to better testing, better optimization, and better ideas, because you are focused on a small group of specific visitors, rather than attempting to improve the large, unfocused group of all visitors. It is glorified people-watching, not number-crunching. If you are not having fun with analytics, then you are certainly doing it wrong.

Thursday and Friday: Develop Segments

Segmentation is the principle of measuring groups of visitors who have something in common. By isolating them from the aggregate numbers, you can begin to see nuances that are particular to that group. By examining smaller groups of visitors based on search terms, behavior, conversion, or other actions, you can isolate each group, examine it, and draw practical conclusions that will enable you to improve the experience for that specific group of people.

Segmentation breaks down all the information into bite-sized chunks, which allow careful examination. Once you have broken down the visitors into segments, then you can compare and contrast those segments. Aggregate numbers (such as unique visitors, visitor sessions, and search engine referrals) treat all the visitors the same. By lumping everyone into the same group, such as "unique visitors," you overlook all the different reasons people come to the website. Your website traffic consists of hundreds to thousands of people looking for their own needs. These needs will be similar, but you can't develop one report that tells the story about all of your visitors.

Use Context to Build Segments

Compare your keyword segments. For example, say you are comparing the search visitors for Blu-ray players and digital cameras on an electronics website.

In Figure 20.3, you have a visitor from a search engine referral for the term *digital camera* on the left. The thought cloud includes all the additional information that is in their head and information that is necessary to satisfy in order to decide to complete the purchase. Some visitors are looking for product information, and others are looking for prices, details, or comparisons. Visitors are different and have different motivations, even if they type the same search phrase into the search engine. The words associated with the digital camera buyer are all the concepts that are typically floating around in the searchers' brains but sometimes are not used in the search. However, these are important concepts to the decision-making process, and they will drive the visitor to visit certain pages, click specific links, and find what they need.

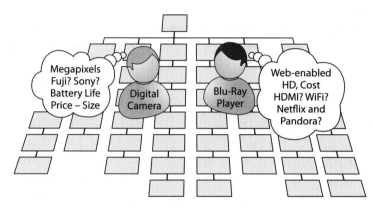

Figure 20.3 Typical visitors to an electronics website

On the other side of the website, a visitor is searching for a Blu-ray player. In doing so, they most likely will enter the site through a different page than the "digital camera" searcher did. You cannot measure the experiences of searchers for digital cameras the same way you can measure the experiences of searchers for Blu-ray players. Those visitors are looking for completely different products, and they have completely different informational needs that will persuade them in the process and have completely different expectations of the process. If you have employed SEO, then you've set up your marketing so that different pages rank for different terms in the search engines and bypass the home page to take the searcher to the site content that is relevant to them.

Measure Outcomes by Segment

By finding segments that are performing well, you can optimize those for even better performance and targeting. Poorly performing segments can be recognized, and conclusions can be drawn about the performance and what can be done to improve those segments. Compare segments and keyword rankings to be sure you are targeting the right words. Get a clear picture of exit rates by finding the segment that is causing you the most trouble. Comparing and contrasting is the basis of learning, and it is the easiest method to find opportunities for growth in your marketing. You may find that your best-ranking keywords, the ones bringing in the most traffic, are also the worst-performing group. Only segmenting and building context will allow that exploration.

If you know that one segment has a 1 percent conversion rate and another segment had a 12 percent conversion rate, you are then able to decide which group you want to work on and improve. One conversion rate doesn't tell the story of who came to the website, what they expected to see, what they did see, and how they reacted to it. But examining multiple conversion rates based on keywords, actions, product types, price points, keyword rankings, or navigation methods can help you build conversion segments.

If you do not have your conversion rate built in Google Analytics yet, then please consult Monday's content in Chapter 21, which covers the aspects of building your conversion rate. This is the critical piece of analysis, because all activity needs to be associated with the outcome in order to make the best decisions about marketing your business and your website.

Segment by Source

Review Chapter 16's Friday topic, which is about evaluating the marketing value of your links. The link analysis performed in this section was the result of attempting to find the best-performing link source for visitors to a website. This was done by creating segments of all the incoming visitors based on source—search engine, website link, blog link, banner ad link, and social-media links. By measuring all the channels through which this website received traffic and the specific outcomes based on the goal, important information was found that provided a confident direction for the online marketing budget over the next year. This analysis allowed the company to find specific tactics to follow and emphasis for link building that would develop the kind of visitors it wanted for the website.

This is a method of developing a clear understanding of the value of a visitor by the source. Most analytics programs will allow you to see how many visitors you receive from various sources, such as from search, external links, ad clicks, and so on. However, by segmenting each source in order to measure the conversion outcomes by source and then comparing each source according to the same measurements, you will find the best-performing segments (the ones that get you the greatest percentage of conversions or leads), not just those who sent a lot of visitors.

Finding the differences within the different visitor sources will enable you to find those high-profit acquisition channels and develop them even more. This analysis will also enable you find low-performing sources and develop an understanding of why they may be underperforming by comparison. This may also optimize your online spending, because you begin investing in sources that are bringing profitable visitors and cutting back in those that aren't.

Segment by Action

Segmenting by actions can be as simple as tracking the navigation behavior beyond the home page. By tracking those visitors who navigate directly to the home page, segmenting the different paths from the page, and measuring against goals or revenue, you can begin to develop an understanding of the content that is requested more, and ideally it is the profitable content as well. Action-based conversions, such as video views and navigation tendencies, point to the behavior of people within a segment and can provide insight as to how people respond when they interact with elements within the website. Understanding the actions and how they affect conversions will provide direction for continued development of interactions within the website.

Actions can be any goal that is measured in the analytics. Any segment has to be evaluated by a goal or by revenue in order to help you make a final decision as to the value of that segment. One business found that visitors who viewed embedded videos on the website tended to convert 20 percent more than visitors who did not view any of the videos. When finding data like that, it's not hard to make determinations about how to improve the visitor experience and increase conversions.

As social media becomes more pervasive in the development and marketing of websites, analytics will be able to track more of the interaction between the visitor, social media, and visitor behavior. Integrating comments on blogs, videos, and articles along with voting, linking, and cross-media promotion, analytics is able to provide integrated views of how visitors are interacting with your information, and additional actions will enable further analysis.

Segment by Content

Publishers can segment their content by author, popularity, links, and any number of other factors that will enable them to determine the types of content that their readers like and respond to favorably. Publishers can also track to see which stories gain the most nonsubscriber traffic in order to see how their content can grow beyond their subscribers and attract new members.

One of the more interesting segments I look at is the page views prior to the conversion, especially on content and lead generation sites. It is always interesting to see the pages that are part of the decision-making process. Sometimes, they aren't what you think. I often see the About Us page as one of the most previewed pages prior to a conversion.

Segmenting by content will enable you to develop an understanding of how your website is actually used by visitors. You will be able to find the content that may have required extensive time and investment to create but isn't critical for the most conversions. Analyzing your content segments by conversion enables you to find direction in developing new content, optimizing current content, and possible interlinking within your own site to enable visitors to find the information they need more effectively.

One of the harder-to-track groups of visitors on the website is those who navigate directly to the home page. Most likely, these visitors have the site bookmarked or are just so familiar with it that they typed it in directly. For these types of visitors, I also like to segment the choice of content (the next page that visitor goes to) from the home page. By segmenting the most selected content from those visits, I can begin to see the preferences of different types of visitors. Most likely, these are returning visitors, so they have seen the site before. Knowing that, segmenting the paths from the home page may provide some enlightenment as to what content is important for a returning visitor.

Review and Hands-On

If you are reporting using the information found on the dashboard of your analytics, stop!

First, get familiar with your choice of analytics programs. How is the data collected? Are you using a page-tagging solution (which is what Google Analytics offers). If so, verify on random pages throughout your website that the code is there. Do this by viewing the source code; on most browsers you can do this by viewing a web page and then selecting View > View Page Source. I typically will press Ctrl+F (PC) or Cmd+F (Mac) and then search for *ga.js*. This will find the Google script on the page.

Next, look at the reports that you are currently tracking, and define visitors, page views, session, bounce rate, exit rate, and conversions. Understand that these are KPIs and report numbers but do not provide analysis that will point to action.

After reviewing your current reports, write down the goals you have for your website. Compare your goals to the reports you are generating or viewing. Are you measuring your goals with your reports? Do your reports include goal completion, conversions, or profitability? How closely do your reports match the stated goals for the website and for your visitors?

Now, move to analysis. This is where you take the goals that you have for the website and for your business and start to develop a report that will enable you to track the success of your goals, and not simply reporting KPIs.

Develop segments that will enable you to break down all of your visitors by their intent and activity. Return to your keyword lists that you developed for your optimization, and review your current keyword visits. Are you getting visitors for the words you are targeting? Segment your keyword phrases into large segments at first, using a single word or concept. You can use a spreadsheet or do this in Google Analytics if you are comfortable at this point. Build large segments at the initial level, and then evaluate each segment's performance against other segments.

Build additional segments based on content that you have on the site and actions available to visitors (videos, downloads, forms, and so on). This will provide insight into the tendencies of visitors while they are on the site.

Build segments based on the content of your website. This is especially effective if you have multiple product categories. By contrasting categories against each other and evaluating based on conversions, you will be able to see the profitable categories against those that simply attract large numbers of visitors.

Remember not to be distracted by the big numbers. The most important thing in segmenting is to associate a group of visitors by a common denominator to the goal and then compare and contrast other segments in order to find the best-performing trends.

Week 18: Analyze for Action

Now that you have gained a proper perspective on analytics, it is time to put that perspective into practice. Apply your business goals to the data, and find the knowledge you need to manage your website more effectively. Get your segments from last week ready—this week everything comes together to give you a true picture of your marketing campaigns and how to improve them.

Chapter Contents

Monday: Set Up Goals and Analysis in Google Analytics

Throughout this entire book, I have been preaching to track your conversions and goals as the means of truly measuring success. This chapter will focus on the steps to accomplish that. In today's section, I will cover how to set up your goals and track conversions, because they are separate actions within Google Analytics.

For purposes of example, I will use Google Analytics for setting up goals and conversions. There are a few reasons for doing this. First, it's free. It's hard to beat a price tag like that. I held out for years, because I didn't want to admit that Google's analytics product was going to be the top in the industry, but the improvements made over the recent years have changed my mind. Second, the tool has the ability to segment. Very few analytics programs offer the ability to segment nearly every aspect of the visitor experience. The speed, ability to create segments on the fly, and ability to develop custom segments is beyond comparison and beats many of the expensive, high-level analytics programs available. Third, the levels of knowledge required to get set up and begin to gain actionable data is very low. You don't have to be an advanced programmer, and you don't need advanced training in analytics to begin setting up reports and analysis on your own. The accessibility of the program is very high when compared to others. Fourth, it is pervasive. Because of the price tag (it's free!), I have found that most people I speak with are using Google Analytics, even when they have already purchased another analytics program. They use them together, because Google Analytics is easier and provides more understandable reports, and the other more expensive, more complicated systems are just that—more expensive and complicated.

Marketers and business owners just want to get their reports and get back to business. They don't want to be burdened with figuring out complicated tracking scripts and setup schemes and finding out that the functionality they need costs more and requires hundreds to thousands of additional investment and setup dollars.

Set Up Your Goals

Here I'll walk you through the steps to set up goals in the most recent edition of Google Analytics. You'll need to log into a Google Analytics account to follow along, and you'll need to be able to identify a specific page on your website that is served only when a visitor takes an action that you've set as a goal. In the Website Profiles screen, click Edit (see Figure 21.1).

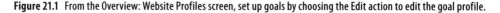

				2010 Nov 12 - 2010 Dec 12		
				Comparing to: 2010 Oct 12 - 2010 Nov 11		
					Day Week **Month** Year	
						+ Add new account
Visits	Avg. Time on Site	Bounce Rate	Completed Goals	Visits ▼ % Change		Actions
12,075	00:01:22	51.71%	1,441	⊕ -0.16%		Edit ←

Figure 21.1 From the Overview: Website Profiles screen, set up goals by choosing the Edit action to edit the goal profile.

This will take you directly to the profile settings for your website. In the second block of settings is the goal setup. Click Add Goal. You are now at the goal page. Name the goal you are creating. In the example in Figure 21.2, the goal is to place a classified ad. This type of goal is based on the visitor completing a process that is able to be tracked because the visitor sees a specific and trackable "thank you" page at the end of the process. Any form completion, task, or event that shows the visitor a "thank you" with a specific URL page can be tracked as a goal. For publishers, pages viewed or time on site may be a goal for visitors. For lead generation or commerce sites, form completion, registrations, downloads, or subscriptions can all be tracked as an event as long as there is a specific URL page for the destination, or "thank you," page.

Figure 21.2 The goal setup page

The URL destination is the goal type for this site, because there is a specific URL "thank you" page for this action. The goal details require a match type—if you have a specific URL page (which most sites utilize), then an exact match will suffice. The *exact match* is when the goal matches the exact URL. This is easily accomplished if your site's URLs are easy to understand and read.

The second type of match is the *head match*. This type of match is necessary if you have a string of numbers or characters after the URL, such as https://www.example .com/checkout.php/?page=1&id=123456789. In this case, the goal can be tracked without the information appended to the URL. You can enter the URL as **https://www.example.com/checkout.php/?page=1** and select Head Match for your goal.

The third type of match is the *regular expression match*. This is for sites that utilize wildcards, use additional parameters, or can show multiple URLs for the same pages. If you fall into this category, you will need assistance from your developers or IT staff in order to identify the constant part of the URL and to relate the inconsistent parts within the match type.

Add the URL of the "thank you" page in the Goal URL field. It's useful to add a value to the goal (in the Goal Value field). This is an excellent method of showing value, based on the priorities of goal conversions, or creating a value for the lead. The value is whatever you set it to be. If you have a set price for any activities in this goal, then you can add the value of that price. If you have a lead generation website, then I recommend entering the value of the lead. This field is not restricted in any way, because it allows you to determine your value for each action set up in the goals.

Save your goal, which will be added as a specific measurement aspect of your reports. You will find the goal in the tabs of your regular reports. Go ahead and add any other goals that you have developed for your website, and rank them accordingly, based on your primary goals and their associated value to your business.

Track Ecommerce Sales

For ecommerce sites, a few considerations need to be addressed in developing the analytics. Initially, your Google Analytics profile settings need to be set as an ecommerce site in the main website profile. Ecommerce websites need to use a special code for tracking sales. Without this code, sales data will not be tracked with your analytics.

The tracking code works best if final checkout pages are on the same domain as the website. Third-party carts, which take users to another website for the checkout pages, are not impossible to track, but each one has its nuances that may or may not allow tracking. The key is if the "thank you" page is on your domain after the transaction is completed and if the sales data is carried through the process as well to enable the data to be tracked.

There are some basic steps contained in the setup instructions for Google, which should be followed. See https://www.google.com/support/googleanalytics/bin/answer.py?answer=55528&hl=en_US. Some third-party shopping carts do not allow tracking, and it is up to each individual third-party cart to decide how integrated they will be with Google Analytics (or any other analytics program, for that matter).

View Your Reports According to the Goals

Now that you have goal conversions set up in your analytics, the reports will take on an entirely different meaning. The Goals tab in the left navigation of Google Analytics will provide conversion information, and other reports will include this data as well.

In the Traffic Sources by Keywords report, the information displays the top keywords by number of visitors and shows the typical information of time on site, pages viewed, and bounce rate for your site as a whole (Figure 21.3a). However, now that you've added your goals, there are new tabs just above the information columns. The Site Usage tab was the only available view prior to adding the goals, so it is now the default tab. If you have named your goals, the tab will reflect the name of the goal, as in the AdSense Revenue tab shown in Figure 21.3a. If you have not named your goals, then they will default to "Goal Set 1." Clicking the tab for one of your goals will display the site usage data, but within the context of the goals you have created. Any individual goals that are part of the goal set will also show up as a field in the information. As shown in Figure 21.3, Place Classified Ad is included as a secondary goal in Goal Set 2.

Search sent 6,116 total visits via 3,043 keywords

Show: non-paid | **total** | paid

Site Usage | Goal Set 1 | Goal Set 2 | AdSense Revenue   Views:

Visits	Pages/Visit	Avg. Time on Site	% New Visits	Bounce Rate
6,116	**2.05**	**00:01:35**	**86.30%**	**60.07%**
% of Site Total: 67.13%	Site Avg: 1.95 (5.43%)	Site Avg: 00:01:29 (6.73%)	Site Avg: 87.72% (-1.62%)	Site Avg: 61.03% (-1.56%)

	Keyword	None	Visits ↓	Pages/Visit	Avg. Time on Site	% New Visits	Bounce Rate
1.	vw beetle		400	2.26	00:02:01	91.00%	52.25%
2.	volkswagen beetle		250	2.51	00:02:47	93.20%	47.60%
3.	vw thing		213	1.58	00:00:25	97.18%	58.69%
4.	volkswagen thing		121	1.59	00:00:21	93.39%	57.85%
5.	vw bug		105	2.38	00:01:42	79.05%	50.48%
6.	vw beetle restoration		86	1.73	00:01:45	81.40%	68.60%
7.	classic beetle		85	2.64	00:02:27	77.65%	47.06%
8.	classic vw beetle		74	2.15	00:00:57	82.43%	51.35%
9.	vw beetle classic		43	2.37	00:01:23	79.07%	62.79%
10.	old vw beetle for sale		38	2.00	00:00:26	86.84%	63.16%

a

Search sent 6,116 total visits via 3,043 keywords

Show: non-paid | **total** | paid

Site Usage | Goal Set 1 | Goal Set 2 | AdSense Revenue   Views:

Visits	Goal6: Place Classified Ad	Goal Conversion Rate	Per Visit Goal Value
6,116	**0.00%**	**10.06%**	**$0.01**
% of Site Total: 67.13%	Site Avg: 0.00% (0.00%)	Site Avg: 15.27% (-34.14%)	Site Avg: $0.01 (-19.32%)

	Keyword	None	Visits ↓	Place Classified Ad	Goal Conversion Rate	Per Visit Goal Value
1.	vw beetle		400	0.00%	11.00%	$0.01
2.	volkswagen beetle		250	0.00%	8.80%	$0.01
3.	vw thing		213	0.00%	0.47%	$0.00
4.	volkswagen thing		121	0.00%	0.83%	$0.00
5.	vw bug		105	0.00%	6.67%	$0.01
6.	vw beetle restoration		86	0.00%	6.98%	$0.00
7.	classic beetle		85	0.00%	11.76%	$0.01
8.	classic vw beetle		74	0.00%	6.76%	$0.00
9.	vw beetle classic		43	0.00%	11.63%	$0.02
10.	old vw beetle for sale		38	0.00%	15.79%	$0.00

b

Figure 21.3 The addition of goal measurement provides the necessary context to evaluate successful (or profitable) visits.

Now the information takes on a completely new meaning. Rather than simply looking at the *number* of visitors for a particular keyword, you can measure the *effectiveness* of a particular keyword in terms of conversions. You are now reporting on performance against goals, rather than reporting mere data! All kinds of valuable information can be drawn from evaluating your data based on goal completion. Adding more data to reports like these also provides a unique outlook, which enables more profitable decisions to be made.

As an example of adding more information, the drop-down box to the right of the keyword drop-down box allows you to view the keywords by source. This additional information enables you to see which keywords in which search engines are doing the most work to provide you the best business. This way, you should be able to find the keywords that are bringing in lots of visitors but converting very few. This provides the direction you need to focus on when developing a plan to improve the experience for this keyword or when choosing more profitable keywords.

To gain perspective on additional keywords and their performance, you can click the column headings to order the information. Clicking Goal Conversion Rate will toggle the order of rows to show you the keywords with conversion rates ordered from highest to lowest or lowest to highest. However, as discussed in Chapter 19, I find that those with the highest rates are usually keywords that bring in very few visitors (see Figure 21.4).

	Keyword ⌄	Source ⌄	Visits	Place Classified Ad	Goal Conversion ↑ Rate	Per Visit Goal Value
1.	"place ad"+"edit ad"+"browse ads"+"search a	yahoo	1	0.00%	0.00%	$0.00
2.	"volkswagen beetle" blogspot	google	1	0.00%	0.00%	$0.00
3.	"vw beetle" "heater channel"	google	1	0.00%	0.00%	$0.00
4.	' 69 vw bus lowering kit	bing	1	0.00%	0.00%	$0.00
5.	'67 beetle brakes diagram	google	1	0.00%	0.00%	$0.00
6.	'hot vws magazine subscription discount'	google	1	0.00%	0.00%	$0.00
7.	+bulding buggys	yahoo	1	0.00%	0.00%	$0.00
8.	+original vw bugs ebay	yahoo	1	0.00%	0.00%	$0.00
9.	+volkswagen +thing	google	1	0.00%	0.00%	$0.00
10.	+volkswagen thing off road	google	1	0.00%	0.00%	$0.00

Figure 21.4 The pages with the highest conversion rates may show only a few visitor referrals.

You may have to page through thousands of keywords in order to gain some perspective on which keywords produced high visitor numbers and high conversion rates. Fortunately, Google provides an ordering mechanism for this massive amount of data called the *weighted sort*. With the weighted sort, the report information is developed based on a threshold of visitors to conversions. Essentially, it eliminates the reports that have 100 percent conversion rates and one visitor, or 0 percent conversion rates and one visitor, and instead displays the information that is most helpful (see Figure 21.5). Seeing that 200 visitors were brought to the site without a single conversion provides a significant direction for a site owner. This direction involves evaluating the content, design, and other factors outlined in this book but directed at a specific segment of visitors based on search term, visit source, entry page, and the purpose of that page.

	Keyword	Source	Visits	Place Classified Ad	Goal Conversion ↑ Rate	Per Visit Goal Value
1.	vw thing	google	208	0.00%	0.00%	$0.00
2.	volkswagen thing	google	120	0.00%	0.83%	$0.00
3.	old beetle	google	32	0.00%	0.00%	$0.00
4.	vw beetle engine	google	30	0.00%	0.00%	$0.00
5.	vw bug	google	97	0.00%	7.22%	$0.01
6.	vw beetle	bing	42	0.00%	4.76%	$0.00
7.	volkswagen classic beetle	google	17	0.00%	0.00%	$0.00
8.	volkswagen beetle	google	220	0.00%	8.64%	$0.00
9.	vw beetle	search	16	0.00%	0.00%	$0.00
10.	classic vw	google	15	0.00%	0.00%	$0.00

Weighted Sort

Figure 21.5 Weighed sort provides a better method for viewing keywords that attract high visitor numbers and high conversion rates.

The most important thing that site managers and owners gain by evaluating data in the context of conversion goals is direction. Too many are simply not able to figure out a direction of where to start in analytics, because they are not sure what to do with the data. This is the "magic" of reporting to the goals. When the goal information is available in the analytics, you find the direction and information that can help you make more informed decisions. Specific words, pages, and information that previously went unnoticed are now highlighted by a lack of conversions or by great conversion rates. You can now determine whether you need to make a specific improvement to your website by viewing a few simple reports based on conversion data.

Tuesday: Analyze by Segments

To me, analytics becomes fun and easy when conversion goals and segments are developed. The information takes on a different life and is more "real." Segments can be based on many things: keywords, sources of visitors (websites, blogs, links, and so on), actions, conversions, events—any form of measureable factor can be used to create a segment. More than simply reporting numbers, using segments and goals provides immediate satisfaction to those who need to find improvements and get a direction.

Nothing to me is more revealing than analyzing segments. The only way to understand the big numbers is to slice them into small segments, which then provide better insight as to the cause and remedy of particular situations. Segments are a way of asking and answering questions. When that happens, learning takes place, which brings results, as discussed last Thursday and Friday in Chapter 20. Today is when you take the segments you created last week and apply them to your analytics.

Of course, because you are viewing the available segments, you should be getting ideas and thoughts about how to use and apply the additional options. I find that the easiest place to get started is to segment by search engine keyword referrals. At this stage, SEO has most likely been part of your strategy, and this is where you measure the results of your efforts. Just this starting point will provide a significant amount of information that can be immediately applied to your marketing strategy.

Today's lesson is not a comprehensive guide to the segments available, but simply beginning with these few segments will be enough to get you started and comfortable with the process. Once you feel comfortable, test and see what else you can find.

Focus on Actionable Information

Remember, setting up segments is great, and you can find a lot of "interesting" information, but that interesting information is not always actionable! Find actionable information, apply it, measure it, and then move on to the next actions.

Analyze by Search Segment

I usually like to start by setting up segments based on keywords and diving into search analytics. Especially when you are spending time on keyword research, optimization, and content development, the desire to see the results for that work is natural. This is particularly true if you have paid someone to optimize your website. Even though you may now have some top rankings, aren't you the least bit curious to know whether those rankings are doing you any good?

So, the principle of setting up segments is based on starting very general at first and then drilling down into the segments, in other words, segmenting the segments. At the very start, you want to segment the primary or core words and keyword phrases. At this stage, do not be concerned about the individual words like the ones shown in the reports in yesterday's section. To start, the informational segments will be based on the core terms you have selected. If you developed the keyword graphs, as explained in Chapter 6, then you know your core terms.

To set up a segment in Google Analytics, navigate to the Dashboard report in your analytics. In the upper right of the page there is an Advanced Segments label with a drop-down that most likely shows the default All Visits; when you click that drop-down, a new window opens to reveal the options (Figure 21.6).

Clicking that drop-down will bring additional segment information. The default segments available to you are the typical KPIs: new visitors, returning visitors, search traffic, direct traffic, paid search traffic, and so on. Although those segments are very good to gain information, the custom segmenting tools provide an easy means of customizing these reports to your website and your business. To the left of the default segments are two links that provide that customization. Click Create A New Advanced Segment. Now, just about every variable is available to you in developing a segment (see Figure 21.7).

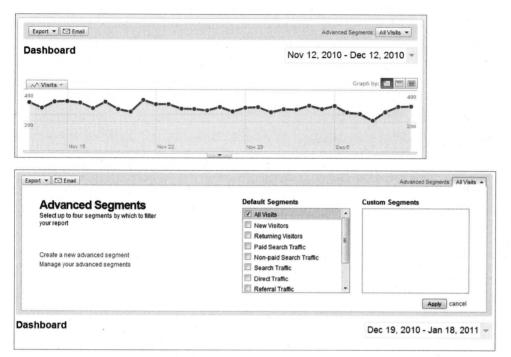

Figure 21.6 Starting to set up advanced segments

Figure 21.7 Creating advanced segments

As I mentioned earlier, the easiest method for beginning segmentation is to work with the search analytics. This is because you have become very familiar with your keywords and rankings, so it is simply a matter of taking that familiarity and applying it to your analytics. The first pass at segmenting search terms will focus on the general terms. The first few segments will be based on your core keywords.

To the left of the page you will see two highlighted terms, Dimensions and Metrics. In this case, the primary objective is to evaluate the source of visitors. This is a dimension—an attribute of the visitors you want to analyze. The sources of the segmentation that have been covered in this chapter and in Chapter 20 are all dimension metrics (by keyword, by action, by content, or by product category). You can think of these as the "intentions" of the visitor. The metrics shown in the report are based on the dimension selected in the segment. Metrics are the pages they viewed, the time they spent on the site, the time and date they visited—all of the "detail" information that are typical KPIs. Get it? You are in the process of adding the context to the KPI.

Now, click and drag the dimension Keyword from the Dimensions list on the left (click the toggle arrow next to Traffic Sources to reveal the Keyword option) into the Dimensions or Metrics box at the top of the page (refer to Figure 21.8). Now, to match the keyword, since this is focusing on the large segment data, simply set Condition to Contains (Figure 21.8), which will provide the broadest variety of keywords available that match the core term. In this example, I am selecting VW in the Value field, since this is a site about Volkswagens. Name your segment, and click the Test Segment button in the upper or lower right to see whether there is any data available. If so, click Create And Apply To Report, and you will see your newly created segment.

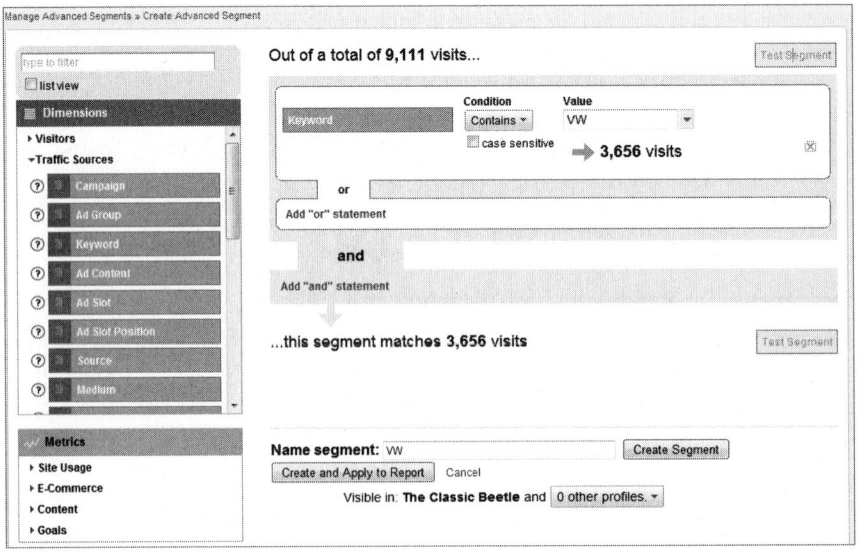

Figure 21.8 Creating the large segment

Dealing with Tricky Keyword Segments

Sometimes, you may have to get creative with matching the search terms. A lighting website may show a dozen or more spelling variations of the search referral *chandelier*. Instead of using the entire word, find a value that contains enough of the core letters of the term, such as *chand*. Alternatively, find a core spelling of the root word that may be consistent enough to gather most or all of the searchers within that keyword segment.

You may have noticed that the screenshots in this section are from a Volkswagen website, and in order to capture brand-name searches, the core term had to be one that used the core letters of *volks* in order to capture anyone who misspelled the brand name. Variations include *Volkswagen*, *volkswagon*, and *Volkswagan*).

The segment shows that about a third of the total search traffic used the core term *VW*. This can be valuable and answers a few questions, but it can be refined further to give a better idea as to what exactly people are looking for and the intent of their searches. This is where creating the subsegments provides a much deeper view of the tendencies of the searchers and the true popularity of keyword concepts within your website. Rather than looking at search rankings and the referrals from individual terms, the keyword-based segments bring in all of the "long tail" terms and provide a more extensive view of the keywords that are attracting high-value visitors to your website.

To create the subsegments, you simply segment the segment. Create another advanced segment, and use your core term. Then, click the Add "and" Statement link, and add your desired term in the Value field. This creates the conditions for a multi-word keyword phrase and begins the process of dividing your search traffic by subsegments and different words.

In Figure 21.9, the subsegment "resto" is meant to isolate all of the keyword referrals that include the two words *VW* and *resto* (*resto* being short for restoration).

Now, start setting up the subsegments that are targeted in your keyword marketing and optimization. In addition, look over your keyword referral reports to get an idea of the keywords that are referring people to the site. You should be able to derive a number of subsegments for each core term, which will enable you to look at your search analytics in a completely different light. How that evaluation is performed will be covered in tomorrow's content.

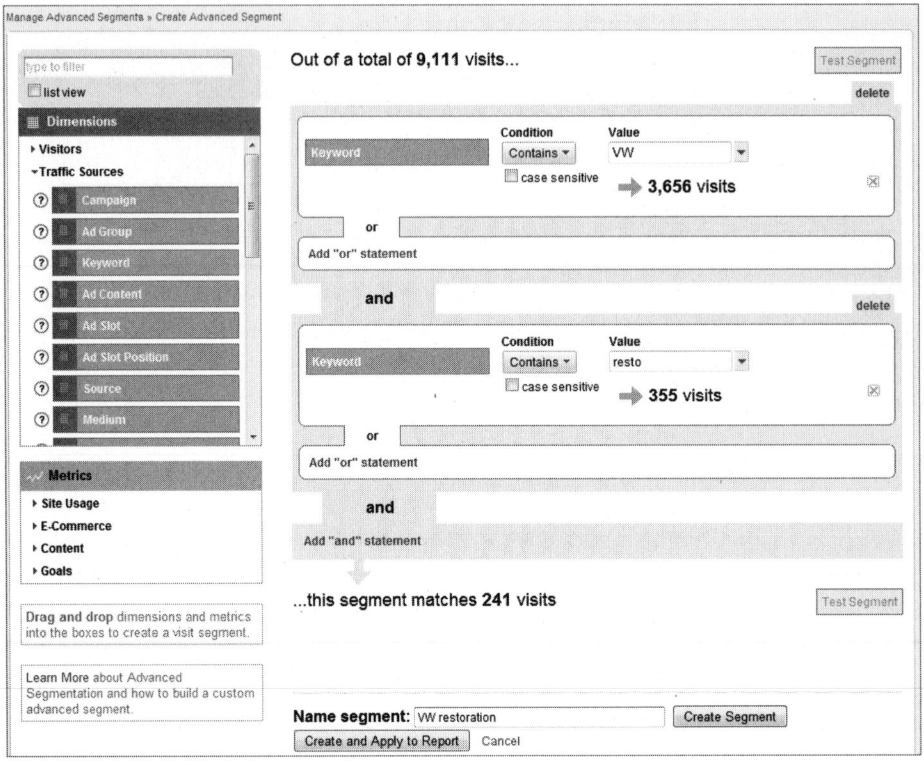

Figure 21.9 Use subsegments to show searcher intent.

Analyze by Page View Segment

Setting up page view segment analysis is similar to setting up your goal analysis, but it's more of a "soft" conversion. The idea for setting up a page view segment is to compare the people who saw a specific page during a visit. By itself, this segmented report may not carry a lot of actionable information, but when combined with another segment, such as the people who searched for the specific page of information, you can gain strategic insight and answer the question, "Did people looking for this information find this page?"

To use the search to do page-view analysis, choose the keyword from the Traffic Sources dimension, and choose Contains. Click the Add "and" Statement in order to associate the two actions. Then choose the page from the page title (in this case I am choosing the For Sale page, as shown in the value box), and set the value to Matches Exactly, because that is the specific page you want to measure. Name the segment, click Test Segment, and you should see how many visitor sessions match these conditions. You then click Create And Apply To Report to see the metrics associated with this group of visitor sessions (Figure 21.10).

Figure 21.10 Set up a segment based on keyword intent and the intended landing page.

Analyze by Support Segment

I call these *support segments*, because they are mainly used for troubleshooting specific areas of site performance. By measuring browser types, screen resolutions, and operating systems, you can detect any early problems with specific issues that may be experienced with a certain computer, operating system, or browser.

As an example, I'll cover how to set up segments based on browser type. Start by dragging the Browser dimension to the segment. Set Condition to Matches Exactly, and select the browser from the drop-down list in the value. Name your segment, test it, and you will see the number of visits that used that browser. In Figure 21.11, I have set up a segment to see how many visits used the Firefox browser to visit the website.

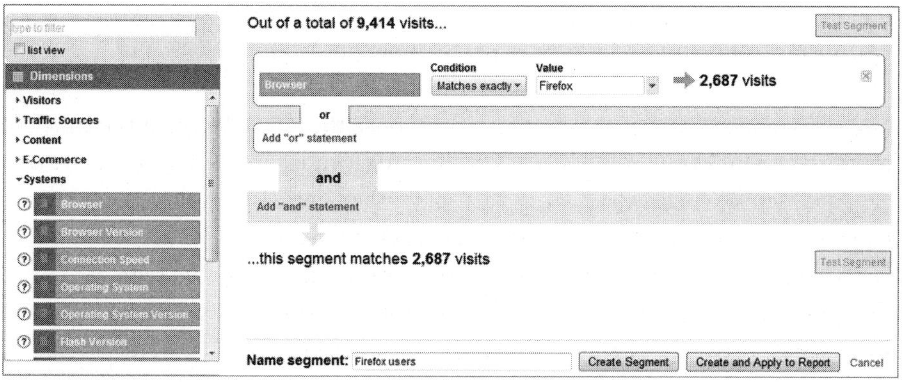

Figure 21.11 Setting up a support segment to view visitors using the Firefox browser

This is a troubleshooting mechanism that can also help you spot potential design flaws that haven't been tested in multiple browsers and operating systems. In one instance, a consulting client was having a significant bounce rate on the product pages. The site was designed to be "stretchy," in that it would flow to fill the entire browser width. In doing so, the content was stretched across the page, and the paragraph became one long sentence that was very difficult to read. Long sentences are harder to read if they require the visitor to move horizontally across the page.

An enterprising analyst found the problem by adding the screen resolution dimension as a segment. In evaluating the bounce rate, he found that visitors using a high resolution (1400 × 1050 and above) were bouncing twice as much as visitors using a more standard resolution (1280 × 800). When testing the problem with the resolution, the cause was confirmed. Visitors on higher-resolution monitors were seeing the design of the pages simply fall apart; nothing looked right. I'll discuss segmenting for bounce rates tomorrow.

A Recap of Bounce Rate

The *bounce rate* is a measure of the visitors who come to your site and immediately leave. They view one page, spend only seconds, and either back out or close the session.

Typically, the visitors who bounce were looking for information and simply do not see it anywhere on the page they enter. If the page has no information or even appears to have the information they want, they will leave. This happens with poor design or unclear information.

Another reason for high bounce rates is in areas where there is more than one meaning for a keyword. Recall the example from Chapter 11: a search for "nested tables" will take a searcher to a furniture store or a programming resource. If the destination does not match the intent, then the visitor will bounce.

Examining causes for high bounce rates is a helpful method of finding problems within your website. The cause could be misleading keywords, bad landing or entry or lack of clear content. This is where viewing the website while performing analytics can help establish causality.

These are areas where many site owners have had to get better at monitoring these issues. Development companies are used to signing off on the website design, and testing is usually included. However, once the site is live, unless there is a maintenance contract in place, this falls to the site owner to detect and correct any problems. If there are major flaws, then it might be possible to get a correction made, especially if you can prove a loss in sales or visitors as a result of a missed test in that area.

Wednesday: Analyze Segmented Search Terms and Bounce Rates

Being able to look at the performance of the entire group of search segments on one report and to view them comparatively enables better evaluation. Conclusions can be drawn based on specific data. I like to download the information into a spreadsheet.

I recommend evaluating the top-performing key phrases and their subsegments. Include the typical performance measures such as pages viewed, time on site, bounce rate, and conversion rate. When looking at the "typical" data in context of the search-term segment, significant differences between the segments should appear. To add another layer of analysis, add the top two or three entry pages for each segment.

By creating a large table of segments and looking at the similarities and differences between the segments, you can draw immediate conclusions concerning well-performing and converting segments and those that may be drawing visitors but not converting them.

Segment Core Search Terms

Look at Table 21.1, which shows the analytics information for two core search terms—*publish* and *write*—for a website with the goal of attracting writers who wanted to publish a book. In comparing the segments of terms that provided registrations on the site, the goal was to find the best usage of the word to properly communicate the business value

▶ **Table 21.1** Analytics information for the core search terms *publish* and *write*

Metric	Data for *publish*	Data for *write*
Segment Visitors	1,941	1,815
Average Segment Keyword Ranking	#8	#5
Average Segment Time on Site	11:53 minutes	9:09 minutes
Average Segment Page Views	4.86	4.4
Segment Bounce Rate	**48%**	**54%**
Segment Conversion Rate	**5%**	**3%**

Simply by comparing the core terms, you can see that the number of visitors generated within the time frame is very similar. The average rankings of the top key phrases in each segment were not too far apart. However, when drilling down into the different segments, there are obvious differences. Both have very healthy usage statistics, but the *publish*-based group of keywords has lower bounce rates and better conversion rates than the *write*-based group of keywords, despite the lower average ranking of keywords in that segment.

By looking deeper than statistical performance (numbers of visitors, time on site, and pages viewed), a group of keywords can be measured in the proper context—success. In this way, you can determine the best place to invest in future marketing. By investing in segments that are already profitable, you know that your search engine optimization campaign will provide even more return on investment, because there is proven return already.

Segment Word Variations

One of the most dramatic realizations was the measurable difference between searchers who used the singular or plural version of a word. The behavior was distinctly different and noticeable across a wide spectrum of other markets, websites, and industries. Based on a single letter, searchers do not have the same intent and tend to act very differently.

In the example in Table 21.2, the comparison is between searchers using the plural version of a term, *vacations*, and searchers using the singular version of a search term, *vacation*. For this travel site, the words *vacation* and *vacations* were used interchangeably throughout the website and in the terminology of the organization. However, when the two terms were analyzed based on rankings and conversions, it is clear that a different approach is needed. This specific segment shows searches that included the word *vacation* or *vacations* in any form or order for a day.

▶ **Table 21.2** Analytics Information for the search terms *vacations* and *vacation*

Metric	Data for *vacations* (plural)	Data for *vacation* (singular)
Ranking in Google	#3	#34
Search referrals	600	1800
Conversion Rate	0%	2%

In comparing the two segments, it became immediately clear that the singular version was the more profitable version of the phrases. Even with being listed in the fourth page of results at #34 (at the time of the analysis) in Google, the singular version far outperformed its plural counterpart, with three times as many visitors and significantly more conversions. More measurement over longer periods of time confirmed this trend.

Some SEO agencies would be very happy to report that they attained a top ranking for a term. This shows that success goes well beyond a good ranking—a lower ranking term was much more profitable (as is often the case), and it showed a trend among the searchers. More investment could be made in growing the content and optimization of the singular term throughout the website. More money and time could be invested in the singular term, because the term was already profitable, and the results were measurable. The more it would increase rankings, the more profit it would produce because it was already proven to be a profit-generating word.

The plural version of the term, despite having a great ranking, was not as immediately profitable. By analyzing the behavior of this segment, we found that plural-version searchers were seeking information but not ready to commit. They had an idea of what they wanted but were not yet ready to commit. They were looking for additional information, more options, and more ideas. The singular-version searchers (sharpshooters) were looking for different types of information than the plural-version seekers.

This finding created implications about the content provided to searchers throughout the website. This simple indicator of intent showed that searchers were looking for different types of information based on this small difference of wording. The behavior of the searchers enabled a content survey to be made, focusing on the types of preferred content by each segment and then customizing the wording within the groups of content to be more focused on the exhibited need.

Segment Entry Points by Search Term

Beyond having the right ranking for the wrong word, it is also possible to have the right ranking but for the wrong page.

One company I worked with had two pages ranking for the same term in Google; the home page ranked at #2 and the product page ranked at #12 (on the second page of results). The average conversion rate for this search term segment was 2.2 percent. However, when breaking down the segment by entry page, a completely different view of this segment emerged (Table 21.3).

▶ **Table 21.3** Analytics Information for a single search term with two different site-entry points

Metric	Data for home page as entry point	Data for product page as entry point
Average ranking in Google	#3	#12
Search referrals	2,682	1,007
Bounce rate	**22%**	**13%**
Conversion rate	**1.8%**	**4.3%**
Number of conversions	48	43

The story of these segments showed that visitors who entered the site at the product page, which ranked on the second page of results, produced a more effective visit in terms of conversions. The number of conversions was comparable to those produced by the higher-ranking home page. What was most telling was the significantly higher bounce rate and the significantly lower conversion rate experienced by the home page compared to the product page.

Impatient visitors did not do well in navigating beyond the home page to the product page. Those visitors who entered the site closer to their intended destination experienced a higher level of success. The mandate as a result of this observation was clear: focus more attention on getting the product page to rank higher, remove the terms from the title of the home page, and make a more visible link to the category page. Doing these things caused the category page to rank higher than the home page and be the primary entry page for this term, which then produced a more profitable ranking, based on conversions.

Segment Bounce Rates

I've already touched on considering bounce rates in analysis this week, but now I'll focus on segmenting specifically by bounce rate. Bounce rates are one of the most aggravating measurements for many marketers. However, I find them to be the best way to improve your website, because they are clear indicators of issues within a particular page of your website. Bounce rates indicate that the content, design, call to action, or other factors do not line up with the expectations of the visitor. Their reaction to the page is found in the bounce rate. A high bounce rate means that they have rejected your site based on the initial impression, and you need to make a better impression in order to improve.

A publisher in one of my seminars was so excited by the analytics training that they went back to their site to discover what they could. They were particularly troubled by a new article that was receiving bad feedback from the readers. This publisher had written an article titled "Holiday Time Travel" with ideas for destinations and low-cost getaways during the winter holidays. It had quickly grown as the highest read article but also the most unfavorable in the comments. After the analytics seminar, she started segmenting her traffic and found the reason for this strange behavior. She found that the top search phrase sending visitors to the article was *time travel*. No wonder the bounce rate was so high! The expectation of nearly 60 percent of the search traffic was information about time travel, and this article did not deliver the information about space-time theories that they wanted; it was about travel during the holidays. (The confusion was in part because the article title was missing a hyphen that makes all the difference in meaning—for the best human-readability, the title should have been "Travel Ideas for the Holidays.") Analytics makes sense because it puts information in perspective!

Thursday: Segment Content

Content segmentation is a valuable method of finding important information as valued by your customer. I find that most organizations evaluate content based on the investment of the content or their own internal organizational value but lack the necessary means to determine the visitor's value of that same content. By using the contextual measurement tools available in Google Analytics, you can gain a better perspective on the content on your website.

Simple content evaluation tools are available in the Content: Content by Title report. They provide different ways of looking at your content and are extremely valuable tools, especially for publishers and content sites, simply by evaluating each page of content (I prefer viewing by the page title) and then comparing and contrasting using the buttons above the rows of information on the right side of the panel (see Figure 21.12). These buttons display the information in different visual formats, which enable a different perspective on the content and how it compares to the other data in the chart.

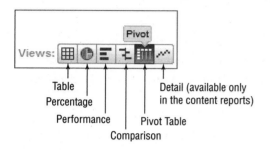

Figure 21.12 The Views buttons in Google Analytics from the Top Content: Content by Title report: Table (default), Percentage, Performance, Comparison, Pivot Table, and Detail

Compare a Page's Metrics to the Site Average

Once the Comparison view is enabled, I suggest viewing the information by Avg. Time on Page. This option then shows each page of content by time on site and compares it to the other pages of content and the site average (see Figure 21.13).

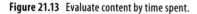

Figure 21.13 Evaluate content by time spent.

The purpose of this report is to identify poorly performing pages and answer "why?" In addition, it will allow you to find the well-performing pages and answer the "why?" These reports, while informative, still require the human interaction of asking questions and finding answers. Searching for the "why?" forces you to develop theories (or causality—what caused this?) of what content that visitors liked and did not like, but you have the added benefit of evidence, rather than guesses and suppositions. Viewing graphs is not the final action; it is the means to developing a targeted approach to website improvements based on the evidence.

Another simple report in Google Analytics allows you to compare content performance by page. When viewed compared to segments, this report allows you to find the content that is more profitable for each segment and to find which content produces a high bounce rate with your visitors and has little or no persuasive value. To get this perspective, simply change the parameter of Avg. Time on Site to Bounce Rate in the Individual Page Title...Compared to Site Average drop-down selection. The graph will change to display the Comparison view with pages, page views, and bounce rates based on the average site bounce rate (see Figure 21.14).

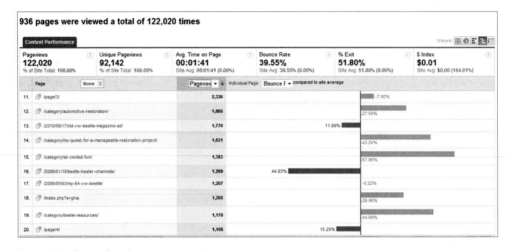

Figure 21.14 Content bounce rates in perspective

This report shows the content that keeps people on the site and interested and shows which content makes people leave. The perspective provided by the positive or negative length of the bar in the graph is the number of visitors who bounced from the content, and when viewed compared to other content, the trends emerge, and the value of content to the visitors becomes clear. This is critical to your content development strategies and building a plan for increasing or addressing the content of the site. By identifying content that drives conversions, the marketing plans become clearer; it becomes less about guessing and more about factually driven information providing clear trends to conversion.

Use Pivot Tables

I find one of the more valuable reports for search analytics is the Traffic Sources: Keywords report. This requires some additional customization, again using one of the buttons in the upper right, namely, Pivot Table. Now, just hearing the phrase "pivot tables" can make some marketers prepare for hours of boring statistics, but this is one pivot table that you'll want to see! Click Traffic Sources: Keywords in the main analytics navigation. Then, click the Pivot Table button. Pivot tables display an amazing amount of data in order to make better comparisons. Simply put, they are another way of viewing data that can help you build a better understanding of your website.

After you have selected the pivot table view, you'll see that the keyword is the heading of the first column, but the second column is unused. Select Landing Page in the drop-down. *Bam!* You now have a pivot table showing you your keyword referrals by landing page and number of visits, grouped by the referring search engine.

The additional customization is the level of context that can be built into this report, based on factors important to you. Click your preferred goal set in the tabs above the table. In this case, I am using my Goal Set 2. Above the data table, on the left side, should read "Pivot By: Source" and to the right of that is a Showing drop-down. This is where you apply your custom business goals. You add your specific goals into this report, which can be compared along with all of this data. In the Pivot By drop-down, select Visits. In the Showing drop-down, select Goal Conversion Rate. This report will be one of the more valuable reports that you will generate about your online marketing efforts. This report (Figure 21.15) has multiple data points that provide an amazing level of information: keyword, visits, search engine, conversion rate by search engine by keyword and conversion rate by search engine and by keyword. Just look at all of that beautiful data! More context equals more understanding!

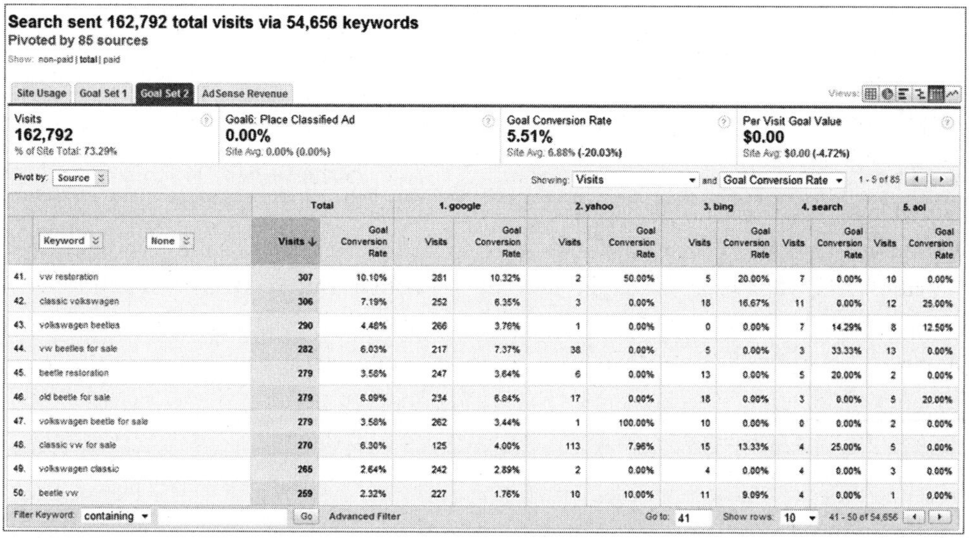

		Total		1. google		2. yahoo		3. bing		4. search		5. aol	
	Keyword / None	Visits ↓	Goal Conversion Rate	Visits	Goal Conversion Rate	Visits	Goal Conversion Rate	Visits	Goal Conversion Rate	Visits	Goal Conversion Rate	Visits	Goal Conversion Rate
41.	vw restoration	307	10.10%	281	10.32%	2	50.00%	5	20.00%	7	0.00%	10	0.00%
42.	classic volkswagen	306	7.19%	252	6.35%	3	0.00%	18	16.67%	11	0.00%	12	25.00%
43.	volkswagen beetles	290	4.48%	266	3.76%	1	0.00%	0	0.00%	7	14.29%	8	12.50%
44.	vw beetles for sale	282	6.03%	217	7.37%	38	0.00%	5	0.00%	3	33.33%	13	0.00%
45.	beetle restoration	279	3.58%	247	3.64%	6	0.00%	13	0.00%	5	20.00%	2	0.00%
46.	old beetle for sale	279	6.09%	234	6.84%	17	0.00%	18	0.00%	3	0.00%	5	20.00%
47.	volkswagen beetle for sale	279	3.58%	262	3.44%	1	100.00%	10	0.00%	0	0.00%	2	0.00%
48.	classic vw for sale	270	6.30%	125	4.00%	113	7.96%	15	13.33%	4	25.00%	5	0.00%
49.	volkswagen classic	265	2.64%	242	2.89%	2	0.00%	4	0.00%	4	0.00%	3	0.00%
50.	beetle vw	259	2.32%	227	1.76%	10	10.00%	11	9.09%	4	0.00%	1	0.00%

Figure 21.15 Multiple data points create better context for making decisions.

This report has implications throughout the marketing strategy. It pinpoints where the best factors for success are happening within the search engine optimization strategy. When this report is applied with PPC data as well, it provides amazing comparative insight as to where the most effective campaign is happening and where to place your budget for best results.

For the site in Figure 21.15, this report shows the keywords that are extremely valuable in providing conversions and those that are not as effective. Going forward, you could evaluate the landing pages for low-performing keywords to see whether the entry page has a high bounce rate. You could also evaluate the reaction of visitors to deduce whether the content they expect to find is the content they see.

Friday: Turn Your Analysis into Action!

This is the final step. My own analysts like to remind me about this, because I tend to get excited about the insights and trends that I find in analytics. *Unless it results in action, it's worthless.*

I could spend all day being fascinated by the user behaviors, bounce rates, search factors, and developing hypotheses about these findings. However, unless I test those hypotheses and focus on a specific action or set of circumstances to improve, looking at the data was a waste of time. Gaining knowledge about your website doesn't improve it; your reaction to that knowledge does.

Each report that you view needs to generate a specific action that will take place. Once trends and opportunities have been uncovered, you need a plan to take advantage of them. Problems need to be fixed. Having the plumber tell you there is a leak doesn't fix it. Someone needs to crawl under your sink and make changes and then test the effect of those changes.

The exciting part of all of this is that what you learn in analytics can be applied to many methods of evaluation and improvement. Identified problems may be in the calls to action, design, color, contrast, optimization, images, copywriting, clarity, or on-page goals. This book should give you the necessary tools to develop causal mechanisms for site performance and improvement. Simply exposing the problems in analytics is the start; finding the causes and corrections are based on the experience you will develop by practicing many of the other disciplines contained in this book.

Don't be afraid of making mistakes—we all make them. The Internet is a very forgiving medium, and mistakes can be quickly mitigated by a quick response. Mistakes are made when changes are made without measurement or the results are neglected. The key is in how you react to those mistakes and what you learn from making them. A simple change can cause ripples across the performance of the website. Of course, a major change can cause waves of uncertainty for a few days or weeks afterward. By keeping track of the changes that were made, when they were made, and the results of those changes, you learn quickly and develop a keen sense of wisdom when it comes to managing the website.

By developing a holistic view of all the elements that create and drive a website to the goals of the business, you will develop a better understanding of the necessary improvements and how they relate to each other. Many factors will affect other elements of the site and the strategy, but by understanding how everything works together, both the management and the troubleshooting become easier to perform and more effective in their execution.

As you dig into the analytics, you will begin to find those trends and opportunities that will enable you to grow. Some changes will provide immediate results, and some will take time to materialize. This is where I always recommend marketers use the annotation function in Google Analytics.

Your memory is not the best mechanism for associating events that may lead to high rankings, better conversion rates, or happier customers. Keep a record so that you always know when you made that design change or navigation option, changed the graphic and the call to action, or even got a link from another website. These are important events in the life of your website, and everything works together to create success. You can't simply make changes and not know when or what was done and expect to learn and gain experience in this business.

The annotation feature is a valuable tool, because it provides perspective to the business. Any changes to the website, content, code, pages, optimization strategy, rankings, or any external factors can be noted in the annotations (see Figure 21.16). Simply click on the data point for that day in the graph, and the annotation feature will appear.

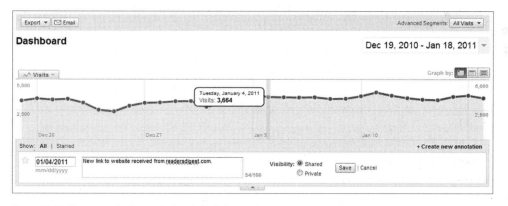

Figure 21.16 The annotation feature in Google Analytics

The purpose of this function is clear. When looking for a causal factor in new visitors, improved conversions, or any other factor on the site, having a record of changes made immediately accessible makes the connection clear. Don't miss making the connection because you can't remember the date that you made a significant change to the website!

Review and Hands-On

So many marketers and business owners tell me that the most difficult part of managing a site is knowing where to start. Do you start with design? Maybe changing the navigation? Or is it the copywriting? Maybe the SEO?

This is why I see analytics as more than the capstone to the online marketing process. For me, it is the central part of marketing your website because it provides the only clear measurement of your efforts. Everything you need to evaluate your site is contained in this book, and analytics helps you see the results of those efforts. Some days I wish I could teach analytics first, because it is so central to setting up the measurement correctly, but you also have to understand what you are looking at and how it all relates.

I always recommend starting with analytics and seeing whether your performance lines up with your marketing goals. I then like to compare the search performance in the analytics compared to the search campaign goals. Start simple, start with the big picture, and look at the goals of your business and the website to see whether you are performing well by your own standards.

The best evaluation is not based on industry averages but on comparing the segments within your own website. This is the best information you will get about your audience and how it views your website. Industry averages are made up of very, very bad sites and very good ones; it is really not a good measure for comparison and, even still, not a practical measure because the comparison does not provide you with a specific direction.

Comparing your own segments provides direction, because it exposes those searchers and trends within your website that need attention. Segmenting shows opportunities and creates knowledge because it provides a significantly new way to look at the numbers, and the context provides actionable ideas for improvement.

The principle of segmentation is simple. Break down your large numbers into highly contextual groups of visitors. In doing do, you can determine their intent and expectancy. By simply viewing their tendencies, where they entered the site, and the results of the visitor, you will begin to find specific areas of difference. Then, this is where your brain power is needed to determine how to apply the information that you have learned.

This is the point where I cannot cover all the variables, alternatives, and specific details for your website. If there is one thing that is obvious to anyone who hears it, it is that not all sites can be compared—none is the same as another. Even within the same industries, messaging is different, target audiences are different, and businesses are different. This is where segmenting creates a highly customized measuring stick for your business and your website.

Here are the final considerations as you wrap up your time with this book:

- Set up your business and visitor goals in your analytics. This is the first step, because every subsequent step relies on comparing the data to the ultimate goals of your business. Set up goals in order of their importance and revenue, and annotate them for your convenience.

- Move on to segmenting your visitors by source, keywords, links, and direct navigation. Further segment those segments by link types and additional keywords and actions. Compare the segments to find differences in behavior, conversion rates, and preferences.

- Start to explore. Look at the data in different ways. Use some of the examples outlined in this chapter to view your data. Most importantly, find what works for your business and your website. Take time with this step. Analytics are not to be used to get quick data for reports. Analytics take time and work to find those valuable insights and opportunities.

- Above all, find action. Developing a deeper knowledge about your website is one thing; taking action on that knowledge is another. Take action, write your actions down, and refer to them often. This way, you will be teaching yourself and gaining valuable experience.

I am sure that as you have been reading this text, you have also been working and making changes to your website. Ideally, you have seen significant improvements. If so, I would love to hear about it. You can contact me with the information found in the introduction of the book. I wish you the best as you take these critical steps to increasing the effectiveness of your online marketing but, most of all, that you gain the experience of working through this book to become a better marketer!

Index

Note to the Reader: Throughout this index **boldfaced** page numbers indicate primary discussions of a topic. *Italicized* page numbers indicate illustrations.

M